THE PAPERS OF
THOMAS JEFFERSON

THE PAPERS OF

Thomas Jefferson

Volume 4

1 October 1780 to 24 February 1781

JULIAN P. BOYD, EDITOR

LYMAN H. BUTTERFIELD AND MINA R. BRYAN,

ASSOCIATE EDITORS

PRINCETON, NEW JERSEY

PRINCETON UNIVERSITY PRESS

1951

London: Geoffrey Cumberlege, Oxford University Press

Printed in the United States of America by
Princeton University Press, Princeton, New Jersey

DEDICATED TO THE MEMORY OF

ADOLPH S. OCHS

PUBLISHER OF THE NEW YORK TIMES

1896-1935

WHO BY THE EXAMPLE OF A RESPONSIBLE

PRESS ENLARGED AND FORTIFIED

THE JEFFERSONIAN CONCEPT

OF A FREE PRESS

GUIDE TO EDITORIAL APPARATUS

1. *TEXTUAL DEVICES*

The following devices are employed throughout the work to clarify the presentation of the text.

[. . .], [. . . .]	One or two words missing and not conjecturable.
[. . .][1], [. . . .][1]	More than two words missing and not conjecturable; subjoined footnote estimates number of words missing.
[ ]	Number or part of a number missing or illegible.
[roman]	Conjectural reading for missing or illegible matter. A question mark follows when the reading is doubtful.
[*italic*]	Editorial comment inserted in the text.
⟨*italic*⟩	Matter deleted in the MS but restored in our text.

2. *DESCRIPTIVE SYMBOLS*

The following symbols are employed throughout the work to describe the various kinds of manuscript originals. When a series of versions is recorded, *the first to be recorded is the version used for the printed text.*

Dft	draft (usually a composition or rough draft; later drafts, when identifiable as such, are designated "2d Dft," &c.)
Dupl	duplicate
MS	manuscript (arbitrarily applied to most documents other than letters)
N	note, notes (memoranda, fragments, &c.)
PoC	polygraph copy
PrC	press copy
RC	recipient's copy
SC	stylograph copy
Tripl	triplicate

All manuscripts of the above types are assumed to be in the hand of the author of the document to which the descriptive symbol pertains. If not, that fact is stated. On the other hand, the following types of manuscripts are assumed *not* to be in the hand of the author, and exceptions will be noted:

FC file copy (applied to all forms of retained copies, such as letter-book copies, clerks' copies, &c.)

Tr transcript (applied to both contemporary and later copies; period of transcription, unless clear by implication, will be given when known)

3. *LOCATION SYMBOLS*

The locations of documents printed in this edition from originals in private hands, from originals held by institutions outside the United States, and from printed sources are recorded in self-explanatory form in the descriptive note following each document. The locations of documents printed from originals held by public institutions in the United States are recorded by means of the symbols used in the National Union Catalog in the Library of Congress; an explanation of how these symbols are formed is given above, Vol. 1: xl. The list of symbols appearing in each volume is limited to the institutions represented by documents printed or referred to in that volume.

CSmH	Henry E. Huntington Library, San Marino, California
CtY	Yale University Library
DLC	Library of Congress
DNA	The National Archives
DeHi	Historical Society of Delaware, Wilmington
MB	Boston Public Library
MHi	Massachusetts Historical Society, Boston
MdAA	Maryland Hall of Records, Annapolis
MdBJ	Johns Hopkins University Library
MiU-C	William L. Clements Library, University of Michigan
MoSHi	Missouri Historical Society, St. Louis
N	New York State Library, Albany
NHi	New-York Historical Society, New York City
NN	New York Public Library
NcD	Duke University Library
NcDAH	North Carolina Department of Archives and History, Raleigh
OFH	Hayes Memorial Library, Fremont, Ohio

PHi Historical Society of Pennsylvania, Philadelphia

PHMC Pennsylvania Historical and Museum Commission, Harrisburg

PPAP American Philosophical Society, Philadelphia

Vi Virginia State Library, Richmond

ViW College of William and Mary Library

ViWC Colonial Williamsburg, Inc., Williamsburg, Virginia

WHi State Historical Society of Wisconsin, Madison

4. *OTHER ABBREVIATIONS*

The following abbreviations are commonly employed in the annotation throughout the work.

TJ Thomas Jefferson

TJ Editorial Files Photoduplicates and other editorial materials in the office of *The Papers of Thomas Jefferson*, Princeton University Library

TJ Papers Jefferson Papers (Applied to a collection of manuscripts when the precise location of a given document must be furnished, and always preceded by the symbol for the institutional repository; thus "DLC: TJ Papers, 4:628-9" represents a document in the Library of Congress, Jefferson Papers, volume 4, pages 628 and 629.)

PCC Papers of the Continental Congress, in the Library of Congress

RG Record Group (Used in designating the location of documents in the National Archives.)

5. *SHORT TITLES*

The following list includes only those short titles of works cited with great frequency, and therefore in very abbreviated form, throughout this edition. Their expanded forms are given here only in the degree of fullness needed for unmistakable identification. Since it is impossible to anticipate all the works to be cited in such very abbreviated form, the list is appropriately revised from volume to volume.

Atlas of Amer. Hist., Scribner, 1943. James Truslow Adams and R. V. Coleman, *Atlas of American History*, N.Y., 1943

Biog. Dir. Cong. *Biographical Directory of Congress, 1774-1927*

Bland Papers *The Bland Papers: Being a Selection from the Manuscripts of Colonel Theodorick Bland, Jr.*

B.M. Cat. British Museum, *General Catalogue of Printed Books*, London, 1931—. Also, *The British Museum Catalogue of Printed Books, 1881-1900*, Ann Arbor, 1946.

B.N. Cat. *Catalogue général des livres imprimés de la Bibliothèque Nationale. Auteurs.*

Burk-Girardin, *Hist. of Va.* John Burk, *The History of Virginia . . . Continued by Skelton Jones and Louis Hue Girardin*

Burnett, *Letters of Members* Edmund C. Burnett, ed., *Letters of Members of the Continental Congress*

C & D See *Va. Gaz.*

Cal. Franklin Papers *Calendar of the Papers of Benjamin Franklin in the Library of the American Philosophical Society*, ed. I. Minis Hays

Cal. Wash. Corr. with Officers Library of Congress, *Calendar of the Correspondence of George Washington . . . with the Officers*

Clark Papers See *George Rogers Clark Papers*

CVSP *Calendar of Virginia State Papers . . . Preserved in the Capitol at Richmond*

D & H See *Va. Gaz.*

D & N See *Va. Gaz.*

DAB *Dictionary of American Biography*

DAE *Dictionary of American English*

DAH *Dictionary of American History*

DNB *Dictionary of National Biography*

Epistolary Record Jefferson's MS Index to Letters Written and Received (in DLC: TJ Papers)

Evans Charles Evans, *American Bibliography*

Ford Paul Leicester Ford, ed., *The Writings of Thomas Jefferson*, "Letterpress Edition," N.Y., 1892-1899

Fry-Jefferson Map *The Fry & Jefferson Map of Virginia and Maryland: A Facsimile of the First Edition*, Princeton, 1950

George Rogers Clark Papers, 1771-1781; also 1781-1784 *George Rogers Clark Papers*, ed. James A. James, Illinois State Historical Library, *Collections*, VIII, XIX

HAW Henry A. Washington, ed., *The Writings of Thomas Jefferson*, Washington, 1853-1854

Heitman Francis B. Heitman, *Historical Register of Officers of the Continental Army*, new edn., Washington, 1914; also the same compiler's *Historical Register and Dictionary of the United States Army* [1789-1903], Washington, 1903

Hening William W. Hening, *The Statutes at Large; Being a Collection of All the Laws of Virginia*

JCC *Journals of the Continental Congress, 1774-1789*, ed. W. C. Ford and others, Washington, 1904-1937

JHD *Journal of the House of Delegates of the Commonwealth of Virginia* (cited by session and date of publication)

Johnston, "Jefferson Bibliography" Richard H. Johnston, "A Contribution to a Bibliography of Thomas Jefferson," *Writings of Thomas Jefferson*, ed. Lipscomb and Bergh, XX, separately paged following the Index

L & B Andrew A. Lipscomb and Albert E. Bergh, eds., *The Writings of Thomas Jefferson*, "Memorial Edition," Washington, 1903-1904

L.C. Cat. *A Catalogue of Books Represented by Library of Congress Printed Cards*, Ann Arbor, 1942-1946; also *Supplement*, 1948

Library Catalogue, 1783 Jefferson's MS list of books owned and wanted in 1783 (original in Massachusetts Historical Society)

Library Catalogue, 1815 *Catalogue of the Library of the United States*, Washington, 1815

Library Catalogue, 1829 *Catalogue. President Jefferson's Library*, Washington, 1829

Marraro, *Mazzei* Howard R. Marraro, *Philip Mazzei: Virginia's Agent in Europe*, New York, 1935

OED *A New English Dictionary on Historical Principles*, Oxford, 1888-1933

Official Letters *Official Letters of the Governors of the State of Virginia*, ed. H. R. McIlwaine

P & D See *Va. Gaz.*

PMHB *The Pennsylvania Magazine of History and Biography*

Randall, *Life* Henry S. Randall, *The Life of Thomas Jefferson*

Randolph, *Domestic Life* Sarah N. Randolph, *The Domestic Life of Thomas Jefferson*

Randolph, "Essay" Edmund Randolph, "Essay on the Revolutionary History of Virginia," VMHB, XLIII-XLV (1935-1937)

Report *Report of the Committee of Revisors Appointed by the General Assembly of Virginia in MDCCLXXVI*, Richmond, 1784

Sabin Joseph Sabin and others, *Bibliotheca Americana. A Dictionary of Books Relating to America*

Swem, "Va. Bibliog." Earl G. Swem, "A Bibliography of Virginia," Virginia State Library, *Bulletin*, VIII, X, XII (1915-1919)

Swem and Williams, "Register of the General Assembly of Va." Appended to: Virginia State Library, *Fourteenth Annual Report*, 1917

TJR Thomas Jefferson Randolph, ed., *Memoir, Correspondence, and Miscellanies, from the Papers of Thomas Jefferson*, Charlottesville, 1829

Tucker, *Life* George Tucker, *The Life of Thomas Jefferson*, Philadelphia, 1837

Tyler, *Va. Biog.* Lyon G. Tyler, *Encyclopedia of Virginia Biography*

Va. Council Jour. *Journals of the Council of the State of Virginia*, ed. H. R. McIlwaine

Va. Gaz. *Virginia Gazette* (Williamsburg, 1751-1780, and Richmond, 1780-1781). Abbreviations for publishers of the several newspapers of this name, frequently published concurrently, include the following: C & D (Clarkson & Davis), D & H (Dixon & Hunter), D & N (Dixon & Nicolson), P & D (Purdie & Dixon). In all other cases the publisher's name is not abbreviated

VMHB *Virginia Magazine of History and Biography*

WMQ *William and Mary Quarterly*

CONTENTS

CONTENTS

CONTENTS

CONTENTS

CONTENTS

CONTENTS

CONTENTS

1781

CONTENTS

CONTENTS

CONTENTS

CONTENTS

CONTENTS

CONTENTS

CONTENTS

ILLUSTRATIONS

ILLUSTRATIONS

VOLUME 4

1 October 1780 to 24 February 1781

JEFFERSON CHRONOLOGY

VOLUME 4

1780 October 5. Gates relieved by Congress of command of Southern Army; succeeded by Greene, 30 October.

1780 October 10. Henry Hamilton paroled.

1780 October 16. General Assembly convened.

1780 October 21. British fleet arrived in Hampton Roads with Leslie's army.

1780 November 3. TJ's daughter, Lucy Elizabeth, born.

1780 November 16. Greene and Steuben arrived in Richmond; Steuben remained in command of Continental troops in Virginia.

1780 November 22. British fleet and Leslie's army left Virginia for Charleston.

1780 ca. November. TJ began preparing answers to M. Marbois' queries (origin of *Notes on the State of Virginia*).

1780 December 29. Benedict Arnold's invasion of Virginia and raid up the James; Richmond and Westham sacked.

1781 January 2. General Assembly adjourned.

1781 January 5. TJ elected a councilor of the American Philosophical Society.

1781 January 17. Morgan's victory over Tarleton at Cowpens.

1781 January 22. George Rogers Clark left Richmond for expedition planned by TJ against Detroit.

1781 January 31. TJ proposed to Muhlenberg a plan to capture Arnold at Portsmouth.

1781 February 14. Greene crossed Dan River at Boyd's Ferry, the most northerly point of his retreat before Cornwallis.

1781 February 14-19. De Tilly's squadron in Virginia waters but failed to reach British vessels supporting Arnold.

1781 February 20. Lafayette ordered by Washington to march to Virginia in an effort to cut off Arnold.

THE PAPERS OF THOMAS JEFFERSON

George Muter to James Kemp

SIR War Office Richmond Octobr 1st. 1780.

You will please to take measures, for immediately establishing an Express at Hampton, one at Williamsburg, and keeping an Express house at York. An Express will be sent from hence to remain at N: Kent Ct. house. Circumstances render it most essentially necessary, that this measure shou'd be at present taken, that the quickest intelligence may be conveyed from Hampton to this place, shou'd there be occasion for it. I must therefore beg for your exertions.

The stove at the House of Burgesses in Williamsburg will be wanted for the House of Delegates. It is his Excellency's wish, that you woud send it up by the first convenient opportunity. I am yours,

GEO: MUTER C.

FC (Vi); at head of text: "[James] Kemp Esqr [A.Q.]M.G: Wmsburg."

The decision of the commissioner of the war office to establish a line of expresses was very probably the result of an oral or written direction from TJ, as the order for the stove certainly was.

From James Barron

[*Richmond?, before 2 Oct. 1780.* Minute in Journal of the Commissioner of the Navy (Vi), under date of 2 Oct.: "Letter from Commodore Barron referred from his Excellency the Governour." An entry of 3 Oct., following, states that a reply was written by James Maxwell to Commodore Barron "inclosing a Form of a List of Seamen employed in the Navy of Virginia." Neither Barron's letter nor Maxwell's reply with enclosure has been located.]

To Thomas Burke

SIR Richmond Oct. 2. 1780.

I am sorry to be obliged to inform you that it is out of our power to have paiment made of Mr. Clay's draught for 225,000 dollars.

Our treasury is at present absolutely exhausted, and no prospect of it's being replenished till the assembly shall have met and have had time to provide supplies. I hope this will reach you in time to prevent the additional disappointment which might arise from your setting out on your journey previous to your receipt of it.

I have the honor to be with the greatest esteem & respect Sir Your most obedt. & most humble servt., TH: JEFFERSON

RC (NcDAH); addressed by TJ: "The honourable Burke esq: N. Carolina." Tr in Thomas Burke's Letter Book (NcDAH).

Burke was at this time a North Carolina delegate to Congress; since he and TJ had engaged in correspondence about legal matters in 1770-1771 and since TJ had taken notes of a speech by him in 1775, it is curious that he should have been in doubt about Burke's first name.

From James Maxwell

[*Richmond, 2 Oct. 1780.* Minute in Journal of the Commissioner of the Navy (Vi), under this date: "Letter written to his Excellency the Governour relative to Capt. Richd. Barron." Not located.]

From Riedesel

New York, 2 Oct. 1780. Acknowledges a letter and congratulates TJ "on Mrs: Jeffersons Health and recovery." Encloses further letters from Brig. Gen. Specht. Postscript (in French): Capt. Geismar had left New York before TJ's letter containing kind remembrances of Geismar arrived; has had a letter from Geismar written from London, and has forwarded TJ's message to him.

RC (DLC); 3 p.; in a clerk's hand; postscript and two signatures in Riedesel's hand. The letter acknowledged by Riedesel is missing.

From John Fitzgerald

SIR Alexandria 3d. Octr. 1780.

I yesterday afternoon received your Excellency's Letter and immediately waited upon Mr. Adam and delivered him the Letters inclosed. We have this Morning laid off the Goods consisting of 45 ps. [pieces] Oznabriggs 5 ps. Drillings 2 ps. coarse white Linen (there being no white Sheeting but what we judged too fine, as it would come at about £30 ℔ yard) 2 ps. blue and 2 ps. red Duffells, 6 ps. Strip'd Blanketting, and 1 piece Sup fine white Cloth. Also 30 pair Shoes. There are 18 or 20 ps. of Ravens Duck which I judged would be a very necessary Article, especially as there is no brown Sheeting. Mr. Adam and I intended forwarding it with the rest, but upon second thoughts have declined it, untill your further Orders, As it is not Specified either in your Letters or Captain Conway's. Mr. Adam desires me to inform you that there are about 2 doz. Coarse Hose, and some Castile Soap which he thinks may be wanted for the Troops. The Goods will be packed up and sent over to Mr. Roger's this Afternoon. I will with pleasure attend to any further orders sent by the Waggons and have the honor to be Your Excellys. Mo Obed Hble Servt., JOHN FITZGERALD

NB There are three ps. of Grey Bath Coating if wanted, and 8 or 9 ℔ Check.

RC (NN). Without indication of addressee, but RC is mounted in an extra-illustrated volume whose provenance (Emmet 13801) supports the evidence given below that the attribution is correct.

Lt. Col. John Fitzgerald, of Alexandria, Va., had served as Gen. Washington's aide, 1776-1778 (see Washington, *Writings*, ed. Fitzpatrick, *passim*; also Heitman). TJ's LETTER here acknowledged and the LETTERS ENCLOSED therein have not been found. It is very likely that the present letter was addressed to TJ (rather than to Washington or another), for in 1781 Fitzgerald performed other missions for TJ in Alexandria. The supplies listed by Fitzgerald may have been for the Virginia troops captured at Charleston and held at Hadrell's Point, S.C.; a capt. Joseph CONWAY of the 10th Va. Line was a prisoner there (Gwathmey, *Hist. Reg. of Virginians in the Revolution*).

From Horatio Gates

SIR Hillsborough 3d October 1780.

I have the honor to inclose to Your Excellency Three Letters from Generals Sumner and Davidson, Commanding the No. Carolina Militia to the Westward. Contrary to my Express Orders Colo. Polk Commissary at Charlotte, collected 1500 or 2000 Bushels of Grain to his Mill there—a Bait I knew the Enemy would catch at, and repeatedly cautioned him against it, directing him never to have more than two Days Allowance for the Troops there, and in the Vicinity, and to have no fix'd Magazine, but collect his Grain at different Farms, West East and North, at Twenty Miles Distance from Charlotte, the Common Centre; but the Blow[1] is now hit, and we must act for the best in the Present Circumstances. Genl. Smallwood and Colonel Morgan will march this Day, with two Hundred Continental Light Infantry to the Ford upon the Yadkin, to form a strong Camp there; and by skirmishing with the Light Troops to be put under Col: Morgan, circumscribe the Enemy's Lines, and protect the surrounding Country. Should the

Enemy Advance in Force from Charlotte, and endeavor to pass the Ford upon the Yadkin, I shall march with all the Troops I can collect to sustain Genl. Smallwood. I expect all of the Continental Cavalry, and Major Nelson's Corps fitt for Service, will be here in to or three Days, they will march directly from hence to the Yadkin. I cannot think Ld. Cornwallis will[2] march further from Chas. Town, unless he is confident that Town, and his communication therewith, will be secured, by Reinforcements from Sir Hy. Clinton. This is a Bon Momment, for a Squadron of our Allies, to make their Appearance at Chas. Town. In that Case, I think it would be easy to carry the place, before The Earl could arrive to save it. But without a naval Armament, nothing can be done there. As Things stand at Present I must request your Excellency to press forward to Hillsborough the Supplies of Men, Provisions Carriages and Stores, so necessary, and so very much in request here. I am &c.,

HG

FC (NHi); endorsed: "Copy to Govr. Jefferson 3d October 1780." Tr (DLC: PCC, No. 71, I), originally enclosed in TJ's letter to Huntington, 8 Oct. 2d Tr (DLC: Washington Papers); 3d Tr (DLC: TJ Papers). Enclosures (missing): presumably (1) William Davidson to Gates, "Capt. Phipher's," 26 Sep.; (2) Jethro Sumner to Gates, Camp at the Yadkin Ford, 29 Sep.; (3) same to same, Camp McGoon's Creek, 1 Oct. 1780; all three are printed in *N.C. State Records*, XV, 83, 89-90, 90-1.

1 All copies read "blot," but "blow" must have been intended.

2 The word "not" is interlined here, but undoubtedly as a mistaken afterthought; it is not in the copies sent to Huntington and to Washington.

From Samuel Huntington

Philadelphia, 3 Oct. 1780. Circular letter to the state executives enclosing a resolve of Congress of 29 Sep. requesting the states "to supply their Delegates with Money for their Support by other Means than drawing on the Treasury of the United States."

RC (Vi); 2 p.; in a clerk's hand, signed by Huntington. FC (DLC: PCC, No. 15). Enclosure (Vi): copy signed by Charles Thomson of resolve of Congress of 29 Sep.; printed in JCC, XVIII, 876.

From Samuel Huntington

SIR Philada October 3. 1780

By the enclosed Copy of an Act of Congress of the 2. Instant your Excellency will be informed, that they approve of the Measures you have taken for remounting the Cavalry with the southern Army and request a Continuance of your Exertions for that Purpose on the same Principles as formerly.

I have the Honor to be with the greatest Regard your Excellency's most obedient Servant, SAM. HUNTINGTON President

P.S. Your Letter of the 26. Ultimo with the Despatches enclosed have been received and laid before Congress. Your Excellency will doubtless have received Intelligence of the aggravated Treason of Genl. Arnold before this comes to Hand.

RC (Vi); in a clerk's hand, signed by Huntington; endorsed: "resolve of Congress approvg the remountg Southern Cavalry. 1780 Oct 3d." FC (DLC: PCC, No. 15). Enclosure (Vi): copy signed by Charles Thomson of resolve of Congress of 2 Oct. approving TJ's measures concerning cavalry; printed JCC, XVIII, 889.

See TJ to Huntington, 8 Sep. 1780.

To Samuel Huntington

SIR Richmond Oct. 3. 1780.

I inclose you the within copies of letters transmitted me by Genl. Gates, according to his desire expressed in the one addressed to me. I shall endeavor as far as shall be in my power to have his several desires complied with.

I have the honor to be very respectfully Your Excellency's Most obedient & most humble servt., TH: JEFFERSON

RC (DLC: PCC, No. 71, I); endorsed by Charles Thomson: "Letter from Govr Octr. 3. 1780. enclosg G Elliot to Genl Gates Sept. 19 Gen Gates to Govr Jefferson—27 do. to col Finnie—27." The letter to TJ is printed above; a transcript of Finnie's letter is in DLC.

This letter and its enclosures were read in Congress on 9 Oct. (JCC, XVIII, 911).

To Edward Carrington

SIR Richmond Octr. 4th. 1780

The Provision Law pointed out no places for storing the provisions to be collected under it. It remained therefore for the Executive to do this. They accordingly, when they first appointed Commissioners, and sent them their Instructions pointed out the places at which they were to store their provisions. Halifax, Charlotte, Prince-Edward, Lunenburg, Mecklenburg Brunswick, Sussex and Southampton, were to Store theirs at any places they thought proper on the road leading from this place to Hillsborough. Richmond, Petersburg, Hoods, the College Landing, Smithfield, Portsmouth and Hampton, were appointed for the Counties on Appamatox and James River. The Counties on or convenient to York River, Rappahanock and Patowmack, were directed to store their Provisions at certain places on those Rivers. The Transportation to all these places, was to be by the Commissioners. Congress having required Sixty thousand ℔s. of Bacon to be sent Northwardly, The Collections on these three last Rivers were appropriated to that purpose. The Collections at the College Landing, Portsmouth, and Hampton, were principally intended for our Garrisons at or convenient to those places. A great deal of what was brought to Richmond, has been sent to the Barracks in Albemarle, and there being no probability of finding means of transportation to the Southward before the Bacon would spoil, I believe considerable part of what was stored at Petersburg, Hoods, and Smithfield, has been sent by Majr. Forsythe to the Northward. So that the part actually received for the Southern service, was only that Stored on the Southern Road, and part of the Collections at Richmond, Petersburg, Hoods, and Smithfield. This State of the Articles and appropriation of them only respects the old stock of the last Year. We have taken measures for collecting a large Quantity of Flour of the present Crop, which is all destined for the Southern service, and is to be collected almost solely on Appamatox and James Rivers. We have moreover sent an Agent, to procure, and send on to the Southern Army, all the Beeves which can be spared by the People. He begins with the Counties of Princess Anne and Norfolk and so is to proceed to others in order as they stand exposed to an enemy, Exhausting them as closely as possible. He has been gone three weeks or a Month, and I cannot but hope he has carried before this good supplies to that Army. He was directed to investigate carefully the Channels of Navigation Practicable from the lower Counties, on the South side of James River, that as soon as Corn shall be fit to be stored in Bulk, we may send Quantities of that by Water into the Neighbourhood of the Army. If some Channel cannot be found out, I am sure no supplies of that Article of any Consequence can be transported from this State. A Letter of mine not come to hand when yours of Septr. 29th was Written, will inform you of our Expectations as to the Batteaux. I wish you to put back as long as you possibly can the Draughts for Money, because we have none at present, and as the Assembly does not meet till the 15th (but say the 30th) instt. You may judge that it will still be later before they have produced a Replenishment to the Treasury. Moody is proceeding with his Waggons; Mr. Hunter can make none. We sent about three weeks ago, Agents to the Westward to buy a hundred Waggons and Teams. I am much pleased with Genl. Gates's Regulation to Stop our Waggons at Roanoke. This will put it visibly in our power, to repair and replace them, to calculate their Returns, provide Loads in time, and will be a great Encouragement to encrease their Number, as their Departure hence will no longer produce the Idea of a final Adieu to them. We are Enabling the Conductor of the Continental Laboratory to get to Work. I am with great respect Sir, Your most obedt hum St, TH JEFFERSON

Tr (DLC); both text and signature in a clerk's hand; endorsed.
A LETTER OF MINE . . . YOURS OF SEPTR. 29: Both missing.

To Horatio Gates

SIR Richmond Oct. 4th. 1780.

My Letter of Sept. 23d. answered your favours received before that date, and the present serves to acknowledge the receipt of those of Sept. 24th and 27th. I retain in mind and recur almost daily to your Requisitions of August; We have as yet no prospect of more than one hundred Tents. Flour is ordered to be manufactured as soon as the Season will render it safe, out of which I trust we can furnish not only your Requisition of August, but that of Congress of Sept. 11. The Corn you desire we could furnish when the New Crops come in, fully, if water Transportation can be found, if not we shall be able only to send you what lies conveniently to the Southern Boundary, in which neighbourhood the Crops have been much abridged by a flood in Roanoak. We have no Rice. Rum and other spirits we can furnish to a greater amount than you require, as soon as our Waggons are in readiness; and shall be glad to commute into that Article some others which we have not, particularly Sugar, Coffee, and Salt. The Vinegar is provided. Colo. Finnie promised to furnish to Colo. Muter, a list of the Spades, Hoes &c. which could be furnished from the continental Stores. This List has never yet come to hand. It is beleived the Continental Stores here will fall little short of your Requisition except in the Article of Axes; which our Shops are proceeding on. Your Information of Sept. 24th. as to the Quality of the Axes was notified to the Workman and will I hope have a proper Effect on those made afterwards. Application has been made to the Courts to have the Bridges put into a proper state, which they have promised to do. We are endeavouring again to collect Waggons. About twenty are nearly finished at this place. We employed about three weeks ago Agents to purchase in the Western Counties a hundred Waggons and Teams. 'Till these can be got it will be impossible to furnish any thing from this place. I am exceedingly pleased to hear of your Regulation for stopping our Waggons at Roanoke. This will put it in our power to repair and replace them, to calculate their Returns, provide loads, and be a great Encouragement to increase their number if possible, as their departure hence will no longer produce the Idea of a final adieu to them. Colo. Senf arrived here the Evening before the last. He was employed yesterday and to-day in copying some actual and accurate Surveys which we had made of the Country round about Portsmouth, as far as Cape Henry to the Eastward, Nansemond River to the Westward, the Dismal Swamp to the Southward, and Northwardly, the line of Country from Portsmouth by Hampton and York to Williamsburg and including the Vicinities of these three last posts. This will leave him nothing to do but to take drawings of particular places and the Soundings of such Waters as he thinks material. He will proceed on this Business to morrow with a Letter to General Nelson and powers to call for the Attendance of a proper Vessel. I suppose that your Draughts in favor of the Q.M. if attended with sixty days grace, may be complied with to a certain Amount. We will certainly use our best Endeavours to answer them. I am only to desire that they may be made payable to the Quarter Master only, and not to the Bearer. This is to prevent the Mortification of seeing an unapprised Individual taken in by an Assignment of them as if they were *ready Money*. Your Letter to Colo. Finnie will go to Wmsburg immediately. Those to Congress, with a Copy of the Papers inclosed to me, went yesterday by Express. I will take order as to the Bacon you mention. I fear there is little of it, and that not capable of being long kept. You are surely not uninformed that Congress required the greater part of this Article to be sent Northward, which has been done. I hope by this time you receive Supplies of Beeves from our Commissary Mr. Eaton, who was sent three weeks or a month ago to exhaust of that Article the Counties below and in the neighbourhood of Portsmouth; and from thence was to proceed to other Counties in Order as they stood exposed to an Enemy. The Arrival of the French W: India Fleet (which tho' not authentically communicated, seems supported by so many concurring Accounts from Individuals, as to leave scarcely room for doubt) will I hope prevent the Enemy from carrying into Effect the Embarkation they had certainly intended from N. York, tho' they are strengthened by the Arrival of Admiral Rodney at that place with twelve Sail of the line and four frigates as announced by General Washington to the Congress on the 19th Ult. The Accounts of the additional French Fleet are varied from sixteen to nineteen Ships of the line besides Frigates. The Number of the latter have been never mentioned. The Extracts of Letters which you will see in our Paper of this day are from Genl. Washington, President Huntington and our Delegates in Congress to me. That from Bladensburg is from a particular Acquaintance of mine whose Credit cannot be doubted. The distress we are experiencing for want of Leather to make Shoes is great. I am sure you have thought of preventing it in future by the Appointment of a Commissary of Hides, or some other good Regulation for saving and tanning the Hides, which the Consumption of your Army will afford.

I have the honor to be with all possible esteem and respect Sir Your most obedient & most humble servt., TH: JEFFERSON

RC (DLC); in a clerk's hand, with corrections, complimentary close, and signature by TJ. Endorsed: "From Govr: Jefferson 4th Octbr: 1780." Tr (DLC: PCC, No. 171), enclosed in Gates' letter to Huntington, 13 Oct.

COLO. SENF . . . WAS EMPLOYED . . . IN COPYING . . . SURVEYS: John (or Jean) Christian Senf, variously said to be of Danish or Swedish nationality but with connections in Saxony, was a military engineer who had held the rank of colonel of engineers in the South Carolina forces from Feb. 1779; he therefore declined an appointment as lieutenant colonel of engineers in the Virginia service offered him by TJ in Feb. 1781 (TJ to Senf, 21 Feb.; Senf to TJ, 26 Feb. 1781). TJ later urged his appointment as colonel (TJ to Harrison, 10 May 1781). It was Senf who brought the news of the disaster at Camden to Richmond late in Aug. 1780 and concerted measures with the Council and Gen. Muhlenberg until TJ's return to the capital (*N.C. State Records*, XIV, 574-5). Gates, who held a high opinion of Senf's abilities, sent him to Richmond early in October to examine the defenses and survey the southerly coastline of Virginia. Senf's first report, written from Portsmouth, 12 Oct., is in same, p. 688-90; he was still there when Leslie's invading force arrived, and he took part in the improvised defense of the Portsmouth region (see note on Gates to TJ, 14 Oct.). In the early part of 1781 he was the principal military engineer serving in Virginia; he supervised the fortifying of Hood's and Yorktown and was in charge of the rebuilding and enlargement of the shops and magazines at Westham after Simcoe's raid in January. After the Revolution Senf settled at Rocky Mount, Chester co., S.C., and was active as a builder and promoter of canals until his death in 1806; in 1799 he was considered by Washington for the post of chief engineer of the U.S. Army (*S.C. Hist. & Geneal. Mag.*, XXVIII [1927], 8-21, 112-31; same XLIV [1943], 69-70; Washington, *Writings*, ed. Fitzpatrick, XXXVII, 224). THE EXTRACTS OF LETTERS . . . IN OUR PAPER OF THIS DAY: In *Va. Gaz.* (D & N), 4 Oct. 1780, are brief extracts of five letters; one is dated from Bergen co. (N.J.), 11 Sep. (from George Washington, q.v., above); three are dated from Philadelphia, 16, 18, and 19 Sep.; and one from Bladensburg (Md.), 26 Sep. The three from Philadelphia cannot be equated with any surviving letters to TJ; all of them report the presumed arrival of "the second French fleet" off the American coast, and those of 18 and 19 Sep. also report the arrival of Admiral Rodney's British fleet off Sandy Hook. The letter from Bladensburg is printed above under 26 Sep. 1780.

From Theodorick Bland

Sr [Philadelphia, ca. 5 October 1780]

Some overtures having been made to Congress, through Mr. Jay our Commissioner at the Court of Madrid, for Building Frigates in America for and on account of his Catholic Majesty and the Proposals having been referred to the Admiralty to Confer with the Navy Boards of the Eastern and Middle district and obtain from them estimates of what would be the Cost of a frigate of forty Guns, and there being no Navy Board in Virginia it was moved in Congress by the Delegates from that State, that the Admiralty should also lay before Congress Estimates of the Cost &c. of Building such frigates in Virginia in which it would be proper to specify the terms, and the time it would take to Compleat one or more such frigates. We have thought it Proper to inform you thereof, that proper persons may be applyed to, to make out such Estimates for Government, in order that they may be given in to the Admiralty to report upon to Congress, as we are not willing that such lucrative, and advantageous contracts, the Execution of which must in the end be attended with so many advantages should be lost to our state and engrossed by others already so far advanced before us in the Establishing a Marine. This Estimate transmitted as early as possible will put it in the power of the Delegates from Virginia to press its being transmitted to our Commissioner at Madrid with the Estimates from the Other States, and the subject itself together with a speedy compliance we have no doubt will strike you in the same important light in which it has us. The perfect tranquility which has reigned here with regard to news has been lately disturbed by a most extraordinary and unexpected event, no less than the sudden defection of Major Genl. Arnold from the American Cause, and his flight to the Enemy. [He o]n the   ultimo[1] Shamefully treacherously and ignominiously deserted the important Post at West point which Garrison he Commanded, after having Concerted Measures with the British Adjutant Genl. Colo. André in the Quality of a spy for delivering it up to the Enemy, with the Blackest Circumstances of treason and Perfidy that ever enterd the heart of any, wretch, but his own. Our Great General Washington, the French Ambassador and the Marquis de la fayette were to have been his Peace offering to the Enemy. But Mr. Andre was accidentally taken, by a small party of Militia and is now in our Hands and has probably before this paid his last tribute of Loyalty to his Royal Master together with his infamous Coadjutor Joseph Smith of N. York, occasioned Arnolds precipitate flight on board a British Man of War, which was ready to receive him in case of Accident. The General and other Gentlemen above Mentiond arrived at Arnolds Quarters a few minutes after his flight, and he has taken effectual measures to prevent further Mischief. Arnold has wrote him a letter dated on Board the Vulture sloop imploring his interposition in favor of his Wife whom he has left behind. His Papers have been seized in this City where he some time ago resided and lay open several scenes of Vilany transacted in the Commercial way while he had the Command here between him and other Miscreants, and have laid a train perhaps for further discoveries. Quid non mortalia pectora cogis Auri Sacra fames? Every Mark of horror and resentment has been expressed by the Army at such atrocious and Complicated Vilainy, And the Mob in this City have burnt the traitor in Effigy after Exposing it through the streets with a long purse in one hand and a Mask in the other and labels descriptive of the Character thus [consigned?] to public infamy and odium. Thus with [. . .] faded the laurels of a hero, and the apellat[ion . . .] Arnold must be everlastingly changed for [. . .]tive of the Blackest infa[my].

Dft (NHi); endorsed: "Rough drt of letter, from Col. Theok Bland Jr to Govr. Jefferson." MS mutilated; signature missing; date conjecturally established from Bland's reference to the treachery of Benedict Arnold on 25 Sep. 1780; moreover, Burnett, who prints part of his letter (*Letters of Members*, v, No. 470), points out that the plan of building frigates was to come before Congress on 5 Oct.; see his note on this matter.

JOSEPH SMITH: Joshua Hett Smith, who lived near Haverstraw on the Hudson; he was acquitted of complicity in the Arnold-André plot (Van Doren, *Secret History*, p. 289-90, and frequently).

1 The day is left blank in MS.

From William Eaton

[*Place not known*, *5 Oct. 1780*. In a letter to Gen. Gates, 15 Oct. 1780, TJ says: "As to provisions, our Agent Eaton . . . informs me in a letter of the 5th. inst. he shall immediately get Supplies of Beef into Motion and shall send some corn by a circuitous Navigation." Not found.]

From Horatio Gates

SIR Hillsborough 5. October 1780.

Since writing my last Letter to your Excellency I have received the inclosed from Genl. Sumner, whose Camp is at Macgoens

Creek one Mile from the ford of the Yadkin. I send my Letter to the President of Congress under a flying Seal that you may peruse it. I beg that with all the Letters and papers, I now send your Excellency may be as soon as possible dispatched to Congress. I am Sir your obedient humble servant, HORATIO GATES

P.S. The inclosed Letter [from Lt. Co]lo. Washington, will acquaint you with all the Continental and Cavalry of your State we have to depend upon.

RC (DLC: PCC, No. 154, II). Endorsed by Thomson: "Letter from Major genl Gates to Govr. Jefferson Octr. 5. 1780 Read Octr. 13." Enclosures (same location): (1) Jethro Sumner to Gates, Camp at the Yadkin Ford, 29 Sep. 1780 which in turn enclosed a (missing) "examination of 4 British prisoners taken at Charlotte"; (2) W[illiam] Washington to Gates, place illegible, 4 Oct. 1780. Gates' letter and enclosures were transmitted by TJ to Huntington, 8 Oct., q.v. Tr of letter is in DLC: Washington Papers.

Sumner's LETTER reports that the enemy continue in Charlotte and are estimated as between 2,000 and 3,000 strong; Sumner has detached two companies of horse to reconnoiter and to prevent their plundering the inhabitants; there have been some small actions; Ferguson (i.e. Maj. Patrick Ferguson) is just reported at Burke Court House, "which seems to indicate an intention of forming a junction with Lord Cornwallis."

To James Wood

SIR Richmond Oct. 5th. 1780.

I received a Letter from General Gates on the 14th. Sept. communicating Intelligence which he had received of a design meditated by the Enemy to make a lodgement at Portsmouth in this State. Tho' I thought it very improbable under the then existing Circumstances it was yet my duty to communicate it to Congress and apprise them of our general Situation. In my Letter was this paragraph. 'another circumstance should be previously determined on Supposition that an Invasion of this State should take place. A Spirit of disaffection, which had never been suspected, has lately discovered itself in the Counties of Washington, Montgomery, Henry and Bedford and had extended so far as that many hundreds had actually enlisted to serve his Britannic Majesty, had taken Oaths of Allegiance to him, and had concerted the time of Insurrection. The last of the Counties above mentioned is within sixty or seventy Miles of the Barracks in Albemarle, and had always been considered as a Barrier to any Enterprise on them from the Southward. Other Counties equally relied on may fail us in the Hour of trial. Should an Invasion of this State take place, and the progress of the Enemy, or other Circumstances render a Removal of the Convention Troops necessary, to what place should they be removed? I would beg the Instructions of Congress on this head, and at this time, that we may at no future Time be at a loss when such a measure shall be rendered necessary.' The Letter of the Board of War of Sept. 21st: was probably in consequence of mine. It has since appeared that the Enemy had meditated a great Embarkation, it's destination unknown, tho' generally beleived for the Southward. The Arrival of the French West India Fleet (tho' not announced by public Authority, yet supported by so many concurring Informations from private Hands as to leave little Room for doubt) has probably prevented this movement, notwithstanding their being strengthened by the Arrival of Admiral Rodney with twelve Sail of the line and four frigates. The Accounts of the strength of the additional French Fleet vary from sixteen to nineteen sail of the line besides Frigates. The arrival of this Fleet must be put out of doubt before the Regiment mentioned in the Letter of the Board of War will have reached Orange Court House. Should it have actually arrived, it will effectually prevent any Embarkation from N. York, in which case that Regiment should make no Halt at Orange Court House or elsewhere, but make the best of their way to Hillsborough, where they are certainly wanted. By this Conveyance I send to Colo. Crockett his final Orders. I take for granted that some time will intervene between his Receipt of them and his actual march; sufficient probably to ascertain us of the Arrival of the French Fleet. Should it however be otherwise, I would be glad to be informed by Express of the day fixed on for his march, whenever it shall be fixed on with any certainty of its taking place, as under our present uncertainties I should think it proper to detain him till the actual Situation of things to the Northward is better known. Should it ever become necessary to remove the convention Troops you may be assured of being strengthened with Militia to your wish. I should be glad to have your disabled Arms sent here for Repair, unless you can have them Repaired at your post. There is no flag going hence to N. York, but Expresses pass on to General Washington every week almost. I will send the Letters of the Convention Officers by this channel and desire them to be forwarded by flag. Captains Jones, Fergusone, Coote, and Mr. McCarty have permission to remove their Quarters to Byram Ballard's in Orange. The necessary change of parole you will of course have made.

I am with great esteem Sir Your most obedient humble servt.,

TH: JEFFERSON

RC (Lloyd W. Smith, Madison, N.J., 1946); in a clerk's hand, with corrections, complimentary close, and signature by TJ; endorsed: "Govr. Jefferson 5th. Oct. 1780." Addressee identified from internal evidence.

A LETTER FROM GENERAL GATES: That of 9 Sep. 1780, q.v. TJ's LETTER to Congress was dated 14 Sep. 1780. THE LETTER OF THE BOARD OF WAR OF SEPT. 21ST (not found) was perhaps written to Wood. FINAL ORDERS to Crockett: See TJ to Crockett, 27 Sep. 1780.

From Horatio Gates

SIR Hillsborough 6th: October 1780.

Forty of your 18 Months Men from Bottetourt County Arrived in this Camp Yesterday, they are intirely unequiped, and unprovided, with every thing that is necessary for the Service they are intended to perform, and for the Term they are engaged to serve. I must beg Sir this may be Seriously consider'd by the Executive, whom I must request, will not send any Men into the Field, or even to this Camp, that are not sufficiently Clad, well furnish'd with Shoes, Blankets, and every necessary for immediate Service, as I have not a Single Article here to Supply them with. Some Tent Cloth, and Linnens, are all that can be procured from the Prize I wrote to your Excellency about sometime ago; nor can the Board of war of This State, from every part of it, find sufficient to Equip their Own—not a Blanket to be purchased at any Price. In regard to the Rendezvous of the Militia, I must entreat Your Excellency will fix upon some place from whence they can be well Supplied with Provisions, and Carriages, for they ought not to Quit the State of Virginia, unless they bring Thirty days of the Bread Kind with them. Inclosed are Copies of Letters received Last night from the Westward, and One Original from Mr. Hooper of this State. I request they may be forwarded immediately to Congress. Surely it is Time, some Determind Resolve of that Honourable Body, should be sent to Lord Cornwallis, to restrict his unjustifiable and Tyranical Proceedings; no part of my Baggage, nor a Single Public, or private paper of mine, fell into Lord Cornwallis's Hands. They were very Fortunately all saved as was every paper and private Letter of all the Gentlemen belonging to my Family. I also inclose Your Excellency a Copy of a Letter of Lord Cornwallis's, and another of Lt. Col. Balfours, taken upon Spy.

I am Sir &c., HG

Dft (NHi); endorsed. Tr (DLC) of Dft. Enclosures: presumably the papers transmitted by TJ to Huntington, 14 Oct., q.v. The missing recipient's copy of this letter must have been dated 7 Sep., since TJ in his acknowledgment of 15 Oct. so dates it; moreover, the text of Dft is evidently incomplete, for

TJ quotes one sentence in his reply that is not in Dft.

On 10 Oct. Gates wrote to Muhlenberg (Dft: NHi) about this "party of Forty three Men under Lieutt. Smith . . . from Botetourt County" who had arrived "in a manner Naked, being intirely unsupported with a Single Article a Soldier ought to Possess," and added: "Colonel Buford says, he Expects More of these Eighteen Months Men will shortly arrive in Camp from the Adjacent Counties." In view of this, Gates requested Muhlenberg either to provide these men with clothing and other materials or else cause them to rendezvous in Virginia where they could be more conveniently fitted out.

From Samuel Huntington

Sir   Philadelphia October 6. 1780

Your Excellency will receive herewith enclosed an Act of Congress of the 21. Ulto. containing a new Arrangement of the Army. Special Reasons have delayed the sending of it until this Time.

By this Arrangement the Number of Battallions is greatly reduced, and of Consequence many of the Officers now retained in the Service must retire for the present; but after just and equitable Compensation is made to them, the Saving of Expence will be very great.

Congress are extremely anxious, not only to avoid the Dangers and Embarrassments heretofore experienced by Delays in recruiting the Army until the Opening of the Campaign; but also to establish a permanent Army, of Troops engaged for the War, to consist of such Numbers as may be adequate to the Service, and at the same Time not exceed the Ability of the States to raise and support, and constantly recruit so as to keep up the Number.

It is recommended to the States in the most pressing Manner to have their Regiments completed and in the Field by the first Day of January next at farthest. The Commander in Chief will cause immediate returns to be made of the Deficiencies of each State according to this Arrangement.

You will observe Sir, that the respective States are to select from the Line of the Army the Number of Officers to command the several Regiments to them respectively assigned; taking Notice that no new Appointment is to be made of higher Rank than Lieut. Colonel Commandant, for substantial Reasons supposed to be known to all the States.

But the first and immediate Object is to complete the Regiments to their full Number of non Commissioned Officers and Privates; which is recommended in the most pressing Manner as of the greatest Importance.

I have the Honor to be with the highest Respect your Excellency's most obedient Servant, SAM HUNTINGTON President

RC (Lloyd W. Smith, Madison, N.J, 1946); in a clerk's hand, signed by Huntington; endorsed: "Congress resolutions &c papers respecting the Arrangement of the Army—referred to in the Governors Letter of Novr: 7th:—November 30th: 1780 Referred to a Committee of Arrangement" (see entry for TJ to Harrison, 7 Nov., transmitting the present letter). FC (DLC: PCC, No. 15); at head of text: "Circular." Enclosure missing.

The debate on the NEW ARRANGEMENT OF THE ARMY was not completed until 3 Oct. 1780; and the enclosed ACT OF CONGRESS OF THE 21. ULTO was presumably a copy of the resolutions as finally passed (printed in JCC, XVIII, 893-7).

From George Mason

DEAR SIR Fairfax County, Gunston-Hall Octob. 6th. 1780.

This will be delivered You by my Son William, who commands the Militia Company ordered from this County to Carolina: The Men are mostly Volunteers; who turned out from the Battalion at large, without any Regard to the Divisions to which they belonged; there are among them Several Soldiers, and three or four Serjeants who had served out their Time in the Virginia Line on Continental Establishment; so that I look upon it to be equal to any Militia Company in the State: I intreat You Sir to order them to be furnished with good Musquets and Bayonets &c. It is a most discouraging Circumstance to a Young fellow to lead Men into Action, without proper Arms; and I fear the former Regiments of Militia, serving to the Southward, have thrown away and lost so many of their Arms, that they can have little Dependence in being properly supplyed on their Arrival at Hillsborough.

The Militia I presume are to be paid in Tobacco which they can't receive until after their Return, and must in the mean time be distressed a good deal for many things they will want in the Service; I don't recollect whether any Money is advanced them on this Account; You will be pleased to give my Son the necessary Information and Orders respecting it.

The late Draught for the regular Service, has been not only quietly, but cheerfully executed in this, and the neighbouring Countys; and the subsequent Requisition from the Militia has, in this County, been complied with, with the utmost Alacrity; I have not yet heard how it has been executed in the adjacent Countys; but I think there is little Danger of Resistance, where the leading Men are true Whigs, and possessed of common Discretion. I understand the Draft has been resisted, and prevented in some of the lower Countys, and some Lives lost; which I am not at all surprized at: if such dangerous Meetings are not effectually quelled, and the Ring-leaders punished, our Government can't subsist: if the Civil Power of the Countys where they have happened is insufficient, I hope the Military Force, lately raised, will afford Means of doing it: if the Truth cou'd be discovered, I doubt not but some of their principal Men are privately at the Bottom of it.

I am much concerned to hear You intend at the End of the present Campaign, to resign the Office of supreme Magistrate; I wish You could be prevailed on to hold it at least 'til after the next general Election; for I really dread the Choice which the present Assembly may make.

As my very ill Health, at present, makes my attendance at the next Session of Assembly rather uncertain, I take this Opportunity, by my Son, of sending You a few of the Portugal, and best kind of Rare-ripe Peach Stones. Almost all my Portugal peaches were stolen this Year before they were ripe; but I saved the few Stones I send you myself, and know they are the true Sort. I have observed this kind of Peach requires more Care than most others, and if the Trees are not tended, and the Ground cultivated, the Fruit is apt to be coarse and harsh; with due Culture the Peaches are the finest I ever tasted.

I beg my Compliments to your Lady; and am with the greatest Esteem and Respect Dr. Sir Yr. most Obt. svt., G. MASON

P.S. The sooner the Peach Stones are planted the better; if it is deferred 'til late in the winter, very few will come up next Spring; they should be secured from the Moles by Slabs, or some such thing, let into the Ground.

RC (DLC). William Mason was appointed captain of the Fairfax militia in 1778 (Gwathmey, *Hist. Reg. of Virginians in the Revolution*).

Petition of Certain Deserters, with Jefferson's Observations

[Before 7 October 1780]

To his Excellency Thomas Jefferson Esqr. Governor of Virginia, and the Honble. Members of the Council.

The petition of sundry persons whose Names are hereto Subscribed, most humbly sheweth,

That your said Petitioners being of the Goochland Militia lately March'd to Hillsborough in divisions, and with shame and Sorrow acknowledge the disgracefull rout your said Petitioners, with most of the Militia soon after sustain'd, but the[y] humbly hope that when plain facts are made known to your Honble Board, it will in some measure take off the Odium your said Petitioners at the time labours under; Being raw and ignorant of discipline and under officers (generally) as undisciplin'd as your Petitioners, who being Order'd not to fire, untill they had the word, and then to advance with charg'd Bayonetts occasion'd the Confusion which soon follow'd. When your said Petitioners arriv'd at Hillsborough, destitute of money, a Shirt to shift th[em,] and even Clothes to wear, apply'd to their Officers for leave to come in and procure such Supplies as their poor families could furnish, altho' such permission was not obtain'd, yet with the Connivance of several of their Officers they came in, and with the utmost diligence were returning back, met sundry of their old Companions who said they would not be receiv'd at Head Quarters, but were deem'd Continental Soldiers for Eight Months.

Your said Petitioners having no intention of desertion, then deliver'd themselves up to the County Lieutenant, and are now under Marching Orders. They wish not to Repine at their Lott, in performing a Tour of duty in so good a Cause, but most of them being very poor Men, with family's of small Children unable to Labour, must enevitably loose great part of their Stocks, by the shortness of their present Crops. What then must be the distresses of their helpless families the ensuing Year, should they be deem'd Soldiers Eight Months longer.

Your Petitioners therefore pray, that your Honourable Board will be Graciously pleas'd to take the premisses under your Consideration and remit the additional service, and your Petitioners shall ever pray &c.

David England	John Askew	[Arthur Slaughter?]
Benjamin [Adams?]	Robert George	William Cosby
David Mitchel	Nathan Wingfield	Buucer Carrol
Aaron [Nash?]	Ruben [Slaughter?]	Humphrey Parrish
Thomas [Minton?]	James Busby	John Gilliam
Robert Groom	Eleaser Williams	William Utley
		⟨*Peter Walker*⟩

Goochd. Sc.

The Subscribers as soon as they came into said County delivered up themselves to me and are, and seem willing to March immedeatly to Hillsborough.

John Woodson C. Lt. Goochd.

I think the within Pettition reasonable and True.

Jno. Hopkins
Jolley Parrish
John Curd

I have no power to remit the sentence of the law, nor do [I] know any power which can, except the General assembly unless the Commander in chief to the Southward shou[ld] think proper to discharge the petitioners at any certain point of time short of the eight months, which it does not appear probable to me he will do.

Octob. 7. 1780 Th: Jefferson

MS (Vi). Body of petition in an unidentified hand; a few of the signers' names are evidently signatures, but most of them were written down by some one person who had good intentions but atrocious penmanship, and hence some are illegible. The officers' certifications are in other hands and are signed in autograph. TJ's note at the end was written, signed, and dated by him.

This interesting document suggests the difficulties faced by both the common citizen when an enemy army was nearby and by a humane executive attempting to enforce laws designed to keep a citizen army in the field. See TJ to Edward Stevens, 19 July 1780. The militia had been embodied to march southward by an act passed early in the May session (Hening, x, 221-6), but a little later, when the enemy actually approached Virginia, the legislature passed an "act for giving further powers to the governour and council," which provided that deserters from the militia should be court-martialed, compelled to serve eight months longer in the state forces, and be subject during that time to the Continental articles of war (Hening, x, 314). To support their petition, some of the deserters from the Goochland militia submitted depositions testifying that their officers had encouraged them to "come in" (i.e., return home), since they were helpless as a fighting force without clothing or arms. In Vi is a group of three such depositions, certified by Thomas F. Bates, a justice of Goochland co. They are all written on one page; the first of them reads as follows:

"Virginia, Goochland County Sct:

"Booker Carrell and William Cosby two of the Militia lately return'd from Hillsborough, being first duly Sworn, deposeth and saith, that at the time some of the Men from said County were about to leave Camp on their way home, Capt. Edmund Curd ask'd the deponent Carrell, if he was coming in with the others. Said Carrell reply'd that he should come if able. Capt. Curd then said, he would be Damned if he did not, was he in the deponents place, and gave said Carrell a Book to bring in, and further these deponents saith not.

his
Booker + Carrell
mark

his
Wm. + Cosby"
mark

Some of the local courts-martial refused to impose the eight-months' penalty; see Gen. Stevens to TJ, 30 Oct. 1780.

Appointment of a Commissioner of the Provision Law

SIR Virginia in Council Octo: 8. 1780.

You are hereby appointed a Commissioner under the act for procuring a supply of provisions and other necessaries for the use of the army, but restrained specially to the procuring the articles enumerated in the said act, and live cattle for the subsistance of the continental regiment of guards marching to the barracks in Albemarle and again to march from there shou'd they be found unnecessary at the barracks. You are in the first instance if it can be done with any convenience to call on the Continental commissaries, or on the commissioners of the same provision law appointed in each county thro' which the said regiment is to march, to furnish provisions for their subsistance during their stay at any place within this state, or on their march thro' the same. Your receipt to such commissioners shall be to them a good voucher for the delivery of any articles you shall call on them for, notwithstanding any former orders we may have given to deliver them otherwise. If neither the said commissioners nor commissaries can furnish you with subsistance you are in that case to exercise the powers hereby given you. When you shall have fully executed this commission or your attendance on the troops for the purposes thereof or[1] this commission shall be dispensed with by any officer having authority so to do, this commission is to determine, and you are to transmit to me by safe conveyances, duplicate Lists of all the certificates or receipts you shall have given for articles hereby submitted to your seizure, specifying the name of the [owner,] the article seized, the price to be paid, and the date of the Certificate. That you may be informed of the manner in which you are to proceed in the execution of this commission you will receive herewith a copy of the provision law, and an extract from another act, relative to the particular article of live stock.

I am sir, Your humble servant, THO: JEFFERSON

Tr in the War Office Letter Book (MiU-C). The following note appears in the margin: "this power was enclosed to major Foresythe; to be directed to any person he thought proper." (The letter to Robert Forsyth is missing.) Enclosures: see note on a similar appointment, 29 Aug. 1780. See also TJ to Messrs. Ball, et al., under date of 2 Nov. 1780.

[1] MS: "of"; an obvious error by the copyist.

To Samuel Huntington

SIR Richmond Oct. 8. 1780.

At the desire of Majr. Genl. Gates I do myself the honour of transmitting you the inclosed papers sent by him to me, and copies also of his letters to me.

I have the honor to be with the most profound respect Your Excellency's Most obedt. & most humble servt., TH: JEFFERSON

RC (DLC: PCC, No. 71, I); endorsed by Thomson: "Letter from Gov Jefferson Oct 8. 1780 Read 13." Enclosures: Gates to Huntington, 5 Oct. (DLC: PCC, No. 154, II); Gates to TJ, 5 Oct.; and presumably the enclosures in the latter, q.v. See JCC, XVIII, 920, 921.

To James Wood

[Richmond, October 8, 1780]

Mr. Martin receives body shirts and hunting shirts for the regiment of guards, clothing for the officers, and some for yourself. Your portion being not equal to what you expected it becomes my duty to explain it. On the discontinuance of the board of War the Executive finding that the method which had been followed of issuing individual orders for clothing had produced great inequality they determined from thence forward to make general issues only and under general rules which should be applied to all cases. . . . I understand from Mr. Martin that it happens that you have received some clothing since the passing of the act, which (however you were in arrears before) it becomes necessary under the regulations to take it into account now.

RC privately owned and not available for publication. Text (extracts only) from Stan V. Henkels' sale catalogue No. 1418, 9 Oct. 1928 (Newbold Sale), lot 24, where the original is described as "A.L.S. 2 pp., small 4to . . . with address."

From Horatio Gates

SIR Hillsborough 9th. October 1780.

As we are much Distress'd for Carriages to Transport Provisions and Stores for this Army; I must beg Leave to request, Your Excellency, will prevail upon the Executive of Virginia to Order a Brigade of Ten Waggons from each of the Neighbouring Counties of this State from Mecklinbourg ⟨*Hallifax*, *Pittsylvania*, *& Henry*⟩ North Westward to Transport Stores, and provisions

⟨*from Taylors Ferry to Hillsborough*⟩; which Service, they shall Bona Fide be employ'd in, and not impress'd, or taken for any Other Use; when they have been One Month upon the Communication, they shall be Discharged. And I trust Your Excellency, and the Executive, will take proper Measures to have them Finally relieved by Others, so that a Succession may regularly take place to assist in Waggoning the Supplies so much Wanted for the Southern Army; I wrote to Your Excellency Yesterday, and inclosed You a Number of Letters, and papers, relative to the State of Public Affairs this way. I wish to hear you have received that Dispatch, as well as all those I have at Times Sent Your Excellency for more than a Month Past.

I am Sir &c HG

Dft (NHi). Tr (DLC) of Dft.

I WROTE TO YOUR EXCELLENCY YESTERDAY: An error; Gates' last letter was that of 6 Oct.—a letter evidently not sent until 7 Oct. (see under the former date). The present letter may, of course, have been drafted on the 8th.

Henry Hamilton's Parole

I Henry Hamilton Lieutenant Governour and Superintendent of Detroit do hereby acknowledge myself a Prisoner of War to the Commonwealth of Virginia and having permission from his Excellency Thomas Jefferson Governor of the said Commonwealth to go to New York do pledge my faith and most sacredly promise upon my Parole of Honor that I will not do, say, write or cause to be done, said or written directly or indirectly in any Respect whatsoever any thing to the Prejudice of the United States of America, or of any of them untill I shall be enlarged from my Captivity by Exchange or otherwise with the Consent of the said Governor of Virginia or his Successors and that I will return when required by the said Governour or his Successors[1] to such place within the said Commonwealth as he shall point out and deliver myself up again to him or the Person acting for or under him.

In testimony whereof I have hereunto set my hand and seal at Chesterfield this 10th day of October 1780. Henry Hamilton

The within mentioned having signed a Parole of which the within is a Copy, has permission to go to New York, and to remain within such parts of that State as are in possession of the Armies of his Britannick Majesty until he shall be exchanged, or otherwise liberated with consent of the Governor of Virginia for the time being, or until he shall be recalled by him. Given under my hand and the Seal of the CommonWealth of Virginia at Richmond date within written. TH: JEFFERSON

MS (Vi). In two different clerks' hands, signed by Hamilton and by TJ; seal accompanies each signature. Endorsed: "Gov Hamiltons Parole."

This parole is not identical in text with that refused by Hamilton on 1 Oct. 1779, q.v., but it does contain the prohibition of speaking against the United States that Hamilton had objected to in 1779. An identical parole (also in Vi) was accepted by Maj. Jehu Hay on the same day. On the Hamilton case generally, see TJ to Theodorick Bland, 8 June 1779, and references there.

[1] Preceding fourteen words interlined in TJ's hand.

To Samuel Huntington

[*Richmond, 10 Oct. 1780.* JCC, XVIII, 957-8 (21 Oct.): "A letter, of 10, from Governor Jefferson was read; Whereupon, *Resolved*, That the reasons assigned by his excellency Governor Jefferson for inviting Oconostota and a few other principal warriors of the Cherokee nation to visit Congress and the Commander in Chief and army are wise and prudent, and that Governor Jefferson's letter with the papers enclosed, be referred to the Board of War, who are directed to take order for the accommodation of the said chiefs on their arrival." TJ's letter has not been found, though a copy of Congress' resolve approving the visit was enclosed in Huntington's reply of 21 Oct., q.v. The visit itself never took place, for the reasons given in TJ's letter to Huntington, 17 Feb. 1781.]

From Samuel Huntington

Philadelphia, 10 Oct. 1780. Enclosing a resolve of Congress of 7 Oct. "appointing Commissioners to endorse the new Bills of Credit to be issued by Virginia, and Letters to the Gentlemen informing them of their Appointment." A postscript acknowledges TJ's letters of 27 Sep. and 3 Oct.

RC (Vi); 2 p.; in a clerk's hand, signed by Huntington; endorsed. Enclosures: 2 copies (Vi) attested by Charles Thomson of resolution of 7 Oct., appointing Charles Fleming and Forster (i.e., Foster) Webb commissioners to endorse bills emitted by Virginia (printed in JCC, XVIII, 910-11); letters of appointment to Fleming and Webb (not found). FC (DLC: PCC, No. 15).

From Walter McClurg

MAY IT PLEASE YOUR EXCELLENCY Hampton Octbr. 10th. 1780.

Having received an Apointment from the Board of Warr First of last March, to A Marine Hospital at Hampton and also have gave my Advice and Assistance to the Small Garrison here in Absence of their Surgeon, I have wrote Col. Muter Inclosing an Invoice for Medicines and Other Necessaries some Months past have received no Answre. As Several patients under my care are now Suffering for want of them I intreat your Excellency to give the necessary Orders to those concerned, to forward them by first Opportunity, as I know not to whom to apply having failed through Col. Muter. Bark. Wine and Vinegar much wanted for an Unfortunate Youth who received a shott in his Breast shatter'd one of Ribbs went through his lungs and cutt Out Just Below his Shoulder blade.

As I have served the State as Surgeon to Sailors and Soldiers ever since June 76. (A small Interval from Your Excellences Dismission on 19th. of Janry. last to the First of March Excepted) I hope and expect that Your Excellency and the Honourable Council will consider me and fix my pay on the first footing of ten Shillings Old Money or Fifty pounds of Tobacco ℔ day, as I Know not at present what I am to receive with the Customary priviledges. I am Your Excellances Obedient humble Servt., WA: McCLURG

RC (Vi); addressed and endorsed. At foot of text (in TJ's hand except the first word): "refd to Colo. Muter. Th: Jefferson."

Walter McClurg, formerly an English army surgeon, lived at Hampton; he was father of TJ's college friend James McClurg (Blanton, *Medicine in Va. in the 18th Cent.*, p. 328). See further, Muter to TJ, 19 Oct.

From George Washington

SIR Hd Qrs near Passaick Falls Octr. 10th 1780.

On Sunday Evening I had the honor to receive Your Excellency's Letters of the 23d and 26th of last Month. I am happy to find by the former and the Letter You were so obliging as to forward from Colo. Wood that the Convention troops are now comfortably supplied. I hope this will be the case and that the mode You have in contemplation to adopt will answer your expectations. Colo. Wood's conduct is highly pleasing to me, and merits the public esteem. It is such as I fully expected. He has not himself suggested the most distant hint of his intentions to quit the post, or I should most strongly urge his continuance. I shall however in a Letter to him of this date take occasion to mention his good conduct, the services he has rendered, and those that will be derived to the public from his continuing in the command.

It gives me pleasure to hear that the New Levies are rendezvousing so generally. I fear they will be but too much wanted, from the measures I think it highly probable the Enemy will pursue this fall and Winter, especially during the latter, as they will not be under any apprehension of the force we shall then have in this Quarter, and will be at liberty to make almost any detachments they please. The dissolution of half our Army last fall and winter enabled them to make the Detachments they did against Charles Town, which has involved so many serious consequences, and the same cause will put them in a condition to push their operations or at least to attempt it, in the course of this, in the Southern States. While we persevere in the system of short inlistments we shall experience misfortune and disgrace, and ultimately if it is persisted in we shall, most probably, lose the cause in which we are engaged. The arrangement You intend of part of the Draughts for Colo. Harrison's Regiment is perfectly agreable and I think proper. The matter did not occur to me, and if it had I should not have thought myself at liberty to have directed the appropriation, as I understood the Object of the Act, by which the Levies were raised, was to apply them to filling or replacing the Regiments of Infantry. It would be a most desireable thing, if we had Magazines of Arms, Ammunition, Cloathing, and Tents formed as Your Excellency mentions, but unhappily this is not the case, nor have we a store of these essential Articles at any point. A Letter I had the honor of addressing You on the 11th of Sepr. will have informed You of our situation in these respects. I am sorry to find that the Southern Army suffers for provision, and from the cause which contributes powerfully to our Embarrasments here—the want of transportation. This is now become a difficulty in our Affairs of the most serious consideration, and, our situation admitting of no alternative, I have been obliged to use coercive measures, such as impresses, frequently in the course of the Campaign, to enable me to move the Army and to bring it supplies. We are at this moment destitute of a drop of Rum for the Soldiery, and cannot obtain some Blankets we have at the Eastward, for want of transportation. As to the provision supplies which You have procured it would be most eligible to keep them for Southern demands. This seems to have been fully the intention of Congress by their Act of the 8th Ulto. for forming Magazines of provision and forage for 15000 Men for 6 Months for the S. Army, and directing Two thirds of the quota of the flour and Beef, which had been required from Maryland, to be retained for that purpose. I took the liberty in my Letter of the 11th of Septr. to recommend to Your Excellency the removal of such as was collected on Navigable Rivers, from the reports which I had then received that the Enemy were about to embark troops and as some supposed for Virginia. As to the French fleet, I don't think it probable that it will winter in the Chesapeak. The Enemy have a superior force to it in these seas and have held it blocked up ever since it arrived. This circumstance, supposing other considerations out of the question, would prevent the measure while it continues inferior.

I thank Your Excellency for the inclosures contained in Your Letter of the 26th which I have not received through any other Channel. Lord Cornwallis's Letter establishes beyond doubt that his loss in the affair of the 16th of August was considerable, tho his report with respect to ours is not admissible. He seems determined to try what severity will do. I hope sooner or later he will be stopped in his career, and that the rigorous policy he is pursuing will contribute to this. It would appear from Genl. Harrington's Letter as if the Enemy had left Campden, but this seems highly improbable unless they were advancing. The information of the Spaniards was premature as to the captures they mentioned, or at least the latest advices I have seen from the Havannah were silent about them. The Count de Guichen has not appeared in this Quarter yet tho he may have been on the Coast as they related. Your Excellency's Letter with respect to Lt. Govr. Hamilton and Major Hay gives the satisfaction I wished. I only wanted information on the point, that I might know how to conduct myself with propriety and agreable to the views of the State.

With respect to the reduction of Detroit I have ever considered it as an event much to be desired, but we have never been in circumstances to attempt it. This will be less the case the ensuing winter than at any period almost before, nor do I conceive myself at liberty to say an expedition may be undertaken against it in the manner You propose. As to Powder our own supply of this Article is very deficient. I was not able with all we have and all I could borrow from the different states to make up near a sufficiency for the operations intended against New York, and must have depended much on our Allies for it, if these had been prosecuted. If however Your Excellency should determine to attempt the reduction of the Post either at the expence of the State, or at that of the United States with the consent of Congress, it is possible the quantity you may have occasion for may be spared, if it is not too great and the means of transportation can be procured.

Your Excellency will have heard probably before this reaches You, of the perfidy of Major General Arnold. On the 25th of

Septr. he went to the Enemy. He had entered very deeply into a combination with them, as far as we can judge, for putting them in possession of the important post of West Point, where he commanded and the command of which he had solicited. For this purpose he had contrived an interview, with Major André Adjutant General to their Army, on the night of the 21st and delivered to him, A Copy of a State of matters I had laid before a Council of General Officers the 6 of Septr. An Estimate of the force at West Point and its Dependencies—of Men to man the Works at West point—Remarks on those works. A Return of ordnance at West point and its Dependencies. Artillery orders for the disposition of the Corps in case of an alarm at West point. A Permit to Major André, under the assumed name of John Anderson to pass our Guards. This Officer, with all these papers in Arnold's hand writing, was taken by a most extraordinary and providential intervention of circumstances, under the assumed name of John Anderson and in a disguised habit, about Fifteen miles from the Enemy's outpost at King's bridge, by a small Militia patrol, who acted with great virtue upon the occasion, as he was returning to New York, having been all the night of the 21st and next day in the vicinity of our posts at Stony and Verplanks points, and passed by them the night preceding his capture. Arnold got information of the event on the morning of the 25th before it was known to any of the Officers under his command or any in authority and pushed down the River in a barge to the Vulture Sloop of War, which lay a few miles below Stony point. Major André was tried by a Board of General Officers, and, on his free and voluntary confession, and Letters, was sentenced to suffer death, agreable to the practice and usage of Nations in like cases, which he has accordingly suffered. He acted with great candor after he avowed himself untill he was executed. Your Excellency will probably see the whole of the proceedings in his case published. We have no doubt now, whatever may be the future objects and measures of the Enemy, that the primary and principal design of the embarkation they were making, was to take West point, which through the preconcerted arrangements between them and Mr. Arnold, in all human probability, would have inevitably fallen into their hands and most likely in the course of a few days after the discovery. The Enemy have not laid aside, from the accounts I continue to receive, their preparations for an expedition, and must now mean to make a push in some other more remote Quarter. Hence Your Excellency will perceive that they leave nothing unessayed to carry their point, but I trust there is more than abundant virtue, as well as means in our hands if these are properly directed, to withstand and baffle easily all their most vigorous and artful efforts.

I have the honor to be with very great respect & esteem Yr Excellency's Most Obedt St.,

G W

Dft (DLC: Washington Papers); in hand of R. H. Harrison; endorsed.

The letters of WOOD, CORNWALLIS, and HARRINGTON mentioned by Washington were enclosures in TJ's letters to Washington of 23 and 26 Sep., q.v. A LETTER TO HIM OF THIS DATE: Washington's letter to Wood, dated 11 Oct., is in *Writings*, ed. Fitzpatrick, XX, 155-6.

From James Maxwell

[*Richmond*, *11 Oct. 1780*. Minute in the Journal of the Commissioner of the Navy (Vi), under this date: "Letter written to the Governor inclosing Mr. Moss's proposals for chartering his Vessel." Not located.]

From James Maxwell

[*Richmond*, *11 Oct. 1780*. Minute in the Journal of the Commissioner of the Navy (Vi), under this date: "Letter written to his Excellency the Governor, informing him of the Return of the Boat Nicholson to the Yard." Not located.]

To Daniel Brodhead

SIR

Richmond, Oct. 12th, 1780.

I received some time ago a Letter from the board of war desiring that provisions might be furnished for the subsistence of the garrison at Fort Pitt, I immediately informed them that our Treasury was utterly without money and could not be replenished till the meeting of assembly, that the line which had been agreed to by the assembly as a boundary between us and Pennsylvania had thrown into that State, nearly the whole settlement in the vicinity of Fort Pitt and being not yet Ascertained, had left it difficult and improper for us to put in force our Provision Law, which might indeed Produce supplies to the Posts but would Probably give umbrage to the state of Pennsylvania, I am therefore able to do nothing more on this head, but to look forwards to the approaching Session of Assembly for the means of Procuring by Purchase suplies for your Post, and to the Ratification of the boundary by Pennsylvania, and its actual Extention to ascertain the ground on which we may exercise the Compulsory measures of our Law on failure of Purchases. Indeed our inabillity to aid you may be well known by the Extreme sufferings to which our Posts on the Ohio have been exposed and of which you cannot be uninformed, as soon as any Powers shall be put into my hands to procure either by volunteer or Compulsory means, any suplies for you, you may be assured they shall be exercised.

I am with great respect Sir, Your most Obedt Servt.

P.S. Since writing the above Colo. Campbell informs me, that the only obstacle to your availing yourself of the Powers given you by the State of Pennsylvania for Procureing Provisions is an apprehension that we might entertain a Jealousy at the exercise of such Power, I assure you that no such apprehension need be Entertained. The inhabitants south of Masons & Dixons line Continued are decidedly in Virginia, over these therefore we cannot authorize you to Exercise any Power derived from the other Government, I make no doubt but you can nearly Judge whereabouts the north line will Run I understand it will but a little to Eastward of the Ohio hence you may Act even there also with Tolerable Certainty.

No MS located. Text from a "Copy" in Brodhead's Letter Book which is printed in *Pennsylvania Archives*, 1st ser., VIII, 641-2, without signature and very ill-punctuated.

The LETTER FROM THE BOARD OF WAR was dated 2 Aug. 1780 and was signed by Timothy Pickering, but has not been found; TJ's reply to Pickering is printed above, 2 Sep. 1780. See Brodhead's answer to the present letter, 17 Jan. 1781.

To George Rogers Clark

SIR Richmond October 12. 1780

We have this moment learnt that there is in possession of Colo. Gibson at Fort Pitt or his Pay-master a quantity of Clothing fit for Soldiers: As Majr. Slaughter's Corps we know is in want, and yours may possibly be, I have given Majr. Moore an Order to receive it, and deliver it to your order.

I am with great respect Sir Your most obedt. humble servt,

TH: JEFFERSON

RC (WHi); in a clerk's hand, with complimentary close and signature by TJ and addressed by him: "Colo. George Rogers Clarke Louisville." Endorsed in two different hands: "Govr. Jefferson 12th Octr. 1780 Clothing for Troops."

From Horatio Gates

SIR Hillsborough 12th: October 1780.

This Instant I received The Great and Glorious News, contained in the inclosed Letter from Brig: Gen: Davidson to Gen: Sumner, who directly dispatched it me by Express. We are now more than even with the Enemy. The moment the Shoes &c. for the Troops here, arrives from Taylors Ferry, I shall proceed with the Whole to the Yadkin. General Smallwood, and Col. Morgan, are on their way to that post; the Latter, with the Light Infantry, was yesterday advanced Eighteen Miles beyond Guilford Court House, the Former with the Cavalry lay last night thirteen Miles on this side that place. I desire Yr: Excellency will forthwith Dispatch copies of all The Letters I now send You to the President of Congress.

I am Sir Your Excellency Obedt: Hble Servt.,

HORATIO GATES.

FC (NHi); endorsed (in part) "Copy." Tr (DLC: PCC, No. 71, I), transmitted to Congress in TJ's letter to Huntington of 15 Oct. 1780, along with the following enclosures (transcripts, same location): (1) Jethro Sumner to Gates, "Camp McGoons Creek," 5 Oct.; (2) Gates to Sumner, Hillsborough, 7 Oct.; (3) Sumner to Gates, "Camp Yadkin Ford," 10 Oct. (2 copies; this letter is printed in *N.C. State Records*, xv, 114); (4) William Davidson to Sumner, Rocky River, 10 Oct.; (5) Davidson to Sumner, "Camp Rocky River," 10 Oct. (a second letter). 2d Tr of Gates' letter to TJ (DLC); 3d Tr (DLC: Washington Papers); 4th Tr (Arch. Aff. Etr., Paris: Corr. pol., E-U, vol. 14), in French, accompanied by French transcripts of Davidson's 2 letters and Sumner's letter (i.e., enclosures Nos. 3-5, above)—these last being translations taken from printed documents "publié par ordre du Congrès."

THE INCLOSED LETTER FROM . . . DAVIDSON was, specifically, enclosure No. 5 listed above; it was transmitted by Sumner in enclosure No. 3, and it conveyed the news, brought by one who was in the action, that "Ferguson the great Partisan" had been defeated at King's Mountain, 7 Oct., by a force of 1600 Americans under "Colonels Campbell, Cleavland [Cleveland], Shelby, Seveer [Sevier], Williams, Brandon, Lacey, &c. . . . Colo. Ferguson fell in the Action, besides 150 of his Men. 810 were made prisoners including the British, 150 of the Prisoners are wounded. 15 hundred Stand of Arms fell into our Hands. Colonel Ferguson had about 1400 Men, Our People surrounded them, and the Enemy Surrendered. We lost about Twenty Men." The American forces will probably "secure their Prisoners in, or over the Mountains, and proceed towards Charlotte."

From Meriwether Smith

DR. SIR Hobbs' hole. Octo: 12h. 1780

Inclosed I send you Copies of the Papers I mention'd to you. You know the Importance of them and therefore will retain them for your *own* satisfaction and perusual.

Pray be so good as to remind the clerk of the Council to send me a Copy of your Letter to the President of Congress with the Account you stated. Your Sentiments with the Respect to the Boundary of Virga. in case of Negociation respecting the Confederation, will be useful to me. I wish you to look on the Map and send me the Lines which in your Judgment will be proper. Adieu! Yrs. &c.

M. SMITH

RC (DLC); addressed: "His Excellency Governor Jefferson at Richmond ℔ mr Ship" (bearer's name not wholly legible). Enclosures not identified.

Smith had been reelected to Congress to serve from the first Monday in November, but he did not attend until Feb. 1781 (Burnett, *Letters of Members*, v, p. lxiv). A COPY OF YOUR LETTER TO THE PRESIDENT: Probably TJ to Huntington, 27 July 1780.

From Oliver Towles

SIR Octr. 12. 1780

This will be handed your Excellency with a Letter from me addressed to Commissary Loring, left unsealed for your perusal, after which you will either retain or transmit it as you think best. The day before I left New York Mr. Loring requested, that if the legislative authority of the State should consent to Governor Hamilton and fellow prisoners going to that City, The following things should be furnished them by the state, (that is to say) a Flag Vessell, also such Money, Shoes and other necessaries that might be wanted for Hamilton and Fellow prisoners, before they set out for New York; that if they should March by Land, then with the necessaries aforementioned proper Passports to enable them to proceed through the several States to New York; he concluded with saying, that he judged it most convenient for the whole of the prisoners to embark together in a Flag Vessel and if the State would furnish them with the proper necessaries to enable them to proceed by Land or Water, (as the case might be) that on the part of the British, a just and generous return should be made in every respect; General Phillips spoke to the same effect with Loring; Now if all this should be complied with, from the conversation that passed between Loring and me, I am of opinion our state may obtain permission to send Tobacco or other Commodities necessary for the sustenance of our Captive Friends, otherwise I suspect the article *Tobacco* will not be allowed to go from us to New York; and I have to observe that however whimsical and capricious the enemy may be in general in matters of this kind, yet on the present occasion from the assurances I have received, I am persuaded a punctual and generous conduct will be held out by them to us, provided the same kind of conduct is observed on our side, respecting the requisitions made in behalf of Governor Hamilton; which I have as fully mentioned as appear to me to be any wise necessary, but should they prove dificient in perspicuity, I shall be ready to assist in explaining them. Should your Excellency apply for a Flag, I judge it may be proper to write General Phillips as well as Mr. Loring respecting it, and to guard against a disappointment it will be necessary to inform among other particulars, *The burthens of the Vessel*, *the name of its Commander*, *the number of Hands to navigate the Vessel; the whole of her Lading or Cargo*, *and to whom consigned*. In regard to the latter it may not be unnecessary to mention, that Lewis Pintard Esqr. has acted as an Agent for American prisoners at New York, and has discharged that Trust with great Fidelity; he is I believe at this time in New York, and continues our Agent; if so I should think him the proper person to consign to, or in his absences &c. then with Liberty for Colo. Geo. Matthews, Majors Wm. Drake and Tarlton Woodson and Captain John Hays prisoners on Long Island or any three of them to nominate and appoint an Agent for this special purpose, to receive and dispose of the Cargo, and to appropriate it to the several Officers [and] Volunteers according to the Resolve of the state; I know of nothing more that [is] necessary to mention at present, should any matter hereafter occur, I will without delay communicate it; and should you find occasion to write me, your Letters lodged at the Fredericksburg post Office, will soon come to hand; I sincerely Wish You Health and happiness, and am with great respect and esteem Your Most obedient, and Most humble servant,

O. Towles

RC (Vi); addressed: "His Excellency Thomas Jefferson Esqr. Governor of Virginia"; endorsed in clerk's hand. Enclosure (Towles to Joshua Loring) not found.

On the case of Henry Hamilton, see TJ to Theodorick Bland, 8 June 1779, and references there. On the problem of furnishing supplies to the captive Virginia officers, see the Officers' Memorial, 24 May; TJ to Harrison, 22? June; and TJ to Washington, 4 July 1780.

To James Wood

Sir — Richmond October 12th. 1780.

Baker was to give notice to Colo. Crockett when he should have ready subsistence and pack horses for him. Colo. Matthew's Suggestions as to the Militia shall be submitted to the Council, and the result communicated to Colo Crockett.

I am sorry to hear that your Supplies of Provision are still precarious. Mr Divers has made a Proposition to victual the troops on contract, which we think to submit to the Assembly. What is your Opinion of such a mode? I would be glad to hear from you, on this Question, together with your Sentiments on the prospect of Subsistence in any other way, as early as possible.

I am Sir with great esteem Your most obedt humble servt.,

TH: JEFFERSON

RC (Lloyd W. Smith, Madison, N.J., 1946). In a clerk's hand, with complimentary close and signature by TJ. Endorsed.

Robert Scot's Invoice

for Executing an Indian Medal, with Jefferson's Memoranda

[Richmond, 13-21 October 1780]

His Excellency Thomas Jefferson Esqr to Rot. Scot Dr.

1781		
Oct 13	To Engraving and making a Medalion mould in Brass and casting paterns	£3150. 0.0
	To Pewter for paterns	15. 0.0
	To Cash payed on Acct Express as pr. receipt	41.14.0
		£3206.14.0
	37 Silver dollars estimated @ 140 for 1. To 37 Silver Dollars	1554.
		£4760.14.0

In Council Oct. 21. 1781

The within service was performed on requisition from the Executive.

TH: JEFFERSON

The within Account of £3206.14 was presented to the Auditors the 21st of October 1780 a warrant for which together with the value of 37 silver dollars will be issued when the Treasurer is in a Situation to discharge it.

Auditors

In Council. Oct. 21. 1780

The Auditors alone have a right to say what Mr. Scott deserves to receive. The Executive think his account not unreasonable. The workmanship was extraordinary good. TH: JEFFERSON

MS in two slips, among Contingent Fund Vouchers (Vi). Scot's Invoice is evidently in his own hand; the first of TJ's two notes, together with the Auditors' statement, is on its verso. TJ's second note is on a separate slip. A covering sheet bears arithmetical calculations on recto and the following endorsement on verso: "April 2d. 1781 Robt. Scott £4760.14. Contingent. [*In another hand*:] Exd." (For a note on the Contingent Fund Vouchers in Vi, see George Brooke to TJ, 25 Jan. 1781.)

From this and related documents it is clear that TJ had called on the Richmond artisan RO[BER]T SCOT to execute the earliest Indian medal issued by the State of Virginia or perhaps by any state of which an example is known to survive (though it will be noted that the term Indian medal is not used in the present paper). There can be little doubt that this was done on the occasion of a visit to Richmond by Potclay and other Cherokee Indian chiefs, whom TJ planned to have continue their travels northward to Congress and Washington's army (see entry for TJ to Huntington, 10 Oct.; Page to TJ, 20 Oct.; and Huntington to TJ, 21 Oct. 1780). Examples of the Virginia Indian medal of 1780 survive but are of great rarity; the illustration of the medal in the present volume is taken from an example in the Appleton Collection in the Massachusetts Historical Society. C. Wyllys Betts, *American Colonial History Illustrated by Contemporary Medals*, N.Y., 1894, p. 261-2 (No. 570), records this and one other example (in the British Museum) and gives the following description:

"*Obv.* REBELLION TO TYRANTS IS OBEDIENCE TO GOD. On a label in the upper part of the field, VIRGINIA. Arms of Virginia; a woman in armor, with a sword in right hand and a spear in her left, presses her right foot on a man lying prostrate, and with her left foot secures a chain, which he clutches with his left hand; on the ground is a crown.

"*Rev.* HAPPY WHILE UNITED. In exergue, 1780. At the right is a strange sort of tree, under which an Indian at the left and a white officer at the right, are seated; the Indian holds a pipe; at the left is an open sea, on which are three vessels; near them is a rocky point with a house."

In design, this medal continued a well-established tradition: the reverse and the loop (calumet and eagle's wing) are quite similar to those found in several Indian medals issued during the colonial period (e.g., Betts, No. 510, dated 1764; compare Nos. 509, 511), but in the obverse Scot substituted the seal of Virginia and TJ's favorite motto, "Rebellion to tyrants . . . ," for the usual portrait of the sovereign.

As for Robert Scot (frequently written Scott, but not by the engraver himself), a contribution to *The Numismatist*, LIV (1941), 84-5, entitled "Robert Scot, First Engraver at the Philadelphia Mint," gives most of the details of his career that are known. He was born in Edinburgh, 1745, and was at first a watchmaker, then an engraver. It is not known when he came to Virginia, but on 12 May 1780 he was paid £2103.8 "for his Services & expences in detectg some persons concerned in counterfietg the paper currency" (*Va. Council Jour.*, II, 257). On 30 May 1781 TJ wrote Scot by express from Charlottesville requesting him to "make a medal of the kind formerly made" and to send it at once so that it could be presented to an Indian chief from Kaskaskia then visiting the Governor. Scot settled in Philadelphia in 1782, where for many years he was active as an engraver of maps, portraits, heraldic devices, diplomas, and book illustrations. See N.Y. Publ. Libr., *Bull.*, LIV (1950), 123. He was appointed engraver to the United States Mint by TJ as secretary of state, 23 Nov. 1793, and died in prosperous condition, 1823.

In an answer to queries submitted by the editors after the present note was in the press, Mr. William J. Van Schreeven, Head Archivist, Virginia State Library, pointed out that on 21 June 1780 Nicholas Gauteir was paid £900 by the state for "5 silver medals made for the Cherokee indians" (*Va. Council Jour.*, II, 258). This clearly indicates that there were earlier medals issued by the state. Of Gauteir nothing is known except that he probably lived in Norfolk. Of Scot, however, more is now known. He wrote a letter from Fredericksburg, [14?] Sep. 1778, to George Webb at Williamsburg urging Webb to send him type metal for use in engraving "Money

Plates" for printing state currency. This letter (in Vi; photostat in TJ Editorial Files) is printed in *Virginia Imprint Series Number 4, Preliminary Checklist for Fredericksburg 1778-1876*, ed. Carrol H. Quenzel, Richmond, 1947, p. 99-100, where will also be found some other biographical data on Scot.

From Horatio Gates

SIR Hillsborough 14th: October 1780.

I have read and attentively considered Your Excellencys Letters of the 23d Ult:, and 4th. Instant and Lest Congress, or the Board of War, should conceive Greater Supplies for the Southern Army, can be furnished by your State than it is in their Power, or Abillity, to give, I have sent The President by this conveyance, Exact Copies of Your Excellencys Two letters to me, that no Plea of not knowing Our Wants may in Future be Urged in Excuse of not Supplying this Army in Time. My Opinion of what *this State will do*, has been long ago transmitted to Congress. Inclosed is a Copy of Letter I received this morning from Col: Polk. The Payment of the Bill he mentions to have deliverd to Mr. Ochilltree should be Stop'd, as that Gentleman is supposed to be a Prisoner by his Own Consent. As the Salvation of our Troops upon the Yadkin, and to the Westward, depends So intirely upon Polks supplying them with provisions I have sent him the Bill he requests upon Your Excellency in Lieu of that Lost, or carried off by Mr. Ochilltree; I am somewhat alarm'd at what Your Excellency says in regard to my Bills, to be drawn in Favour of The Quarter Master; I have only yet drawn in Favour of The Purchasers of Provisions, Supplied to the Army; and in favour of Persons furnishing Cloathing; I must have a much better Opinion of the Qr: Mastr: Department before I give them a Single Draught either upon Your Excellency, or Maryland, but if my Bills for Victualling and Cloathing the Troops are not paid, the consequence will I have reason to fear be most injurious to Our Affairs. I am to thank Your Excellency for your great Care and Assiduity for this Army. It is some releif to my Mind, to have so good a Friend in my Rear. I beg you to forward the inclosed to Col. Senf. I am &c

HG

FC (NHi). Tr (DLC) of same. Enclosures: (1) Thomas Polk to Gates, 10 Oct. (not found, but see Gates' reply, 13 Oct.; Tr in DLC); (2) Gates to J. C. Senf, 14 Oct.; Tr (DLC); RC of Gates to Senf was sold at Parke-Bernet Galleries, Inc., Catalogue of Oliver R. Barrett Sale, 30 Oct., 2 Nov. 1950, Item No. 455.

Gates' letter to THE PRESIDENT (Samuel Huntington) enclosing copies of TJ's letters to Gates of 23 Sep. and 4 Oct. is dated 13 Oct. 1780 in RC (DLC: PCC, No. 154, II), but 14 Oct. in a transcript in DLC: TJ Papers. Gates' letter to Senf, enclosed in the present letter, ordered Senf to obtain TJ's "directions in respect to the Survey you are to make of the Coast and posts on the South side of Virginia" (see TJ to Gates, 4 Oct. 1780) and to "keep an Attentive Eye upon the Sea Board" for "the Fleet of our Allies"; if the fleet (which was transporting the daily-expected second division of the French forces) arrived, Senf was to go aboard and to conduct any French officer that might be sent to Gates' headquarters; on the other hand, if a British fleet appeared, Senf was "instantly" to notify TJ, then to determine its strength and return to Gates. This letter, as TJ told Gates on 28 Oct., was never delivered, "as it did not come till the enemy had taken possession of the ground on which I knew him to have been." On 20 Oct. Senf wrote Gates from Portsmouth (RC in DLC) informing him that "Yesterday I had finish'd with Surveying the Situation of this place, and was to go to morrow Morning to Cape Henry, but prevented. Genl. Nelson received last Night an Express from Cape Henry, says, that a fleet of about Sixty Sails . . . came to Ancher without Cape Henry. This Morning some of the Ships were discovered standing in for Cape Henry. It is generally believed, that they come from the Northern and are Ennemy. . . . This Place is in no kind of Defence, we hardly can muster forty Militia Men, and the greater part of the Inhabitants are about securing their effects." Nelson is nevertheless determined, continues Senf, to make a stand with what men he can muster "till supported by the Country. It seems the Mean Arnold has given good Intelligence to the Ennemy of our Situation." For further reports by Senf on the actions around Portsmouth, see *N.C. State Records*, XV, 112-13, 144-5.

To Samuel Huntington

SIR Richmond Oct. 14. 1780.

At the desire of Majr. General Gates I transmit you the inclosed papers which he put under cover to me. He complains of the arrival of our troops without clothes, tents, or arms at Hilsborough: and desires they may not be sent on at all unless completely equipped with every necessary. This would indeed put an end to the marching a single man there. They go clothed as militia. Few of them carry blankets. Nor shall we be able to furnish tents or arms for more than half of them. However they will go on in hopes of supplies from Congress. I have the honor to be with the most profound esteem & respect Your Excellency's Most obedt. & most humble servt.,

TH: JEFFERSON

RC (DLC: PCC, No. 71, I); endorsed: "Letter Govr. Jefferson Octor. 14th. 1780." Enclosures (same location), originally enclosed in Gates' letter to TJ, 6 Oct.: (1) [Gen. Sir Henry Clinton] *Orders*, dated "Head-Quarters, Charles-Town Neck," June 1, 1780, congratulating Cornwallis and Tarleton on their success against the Americans in the back country (broadside, "Charles-town printed: New-York, Reprinted by James Rivington"). (2) Cornwallis to [Clinton?], no place or date, reporting the British victory at Camden, 16 Aug. ("Copy"). (3) Lt. Col. Nisbett Balfour, "Comdg. at 96," proclamation against plundering loyalists ("true Copy"). The last bears the following endorsement: "Lord Cornwallis's & Lt. Col. Balfours Letters; taken upon a Spy —17th. Sepr. 1780.—at Hillsborough" (see also Gates to TJ, 6 Oct. 1780); it is not certain whether the date and place given refer to the capture of the spy or to the making of the endorsement. (4) Col. James Williams to Gates, dated "Burk County [N.C.] 2nd October 1780" (RC). (5) William Davidson to Jethro Sumner, "Camp near Phyfers," 3 Oct. 1780 ("Copy"). (6) W. R. Davie to Davidson, "Flying Camp," no date ("Copy"). (7) William Preston to Gates, "Bottetourt Court House," 18 Sep. 1780 ("Copy").

To Thomas Burke

SIR Richmond Oct. 15. 1780.

Your favor of the 5th. covering a draught of Mr. Clay's for 106,775 D. came safely to hand last night. I am sorry that Mr. Clay adopts this method of negotiating money claims on our treasury which is not and I fear will not again be in a condition to answer his draughts with any kind of punctuality which might justify his drawing and negotiating in the mercantile way. In my letter to you of the 2d inst. acknowledging the receipt of the draught for 225,000 D. I informed you of the exhausted state of our treasury. There is as yet no symptom of replenishment. I really therefore do not know what to recommend to you. If you find it better to retain those bills on us, we expect to pay money to or for Mr. Clay, and shall with great chearfulness do it through you: but I am bound at the same time to inform you that we are so far from being in arrears on the general requisitions of Congress for money (in which case depreciation might perhaps be chargeable to us) that we have overpaid their requisitions till the close of the present year upwards of six millions of dollars. Mr. Clay's draught from Congress is supererogation. Yet we do not mean to count or weigh our contributions by any standard but that of our abilities. If you find you can better secure yourself against depreciation by recalling these draughts they shall be delivered to your order and in the mean time safely kept.

I am with great esteem Sir Your most obedt humble servt.,

TH: JEFFERSON

RC (NcDAH). Addressee not indicated in MS. Though the original is in Governors' Papers, Vol. VI, Abner Nash, 1780-1781, p. 80, the text appears clearly to refer to TJ's letter to Thomas Burke of 2 Oct. 1779, q.v. It is possible, of course, but unlikely that TJ wrote also to Nash on 2 Oct. on the subject of Joseph Clay's draft on Virginia and that that letter is missing. No letter of 5 Oct. to TJ from Burke has been found.

To Horatio Gates

SIR Richmond Oct. 15th. 1780

I am rendered not a little anxious by the Paragraph of yours of the 7th. Inst: wherein you say 'it is near a Month since I received any Letter from your Excellency; indeed the receipt of most that I have wrote to you remain unacknowledged.'[1] You ought within that time to have received my Letter of September 3d. written immediately on my return to this place after a fortnights Absence; That of September 11th. acknowledging the receipt of yours which covered Draughts for Money; that of Sept. 23d. on the Subject of Batteaus at Taylor's Ferry, Waggons, Maps of Virginia, wintering the French Fleet in Chesapeake, our new levies, and Provisions from our lower Counties; and that of Oct. 4. in Answer to yours of Sept. 24th. and 27th. I begin to apprehend Treachery in some part of our Chain of Expresses, and beg the favor of you in your next to mention whether any and which of these Letters have not come to hand.

This acknowledges the receipt of yours of Sept. 28. and Oct. 3. 5 and 7th. The first of these was delivered four or five days ago by Capt. Drew. He will be permitted to return as you desire, as we would fulfill your wishes in every point in our power, as well as indulge the Ardor of a good Officer. Our Militia from the Western Counties are now on their march to join you. They are fond of the kind of Service in which Colo. Morgan is generally engaged, and are made very happy by being informed you intend to put them under him. Such as pass by this place take Muskets in their hands. Those from the Southern Counties beyond the Blue Ridge were advised to carry their Rifles. For those who carry neither Rifles nor Muskets, as well as for our 18 Month's Men we shall send on Arms as soon as Waggons can be procured. In the mean time I had hoped that there were Arms for those who should first arrive at Hillsborough, as by Genl. Stevens Return dated at his Departure thence there were somewhere between 5 and 800 Musketts (I speak from Memory not having present Access to the Return) belonging to this State either in the hands of the few Militia who were there or stored. Capt. Fauntleroy of the Cavalry gives me hopes he shall immediately forward a very considerable Supply of Accoutrements for White's and Washington's Cavalry. He told me yesterday he had received 113 Horses for that Service from us. Besides those he had rejected sixty odd after we had purchased them at £3000 a piece. Nelson's two troops were returned to me deficient only 12 Horses, since which 10 have been sent to him by Lt. Armstead. I am not a little disappointed therefore in the Number of Cavalry fit for Duty as mentioned in the Letter you inclosed me. Your request (as stated in your letter of the 7th.) that we will send no Men into the field, or even to your camp that are not well furnished with Shoes, Blanketts, and every necessary for immediate service, would amount to a stoppage of every Man: as we have it not in our power to furnish them with real Necessaries completely.

I hope they will be all shod. What proportion will have Blanketts I cannot say: we purchase every one which [can] be found out, and I now begin to have [a] prospect of furnishing about half of them with Tents as soon as they can be made, and forwarded. As to provisions, our Agent Eaton, of whom I before wrote, informs me in a Letter of the 5th. inst. he shall immediately get Supplies of Beef into Motion and shall send some Corn by a circuitous Navigation. But till we receive our Waggons from the Western Country I cannot hope to aid you in Bread. I expect daily to see Waggons coming in to us. The Militia were ordered to rendezvous at Hillsborough, expecting they would thence be ordered by you into Service. I send you herewith a copy of Henry's map of Virginia. It is a mere cento of blunders. It may serve to give you a general idea of the courses of rivers and position of counties. We are endeavoring to get you a copy of Fry & Jefferson's; but they are now very scarce. I also inclose you some newspapers in which you will find a detail of Arnold's apostacy and villainy. I am with sentiments of sincere respect & esteem Sir Your most obedt. & most humble servt.,

TH: JEFFERSON

P.S. Just as I was closing my letter, yours of the 9th. instant is put into my hands. I inclose by this express a power to Mr. Lambe Q.M. to impress for a month ten waggons from each of the counties of Brunswick, Mecklenburg, Lunenburg, Charlotte and Halifax and direct him to take your orders whether they shall go first to you, or come here. If the latter, we can load them with arms and spirits. Before their month is out I hope the 100 waggons from the Westward will be come in. We will otherwise provide a relief for these. I am perfectly astonished at your not having yet received my letters before mentioned. I send you a copy of that of the 4th. of Octob. as being most material. I learn from one of Genl. Muhlenburgh's family that five waggons have set out from hence with arms &c. However the General writes to you himself. TH: J.

RC (DLC); partly in a clerk's hand and partly in TJ's (from the sentence beginning "I send you herewith a copy of Henry's map" in the third paragraph); TJ also made corrections in the portion written by the clerk. Endorsed: "Richmond 15th. Octr. 80 Govr. Jefferson rec'd 19th Octr." Enclosures missing except for TJ's Commission to Lambe (or Lamb), printed under the present date.

TJ acknowledges two letters (among others) from Gates (28 Sep. and 7 Oct.) which are printed above under dates one day earlier in each instance, our texts being taken from drafts written the day before the recipients' copies were sent; see note on Gates to TJ, 6 Oct. 1780. HENRY'S MAP OF VIRGINIA: John Henry, *A New and Accurate Map of Virginia. . . . Engraved by Thomas Jefferys*, London, 1770 (Swem, "Maps," No. 222). FRY & JEFFERSON'S map: *A Map of the Inhabited Part of Virginia . . . Drawn by Joshua Fry & Peter Jefferson in 1751—Engrav'd . . . by Thos*

Jefferys, London [1754?], and several times reissued (same, No. 175, and see especially *The Fry & Jefferson Map of Virginia and Maryland: A Facsimile of the First Edition in the Tracy W. McGregor Library*, Princeton, 1950).

1 This sentence is not in Gates' letter of 7 Oct. as printed above from the draft, dated 6 Oct. It was probably added as a postscript in the (missing) recipient's copy.

To Samuel Huntington

SIR — Richmond Oct. 15. 1780. 6. o'clock P.M.

I do myself the pleasure of congratulating your Excellency on the small dawn of good fortune which at length appears in the South, as you will find by the dispatches I have the honor of inclosing to you, and which I this moment receive from Genl. Gates. There seems to be a confusion between the numbers 810. and 1400. However the smaller one is not to be despised. The line of expresses having been set in motion last night, I wish that no delay may be occasioned by their missing one another on the road.

I have the honor to be with great esteem & respect Your Excellency's Most obedt. & most humble servt, TH: JEFFERSON

RC (DLC: PCC, No. 71, I); endorsed by Charles Thomson: "Letter from Gov Jefferson Octr. 15. 1780. Read 23. Comee. of intelligence." Enclosures: Gates to TJ, 12 Oct. 1780, and enclosures as listed with that letter; see also JCC, XVIII, 963. Tr (Arch. Aff. Etr., Paris: Corr. pol., E-U, vol. 14); in French.

Commission to Richard? Lamb

VIRGINIA TO WIT.

Whereas by an act passed at the General Assembly holden in the month of may in the present year, and intituled an act for giving further powers to the Governour and Council and for other purposes authority was given for obtaining by impress among other things so many horses, waggons and necessaries as might be wanting to supply the militia or other troops ordered into actual service from this commonwealth, and fifty waggons with their gear and drivers are now wanting for those purposes.

These are therefore to authorize you to obtain by impressing in the counties of Brunswick, Mecklenburg, Lunenburg, Charlotte, and Halifax, fifty waggons with their teams and gear, that is to say ten in each of the said counties and the same to detain and employ for the term of one month in transporting provisions and other necessaries for the troops from this commonwealth under the command of Genl. Gates in such manner as he or any person authorized by him shall direct drawing on the treasury of the Commonwealth for paiment of the hire to be made on or before the 31st day of december next. And all officers civil and military and other the good citizens of this commonwealth are hereby required and commanded to be aiding and assisting to you in the execution of this warrant. Given under my hand and the seal of the Commonwealth at Richmond this 15th day of octo: 1780. THO: JEFFERSON

Tr in the War Office Letter Book (MiU-C); copy of seal at foot of text. At head and in margin of text: "To Mr. Lamb." Original enclosed in TJ's letter to Gates of this date, q.v.

The addressee was probably Richard Lamb, who was associated with the quartermaster's department in Mch. 1781 (*Va. Council Jour.*, II, 322).

From the Commissioners of the Specific Tax in Essex County

May it please your Excellency [After 16 October 1780]

Your Letter of the 6th of Septr. requisting a delivery of the Tobacco Notes in our Hands of the Specific Tax, came to hand the 16th. of October. The bearers Name not being specified, in the Letter, we were unable to tell by whom it was sent, or to whom the Notes were to be delivered; fortunate for us, that it did not in its slow conveyance, get into the hands of some of our public plunderers, as the letter was unsealed and the contents known to all, thro' whose hands it passed. We embrace this favourable opportunity by Mr. to send you the Notes of the Tobacco, in our hands, which after the necesary deductions, of 6 Pt. for crop and 30lb Tobo. for Cash amounts to 44444 Nett. Tobo., which we hope will be safely delivered to your Excellency. We observe that the commissioners have received 2 notes older than the date mentioned in Your letter; the Law not specifying the date, or age of Tobacco the Commissioners judge from that old Tobacco wou'd answer the intention of the Law.

RC (Vi); unsigned; written on address leaf of TJ's letter to the Essex Commissioners, 6 Sep. 1780, q.v.

From James Maxwell

[*Richmond, 17 Oct. 1780.* Minute in the Journal of the Commissioner of the Navy (Vi) under this date: "Letter written to the Governor inclosing Capt.: Dean's proposals." Not located.]

From Horatio Gates

SIR Hillsborough 18th. October 1780.

Inclosed I send Your Excellency my dispatch of this [Date?] to the President of Congress under a flying Seal for your Persual. I must entreat you to forward it with all its contents, directly by Express to Philadelphia. If the News from General Fleming is Confirmed I think A Speedy recovery of South Carolina and Georgia must be the Consequence, but we are so often disappointed in Reports that I should pay little attention to it, did not the precipate Retreat of Lord Cornwallis give A Sanction to this. I request your Excellency will send the enclosed to Colonel Hunter. HG

Tr (DLC). Enclosures: Gates to Huntington, 16-18 Oct. (Tr in DLC); a letter from Gen. Fleming to Gates not further identified; Gates to James Hunter, 18 Oct. (Tr. in DLC). These enclosures were transmitted by TJ to Huntington, 25 Oct. 1779, q.v.

From Samuel Huntington

SIR Philada October 18. 1780

Your Excellency will receive herewith enclosed the Copy of an Act of Congress of the 10. Instant wherein they have resolved that the unappropriated Lands that may be ceded or relinquished to the United States pursuant to the Recommendation of the 6. of September last *shall be disposed of for the common Benefit of the United States*, be formed into distinct Governments, and granted and settled as expressed in the Act and the reasonable Expences incurred in subduing British Posts &c. on such ceded Land shall be reimbursed.

I have the Honor to be &c. &c. &c., S. H.

FC (DLC: PCC, No. 15). Enclosure (not found): resolve of Congress, 10 Oct., respecting cession by the states of their western land claims, printed in JCC, XVIII, 915. Huntington had addressed a circular letter to the state executives on 16 Oct. (FC, same location) with a similar message, but the circular was probably not sent to TJ and is omitted here.

On the controversy over the states' western land claims, see Huntington to TJ, 10 Sep. 1780, with references there.

To George Skillern

[*Richmond, 18 Oct. 1780.* A letter from George Skillern to the Governor of Virginia (Benjamin Harrison), dated Botetourt, 29 Apr. 1783 (Vi), states: "I would beg Leave to inform your excellency that in the year Eighty I Received an order of council, dated Octr. 18th. together with a very pressing letter from his Excellency Thos. Jefferson (who was then governor) which I inclose you, requisting me to use my utmost indeavours to rais a Number of Volunteers to be sent to the aid of the southern Army, And that they ware to be allow'd the same pay as the melitia ordered there on a former occation, this requisition together with my own feelings for the defence of my Country, Induced me fourth with to proceed on the Prosecution thereoff, and after attending sundry places in the County where the melitia ware ordered to meet as might be necessary for the purpose of recruting, and Expending a considerable sum of money out of my own Private property by way of treats and other Expences, I at last Effected my purpose and marched off a Majors Command and sent with them two waggons Loaded With provisions; these poor men suffered a Very hard Campaign numbers of them returned almost Naked And some lost their lives, Nothwithstanding They have Never been payed a farthing for their brave and Spirited beheavour, Numbers of them at this time has not wherewith to pay their taxes, and yet will not be allowed credit for this just demand they have against the Public." Skillern, who is threatened with suits by some of the claimants, asks "to have something done In this case." TJ's letter and the Council order of 18 Oct. 1780 have not been found. See also TJ to Gates, 10 Nov. 1780, Skillern to TJ, 14 Apr. 1781.]

From George Washington

Headquarters near Passaic, 18 Oct. 1780. "Circular." "In obedience to the Orders of Congress, I have the honor to transmit Your Excellency the present state of the Troops of your line, by which you will perceive how few men you will have left after the first of January next. When I inform you also that the Troops of the other Lines will be in general as much reduced as Yours, you will be able to judge how exceedingly weak the Army will be at that period; and how essential it is the States should make vigorous exertions to replace the discharged men as early as possible." Congress' new plan for a military establishment will soon be sent to the states "with requisitions for their respective quotas." New levies should be for the war, as "I am religiously persuaded that the duration of the war, and the greatest part of the Misfortunes, and perplexities we have hitherto experienced, are chiefly to be attributed to temporary inlistments. . . . A moderate, compact force, on a permanent establishment capable of acquiring the discipline essential to military operations, would have been able to make head against the Enemy, without comparison better than the throngs of Militia, which have been at certain periods not in the feild, but on their way to, and from the feild: for from that want of perseverance which characterises all Militia, and of that coercion which cannot be exercised upon them, it has always been found impracticable to detain the greatest part of them in service even for the term, for which they have been called out; and this has been commonly so short, that we have had a great proportion of the time, two sets of men to feed and pay, one coming to the Army, and the other going from it." Instances cited of the disasters and near-disasters caused by the constant "fluctuations" in the number of troops in the field. Besides, "It is impossible the people can endure the excessive burthen of bounties for annual Drafts and Substitutes, increasing at every new experiment: whatever it might cost them once for all to procure men for the War, would be a cheap bargain." Not without reason, the enemy themselves look forward to our eventually sinking "under a system, which increases our expence beyond calculation, enfeebles all our measures, . . . and wearies and disgusts the people. This had doubtless had great influence in preventing their coming to terms." Through infatuation with "an error which the experience of all mankind has exploded, and which our own experience has dearly taught us to reject, . . . America has been almost amused out of her Liberties." Those who favor militia forces are those "whose credulity swallows every vague story, in support of a vague hypothesis. I solemnly declare I never was witness to a single instance, that can countenance an opinion of Militia or raw Troops being fit for the real business of fighting. I have found them useful as light Parties to skirmish in the woods, but incapable of making or sustaining a serious attack. . . . The late battle of Camden is a melancholly comment upon this doctrine. The Militia fled at the first fire, and left the Continental Troops surrounded on every side, and overpowered by numbers to combat for safety instead of victory. The Enemy themselves have witnessed to their Valour." Let the states, then, in providing new levies "abandon temporary expedients, and substitute something durable, systematic, and substantial." A few remarks follow on the army's lack of money, clothing, and stores, and the letter concludes: "The present crisis of our affairs appears to me so serious as to call upon me as a good Citizen, to offer my sentiments freely for the safety of the Republic. I hope the motive will excuse the liberty I have taken." Postscript: "The foregoing is circular to the several States. The circumstances of Your Line put it out of my power to transmit a Return."

RC (Vi); 11 p.; in hand of David Humphreys, signed by Washington (postscript signed with initials); printed in Washington's *Writings*, ed. Fitzpatrick, XX, 204-12, from Dft (DLC: Washington Papers).

To James Wood

SIR Richmond Oct. 18. 1780.

Your letters of the 11th. and 14th. inst. are now before me. I inclose you four blank powers to be directed to any person or persons you shall think proper for Green briar or any other county. I am informed beef may be had in Frederic and Hampshire. I am only to desire that when you fill up any of these powers you immediately communicate to me the name of the county and persons inserted therein that it may be entered as our act in our books.

Lt. McNeill has our consent to go to N. York on parole. A flag will go from this place to N. York in about four or five days or a week to carry Govr. Hamilton and Majr. Hay. Perhaps he can be here in time. Besides this Capt. Lamothe, Doctr. Mcbeath and some others are going from Winchester by land. He will therefore chuse between the two modes, or any third which you please. Capt. Winchester has the permission desired to go to Colo. Cary's, and Mr. Maxwell to reside in Culpeper.

I am with great esteem Sir Your most obedt. humble servt.,

TH: JEFFERSON

RC (Lloyd W. Smith, Madison, N.J., 1946); endorsed. Enclosures not found. Addressee identified from internal evidence; the endorsement is similar to those found on other letters from TJ to Wood.

YOUR LETTERS OF THE 11TH AND 14TH INST.: Missing. A FLAG . . . TO N. YORK: In War Office Letter Book (Vi), under date of 19 Oct., there is a letter from George Muter addressed to "Mrs. Burnley, Hanover," as follows: "I laid before the Governor and Council your requisition for leave to send by the flag going to New York for Cloathing; and have this moment received in Answer—That it is refused." Mrs. Hardin Burnley's husband was a loyalist.

From James Maxwell

[*Richmond, 19 Oct. 1780.* Minute in the Journal of the Commissioner of the Navy (Vi) under this date: "Letter written to the Governor inclosing one from Capt. Markham." Letter and enclosure not located, but see entry for Orders to Markham, 20 Oct. 1780, below. James Markham was captain of the state brig *Jefferson* (minute in same, 11 Nov. 1780).]

From George Muter

[SIR] War office Octr. 19. 1780.

I have the honour of inclosing to your Excellency, an order to the Commissary of stores to deliver Dr. Foushee Linnen and rags; and an order to Dr. Foushee to put up a small box of medicine for Hampton.

I cannot recollect ever having received from Dr. McClurg such a list as he Speaks of, nor is there any Such letter or list to be found among my papers.

The board of War the 21st of March last write to Dr. McClurg as follows.

"You are appointed one of the surgeons of the Navy, your Station Hampton, for the purpose of taking care of the seamen at that place. You are to draw the same pay and rations of Naval surgeons and enjoy the same privileges, your appointment to take effect from the first day of this month."

No mention is made of any allowance for his care of the garrison.

I have the honour to be Your Excellency's most humble Servant,

GEORGE MUTER C

RC (Vi); addressed and endorsed. See Walter McClurg to TJ, 10 Oct. 1780.

From Timothy Pickering

SIR Camp at Totowa 19 October 1780

I was honoured with your letter relative to a deputy quarter master for the State of Virginia, and from the information it contained expected Colo. Finnies arrival in Philadelphia before I left it; but I have not seen or heard from him, And as I was so soon going to the Army I suspended my answer till I should have an opportunity of enquiring of the Gentlemen from your State if they could recommend to me a suitable character. That enquiry I have now made and find they are equally at a loss with your Excellency to hit on a person altogether fit for the post.

Two days ago I received a letter from Colo. William Davies of the Virginia Line making a tender of his services in case Colo. Finnie resigned or was not appointed. Colo. Davies's abilities are indisputable, and I do not know that his Integrity is suspected: but whether he is industrious I am altogether uninformed. It seems too that he is of an uneasy disposition, and less accomadating than could be wished at a time when by every just means we should conciliate the affections of the people, as so much depends on their good will. Yet upon the whole, from the vast superiority of his abilities, he may merit a preference to Colo. Finnie. However, I would not wish to decide in the Case. Colo. Mead who will deliver you this can give more particular information relative to both the Gentlemen, and he has kindly consented in my behalf, to speak to your Excellency upon the Subject. Perhaps some Gentleman may have occurred to your Excellency, since you honoured me with a Letter, whom you will prefer to either: in this case I beg leave again to submit the appointment to your Excellency's determination: Or if otherwise and Colonel Meade shou'd think of such a character, I should be perfectly satisfied with his recommendation. At all events I should be happy to have some one appointed without further loss of time that the business of the department may no longer be in suspense; and with your Excellency's choice shall be well pleased. I have the honour to be &c.,

TIM: PICKERING Q M Gl

FC in Pickering's Letter Book (DNA: RG 93). YOUR LETTER RELATIVE TO A DEPUTY QUARTER MASTER: TJ to Pickering, 6 Sep. 1780.

From Horatio Gates

SIR Hillsborough 20th. Octr. 1780.

I wrote Your Excellency the 18th. which was sent from hence By Express, on the Evening of that Day, and would proceed to Taylor's Ferry, as Mr. Cooper the Stationed Express at Harrisbourg, was, at the Same Time on his Way to this place; the Latter arrived here Yesterday about One oClock A.M. and brought me Your Excellency's Letter of the 15th. Inst. This Letter, came in Time, which was not the Case with several Others written before, from you, as I observe, some of them were, from a week to Twelve Days in coming to this place. The following is the State of the correspondence since the 1st. of Sepr. 1780.

Genl. Gates		Govr. Jefferson	
Sepr.	5	Sepr.	3
	9		11
	14		23
	20	Oct.	4
	24		15
	27		
Oct.	3		
	6		
	9 so far acknowledged		
	12		
	14		
	18		

It appears from the above State and the Contents of Both our Letters, that none have miscarried; for although Your Excellency has not expressly said the Letters of the 9th. and 20th. September were received by you, yet your Letters of the 23 Sepr. and 4th October imply as much. Mr. Cooper the Express, complains much of the Want of Money. I have for the Present Advanced him Dollars with which you will please to have him Charged. I observe what Your Excellency says in regard to your Order for impressing

Waggons sent to Mr. Lamb. I shall therefore give Orders to Mr. Lamb to send half of the Waggons to Richmond to load with Arms Accoutrements and Rum or Cloathing if any should have arrived. The Other half to Petersburgh, to bring Salt and flour from thence, or such Stores which may be there and more immediately wanting. With these Loads they are to proceed to Hillsborough, One Trip only, and afterwards return to Virginia to be employed in transporting Stores to Taylors Ferry and no further. It is absolutly necessary that this should be the Case, for once, as no Waggons can be procured here immediately, to bring Goods on from Taylor's, but it is possible by the Time, your Waggons shall have performed this Duty, a Sufficient Number will be provided in this State, to do the Business between Roanoak, and this place and the Army; when the Rout of the Army is changed, other Modes of transportation may be adopted.

I understand that Mr. Lamb is Quarter Master and Commissary; these Offices are incompatible, as they ought to be checks upon each other. I wish your Excellency would fix upon a Man of tried Fidelity to this Country, to reside at Mr. Lamb's as Commissary, and I desire that he may have your Private Instructions to have an Eye of Circumspection upon the Conduct of Mr. Lamb. Since the State Stores for Cloaths, and Equipment, are so deficient with you, I much desire your Excellency will adhere to your original plan, and assemble the troops to be commanded by Genl. Stevens at Hillsboro; and as I shall leave this place on Tuesday, I wish General Stevens could come directly and take the Command here; in the mean Time, I entreat you Sir to press Congress to forward all such Articles as your State cannot Supply. Men merely Armed but without Cartridges, Boxes Blankets or Tents, are but a poor Support to an Army. I am &c.,

HG

Dft (NHi). Tr (DLC) of Dft.

ORDERS TO MR. LAMB: Gates wrote this day to Commissary Lamb; a transcript of his letter, in a clerk's hand but with corrections by TJ, is in DLC.

From Samuel Huntington

Philadelphia, 20 Oct. 1780. Circular letter to the state executives enclosing a proclamation recommending that Thursday, 7 Dec. next, be observed as a day of thanksgiving and prayer.

FC (DLC: PCC, No. 15); 1 p. Enclosure missing; printed in JCC, XVIII, 950-1, under date of 18 Oct. This proclamation was printed in *Va. Gaz.* (D & N), 4 Nov. 1780, signed by Huntington and attested by Thomson.

Orders to James Markham

[*Richmond, 20 Oct. 1780.* Minute in the Journal of the Commissioner of the Navy (Vi) under this date: "Orders given to Capt. Markham to proceed to Hampton and wait on the Commodore for Directions, countersigned by His Excellency The Governor." Not located.]

From Philip Mazzei

[Florence, 20 October 1780]

In letter 20, dated Paris, June 22d., I said that I should set out for Genoa and Florence, and do all my endeavors to pave the way for executing such orders as I might receive. So I have done, and with as much success in both places, as I could almost wish, considering that I have nothing to show to corroborate what I say in regard to my Commissions. I have greatly lessen'd here and there the Credit of British reports to our disadvantage; and had I my powers, a loan office would probably have been opened in Genoa, to take in subscriptions for us before I left it. Some money men there, and an eminent Merchant were determined to send you on your terms the Goods I was ordered to purchase for Tobacco, and to make use of the Emperor's flag, which they say they can easily obtain; but they wanted to be assured, that after so long an interval, you might not have altered your mind. This you know, Sir, is more than I can do; and my ignorance of the footing, on which our State and Continental loan offices are at present, puts out of my power to encourage adventurers in any thing, as they cannot expect an advantage by it, unless they send a much larger Capital than they can fetch back, for the reasons I mentioned in letter 8.; and I cannot tell them how they can now dispose of their money in America. Here, where I am since the 13. of September, I have been assured that every thing will be done in our favour which prudently can be done. It is very mortifying for me to be still deprived of my Commissions and Instructions; and was not my Character well Known, it is probable that I should be looked upon as an imposter, since so many ships are arrived from America, and even from Virginia, without ever a letter for me. I must soon return to Genoa, to keep in good humour our new friends, as writing alone don't answer the purpose as well as I could wish. I shall soon after come back, and then go to Rome, Naples, and Sicilly, having been assured, that something can be done in all those places. Untill I receive your posotive Orders, I have no other rule to go by, than to act to the best of my judgment. You know, Sir, my situation, and my feelings for my Country. To be deprived of the power of being of real service at this time is cruel, and my state of uncertainty gives me more uneasiness than I can express. Permit me to remind you, Sir, that I live on credit; I wish at least that I may not be censured by my Countrymen, which I dare say, will not be the case, if they are fairly informed of my actions and true situation, ever since I left Virginia. I have the honor to be most respectfully, &c.

Original not located. Text from Mazzei's "Representation" of 1784 (NN), which gives in full or partial form many of Mazzei's dispatches from Europe. The missing original was Mazzei's Dispatch No. 22, and was copied entire in the "Representation."

From John Page

MY DEAR JEFFERSON Rosewell Octr. the 20th. 1780

The Inscription on my Friend Potclays Badge would be a most delightful Morsel for a Member of the Antiquarian Society, or a Member of the Society [of] Inscriptions and Belles Lettres; and had it not been too soon submitted to the Examination of the Connoiseurs of our Society might have been thereafter deposited in our Museum, and numbered amongst the most Precious of our Curiosities. For I should suppose as there is no Date to fix the Æra in which this Badge was given, nor any Symbols descriptive of the Time when, Place where, or Occasion of giving it; and as History is silent on this Head, it would puzzle the most accute Antiquarians in the World to find out even the Meaning of the Inscription, and much more to discover the Occasion of its being presented by the Governor of Virginia to a Cherokee Chief. But unluckily for the Virtuoso who might wish to puzzle himself and the World with ten thousand ingenious Conjectures concerning this same Badge, on shewing it to Doctr. McClurg and my Son Mann they recollected that they had seen it worn at College by the Censor, under Mr. Madisons Institution. The Doctr. bursting into one of his Fits of Laughter swore he thought he remembered when Madison presented it to Potclay, being at a Loss what to give him, when he happened to pick up this Badge of an Office then just laid aside. The D. O. ne B. M. Q. D. C. they say, stand for "Da Operam ne boni Mores Quid Detrimenti Capiant." This I take to be the true Reading of the Inscription. Potclay or his Friend only mistook the

President for the Governor, so that I think we have fairly solved the Difficulty, but which I confess without some Recollection of having seen the Badge, and the Light which the Doctr. and my Son threw on it I alone could never have done. I have no Objection to such Employment as this, but the arduous one you before alluded to especially after having declined a lighter Toil, would be very inconsistent. I beg therefore you will not think of proposing it to me again. Consider how inconsistently we shall act, if you should leave the Helm when it requires such Vigil[ance,] Activity, Spirit, and Dexterous Skill to steer us through the Storm; and if [he] who had quitted the Ship confessedly because worn down with Fatigue, and unable to hand a Rope or keep the Deck, even in a Calm, should presume to take your Helm out of your Hands. It will never do indeed. As many Riddles or *Puzzles* as you please but no ——— —— for your Friend JOHN PAGE

RC (DLC).

MY FRIEND POTCLAYS BADGE: TJ had evidently written to Page (in a missing letter) describing a visit to the governor by the Cherokee chief Potclay (of whom nothing further is known) and asking Page to explain a curious badge or medal worn by the chief. Page's letter contains a full explanation as well as revealing comments on a proposal by TJ that Page stand as a candidate to succeed TJ in the governorship. Potclay and his companions probably received new Virginia Indian medals from TJ: see Robert Scot's Invoice for Executing an Indian Medal, 13 Oct. 1780.

From Horatio Gates

Hillsborough, 21 Oct. 1780. The bearer, Mr. Thompson, has a bill from Col. Polk on TJ for £100,000 in lieu of the bill Mr. Ochiltree had with him when he stayed in Charlotte with the enemy. Ochiltree's bill will be canceled. Thompson is anxious for payment.

Dft (NHi); 1 p. Tr (DLC) of Dft.

From Samuel Huntington

SIR Philada October 21. 1780

Your Excellencys several Letters of the 8. and 10. Instant with those covering the Dispatches from General Gates have been duly received.

The Expedient you have adopted to invite some of the Chief Indian Warriors to visit Congress and Genl. Washington appears to me good Policy. Your Despatches on that Subject which are just received, will be laid before Congress this Day, and their

Sentiments thereon shall be communicated to your Excellency as soon as possible.

I have enclosed for your Information a Copy of a Letter this Moment received from General Washington.

I have the Honor to be with the highest respect &c. &c. &c.,

S. H.

P.S. The enclosed Resolve this Moment passed contains the Sense of Congress respecting the Indians.

FC (DLC: PCC, No. 15). Enclosures: (1) copy of a letter from Washington to Congress, not identified; (2) resolve of Congress, 21 Oct., approving proposed visit by Cherokee chiefs to Congress and the army (attested copy in Vi; printed in JCC, XVIII, 957-8, and also above in entry for TJ's missing letter to Huntington of 10 Oct. 1780, q.v.).

From Thomas Nelson

SIR Halls Mill October 21st. 1780.

I was this morning informed that the Enemy had landed. A party of light Horse who was at Kemps landing about break of day on their way to the Great Bridge, which I fear they have taken possession of by this time, there being no Militia collected. I had ordered Capt. Bradley with two four Pounders to that post; but it will not be in his power to defend it with the few Men he had. The Enemy will Undoubtedly secure all these passes, there being no possibility of preventing it with the Militia of [that] part of the Country who are not armed at all. I hope you will lose no time in ordering a body of Men down, that we may at least attempt an Opposition. I shall endeavour to collect a force from these Counties, but the Confusion is so great that much cannot be expected. Light Horse are absolutely necessary, and I have a poor prospect of raising any number among these people, their horses being unfit for that service. Will it not be a good plan to raise, from the Militia, as many Volunteers as can be got to serve during the Invasion? The public Stores at Portsmouth are very trifling. The Cattle that were collected in the County of Princess Anne for the Commissary I am told have fallen into the Enemies hands. I never was in so bad a part of the Country for Intelligence. The Enemy might have secured every pass before I had any Account of their landing. Their numbers I cannot learn, but from their Ships and bringing light Horse with them, I suppose they mean to make their Winter Quarters in this State.

I am Sir with due Respect Your mo: Obt. & hble Servt.,

THOS. NELSON JR.

We have not a single piece of Artillery. They were all carried to Richmond with the Ammunition.

Tr (DLC); endorsed: "Copy of Letters to Govr. Jefferson." 2d Tr (DLC: PCC, No. 71, I), enclosed to Huntington in TJ's letter of 22 Oct. 1780.

From James Innes

Dear Sir [21? October 1780]

Ere this reaches you, you will doutless have heard of the arrival of an inimical fleet in our Bay. Being vested with no public authority, I do not presume to address you officially. Yet as a friend, an appellation I shall allways wish to merit, I will venture to offer you my Sentiments on the present Critical Conjuncture. From a close attention to the Dispositions of the people in the Lower Country, I think I know them well. Their attachment to the great Cause in which they are engaged is I am certain as unanimous and firm, as of any Class of people upon the Continent, but the extremely exposed Situation of their properties and families, and the anticipation of Captivity or famine may act so strongly upon them in the hour of alarm and danger, when their Hearts too are soften'd by the forebodings of the miseries, impending over their dearest domestic connections, as to produce a Languor, and Indecision, totally incompatible with the rapid and determinate movements of War. The feelings of the man, may in a fatal moment, swallow up the sentiments of the patriot. During my little experience in the Northern Army, I learnt by observation one Truth—which I ever found invariable—which was that no aid of militia could ever be drawn from the part of the Country immediately invaded. The strong Impulses on the Heart, I have just now described, forever produced Inactivity, but transfer the Scene of war from their own Doors, and the very men who before had been so tame and inactive, flew to arms with ferceness and unanimity, and were of very important Service. This was truly the Case with the now famed Jersey militia in 1776-1777. In 1777 I very well remember, when Sir William Howe's Army was on the Banks of the Skuylkill, the populous City of philadelphia and the thickly inhabited Counties immediately around it, did not furnish three hundred men alltogether to Genl. Washingtons army. Yet I observe that the other Day Govr. Reed marched three thousand men from the city of philadelphia only, to join our army, in offensive operations against N. York. I mention these instances only to evince the propriety of the observations I have made above, and to shew too, the impolicy of estimating in the number requisite to repel the invading foe, the militia on the Spot of Invasion. It follows of Course then that the only effectual Service in our present Circumstances must be derived from the aid of militia's less exposed in their Situations than the Counties on the Bay and sea shores. If such aid should be speedily sent, I am Confident it would animate the lower Counties to make that proper Stand, which, without such Support I fear they will not be equal to. Besides a speedy assistance from above will inspire them with a proper Confidence in Government and banish from their minds the baneful Idea (which has been too prevalent since the Removal of the Seat of Government) of being abandoned and deserted by their upland Brethren. These opinions, believe me, I consider as foundationless, and reprobate as pernicious to the common weal. Yet as they are but too popular, I humbly concieve it might be productive of beneficial Consequences to eradicate them entirely, tho the accomplishment of so desirable an object, might be attended with some trouble and Expense. These crude Sentiments written amidst much Haste and Confusion I submit to your better Judgement, happy, if upon perusing them you shall find one Hint worthy adoption. I trust you will consider me on this occasion as divested of all local partialities and governed solely by disinterested attachment to the general good. Should you not coincide with me in opinion, I pray to Heaven, my augury may prove false. Do not concieve from the style of this letter that I am appal'd at approaching Danger, or that my soul feels one sentiment of Despair. I thank my God, I am free from such Influences. My poor Exertions shall not be wanting to animate the people to action tho' my present Decripitude will not permit me to be so active, as I could wish. I hope this letter will be understood as I wish it, I mean, as originating from Duty to my Country, and affection for your Excellency.

I have the honor to be most respectfully Yr friend & Sert.,

JAS INNES

RC (DLC); without place or date, but unquestionably written by Innes upon the arrival in Virginia waters of the British invading force under Gen. Alexander Leslie, a fact clearly established by Innes' reference to Joseph Reed.

THE OTHER DAY GOVR. REED MARCHED: In August 1780 Joseph Reed, president of the Executive Council of Pennsylvania, assumed personal charge of the militia raised for Washington's projected attack upon New York (Washington, *Writings*, ed. Fitzpatrick, XX, 263, 398-400, 442). By mid-August Washington was obliged to abandon the plan and Reed's militia, encamped at Trenton, were dismissed; an extract from a Philadelphia newspaper under the dateline 5 Sep. was published in the *Virginia Gazette* (D & N) for 20 Sep. announcing that "On Friday last [i.e., 1 Sep.] the camp which had been formed at Trenton by the militia of this state, by orders of his Excellency General Washington, broke up in consequence of a countermand from him, on advices received from Europe." A brief official account of the invasion appeared in *Va. Gaz.* (D & N), 25 Oct., and may have been communicated by TJ. It reads as follows:

"On the 20th instant arrived in Chesapeake bay a British fleet of 54 ships, 25 of which are large, the residue small. On the 23d they landed 1000 infantry and 100 horse at Newport news, who immediately proceeded to Hampton, of which they took possession. Part of them are gone into Elizabeth river, but whether they have effected any landing there is not certainly known. It is supposed the whole land force is 5000 men, commanded by General Leslie, and the fleet is said to be commanded by Commodore Rodney, son of the Admiral of that name. The people in the neighbourhood of the invasion, turn out with great alacrity and spirit, and trust they will be immediately supported by their upper brethren."

See also J. C. Senf's letter to Gates from Portsmouth, 20 Oct., quoted in note to Gates' letter to TJ, 14 Oct. Leslie's invasion of Virginia proved abortive because he was soon afterward summoned to Cornwallis' rescue following the British defeat at King's Mountain (see Muhlenberg to TJ, 18 Nov., and TJ to Huntington, 10 and 19 Nov. 1780).

To Horatio Gates

SIR In Council Oct. 22d. 1780

The Letters which accompany this will inform you of the Arrival of a large fleet of the Enemy within our Capes, and that they have begun their Debarkation. We are taking Measures to collect a Body to oppose them; for which purpose it seems necessary to retain such Regulars Volunteers and Militia as have not yet gone on to you. We have left the Counties of Lunenburg, Mecklenburg, Halifax, and all above them on the South Side of James River uncalled on, that they may be in readiness to reinforce you as soon as Arms can be procured. I am in hopes the 18 months Men and western Militia, who will have joined you with the Volunteers from Washington and Montgomery, as proposed by Colo. Preston, and the 8 Months Militia, will be a useful reinforcement to you, and shall continue to divide our Attention both as to Men and Provisions between the Army in your Front, and that which is posting itself within our own Country.

I have the Honor to be with the greatest Esteem Sir Your mo. obedient & most humble Servt., TH: JEFFERSON

P.S. Colo Carrington is arrived since writing the above, and says you want 30 horses to move your Artillery. They shall be immediately sent to you.

RC (DLC); in a clerk's hand, with postscript and signature by TJ. Enclosures missing. They were probably the same as those enclosed to Huntington in the following letter. On 26 Oct. Gates forwarded this letter to Gen. Smallwood with the note: "I have just this moment recd the Letter on the other side from His Excelly Govr. Jefferson. I send it to you instantly by specal Expriss. I have kept this News as secret as possible" (DLC: TJ Papers).

To Samuel Huntington

SIR In Council Oct: 22d. 1780

The inclosed Letters which came to hand this morning will inform your Excellency that a Fleet of the Enemy has arrived in our Bay; and that a Debarkation of some light Horse in the Neighbourhood of Portsmouth seems to indicate that as their first Scene of Action. We are endeavouring to collect a Body to oppose them as numerous as the Arms we have will admit. We are obliged of Consequence to divert to this New Object a considerable Part of the Aids we destined for Genl. Gates. We shall not however by any means consider his reinforcement as no longer interesting, but clearly see the Necessity of supporting him with our utmost Abilities. We have therefore left that part of our Country which is more convenient to him uncalled on at present, which with the Proportion of Regulars, Volunteers, and Militia already with him, or not meant to be diverted will I hope be a seasonable aid. The want of Arms prevents every hope of effectual Opposition. I have perfect Confidence in Congress that this Want will be suffered to fetter us not a Moment after they can supply it. Generals Weeden and Muhlenburg of the line, and Nelson and Stevens of the Militia are called into Command. Congress will please to consider whether these can be aided by any other Officer of higher Rank and of approved Abilities and Trust. We have come to no determination on the Subject of the Convention Troops. Should the Enemy be in force, every Circumstance will render their Removal essential. This shall in that Case be done as directed by Congress and due Notice given to them as well as Governor Lee.

I have the honor to be with the most perfect Esteem and Respect Your Excellency's mo. obedient & Mo. humble servant,

TH: JEFFERSON

RC (DLC: PCC, No. 71, I); in a clerk's hand, signed by TJ. Endorsed: "Letter October 22d. 1780 Govr. Jefferson. Read October 30th." Enclosures: copies of Nelson's letter to TJ, 21 Oct., q.v., and of two letters from E. Moody to George Muter, the first without place, 20 Oct., and the second from York, 21 Oct., reporting the arrival of 50 British vessels within the Virginia Capes (transcripts of all three letters are in DLC: TJ Papers and also in DLC: PCC, No. 71, I).

TJ's letter and its enclosures were read in Congress on 30 Oct. and were "referred to the committee on the letters from General Washington, Major General Greene and Colonel Pickering, Q.M.G." (JCC, XVIII, 994).

To John Smith

SIR In Council October 22d: 1780.

Certain information being received that a considerable Fleet of the Enemy has arrived within our Capes, and have begun their debarkation, I have thought proper with advice of the Council of State to require one fourth of the Militia of your County to repair immediately to Richmond armed and accoutred in the best manner possible. Let every Man bring his own Blanket. It is not necessary that any field Officer should come with them, as field and General Officers will be provided by the Executive. They are to [be] furnished with provisions by impressing it as directed by the provision Law, giving to the persons from whom they take it, a Certificate of the Article, Price and purpose and transmitting to me a List of all such Certificates. I am to request that you lose not a Moments Time in the execution of these Orders. I am with great Respect Sir Yo. Mo. Obdt Hble Servt:, TH: JEFFERSON

RC (Vi); in a clerk's hand, signed by TJ. Addressed: "On public service To the County Lieutenant of Frederick." Endorsed, probably much later: "Governor Jefferson Cy. Lt. I do not recollect any thing about this. J. Smith."

John Smith was lieutenant of Frederick co. from 1777 (*Official Letters*, III, 156, note).

To Edward Stevens

SIR In Council Octr. 22. 1780

We this Morning received certain Information of the Arrival of a Considerable Fleet of the Enemy in our Bay, and that they had begun their Debarcation. We have taken measures for Assembling a Force to oppose them, and must take the liberty of desiring you to return imediately and assist in the Command of them. I am with great respect Sir Your Most Obt Servt., TH JEFFERSON

Tr (DLC); endorsed: "Copy of a Letter from Governor Jefferson to Edward Stevens dated October 22d. 1780."

To George Washington

SIR Richmond October 22d. 1780.

I have this morning received certain information of the Arrival of a hostile fleet of about Sixty Sail in our bay. The debarkation of some light Horse in the Neighbourhood of Portsmouth seems to indicate that, as the first scene of their action. We are endeavouring to collect as large a body to oppose them as we can arm: this will be lamentably inadequate if the Enemy be in any force; it is Mortifying to suppose it possible that a people able and zealous to contend with their Enemy should be reduced to fold their Arms for want of the means of defence; yet no resources that we know of, ensure us against this event. It has become necessary to divert to this new object a considerable part of the Aids we had destined for General Gates: we are still however sensible of the necessity of supporting him, and have left that part of our Country most Convenient to him uncalled on at present, that they may reinforce him as soon as Arms can be received. We have called to the Command of our forces, Generals Weeden, and Muhlenburg of the line and Nelson, and Stevens of the militia. You will be pleased to make to these such addition as you think necessary. As to aids of men I ask for none, knowing that if the late detachments of the Enemy should have left it safe for you to spare aids of that kind you will not await my application. Of the troops we shall be able to collect there is not a single man who ever saw the face of an Enemy. Whether the Convention Troops will be removed is not yet determined; this must depend on the force of the Enemy and the aspect of their Movements.

I have the honor to be, with the most perfect esteem & respect your Excellencies mo: Obt. & mo: hble Servt, TH: JEFFERSON

RC (DLC: Washington Papers); in a clerk's hand, corrected, signed, and addressed by TJ: "On public service His Excellency General Washington Head Quarters"; endorsed: "Richmond 22d. October 1780 from Govr. Jefferson. Ansd. 8h. Novem." Tr (DLC); text defective.

From George Washington

SIR Head Quarters 22d. Octobr. 1780

Major General Greene, who goes to take command of the southern Army, will have the honor of presenting this to your Excellency. I have advised him to take the several States in his way which are immediately concerned in furnishing Men and supplies for the department committed to his direction, that he may gain a more accurate knowledge of the forwardness they are in, a tolerable Idea of what may be his future expectations, and endeavour to settle some plans for the regular support and subsistence of the Army in provisions, Forage and transportation.

I am well aware of the embarrassments under which the southern States labor, and of the many difficulties which are to be surmounted: But I have a very full dependance that the most vigorous exertions will be made by them upon the present occasion, and the entire confidence I have in the abilities, fortitude and integrity of Genl. Greene, founded on a long and intimate experience of them, assures me that he will do every thing his means will enable him to do; and I doubt not, candid allowances will be made for the peculiar difficulties he has to encounter.

I recommend him to your State as worthy of its utmost confidence and support, and to Your Excellency personally as one whom I rank among the number of my friends.

With the greatest Respect and Esteem I have the honor to be Your Excellency's Most obt. and humble Servt.

Dft (DLC: Washington Papers); in hand of Tench Tilghman; endorsed. At foot of text the several recipients of this letter are named: "Govr. Lee. Maryland Gov Jefferson Virginia Gov. Nash. No. Carolina." In Washington's *Writings*, ed. Fitzpatrick, xx, 247-8, the copy sent to Gov. Lee of Maryland is printed from the original in MdHi; it bears the date 23 Oct.

To George Weedon

Sir — Richmond Oct. 22d. 1780.

We this morning received certain Information of the Arrival of a considerable Fleet of the Enemy in our Bay and that they had begun their Debarkation. We have taken Measures for assembling a force to oppose them and are to beg the favor of you to come immediately on to aid in the command of them. Generals Muhlenburg, Nelson, and Stevens are also called on to lend their Assistance.

I have the honor to be with great Respect Sir Your mo. ob. & most humble Servt.,

Th: Jefferson

RC (PPAP); in a clerk's hand, corrected and signed by TJ. At foot of text: "General Weeden."

Steps to Be Taken to Repel General Leslie's Army

[22? October 1780]

Call on Lawson's troops of horse.

Call 10,000 troops. viz.

Chestfd. C.H. 1000.

Lawson. 500.

⅓ militia Prss. Ann 594. Norf. 800. Nansemd. 644. Eliz. City 182. Warwick 100. York 244. James City 222.

Gloster 805. Middlesex 210. K & Queen. K. William. N. Kent. Chas. city. Surry. Southampton. Sussex. Dinwiddie. Pr. Geo. Chestfd. Henrico. Hanover

The counties nearer or as near to Portsmouth than Hillsborough are Brunswick, Amelia, Powhatan, Goochland, Louisa. Orange, Culpepper. The proprietary counties and all below those which should not be called out I. Wight. Surry. Pr. Geo. Jas. City. Gloster. Middlesx. Richmond. K. Geo.

Stop troops going on to Southward

viz. new levies.
Lawson's lower battalion
garrison for Hobbs' hole } because will carry public arms.

but not Lawson's upper battalion
Western volunteers. } becaus carry their own

Call vessels and stores from Ship yard.

Provide batteaux at Foundery.

Order away Conventioners.

Crockett's battaln. to attend till Maryland battaln. joins. Then to return.

Beeves from Warm springs to come to Barracks.

Colo. Wood impress waggons
provision

Officers. Genl.
Feild.
Subaltern.

Commrs. of provn law

Stores &c. at Wmsburg.

Write to Genl. Nelson
Gates
Congress

Hamilton

New recruits gone forward	5
Do. rendezvousing at Hillsboro	5
Western militia	10
⟨*Lynch's volunteers*⟩	⟨*3*⟩
Campbell's &c.	7
Delinquents	10
	37
New recruits not gone forward	20
Lawson's volunteers	7
Crockett's battalion	

FOR CAROLINA.

Washington	829
Montgomery	750
Botetourt	589
Henry	600
Pittsylva.	923
Bedford	1369
Buckingham	650
Cumberland	384
Prince Edward	570
Charlotte	625
Halifx	987
Mecklbgh	850
Lunbgh	550
	9676
Southampton	1000
Brunswick	1300
Sussex	700
Dinwiddie	700
Amelia	1100
Chestfd.	750
Powhatan	285
	5835
Chas. City	286
N. Kent	418
Hanover	980
Henrico	619
Goochland	580
Louisa	600
Fluvanna	260
Albemarle	911
Amherst	800
	5454

NOT TO BE CALLED OUT

Accomack	1208
Northampton	430
Prss. Anne	594
Norf.	880
Nansemd.	644
I. Wight	600
Surry	380
Pr. Geo.	500
El. City	182
Warwick	100
York	244
Jas. City	222
Gloster	805
Middlesex	
Essex	550
Lancaster	292
Northumbld.	739
Richmd.	573
Westmld.	663
K. Geo.	350
	9956
K. & Q.	500
K. Wm.	436
Caroline	1039
Spotsylva.	480
Orange	580
	3035
Stafford	500
Pr. Wm.	800
Fairfx	831
Loudon	1700
Fauqr.	1222
Culpeppr.	1600
	6653
Frederick	1000
Hampshire	829
Berkeley	1301
Shenandoah	1000
Rockingham	875
Augusta	
Rockbridge	395

N (DLC); 2 p.; entirely in TJ's hand.

This is a memorandum of executive agenda, together with militia estimates, probably drawn up immediately after TJ received news (see Nelson to TJ, 21 Oct.) that enemy troops had landed from the British fleet in Hampton Roads and were occupying adjacent points. A number of letters of the present and following dates show that TJ promptly carried out the plans here formulated.

To Robert Lawson

SIR Richmond October 23. 1780.

Knowing that you were not about to leave this place, and that the preparations for your corps were still going on, I have referred till some other very necessary orders were issued the communicating to you the desire of the Executive to divert the engagements of the volunteers raising under your auspices to the new object presented by the invasion of our own country. The troops of cavalry we shoud be very glad to have sent into the neighbourhood [of] the enemy as soon as their accoutrements can be obtained: and the infantry repair also in such bodies as you shall direct to the general Rendezvous at Cabin point. I inclose you blank powers for subsisting them [o]n their march, being the only resource we can recur to. We shall be glad to proceed to issue commissions conferring the several degrees of command [necessary?] for your corps as soon as your returns shall enable us. We concur in approving your choice of Major Jones to command the troops of horse. Any volunteers who may hereafter be engaged to take the places of the militia called from your county by the order of yesterday may enter if they chuse it into your corps.

I am with great esteem, sir, Your most obedient Servant,

TH JEFFERSON

RC (NcD); in a clerk's hand, signed and addressed by TJ: "Colo. Robert Lawson Richmond." Text damaged. Enclosures missing.

To James Maxwell

[*Richmond, 23? Oct. 1780.* Minute in the Journal of the Commissioner of the Navy (Vi) under date of 23 Oct.: "Waited on the Governor and Council in Consequence of a Letter received from his Excellency, and then proceeded to the Shipyard in order to have the state Vessels lying there brought up the River should Occasion require it." TJ's letter not located, but see an entry in his memorandum on the invasion, 22 Oct., reading: "Call vessels and stores from Ship yard."]

To James Wood

SIR Richmond, Octr 23d. 1780.

Certain information being received of the arrival of an enemy's fleet in the bay, it is thought expedient to decline for a time at least the sending Colo. Crocketts battalion to the Westward, as it is possible their services may be wanting elsewhere. Be pleas'd therefore to forward the inclosed to Mr. Madison requiring him to bring the beaves he had collected for that battalion to the barracks. If you think the pack-horses may be of service at your post either to perform ordinary duties, or in the event of removing the Convention prisoners, you will be pleas'd to require them to be brought at the same time.

I am with great esteem, Sir, Your Most obedt. hum. Servt.,

TH: JEFFERSON

PS It is probable you will hear from us very shortly. We wait to know the force of the Enemy before we write to you further.

RC (Lloyd W. Smith, Madison, N.J., 1946); in a clerk's hand, signed by TJ; endorsed.

From Edward Stevens

SIR Taylors Ferry October 24th. 1780.

On my getting to this place I fell in with the Bearer Majr. Lee on his way from Hillsborough to Richmond. He informs me the Troops at Hills Borough has been much distressed for Provisions and no prospect of its being much better for some time to come. He tells me no Cattle has yet gone to the Southern Army from the lower parts.

From this Information I shall order all the Militia that would pass this place to halt here and shall immediately go on myself to Hillsborough to advise with Genl. Gates.

Since my Arrival here I am informed and am afraid from too good Authority that a Considerable British Fleet is in the Chesapeake and an invasion of this State is certainly intended. If that should really be the case perhaps the haulting the Militia here would not be amiss on that Account. I am rather persuaded Genl. Gates had some apprehensions of an invasion of the State when he wished the Militia to Rendevous on this side of the Roan Oak.

The Provision Magazines at this place is quite empty. I have conversed with the Commissioners on the Subject of Supplying the Militia while they remain here; they say their powers this day ceases, as it is Ten days since the meeting of the Assembly tho' They seem disposed to render every Service in their power, in having the Militia provided for, till they hear from you on the Subject, which I hope will be as soon as possible.

I can get no information of the Success the Person has had who was empower[ed] to get the 50 Waggons in these parts. I am afraid but bad as none of them has yet gone Forward. I am &c.

Tr (DLC); endorsed (in part): "Copy."

From D'Anmours

SIR Montecielo 8bre 25. 1780

It will appear to you very strange that I should Communicate You Pollitical news from this place, where I expected to hear of none but of the Rural sort. Yet I have one which, though it may at first seem rather extraordinary, is not altogether quite improbable.

Yesterday, after I had finished my letter to Mrs. Jefferson, I went to dine with Dr. Gilmer. In the evening Just as I left the town, I overtook a British officer who was Riding the same Road I did. As he heard me speak french to my servant, he addressed me in that language and asked me what news? I told him what I knew. He then asked me where I thought general Clinton was? I answered him in new york. He then told me, that that very same Day they had Received news at the Barracks that he was gone to Halifax, on account of a french fleet having landed at Annapolis, in the Bay of fundy, with views of attacking the first of these Places. The following circumstances immediately occurred to my mind, and may serve as a Basis for the probability of that intelligence.

1st it is certain that the fleet under the Ct. De Guichen sailed from the Debouquemens of Hispaniola on the 20th of August, and that after he had ordered a small Division of men of war as a Convoy to a merchant fleet for Europe, and another for the Station of that island he Directed his course to the East as close the wind as he could.

2ly it appears no less Certain that in the Beginning of September, that fleet was Seen and Spoke to near the Continent By some american vessels after which we heard no more of it.

And lastly the Great numbers of friends we have still among the inhabitants of acadia, and the neighbouring indians, may have induced the admirals and Generals to plan that operation, which, in Case of Success, would occasion a Powerfull Diversion in favour of the united States By paving the way to Canada where we also have a very great party in the people of that Province. I say, all this considered inclines me to give some Credit to that Report. The officer told me it Came from Philadelphia by some People who had arived from there at the Baracks; and I had heard in the Course of the Day that Really there were some Quakers arived there.

You will learn By my letter to Mrs. Jefferson how I was Punished for having neglected the advice you Gave me of getting a good Dinner before I went to Mr. [*name scratched out*].[1] This is the only instance of inhospitality I ever met from virginians, and another proof that national virtues, as well as Rules, though ever so General, have their exceptions. I leave monte-cielo to day to Continue my Journey By Staunton and winchester to Baltimore, where I will be obliged to you to send me by the Expresses you send to the northward any Packets that might be Directed to me by your means.

I am with Great Respect and a most sincere attachement, sir Your most humble & obliged servant, LE CHEVR D'ANMOURS

RC (DLC); text faded.

MY LETTER TO MRS. JEFFERSON: Not found.

1 The editors have made an earnest effort to decipher the obliterated name, but without success. The ink in which the letter was written has faded to a pale yellow, whereas the ink employed in scratching out the name is a different, unfaded ink (it is possible that TJ himself blotted out the name). Nevertheless, it is apparent that the name consists of two syllables of four letters each, the first of which seems to end with a double "l" and the second with a "d" (the second part of the name is almost certainly "wood"). Yet the editors cannot identify any Albemarle name that seems to fit these conditions (see, for example, the lists of Albemarle names given above. Vol. 1: 664; 2: 128). For assistance in this disappointing attempt to reveal a host whom TJ regarded as deficient in hospitality the editors are obligated to Mr. Donald H. Mugridge, Fellow in American History, Library of Congress (communication to the editors, 30 June 1950).

To Samuel Huntington

SIR Richmond Octr. 25. 1780.

I do myself the pleasure of handing on the dispatches from General Gates accompanying this.

Since my last informing you of the appearance of an enemy's fleet they have landed 800 men in the neighbourhood of Portsmouth and some more on the bay side of Princess Anne County. On the 23d. in the morning they landed 1000 infantry and 100 cavalry at New Port's news who immediately took possession of hampton. The horse were proceeding up the road at the time of our last intelligence. The residue of their force remained still on board.[1] The unarmed State of the people leaves it not in our power to say precisely where one hundred horse will be stopped. The few who have arms have turned out with the greatest alacrity but they are not of a nature proper to oppose horse. Such a Corps as Major Lee's would now be of infinite value to us. Our Cartridge paper has been nearly exhausted by the Southern army, and 2000 Cartouch boxes which we had bought in Baltimore we have reason to believe were on their way down the bay when the enemy came in and have probably fallen into their hands. The want even of these small articles will be of great disadvantage. The Spirit which has shewn itself among the people on this occasion has given me the greatest pleasure, but I must not-withstanding assure you Sir that if great supplies of arms are not immediately sent on there is no event which may not be expected.

I have the honor to be with the greatest respect & esteem Your Excellency's most obedt. & most humble servt, TH: JEFFERSON

RC (DLC: PCC, No. 71, I); in a clerk's hand, with complimentary close and signature by TJ. Endorsed by Charles Thomson: "Letter from Govr Jefferson Octr. 25. 1780 Read 31." Enclosures: Gates to Huntington, 16-18 Oct. (Tr in DLC; original in DLC: PCC, No. 154, II), together with its enclosures (see Gates to TJ, 18 Oct.).

When this letter was read in Congress, 31 Oct., that body at once resolved that "Major Lee's corps be ordered to proceed immediately on their route to join the southern army" (JCC, XVIII, 997).

[1] This sentence interlined in TJ's hand.

To George Washington

SIR Richmond Octo. 25th. 1780.

I take the liberty of inclosing to you Letters from Genl. Hamilton for New York. On some representations received by Colo. Towles that an indulgence to Governor Hamilton and his Companions to go to New York on parole would produce the happiest effect on the situation of our Officers in Long Island we have given him, Majr. Hay and some of the same party at Winchester leave to go there on Parole. The two former go by water, the latter by land.

By this express I hand on from Genl. Gates to Congress intelligence of the capture of Augusta in Georgia with considerable quantities of Goods; and information which carries a fair appearance of the taking of George Town in So. Carolina by a party of ours, and that an Army of 6000 French or Spaniards had landed at Sunbury. This is the more credited as Cornwallis retreated from Charlo[tte o]n the 12th. inst. with great Marks of precipitation.

[Since] my last to you informing you of the appearance of an enemy's fleet they have landed 800 Men in the neighbourhood of Portsmouth and some more on the Bay side of Princess Anne. One thousand Infantry landed at New Ports News in the Morning of the 23d. and immediately took possession of Hampton. The horse were proceeding up the Road. Such a Corps as Major Lee's would be of infinite service to us; next to a naval force, horse seem to be most capable of protecting a Country so intersected by waters.

I am with the most sincere esteem Your Excellency's Most obedt. & most humble servt, TH: JEFFERSON

RC (DLC: Washington Papers); in a clerk's hand, with complimentary close and signature by TJ; endorsed (in part): "Ansd. 8h Novem." FC (DLC). Enclosures not found.

On the Henry Hamilton case, see TJ to Theodorick Bland, 8 June 1779, and references there.

To William Frazer

SIR Octob. 26. 1780.

You are at liberty to make use of the cannon and other public Stores for defence of the branches of York River. Any powder which may be necessary and can be procured from private hands, shall be paid for by the publick on your certificates. Commissaries, Commissioners of the provision Law and others having public provisions in their hands shall be justified in delivering a sufficient quantity for the subsistence of those aiding you in this defence so long as they shall be on that Service. I am Sir Your very humble servt., TH: JEFFERSON

RC (Vi); in a clerk's hand, with complimentary close and signature by TJ; endorsed: "Octor. 26. 1780 Thos. Jefferson's Letter."

On this day, according to a marginal note in TJ's letter to the Commissioners of the Provision Law in Hanover and Certain Other Counties, 29 Aug. 1780, q.v., TJ addressed "Similar Lres . . . to the comrs. of Caroline N[ew] Kent C[harles] City." These letters are missing.

To Samuel Huntington

Richmond, 26 Oct. 1780. This letter is almost identical with TJ's letter to Thomas Sim Lee of this date, q.v.

RC (DLC: PCC, No. 71, I); in a clerk's hand, signed and addressed by TJ; endorsed: "Letter from Govr Jefferson Octr 26. 1780 Read Novr 2 Referred to the board of War to take order." For variations from the text of the letter to Lee, see note there.

From Samuel Huntington

Philadelphia, 26 Oct. 1780. Circular letter to the state executives enclosing a resolve of Congress of 21 Oct. "which makes some Alteration in the late Arrangement of the Army . . . requested by the Resolution of the 8. Instant. . . . The whole of the Troops are to be enlisted during the War, and join their respective Corps by the first Day of January next." This resolution "was adopted in Consequence of a Letter from the Commander in Chief expressing his Sentiments on the Subject in pressing and explicit Terms."

FC (DLC: PCC, No. 15). Enclosure (Vi): copy written and attested by Charles Thomson of Congress' resolve of 21 Oct.; printed in JCC, XVIII, 959-60.

A LETTER FROM THE COMMANDER IN CHIEF: Washington to Huntington, 11 Oct. 1780 (*Writings*, ed. Fitzpatrick, XX, 157-67).

From Samuel Huntington

SIR Philada October 26. 178[0]

Your Excellency will receive herewith enclosed the Copy of an Act of Congress of the 24. Instant, directing that the Commissary General make accurate Returns to Congress of the Supplies furnished by each State since the last Day of December last, and that the State Agents transmit to the Commander in Chief and Commissary General respectively monthly Returns of all the Provisions which shall be drawn into their Hands, specifying the Articles and Places where they shall be deposited, and also earnestly recommending to the several Legislatures to enjoin it as a Duty on their State Agents in such Manner as to enforce a punctual Obedience.

I am also directed to transmit you the enclosed Copy of Col. Blaine's Letter and Papers to which it refers, and to request the serious Attention of the States to the present Wants and Distresses of the Army, and the most efficacious Means in their Power to furnish the Supplies requested with unremitted Attention.

I have the Honor &c. &c., S. H.

FC (DLC: PCC, No. 15); at head of text: "Circular." Enclosures (Vi): (1) attested copy of Congress' resolve of 24 Oct. on Ephraim Blaine's letter of 17 Oct. (resolve printed in JCC, XVIII, 970-1); (2) copy of letter from Ephraim Blaine, commissary general of purchases, to Samuel Huntington, 17 Oct. 1780, describing his difficulties in securing provisions of food from the states. Blaine's letter transmitted other letters from his deputies in the southern department describing conditions there, but these have not been located.

To Thomas Sim Lee

SIR Richmond Octo: 26. 1780.

The Executive of this State, think it expedient and necessary that under our present circumstances the prisoners of war under the Convention of Saratoga, be removed from their present situation. Many circumstances have led to this necessity. It will be utterly impracticable as long as they remain with us to prevent the hostile army now in this State from being reinforced by numerous desertions from this corps and this expectation may be one among the probable causes of this movement of the enemy. Should moreover a rescue of them be attempted the extensive disaffection which has been lately discovered, and almost total want of arms in the hands of our good people, render the success of such an enterprize by no means desperate. The fear of this and of the dangerous convulsions to which such an attempt wou'd expose us, diverts the attention of a very considerable part of our militia from an opposition to the invading enemy. An order has therefore been this day issued to Colo. Wood to take immediate measures for their removal[1] to fort Frederick in your State agreeable to a resolution of Congress of september 20. 1780. of which your Excellency has I believe been apprized. Every aid has been and will be given him for transporting, guarding and subsisting them on the road, which our powers could accomplish. Notice of this measure is sent by the present conveyance to their Excellencies the President of Congress and General Washington.[2]

I have the Honor to be with the most perfect esteem and respect Your Excellency's most obedient and most humble servant,

TH: JEFFERSON

RC (MdAA); in a clerk's hand, signed by TJ. TJ sent almost identical letters on the same day to Samuel Huntington and George Washington.

THE EXTENSIVE DISAFFECTION WHICH HAS BEEN LATELY DISCOVERED: See TJ to the Virginia Delegates, 27 Oct.

1 The rest of this sentence does not appear in the letters to Huntington and Washington.

2 In the letters to Huntington and Washington this sentence reads: "Notice hereof is sent by the present conveyance to his Excellency Governor Lee, on whose part I doubt not necessary preparations for their reception will be made."

To Josiah Parker

SIR Richmond October 26, 1780.

The invasion of our country, lately taken place has rendered it necessary to call into the field a large body of militia to oppose them. The Executive are very anxious as far as it can be done, to substitute in place of the militia officers, others who to equal zeal join experience in military duties. Should your present situation admit you to take over them the same command you held in the regular service, I am now to ask the favor of you to do it; and trust that your wish to expel the invading enemy from among us will overweigh many domestick inconveniences which might attend it. I wish to receive your answer by the bearer or any speedier opportunity, and that you may join the Commanding officer as soon as possible if you can undertake the charge, as I suppose the whole force will assemble between this date and the 12th of the ensuing month. I readily apprehend that difficulties about relative rank between the gentlemen who have resigned, and those who have continued in service may arise; The removal of these is beyond the reach of our powers; and I shall think it unfortunate indeed, if our country should for that cause lose the services of gentlemen in a crisis where they are so vitally important. I cannot but rely that those who have so far changed their line of life, as that military rank is no longer their object, will cheerfully take their stand at the most useful place in which the laws have left it in our power to employ them.

I am, with great respect, Sir, Your Most Obt humble Serv,

Th. Jefferson

MS not located. Text from *Virginia Magazine of History and Biography*, xxii (1914), 257-8, where it is printed with other "Revolutionary Correspondence of Col. Josiah Parker of Isle of Wight County, Va.," from originals then in the possession of Robert M. Hughes of Norfolk, Va. This letter is not among the Hughes Papers that were later acquired by the College of William and Mary.

There is a biographical sketch of Josiah Parker of Macclesfield, Isle of Wight co., in vmhb, vi (1898-1899), 421-4; he had served as colonel of the 5th Va. Line, 1777-1778.

To George Washington

Richmond, 26 Oct. 1780. This letter is almost identical with TJ's letter to Thomas Sim Lee of this date, q.v.

RC (DLC: Washington Papers); in a clerk's hand, signed by TJ; endorsed. Tr in DLC: TJ Papers. For variations in the text from the letter to Lee, see note there.

To James Wood

Sir Richmond Octo. 26. 1780

The Enemy invading us appearing now to be in force the Executive have determined that the Convention Troops be removed without delay. You will therefore take immediate measures for their removal to fort Frederick[1] as directed by the Board of War.

Previous to the publication of this measure another is expedient: The Regiment of Guards you know is enlisted to serve only till the departure of these Troops from the county or Country. We wish to have them enlisted to serve in the State and during the present Invasion only, at the determination of which they shall be discharged. I pray you therefore to communicate this matter to Colo. Taylor, and with him so to concert Measures as that while you are making the necessary preparations for removal, he may be taking Measures to engage both his Officers and Men for the purpose above mentioned.

I inclose you blank Powers for impressing Waggons Beef, Flour and Indian Corn; these you will fill up with the Names of Persons whose activity you can rely on. They will proceed on the rout you propose to take and have the necessary Provisions ready by certain days at certain places all along the road. The Beeves you will probably find it best to take with you on the Hoof from the different places where they are laid in, and kill them as you want them. I suppose those from the Warm-Springs will be with you before you march and perhaps others from other places. I inclose you the extracts which were omitted before but doubt whether it will be now necessary to send to Green Briar &c. as formerly proposed. Still I take for granted some Money will be necessary for you. We have not a shilling now, but expect some in a few days of which we will communicate to you a part.

As to the Guard to move the Troops on you know that a Regiment from Maryland is now on their march to assist you. I have not heard where they are, but you can probably take Measures for finding that out, and causing them to bend their course so as to fall in with you. The aid of the Regiment of Guards (if enlisted) and of Colo. Crocketts Batallion is extremely wanting here, the moment you can do without them. If Militia will do to conduct the Prisoners in conjunction with Capt. Reades Troop, you would render the State essential and critical Service by sending down these two Regiments. In that event make use of Letter No. 2. which calls on the County Lieutenant of Albemarle to furnish you with as many Militia as you shall require. Perhaps you may better answer your purpose by raising volunteer Horse to serve on this special occasion and be discharged on their return, or perhaps it may be useful (if you cannot raise Horse) to get your Militia or part of them to mount themselves: in either of these cases forage should be allowed. If you think that the attendance of Crocketts Batallion and the Regiment of Guards or a part of them cannot be dispensed with you will in that case I am sure send them back to us as soon as you can safely spare them and in the mean time send Letter No. 1. to the County Lieutenant of Albemarle.

It will possibly happen that the Officers cannot be so soon ready as the Men: In which case we would wish the Men not to be delayed a Moment, but that the Officers should be allowed what time you think reasonable for following you.

It is probable you may have occasion to make further application to the Executive before you march: For this reason I think it will be expedient to keep a Horseman at Rutherfords. Indeed it is pretty remarkable that the Enemy retain a large Body of their Troops on board their Vessels. When the Stake is so great we are apt to fear every thing which is not impossible. You will cross Patowmack some distance above Alexandria; to that place the Enemy can go with their largest Ships in a very short time from where they now are. Suppose them landed at that place, Great improbabilities indeed are opposed to the Success of their enterprize; but how often have we seen the greatest improbabilities surmounted by bold adventure. It would take the people of the Vicinities some time to recover from their first consternation and to get their Arms and Accoutrements into a state fit for use: Experience has shewn how very long it is from the landing of an Enemy before we can collect a force sufficient to oppose them: Might not this danger be lessened by leaving a chain of expresses from this place to you; still dropping one every 40 Miles as you march; and forming another from the Mouth of Patowmack up by the Place where you will cross it, and so continued along your road till it should meet you. The former would convey to you the most speedy intelligence of the Enemy's moving from their present Station; and the latter, if they should enter Patowmack; both might be discontinued on your crossing that River as all Danger would then cease. I suggest this matter merely for your consideration; perhaps it might take more horsemen than you have to spare,[2] or perhaps your rout may be so much more to the Westward than I have expected as to render this precaution altogether useless.

The inclosed letter to Colo. Crockett you will deliver when you think proper.

I am with great esteem Sir Your most obedt. humble servt.,

TH: JEFFERSON

RC (Lloyd W. Smith, Madison, N.J., 1946); in a clerk's hand, signed and with additions by TJ; endorsed. Enclosures: Powers for Impressing Supplies (six blank copies; see the following document); others not certainly identified. An extract of the letter (first paragraph only) was enclosed in TJ's letter to Harrison, 29 Dec. 1780, q.v. THE EXTRACTS WHICH WERE OMITTED BEFORE: This may possibly refer to the "four blank Powers to be directed to any person . . . for Green Briar or any other county" (see TJ to James Wood, 18 Oct. 1780). LETTER NO. 1 and LETTER NO. 2 have not been found, but both are adequately described in the present letter as being addressed to the county lieutenant of Albemarle and as providing against either of two contingencies.

1 The place was left blank by the clerk and filled in by TJ.

2 The rest of the letter is in TJ's hand.

Warrant for Impressing Supplies

for the Convention Army on Its March to Maryland

VIRGINIA TO WIT,

Whereas the present invasion of this state by a powerful enemy has rendered it necessary for the safety thereof that the prisoners of war under the convention of Saratoga, be instantly removed, for which purpose great numbers of waggons and quantities of provisions and forage will be wanting. These are therefore to authorize and empower you to impress so many waggons, teams and drivers and so much beef living or slaughtered, bread, meal, flour and forage as by the commanding officer having charge of the said prisoners shall be deemed as necessary for the transportation of baggage and subsistance of the said troops their guards and attendance, giving to the persons, whose property shall be so taken or employed a certificate of the price due to them for such property or the hire thereof, such price being first settled by valuation as by law directed in other cases of impress, of which certificates you are to return a perfect list to the said commanding officer, by him to be forwarded to me, specifying in such list the names of the persons, articles seized, prices and dates. You are moreover authorized and in the first instance required to call on the Continental commissaries and quarter masters at the posts by which the said troops shall pass and also on the commissioners of the provision law in the several counties thro' which their route lies (if with any convenience it may be done) to furnish any transportation and subsistance for the said troops which may be within their power; and your receipts to such commissioners shall be to them a good voucher for the said troops which may be within their power; and your for what you shall call on them, notwithstanding any former orders we may have given to deliver them otherwise. And all the good citizens of this state, and others civil and military within the same are hereby required to be aiding and assisting to you in the execution of this warrant. Given under my hand and the seal of the Commonwealth at Richmond this 26th day of octo: 1780.

THO: JEFFERSON

Tr in the War Office Letter Book (MiU-C); place for seal indicated at foot of text. In the margin: "six copies enclosed to Colo Wood" (i.e., in TJ's letter to Wood of this date, preceding).

From Edward Stevens

SIR Hillsborough October 27th. 1780

On my arrival here last Night I found your Letter of the 22 Instant giving me Information of the Arrival of a British Fleet in the Cheasepeak Bay, and desiring my Return immediately.

General Gates seems to wish I would remain here a day or two to make some regulation among the Militia that has already got in by which time he expects to hear farther from you, and be certainly informed whether the Enemy mean to take Post in Virginia or not. If they should my return shall be the nearest way to where I shall understand our force may be assembled. It is not in my power yet to give you any Just State of the Militia or 8 Months men, that has got to this place. Am afraid from what I have already understood there will be but little chance of getting Arms and Accoutrements for such of those as come without.

The General seems to be perfectly pleased with respect to the Orders I have given to the Militia that was to pass Taylors Ferry.

This will be delivered you by Lieutenant Chew of the Virginia Militia who was unfortunate enough to loose an Arm in our unfortunate affair near Camden. I am &c.

Tr (DLC); endorsed (in part): "Copy."

To the Virginia Delegates in Congress

GENTLEMEN Richmond Octo. 27. 1780.

I must beg the favor of you to solicit the sending on to us immediately a good supply of Cartridge Paper and Cartouch Boxes. Nearly the whole of the former Article which we had bought at Alexandria, Baltimore &c. and what the Board of War sent from Philadelphia has been made up and forwarded to the Southern Army; there remains now but a few Ream to make up. I fear we have lost 2000 cartouch Boxes on the Bay which we had had made at Baltimore. Our distress for these is also very great Muskets being really useless without them. I must entreat the greatest dispatch in forwarding these Articles.

A very dangerous Insurrection in Pittsylvania was prevented a few days ago by being discovered three days before it was to take place. The Ring-leaders were seized in their Beds. This dangerous fire is only smothered: when it will break out seems to depend altogether on events. It extends from Montgomery County along our Southern boundary to Pittsylvania and Eastward as far as James River: Indeed some suspicions have been raised of it's having crept as far as Culpepper. The rest of the State turns out with a Spirit and alacrity which makes me perfectly happy. If they had Arms there is no effort either of public or private Enemies in this State which would give any Apprehensions. Our whole Arms are or will be in the hands of the force now assembling: Were any disaster to befall these, We have no other resource but a few scattered Squirrel Guns, Rifles &c. in the Hands of the western People.

I am with the greatest esteem Gentlemen Your most obedt. humble servt, TH: JEFFERSON

RC (DLC: PCC, No. 71, I); in a clerk's hand, with corrections, complimentary close, and signature by TJ. Endorsed by Charles Thomson: "Letter from Govr Jefferson to the Delegates. Oct 27 1780 Read Novr 2. Referred to the board of War to take order [*In another hand*:] Acted upon."

To Horatio Gates

SIR Richmond October 28. 1780.

Your Letters of the 14th, 20th, and 21st are come to hand, and your dispatches to Congress have been regularly forwarded. I shall attend to the caveat against Mr. Ochiltree's bill. Your Letter to Colo. Senf remains still in my hand as it did not come till the enemy had taken possession of the ground on which I know him to have been, and I have since no certain information where a Letter might surely find him. My proposition as to your Bills in favor of the Quarter Master referred to yours of sept. 27. I have notified to the Continental Quarter master your advance of 900 dollars to Cooper. As yet we have received no waggons. I wish Mr. Lamb may have supplied you. Should those from the western quarter not come in we will authorize him or some other to procure a relief in time for those first impressed. We are upon the eve of a new arrangement as to our Commissary's and Quarter Masters departments as the want of money, introducing its substitute force, requires the establishment of a different kind of system.

Since my first information to you of the arrival of an enemy, they have landed about 800 men near Portsmouth, some on the bay side of Princess Anne, one thousand at Hampton, and still retained considerable part on board their ships. Those at hampton after committing horrid depredations have again retired to their ships which on the evening of the 26th were strung all along the road from Newports news to the mouth of Nansemond, which seems to indicate an intention of coming up James river. Our information is that they have from 4 to 5000 men, commanded by Genl. Leslie, and came under convoy of one 40. gun ship and some frigates (how many has never been said) commanded by Commodore Rodney. Would it not be worth while to send out a swift boat from some of the inlets of Carolina to notify the french Admiral that his enemies are in a net if he has leisure to close the mouth of it? Generals Muhlenburg and Nelson are assembling a force to be ready for them, and General Weedon is come to this place where he is at present employed in some arrangements. We have ordered the removal of the Saratoga prisoners that we may have our hands clear for these new Guests.

I have the honor to be with the most perfect esteem & respect Sir Your most obedient & most humble servt., TH: JEFFERSON

RC (DLC); in a clerk's hand, with corrections, complimentary close, and signature by TJ; endorsed.

YOUR LETTER TO COLO. SENF: Dated 14 Oct. and enclosed in Gates' letter to TJ of that date, q.v.

To J. P. G. Muhlenberg

SIR Richmond Octr. 28. 1780.

I inclose you my last intelligence from the north side of the river: also an advice of Council for regimenting the militia. Some difficulty will arise under the 3d head between the militia and the regular Captains and subalterns. I must leave it to yourself to get over it by permitting those of the militia officers who shall be willing to return home, or by double officering, that is putting a set of regular officers into the Company with those of the militia or making the Companies small and increasing their numbers, or such other expedient as shall be most practicable and useful and will give least uneasiness.

I inclose you the names of such resigned and supernumerary

officers as occur to us with the dates of their original appointments; also letters to be Directed to such of them and such others as you think can be got. If you will direct them we will send expresses out with them.

The above is a copy of a letter from me to Genl. Muhlenberg.

TH: JEFFERSON

Tr (PPAP); endorsed: "Govr. Jefferson." The final sentence was added, with signature, in TJ's own hand. Enclosures not found: Minutes of the Council for the latter half of 1780 are, of course, lacking (see *Va. Council Jour.*, II, v-vi).

To James Wood

DEAR SIR Richmond Oct 28. 1780

My letter by Cap. Read which could not be come to hand when yours of the 26th came away will have answered beforehand the several matters stated in that except as to the division of the Convention troops into three parts. This I apprehend is contrary to the Convention, and I should expect would render their government and safe custody more difficult.

My last intelligence is that the troops who had landed at Hampton had again embarked, and that the Vessels of the Enemy were strung along the road from Point Comfort to the mouth of Nansemond River, which indicated a design of coming up James River. The information of Deserters and others concurs in this. No force is yet assembled which could venture to oppose them. These movements will of course [sho]w the necessity of quickening the execution of our desires [com]municated in my last.

Since writing so far the inclosed letter from the board of War came to hand. I wish the information of the General may be right as to the numbers. Our intelligence is that they are from 4 to 5000. I send you also an extract from their letter to me which covered it.

I am with great esteem Sir Your most obedt. humble servt.,

TH: JEFFERSON

RC (Lloyd W. Smith, Madison, N.J., 1946); in a clerk's hand, with complimentary close and signature by TJ; endorsed. Enclosures missing. Addressee identified from internal evidence.

MY LETTER BY CAP. READ: Doubtless TJ's letter to Wood of 26 Oct., q.v. YOURS OF THE 26TH: Not found. THE INFORMATION OF THE GENERAL: On 17 Oct. Washington advised the President of Congress that "the Fleet fell down from New York on Sunday last" and added that the "numbers gone are, by the best information I have yet obtained, about 2500 Foot and thirty or forty Horse, but they have taken spare furniture for a considerable number of Horse" (Washington, *Writings*, ed. Fitzpatrick, XX, 203).

From Thomas Sim Lee

SIR In Council Annapolis 30th Octr. 1780

We received your Favor of the 26th. Instant and can assure your Excellency our Inclination to relieve your State from its present embarrassing Difficulties and to prevent the Attention of the Militia being diverted from a vigorous Opposition to the invading Enemy will prompt us to render, most chearfully, every necessary Aid in accommodating the Convention Troops, when removed to Fort Frederick, with what Provisions we can spare; but the eventual Measures taken by this State for Supplying them, were only calculated for a partial Subsistence, because we expected your State would provide Magazines, at or in the Neighbourhood of the Post according to the Resolution of Congress referred to by your Excellency. We are &c.

FC (MdAA).

From Daniel Morgan

[Twelve Mile Creek, S.C., 30 October 1780]

The Enemy are retreating toward Charles Town, they are at present in the Neighbourhood of the Congarees, and General Smallwood and myself at some distance in their rear, but our forces too small to attempt any thing offensive; the Enemy's intentions seem to be destroy the provision in the Country, which I am afraid will render the operations of an extensive Army extremely difficult, if not impracticable for the want of provisions and Forage, supplies of which are at present attended with some share of distress to the Inhabitants.

Tr (DLC: PCC, No. 71, I). At head of text: "Extract of a Letter from General Morgan dated Camp at twelve Mile Creek October 30th: 1780 To Governor Jefferson." Enclosed in TJ to Huntington, 19 Nov. 1780.

Warrant to Thomas Russell to Impress Boats

VIRGINIA TO WIT.

Whereas the present invasion of this state by a Powerful enemy renders it necessary to collect Boats and other vessels sufficient for occasional transportation of troops across the rivers and water courses. These are therefore to authorize and empower you to impress so many boats and other vessels with crews and appendages as by any commanding officer acting with a distinct corps shall be thought necessary, giving to the owners thereof a certificate of the worth and rate of hire of the said vessels, such worth and hire being first settled by appraisement as by law directed in others cases of impress. And all the good Citizens of this state, and others civil and military within the same are hereby required to be aiding and assisting to you in the execution of this warrant. Given under my hand and the seal of the Commonwealth at Richmond this 30th day of October 1780. THO: JEFFERSON

Tr in War Office Letter Book (MiU-C); location of seal indicated at foot of text.

In PPAP (Weedon Papers) there is a letter from Weedon to Major P. Cooke, dated at Richmond, 31 Oct. 1780, stating that "The Executives have authorized me to assemble a Fleet of flatt bottom boats at Hood for the purpose of transporting Troops from either side of the River as the service may require. Mr. Thomas Russell A.D.Q.M.G. is now on the business of empressing Boats and will assemble them at that place. . . . His Excellency the Governor informs me you have a body of militia stationed at that place, so that a strong guard may be kept over them by your direction. . . . PS I must again beg your utmost care in keeping this little fleet always ready and well found—a large smoke on this side made on the shore will be a signal for them to come over."

From Edward Stevens

SIR Hillsborough October 30th. 1780

Since your last giving an Account of a British Fleet in the Cheasepeak Bay, reports here has been Various with respect to them. Genl. Gates and the Troops here are waiting with the greatest impatience to hear something certain about them, and expect hourly to receive information from you. Till then, he desires my stay at this Place, tho' this I informed you of a day or two agoe. The General seems to be embarrassed with respect to his movements, till he can receive certain Accounts of the Intention of that Fleet, and for that purpose he has sent Capt. Singleton to Virginia but at the same time is Confident he will hear from you before Captain Singleton can get to Richmond. Had the General received no information of the Fleet, I believe he would have marched from here before now.

Inclosed you have a return of the number of Militia that is at this place. From what I can already discover without some other steps are taken I fancey but very few of the 8 Months men will ever be Collected. Some of them who have had their Trials in their Counties are sent here and are only Condemned to serve out the Term of Three Months. Where the Court Martial found Law to Govern them in this I am at a loss to know. Others are allowed to Inlist in the Volunteer Service. Certainly the whole of these fellows ought to be on the same footing. Many of them alledge that their Officers countenanced their deserting and gave them leave, but this ought to be no plea for them for they well know they were doing wrong, and that their Officers had no right to give them leave to return Home, As I had expressly forbid any furloughs or Discharges being given without Countersigned by me and this they all knew. Any of the Officers who have been guilty of the accusation and I am pretty well Satisfied there are many of them that are, ought to be broke and turned into the Ranks to serve 8 Months. I never shall be reconciled with these fellows till I can get them altogether again, and put them into a situation where they may wipe off the stain they have brought on themselves, and their Country, and make some atonement for the Distresses that their Rascally Behaviour has occasioned, and at a time when if they had behaved like Men they might have releaved Thousands and immortalised their own Names.

I find there is about a 1000 Stand of Arms at this place tho they have been picked and Culled in such a manner that there is not one of them fit for Service till they are repaired, and they have no conveniences here for doing it. I believe will be sent back to Virginia; there is not a single Cartouch Box or Bayonett Belt here. How or where the Militia that is now without is to be equiped, I am at a loss to know.

There has been nothing from the Southward since Genl. Gates wrote you last. The Enemy are Retreating towards Camden where they are throwing up redoubts. I am &c.

Tr (DLC); endorsed (in part): "Copy." Enclosure not found.

On THE 8 MONTHS MEN, i.e., deserters from the militia after the battle of Camden who were condemned by courts-martial in their own counties to serve under the Continental articles of war for eight months longer than their normal militia service, see Petition of Certain Deserters, printed above under date of 7 Oct. 1780.

Advice of Council Embodying the Militia of Three Western Counties

In Council Octr. 30. 1780.

The board having reason to believe that a number of spirited citizens in the Counties of Botetourt, Montgomery and Washington are willing to proceed on Service to the Southward, and being of Opinion that large succours thrown in to General Gates may enable him to recover possession of the Country lately assumed by the enemy and put a speedy termination to the evils of conquest under which our brethren are suffering, that it will be less burthensome to the good people of the State to concur in one great effort at this season of the year when they may be best spared from their farms than by going in such numbers only as by barely opposing the progress of the enemy may protract the necessities for their service through the course of another year, advise the Governor to accept of their services on the following terms that is to say;

Each Company shall consist of 50 men at the least, the Captains, Lieutenants and Ensigns shall be appointed by the County Lieutenants from whence the men they are to command shall go. The whole to be in one regiment to be commanded by Colo. Wm. Campbell and such Lieutenant Colonal and Major as himself and the County Lieutenants of the said three counties shall appoint.

They shall be at head quarters of the Southern army or such other place of rendezvous as shall be appointed by the southern commander in chief or the Governor of this State by the 1st. of December or as soon after as possible and shall serve three months from the time of their getting there. The individuals going on and actually performing this duty shall be entitled to have it considered as their tour of duty whenever the Militia division of which they happen to be shall be next called into service.

They shall be subject to the Continental rules of war.

They shall as militia be entitled to the same pay as other militia sent from this State to the Southward, to commence at the time they march from their County.

Each man shall carry a good rifle, and it is recommended to those who can procure them to carry Spears: that they take with them as much provisions as they can to victual themselves for which they shall be allowed (on proper Certificates from their Commissary) at the rate of rations according to the time; that they do not encumber themselves with any baggage which can possibly be done without; let them carry their Waggons into Service to continue as long as the corps remains on duty, to be employed under the orders of the Commander in chief in bringing in provisions for themselves in the first instance for which a reasonable hire is allowed by law. On this their Utility and their Subsistence will depend; a waggon to each Company may perhaps suffice, tho' more would be better:

It is expected that when the men shall be raised and the arrangement of Officers fixed a person shall be sent to the Executive to receive such new Commissions as may be wanting, with instructions to meet or fall in with the Corps at some concerted place; the Officers to be appointed as beforementioned may either be of those already bearing Commissions in the Militia or such other persons as may be thought most proper for the service.

A Copy ARCHD. BLAIR C.C.

MS (Vi); in Blair's hand and signed by him. Endorsed in another hand: "Order of Council Octr. 30th. 1780." Copies of this Advice were enclosed in TJ's letters to the lieutenants of these counties, 1 Nov. 1780, q.v.

From William Campbell

SIR Hillsborough, October 31, 1780.

I came to this place last night to receive General Gates' directions how to dispose of the prisoners taken at King's Mountain, in the State of South Carolina, upon the seventh instant. He has ordered them to be taken over to Montgomery county, where they are to be secured under proper guards. General Gates transmits to your Excellency a state of the proceedings of our little party to the westward. I flatter myself we have much relieved that part of the country from its late distress.

I am your Excellency's most obedient and very humble servant,

WILLIAM CAMPBELL

MS not located. Text from a typescript in ViU: Summers Collection.

GENERAL GATES' DIRECTIONS: In DLC is a transcript of Gates' instructions to Campbell of this date; (much of its text faded to the point of illegibility) containing some corrections in TJ's hand.

From Samuel Huntington

SIR Philadelphia October 31. 1780

By the Act of Congress of the 30 Instant, herewith enclosed, your Excellency will observe that Majr. Genl. Greene is appointed to take the Command in the southern Department; and you will also receive the necessary Information of the Powers and Instructions given to him by Congress, and that it is earnestly recommended to the Legislatures and Executives from the Delaware State to Georgia inclusive to afford him all necessary Aid and Assistance.

With the highest Respect I have the Honor to be your Excellency's most obedient servant, SAML. HUNTINGTON President

P.S. Your Several Letters of the 10th: 15th 22nd & 25th ulto. have been received.

RC (Vi); in a clerk's hand, with postscript and signature by Huntington; endorsed. FC (DLC: PCC, No. 15) is captioned "To the Supreme Executive Powers from Delaware to Georgia inclusive" and lacks the postscript. Enclosure: attested copy of Congress' resolve of 30 Oct. approving Washington's appointment of Gen. Greene to replace Gen. Gates in the South and of Inspector General Steuben's being ordered to serve in the southern department; this resolve is printed in JCC, XVIII, 994-6.

To the County Lieutenants of Botetourt and Montgomery

SIR Richmond Novr 1. 1780

The propositions of the Executive for raising in the counties of Botetourt, Washington and Montgomery, a corps of volunteers to proceed to the southern army having on account of some circumstances contained in them failed to induce the engagement of such a corps, they have put them into a form in which they hope they will be more successful. The necessity of vigorous exertions to repel the enemy to the seashores and thereby to prevent the necessity of disturbing the operations of husbandry in more interesting seasons, and the peculiar aptitude of the mode of warfare to which your people are habituated for effecting this desirable purpose, induce me to apply in the warmest terms to your well known zeal for the American Cause to use your most strenuous endeavours for promoting the object of the inclosed advice of Council, and thereby giving a decisive blow to the southern operations of our enemies. I shall be glad to hear from time to time of your successes and prospects, and am with great respect sir, Your most obedient humble servant, TH: JEFFERSON

Nov. 11. 1780.[1] P.S Shoud you find that the service will be promoted by sending on the men by company or companies to be regimented there, you will be pleased to do so. Since writing the above Colo. Campbell informs us he can not proceed shortly to the southward. The Lieutenant colonel and major may therefore suffice for the command till Colo. Campbell can come on.

RC (WHi); text and postscript in different clerk's hands; signed by TJ; at foot of text: "Lt. Montgomery"; endorsed: "Governour's Letter Novr. 1780." William Preston was lieutenant of Montgomery co., and the original is among the Preston Papers. The text printed here is from this original, but a letter identical in substance, including the postscript, is in Vi, signed by TJ and addressed: "County Lieutenant of Bottetourt"; endorsed "Copyd." No doubt a third letter to the same effect was sent at this time to the lieutenant of Washington co.; and all three letters must have enclosed copies of the Advice of Council of 30 Oct. 1780, q.v.

[1] The date is clearly "Nov. 11. 1780." This must, however, have been an error.

From Horatio Gates

Sir Hillsborough 1st: November 1780.

I recd Your Excellency['s] Favour of the 20th: Ult. Just as I was upon the Point of Marching to the Westward. Upon communicating the Contents to Generals Huger and Stevens, and the principal Officers here, they Unanimously gave it as their Opinion, that I should not march from hence, until I received further intelligence of the Enemys movements, as well South Eastward, as Westward. I therefore Commanded a Halt, until the desired information was Obtained. Last Night Colo: Campbell, who Commanded Our Victorious Troops, in The Action of the 7th Ult. at Kings Mountain, arrived here. He has delivered me the inclosed Authentic, and Particular Account of that affair. I beg your Excellency will immediately after perusal, forward it to Congress. I have ordered the Prisoners who were taken at Kings Mountain, and who are now at the Moravian Town in this State, to be march'd immediately to Fincastle C House, also requested Colo. Preston to Supply them, and their Guard with provisions, and directed Him to have a Stockade immediately Set Up, to Secure them in. I have engaged that the Continent, or the Executive of Virginia, will Satisfie the Expence necessarily incurred upon this Occasion. I doubt not but Your Excellency, and the Executive will give proper Sanction to my Orders to Colo. Preston. I have wrote to Congress in regard to an Exchange of prisoners, if they send me Instructions to Treat with Lord Cornwallis thereupon, it will not be long before we shall get rid of the Burthen now upon Our Hands. Lord Cornwallis Cross'd The Catawba the 22d. Ult, at Langs Ford, Forty Miles below Charlotte. He was himself Dangerously Ill and is gone in a Waggon Escorted by a Guard of 300 Men Down the Country. Lord Rawdon on whom the Command Devolves was encamp'd on the West Bank of the River the 23d: Ult. I hourly Expect further intelligence, which shall be immediately sent to Your Excellency. The enemy have Fortify'd Camden, by surrounding it with Redoubts; apparently shewing they mean to Establish it as a place of

Arms; when their Army Arrives there, they are nearer X [Cross] Creek by Sixty Miles, than when they were at Charlotte. I shall therefore be very Exact in Observing their Movements, and very particular in acquainting Your Excellency therewith: and I must request You will direct every information to be sent me, of The Operations of The Enemys Troops in Virginia—as by good intelligence, on both sides, proper Measures may be taken to Distress, and Defeat the Enemy. I have this moment received the inclosed Letter from General Smallwood dated the 27th: Ult. Upon reconsidering the difficulty of properly disposing the prisoners taken by Colo. Campbell, he is of Opinion with me, that it will be better for him to go by Richmond Home and take the Orders of the Executive upon the Subject; He has therefore the Honour to Deliver your Excellency this Dispatch—he also takes a Copy of my Letter of the 13th Ult. to Colo. Preston of Fincastle County. I suspect we shall be much Distress'd here to Arm the Militia that are come in from your State. I beg Sir, what can with Safety be spared from Virginia, may be sent forward to Hillsborough. I have directed Eight Hundred Arms out of repair in the Stores here, may be sent by return'd Waggons to Richmond, where they can easily be put in Order. With every Sentiment of Esteem & regard I am Sir &c., HG

Dft (NHi). Tr (DLC) of FC. Tr (DLC: PCC, No. 71, I), transmitted to Huntington in TJ's letter of 7 Nov., together with copies (same location) of Gates to Preston, Hillsborough, 13 Oct.; Smallwood to Gates, "Camp Newprovidence," 27 Oct.; and a MS account of the battle of King's Mountain. See JCC, XVIII, 1048-9.

Gates' letter to Preston of 13 Oct. expressed the following opinion: "I think the neighbourhood of Fincastle Court house the most eligible part of the back Country for this edifice [a stockade for the prisoners taken at King's Mountain], not only on account of its being a good Whig Country, and well stored with provision; but also of its difficulty of access to the enemy, and nearness to the states where the scene of action now lays." Both Preston and TJ disagreed with this view and the arguments on which it was based; see TJ to Samuel Huntington, 7 Nov. 1780.

YOUR FAVOUR OF THE 20TH: This must have referred to TJ's letter to Gates of 22 Oct.; none of 20 Oct. has been found.

To James Wood

SIR Richmond November 1. 1780.

No movement of the enemy since my last has contributed in the least to declare their object. They have left the north side of James river, and taken possession of the Country on the south side as far up as Suffolk. Still we are told they keep a considerable part of their troops on board their Ships. They are making great collections of horses to mount their men on, and taking possession of all the Carts, draught horses and oxen they can find. The Refugee families who have returned from N. York to Virginia with them have taken possession of their own houses and farms in the Country now occupied by the enemy and seem to be settling themselves. Very little blood has been yet drawn; three of our Militia were killed in a small rencounter and one of their men. As yet we have no force together which may face them. This is the situation of things below: from the South, report brings great news, but it wants authentication totally.

The Executive are still impressed with the necessity of the measures formerly pointed out. The disaffection which has been lately discovered in the middle country, and the incertainty what is it's true extent, leaves no grounds for sure confidence in the opposition which ought to have been expected. The presence of the convention troops furnishes perpetual fuel to that smothered fire. The discontented build on their assistance whether they have or have not a right to expect it. We are not without hopes that their removal will contribute greatly to the cure of that spirit. Besides this it is believed that no cautions can prevent the British Conventioners from deserting and reinforcing this army, and this may be one among the probable objects which brought them here. We are in hopes the Convention Officers will think better and give a proper parole on their removal. Should they however refuse, it is our opinion they may remain where they are, until you shall have got the men on safe, and be in condition to make the conducting the Officers a single and separate undertaking. As their separation from the men will in this case be voluntary, they cannot complain of it as a breach of the Convention. I am therefore only to repeat to you that though no present appearances indicate a necessity of removing the troops so hastily as to leave their baggage, yet we wish every exertion to be used for removing them with their baggage as speedily as possible. Whenever you shall think proper to make public the determination, perhaps the Officers may require so long a time to settle their affairs as to allow the same waggons to come back for their baggage. Should the Exchange take place which is mentioned in the letter of the Board of War, the troops will be so far advanced on their way.

I am with great esteem Sir Your mo: obedt. Hble Servant,

Th: Jefferson

RC (Lloyd W. Smith, Madison, N.J., 1946); in a clerk's hand, corrected and signed by TJ; endorsed. Addressee identified from internal evidence.

THE LETTER OF THE BOARD OF WAR concerning an EXCHANGE has not been found.

To Messrs. Ball, Elliott, Morris, and Southall

[*Richmond, before 2 Nov.*] *1780.* Appointment of these men as commissioners "under the act for procuring a supply of provisions and other necessaries for the use of the army, but restricted specially to the procuring the articles enumerated in the said act, and live cattle, horses, waggons, and their gear for the subsistance and transporting the baggage of the troops marching to oppose the enemy." Instructions follow which are the same as those in the appointments dated 29 Aug. and 8 Oct. 1780, qq.v. A special instruction appears in a postscript to the present letter: "Waggons employed by the commissioners of the provision law or by others to perform public services shou'd not be impressed under the power above given."

Tr in the War Office Letter Book (MiU-C). At head of text: "To mr. Ball of Chesterfield and messieurs Elliot and Morris of Petersburg." In the margin: "Three copies of this put into the hands of General Muhlenburg." Dated: "Virginia in Council 1780." At foot of text is the following: "N.B. a Copy of the above delivered to Mr. Stephen Southall, only leaving out the words 'horses, waggons and their gear,' dated novemr. 2nd 1780," whence our approximate date is derived.

From Samuel Huntington

Philadelphia, 2 Nov. 1780. Circular letter to the state executives enclosing a copy of a resolve of Congress of 25 Oct. "recommending to the respective States, to exert their utmost Endeavors to furnish their Troops with Cloathing, on the Terms formerly mentioned."

FC (DLC: PCC, No. 15). Enclosure missing; printed in JCC, XVIII, 973-8.

To Thomas Sim Lee

SIR Richmond Nov. 2. 1780.

In the course of examination of a British deserter this morning some information was given interesting to the state over which your Excellency presides and which therefore I think it my duty to communicate. He calls himself Peter Christian; says he is a native of New York, was taken in Fort Montgomery; that after being kept two years in prison he was induced to enlist into the British service in hopes it would give him an opportunity of making his escape: that he was then carried to Long island where he has been kept on duty till he was embarked on board the fleet now in this state, and made his escape the first day he was put on shore. Being questioned as to the object of this expedition he said he could not pretend to affirm what it was but that it was commonly said in the army that after they should have drawn the force of this state down to Suffolk, where they now are, they meant to go up to Baltimore, and that he particularly heard Colo. Fanning (in whose regiment he was a Serjeant) say that he had no doubt of eating his Christmas dinner in Baltimore. The man appears credible and affectionate to his country as far as we can judge from his appearance; but how far we are to credit the reports prevailing in their army, or what his Colo. might say in his presence is a very different question. Your Excellency will judge in this for yourself. The removal of their plunder on Ship-board has induced an opinion with some that they are about to embark. The settlement of the refugees in their own houses and other symptons contradict this opinion. Their movements here have been truly incomprehensible. I rather believe that Ld. Cornwallis had expected to have been in this state at this time, that they were intended to join him here; that his precipitate flight has left them without an object, and that they wait for further orders. But we have not data enough to confide in any opinion. They are beleived to be from 2500 to 3000 strong under the command of Majr. Genl. Leslie and convoyed by the Romulus of 40 guns, the Blonde of 32, the Delight sloop of 16 guns and a 20 gun ship of John Goodrich's, and two row gallies under Commodore Gayton. On this contemptible naval force hangs the fate of an army; and yet comtemptible as it is and without a possibility of protection but from itself it does not appear to be in danger. Should any further intelligence be received corroborating the information from the deserter it shall be immediately forwarded.

I have the honor to be with all possible respect Your Excellency's most obedt. & most humble servt, TH: JEFFERSON

RC (John Work Garrett Library, Baltimore, 1946; now MdBJ); endorsed: "Novr. 1780 Govr. Jefferson."

A copy of TJ's letter was enclosed in a letter from the Maryland Council of 6 Nov. 1780 to Andrew Buchanan, lieutenant of Baltimore co., Md., advising Buchanan to hold the militia of Baltimore Town and its vicinity "in Readiness, at a short Notice" (*Md. Archives*, XLIII, 351). See also Maryland Council to Col. Moses Rawlings, 6 Nov. 1780, containing instructions for provisioning Fort Frederick (same, p. 350-1).

To George Muter

In Council Novr. 2d. 1780

It is the opinion of the board that Mr. Anderson continue to discharge the Duties of Keeper of the public arms till further order

449

Head-Quarters, Charles-Town Neck, June 1, 1780.

Orders,

THE Commander in Chief congratulates the ARMY on the Succeſs that has attended the Corps in the Back Country, under Lieutenant General Earl CORNWALLIS.

Lieutenant Colonel TARLETON, with the Corps of Cavalry, and with the Infantry of the Legion, (mounted) being detached by his Lordſhip, reached the REBELS, after a March of near one Hundred Miles in two Days.---They rejected the Terms on which he required them to ſurrender, and were in Conſequence attacked.

One Hundred and Seventy were cut to pieces, and the whole Cannon, Baggage, Colours, &c. of the Corps, were taken.

The General, however ſmall the Loſs of Britiſh, has been compared to the Advantage obtained, cannot mention it without concern, two Officers are killed, and twenty Officers, Non-Commiſſion Officers, or Privates, wounded.

Charleſtown printed: New-York, Reprinted by JAMES RIVINGTON, Printer to the King's Moſt Excellent Majeſty.

Sir Henry Clinton's General Orders, Charleston, South Carolina, 1 June 1780

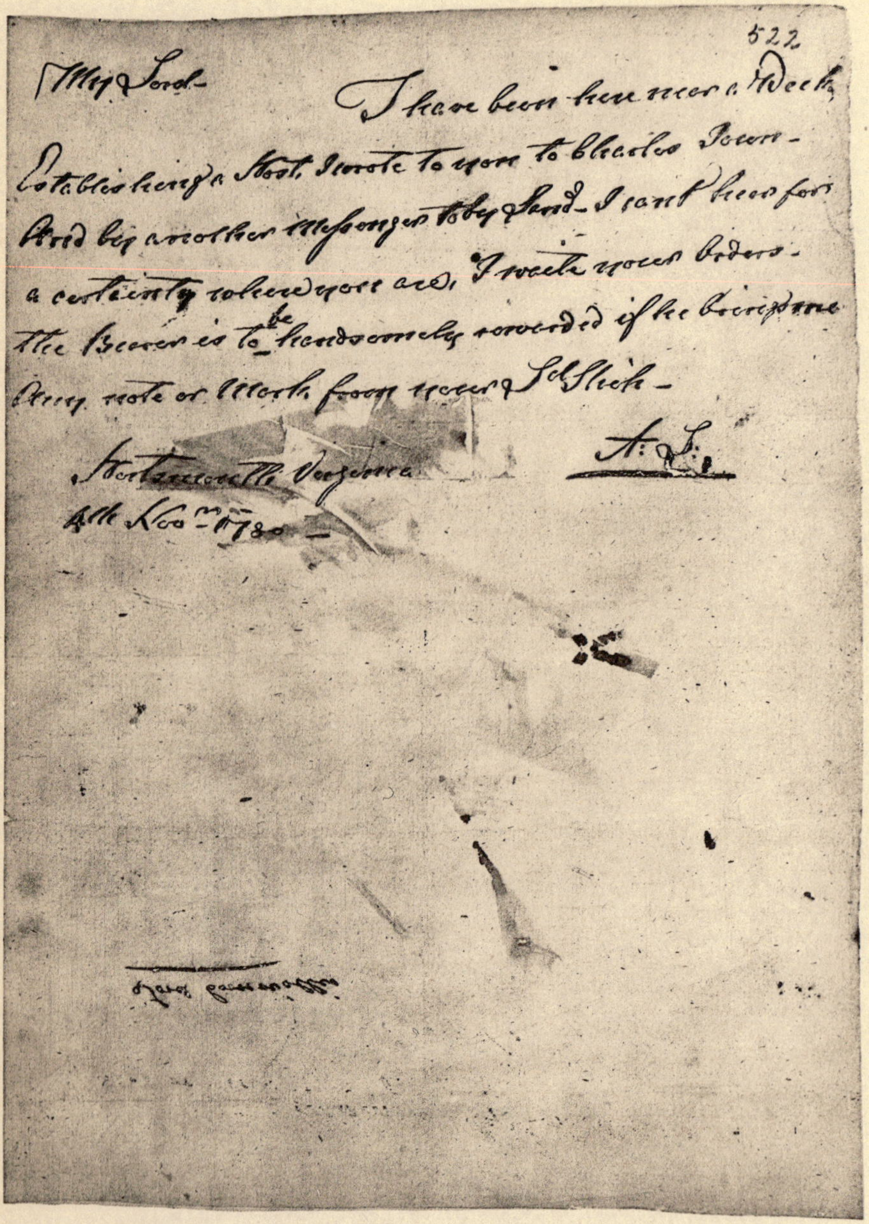
My Lord—

I have been here near a Week, Establishing a Post. I wrote to you to Charles Town—and by another Messenger to my Lord— I can't hear for a certainty where you are. I wait your orders— the Bearer is to be handsomely rewarded if he brings me any note or Mark from your Ldship—

A: L:

Portsmouth Virginia
4th Novr. 1780—

Intercepted Letter from Leslie to Cornwallis, 4 November 1780 shall be taken therein for which the board will allow him proper compensation. TH JEFFERSON

Tr in War Office Letter Book (MiU-C). At head of text: "In answer to Colo Muters Lr. of Nov. 2d. 1780"; Muter's letter has not been found.

To George Weedon?

SIR In Council Nov. 2. 1780

Genl. Muhlenberg having found it necessary to employ in this state some Continental arms, we are much dispos[ed] to have the 50. Marylanders pressing to the Southward armed here, if you suppose that they will not be armed of the 1200 stand taken at King's mountain and the 600 stand taken by Colo. Davie on Cornwallis's retreat.

We shall immediately countermand all the militia called from the Proprietary counties, these being more remote from us, and most convenient to Alexandria should the scene of invasion be shifted to that quarter. After this deduction the militia called on will amount to about 4150, which with the new levies and volunteers (of whom Colo. Lawson writes me *he* shall have 1500) will be sufficient, and will lighten the difficulties of covering and feeding.

I am with great respect Sir Your most obedt. humble servt.,

TH: JEFFERSON

RC (PPAP). MS contains no evidence of recipient's name; the original is among the Weedon Papers in PPAP, and though there indexed as to "P. Cooke" (one of Weedon's officers, at this time stationed near Hood's, Prince George co.), the substance of the letter strongly suggests that it was addressed to Weedon.

From Horatio Gates

SIR Hillsborough 3d: November 1780

Yesterday afternoon I had the Honour to receive your Excellencys Letter of the 28 Ult. from Richmond, and a few Minutes after the inclosed from Colo: Preston. I send it to Your Excellency that the Executive may determine, as they think proper upon the Subject. I had no conception that the Setting Up Two hundred Yards of Picketing, could Cost 100,000£, as to the Log Huts within side, the Prisoners might do that for themselves; Colo: Campbell being now at Richmond, will enable Your Excellency to decide, what is the best mode to be pursued, to Subsist, and Secure these Fellows, but it shews a Strange Imbecillity, not to be Able to keep the Prisoners we take. If they are left at large be assured numbers will get off, and Our poor Friends in Captivity, must remain without hope of Exchange. I have no news from the Westward since my Letter of the 1: Instant to Your Excellency. The Infantry march'd Yesterday, I shall follow them as soon as the Cavalry can March. I am Sir &c., HG

Dft (NHi). Tr of same (DLC). Enclosure not found.

To Samuel Huntington

Sir Richmond November 3rd 1780.

Since I had the honour of writing to your Excellency on the 25th ult, the enemy have withdrawn their force from the north side of James river, and have taken post at Portsmouth, which we learn they are fortifying; their highest post is Suffolk, where there is a very narrow and defensible pass between Nansemond river and the dismal swamp, which covers the country below from being entered by us. More accurate information of their force than we at first had, gives us reason to suppose them to be from 2500 to 3000 of which between 60 or 70 are cavalry. They are commanded by General Leslie and were convoyed by the Romulus of 40 guns, the Blonde of 32, the Delight sloop of 16, a 20 gun ship of Jno. Goodrichs, and two row gallies: commanded by Commodore Gayton. We are not yet assured that they have landed their whole force. Indeed they give out themselves that after drawing the force of this state to Suffolk they mean to go to Baltimore. Their movements here had induced me to think they came in expectation of meeting with Lord Cornwallis in this country, that his precipitate retreat has left them with out a concerted object, and that they were awaiting further orders. Information of this morning says that on being informed of Lord Cornwallis's retreat, and a public paper produced to them wherein were printed the several dispatches which brought this intelligence from General Gates, they unladed a vessel and sent her off to Charles Town immediately. The fate of this army of theirs hangs on a slender naval force indeed.

The want of Barracks at Fort Frederic, as represented by Colo. Wood, the difficulty of getting waggons sufficient to move the whole convention troops at once, and the state of unreadiness in which the regiment of guards is, having induced us to think that it will be better to remove those troops in two divisions: and as the whole danger of desertion to the enemy and of correspondence with the disaffected in our southern counties, is from the British only (for from the Germans we have no apprehensions on either head) [we h]ave advised Colo. Wood to move on the British in the first division and to leave the Germans in their present situation to form a second division, and to be moved so soon as barracks may be erected at fort Frederic. By these means the British may march immediately under the guard of Colo. Crockets battalion, while Colo. Taylor's regiment of guards remain with the Germans. I cannot suppose that this will be deemed such a seperation as is provided against by the Convention, nor that their officers will wish to have the whole troops crouded together into barracks, which probably are not sufficient for half of them. Should they however insist on their being kept together, I suppose it woud be the opinion that the second division should follow the first as closely as possible, and that their being exposed to a want of covering woud in that case be justly imputable to themselves only. The delay of the second division will lessen the distress for provisions which may perhaps take place on their first going to the new post, before matters have got into a regular train.

I have the honor to be with the most profound respect Your Excellency's Most obedient & most humble servt,

TH: JEFFERSON

P.S. By a letter from Colo. Wood received since writing the above I am informed the British Conventioners are 804 rank and file. He does not mention the present number of the Germans. In May last they were 1503 including officers.

RC (DLC: PCC, No. 71, I); in a clerk's hand, with corrections, complimentary close, signature, postscript, and address (to Huntington as President of Congress) in TJ's hand. Endorsed by Charles Thomson: "Letter from Gov Jefferson Novr. 3. 1780 Read 13"; see JCC, XVIII, 1048. An identical letter was sent by TJ to Washington this day, and another, lacking only the postscript, was sent to Gates on 4 Nov.

A LETTER FROM COLO. WOOD: Not found.

To Thomas Sim Lee

[*Richmond, 3 Nov. 1780.* A letter from the Maryland Council to Col. Moses Rawlings dated 10 Nov. states: "we have received one from Governor Jefferson, of the 3d informing us that he had given Directions for the March of the Convention Troops, in two Divisions, the first to consist of the British, amounting to about 804 Rank and File, the second consists wholly of Germans, in Number, the Governor Supposes, about 1503 including Officers. The first Division must have been some Time in its March and of Course may shortly be expected at Fort Frederick, the second certainly will not follow immediately and probably may remain at their present Barracks a considerable Length of Time; As the Motives for removing the former do not, at present, operate so powerfully for removing the Latter" (*Md. Archives*, XLIII, 357). TJ's letter not found.]

To George Washington

Richmond, 3 Nov. 1780. This letter is almost identical with TJ's letter to Samuel Huntington of this date, q.v.

RC (DLC: Washington Papers); in a clerk's hand, with corrections, complimentary close, signature, postscript, and address in TJ's hand; endorsed: "No. 19. Richmond 3d: Novr. 1780 from Governor Jefferson Ansd. 9th. Decr." PrC (DLC: TJ Papers), lacking postscript.

From George Weedon

DR. SR. Richmond Novr. 3d. 1780

I take the liberty of laying before your Excellency a return made me this morning of our Provision Stores. As the Militia are now coming in fast, and a considerable body may be Expected here in a few days we shall be much distressed to feed them unless steps are taken previous to their Assembling. And tho' they will not remain here long, yet some delays may happen in Acquiping that cant possibly be prevented. Your Excellency will Observe the stock on hand to be very inconsiderable, and no doubt give such Directions as will obviate any evil to be Apprehended from want.

I am Yr. Excellencies Most Obt Servt., G WEEDON

P.S. My dispatches to Genl. Gates is reporting to him a state of our operations and Defences making in Consequence of the present invasion. They will not require a particular Express. GW.

FC (PPAP); in Weedon's hand; endorsed.

To George Weedon

SIR Richmond Novr 3. 1780.

The State of our Magazine renders it essential that we do not lose a single arm. There is no point therefore in which we are obliged to be so rigid as this and the salvation of our country renders that rigour indispensible. We have determined that no militia man who has received a public arm shall ever be discharged from duty till he has delivered such arm to the officer appointed to receive it and obtained his receipt which receipt is to be taken in, to found a debit against the receiving officer, or until he shall give satisfactory proof to the commanding Officer that such arm has been lost by unavoidable accident. We therefore wish you to give notice of this and to act in conformity with it, and if any of them go off without having returned their arms or given satisfactory account of them, be so good as to declare them deserters and to forward a list of them to me and no exertions shall be spared to recover them.

I have the honor to be with great respect Sir Your most obedt. humble servt, TH: JEFFERSON

RC (PPAP); in a clerk's hand, with complimentary close and signature by TJ.

To James Wood

SIR In Council Novr 3d 1780.

Your representation on the want of barracks at Fort Frederick has been again the subject of consideration with the board, together with a Letter from Govr. Lee informing me it is not in their power to make more than a partial provision for the Subsistence of the Convention troops. Our apprehensions as to desertion to the enemy and corresponding with the disaffected arise from the British altogether. We have no fear of either from the Germans. That the former should be removed immediately we think very essential; and we have no objections to the latter remaining until Barracks may be provided for them at Fort Frederic. I suppose that the marching them in two divisions, to wit, the British first and Germans next cannot be considered as such a separation as is provided against in the Convention and that themselves would chuse that the German Division should not go on till barracks are provided, as their going would of course so much the more streighten the British accommodations. This mode of removal will put it in your power to push off the British division instantly, because they will require but half the waggons and half the guards; the former of which we suppose you will have procured and for the latter Colo. Crocketts battalion is in readiness. With which division you would chuse to proceed is left to yourself.

I am with great esteem Sir Your most obedt. servt,

TH: JEFFERSON

RC (Lloyd W. Smith, Madison, N.J., 1946); in a clerk's hand, with complimentary close and signature by TJ; endorsed. A copy of this letter was enclosed in TJ's letter to Harrison, 29 Dec. 1780, q.v.

YOUR REPRESENTATION: Not found. A LETTER FROM GOVR. LEE: Dated 30 Oct. 1780, q.v. It is to be noted that, in his letter to Wood of 28 Oct., TJ had expressed the opinion that dividing the Convention prisoners was contrary to the terms of the Saratoga Convention, an opinion which he now revised in letters to Wood, Washington, and Huntington of 3 Nov.

To Horatio Gates

Richmond, 4 Nov. 1780. This letter is almost identical with TJ's letter to Samuel Huntington of 3 Nov., q.v., except that it lacks postscript.

RC (DLC); in a clerk's hand, signed by TJ; endorsed (in part): "Recd 11 Novr. 80."

From Abner Nash

[*Newbern (New Bern, N.C.), 5 Nov. 1780.* TJ in a letter to Samuel Huntington, 19 Nov., q.v., transmits information respecting "a very large fleet" of vessels off Charleston, sent in a letter of this date from Nash. Letter not found.]

From the Virginia Delegates in Congress

[Philadelphia, 5 November, 1780]

The great depreciation of money and the extravagant prices of every thing here together with the difficulty of negociating Bills renders it absolutely necessary that some stable provision shoud be made, and some fixed mode adopted for supplying us with money. Other wise we shall not be able to exist. We shou'd be glad to be informed on this head as soon as possible.

Tr (Vi), bearing notation "Extract of a lre from the Virga. Delegates in Congress to his Excellency the Governour dated at Phila: nov. 5. 1780," and enclosed in TJ's letter to Benjamin Harrison, 17 Nov. 1780.

See TJ's reply, 17 Nov., and also Burnett, *Letters of Members*, v, No. 504, note 2.

To George Weedon

SIR In Council Novr. 6th. 1780.

The Act of Assembly having expired under which we have hitherto proceeded to impress waggons and provisions, we think it safest to recur to the directions of the invasion law which give a standing power to the commanding Officer to authorise any Commissioned Officer to impress every kind of necessary. We have therefore directed 100 Copies of the Clause in the invasion law on this subject to be printed, part of which we shall take the Liberty of putting into your hands. Should Mr. Triplett and the person you would wish to act as Brigade Q.M. or any other person whom you would call to their aid be not commissioned Officers we will give them Militia Commissions to make their proceedings strictly legal.

We have directed the State Quarter Master to spare to Mr. Southall two of the three waggons he has, and given Mr. Southall some directions under which we hope he may add to the number. We before declined appointing the Surgeons mate thinking the right of appointment in the Surgeon himself. Is not the right of appointing the Surgeon in the field Officers of every regiment? If it be so, they will of course apply to Dr. Pope the State Apothecary for whatever they want.

I do myself the pleasure to inclose you a warrant for £125. new money equal to £5000. old, there being none but the new which can be issued from the treasury.

We will do anything in our power to promote the operations in the Laboratory.

I have the honor to be with great respect Sir Your most obedt humble servt, TH: JEFFERSON

RC (PPAP); in a clerk's hand, with complimentary close and signature by TJ.

THE INVASION LAW: Act for providing against invasions and insurrections, passed in the May 1777 session; for the power to impress necessities under this law, see Hening, IX, 293-4; see also TJ to Weedon, 7 Nov. 1780.

From Richard Elliott

MAY IT PLEASE YOUR EXELENCY Cabin point 7th Novemr. 1780

I am at this place with Two Hundred and Twenty five Men from Brunswick County and only fifteen Guns with out any other accutryments should Be glad you would please to inform me in what manner We are to Be accuterd as I do not think it prudent to March any lower with out arms shall remain here till Your Exelencys Orders and assistances Comes. As my men were Very Anxious that I should Command them I have proceeded this far as there Colo. and as I have on every occation heretofore Commanded when the men under me has been Calld for I hope Your Exelency and Counsil will not take from me the Command unless You find reason to take the Commission I confess I Am not so Skilld as those who Have Been Continually in the service but am Desirous of ganing Experiance that I may be ready at all times to Serve and Defend my Country I am Sr. your Exelencys Most Obt: Humle. Servt.,

RICHD. ELLIOTT

RC (Vi); addressed: "His Excelency Thos. Jefferson"; endorsed: "Col Rd. Elliotts letter to the Governeur Nov. 7h. 1780."

Gwathmey, *Hist. Reg. of Virginians in the Revolution*, gives Richard Elliott's record as "Captain, Brunswick Militia in 1777." CABIN POINT, whence Elliott wrote, was a settlement in the western part of Surry co. (Martin, *Va. Gazetteer*, p. 286).

To Benjamin Harrison

[*Richmond, 7? Nov. 1780.* JHD, Oct. 1780, 1827 edn., p. 10 (7 Nov.): "The Speaker laid before the House a letter from the Governor, enclosing several others addressed to the executive, and sundry resolutions of Congress, with other papers, and stating several matters for the consideration of the General Assembly; and the said letters, papers, and resolutions were read, and ordered to lie on the table." TJ's letter not located; one of its enclosures was Huntington's letter of 6 Oct. 1780, q.v.; see also entry for TJ to Harrison, 30 Nov. 1780.]

To Samuel Huntington

SIR Richmond Novr. 7th. 1780.

I have the honor of forwarding to your Excellency sundry dispatches received from Majr. General Gates. You will observe in these what the General had at first proposed to do with the prisoners taken at Kings Mountain, and that difficulties suggested afterwards had produced subsequent doubts. As to the regulars among those Captives I should think them properly disposed of if joined to the others of their nation now at Winchester. But it is not so easy to decide what should be done with the Tories. To place them at Montgomery (formerly called Fincastle) courthouse wou'd be very improper indeed. They would there be in the midst of the most disaffected part of our State, and so near the Country possessed by the enemy that their escape would be certain should they not be rescued. Nor could that post be recommended as likely to be furnished with provisions. It is also within 8 miles of our Lead Mines the destruction of the works and utensils at which wou'd do us vital injury. It does not seem expedient to join them to the prisoners in Albemarle or at Winchester because such an addition would render either of those bodies still more formidable and greatly increase the difficulty of subsisting them. Colo. Campbells proposition is perhaps the least objectionable and having been suggested by him to General Gates was probably the cause of his referring him to us. He sais that the spirit of this part of the Captives is so absolutely broken that they will agree to inlist in our armies for the war or to do any thing else which shall be required of them. He thinks that if employed to the Northward at a distance from their own Country they will never attempt to return and still less to join the enemy. He therefore advises that they be sent on to the northward and there inlisted and employed either with General Washington's army or still further north if there be occasion. There are enough of them to form a strong battalion. This matter being altogether proper for the determination of Congress I beg leave to submit it to them and to receive their orders as early as possible in what manner to dispose of them. In the mean time as the season is fast advancing which would render it impracticable to move them any distance were they to delay setting out, and it is apparent they must be removed northward of their present situation and indeed they are now in motion towards the Flower gap and Montgomery County by order of General Gates, I shall immediately take measures for continuing their march Northwardly along the valley between the Blue ridge and the North mountain until I shall be informed where you will chuse to terminate their journey. Considering that they are now under the care of occasional guards of militia only, and that they must be handed on by successive relieves of the same kind, I fear that but too many of them will find means to escape.

I have the honor of being with the most perfect esteem & respect Your Excellency's most obedt. & most humble servt.,

TH: JEFFERSON

RC (DLC: PCC, No. 71, I); in a clerk's hand, with complimentary close and signature by TJ. Endorsed by Thomson: "Govr Jefferson's Letter Novr. 7. 1780 Read 13. Referred to Mr Bland Mr Sharp Mr Bee." Enclosures (same location): copies of Gates' letter to TJ, 1 Nov., q.v., and its enclosures.

On 14 Nov. the committee appointed by Congress to report on this letter brought in its report, which on 20 Nov. was adopted in the form of a resolve; this was transmitted to TJ in a letter from Huntington of 21 Nov. 1780, q.v.;

see also JCC, XVIII, 1053, 1073. THE MOST DISAFFECTED PART OF OUR STATE: Gates, in his instructions to Preston, had advanced as a reason for selecting "Fincastle Court House" the fact that it was located in "a good Whig Country, and well stored with provision"; see Gates to TJ, 1 Nov. 1780, note.

To George Weedon

SIR In Council Nov. 7. 1780.

I inclose you a militia commission to Mr. Triplett merely to comply with the letter of the law, and to lay a ground work for arming him with your warrant under which he will conduct himself according to the inclosed extract from the act of assembly. I am with great esteem Sir Your most obedt. servt., TH: JEFFERSON

RC (PPAP); endorsed. Enclosures missing; no copy of the extract from the invasion law printed at this time has been located; see TJ to Weedon, 6 Nov. 1780, and Swem, "Va. Bibliog.," No. 7242.

To James Wood

DEAR SIR Richmond Novemr. 7. 1780

Your Letters of the third and fifth instant are now before me. My last to you which you could not have received on the fifth will I think have anticipated some parts of these letters. The terms of the Officers paroles, being that they will not say or do any thing to the prejudice of the united States while they are under the convention of Saratoga, and that they will remain within certain bounds, they cannot be released from the obligation of that parole by a removal of the troops, an event not mentioned in the parole. However I trust it will not be difficult for you to march them safely under guard (as the british alone will be moved as yet) with Capt. Reid's troops and Crockets battalion aided by militia. Genl. Hamilton's agreeing that the troops shall be seperated for their better accommodation will remove the only difficulty in the plan proposed in my last Letter. Congress having foreseen the possibility that a removal of these troops might shortly become necessary, determined that fort Frederick shou'd be the place to which they shou'd be removed. They desired Governour Lee and myself therefore to make provision for them shou'd it become necessary. The moment we found it necessary I communicated it to Congress and to Govr. Lee. I have had an answer from the Latter, who assures me he will immediately do every thing he can to prepare for them, but informs me of the necessity of our contributing provisions. This first suggested the sending on the british only as yet, that there might not be more thrown on that state than could of a sudden be provided for. We shall take measures for subsisting the Germans in their present situation, and have no objections to your enlarging your demands on the county of Berkeley to ensure a sufficient subsistance for the british. I have no doubt of the candour of Genl. Hamilton's endeavours to prevent desertions by his orders, but nothing less than stone walls can effectually do this among the british, while a british army is cantoned in our country. General Hamilton's request to leave non commissioned officers to take care of their houses and gardens, having been probably founded on the idea of their returning to this state when the present invasion shall be over he will probably think it unnecessary when he is assured that they will not be moved back again. No Citizen is at liberty to take forcibly from the Officers of convention their effects in satisfaction for debts. These persons, tho prisoners, are under the protection of the laws and those who injure either their persons or property are liable to indictment, and to have such property rescued wherever found. Justice nevertheless ought to be done both to citizens and their debtors. We recommend that yourself and General Hamilton appoint a Convention officer and a Citizen and also a third person of either character, of the most discreet, candid, and sensible, and that they liquidate all debts due to or from the Conventioners. This being fairly done, justice requires that their property be subjected to make good their debts, they may be arrested on the order of the state and not otherwise: but we shall not by any slight matter be led to order such an arrest.

As to the horses of the officers, the resolution of Assembly of June 8th, was made while an exchange was in contemplation, and under the apprehension that if permitted to be carried out of the state, they were of course to be carried into New york and might be employed by the enemy greatly to our prejudice as the resolution sais. That of July 7th dispenses with the former so as to permit them to retain them while in this State, the former idea still prevailing that the carrying them into New york was to be a consequence of their carrying them out of the state. But as the removal proposed, is but just across our boundary and they are not to proceed to New york, and as the reason on which the resolution of July 7th was founded will most certainly be equally cogent at least in their new situation, viz. that 'the Officers will not be able to supply themselves with provisions unless they are permitted to retain their horses,' we must give it as our opinion (there being no Assembly yet met to advise with on this point) that they ought not to be compelled to part with their horses. Capt. Reid receives a warrant for £250 money of Mar: 18. equal to £10,000 old to be forwarded to you for incidental charges in moving on the convention troops. I am with great esteem & respect Sir Your most obedt. humble servt,

TH: JEFFERSON

RC (Lloyd W. Smith, Madison, N.J., 1946); in a clerk's hand, with complimentary close and signature by TJ and addressed by him: "Colo. James Wood Charlottesville." Endorsed.

Wood's letters of 3 and 5 Nov. have not been found. MY LAST TO YOU: Possibly TJ's letter of 3 Nov., q.v.

To James Wood

DEAR SIR Richmond Nov. 7. 1780.

We think with you that the Germans you have furloughed to Augusta Rockingham &c. may be permitted to remain. My opinion of Pastor Kohlé is the same with yours, that is that he is more American than British. He never wrote a letter to me which could be exceptionable to me. I beleive that with a proper opportunity for explanations he might be rendered useful.

I am with great [estee]m Dr Sir Your most obedt. servt.,

TH: JEFFERSON

RC (Lloyd W. Smith, Madison, N.J., 1946); addressed by TJ: "Private Colo. James Wood." Endorsed.

PASTOR KOHLE: Chaplain of the Regiment Specht in the Brunswick service (Riedesel, *Memoirs*, II, 272); his further record is given as "unknown" in Eelking's roster, and he may well have remained in America like many of his compatriots. No correspondence between him and TJ has been found, but see Unger to TJ, 13 Nov. 1780.

To a County Lieutenant

SIR In Council Novo 8. 1780

Captain Patrick Lockhart being appointed to conduct the prisoners of war taken at Kings mountain in north Carolina to their place of destination, and your county lying in their route, he has received authority to call on you for such guard of your militia as he may find necessary for their safe custody and to continue with them such distance as he shall find expedient. The advanced season of the year and naked condition of the prisoners induce me to press you to have such guard ready at the time and place specified by him that not a moments delay may take place. You will of course give orders that your guard be properly armed.

I am Sir, Your mo. ob servt, TH: JEFFERSON

RC (MoSHi); in a clerk's hand, signed by TJ. On cover: "Mr Anderson B"; if this is the addressee, a point far from certain, he has not been further identified.

See TJ to Patrick Lockhart, this date, empowering Lockhart to call for provisions on the county lieutenants and others through whose counties Lockhart is to march. Very likely copies of the present letter were enclosed to Lockhart.

From Horatio Gates

SIR Guilford Court House 8th: Novbr. 1780

My Letter of the 3d. Inst. to Your Excellency, Own'd the Receipt of yours of the 28th. Ult. I marched the 6th. Inst. with all the Cavalry that were fit to move from Hillsborough; and that day received the enclosed Letter of the 31st Ult: from General Smallwood. I apprehend the Tardiness of Col. Polk in supplying Provisions, must be occasion'd by the Delay of payment my Bills in his favour have met with. I hope to see him in a few Days, when all the Encouragement in my Power shall be given him, to continue his Services in supplying Provisions to the Army. The moment I Join The Troops to the Westward and know with certainty the Movements of the Enemy, I shall consult with the rest of the General Officers, and Determine the Future Operations of this Army. The Maryland Regiment under Col: Williams, will reach Salisbury Tomorrow; but the Most of the Virginians, Eighteen, Eight Months Men, and Militia, are left under General Stevens at Hillsborough, to be Arm'd and Accoutred, and in some Degree equip'd, before they can March from thence. Axes, and Intrenching Tools, I must beg your Excellency will forward to us with the Utmost Dispatch. Instead of Thirty Horses, which Your Excellency inform'd me were to be sent to Hillsborough for the Artillery; only Nineteen Arrived, and those very bad, and poor. I entreat You will Order the Deficiency to be immediately Supplied.

I am Sir Your Excellencys most Obedient Humble Servant,

HORATIO GATES

Dft (NHi). Tr of same (DLC). Tr (DLC: PCC, No. 71, I) of missing RC transmitted by TJ in his letter to Huntington, 19 Nov., together with a copy (same location) of Gen. William Smallwood's letter to Gates, "Camp New Providence," 31 Oct. 1780. Another Tr (MdAA).

To Patrick Lockhart

SIR Richmond Novr. 8. 1780.

It being necessary to remove Northwardly the Prisoners taken on Kings mountain in Carolina and that they be under the charge of some careful person I am to beg the favor of you to undertake that charge. It will be necessary for you to proceed immediately to meet them. They are to cross the mountain at the Flower Gap and to proceed Northwardly: you will please to continue them along the valley between the blueridge and North mountain till you shall have delivered the regulars at Winchester and received further instructions what to do with the tories. You will call on the Lieutenants of such of the Counties thro' which you pass as you think best under authority of the Letters herein inclosed and which you will direct as you shall have occasion to furnish such guards as you find necessary, relieving the said guards from time to time as you shall find practicable and expedient. You are hereby authorized to call on any Commissaries, Commissioners of the provision law or holders of specific tax grain for provisions and forage necessary for the prisoners or guards and where you cannot with tolerable convenience obtain them in any of these ways you are to impress them according to the directions of the invasion law of which I inclose you an extract. In like manner if you cannot hire necessary waggons you are to impress them according to the same directions. Whatever you hire or purchase, shall be paid for on your order on the Auditors attended by an account certified by you. I expect within a few days the directions of Congress as to the ultimate destination of the Tory prisoners which I will immediately communicate to you by express. The very advanced season of the year, and naked condition of the prisoners induce me to press all the expedition you can possibly use. For this purpose you [will] find it necessary to keep Agents advanced before you that your provisions may be laid in at every day or twos stages and to send forward in time expresses to the County Lieutenants that they may have their guards at specified times and places ready to receive you. Pay the greatest attention to the safe custody of the prisoners using for that purpose all those cautionary means practised on such occasions.

Tr (DLC: PCC, No. 71, I); endorsed: "Govr. Jefferson's instructions to Capt. Lockhart." (This copy was enclosed, together with Lockhart's reply of 4 Dec., in TJ's letter to Huntington, 25 Dec. 1780.) Enclosures not found, though see TJ to an unidentified correspondent, this date, and TJ to Weedon, 7 Nov. 1780.

To James Maxwell

[Richmond, 8 November 1780]

The flagg is to go as soon as we receive some Bills of Exchange to be sent by her, which we daily expect. I think it would be not amiss for her to be taking in her loading, which is to be Flour, Spirit, some Tobacco and the Officers Baggage.

Tr in Journal of the Commissioner of the Navy (Vi).

From James Maxwell

[*Richmond, 8 Nov. 1780.* Minute in the Journal of the Commissioner of the Navy (Vi) under this date: "Letter written to his Excellency the Governor on the subject of the Flagg going to Charlestown." Not located.]

From George Washington

Headquarters, Passaic Falls, 8 Nov. 1780. Acknowledges TJ's letters of 22, 25, and 26 Oct. Reports have been received that the enemy have already left Portsmouth, and the cause assigned is "the appearance of a French or Spanish Fleet upon the Coast of Carolina." But if this account is premature, the Convention troops should certainly be moved. Gen. Phillips' application for a flag-of-truce vessel is to be granted; if the Convention troops, for which it carries supplies, have already been moved, TJ is to direct the vessel where to proceed. "I am glad to hear that you have permitted Govr. Hamilton and Major Hayes [Hay] to go to New York. While they remain there upon parole, they will be less capable of concerting mischief than in Virginia, and it will deprive the enemy of a pretext for complaining that they are treated with rigor." The report of another embarkation preparing at New York is probably correct, for the enemy will of course take advantage of "the expiration of the times of the better half of our Army" late in December. Should the enemy continue in lower Virginia, it would be a good expedient to have a number of flatboats on traveling carriages accompany our army in order to watch their motions and enable our forces to cross the rivers; Gen. Greene "is perfectly acquainted with the kind of Boats I have mentioned" and will give "proper directions for having them constructed"; New Castle would be "a good and safe place to build the Boats."

Dft (DLC: Washington Papers); in hand of Tench Tilghman; 4 p.; endorsed. Printed in Washington, *Writings*, ed. Fitzpatrick, xx, 325-7.

From Samuel Huntington,

enclosing a Table of Continental Requisitions of Food

SIR In Congress Novr. 9th 1780.

Fully convinced of our inability to obtain the grand object of the fœderal Union without the vigorous exertions of the several States we have thought it our duty to make the requisitions contained in the enclosed resolutions; and we wish our constituents to be impressed with the necessity of a speedy and punctual compliance. For although by the blessing of providence we have been conducted thus far in a War with a powerful and enraged Enemy, yet the events of the present year have not enabled us to speak the language of triumph. This indeed may be attributed to a variety of causes, but we cannot refrain from observing that the unpunctuality of the States in their supplies of Men, Money and provisions is not one of the least.

It is unnecessary to point out the public wants and distresses. They are too well known, too generally felt. Hitherto the war has been carried on principally by emissions of paper Money. This being depreciated and Congress having in Compliance with the general inclination and voice of their Constituents, resolved to stop farther Emissions, we are compelled to call upon the States for taxes and specific supplies.

An opinion seems to prevail that foreign Loans can be obtained, and we perceive with regret that some are disposed to place too great reliance on this resourse. Duty compels us to be explicit with our Constituents on a subject of such interesting importance. Every effort has been made for the purpose of procuring Loans; but without sufficient success to justify a relaxation of our own most vigorous exertions.

It is to be observed that a powerful armed Neutrality appears to be formed in Europe determined to support the freedom of Commerce. Should overtures of peace be the result of a Convention of the neutral powers, is it not our interest, is it not our indispensible duty to be prepared for such an event? Our object is of the greatest magnitude, the security, freedom and Independence of the United States: and experience evinces that no Nation can promise itself a safe and honourable peace which is not in condition to maintain a War with vigour. We are confident there is no want of ability in the States to do this. Can arguments then be necessary to call forth every internal resourse which may contribute to put a happy period to the War? Is it not high time to expel from our Country an Enemy whose progress is marked with blood and desolation and whose successes inspire them only with redoubled vengeance?

The estimates may appear large but we conceive them to be absolutely necessary. To the utmost of our power we have endeavoured to correct abuses in the public expenditures. We have called for the aid of the respective Executives. Again we recommend this

Indian Medal Struck for the State of Virginia, 1780

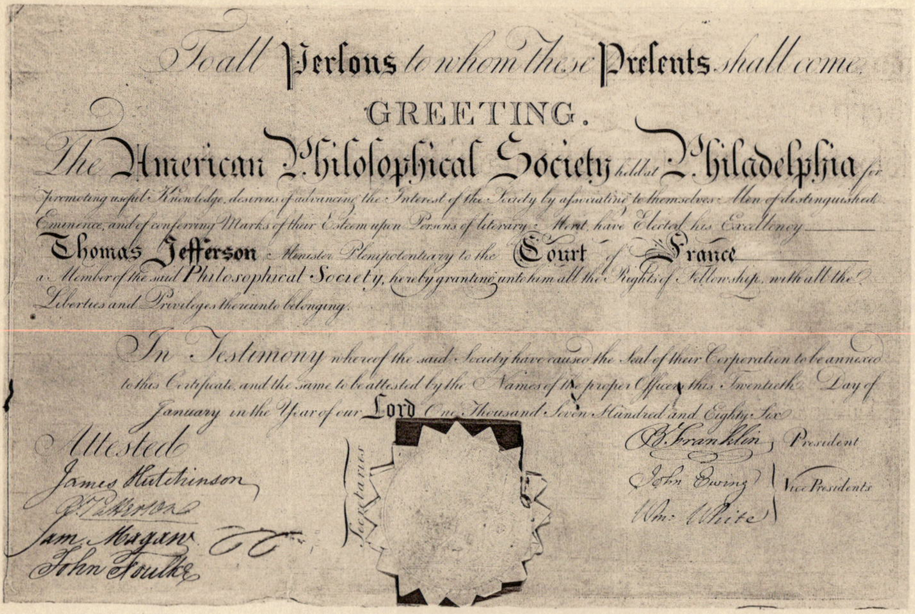

To all Persons to whom these Presents shall come.

GREETING.

The American Philosophical Society held at Philadelphia for promoting useful Knowledge, desirous of advancing the Interest of the Society by associating to themselves Men of distinguished Eminence, and of conferring Marks of their Esteem upon Persons of literary Merit, have Elected his Excellency Thomas Jefferson Minister Plenipotentiary to the Court of France a Member of the said Philosophical Society, hereby granting unto him all the Rights of Fellowship, with all the Liberties and Privileges thereunto belonging.

In Testimony whereof the said Society have caused the Seal of their Corporation to be annexed to this Certificate, and the same to be attested by the Names of the proper Officers this Twentieth Day of January in the Year of our Lord One Thousand Seven Hundred and Eighty Six

Attested

James Hutchinson

[illegible]

Sam Magaw

John Foulke

Secretaries

B. Franklin President

John Ewing

Wm. White Vice Presidents

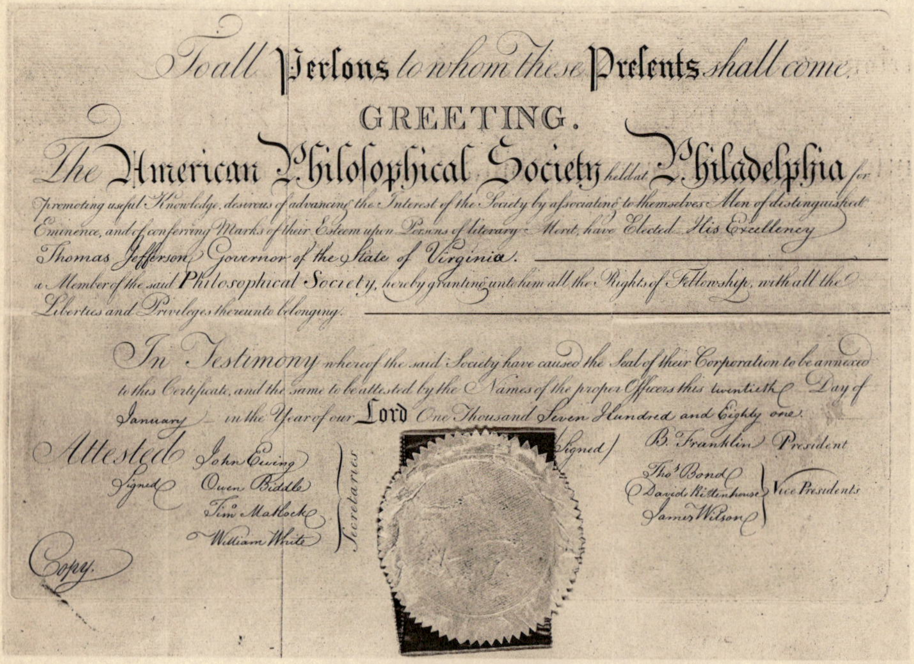

To all Persons to whom these Presents shall come.

GREETING.

The American Philosophical Society held at Philadelphia for promoting useful Knowledge, desirous of advancing the Interest of the Society by associating to themselves Men of distinguished Eminence, and of conferring Marks of their Esteem upon Persons of literary Merit, have Elected His Excellency Thomas Jefferson Governor of the State of Virginia a Member of the said Philosophical Society, hereby granting unto him all the Rights of Fellowship, with all the Liberties and Privileges thereunto belonging.

In Testimony whereof the said Society have caused the Seal of their Corporation to be annexed to this Certificate, and the same to be attested by the Names of the proper Officers this twentieth Day of January in the Year of our Lord One Thousand Seven Hundred and Eighty one.

Attested

Signed

John Ewing

Owen Biddle

Tim. Matlock

William White

Secretaries

Signed

B. Franklin President

Thos Bond

David Rittenhouse

James Wilson Vice Presidents

Copy.

Jefferson's Certificates of Membership in the American Philosophical Society

ENCLOSURE

Continental Requisitions of Food, 4 November 1780

	Barr. beef. 240℔ @ 17½ D. pr. barl.	Hundred wt. @ 5½ D. pr. C.	Hundred wt. @ 8.D. pr. C.	galls. W. India rum.	bush. salt.	bar. pork 220.℔. 22 D.	barr. flour 224.℔	Dollars
New Hampshire	2,500	6,000	2,000	20,124				47,623
Massachusets	16,000	29,250	9,750	74,576	13,000	2,000		273,831⅔
Rhode island	900	1,500	500	20,000		83.		23,797⅔
Connecticut	15,000	18,750	6,250	25,000	813	3,500		202,399⅓
New York	2,800	1,320	441½			1,500	16,000	89,295
New Jersey	3,000	4,000	1,333		996	4,000	12,000	107,152
Pennsylvania	3,000	1,500	500	50,000	13,028	2,000	55,000	27,383⅓
Delaware				2,000	500	800	3,471	20,240⅔
Maryland	4,800	9,000	3,000	17,007	4,000	5,500	20,000	188,111
Virginia	9,000	23,670	7,890	70,292	6,673	10,617	7,529	297,645
N. Carolina	3,000	7,500	2,500	24,000	991	5,000	6,000	119,060
Total								
Virginia to deliver								
Jan. 1. 1780.	9,000			11,000	1,000	10,617	2,500	
Mar. 1.				5,500	500		1,250	
May. 1.				11,000	1,000		2,500	74,411¼
July 15.				42,792	4,173		1,279	
Aug. 1.								74,411¼
Nov. 1.								74,411¼
Feb. 1.								74,411¼

Nov. 4. 1780.

essential object to their attention. Nothing on our part shall be wanting which may contribute to promote the strictest Oeconomy in dispensing the supplies now required.

We have only to add our earnest desire that no time may be lost, and should the Legislature of your State not be in Session on the receipt of this Letter that it may be immediately convened.

By order and on behalf of The United States in Congress Assembled, SAM. HUNTINGTON President

RC (Vi); in a clerk's hand, signed by Huntington; at head of text: "(Circular)." The original enclosure, an attested copy of an 8-page resolution of Congress, 4 Nov., is also in Vi (and there is also a copy, sent later), but the text presented here derives from a condensed form of the resolution in TJ's own hand (also in Vi), arranged by him somewhat differently from the original for the purpose of ready reference. Huntington's letter and its enclosure were transmitted by TJ to Speaker Harrison on 20 Nov. 1780, q.v.

Huntington's circular letter was drawn by a committee of Congress and agreed to on the day it was sent; several versions are to be found in PCC; see JCC, XVIII, 1038-40, especially p. 1040, note. The requisitions on the states, approved 4 Nov., are printed in full in same, p. 1011-18.

To Horatio Gates

SIR Richmond November 10th. 1780.

Your favour of the third instant Enclosing Colo. Preston's Letter, came to hand on the eighth. The proposals mentioned in the colonel's Letter for sending volunteers to you were accepted and put as was necessary into such precise form as that all parties might know what they had right to expect. In doing this two circumstances happened to interfere with what had been expected. 1. We required that they shou'd be subject to your orders, and those of such other officer as you shoud place them under: this was to enable you to make use of them in constituting the corps you had proposed under General Morgan. 2. That there shoud be two companies of rifles only to each battalion: this was the advice of Genl. Morgan in a conversation with me. We have since dispensed with the last of these conditions and allowed every man to carry his rifle as we found that absolutely necessary to induce them to go. Colo. Skillen of Botetourt writes me he has 150. engaged and we shall endeavour to prevail on Colo. Campbell to raise another corps, in which, if he undertakes it, I trust he will succeed. I am much at a loss what shoud be done as to the prisoners taken at Kings mountain. I do not think Montgomery courthouse a good place because it is very disaffected, it is too near their own country, and would admit their cooperation in any enterprise on our lead mines which are about eight miles from thence. I have taken measures for continuing their march under a guard northwardly and in the mean time for receiving instructions from Congress where to terminate their journey. The British Convention troops will proceed immediately to Fort Frederick in Maryland. The Germans will remain in Albemarle till accommodations can be provided for them in the same place. From them we have no apprehensions of desertion to the enemy. Some British were taken yesterday who are said to have been with the enemy and were returning to the barracks. Two or three days ago a british emissary from Portsmouth, was taken endeavouring to proceed towards Carolina. On a proposal to search him they observed him to put his hand in his pocket, and put something to his mouth like a quid of tobacco. On examination it was found to be a letter, of which the inclosed is a copy, written on silk paper, rolled up in gold beaters skin, and nicely tied at each end, the whole not larger than a goose quill. By this you will find our conjectures verified that they expected to meet with Lord Cornwallis in the neighbourhood at least of this country, and are disappointed and without an object. Can you not take measures for finding out the other messenger to Lord Cornwallis who went by Land? The force we shall now immediately have together authorizes me to assure you, you need not apprehend their penetrating any distance southwardly. I only lament that this measure shou'd have intercepted our reinforcements to you. We have left all the counties south of James river and nearer to Hillsborough than portsmouth uncalled on that they may be ready to go to the aid of our southern friends [when]ever arms can be procured. I am with the greatest esteem & respect Sir Your most obedient & most huble servt,

Th: Jefferson

RC (DLC); in a clerk's hand, with complimentary close and signature by TJ; endorsed. Enclosure (missing): Copy of Leslie to Cornwallis, 4 Nov. 1780. The original of Leslie's letter was enclosed in TJ to Huntington, following, and is printed with it. The present letter is probably that to which Gates refers in his to General Smallwood of 13 Nov., enclosing "a Copy of a Letter I received last night from Governor Jefferson" (Tr in DLC).

The letter from COLO. SKILLEN (George Skillern) to TJ is missing, but see entry for TJ to Skillern, 18 Oct. 1780. The MESSENGER . . . WHO WENT BY LAND: It is very likely that the other messenger is referred to in a letter from Robert Bulfill to Cornwallis, undated and without place, in Vi, which states in part: "I have the Honor to inform your lordship that agreeable to Major General Leslie orders I have proceeded up the rapahanok in order to procure the enclosed letter a safe conveyance to your lordship." The writer stated that he would wait for a reply on the Rappahannock.

To Samuel Huntington, enclosing an Intercepted Letter from Leslie to Cornwallis

SIR Richmond November 10. 1780.

I inclose your Excellency an intercepted Letter from Major General Leslie to Ld. Cornwallis. It was taken on a person endeavouring to pass through the Country from Portsmouth towards Carolina. When he was apprehended and a proposal made to search him, he readily consented to be searched but at the same time was observed to put his hand into his Pocket and carry some thing towards his mouth as if it were a quid of tobacco. It was examined and found to be what is now inclosed.[1] As this is the first authentic disclosure of their purpose in coming here and may serve to found with somewhat more of certainty conjectures of their future movements while their disappointment in not meeting with Ld. Cornwallis may occasion new plans at New York, I thought it worthy of being communicated to your Excellency by Express.

Some Deserters were yesterday taken, said to be of the British Convention troops who had found means to get to the enemy at Portsmouth and were 70 and 80 Miles on their way back to the barracks when they were taken. They were passing under the guise of deserters from Portsmouth.

I have the honor to be with every sentiment of respect Your Excellency's most obedt. & most humble servt, TH: JEFFERSON

ENCLOSURE

Alexander Leslie to Cornwallis

My Lord Portsmouth Virginia 4th. Novr. 1780.

I have been here near a Week Establishing a Post. I wrote to you to Charles Town, And by another Messenger by Land. I cant hear for a certainty where you are. I wait your Orders. The Bearer is to be handsomely rewarded if he brings me Any note or Mark from your Ldship. A: L:

RC (DLC: PCC, No. 71, I); in a clerk's hand, with complimentary close, signature, and address by TJ; endorsed by Charles Thomson: "Letter from Govr Jefferson Nov 10. 1780. Read 17." The cover also bears the following series of notations, indicating that TJ must have sent this important information northward immediately by special express: "Delivered in Annapolis the 13th. November at half after five P.M. Delivered at Baltimore 14 Novemr. 1780. at one oClock P.M. Delivered at Hartford 14th. Novemr. 1780. 25 minutes Past five P M. Reced at Elk 15th; four oclock P M and forwarded 16th; in the Morning HH." ("Hartford" must be Harford Town, Harford co., Md., a station on the express line from Richmond to Philadelphia; see Maryland Council to Col. Henry Hollingsworth [whose initials appear above], 7 July 1780, *Md. Archives*, XLIII, 214. "Elk" is Head of Elk, modern Elkton, Cecil co., Md.) Enclosure (filed with the letter in PCC, No. 71, I); this is the original intercepted letter, bearing the direction "Lord Cornwallis" on cover. Tr of part of TJ's letter to Huntington (as indicated in note below) is in CtY; it is endorsed: "[. . . Th]omas Jefferson, Governour of Virginia, to the President of Congress, dated 10 Novr. 1780. No. 1 enclosing No. 2.

TJ gave both Gates and Washington more details on how the messenger attempted to conceal Leslie's letter; see letters to them of this date. The intercepted letter was printed in *Va. Gaz.* (D & N), 11 Nov. 1780, with caption: "An intercepted letter taken by one of our out posts from a person in disguise."

[1] Tr ends at this point.

To Edward Stevens

SIR Richmond November 10. 1780

Your two Letters of Octr. 24 and Octr. have been duly received. I have been informed that the Beeves which had been collecting in Princess Anne and Norfolk to be sent Southwardly were the first things which fell into the hands of the Enemy. We received notice of this invasion a few Hours after you left this place, and dispatched a Letter to recall you which we expected would have found you in Petersburg. However you had gone on, and as there should be a General Officer with the men from this State in the Southern Service, and we have here three General Officers we have not repeated our call for Your Assistance. The force called on to oppose the Enemy is as yet in a most Chaotic State, consisting of fragments of 3 Months Militia, 8 Months Men, 18 Months men, Volunteers and new Militia.

Were it possible to arm men we would send on Substantial reinforcements to you notwithstanding the presence of the Enemy with us, but the prospect of Arms with us is very bad indeed. I have never received a line from Mr. Lambe as to his Success in pressing Waggons, none have yet Come in from the Westward. The Executive were so far from allowing the 8 Months Men to Enlist into the Volunteer Corps, as you say they pretend, that they were expressly excluded from it in the several propositions we made for Raising Volunteers. Nothing of Moment has happened here since the arrival of the Enemy. Genl. Muhlenburg is at Stoners Mills, at the head of Pagan Creek with our main force. Genl. Nelson is on the Northern side of James River with another Body. Genl. Weedon is gone to Join the one or the other. A British emissary was taken two or three days ago with a Letter from Genl. Leslie to Lord Cornwallas, informing him he was at Portsmouth but could not learn where his Lordship was; that he had sent one Letter to him to Charlestown by Water, another by land and waited his orders. Cannot measures be taken to apprehend the messenger who went by Land. I am with the greatest Esteem Sir your most Hum: Servt,

TH JEFFERSON

Tr (DLC); endorsed. 2d Tr (NHi); endorsed. One or two copyist's errors have been corrected and one or two faded passages have been supplied from 2d Tr.

YOUR TWO LETTERS: Stevens wrote TJ on 24, 27, and 30 Oct. TJ's letter recalling Stevens is dated 22 Oct.

From Edward Stevens

SIR Hillsborough November 10. 1780

This will be handed you with a Letter from Genl. Gates, by the latter I presume you'll be informed that on Monday last the General left this for the westward with about 120 Cavelry, composed of detachments from Whites, Washingtons Armongs [Armand's] and Nelsons Corps. The Maryland Troops with a detachment of the Virginia regulars under Colo. Buford, the whole consisting of about 800 moved from here on the Thursday befor the General. The Virginia Malitia and the 18. Months new Levies that are here the Numbers[1] of each I now Inclose you a return of, are to follow on, as soon as the Arms and Accoutrements can be got from Taylors Ferry. The two Companies of Malitia from Fairfax and Prince William halted at Taylors Ferry are ordered hence.[2] The Numbers of the Malitia is small, all those that was ordered (or at least such as intended to come) must have got here by now, without they have been Countermanded. I have been somewhat uneasy since I received your Letter desiring my return to Virginia least you should think by my not returning immediately it might proceed from the want of respect to your Orders, but what I wrote you the 27th and 30th of last Month, I hope will Satisfy you of the Princeples I was actuated from, and since then your Information to the General of the Enemies embarking from Hampton gave some reason to hope they were only a Forageing party, and that they were about to leave Virginia. But at the same time I have waited here with much impatience, and daily in Hopes I might hear from you.

I expect Genl. Gates Letter may give you the same Intelligence, tho' least it should not I inclose you a Copy of a Letter from Genl. Harrington to the Board of War at this place. It contains the latest Intelligence we have from the South.

The greatest part of the 18th Months Men that are here, and indeed all the Virginia Regulars are in a most Pitifull condition. Many of them cant Hide their nakedness, and scarce a Blankett among them. When they come to March without Tents to Shelter under in Bad Weather; their Distresses will be greater, than ca[n] possibly be conceived.

The Troops here, for three days past, has been entirely without Bread; their Behaviour on the occasion does them great Credit, as scarce a Murmer was heard amongst them. They are for the present relieved. Nothing is more dispiriting to Troops than to be badly supplied, especially when in a Country where plenty might be had.

I am &c.

Tr (DLC); endorsed (in part): "Copy." 2d Tr (DLC: PCC, No. 71, I), transmitted by TJ to Huntington in a letter of 19 Nov. 1780; this Tr is incomplete but contains notations in TJ's hand which provide the substance of one of the (missing) enclosures; see below.

A LETTER FROM GENL. GATES: Gates to TJ, 8 Nov. YOUR LETTER DESIRING MY RETURN: Dated 22 Oct. A LETTER FROM GENL. HARRINGTON: Presumably H. W. Harrington to the North Carolina Board of War, dated from Camp near Kershaw's Ferry East Side P.D. [Peedee], 3 Nov. 1780, printed in *N.C. State Records*, XV, 139-41.

1 In 2d Tr an asterisk precedes this word, and TJ has written in the margin, under a corresponding asterisk, these notes: "293. eighteen months men [besides those gone on with Bufort]. 193. eight months men. 248. three months do. 4. companies of which no return." (The square brackets are TJ's.)

2 In 2d Tr the passage from here to the end of the paragraph was for some reason omitted. The copyist transcribed almost the whole of the first sentence in the omitted portion but then scored it out.

To George Washington

Richmond, 10 Nov. 1780. Encloses copy of intercepted letter from Gen. Leslie to Lord Cornwallis; describes circumstances of its capture in same terms as in letter to Gates of this date, q.v. An added paragraph reports the capture of deserters from the Convention army in same terms as in letter to Huntington of this date, q.v.

RC (DLC: Washington Papers); 2 p.; in a clerk's hand, with complimentary close and signature by TJ; endorsed (in part): "from Governor Jefferson with intercepted letter from Genl. Leslie to Ld. Cornwallis. Ansd 9th Decr." Printed: L & B, IV, 129-30; *Official Letters*, II, 231-2; and elsewhere. Enclosure (same location): Tr of Leslie's letter to Cornwallis, 4 Nov. 1780. Tr of both letter and enclosure are in DLC: TJ Papers. The enclosure is printed above in full with TJ's letter of the present date to Huntington.

To the Auditors,

with Account of Goods Furnished to the Indians by Major Linctot

GENTLEMEN — In Council Nov. 11. 1780.

Be pleased to issue on the within certificate from Colo. Broadhead a warrant for the sum due on the within account in specie or it's value in paper money at the current exchange, to be paid to Majr. Lintot or order and charged to the Continent. TH: JEFFERSON

ENCLOSURE

An Account of what goods Mr. Godfrey Linctot Major and Agent General of all the Indien Nations have Furnished to the Indiens for the Service of the United States of America.

Furnished at Fort Pitt the 26th. of Aprill 1780	To fourteen Shirts Giveen to the Dallaway Indiens	45/	£31	10	
	To three Pistols	70/	10	10	
	To Seven Yards of Blue Cloth	60/	21		
	To one Riffle Gun		9		
	To one Powder Horn and Shot Bag		1		
	To two Horses	£25	50		
Givven at the Indiens Town the 12th. of may 1780	To Eight Yards of Cloth for a Flag	5/	2		
	To three Coats		18		
	To one Great Coat		5		
	To one Silver Lace Waiscoat		6		
	To Six Shirts	45/	13	10	
	To five yards of Blue Cloth	60/	15		
	To four Blanketts	30/	6		
Giveven at Fort Pitt June the 24th. 1780	To two Horses		50		
	To four Shirts	45/	9		
	To Six Yards of Blue Cloth	60/	18		
	To Eight yards of Cloth for a Flag	5/	2		
	To three gold Laced Hatts	90/	13	10	
Giveen at Fort Pitt June the 26th. 1780	To three Silk Handkerchiefs	15/	2	5	
	To twenty four Yards of Blue Cloth	60/	72		
	To twenty four yards of Cloth	60/	72		
		Spicie	£427	5	
	Exchange at / add ¼		106	16	3
	Pennsylvania Currency		£534	1	3

Fort Pitt July the 2d. 1780. G.f. Linctot

Fort Pitt July 3rd. 1780.

I certify that to the best of my knowledge Major Lanctot has given the above Articles to the Delaware Indians with a view to serve the United States. DANIEL BRODHEAD

Colo. commandg. W.D.

RC (Vi); in TJ's hand. The enclosure, presumably in Linctot's hand, has certification signed by Brodhead on face of document (Vi). Letter and enclosure are endorsed: "Fort Pitt July 3rd. 1780 Indian affairs . . . £534.1.3."

On Linctot as Indian agent see Wis. Hist. Soc., *Colls.*, XXIV, 176, note.

To James Wood

SIR — In Council Novr. 11. 1780.

It will be inconvenient for you to go to Annapolis, yet if not very much so, we think it much more probable that you will get every thing properly settled by personal representations to the fountain of power, than on conferences with persons who might be substituted by them. The former could adapt their orders to actual circumstances, the latter would be bound by orders entered into without the information you would personally give. We think it perfectly reasonable that your travelling expences shoud be paid as proposed in your letter of the 9th instant, and will immediately lay it before Congress for their determination, as with them alone rests the power of determining ultimately. I have delivered to Capt. Read a warrant for £30, currency of Mar. 18 according to your desire. He will be so kind as to receive either the money or such a Certificate as you desire. We suppose Capt. Read's services may be more wanted with you than here, and therefore advise him to return. The line of riders shou'd still be continued. An intercepted letter from Genl. Leslie of which a copy is in the paper of this day inclosed, informs Ld. Cornwallis he is establishing a post at portsmouth which seems as if they meant it to be permanent.

I am with great esteem Sir Your mo. ob. servant,

TH: JEFFERSON

RC (Lloyd W. Smith, Madison, N.J., 1946); in a clerk's hand, signed by TJ; endorsed. Addressee identified from internal evidence.

YOUR LETTER OF THE 9TH: Not found; a copy was forwarded by TJ to Huntington on 13 Nov. Leslie's INTERCEPTED LETTER to Cornwallis: See TJ to Huntington, 10 Nov., where the text of Leslie's letter is printed as an enclosure. THE PAPER OF THIS DAY: The intercepted letter was printed in *Va. Gaz.* (D & N), 11 Nov.

To Samuel Huntington

SIR — In Council Richmond Nov. 13. 1780

I take the liberty of enclosing your Excellency a copy of a letter I received from Colo. Wood. As the determination whether he shall be allowed travelling expenses rests with Congress alone, we could only communicate his application to that honourable Body.

I have the honor to be with the greatest Respect &c &c.,

TH: JEFFERSON

Tr (DLC: PCC, No. 71, I); entirely in the hand of George Taylor (clerk in the Department of State) and endorsed by him: "No. 91. Gov. Jefferson to the Presidt. of Congress Nov. 13. 1780. read 27." The following memorandum, in Taylor's hand, appears on the face of Tr: "Mr. Jefferson in the year 1791 wishing to supply any chasms which might be found in the copies of his public letters while Gov. of Virga. requested that those written to Congress during that period should be sent to Mr. Eppes his nephew for that purpose. On examination after the files had been returned to the office in 1792 the following numbers viz. No. 91 of Nov. 13. 1780 and No. 94 of Nov. 26. 1780 were found wanting, but copies of them having been preserved by Mr. Jefferson, this (No. 91) and No. 94 have been carefully copied from them as substitutes for the originals by Geo. Taylor Jr." Enclosure not found; this must have been James Wood's letter of 9 Nov. acknowledged in TJ to Wood, 11 Nov., q.v.

This letter and its enclosure, having been read in Congress on 27 Nov., were referred to the Board of War (JCC, XVIII, 1095).

From Samuel Huntington

SIR Philadelphia November 13. 1780

Congress having received Information from the Honorable the Minister of France, of Inconveniencies and Injuries received by our Allies, resulting from the Abuse the British make of Papers and Clearances they take in American Prizes, by personating the Officers and Commanders named in such Papers, being fully acquainted with the Language and Manners of our Officers and Seamen &c.

In Compliance with the request of the Minister of France, Congress have adopted the enclosed resolution; and I am to request your Excellency's Attention to the necessary Measures for carrying the same into effectual Execution.

I have the Honor to be with the highest respect your Excellency's most obedient Servant, SAM. HUNTINGTON President

RC (Vi); in a clerk's hand, signed by Huntington; at head of text: "Circular." FC (DLC: PCC, No. 15). Enclosure (Vi, 2 copies): attested copies of resolve of Congress, 10 Nov., respecting clearance of armed vessels from American ports. This resolve (printed in JCC, XVIII, 1043) recommended "that on the back of the Commission [of every private vessel of war] there be inserted a minute description of the persons of the Captain and his Lieutenant with their Age, Stature, Complexion &c. respectively, certified by the Governor . . . under his seal of Office," &c.

From Johann Ludwig de Unger,
with a List of Books Returned

MONSIEUR! Aux Barraques, ce 13me. du Novembre, 1780.

Comme nous avons reçu les Ordres de quitter cette Place, j'ai cru qu'il dût etre un de mes premiers Devoirs de Vous rendre mes Remerciements pour toutes les Marques de Bienveillance dont il Vous a plût me daigner, et de Vous demander tres humblement la Continuation de Vos bonnes Graces.

Ayant aprit que Vous avez toujours honnoré Mons: le Docteur Gilmer avec une Amitié particuliere je ne crois pas d'avoir eu manquer le But que je me suis propose de Vous remetre en bon Etat ces Livres qui m'ont fait passer bien des Jours agreablement et utilement; ci je les ai deliveré a ce Monsieur. Le Lieutenant du Roï et le Ministre Colly m'ayant chargé de remetre les Livres que Vous avez eu la Bonté de leur preter, pareillement au Docteur Gilmer, c'est pour cela que je me donne l'Honeur de joindre-ci un Catalogue du tout pour eviter tout Erreur.

Je Vous prie d'etre assuré que je suis incapable d'oublier toutes les Bontes dont il Vous a plût m'honnorer pendant notre Séjour en Virginie; et quoique il-y-a beaucoup des Persones qui perdent en quittant cette Province, ma Perte est la plus considerable lorsque je serai prive (peut-etre pour jamais) de la Satisfaction de converser avec une Personne en qui se trouvent toutes les Qualités qui peuvent donner de l'Estime et d'Affection. Quel Bonheur serai-ce pour moi ci a la Place ou nous allons etre conduite, je trouverois un Bienfaiteur comme Vous! Ce seroit un Bien qui me donneroit en quelque Façon du Soulagement. Il ne me reste qu'a addresser à la Providence les Voeux les plus sincere pour Vous et Votre chere Famillie. Le Cieul veuille Vous combler de toutes Sortes de Prosperités et Vous faire jouir d'une longue Suite d'Années en parfaite Sante et Contentement. Si apres cela je fais quelques Souhaits particuliers pour moi, c'est que je puisse avoir l'Honneur de Vous temoigner, Monsieur que je ressens comme je le dois les solides Obligations que je Vous ai, et qui m'obligent d'etre avec le plus grand Respect Monsieur, Votre tres-humble, et tres-obeissant Serviteur,

JOHN LEWIS DE UNGER

ENCLOSURE

Catalogue des Livres deliveré a Monsieur
le Docteur Gilmer le 13me. du Nov 1780

par moi:

1.	Cours de Mathematique de Bezout	6 Vol.
2.	Boileau Works	2 Vol
3.	Plays of Vanbruck	2 Vol
4.	Candide	1 Vol
5.	Contes Moreaux de Marmontel	3 Vol

par Lieutenant du Roi

1.	Farquars Plays	2 Vol:

par le Ministre Colly

1.	Originis Contra Celsum	1 Vol
2.	Salmon's Geographical Grammar	1 Vol.

John Lewis de Unger

RC (DLC). Enclosure (MoSHi).

Unger was lieutenant in the Regiment Rhetz of the Brunswick forces (Riedesel, *Memoirs*, II, 269). LE LIEUTENANT DU ROI: August Wilhelm du Roi, lt. and adjutant in Prince Friederich's Regiment (same, II, 268); he kept a journal of his American service which is uniquely valuable for its account of the march of the Convention troops from Boston to Charlottesville, 1778-1779, and its description of the quarters and life of the German Convention prisoners in Virginia: *Journal of Du Roi the Elder* . . . , transl. by Charlotte S. J. Epping [Americana Germanica, No. 15], N.Y., 1911). LE MINISTRE COLLY: Chaplain Kohle; see TJ to Wood, 7 Nov. 1780 (second letter to Wood of that date).

To the Virginia Delegates in Congress

GENTLEMEN Richmond Nov. 14. 1780.

I do myself the pleasure of inclosing to you a draught of Mr. Ben: Harrison jur. and co: on Messicurs Turnbull and co: merchants of Philadelphia for 66,666⅔ dollars for which we have had transferred to Mr. Harrison the Auditors warrant of aug. 9. 1780. for £20,000 Virginia money with which you stand charged in their books.

I have the honor to be with the greatest esteem and respect Gentlemen, Your most obedient & mo. hble. servant.

RC (ViW); in a clerk's hand, presumably signed by TJ, but signature has been cut out. Addressed by TJ: "The honble. The Virginia Delegates in Congress." Endorsed: "Gov. Jefferson's Letter to Delegs. in Congress." Enclosure not found.

To Benjamin Harrison

[*Richmond, 16? Nov. 1780.* JHD, Oct. 1780, 1827 edn., p. 19 (16 Nov.): "The Speaker laid before the House a letter from the Governor, enclosing a return of the present state of the navy, and stating additional matter for the consideration of the General Assembly; and the same were read. *Ordered*, That the Governor's letter do lie on the table. *Ordered*, That the return of the state of the navy, be referred to the committee appointed to prepare a plan of defence for the eastern frontier." Neither letter nor enclosure has been located.]

From George Muter, with Reply

SIR War office Novr. 16. 1780.

One of the workmen at the manufactory of small arms at Fredericksburgh is now here, who says, he has been employed by the other workmen at that place to enquire if they were to receive any additional pay, which they have been informed, was ordered by a resolution of Assembly during the last session. Mr. Dick (he says) has refused to give the workmen any additional pay, because he has received no orders for that purpose.

I have the honour to be Your Excellency's most hl Servant,

GEORGE MUTER. C.

In council Nov. 16. 1780

We know of no resolution for advancing their pay.

TH: JEFFERSON

RC (Vi); addressed: "His Excellency The Governour"; endorsed: "Colo. Muters Letter to the Govr. respecting a workman belonging to the Fredksbg Manufactory Novr. 16th. 1780." The reply is in TJ's hand.

John Smith to Isaac Zane

DEAR SIR Winchester Novem: 16th. 1780.

Through your means I beg leave to renew an application, formerly made to Governor Jefferson, on a proposed plan, for the more easie and safe keeping the prisoners of war in the town of Winchester. By the prisoners of war, you will please to understand, that I do not mean to include the prisoners of the convention of Saratoga, as those troops will be under the imediate inspection of a continental officer. The irregularity of a militia guard, and the want of power in the officers to compel them to abide by the necessary regulations of a military arrangement are too notorious to every man who has read the militia laws, and who has seen the trained bands drawn into service, so that I shall say nothing to you upon this head. I have recruited a company as a Guard to serve at this post, by the permission of Governor Jefferson, tho' not strictly agreeable to the powers he allowed of; I have done more than engaged them as militia, I have engaged them for a twelve month, subject to the continental rules of war, on a promise of a discharge at the expiration of three months, unless I procure them the usual clothing of a soldier within that space of Time. A letter from Col. Grayson in answer to one I had written to the continental board of war, will inform you of their sentiments on this subject. Our friend Col. Holmes has it in possession and to him I must refer you for further particulars on this matter. A guard house is necessary, I would recommend one to be built of loggs, near to the house now applyed to the purpose of barracks. Four sentry boxes are necessary —you well know they can't be dispensed with. In case of any of the guard being sick I should be glad to have the power of imploying a doctor. I assure you my humanity has sufferred upon this account already. Inclosed you will receive an account for ammunition furnishd to the guard. Guns are of small avail without this article. You will be pleasd to get the account paid and procure me a small quantity of ammunition from the public magazine. You will likewise receive a militia pay role and an account of kettles and dutch ovens purchased from yourself, both of which you will procure the payment of. You will be pleased to let me hear from you as soon as possible & am Sir Your mt. obt. Servt, JOHN SMITH

RC (Vi); addressed: "Isaac Zane Esq."; endorsed: "Jno. Smith's Lr. to Mr. Zane Novr. 1780." See TJ to John Smith, 9 Sep. 1780.

To James Wood

In Council, November 16, 1780

I shall be exceedingly glad to hear the British division is gone, as their presence gives uneasiness. I hope the waggons will come in as you expect. Your orders for receiving the forage of the Officers and repaying them specifically are approved as being perfectly just. We wish in every possible circumstance to lighten the inconveniences which will attend their removal, a measure which we think essential for our safety. If the staff officers will make out to you a state of the balances they owe to those soldiers, women, &c. about to remove we will endeavor to send them money to the amount. . . . We have no objections to Lt. Croft's going to New York on parole, as far as we have a right to meddle in it. We recommend it to you to have the pack horses sent on by Baker and unfit for service sold at public auction.

MS not located. Text from extracts in American Art Association, sale catalogue, 30 Nov. 1927 (Henry Goldsmith Sale), lot 24, where the original is described as a letter signed, with "a seven line postscript in [TJ's] autograph."

To Benjamin Harrison

SIR In Council November 17th 1780.

At the request of the honorable Theodorick Bland I take the liberty of laying before the General Assembly the inclosed paper in which he states a difficulty which has arisen in reconciling his qualification as a delegate to the peculiar channel into which he had previously turned his private fortune.

From the inclosed extract of a Letter from our Delegates in Congress you will also perceive that they suffer some inconvenience from precarious remittances. Tho this be not within the line of our immediate care we have never been wanting in furnishing such facilities as we were able towards effecting remittances to them. But these we believe have been rendered irregular sometimes by the want of conveyance, and sometimes by the state of the treasury.

I have the honor to be with the most perfect respect Sir, Your most obedient & most humble servant, TH: JEFFERSON

RC (Vi); in a clerk's hand, signed and addressed by TJ to Harrison as Speaker. Endorsed: "Governors Letter November 17th: 1780. Enclosing Extract of Colo: Blands—and from the Virginia Delegates. Novr: 18th: 1780. referred to Mr: Richard Henry Lee. Fleming. Starke." Enclosures: (1) extract of Virginia Delegates in Congress to TJ, 5 Nov., printed above under date; (2) extract of a (missing) letter from Theodorick Bland to TJ, date not known.

From Samuel Huntington

SIR Philadelphia November 17. 1780

Your Excellency will receive herewith enclosed, the Copy of an Act of Congress of the 14th Instant, representing the criminal Practice carried on by Individuals from some of the States in supplying the Enemy with Provision.

And recommending to the Legislature of the respective States; by whom it hath not been already done; to enact Laws inflicting Capital Punishment on all such Persons as shall directly or indirectly supply the Enemy with Provisions, or military or naval Stores; and adopt the most vigorous Measures for the Execution of such Laws.

I have the Honor to be with the highest Respect your Excellency's most obedient & humble Servant,

SAM. HUNTINGTON President

RC (Vi); in a clerk's hand, signed by Huntington; at head of text: "Circular"; endorsed. FC (DLC: PCC, No. 15). Enclosure (Vi): attested copy of Congress' resolve, 14 Nov., concerning trading with the enemy at New York. This resolve was passed in consequence of information in a letter from Washington to Huntington, 7 Nov. (*Writings*, ed. Fitzpatrick, XX, 311-15) and is printed in JCC, XVIII, 1052-3.

From Samuel Huntington

SIR Philada November 17. 1780

The Intelligence contained in the enclosed Copy of a Letter just received from General Washington is of such a Nature, I have thought proper to transmit the same to your Excellency by Express.

Your several Dispatches of the 26. Ulto. 3d, 7. and 10. Instant have been duly received.

I have the Honor to be &c &c, S.H.

FC (DLC: PCC, No. 15). At foot of text: "N.B. Similar Letters, excepting the last Clause, to Governor Lee and General Greene." Enclosure not found, but it was undoubtedly a copy of Gen. Washington's letter to Huntington of 14 Nov., reporting the movement of the British fleet in New York Harbor. The nature of Washington's information was to be an issue in the inquiry into TJ's conduct as governor (see Nicholas' Charges and Jefferson's Answers, printed under 31 July 1781), and his letter is therefore quoted here in full:

"Sir: I have just received advice that Admiral Rodney's Fleet, with the transports which have been sometime preparing, fell down to the Hook on Saturday last. The number of troops on board is not yet ascertained. It is said that Major General Phillips commands the detachment, but I have it not sufficiently vouched, to make it a matter of certainty. Their destination is generally believed to be to the Southward. I expect more circumstantial intelligence shortly" (*Writings*, ed. Fitzpatrick, XX, 346; TJ received this information on 26 Nov.; see his letter to Gen. Greene of that date).

To the Virginia Delegates in Congress

GENTLEMEN Richmd. Novr 17th. 1780

With respect to the payment made on behalf of Mr. Braxton into the Continental treasury in Part of our Quota of the fifteen Million tax, the Executive having been Charged with the raising and remitting that money, we have thought it unnecessary to lay it before the Legislature. The Sum to be sent, was sent, partly in Money and Partly in Bills. These Bills were drawn in *Continental Dollars*, and paiable in such, and not in Specie. Of this nature was Mr.

Braxtons Bill desiring his Correspondent to pay so many Continental Dollars into the Treasury. If the treasurer has received payment in another kind of money at an Arbitrary rate of Exchange, this must have been either under the Rules of his office or against them. The former I can Hardly suppose, and in the latter case it has become his own Private act, and he should be deemed to have received (no[t] £1318-15 hard Money but) 263750. dollars Continental Money as he has I suppose given a discharge on the Bill for so much of its Contents. Had he rejected the Tender of the Hard Money would not Continental dollars have been paid? If they had not, then indeed the demand should have reverted on the State, and we would have fallen on means for compelling payment. We were really concernd on the return of our agent who Carried the Money and Bills that he did not have them regularly protested as there appeard some doubts on them. But he acted for the best in his own Judgment, and in that point of view was to be approved. I am exceedingly sorry that this want of Punctuality has arisen in these remittances. We sold Tobacco for these Bills, which would in Much less time have produced us money here. But the responsibility and known Connection between the drawer and drawee induced us to consider them as were Better than Money which would have been liable to Accidents in transportation. Had a tender of Specie been made to us here we would certainly have rejected it. But the payment being now to be transacted between the Drawee and Congress (passing us over) neither the Tender or receipt can be considerd as our act, but the former the act of the Drawee, and the latter of the Treasurer of Congress. We do not therefore think ourselves concernd immediately in this transaction. If Congress please to Consider the Payment of £1318-15 hard Money as a discharge of 263750 dollars paper which was to be paid by the drawee, well: if not on rejecting it he will make payment in the Specific Money he was Calld on to pay or we will resort to the Drawer and Compell such payment.

Since writing thus far I note more particularly than I had before done, that the treasurers return sais that he had *received from the Commonwealth of Virginia a Sum of Money in Specie* &c. This indeed stating it as the act of this Commonwealth renders it necessary for me to disavow it, which I hereby do. It was the Act of the drawee of which the Commonwealth had neither knowledge or Intimation; and this return fixing the act on the Commonwealth instead of the Drawee is so far wrong. THOS. JEFFERSON

Tr (DLC: PCC, No. 71, I); in Theodorick Bland's hand and attested by him as a delegate from Virginia. Endorsed: "Extract of a letter from the govr. of Virginia dated November 17 —80 referred to the Board of Treasury. [*In another hand*:] Treasury Board 21st. Decr. 1780 Make two Copies of the Order of Congress of the 15th. [*error for 19th; see below*]. Instant respecting Specie from the State of Virginia. One for the Audr. General and one other for the Treasurer." Cover also bears arithmetical calculations converting £1318/15 specie into 263,750 Continental dollars.

Under date of 19 Dec. 1780, the Journal of Congress records the following:

"Mr. Bland laid before Congress a letter from the governor of Virginia, dated 17 November, 1780. On motion of Mr. Madison, seconded by Mr. Bland, *Ordered*, That so much of the said letter as respects the receiving into the continental treasury, specie, at the rate of 75 continental dollars for one of specie, be referred to the Board of Treasury, and that they be directed to have the transaction stated in their books, and in the books of the treasurer, in such manner that the State of Virginia may not be included in it" (JCC, XVIII, 1174).

From D'Anmours

SIR A Baltimore. Le 18 9bre 1780

I have the honour to Acquaint your Excellency with a Piece of intelligence, Which if true Can not fail of Being Agreable to you in the present Circumstances. A Gentleman of this town Received last night a letter informing him of our ship Washington at Boston and tels him also that that ship parted in a storm from a french Squadron and fleet of transports in the latt. 32. which were intended for this Bay. As I arrived But six Days ago at this place, I have yet no official letter from the Minister. In Case that force did arrive in your Bay, I Suppose you will immediately Send an Express to the northward to acquaint him with it. I will take it as a Particular favour to inform me by that same opportunity of that Event. The moment I Know it I shall throw Myself on the first armed vessel to go down the Bay and Join the admiral.

You know the sincerity of the Attachment and Respect with which I am Sir Yr most obedt & huble servt,

LE CHEVR D'ANMOURS

RC (DLC).

From J. P. G. Muhlenberg

SIR Bakers Mill Novr. 18th. 1780

Enclosd I have the Honor to transmit Your Excellency my latest intelligence from Portsmouth. Part of the Brittish Fleet are now in Hampton road, and from every circumstance I am inclind to believe, they intend to Sea. Upon the Enemys moving from Portsmouth, I requested General Nelson to return to the [North] Side of James River, in order to [prep]are for any event that might happen.

I have the Honor to be with the highest respect Your Excellencys Most Obedt hble Servt, P: MUHLENBERG

RC (Vi); addressed: "*On public Service* His Excellency Governor Jefferson Richmond"; endorsed: "Nov: 18th 1780 Genl Muhlenberg to Governor Jefferson —communicating the presence of Part of the British fleet in Hampton Roads." Enclosure not identified.

From Edward Stevens

SIR Hillsborough November 18. 1780

Yours of the 10th Instant, I received. It relieved me from a State of Suspence, and uneasiness. The latter was occasioned from a fear you might have thought unfavourable of my not immediately obeying your order, tho' the Inclosed Copy of a Letter from Genl. Gates will Convince you that the principles I was actuated from was for the good of the Service, for when I first got here there was not a Field Officer present nor was there, till some time after. Their is now only two. I supposed they had been Stoped in Virginia, tho' two more will be sufficient for the number of men we have out at present. Those two, I have sent a positive order to repair hither immediately without they have received your orders to the Contrary.

A Part of the Captains and subalterns who came out now with the Militia, was indeed a worse set than formerly. Such of those I have given much Satisfaction to by permiting them to return home and I trust I have rendered a Service to my Country by so doing. This oblidged me to appoint some others in their room. The Blank Commissions you told me I should have I would be glad of.

I have Just now sent on a detachment of the 18 Months men to Genl. Gates. It has given me much pleasure to see them off as I was once afraid they would not move. Majr. Redley who commands them deserves much Credit for his Conduct in this matter. It is too true that their situation is a deplorable one and I wish they could in some measure be relieved by being furnished with some part of the Articles that they stand in most need of. I have assured them that you are doing every thing in your power for them, and to appease and quiet them I have allowed the Bearer
to Return to Virginia on this Business. I shall in two or three days

with the Militia and the rest of the Troops here, that is in a Condition to march go forward to the Westward.

At last I have with much ado got tolerable Musketts into the hands of the Militia, and furnished the great[er] part of them with Cartouch Boxes. My Command will be but small tho' small as it is, My wish is to have an Opportunity of recovering wha[t] the Virginians on the 16th so ungloriously lost, and at a time when they had so much in their Power. Your letter gives much Satisfaction to the People of the South (at least of those who knows the Contents, and I make a point of Communicating it) to understand that Virginia is determined to send aid to them altho' she is invaded herself Tho you will observe that Genl. Gates is still Clearly of Opinion that the party of the Enemy now in Virginia is only a Prelude to something that is to follow.

I observe you say the Executive has not given permission to the 8 Months men to enlist in the Volunteer Service tho' certain it is numbers of them have done it. I have been told it will excuse them from the[ir?] 8: Months Service. I am afraid few of them will ever be Collected again. I wish Colo. Faukner may not have done much Mischief in preventing the Collecting them and giving the number of Certificates he Did. The meaning of them and what was his Motives for so doing, I cant understand. I hope he has informed you.

All the Arms here which are out of repair will be sent back to Virginia, as they have no way of repairing them here. Five Hundred and odd has already gone to Taylors Ferry by the return Waggons of that place.

Our latest Accounts from the Westward is Contained in a Paragraph of a letter that I now inclose you, tho I expect General Gates has given you an Account of it.

I am &c.

Tr (DLC); endorsed (in part): "Copy." The enclosure mentioned toward the end of the letter has not been identified; the other enclosure was a copy of Gates' letter to Stevens, 12 Nov., of which a Tr containing corrections by TJ is in DLC.

Gates' letter to Stevens pronounced the opinion "that the Troops arrived in Virginia, are only the advance of a more considerable force, which may, as the season for campaigning to the Northward ceases, be sent to Virginia." Gates continued: "I desire you will not think of returning to Virginia, untill you have marched all the Troops now at Hillsboro' belonging to that State to Salisbury. Your presence with them is so far absolutely and indispensibly necessary, and I request you will immediately send the Governor a Copy of this Letter, to covence him it was my Orders that detained you in North Carolina." MAJR. REDLEY: Probably Thomas Ridley, maj., 6th Va. Line (Gwathmey, *Hist. Reg. of Virginians in the Revolution*). COLO. FAUKNER: Probably Ralph Faulkner, a retired Continental lieutenant colonel (same).

To Horatio Gates

SIR Richmond Nov. 19. 1780

The vessel which had been sent by Genl. Leslie, to Charles town as we supposed, returned about the 12th. inst. The enemy began to embark soon after from Portsmouth, and in the night of the 15th. compleated the embarkation of their whole force. In the morning of the 16th. some of our people entered Portsmouth. They had left their works unfinished and undestroyed. Great numbers of negroes who had gone over to them were left either for want of ship room, or through choice. They had not moved from Elizabeth river at 11 o'clock A.M. of the 16th. They gave out that they intended up James river but the precipitate abandoning of works on receipt of some communication or other from Charlestown, was not likely to be for the purpose of coming up James river. I received this intelligence by express from Genl. Muhlenberg yesterday morning. As the enemy's situation was such as to give reason to expect every moment a moveme[nt] in some direction, I delayed sending off notice to you in hopes that that movement would point out their destination. But [no] such information being yet come to hand I think it proper no longer to delay communicating to you so much.

Since writing so far your favor of the [8]th inst. comes to hand, accompan[ied] by one from Genl. Stevens at Hillsborough of the 10th. A strange derangement indeed our riders have got into to be 9 days coming from Hillsborough. I shall be very happy if the departure of the enemy which I hourly expect to have confirmed, shall leave us at liberty to send you a substantial reinforcement. The men being now in the feild may be marched directly Southwardly. What may be it's precise amount I can[not] say till I get from Genl. Muhlenberg a return of the 18 months m[en], the 8 months men and militia who had been stopped here on their way to the Southward, and from Genl. Lawson a return of the volunteers he has engaged to go to the Southward.

I have the honour to be with the greatest esteem & respect Sir Your most obedt. & most humble servt, TH: JEFFERSON

RC (DLC); text faded and at some points nearly illegible. At Charlotte on 29 Nov. Gates wrote to Gen. Smallwood: "I have within these few Minutes received a Letter from the Governor of Virginia, of which the inclosed is an exact Copy."

To Samuel Huntington

Sir Richmond Nov. 19. 1780.

The vessel which had been sent by General Leslie to Charles town as we supposed, returned about the 12th. inst. The enemy began to embark soon after from Portsmouth, and in the night of the 15th. compleated the embarkation of their whole force. In the morning of the 16th. some of our people entered Portsmouth. They had left their works unfinished and undestroyed. Great numbers of negroes who had gone over to them were left either for want of ship-room, or through choice. They had not moved from Elizabeth river at eleven o'clock A.M. of the 16th. They gave out that they intended up James river; but the precipitate abandoning of works on receipt of some communication or other from Charles town, was not likely to be for the purpose of coming up James river. I received this intelligence by express from Genl. Muhlenberg yesterday morning. As the enemy's situation was such as to give reason to expect every moment a movement in some direction, I delayed sending off notice to you in hopes that that movement would point out their destination: but no such information being yet come to hand I think it proper no longer to delay communicating to you so much. As our riders will be two days going their distance and returning to their post, it will necessarily be so long before any thing further can be communicated.

By a letter from Govr. Nash dated Newbern Nov. 5. I am informed that on the 28th. Ult. a Capt. Howell of that place in a small privateer passed in the night off Charles-town a very large fleet, but of what nation he knew not. In a vessel he took the same day directly out of Charles town were South Carolina gazettes which mentioned this fleet and that they had for several days been off firing signal guns. A gentleman on board her said Ld. Cornwallis returned to town that day. This is the only intelligence I have received from the Southward since that of Ferguson's defeat which I had the honor of forwarding to your Excellency.

Since writing so far I have received the inclosed dispatches from the Southward. The moment the enemy leave us I hope a good reinforcement may march from their present encampment to the Southward. I have the honor to be with the most perfect respect Your Excellency's Most obedt. & most humble servt,

Th: Jefferson

RC (DLC: PCC, No. 71, I); endorsed by Charles Thomson: "Letter from Govr Jefferson Nov 19. 1780. Read 27." Enclosures (same location): (1) Morgan to TJ, 30 Oct., extract, printed above; (2) Stevens to TJ, 10 Nov., printed above; (3) Gates to TJ, 8 Nov., printed above; (4) Gen. William Smallwood to Gates, "Camp New Providence," 31 Oct.; (5) Gen. M. W. Harrington to [North Carolina Board of War?], "Camp near Kershaw's Landing," 5 Nov., enclosing the following paper; (6) Cornwallis' orders to Col. Jynes, "Commanding a Battalion of Militia at the high hills at Santee," dated at Headquarters, Camden, 25 Aug. 1780.

A LETTER FROM GOVR. NASH: Not found.

To Thomas Sim Lee

Richmond, 19 Nov. 1780. The first paragraph of this letter is identical with the first paragraph in TJ's letter to Gates of this date, except that after "coming up James river" TJ here adds: "or I suppose any other of the waters of the Chesapeake." The second paragraph of the letter to Lee is identical with the second paragraph of TJ's letter to Huntington of this date, except that it lacks the last sentence of that paragraph as written to Huntington. The third paragraph is the usual complimentary close.

RC (Herbert R. Strauss, Chicago, 1950); addressed. See Maryland Council to James Calhoun, 24 Nov. 1780, mentioning a letter of this purport received "yesterday from Governor Jefferson" (*Md. Archives*, XLV, 223).

To Edward Stevens

Richmond, 19 Nov. 1780. The first paragraph of this letter is identical with the first paragraph in TJ's letter to Gates of this date. The second and last paragraph (except for the usual complimentary close) reads: "Since writing so far, your favour of the 10th comes to hand with the Letter from Genl. Gates and Genl. Morgan. Strange derangements indeed our Riders are got into to be comeing 9 days from Hillsborough here. Is it not possible to have this enquired into? I will give orders for it at this end of the line if you will do the same at yours. I hope we may now March off an immediate and substancial reinforcement to the Southward. What will be its amount I cannot precisely say till I get a return from Genl. Muhlenburg of the 18 Months Men, 8 Months Men and Militia who were stoped here on their March to the Southward. These two last with those of the same description already gone on will form your Command. Genl. Lawson will come on with a Corps of Volunteers raised by himself."

Tr (DLC). The letter from GATES was dated 8 Nov., and the letter from Gen. Daniel MORGAN was dated 30 Oct., qq.v.

From Nathanael Greene

SIR Richmond Nov. 20. 1780.

My Appointment to the Command of the Southern Army, with Powers to call upon the southern States for Supplies and Support, Your Excellency is already Acquainted with.

The Present state of the southern department and the future Operations that must Necessarily be carried on in that Quarter induces me to lay before You the Inclosed Requisitions for men and Supplies of different kinds.

Uninformed as I am at this time of many things necessary to explain the extent of our wants, I have Confin'd myself in this Application to some principal Articles which will be Requisite under all Circumstances, but as the Scene of Operations may change and as the Emergencies of War are Numerous and Various from which New and Pressing demands may arise, I hope the Legislature will vest You with full and Ample power to Comply with such as they happen. Without this I foresee the Most fatal consequence may attend the Army for want of timely support. It will be my province to Inform You from time to time of the Men and Supplies Necessary to the Operations, and to Conduct the force and direct the men when they are sent to the field. But the Levying of One and Collecting the Other must depend upon Yourselves and on Your exertions hang the Independence of the Southern States. It is perfectly Consistent with sound policy in our Countries to carry on a War rather Abroad than at home as well in Matters of Expence and from Principles of Humanity to the Inhabitants, but this Policy is renderd doubly Necessary to Virginia from the ease with which the Enemy can penetrate the Country and the Numerous Blacks and Other valuable Property which must Eventually fall in to their Hands in Consequence of it. It is pretty evident that it was the Enemys original plan of Operations to penetrate through North Carolina and possess themselves of all the lower Country of Virginia and Notwithstanding they may have a temporary Interruption to their present plan, I make no doubt they will prosecute their design as soon as the prevailing Obstacles are removed unless they are convinced by the exertions of the Southern States that the Thing has become Impossible. Nor will they relinquish the Project from the feeble Opposition which can be given by the present force that may be Opposed to them.

It Affords me great Satisfaction to see the Enterprize and Spirit with which the Militia have turn'd out lately in all Quarters to

Oppose the Enemy; and this Great Bulwark of Civil Liberty promises Security and Independence to this Country, if they are not depended upon as a principal but employed as an Auxilliary but if you depend upon them as a principal the very nature of the War must become so ruinous to the Country that tho numbers for a time may give security yet the difficulty of keeping this order of Men long in the field and the Accumulated expences attending it must soon put it out of your Power to make further Opposition and the Enemy will have only to delay their Operations for a few months to give Success to their measures. It must be the extreme of folly to hazard our liberties upon such a precarious tenure when we have it so much in our power to fix them upon a more solid basis.

I hope therefore the most steady and Effectual measures will be taken to fill up the Army agreable to the new Arrangement and I have only to remark that the reduction of the Regiments renders it absolutely necessary that those remaining be compleated to their full establishment. It is not only necessary to furnish the numbers required but that the men be of a proper Size perfect in their Limbs of a good sound constitution and not exceeding fifty five Years of Age.

I could wish a Law relative to this matter might be made with proper directions to the County Lieutenants not to receive any recruits unless they are agreable to the foregoing description as the Continental Officers Stationed at the different places of Rendezvous will be instructed to this purpose.

Officers are the very Soul of an Army and you may as well attempt to animate a Dead Body into action as to expect to employ an Army to advantage when the Officers are not perfectly easy in their Circumstances and happy in the service.

I am sorry to find that great dissatisfactions prevail among your Officers. I am not fully informed of the several grievances but would beg leave to recommend an enquiry and that immediate and reasonable satisfaction [be given][1] to their Just demands.

The late distressing accounts from the southern Army, claim the immediate attention of Government, both with respect to provision and Clothing. It is impossible for men to continue long in the Field, unless they are well furnish'd with both those articles. And to expose them to the want of either will soon transfer them from the Field to the Hospital or lay them under the Necessity of deserting; in either case government is burthen'd with the expence of raising men without the benefit of their services. Clothing is more important to an Army than at first View may be imagined; and to send troops into the Field without it, is devoting them to certain Distruction.

The Business of Transportation is accompanied with so many Difficulties, that I think great pains should be taken to fix upon some place for Feeding the Army with *Live Stock*, and I can think of none, unless it is puting up a Large number of Cattle to *Stall feed* which may be drove to the Army from time to time as the Service may require. I wish that some person might be commissioned from this State to consert with North Carolina the most proper measures for carrying such a plan into execution.

There [is][1] a variety of Stores, of different Kinds, coming from the Northward; which I am afraid from the present deranged State of the Qr. Masters department, will meet with great difficulty in geting on. I must therefore earnestly recommend that the most Speedy and effectual Support be given to the Officer at the head of this Business; and that he without loss of Time make the proper arangement for forwarding the Supplies as they arrive.

I have this moment received Letters from Genl. Washington and from Mr. Mathews Chairman of a Committee of Congress, appointed to correspond with the Commanding Officer of the Southern Department, which mention the Enemys preparations for making another Detachment to the Southward.

The Distress and Sufferings of the Inhabitants of *North and So. Carolina* deserve the most speedy support to keep alive that Spirit of Enterprize which has prevail'd among them lately, So much to their *Honor*. And it is much easier to oppose the Enemy in those States while the tide of Sentiment is in our favour, than it will be to secure *Virginia* after they are over run: a misfortune which may prove fatal to the Hapiness and Independence of America.

I propose to sett out in the morning for *Hilsborough*, but shall leave *Major Genl. Baron Steuben* to command in this State for the present, and to put things in the most proper train for forwarding the Reinforcements of Men, and supplies of every Kind to the Southern Army. He will advise with your Excellency.

I have the Honor to be with great Respect Your Excellency's most Obed Huml Ser[vant,] NATHL GREENE

Tr (NHi); signed by Greene; endorsed: "Cop. Letter from Gen Greene to Gov Jefferson." This copy was made for Gen. Gates and is among his papers; TJ transmitted the (missing) original in a letter to Speaker Harrison on 24 Nov. 1780, q.v. Enclosure missing, but see the following document.

It is fairly certain that this important letter was drafted (1) after consultation with Jefferson and (2) with a view to influencing legislative action, just as Greene and Jefferson later collaborated to persuade the General Assembly to a proper course concerning the procurement of horses.

[1] Omitted in MS.

General Greene's Requisition for the Southern Army

[20 November 1780]

Requisitions made to the State of Virginia by Genl. Greene for the Establishment and Supplying the Southern Army.

1. That the State immediately furnish its quota of Troops agreable to the new Establishment, and that the Men be supplied with cloathing Blankets, Arms, and every Accoutrement necessary for equipping them for a Winters Campaign, and that Lawsons Corps, and Stephens's Brigade of Militia Continue in Service till the regular Regiments are formed.

That the State immediately lay up a Magazine of 10,000 barrels of Flour and 5,000 Barrels of Beef and Pork, at Taylors Ferry and upwards upon the Roanoke and if it shall be found that provisions can be conveyed down the Watree River in Boats, that they take Measures for lodging the whole upon the Waters of the Yadken near Bethena.

That the State put up 3000 heads of Cattle to be Stalled, for the use of the Southern Army, to be drove to Camp for Slaughter, as they are called for, and that some person be appointed to set about this business without loss of time as it will be impossible to feed the Southern Army altogether upon Salted provisions, for want of the means of Transportation.

That the State furnish 100 good road Waggons with a driver, four good Horses and Harnish Compleat to each Waggon, and that these be got ready for service as soon as possible.

That the State furnish forty Artificers for the use of the Southern Army. That 12 of them be ship Wrights, or Boat Builders. 12 House Carpenters, 4 Wheel Wrights, Six Smiths, three Armorers, two Sadlers, and one Harnish Maker. These may be Negroes if to be had.

That the State furnish two Hundred hhds. of rum or Brandy to be deposited with the provisions upon the Roanoke.

That the State furnish such quantity of provisions at the different places of rendezvous, for receiving recruits, as the Officers superintending this service in the State may require, and that the full and ample supplies of Forage be provided for the use of the Quarter Master Generals department to enable him to perform the business of Transportation, and other services that may be required of him.

That the State supply the Military Chest with 5000£ specie or the Value thereof to defray the Contingent expences of the Army, and that such sums be advanced to the Officers of the Virginia line, as will enable them to equip themselves for the Feild.

The foregoing appears to me absolutely necessary to put the Army in a Condition to oppose the enemy.

MS (Vi); endorsed in several different hands: "For Governor Jefferson from Ed Carrington. Taken from bundle containing papers prior to June 81. Requisitions by Genl Green to the State of Virginia. Autograph of Col. E. Carrington."

Presumably this is a copy by Carrington of the requisitions submitted by Greene in the letter preceding. Carrington's copy is doubtless later, for he was not appointed deputy quartermaster general for the southern army until 4 Dec. (see Greene to TJ, 6 Dec. 1781).

To Benjamin Harrison

[*Richmond, 20? Nov. 1780.* JHD, Oct. 1780, 1827 edn., p. 22 (20 Nov.): "The Speaker laid before the House a letter from the Governor, containing information respecting the embarkation of the enemy from Portsmouth, which was read and ordered to lie on the table." Not located.]

To Benjamin Harrison

SIR In Council November 20. 1780.

The enclosed Letter from the President of Congress with the resolutions of that honourable body of the fourth instant, having come to hand yesterday and being intended for the consideration of the Legislature, I beg leave through you to transmit them to the General Assembly, and have the honor to be with every sentiment of esteem and respect, Sir, Your most obedient and most humble servant,

TH: JEFFERSON

RC (Vi); in a clerk's hand, signed and addressed by TJ to Harrison as Speaker; endorsed: "Governors Letter Enclosing Congress requisition of 4th: Novr:—for specific Supplies. 21st: Novr: 1780—referred to Commttee of whole on State of the Commonwealth." Enclosures (Vi): Huntington to TJ, 9 Nov. 1780, with enclosed requisitions.

From James Francis Moore

SIR Monongahalia Novr. 20th. 1780.

Finding that a Sufficient Quantity of Flour may be procured in this Country for our purpose and that too considerably Cheaper than if it was purchased below the Mountain, I have prevaild on

Mr. Nathl. Randolph to remain in this country to compleat the Purchase of such a Quantity as may be sufficient for the Western Illinois Department, and have legally authorized him to do so. You will therefore please to consider his drafts in the same manner as if made by my self.

The Situation of the Troops below makes it Necessary for me to proceed down with the greatest expidition with about 10000 Weight of Flower purchased since I have been here.

Mr. Randolph I expect will have his purchases compleat and his Boats ready to proceed down the river some time early in March. If no earlier opportunity should offer for your sending the Money for the Purpose of the Meat purchase, he will afford a very good one, and I would beg leave to Mention, that I think it much safer by water than sending it by land. I am with much respect Your Excellencys Most Obt. & very Hble servt., JAS. FRS. MOORE

RC (Vi); addressed; endorsed in two different hands: "Jas F. Moore letter Jany 81. From Monongalia County in Virginia."

Moore, born in Maryland, later lived in Pennsylvania, Virginia, and Kentucky; at this time he was acting as commissary for George Rogers Clark's troops (Wis. Hist. Soc., *Colls.*, XXIV, 310 and note; see also Brodhead to TJ, 17 Jan. 1781).

From Samuel Huntington

SIR Philadelphia November 21. 1780

In Answer to that Part of your Excellency's Letter of the 7. Instant respecting the Prisoners taken at Kings Mountain, I have enclosed a Copy of the Act of Congress of the 20. Instant, recommending, that those Prisoners be secured in such Manner, and at such Places as your Excellency may judge proper.

That a List of the Names of the Tory Prisoners be taken, distinguishing the State, County or District to which they severally belong, and transmitted to the Executive of their several States, who are requested to take such Order respecting them as the public Security and the Laws of the respective States may require.

I have the Honor to be with the highest Sentiments of Esteem & Respect your Excellency's most obedient humble servant,

SAM. HUNTINGTON President

RC (Vi); in a clerk's hand, signed by Huntington. FC (DLC: PCC, No. 15). Enclosure (Vi); resolve of Congress (2 attested copies), 20 Nov., respecting prisoners taken at King's Mountain.

See TJ to Huntington, 7 Nov. 1780, and note; also JCC, XVIII, 1048-9, 1053, 1073-4, where the resolve of 20 Nov. is printed as drafted and amended.

From Thomas Newton, Jr.

Sir — Suffolk Novr. 21. 1780

Your Excellencys favor of the 11th came safe to me this day. I shall have no objection to act in conjunction with Mr. Divers, and render every assistance in my power to my Country but if I cou'd serve in any office in the state had much rather do it, than act in a Continental office as I take Mr. Divers to be in that department; I can assure your Excellency I have no views of making a fortune out of my Country. If they should hereafter think that my services deserve any recompence I shall be satisfied, if not shall be contented. The mode I have fallen, to procure necessarys is to give Certificates and issue out according to plenty or scarcity. If I was to produce issues as vouchers for quantitys deliver'd belive they wou'd amount to ten times the purchases; the troops have been on scanty allowance for bread these two days past and if no other mode is fallen on than by depending on commissioners procuring I am of opinion the army will often want. I think purchases cou'd be made on equal if not better termes than seizing and proper plans fixed on for laying in magazines of provisions and stores on the other side Blackwater river where they wou'd be safe and convenient to Army. This I think wou'd save the Country much money and it is as near to this post or Smithfield by coming a back road as it is to come by the river road. Whatever your Excellency may think proper to command me in I shall with pleasure obey. The fleet is not yet gone and I am of opinion they will land again as they had yesterday as fine a wind as Cou'd blow and did not make use of it. I am Yr. Exclly Most Obt Servt,

Thos Newton Jr

RC (PHi); addressed to TJ in Richmond; endorsed: "Letter fm Thos Newton Feby 81."

Thomas Newton, Jr. (1742-1807), of Norfolk co., colonel of militia, was for many years a member of the Virginia General Assembly and held other important posts during and after the Revolution (VMHB, XXX [1922], 86-7; Swem and Williams, "Register of the General Assembly of Va.," p. 412). TJ's favor of the 11th to Newton has not been found.

From Theodorick Bland

Sr. — Philadelphia Novr 22d 1780

Mr. Walker, who sets off to Virginia tomorrow, affords us this opportunity of Enclosing your Excellency a Copy of a letter Presented to us the 16th Inst. together with a Copy of our Answer, concerning the affair of the Indiana Company.

It may not be improper to Inform Your Excellency and, (through Your Excellency) the Legislature who we suppose may be now Siting, that every art has been and tis probable may be used, by that Company to extend their influence and support their pretensions, and we are sorry to say that we have Suspicions founded upon more than mere Conjecture that the land Jobbs, of this Company, the Vandalia, and the Illinois Companies, have too great an influence in procrastinating that desireable and necessary event of completing the Confederation, which we hope the Wisdom, firmness, candor and Moderation of our Legislature now in Session will remove every obstacle to.

We Could wish also and we think it a duty we owe to our Constituents to call their attention to a revision of our former instructions relative to the Navigation of the Missisipi that, Should any overtures from Spain be offerd which are advantageous to the United States, and which might contribute not only to releive our present necessities, but promise us peace and a firm establishment of our Independance, it might not be considerd as an object that would counterbalance the distant prospect of a free Navigation of that River, with Stipulated ports, which may perhaps under another form or at some more convenient opportunity be obtaind from that Nation in behalf of our Citizens settled on its Bankes and Waters. Having Shewn the above to my Colleague Mr. Madison, he has thought it unnecessary to Join in that Part of it relating to our Instructions on the Subject of the Navigation of the Missisipi. I am sorry to say that notwithstanding the high Idea I entertain of that Gentlemans good sense, Judgment and Candor; I feel myself, irrisistably impelld by a Sense of my duty, to State a Matter and to communicate it through the Proper Channel which *may* eventually affect so greatly the Prosperity and mere existence of the United States at large, and feeling myself willing to receive the Censure of my Constituents if I have done wrong, or their applause if I have done Right in Suggesting to them so important a matter I am under the necessity (as to that matter) of standing alone in my opinion; which I would not wish, should in the Minutest degree, be interpreted, as obtruding or dictating a measure however necessary I as an individual Representative of the State may conceive a relaxation of our instructions on that head to be, nor do I conceive that any Member either of the Executive or Legislature of our State, who is acquainted with my wish to promote the Public good, and to conform to the strict tenor of their instructions, can attribute my suggestion to any wish to swerve from them in my Vote in Congress, having pledged myself both in Principle and in promise Steadily to adhere to them on all occasions. I have the Honor to be Yr. Excellys Most obedt. & very H: Svt., THEOK. BLAND

RC (Vi). Tr (DLC): Madison Papers); certified by William Munford, Keeper of the Rolls, 30 Sep. 1820. Enclosures (Vi): George Morgan, "Agent for the Indiana Compy.," to the Virginia Delegates, 16 Nov., and reply; Morgan's letter is summarized by Burnett, *Letters of Members*, No. 521, note 2, and the reply is there printed in full; see Burnett's further annotation of this letter, which was transmitted by TJ to Speaker Harrison, 5 Dec. 1780.

On the controversy over Virginia's cession of her western land claims, see Huntington to TJ, 10 Sep. 1780, note.

From William Bradford, enclosing Proceedings of the Hartford Convention

SIR Hartford Nov 22d 1780

By the direction of the Convention held at this Place, I have the Honour to transmit to your Excellency their Proceedings with a Request that you will please to lay them before the Legislature of your State.

As the measures we have recommended to the States by whose Appointment we met will depend for their Effacacy upon the Concurrence of the other States, we conceive it our Duty to communicate them Immediately in order that if they should be deemed Elegible they might with the greater Dispatch be carried into Effect.

I remain with the most sincere Wishes for the Success of our Common Cause and the Peace and Prosperity of our sister States Your Excellencys most Obedt. Servant.

By order of the Convention

WILLIAM BRADFORD, President.

ENCLOSURE

Proceedings of the Hartford Convention of November 1780

At a Convention of the Commissioners from the States of New Hampshire Massachusets Rhode Island and Providence Plantations Connecticut and New York holden at Hartford in the State of Connecticut on Wednesday the eighth Day of Novembr 1780.

Commissioners from all the States abovementioned not appearing, The Convention Adjourned from Day to Day untill Saturday the eleventh Day of Novembr. 1780, when the following Gentlemen appeared and produced Credentials from their respective States which were read and accepted, viz.

John Taylor Gilman Esqr.	from New Hampshire
The Honorable Thomas Cushing Esqr. The Honorable Azor Orne Esqr. George Partridge Esqr.	from Massachusets
The Honorable William Bradford Esqr.	from Rhode Island
The Honorable Eliphalet Dyer Esqr. The Honorable William Williams Esqr.	from Connecticut
The Honorable John Sloss Hobart Esqr. Egbert Benson Esqr.	from New York

The Honorable William Bradford Esqr. Chosen President of the Convention.

Hezk Wyllys Esqr. Secretary.

The Convention met from Day to Day and after having discussed several Matters which were deemed proper Subjects of Deliberation came to the following Resolutions

No. 1. Resolved That it be recommended to the States of New Hampshire Massachusets and Rhode Island and Providence Plantations to raise as soon as possible the number of Troops required of them by Congress to serve in the Continental Army, in a mode as nearly simular as their respective Circumstances will admit to that observed by the States of New York and Connecticut.

Resolved that the President forthwith transmit a Copy of the above Resolution with a Circular Letter upon the subject to the Executives of the States of New Hampshire Massachusets and Rhode Island and Providence Plantations. . . .

No. 2. Resolved That it be recommended to the several States Represented in this Convention punctually to Comply with any Requisitions which the Commander in Chief of the Army shall find it necessary to make for Detachments from the Militia to strengthen the Battalions of the Lines of the respective States untill they shall be filled up with Recruits for three Years or during the War.

No. 3. Resolved That it be most earnestly recommended to the several States represented in this Convention punctually to Comply with every Requisition from Congress for Men Money Provisions or other supplies for the War.

No. 4. Whereas in Consequence of the neglect of many if not all the United States in not seasonably furnishing their respective Quotas of Supplies required by Congress the Army has greatly suffered and been frequently brought into a very Critical and dangerous situation, and those Offensive Operations against the Enemy have been prevented which might otherwise have been prosecuted to great advantage, And Whereas there is great Danger that in Case some of the States should be deficient in their Supplies while others furnish their full Quotas, such Jealousies and distrusts will arise as may prove very detrimental to the common Cause and possibly destructive of the Union. Therefore

Resolved That it be earnestly recommended to the several States represented in this Convention to Instruct Their respective Delegates to use their Influence in Congress that the Commander in Chief of the Army of the United States be Authorized and Impowered to take such Measures as he may deem proper and the public Service may render necessary to induce the several States to a punctual Compliance with the Requisitions which have been or may be made by Congress for Supplies for the Years 1780 and 1781.

No. 5. This Convention having received Information That large Quantities of Cloathing for the Army are lying in Store at Boston and Springfield, Resolved That it be recommended to the States of Massachusets Connecticut and New York to Impress Teams if they cannot be otherwise readily obtained and forward the Cloathing by the most direct Rout through their respective Territories to the Army.

No. 6. Resolved That it be recommended to the several States represented in this Convention to Instruct their Delegates to propose and agree in Congress That an Estimate should be made of the annual Amount of the Interest of the Loan Office Certificates heretofore Issued, and also of all other Debts already due from the several Continental purchasing Officers, and which can conveniently be funded. That Congress should then propose certain Taxes upon Specific Articles or Duties or Imposts or all or Either of them as Congress may think proper and Deem to operate in the most equal Manner among the several States the nett product of which Congress may Judge sufficient for discharging such Interest. That the several States should thereupon make the necessary Provisions by Law to enable Congress to Levy and Collect such Taxes Duties or Imposts within them respectively and that the Delegates should be Authorized to Pledge the Faith of their respective States that they will pass the requisite Laws for the purpose with a Restriction that the Delegates shall not have Authority to bind their respective States unless the Delegates from all the States except such who are so in the Power of the Enemy as to be deprived of a Legislature should have simular Powers. That such Taxes Duties or Imposts should be applied solely to the Payment of such Interest. And that inasmuch as it will be Impossible to ascertain precisely the sum, which such Taxes Duties or Imposts may annually Yield, That therefore if during any Year the product should exceed the Amount of such Interest that such excess shall nevertheless be retained in the Continental Treasury, and in the ensuing Years to be appropriated to the payment of such Interest, as shall then have accrued and to no other purpose.

No. 7. Whereas through the neglect of many States in the Union in a full and seasonable compliance with the Requisition of Congress of the 18th of March last Congress have not been able to avail themselves of the Money which they expected to pay their Troops, and transport the necessary supplies to the Army which has Occasioned not only discontent in Our Army but Great Embarrasments in Our Affairs, Therefore Resolved that it be most earnestly recommended to the several States represented in this Convention to take effectual Measures to sink their Full Quotas of the Continental Bills by the Time and in the manner prescribed by Congress.

No. 8. Whereas the Laws heretofore passed by the several States have proved ineffectual for the purpose, Resolved that it be earnestly recommended to the States represented in this Convention to take such farther Measures as may be effectual to prevent any unlawfull Commerce or Intercourse with the Enemy.

No. 9. Resolved That it be recommended to the States represented in this Convention to appoint a Commissioner or Commissioners to meet for the purpose of entering into Contracts for supplying the Fleet and Army of his most Christian Majesty with Provisions, that the Commissioners from the respective States should be fully Authorized to enter into such Contracts and that the Commissioners should meet at such Time and Place as the Governor of Connecticut shall Certify for that purpose.

No. 10. To the End that Congress untill the Confederation shall be agreed to, may be furnished with a Rule for making an appointment [apportionment?] of Men Money or other Supplies among the several States, Resolved that it be recommended to the States Represented in this Convention to Instruct their Delegates to propose and agree in Congress That Congress should require of the several States forthwith to return the number of persons Blacks as well as Whites within them respectively. . . .

A true Copy Attest Hez Wyllys Secrty.

RC (NN); in a clerk's hand, signed by Bradford; endorsed: "Proceedings of a Convention of Commissioners from Sevl. States recd Jany 81." Enclosure (Vi): attested copy (20 p.) of the Proceedings of the Hartford Convention of Nov. 1780, printed herewith (but only in part; see below).

The Hartford Convention of Nov. 1780 was called "principally to confer upon the most eligible Mode for compleating the Army and drawing forth the necessary Supplies from the States" there represented (quoted from the letter sent by the Convention to the executives of the states represented, which appears in the Proceedings but is omitted above). Its proceedings and resolves have apparently not been printed; Burnett (*Letters of Members*, v, No. 545, note 3) is mistaken in citing *Conn. State Records*, II, 562, which prints the proceedings of the better-known Hartford Convention of Oct. 1779, the purpose of which was to devise a general plan of price limitation in order to support Continental currency. As printed above, the following items have been omitted from the Proceedings: (1) a long circular letter from the Convention to the executives of the states represented in the Convention, explaining the first resolve and including copies of the relevant Connecticut and New York acts; (2) another circular to the same concerning the Proceedings as a whole; (3) a letter to Pres. Huntington accompanying a copy of the Proceedings; and (4) a letter to Gen. Washington accompanying another copy. Congress received and read the Convention's letter and proceedings on 12 Dec. and referred them to a committee of five (JCC, XVIII, 1141); one of the members was John Witherspoon, who on 16 Dec. wrote very caustically to Gov. William Livingston of New Jersey concerning the Convention's recommendations, particularly the fourth resolution (Burnett, *Letters of Members*, v, No. 545; see also James Warren to Samuel Adams, 4 Dec., cited by Burnett, as cited, note 3). The committee apparently never reported. The copy of the proceedings sent to TJ was transmitted by him to Speaker R. H. Lee in a letter of 1 Mch. 1781.

To Benjamin Harrison

Sir In Council November 22d. 1780.

Major Nelson, commanding officer of the three troops of cavalry belonging to this state but in continental service informs me on the part of his officers that they find the service extremely discouraging on account of the preference in command given to Continental officers of the same rank tho junior in their appointments, and pray that they may be placed on continental establishment without which they can not reconcile a longer continuance in the present service with their ideas of propriety. At his request therefore I beg leave to refer this matter to the pleasure of the General Assembly with whom alone rests the power of negociating such a transfer with the continental Congress. I have the honor to be with the greatest respect sir, your most obedient & most humble servant,

Th: Jefferson

RC (Vi); in a clerk's hand, corrected, signed, and addressed by TJ to Harrison as Speaker. Endorsed: "Governors Letter Novr. 22d: 1780. referred to the Committee on the recruit Bill." See JHD, Oct. 1780, 1827 edn., p. 25.

To George Muter

In Council, Novr. 22d. 1780.

Colo. Muter will be pleased to have an account made out of all the powder &c. lent or delivered for Continental use since the establishment of the Board of War that we may require a return of it. Also to call on Mr. Maupin for a state of all the powder which has been lent to individuals and never repaid. Th: Jefferson

RC (Vi); endorsed: "Govr. requiring X of all the Powder lent or delivered since the Establishment of the Board of War. Novr. 22d. 1780."

From Thomas Nelson

[*Rich Neck, 22 Nov. 1780.* In a letter to Gen. Robert Lawson, 24 Nov., TJ reports having received a letter of 22 Nov. from Gen. Nelson enclosing intelligence from Newport News Point that the British fleet lately at Portsmouth "appeared to be standing out for the Capes." Neither Nelson's letter nor its enclosure has been found.]

From Samuel Nightingale

Honorable Sir Providence Novr. 22nd 1780.

I have wrote Two Letters dated the 18th and 29th of Sepr. last, to Virginia, which I can have no doubt but your Excelency has Received. They gave an Account of the Schooner Committee (Owned by Messrs. Penet Da Costa Brothers & Comp.; Brisson late Master) Haveing on board a Quantity of Goods for your State; being taken on her Passage from Nantz to Virginia, and Retaken by Two American Privateers, and Sent into this Poart, and here Condemned, the one half to the Former Owners, the Other Half to the Recaptors.

I have now to Inform Your Excelency, That the Schooner and his appurtenances Stores &c. were sold at Publick Vendue on the 26th Sepr. I proposed that there should be no Sale of any thing, untill some Person, concerned in the Schooner, or Ortherised by the Owners, Should be Present, but to no purpose. An Account Sales I now Inclose. An Equal Divition of the Cargo was made, by Thomas Coit in behalf of the Recaptors, my Self in behalf of the Former Owners, and a Third Person Appointed by the Judge of Admiralty. An Invoice of that half belonging to the Former Owners is Also Inclosed. In it you will Observe that the marks and numbers found on the Bales, Boxes, &c, are mentioned. I chose this manner of makeing the Invoice, rather than the manner they are now Packed. These Goods are now Stored and wait your Orders, Except the Salt, Powder, and Shott mentioned below. Monsr. Coulaux la Vigna from Philadelphia came here, after the Cargo was divided and the Vessell sold, and wated a considerable time before the Judge of Admiralty, or my Self, knew what he had a Right too, or ment to do concerning this Recaptor. He mentioned he had a Power of Attorney wrote in the French Language. We desired the privaledge of gitting it Trancelated, but he did not give us Opertunaty, until very lately, but after it was Trancelated, he Proposed receiving the neat Proceads of all that was sold, also the Salt, Powder and Bird Shott, which is delivered, Viz. Thirty One Thousand Seven Hundred Fifty & Four Pound 12/ Continental Money, and Five Cask Powder waying Five Hundred Thirty & Seven Pound American wt. Tare not Taken out; Those he gave his Receipt for, but would not give any Receipt for the Salt and Shott, but Said Capt. Brisson must Receive them. I have by the Advice of the Judge of Admiralty delivered the Salt and Shott to the Said Capt. Brisson, and took his receipt for them; as it did appear by Instructions from

Messrs. Penet Da Costa Brothers & Compy. that he had a Right to receive the Salt.

The Captain of the Randolph Privateer took out of the Schooner at Sea, One Hundred & Eighty wait Cordage, Four Hundred wait Bread, and Two Barrels Beef. The owners of said Privateer have a bill against said Schooner which will ballance part of the above. I have their Promisse for the Paying the remainder. There also was some Other Goods Taken out at Sea, and Carried to New London, in the State of Connecticutt, by the Recaptors. Monsr. Coulaux La Vigna, Capt. Brisson and the Second Captain have all ben up there, and have received some Goods, but no Account has yet bin given me, but I soon Expect an Account from New London. Monsieur La Vigna has a Copy of all the Papers. A Copy shall also be sent to your Excelency & in the Mean time I am with much Respect your Excelencies most Humbl Servt,

SAML NIGHTINGALE Junr.

RC (Vi); addressed: "To His Excellency Thomas Jefferson Esqr Virginia"; endorsed: "Mr. Nightinale Letter March 81 recd." One enclosure has been located in Vi: a 3-page "Account of Sales of Schooner La Comité & appurtenances sold at Public Vendue. Providence September 26th. 1780."

TJ's TWO LETTERS to Nightingale of 18 and 29 Sep. are missing. Another letter from TJ, 28 Oct., also missing, is mentioned in Nightingale's letter of 6 Dec. 1780 to Theodorick Bland, but the date may be in error. The correspondence between Nightingale and TJ was carried on through Bland, a Virginia delegate in Congress. In his letter of 6 Dec. Nightingale is not enthusiastic about sending the goods belonging to Virginia by land (*Bland Papers*, II, 39). Concerning THE SCHOONER COMMITTEE (i.e., *La Comité*), see, further, Penet, D'Acosta Frères to Virginia Board of Trade, 25 Nov. 1780; JCC, XVIII, 890 (2 Oct.).

From Peter Penet

GENTLEMEN Nantes Nov 22nd 1780

You have, no doubt, occasion to be anxious, having received no other supplies yet, but that by our vessel the Committee. Such a misfortune can only be attributed to the Revolutions of time and the actual circumstances of this kingdom in war. I have apply'd several times to the Ministry in Paris for Licence to raise a number of sailors sufficient to man two vessels; my applications were unsuccessful.

In one of my letters I have advised you that I was on the point of concluding a Treaty for supplies conformable to your orders, amounting to about the sum of eight hundred thousand livres Tournois. The Bargain was near being closed under the Guarantee of my house, on conditions that the said sum should be paid at the expiration of one year from the date of the delivery of the goods in Nantes. But previous to my acquiescing to them, I try'd to secure a number of mariners. Notwithstanding my frequent and earnest applications I was put off to the arrival of the West India fleet, which is now near our coasts detained by contrary winds. An embargo was laid on vessels. Those that were provided with sailors were obliged to let them go to Brest to serve in the Royal Navy. Seeing we could neither expedite our vessels nor find freight on foreign ones, I was enforced to suspend my contract for said goods untill the Government will allow us to inlist seamen. The chief motive which actuated me to put off my Treaty, was, that the Manufacturers being willing to give only one year's credit from the day I should receive their merchandises in Nantes, I foresaw they might have remained eight or nine months in our ware-houses before they could be shipped. The time of payment had been expired before the goods had reached you; then you would have been compelled to make sudden and considerable Remittances; which being intercepted, my House had been troubled about those Payments, which became the more onerous, that we receive no remittances of the considerable sum due us by the Northern States. On the other hand, the Loan that I was authorised to negotiate for you, as I mentioned in my letter of the 20th May ult. not being executed, I was deprived of other facilities.

Business transacted in France on terms with the Manufacturers requires time and Instructions. Had I obtained the hundred thousand pounds sterling in question, considering I were not able to get men in this country to equip our vessels, I would have forwarded supplies by way of Holland. I must own I found everything contrary to my views and your advantage, especially after the taking of Charlestown, by which the commerce of France was thrown in great consternation. In a few days I will set off again for Paris to solicit the new Minister at the head of the Navy Department for a number of sailors sufficient to man two vessels that have been ready for some time to take a cargo and set sails. I hope I shall meet with success. Immediately they shall be loaded with the Articles according to your memorandum, and they may arrive with you in the month of february or march.

Government wanting funds in America for the maintenance and the subsistence of the French Army and Fleet, I have furnished them with twelve bills of exchange drawn on you at different Terms, making together the sum of five hundred thousand livres Tournois, to be paid in paper money exchange current or in provisions. The

Treasurer General of the War Office, to whose order I have drawn the bills above mentioned, is directed to pay me the amount of them as soon as he or I shall receive advice that you have been pleased to accept and pay them.

When I saw I could not obtain the Loan, that it was very difficult or rather impossible for you to procure ships and send them safe to France with tobacco, that freight from America here was at an exorbitant rate, I was determined to give Bills of Exchange. By that mean I may be able to raise the hundred thousand pounds sterling agreeable to your desire and powers. Circumstances being alter'd I shall find a favourable opportunity. Be pleas'd, Gentlemen, to acquaint me with your intentions, and have them transmitted as soon as possible. My drafts were preferred to those proposed by the Doctor Francklin and several other People who have great friends in America. The Preference granted to me must be looked upon as a favor. As soon as I am informed those drafts have been accepted I will then resume the Business of my Engagements in order to comply with your orders in expediting all the merchandise you demand and paying the rest of the Bills you have drawn on my House.

I have just received authentic information that a second squadron of men of war is soon to sail in order to joyn that of Mr. D C Ternay. We will use our best efforts to prevail on the Minister that he would permit us to ship all the new stands of arms that have been so long detain'd in our store-houses, principally on account of the difficulties suscitated by Messrs. Lee. At the same time we shall dispatch the other Articles consisting in woollens, linens, shoes, hats, shirts, stockings etc. We have already made the necessary dispositions for it. As soon as we obtain leave you may rest assured that they shall safely be conveyed to America; our intention being to have them put on board some frigates or other ships under the convoy of the Fleet.

It may be attested that since my arrival in France I have lost no time in discharging faithfully the trust you reposed in me. I have undergone the greatest difficulties. On account of the want of mariners and the unhappy circumstances of War my troubles and care were not very fructuous. Your sollicitudes must be great; I share them with you. If anything can assuage the grief I feel at your disappointments, it is the inward persuasion I have of my not being remiss in your service and that my future operations can still indemnify you. Nobody else, I dare say, in my stead, could have conducted your Business with more Prudence and Zeal. The Influence of my friends at Court, their extensive connections had the Preponderance, but what advantage could thirty or forty thousand pounds sterling invested in goods remaining eight or nine months in our ware-houses have procur'd. After the expiration of a year I should have been oblig'd to make payment by virtue of my engagements for the State. My Interest then, and your Credit had suffer'd.

If it be possible for you to expedite some American vessels here, they shall be loaded in return with your Articles. Be pleased to take a Determination. I will never lose sight of your Interest, and am so much attach'd to your Business, that on the Departure of the French Army and Fleet for your continent, having been proposed to take the Post of Commissary for victualling and supplying them with necessaries, I thought it was my duty to refuse it. I belong to you and am bound to exert my utmost endeavours to bring your Affairs to a happy Issue.

I have the honour to be with profound Respect Gentlemen, your most obedient and devoted humble servant, J. P. PENET

MS not located. Text from *Virginia Magazine of History and Biography*, XXII (1914), 91-3, which gives no source. At head of text: "To His Excellency the Governor and the Honorable Council of the State of Virginia Williamsburg or Richmond Virginia."

This is the last letter on record from Penet to TJ. From Benjamin Franklin's correspondence it appears that Penet persisted for a time in his efforts to obtain a French loan for Virginia, but on 14 Dec. 1782 Franklin told Robert Morris that "Penet . . . is broke and absconded. . . . I have long since mentioned the Inconvenience of the Attempts of separate States to borrow Money in Europe. They have hurt our Credit, and produced nothing" (*Writings*, ed. Smyth, VIII, 640). TERNAY: Chevalier Charles-Louis d'Arsac de Ternay, commander of the French squadron that convoyed Rochambeau's army to America earlier this year; he died at Newport, R.I., 15 Dec. 1780 (D. R. Keim, *Rochambeau: A Commemoration by the Congress of the United States*, Washington, 1907, p. 186-7).

From Nathaniel Randolph

GENTLEMEN [Monongahly] Novr 22: 1780

I am to inform you that Mr. James Enis [is] one of those Gentlemen that Your Honours proposed Sending the Money by to this Quarter to Compleat the purchasis for the insuing Campeign to the Westard.

I finde but little to be done without cash here; its true I thought when I first came to this Quarter that the purchasis mite been compleated upon Creadit of Some private Gentlemen in this country but I finde myself in Some Instancis deceiv'd for when I had been informed that they had rather have a draft upon your Treasury than the Money: but I was Since tolde by one of those Gentlemen, to bare [bar] axidence he would rather have the money and would-not wish to take a draft if they could by any means avoid it; by which means the cash sent out by Capt. More is nearly expended.

I Shall leve you to Judge of the neadcessaty of furnishing me with a considerable Quantity of Money to answer your designs here. There is a considerable quantity of Wheat in this Country Sufficient to Supply both Departments.

The Supplies of Flower or eather Wheat mite been had upon good tirms if I had, had a plenty of cash when I first arove here but how it will rate by the time your Supplys comes to hand I cannot pretend to Judge.

I am at times almost tempted to Borrow a considerable Sum upon my own creadit and make what Purchaisis I possably can immediately which I am of opinion would Save the State Sixty or Seventy procent in their Purchaisis here; but if any thing Should happen I have only myself [to blame and I am at t]he hite of my arrens [errands]; I have no orders to proceed [by . . .] and I possibly must Suffer Redicule for [having mo]re Zeal than policy.

There is a repoart prevailing here that the French has laid Siege to Quebeck and carried it. If there Should be any truth in this repoart no doubt but you will be acquaint with the perticulars before this will come to hand; it may alter your plan of proceadings in this Department from this consideration that the conquest Frans has made over the only Capital poart the British has in that Quarter will so effectually Subdue the British Power in that whole Country that the Savage will become Allies to the French. If what is repoarted be true there is nothing more likely for there is no people that we know can do more than half as much with Indians as the French; which is the very Reason we Should devide the Westron country with them and of course the power; which will appear more plane in future than at peasant [present]. You may smile at my peasant [present] caution for future events, and what you laugh at here may caust you anexity and care hereafter.

Capt. More is impatient [to] see the Water a little hire. It rises but Slow and for want of Water to the Mills his Flower is not quite ready but will by the time the water is high anoughf to procead down the River. Colo. Clark has made a Large purchase of Salt at the Fawls (the auther may be dpened [depended] on) which makes me hope that he has receiv'd a Letter from Capt. More (wrote at Richmond the Morning we left that place) advising him of his success as to his Business and likewise a line from me informing him of the favourable disposition of Your Board.

I shall Send a coppy of my own proceadings with the verbia[l] instruction you gave me as near as I can recolle[ct . . .] his to Colo. Clark by Capt. More (which will be [. . .] that will go from this Quarter) which will [. . .] the Colonel to send in an Express: if that Should be the case I shall desire him to send me a few lines to direct me when I move from this place and if any Such letter shoud fawl into your hands I Should take it as a Singular favour if yould would forward it to me.

The Smawl Boats that will be wanting to Compleat the Expedition may be built here at less expence an grater dispatch than any where else as here is Sawmills plenty, and if they donot miss my expectation they will answer an exceading good purpose to transpoart the Troops and provision from this down the Ohio for they must be under Such instruction as to carry Six men for three Monthes cruse.

I have talked with three different men here that profess the Boatbuldind Business. They all agree as to the price and form but not exactly to the Sise (these men I talked with Seperately). I like their construction because they draw but little water and they are much the least Expence: but as to the prise You will have to Judg of which is twenty pounds as they caul it the oald way; every expence is here included. As I am detained here this winter weaght your commands either to make purchasis here of flower which by the time all expence is paid of casks flatbotoms boats to transpoart it from this it will amount to twenty Shilling a pound so I mea'd no [*thus in MS*] of the Sum for you will be Judges of that. I have proposed two Hundred and fifty Thousand weight and if I am to do any thing with the Boats Send casks and your instructions and I weght your command and do my Self the honour of Subscribing my Self your much obliged and very humble Servant,

NATHL. RANDOLPH

[. . .] Letter will acc[ount for] my fredom of drawing [. . . .]

RC (Vi); addressed: "To his Excellency Thomas Jefferson Richmond"; endorsed: "Nathl Randolph Letter Jany 81." Text mutilated; several readings, including the place at head of letter, taken from CVSP, I, 389-90, which prints several extracts.

This letter was sent with another letter from Randolph to TJ, 27 Nov. 1780, q.v.

To George Muter

In Council Novr. 23d. 1780.

The Board agrees to give Capt. Groer a Guinea ℔ Month for each person they shall put under him to be taught the duties and operations of a Laboratory, but if the number shall exceed four, no more than four Guineas a Month.

Tr (Vi); quoted in Muter's letter to Groar of this date entered in War Office Letter Book.

CAPT. GROAR (whose name is variously spelled) has not been further identified, but see TJ to Muter, 4? Feb. 1781.

To Benjamin Harrison

SIR November 24th 1780.

I received yesterday evening a Letter from General Nelson dated Rich neck november 22nd at half after five P.M. inclosing a note by which we learn that the vessels of the enemy were all under way except one which was getting under way, and the whole standing out for the Capes. This event tho' relieving us in a certain degree by opening again the door of our commerce and also by putting it in our power to avail ourselves of the whole resources of our country, seems yet to call for an increase rather than abatement of military preparation. Shou'd those now leaving us proceed to reinforce the hostile army already in the south: shoud the same be the object of a new embarkation said on good authority to be preparing in New york; we shall but too probably and speedily see our retreating enemy treading back their footsteps and menacing this country with a force to which the southern states have yet seen nothing equal. South Carolina and Georgia we are to consider as weighing nothing in our scale. N. Carolina has been exhausted by the ravages of two armies. On this state therefore rests the weight of the opposition; and it is infinitely important that our efforts be such as to keep the war from our own country. Nor does it seem that we have a moment to lose, should the enemy be disposed to lose no time on their part. Men to form a permanent army, clothing, covering, arms, subsistance, transportation and money are to be provided. We have left no measure unessayed for procuring supplies of these different kinds as far as the circumstances of our country wou'd admit. Of tents we have a tolerable prospect; and better hopes of supplies of arms than we some time ago entertained. We shall press them forward with unremitting endeavours. Our country affords sufficient subsistance and we are in a train of obtaining it so far as the late powers given by the Legislature extended and the advanced season of the year permits. But these went to one or two articles only. Cloathing, blankets, and transportation are objects of immense difficulty, and money is necessary to set every wheel in motion.

I thought it my duty so soon as the motives of the enemy indicated the point to which our efforts would probably be called to suggest to the General Assembly these several matters, not doubting but they will give them all the attention they deserve and adopt such measures as in their wisdom shall appear best calculated for making effective opposition wherever the enemy may think proper to shew themselves. The inclosed papers on the same subject from Major Genl. Green, appointed to take command of the southern army, I beg leave to lay before the General Assembly, and am with every sentiment of esteem and respect, sir, Your most obedient and most hble. servant, Th: Jefferson

RC (NN); in a clerk's hand, corrected and signed by TJ. Enclosures: Nathanael Greene to TJ, 20 Nov. 1780 (copy from Gates Papers printed above under date), and Greene's requisition for men and supplies (same).

The letter from general nelson of 22 Nov. has not been found. On 24 Nov. "The Speaker laid before the House a letter from the Governor, enclosing a letter and requisition from Major General Greene, on the subject of men and supplies for the southern army; which were read, and ordered to be referred to the committee for Courts of Justice" (JHD, Oct. 1780, 1827 edn., p. 28).

To Robert Lawson

Sir Richmond Nov. 24. 1780.

Since writing the letter which accompanies this I have received a letter from Genl. Nelson dated Richneck. Nov. 22. 5. o'clock P.M. inclosing a note from New-port's news point probably of the same day which gives information that the enemy's vessels were then all under way except one which was also getting under way, and that the whole appeared to be standing out for the Capes. It is now therefore incumbent on us to resume the business of reinforcing the Southern army as the army which has left us will probably be marched immediately up towards Cambden and Ld. Cornwallis will then have a prospect at least of treading back his lost steps and penetrating further Northwardly. I am Sir with great respect Your most obedt servt., Th: Jefferson

RC (O. O. Fisher, M.D., Detroit, 1950); addressed by TJ: "Brigadr. Genl. Lawson Petersburg." Endorsed: "Governor Jefferson letter No. 3"; also, in a later hand: "Presented to Thomas U. Leefe Esqe by his friend, the Grandson of Genl. Lawson. New Orleans 18 April 1841. John Lawson Lewis."

To Steuben

SIR November 24th 1780.

As you have been so kind as to remain here, among other purposes, for that of organizing our troops meant to be forwarded to the south, I beg leave to inclose to you a resolution of the Executive of this State, entered into previous to your arrival here appropriating such of the men as were before unappropriated to any particular corps, and directing in what manner they shou'd be officered. I have written to General Muhlenberg for a return of the numbers of men of the several descriptions contained in the resolution, which when received shall be immediately communicated to you. I moreover now inclose a return from General Stevens for the purpose of informing you how many eight months men are with him. These you will observe were to be regimented under the command of the same field officers, who commanded them before by election of the General Assembly. In order to procure proper captains and subalterns we desired by advertisement that such officers as had before been in regular service, had resigned, or become supernumerary, and were willing now to take command in the same rank they formerly held, wou'd give in their names. A list of those who have sent in their names I now inclose to you as I had formerly done to Brigadier Genl. Muhlenburg, to which I beg leave to add the name of the Bearer Captain Webb who is desirous of obtaining a command. I also inclose you a number of commissions for the officers to be appointed to command these eight months men, which you will please to fill up as you think proper. It was our idea that they should all bear the same date, that their rank under these new commissions might be determined by the priority of their former ones. I must further [inform] you that before you came Genl. Muhlenberg had been desired to carry this arrangement into execution. No commissions have been yet applied for, but it is possible he may have made some appointments which it wou'd be well he should inform you of. I have the honor to be with the greatest esteem and respect, sir, Your most obedient and humble servant,

TH: JEFFERSON

RC (NHi); in a clerk's hand, signed and addressed by TJ: "The honourable Majr. Genl. Baron Steuben Richmond." Endorsed: "lettre du Gouvern. Gefferson concernant la [. . .] des Trouppes. Richmond 22. Nov." Enclosures missing.

From Edward Stevens

SIR — Hillsborough November 24th. 1780

Yours of the 19th Inst. I received last Evening. It gave me much pleasure to understand the Enemy were about to leave Virginia, altho' I have my doubts and Fears from present prospect[s] here that we shall not be able to support an Army this Winter (with Provisions) sufficient to oppose them to the South. It affords me much Satisfaction that I have it in my power to inform you, I am now moving from hence to Join Genl. Gates with about Seven Hundred Rank and file Virginians and better than a Hundred Marylanders with two Peices of Artillery. Since my last we have no Accounts from the Westward that can be depended on.

I hope the Articles that I left a list of with Colo. Muter will now come on, agreeable to your wish. I shall put on foot an enquiry into the cause of the derangement of the Riders from this to you.

I am &c.

Tr (DLC); endorsed (in part): "Copy."

From Nicholas Eveleigh

SIR — Mecklenburg County Novr. 25. 1780.

I am one of those, who fall under the description of an act of the General Assembly of May last, respecting the Citizens of South Carolina and Georgia, being expell'd from the former State by the Enemy. A few Negros, 14 in number, were remov'd from thence into this Commonwealth, on my account, about 4 months ago; they reach'd it sooner than I did, and by a very different route. They had directions to remain at Colo. Coles on Staunton river: from thence about five weeks ago, when I first saw them after their arrival, they were remov'd into this County. At that time, Sir, it was not in my power to comply with the purport of the act above referr'd to, as I was altogether ignorant of its existence; nor is it, 'till within These 10 days, that I have been made acquainted with it; as soon as this was the case, I repair'd immediately to the Clerk of the Court, in order to inform myself of its contents, which I accordingly did; and was told by him, that it was but a very few days since its arrival in the County. However immediately on its reaching my knowledge I paid a ready obedience to it. I trust therefore that my ignorance of the law, will in this case be readily admitted as an excuse for not having sooner complied with it. Should that be the case, Sir, permit me now to inform you, that I am desirous of taking the benefit of that act. The whole of my Negros in this State consists only of 2 families; (with the exception of 2 house servants). These 2 families contain 7 each, almost all very old or very young, as may be seen by having recourse to the list or schedule; I possess no land here, nor, if I did, have I force enough to render it worth my while to work it. My intention was to hire them out. 'Till within this month nothing was farther from my thoughts, than the disposal of them: but, they are almost intirely without covering, nor is it in my power to procure any for them; and without cloaths I find it also out of my power to hire them. Under these circumstances, Sir, you will, I hope, not think me unjustifiable, in requesting, as I now do, permission to sell them. Humanity gives rise to the request. If it be granted, I have the opportunity of disposing of them, to a person, who will immediately clothe them, and, I am confident from his character, will treat them much better, than it is at present in my power to do. I am Sir Your Excellency's most obedt. servt.,

NICHS. EVELEIGH

RC (PHi). Original enclosure not found, but in Vi is a copy, dated "December Court 1780" and attested by H. Goare, deputy clerk, Halifax co., of "An exact list of all the Slaves brought into the Common Wealth of Virginia by Nicholas Eveleigh of South Carolina"; 12 "Field Negroes" and 2 "House Negroes" are listed. (To this is added a copy of a similar list of the slaves brought from South Carolina by Charles Simes, or Sims, Feb. 1781.)

By "An act to authorize the citizens of South Carolina and Georgia to remove their slaves into this state," passed in the May 1780 session of the Assembly, refugees from these states were allowed to keep their slaves, provided they promptly registered them, until a year after the expulsion of the enemy or the restoration of civil government in their home states (thus in effect excepting refugees from the statute of 1778 prohibiting further importation of slaves into Virginia); furthermore, by specific permission of the executive, the owners were allowed to sell in Virginia "any or all such slaves as shall appear necessary for the comfortable support and maintenance of such citizen, or his or her family" (Hening, X, 307-8).

To Benjamin Harrison

SIR Richmond Nov. 25. 1780.

Since I had the honor of informing the General assembly of the instructions which had been given on the subject of the British Convention officers and their horses, Colo. Wood writes me that he has received a notification from Genl. Washington of the exchange of eighty eight of them, and that they are to proceed to Elizabeth town immediately where they will receive the General's further orders. The whole of the British having marched from the barracks, Colo.

Wood leaves that place tomorrow, and wishes to be immediately informed whether the new destination of these officers will make any alteration in the permission as to their horses. I have no doubt but that Genl. Washington would of course prohibit their carrying within the enemy's lines horses which they have purchased since the convention of Saratoga: but as an express sets out this day with dispatches for Headquarters, I propose to mention the matter particularly to him that we may ensure it's not escaping attention; unless the General assembly should think proper to advise any other measure. The express returning to Colo. Wood will await their pleasure.

I have the honor to be with the greatest respect Sir Your most obedient & most humble servt., TH: JEFFERSON

RC (CSmH). Addressee identified from internal evidence.

James Wood's letter to TJ, here mentioned, has not been located; see, however, TJ to Wood of this date, and TJ to Washington, 26 Nov. The present letter was read in the House of Delegates on the day written, but the Journals record no action on it (JHD, Oct. 1780, 1827 edn., p. 29).

Penet, D'Acosta Frères & Cie. to the Board of Trade

GENTLEMEN Nantes Novr. 25th: 1780

Before this time you have, we hope, been inform'd of the Capture of our schooner the Committee near Cape Henry and her rescue five days after by an American Privateer which carried her into Providence. The Cargo being your Property as Per Invoice and Bill of Lading (Copies of which are here annexed) you have no doubt put a claim on the half which was left unsold after 'tother had been adjudged to the Captors. We are very much concern'd at that unfortunate accident as it deprives you of half of a supply you stand in immediate want of: we expect however, that your Commercial spirits will not be depressed; our future Operations shall be attended with better successes and we are using our best endeavours for that end. We remain Respectfully Gentlemen Your most obedient & very humble Servants,

PENET D'ACOSTA FRERES & CIE.

RC (Vi). At head of text appears the word "*Copy*," but it probably means "duplicate."

OUR SCHOONER THE COMMITTEE (i.e., *Le Comité*): See Samuel Nightingale to TJ, 22 Nov. 1780. It is very likely that Penet knew of the fate of *Le Comité* when he wrote his long, fulsome, and boastful letter of 22 Nov. and if that communication had not aroused TJ's suspicions, the present letter, coming so soon after, must have.

To Steuben

Sir Nov. 25. 1780.

The Officers were desired to give notice to the militia when arms were delivered them that no man would *ever be discharged* till he had returned his arms or given justifiable reasons for not doing it, and this was given out in general orders by the commanding officers. Nothing was said at that time about other stores, but I shall when the order for their discharge is given out, desire that strict account be rendered by every man of what has been put into his hands, before he shall be discharged.

I shall be happy at all times to receive from you every intimation which may tend to secure the public stores or to promote the common good in any other way, and nothing in my power shall be omitted to promote those objects.

I have the honor to be with the greatest esteem Sir, your most obedt. servt., Th: Jefferson

RC (NHi); addressed by TJ: "The honble. Majr. Genl. Baron Steuben"; endorsed: "Govr. Jefferson Nov 25."

From Johann Ludwig de Unger

Monsieur! Aux Barraques ce 25me. de Novembre 1780.

L'ordre que nous reçumes de quitter cette Province, me fit prendre la Liberté, de Vous envoyer la semaine passée une Lettre pour m'aquiter de mes tres humble Devoirs, en me recommandant a Vos bonnes graces. Maintenant un Echangement de quelques Officiers vient de ce publier, parmi quel nombre ma Personne a le bonheur de se trouver; cela m'oblige de repeter mes protestations et de prendre pour une seconde fois et peut-etre pour jamais mon adieu de Vous Monsieur; une Personne que je ne perdrai jamais de Souvenir.

Permettez moi de Vous faire encore une tres humble Priere, car Vous m'avez fait si hardi, puisque jamais Vous m'avez donné un Refus. Je Vous supplie donc Monsieur de me donner la Permission, de prendre hormis mon Valet encore une seconde Personne avec moi jusqu'à la nouvelle York. C'est mon Ecrivain, lequel j'ai prit avec moi de l'Europe; il est païyé particulierement de moi, et n'a jamais porté et ne portera jamais des Armes. Serai-je si heureux que Vous m'accordez cette tres humble priere, mes obligations que je Vous ai s'augmenteront, mais aussi en suis-je convaincu, que si Vous me la refusez, Vos raisons en sont juste, et ainsi je ne craindrai pas que j'aye perdu de Votre Affection.

Je craind en verité de Vous avoir importuner par ma hardiesse mais permettez moi Monsieur de Vous dire, que Vos merites aussi bien que Vos qualités Vous rendent si recommendabe et si necessaire que chacun est en etat de Vous importuner.

En Vous priant d'assurer mes tres humble respects a Madame Votre Epouse et la jolie Betsy [Patsy], j'ai l'Honneur d'etre avec le plus profond Respects, Monsieur, Votre tres-humble et tres obeissant Serviteur, JOH: LOUIS DE UNGER

RC (DLC).

To James Wood

SIR Nov. 25. 1780

Your Dragoon did not get here till last night. I this day submitted the matter as to the horses of the exchanged officers to the House of Delegates informing them that I had no doubt but Genl. Washington would take the proper measures as to those purchased since the Convention, but as an express was this day setting out with dispatches to him, I would mention the matter to him specially unless they chose to have any other measure taken. They desired I would write to the General which I have accordingly done.

As to the pack horses, sell them as you propose to the public creditors, or do whatever else you shall find most for the public good.

Your messenger is detained till two o'clock P.M. I wish this may get to hand before your departure. I am with great esteem Sir, Your most obedt. sert., TH: JEFFERSON

RC (Rev. David H. Coblentz, Fincastle, Va., 1951); endorsed: "Govr. Jefferson 25 Novr. 1780."

Wood's letter, here acknowledged, is missing, but see TJ to Harrison of this date and TJ to Washington, 26 Nov.

To Nathanael Greene

SIR Richmond November 26. 1780.

I received advice that on the 22d. inst. the enemy's fleet got all under way and were standing towards the Capes. As it still remained undecided whether they would leave the bay or turn up it I waited the next stage of information that you might so far be enabled to judge of their destination. This I hourly expected; but it did not come till this evening when I am informed they all got to sea in the night of the 22d. What course they steered afterwards is not known.

By a Letter from General Washington to the President of Congress just come to hand I am informed that Admiral Rodney's fleet with the transports which had been some time preparing fell down to the Hook on the 11th instant.

General Washington referred me to you for instructions as to the mode of building light boats portable on wheels and which would be singularly useful in this Country in case of its invasion. This Letter unfortunately did not come to hand till you had left us. Any information you can have time to give on this head will much oblige me. I have the honor to be with the greatest respect, Sir your most obedt. servt.,

TH: JEFFERSON

RC (MB); in a clerk's hand, with complimentary close and signature by TJ. Addressee identified from internal evidence; see Washington to TJ, 8 Nov. 1780, suggesting that Greene be asked about constructing traveling flatboats.

A LETTER FROM GENERAL WASHINGTON TO THE PRESIDENT OF CONGRESS: Dated 14 Nov. and printed above in note to Huntington's letter to TJ of 17 Nov. 1780.

From Alexander Spotswood

SIR Novr. 26th. 1780

This will be handed you by Major Richard Claiborne, a Gentleman of uncommon merrit.

At the commencement of this War, anxious to serve his Country, he entered as a private in the 2d. Virginia Regiment. His diligence soon prefered him to the Rank of a serjeant, in which character he acted with such propriety, that he drew my attention towards him, and as soon as I had it in my power, appointed him Adjutant to the Regiment. Here his conduct drew the attention of his Brigadier, who appointed him Major of Brigade, in which post he acted until his Brigadier quitted the army, when General Greene appointed him deputy Quarter Master General, which post he held when General Greene resigned his Office as Quarter Master General. He is a Gentleman of good Family and morals. He wishes for a Majority in the new raised troops in which character I am certain he will shine and do honor to his State. I make not the least doubt but your Excellency will use your interest in getting him the appointment.

I am with esteem Your Excellency's Most obt. Servant,

A: SPOTSWOOD.

Tr (DNA: RG 93); at foot of text: "Copy. . . . A similar letter was written to Mr. Henry by Colo. Spotswood." Alexander Spotswood had retired from the colonelcy of the 2d Va. Continental line in 1777 (Heitman).

To Steuben

SIR Nov. 26. 1780.

Brigadr. Genl. Lawson now waits on you for the purpose of informing you of the state of his corps. I would have done myself the pleasure of introducing him to you personally, but am engaged in the council chamber and shall be so till three o'clock. When yourself and Genl. Lawson shall have settled those essential wants without which his corps cannot proceed I shall be happy to do every thing in my power to have them furnished.

I have the honor to be with great respect Sir Your most obedt. & most humble servt., TH: JEFFERSON

RC (NHi); addressed and endorsed.

To Edward Stevens

SIR Richmond November 26. 1780

The Enemy which lately invaded us left our Capes in the Night of the 22d Instant. What course they steered afterwards is not known. Another Fleet of Transports under the Command of Admiral Rodney fell down to the Hook on the 11th Instant. As this as well as the Fleet which lately left us is destined for Charles Town we shall March from their present Encampments all the forces who are so equipted as that they can proceed to distant Service. With them will go on between three and Four Hundred Tents belonging to this State. Three Hundred more are on the Road from Philadelphia and as many to follow. As Baron Steuben remains here to organize our forces I shall be obliged by special Returns of the 18 Months Men, 8 Months Men and three Months Militia which have or shall Come unto you as frequently as convenient. The Assembly being now met will shortly I hope furnish us with Money so that we may once more be able to send Supplies to the Southward. We have Collected here at length, by impress principally, about thirty Waggons which have been delivered to the Continental Q.M. to be sent on with Stores to Taylors Ferry.

I am with Great esteem Sir your most Obt hum: Servt,

TH: JEFFERSON

Tr (DLC); endorsed (in part): "Copy."

To George Washington

SIR Richmond Nov. 26th. 1780.

I have been honoured with your Excellency's Letter of the 8th instant. Having found it impracticable to move suddenly the whole Convention Troops, british and germans, and it being represented that there coud not immediately be covering provided for them all at fort Frederic we concluded to march off the British first from whom was the principal danger of desertion and to permit the germans who shew little disposition to join the enemy to remain in their present quarters till something further be done. The British accordingly marched the 20th instant. They cross the blue ridge at the Rock fish gap and proceed along that valley. I am to apprize your Excellency that the Officers of every rank both British and german but particularly the former have purchased within this State some of the finest horses in it. You will be pleased to determine whether it be proper that they carry them within their Lines. I believe the convention of Saratoga entitles them to keep the horses they then had; but I presume none of the Line below the rank of field officers had a horse. Considering that the british will be now at fort frederic, and the Germans in Albemarle, Alexandria seems to be the most central point to which there is navigation. Would it not therefore be better that the flag vessel solicited by Genl. Philips shoud go to that place? It is about equally distant from the two posts. The roads to Albemarle are good. I know not how those are which lead to fort frederic.

Your letter referring me to General Green for the mode of constructing light portable boats unfortunately did not come to hand till he had left us. We had before determined to have something done in the way, and as they are still unexecuted, we shou'd be greatly obliged by any draughts or hints which could be given by any person within the reach of your Excellency.

I received advice that on the 22nd instant the enemy's fleet got all under way and were standing towards the Capes. As it still remained undecided whether they woud leave the bay or turn up it, I waited the next stage of information that you might so far be enabled to judge of their destination. This I hourly expected but it did not come till this evening, when I am informed they all got out to sea in the night of the 22d. What course they steered afterwards is not known. I must do their General and Commodore the justice to say that in every case to which their influence or attention coud reach as far as I have been well informed, their conduct was such as does them the greatest honor. In the few instances of unnecessary and wanton devastation, which took place, they punished the aggressors.

I have the honor to be with every sentiment of esteem & respect Your Excellency's most obedient and most humble servant,

TH: JEFFERSON

RC (DLC: Washington Papers); in a clerk's hand, corrected and signed by TJ; endorsed (in part): "Ansd. 9th Decr." Tr (DLC). Another Tr (DLC: PCC, No. 71, I); this copy is in George Taylor's hand and is endorsed (in part): "No. 94"; it was supplied at TJ's instance while he was secretary of state (see TJ to Huntington, 13 Nov. 1780).

The (missing) copy of this letter directed to Pres. Huntington was read in Congress on 4 Dec. (JCC, XVIII, 1120); Huntington's acknowledgment of 9 Jan. 1781 indicates that it was dated 25 Nov. 1780.

From George Muter

[*Richmond, before 27 Nov. 1780.* Extract of a letter from George Muter to William Davies, 27 Nov. 1781, in War Office Letter Book (Vi): "From my earnest wish to do all manner of Justice to the Continent as well as the State, and thereby comply with your requisitions, everything in my power shall be done in concert with and under the General's [*i.e., Steuben*] direction, in the quickest and best manner possible, and every assistance I can afford Capt. Reed in the execution of his duty shall be most readily afforded. I have already written to the Governor on the Subject, but have not yet received his Answer." Muter's letter to TJ has not been located.]

From Samuel Huntington

Philadelphia [27] *Nov. 1780.* Acknowledges dispatches of 13 and 19 Nov., received this day and laid before Congress. Authentic intelligence reports the dissolution of the British Parliament and the calling of a new one. Deputies from Holland are on their way to Petersburgh [St. Petersburg] to attend the convention of neutral powers on the armed neutrality.

FC (DLC: PCC, No. 15); 1 p. No day of the month appears in the date line, but TJ's letters of 13 and 19 Nov., qq.v., were read in Congress on 27 Nov. (JCC, XVIII, 1095).

From James Maxwell

[*Richmond, 27 Nov. 1780.* Minute in Journal of the Commissioner of the Navy (Vi) under this date: "Letter written to the Governour on the Subject of the procuring Specie for the Flag going to Charlestown." Not located.]

From Nathaniel Randolph

GENTLEMEN — Monongohala Novr 27. 1780.

After I had seald the Letter that you will receive with this I found that I had in my hurry been too Jeneral.

I mean by this to remove that objection by explaining some particulars Your Honours may be Surprised to hear of my undertakeing this business when you consider the arrend you Sent me upon but as no opportunty has offered till at preasant which is imbrased by Capt. More who straneouly insists he must return to his Family; it likewise is as greate a neadcessaty for him at the Fawls as here. This consideration knowing the Safety of whatever is commited to his charg will be in, was the arguments which prevailed with me to con[tinue] here [on] this Business.

Your Honours will please to remember your frequent Orders in favour of the Kentucky in what manner we have been benefited by your designed Favours. Which deceptions I mean to remove if your Honours is pleased to put it in my power.

And as to the Boats I am fully convinsed of your being acquainted with the neadcessaty of pushing the Boat-building business to Compleat the designed Expedition, but your Honours attention being drawn of [off] by a continued succession of business of like Importance makes me hope that, when it is considered by You Gentlemen it will operate as an excuse for my prosumption to put you in minde of what you would wish to doo.

300 Boats is the Number that is wanting. £20 the oald way will be the expence of each Boat: the plank and timber and the meterials may be had here upon reasonable terms: about one half the Artificers likewise, with all the common labourars. 8 or 9 Boat writes which is Masters of their business furnished with a Sufficient Quantity of Tools; 30℔. of nales and 4 Gallon of Tare [Tar] for each Boat, which is all the meterials that will be wanting from that Side the Mountan, that I can recollect as to the [boats?]. I am Gentlemen your much Obliged and very Hml Svt,

NATHL. RANDOLPH

RC (Vi); addressed: "To His Excellency Thomas Jefferson *Richmond* Pr favour Mr Ennis"; endorsed: "Mr. N Randolph Jany 81."

Sent with Randolph's letter of 22 Nov. 1780, q.v.

From Steuben

SIR Richmond Novr 27th. 1780

I cannot help expressing to Your Excellency the anxiety I am under occasioned by the delay of Genls. Muhlenberg and Lawson, nor, when I consider the unhappy Consequences that this Delay may Occasion, can I avoid justifying myself from having any part in it.

Instead of forwarding Genl. Green the reinforcements he Expected, we are Keeping a Number of Corps dispersed about the State, where no Enemy has been these Eight Days thereby Exposing General Greene with an inferior force to the Enemy, and exhausting what little provision was Collected in this State.

The Expences of Keeping Such a Number of Corps must be enormous, and I should think wholly unnecessary, especially Genl. Nelson's Corps, which can no longer be of any Service, and I am firmly of Opinion that it would be for the Interest of the Country at large and more particularly of this State, immediately to discharge all the Militia who are not destined to go to the Southward.

There are about this Town near 700 Men under a Variety of Commanders. Those who are destined for the Southward Should be Selected under the Command of some Colonel and ordered to Chesterfield Court House and the rest discharged as soon as possible.

FC (NHi). Tr (MiU-C); enclosed in Steuben's letter to Greene, this date.

To Benjamin Harrison

[*Richmond, 28? Nov. 1780.* JHD, Oct. 1780, 1827 edn., p. 31 (28 Nov.): "The Speaker laid before the House a letter from the Governor, enclosing extracts of letters from Major Kirkpatrick and General Nelson, respecting certain persons who had aided and countenanced the enemy, which were read, and ordered to lie on the table." Letter and enclosures not located.]

From William Phillips

SIR New York November 28th. 1780

I have the honour to acknowledge the receipt of Your Excellency's letters of the 3rd. and 19th. of October. I observe, with peculiar satisfaction, the acts of kindness you have extended to several of our Gentlemen whose situations have required such indulgencies; your attention to them claim my best thanks which I now beg leave to present you, and in a more particular manner I am obliged to you for your ready acquiescence to my wishes in sending in Lieutenant Governor Hamilton and the Officers connected with his situation upon their paroles. I find by the Lieutenant Governor's report to me that he is opposed to Lieutenant Colonel Porterfield.

What you are pleased to mention with respect to my interpositions in favour of Your Officers here, I am happy to assure you is only a continuance of that uniform principle I have invariably pursued, in my endeavours to serve persons in captivity, founded upon the purest motives of humanity to mitigate the unavoidable hardships incident to that state.

I shall always be glad to continue my good offices in behalf of the Virginian Officers, and your offers of a corresponding attention to my applications in favour of the Troops of Convention cannot but be very pleasing to me.

Colonel Mathews will have permission to go out upon his parole so soon as some propositions now in agitation for the benefit of the American Officers Prisoners of War on Long Island are digested, and which he is to carry to Virginia for the concurrence of Your Government; I shall write fully to You, Sir, upon the subject by him but I must anticipate part of his Commission which, I apprehend, he will be desirous of effecting. It is that whatever Money in Specie may be given to the order of the Commanding Officer of the Troops of Convention in Virginia for their use, supposing that mode should be adopted by you, Sir, an equivalent sum to the amount of one, two, three, four or five thousands pounds Sterling shall be paid to any person you shall please to nominate for the Virginian Officers prisoners of war here, and this shall be done by me directly upon an acknowledgement from Brigadier General Hamilton or the British Officer Commanding the Troops at Albemarle Barracks of what Monies he may receive. I shall empower the Brigadier to draw Publick Bills for the amount thereof; such publick bills to be paid to whatever order you may send to receive them at this place in Sterling Money to the full Value of the sums specified in them. As this proposal appears of so equitable a nature, and tending to the conveniency of both parties I should wish it might be adopted.

Concerning Mr. Elligood I can only say that I shall ever be desirous to shew such indulgence to Colonel Mathews as my influence can procure him, without bringing him into competition with that Gentleman, who, I confess, I never heard of until he was produced in a conversation I had with Colonel Mathews and some other American Officers. Being, on our part, entirely ignorant of every circumstance relating to Mr. Elligood it renders it not possible to enter upon his subject.

The Vessel which brought Lieutenant Governor Hamilton not being of sufficient tonnage to carry the stores designed for the Troops of Convention, I propose to send a Ship that will answer the purpose in a short time.

I have the honour to be, Sir, with great personal respect, Your Excellencys most obedient and most humble servant,

W PHILLIPS

RC (NHi); in a clerk's hand, signed by Phillips; endorsed: "Major Genl Phillips Lr. recd Feby 81."

TJ's letters of 3 and 19 Oct. to Phillips have not been located. MR. ELLIGOOD . . . COLONEL MATHEWS: See note on TJ's letter to Steuben, 17 Feb. 1781.

From George Muter,

with a Return of Ammunition on Hand

SIR War office Novr. 29. 1780.

My duty obliges me to inform your Excellency, that there are only twelve pigs of lead at Richmond and five at Westham, weighing about 150℔. each. I beg leave to add, that there is the most urgent necessity for a considerable quantity of lead's being soon procured, otherwise the making of musket catridges must soon be at an end. There is only about 200℔. of ball and buck shott in the laboratory to make up.

I have the honour to be Your Excellency's Most humble servant,

GEORGE MUTER. C.[W.]

ENCLOSURE

[1]780	Ammunition for musketts now on hand		
Novr. 29.	Ball catridges packed	1779 done	21.348
	Ball & buck shott catridges packed	5119.	61.428
	Do. Not yet packed	1200.	14.400
		6319	75.828
	Ball & buck shott ready to make up about 200℔.		

George Muter. C.W.

Capt. Irish (Contl. Comy. [Commissary] of Military stores) has an order for all the ball catridges.

RC, with MS Return of Ammunition on separate page (Vi).

Marbois' Queries concerning Virginia

[Before 30 November 1780]

Articles of which you are requested to give some details

1. The Charters of your State.
2. The present Constitution.
3. An exact description of its limits and boundaries.
4. The Memoirs published in its name, in the time of its being a Colony and the pamphlets relating to its interior or exterior affairs present or ancient.
5. The History of the State.
6. A notice of the Counties Cities Townships Villages Rivers Rivulets and how far they are navagible. Cascades Caverns Mountains Productions Trees Plants Fruits and other natural Riches.
7. The number of its Inhabitants.
8. The different Religions received in that State.
9. The Colleges and public establishments. The Roads Buildings &c.
10. The Administration of Justice and a description of the Laws.
11. The particular Customs and manners that may happen to be received in that State.
12. The present State of Manufactures Commerce interior and exterior Trade.
13. A notice of the best Sea Ports of the State and how big are the vessels they can receive.
14. A notice of the commercial productions particular to that State and of those objects which the Inhabitants are obliged to get from Europe and from other parts of the World.
15. The weight measures and the currency of the hard money. Some details relating to the exchange with Europe.
16. The public income and expences.
17. The measures taken with regard of the Estates and Possessions of the Rebels commonly called Tories.
18. The condition of the Regular Troops and the Militia and their pay.
19. The marine and Navigation.
20. A notice of the Mines and other subterranean riches.
21. Some Samples of these Mines and of the extraordinary Stones. In short a notice of all what can increase the progress of human Knowledge.

22. A description of the Indians established in the State before the European Settlements and of those who are still remaining. An indication of the Indian Monuments discovered in that State.

MS (DLC); in hand of Joseph Jones, who transmitted these Queries to TJ after his return to Virginia from Congress in Sep. 1780, though perhaps not until Jones came to Richmond to attend the Assembly on 31 Oct. (see Burnett, v, p. lxiv; and especially Jones to Madison, 5 Nov. 1780, *Letters of Joseph Jones*, Washington, 1889, p. 40). At any rate TJ had had the Queries in hand some little time before he mentioned to D'Anmours in a letter of 30 Nov., following, that he was "at present busily employed for Monsr. Marbois without his knowing it," which implies that Marbois had asked Jones to furnish answers and Jones had turned to TJ for help. The problem challenged TJ's whole being, and his completed answers were to constitute one of the classic literary and scientific books of the eighteenth century—the *Notes on the State of Virginia*, first printed in an edition of 200 copies at Paris, 1785.

Marbois (François Marbois, secretary to the French minister, La Luzerne, and later Marquis de Barbé-Marbois) told Thomas McKean, in a letter of 10 Feb. 1781 enclosing a like set of queries for McKean to answer concerning Delaware, that he was preparing "un mémoire sur les treize Etats en générale" (MS: PHi; photostats in TJ Editorial Files). TJ in his Autobiography stated that Marbois "had been instructed by his government to obtain such statistical accounts of the different states of our Union, as might be useful for their information" (Ford, I, 85). At about the same time that he asked Jones to obtain answers for Virginia, Marbois asked John Sullivan to do likewise for New Hampshire. Sullivan's answers are in a letter to Marbois dated Philadelphia, 10 Dec. 1780 (*Sullivan Papers*, N.H. Hist. Soc., *Colls.*, xv, 229-39). Sullivan also transmitted both questions and answers to Pres. Meshech Weare of New Hampshire, 25 Dec. 1780, observing that "This Gentleman [Marbois] is one of those usefull Geniuss who is Constantly in Search of knowledge he is about to write the History of America or rather to give a Geographical Description of it. As much advantage will arise from our Commerce & Constitutions being well known: As Mr Adams has wrote from Holland to Congress pressing upon them the necessity of Taking measures for this purpose I wish you to Lay these papers before the assembly & request a Committee to furnish Such answers as they may find I have omitted and to Correct Such mistakes as I may have made & I wish a sample of our Glass may be forwarded" (same, p. 249). For New Jersey John Witherspoon was appealed to, and he prepared a fragmentary set of answers posthumously printed in his *Works*, Phila., 2d edn., 1802, IV, 403-12. When Joseph Jones had returned to Congress at the end of Jan. 1781, he told Marbois that the Queries for Virginia had been turned over to TJ; Marbois wrote TJ on 5 Feb. (this letter is missing), and TJ replied on 4 Mch., saying that "Hitherto it has been in my power to collect a few materials only, which my present occupation disables me from compleating"; see the whole letter and the note thereon.

To D'Anmours

Dear Sir Richmond Nov. 30. 1780.

I received your favor from Baltimore and shall carefully attend to the notifying you of the arrival of any fleet here from your nation or other circumstance which I may think interesting to you. The enemy have left us as you will before have heard. Tho' I do not wish for new occasions of calling together my countrymen to try their valour, yet I really wish, as they were called together that the enemy had staid to give them a little exercise and some lessons in real war. Were it not that an invasion of our state at Portsmouth shuts the only door of our commerce, I had rather fight our share of them here than send 300 miles to seek them in a climate more fatal than their sword. I am at present busily employed for Monsr. Marbois without his knowing it, and have to acknolege to him the mysterious obligation for making me much[1] better acquainted with my own country than I ever was before. His queries as to this country put into my hands by Mr. Jones I take every occasion which presents itself of procuring answers to. Some of them however can never be answered till I shall [have] leisure to go to Monticello where alone the materials exist which can enable any one to answer them. I am exceedingly anxious to get a copy of Le grande Encyclopedie, but am really frightened from attempting it thro' the mercantile channel, dear as it is originally and loaded as it would come with the enormous advance which they lay on under pretext of insurance out and in. You once thought that some means might be fallen on of effecting this importation by some vessel of war and perhaps of making the remittance in tobacco in the same way. Should any such occur I shall be greatly obliged by your availing me of it, and will surely answer every engagement you can make for me.

I am with great sincerity Your friend & servt.

Dft (DLC); endorsed: "D'Anmours Chevalr." A number of deletions and revisions occur in the text, one of which is noted below.

For the QUERIES AS TO THIS COUNTRY transmitted to TJ by Joseph Jones in behalf of MONSR. MARBOIS, see the preceding document. D'Anmours' FAVOR FROM BALTIMORE was dated 18 Nov. 1780, q.v.

[1] TJ first wrote "infinitely."

To Benjamin Harrison

SIR Novr. 30. 1780.

In consequence of the resolutions of General Assembly at their last Session on the rank of the officers of the two State regiments, I wrote to the Continental board of war on that subject; an extract from my Letter is now inclosed. To this I have never received an answer. Brigadier General Muhlenberg has desired me to lay before the General Assembly the inclosed letter to him from Colo. Brent and Majr. Meriwether on this subject which I apprehend to be the more proper as the arrangement of our Continental line as well as of the forces of the State will be under the consideration of the assembly.

The executive have had in contemplation the placing two or four guns at the principal ports within the State to protect the shipping which should be lying in them for trade or other purposes from the sudden enterprizes of privateers or other armed vessels. Portsmouth, Hampton, York, Hobbs hole and Alexandria were considered as ports which should be thus protected. We also wished to take advantage of any narrow pass on James or Patowmack rivers where hopeful opposition might be made to the passage of such Vessels, and all the trade above these passes be thereby protected. It seems very doubtful whether there be any such pass on Patowmack. Hoods on James river has been considered as very capable of opposing the passage of Vessels. In pursuance of this plan all supernumerary Guns have been withdrawn from Portsmouth, Hampton and York, and some progress has been made in constructing a battery at Hoods. Major General Gates having sent Colo. Senf, Engineer, to the Southern army to make observations, previous to the late invasion, on such places as might probably be contested in case of an invasion, I asked the favor of him to take Hoods in his way and to oblige us with his observations on it. His report on this subject to Major General Baron Steuben has by this last Gentleman been transmitted to me with a request that I would lay it before the General Assembly which I now take the liberty of doing.

I have the honor of being with the greatest respect Sir Your most obedient & Most hble. Servant, TH: JEFFERSON

RC (Vi); in a clerk's hand, signed by TJ; endorsed: "Governors Letter. Enclosing Papers relating to the Rank of Officers of the two State Regiments Novr: 30th: 1780. Referred to Committee of Arrangement. Mr: Richard Henry Lee. Jno. Taylor. Stevens. Hunter. Fitzhugh. Holmes. Baker. Braxton. Fras: Peyton." Enclosures not located.

This letter was read in the House of Delegates on the day it was written; most of the enclosures were referred to the new committee of arrangement, which reported on 2 Dec.; see TJ to Washington, 13 Dec. 1780. J. C. Senf's REPORT to Steuben was ordered to lie on the table (JHD, Oct. 1780, 1827 edn., p. 33; for further action on the fortification of Hood's, see Senf to TJ, 29 Jan. 1781). The failure of the Assembly to act on the proposed fortification at HOODS had violent repercussions; see Steuben to TJ, 11 Feb., and TJ's reply, 12 Feb. 1781.

From John Todd

MAY IT PLEASE YOUR EXCELLENCY Lexington Nov. 30. 1780

We have been for some time past and are still dreading an Invasion from the neighbouring Northern Indians. Intelligence by the

Way of St. Vincent informs us that late in Octo. a great Number of Indians and English were at the late-destroyd Shawnese Towns waiting the rise of the Waters to make a Descent either against the Falls or this Place. I have ordered upon Duty part of the Militia of this County (Fayette) at three of the most exposed forts and am purchasing up a Quantity of Corn. The people seem fond at present to sell to the Country and Corn will be almost the only article which Government may expect from this Quarter. I expect to procure between One and two Thousand Bushels by giving Certificates to be settled by the Auditors or agreed upon by the Commissary for 40 or 50£ ℔ Barrell or 2/6 hard Money. I hope I have not Acted amiss in this Respect Altho' I have no Instructions. As the assembly at last session recommended the plan laid by the several County Lieutenants and there is a Certainty of a Vigourous attack next Spring, I conclude that a Delay for Orders is unnecessary.

The Indians are annoying us every Week in small parties. Two small detachments of Militia are now in pursuit of some who stole Horses two nights ago from McConnells Station.

A Cargoe of Goods I have heard is arrived at Fort Jefferson for the Use of the State said to be consigned by Mr. Pollock to myself as Co. Lieutt. of Ilinois. I purpose writing to Capt. Dodge to Store them up until further Orders from your Excellency as soon as I shall have an Opportunity and the Report shall be authenticated.

I hope to be excused in expressing my Desires that Your Excellency may have in Contemplation an Early Expedition next Spring against our Savage Neighbours. I will venture to assure you that Any Orders which may tend to that purpose will be executed with the greatest Alacrity by Officers and Men.

Capt. Quirk I hear is on the Way with 30 or 40 Men and I can hear nothing from Col. Crockett. I have the Honor to be with the greatest Respect your Excellencys Mo. obedt. & humble Servant,

JNO. TODD jr.

P.S. Decr. 4th. Since writing the above I hear that a Lieut. Montgomery with 24 Men the whole of Quirk Co. have arrived the other side of the River.

J. TODD jr

RC (Vi); addressed: "His Excellency Tho. Jefferson Esq; Governor of Virginia sent to Col. A. Campbell"; endorsed: "Mr. Fords [*sic*] Lr. Feby 81."

To Johann Ludwig de Unger

SIR Richmond Nov. 30. 1780

The letter which covers this being of a public nature I wished separately to acknolege the many things personally obliging to me expressed in your two letters. The very small amusements which it has been in my power to furnish in order to lighten some of your heavy hours by no means merited the acknolegements you make. Their impression must be ascribed to your extreme sensibility rather than their own weight. My wishes for your happiness give me participation in your joy at being exchanged, sensibly however alloyed by a presentiment of the loss I shall sustain when I shall again be permitted to withdraw to that scene of quiet retirement abstracted from which I know no happiness in this world. Your line of life must have given you attachments to objects of a very different nature. When the course of events shall have removed you to distant scenes of action where laurels not nurtured with the blood of my country may be gathered, I shall urge sincere prayers for your obtaining every honor and preferment which may gladden the heart of a souldier. On the other hand should your fondness for philosophy resume it's merited ascendency, is it impossible to hope that this unexplored country may tempt your residen[ce] by holding out materials wherewith to build a fame found[ed] on the happiness and not the calamities of human nature? Be this as it may, whether philosopher or souldier, I wish you many felicities and assure you that I am with great personal esteem Sir Your most obedt. & most humble servt.

Dft (DLC); at foot of first page of text: "Lt. John Louis de Unger." This graceful letter was not written without considerable literary effort; the draft shows numerous small but highly effective polishing strokes.

THE LETTER WHICH COVERS THIS: Not found; it must have been TJ's official reply to the request contained in the second of the TWO LETTERS—that is, those of 13 and 25 Nov., qq.v.

To ——— ———

[*Richmond, 30 Nov. 1780.* Etienne Charavay, comp., *Inventaire des autographes et documents historiques réunis par M. Benjamin Fillon*, Paris, 1878, I, item 295, lists a letter signed by TJ of this date, 2 p. folio, and summarizes it as follows: "Il mande que le pouvoir exécutif a l'intention de placer, dans les principaux forts, quatre canons pour protéger les vaisseaux qui sont dans les ports de l'Etat." Letter not found, and addressee not identified. It is possible, however, that the letter here described was a copy of TJ's letter to Benjamin Harrison of this date, for the description closely parallels the first sentence of the second paragraph of that letter.]

To John Gibson

[*Richmond, Nov.? 1780.* A letter from Col. John Gibson to Col. George Rogers Clark, Fort Pitt, 17 Dec. 1780, states that Gibson "received a Letter from his Excellency the Governor of Virginia wherein he informed me that Colo. Campbell had told him that I had a quantity of Cloathing which I received last summer for the men of my Regiment and that I had no immediate use for it as he expected we should be supplied by the Continental Store, upon which his Excellency wrote me and ordered me to deliver it to Capt. [James Francis] Moore for the use of the Troops on the Ohio." Gibson is unable to comply because his men are "quite naked." Intends setting off for Richmond in a few days, and "should the Governor and Council adopt any method of furnishing Cloathing for you I shall use my utmost endeavours to have it Transported to you" (*George Rogers Clark Papers, 1771-1781*, p. 474). Neither of TJ's letters has been found.]

Impressment Warrants to Various Persons

VIRGINIA TO WIT,

Whereas by an act passed at the General Assembly holden in the month of may in this present year and intituled an act for giving further powers to the Governeur and Council and for other purposes, authority was given for obtaining by impress among other things so many horses waggons and necessaries as might be wanting to supply the militia and other troops ordered into actual service. These are therefore to authorize you to obtain by impressing fifty waggons with their teams and gear and the same when impressed to bring to this place, having them previously appraised according to law; for the hire of which said waggons teams and gear, paiment will be made at the public treasury[1] and all officers civil and military and other the good citizens of this commonwealth are hereby required and commanded to be aiding and assisting to you in the execution of this warrant. Given under my hand and the seal of the Commonwealth at Richmond this day of november in the year of our Lord one thousand seven hundred and eighty.

THO: JEFFERSON

Tr in the War Office Letter Book (MiU-C); copy of seal at foot of text; in margin: "two copies sent to mr Southall to be sent to Fredericksburg and Alexandria" (this was probably Stephen Southall, assistant quartermaster general for the state; see *Official Letters*, II, 356; Gwathmey, *Hist. Reg.*

of Virginians in the Revolution). These warrants were doubtless issued early in November during Leslie's invasion threat; a variant one issued at the same time is summarized below.

1 Following the text of this document there is in the War Office Letter Book another warrant docketed as "delivered to mr. Robert Boush." It begins and concludes identically with the text above, but the second sentence, to the point noted, reads as follows: "These are therefore to authorize you to obtain by impressing so many waggons, carts, horses, drivers and gear, boats [and] other vessels with their tackle and crews as may be necessary for removing into a place of security any arms ammunition or other public stores, on the south side of James river, giving certificates of all sums which become due for the hire or use of any of the said articles or services, and returning to me a list of the certificates you shall so give specifying the sum due and to whom and for what due."

From Geismar

[November? 1780]

I have leave to go in to N. York and Shall let get of [off] as soon as I can Settle my Affairs; You will oblige me in writing to [. . .][1] French in fredriksburg who has a goald repeater, he was So Kind as to have it repaird for me. I shall be thankfull to you if you will Sell it and Send me the value of it by Some means to Europe. Adieu. Be my friend, do not forget me and persuede Yourself of my Sincerity. My Respects to Mdm and the little Misses; Doriano has all my Musik for You. GEISMAR

RC (DLC). The assigned date is open to question, but presumably Geismar accompanied the other German officers who were paroled at this time.

DORIANO: Torriano?; see Pass for Torriano, printed at the end of 1780, below.

1 Illegible; perhaps "Paitor." The reading of the second name is not altogether certain.

From George Muter

SIR War office Decr. 1st. 1780.

I beg leave to observe to your Excellency that as the Quarter master general's office is to be immedeatly removed to this place (Richmond) it becomes necessary to dispose of the houses in Wmsburgh, lately used for that office, to some other use. Mr. Kemp who is obliged to goe to Wmsburgh as soon as the arangement of the Quarter master generals department takes place, to finish the business there and remove the papers from thence, wishes to be honoured with your Excellency's orders, how to despose of the houses.

I have the honour to be Your Excellency's most hle servant,

GEORGE MUTER

RC (Vi); addressed; endorsed: "Colo Muter To the Govr. respecting the Houses occupied in Wmsburg for the QMG's Office being applied to some other purpose. 1st Dec. 1780. QM.G's office in Wmsburg."

From Jacob Rubsamen

Sir! Decembr 1th 1780

The enclosed Letters contain not any thing in the least injurious to the states. General Riedasel has in on [one] of his Letters the following Passage—

I hear with Pleasure that Some of the deserted Dragoons are desirous to join Corps again. For my part I cannot advice any thing in the present posture of Affairs. Should a General exchange take Place wich is at present more probable then ever, owing to the greater Equality of Prisoners on both Sides, the deserters may be advised of it, and should they prefer joining their Corps, to staying behind, may be exchanged with the Rest.

In a News paper printed at Hamburg and enclosed in one of the Letters, I find the following extract of a German Officers Letter dated barracks—

My only Occupation at present, is, to learn the English Language, it is the easier for me as I have free Access to a Copious and well chosen Library of Colo. Jefferson's Governor of Virginia. The father of this learned Man's was also a favourite of the Muses. There is now a Map of his of Virginia extant, the best of the Kind. The Governor possesses a Noble Spirit of Building, he is now finishing an elegant building projected according to his own fancy. In his parlour he is creating on the Cieling a Compass of his own invention by wich he can Know the strenght as well as Direction of the Winds. I have promised to paint the Compass for it. He was much pleased with a fancy Painting of mine and particularly admired the Paper Money brought on in the piece, and in Joke often rebuked me for my thoughtlessness to shew him counterfeit money for wich I Knew many had been hanged allready. As all Virginians are fond of Music, he is particularly so. You will find in his House an Elegant Harpsicord Piano forte and some Violins. The latter he performs well upon himself, the former his Lady touches very skilfully and who, is in all Respects a very agreable Sensible and Accomplished Lady.

I am Your Excellency most Obt hble svt, Jacob Rubsamen

RC (DLC). Enclosures not further identified.

On Jacob Rubsamen (variously spelled), of Manchester, who married into the Bland family, see a number of references in Swem, *Index*. The german officers letter describing TJ's domestic establishment may very well have been written by Geismar or Unger.

From Steuben

SIR Richmond, Decr. 1st. 1780

Your Excellency was acquainted with My Intention of sending on Genl. Lawson's Corps, and I can now inform you that I expect they will march from hence to morrow, tho' not in such Numbers as I Expected, only 340 Rank and file appearing under Arms at the review Yesterday, including Infantry and Cavalry.

The next Object is sending on as speedily as possible 400 Continental Troops and as many Militia, and this I am in hopes of accomplishing in a few days, for this some Preparation is necessary as well to set them off as to Provide for them on the March. Your Excellency's Assistance will I apprehend be wanting at least to empower Mr. Elliot for that purpose.

This Gentleman has represented to me his want of the necessary Authority, and I have promised to write to Your Excellency on the subject.

I know Your Excellency is equally Anxious with me in this Affair and therefore doubt not your giving him all the Assistance in your Power.

FC (NHi).

To Steuben

SIR Richmond Dec. 1. 1780.

I this moment received your letter, and have extended Mr. Elliot's powers to the procuring subsistence for the marching troops.

You will perceive by the inclosed resolution of assembly (which was put into my hands about two o'clock to-day) that they doubt whether the time, for which Genl. Lawson's corps is enlisted, will not be so nearly expired before they reach the scene of action as, under our present circumstances, to render the sending them on ineligible on the whole. The confidence they deservedly repose in you, authorises me to ask the favor of your judgment on this subject, which I know will be formed on a general view as well of the urgency of the present call for reinforcements to the Southward, as of the necessity of oeconomising our resources to a certain degree, even under the most urgent calls. If the corps can be engaged to serve through the campaign as mentioned in the resolution, I suppose there can be no doubt but their services will be valuable. I presume therefore you will think it expedient to ask the favor of Genl. Lawson to make this experiment first: should he fail in engaging them, an exact return I suppose will be thought necessary of the numbers, and times they have to serve: and, on view of this the ultimate judgment will be formed. As the present resolution of assembly was unexpected to me, and my reflections had hitherto run only in the channel of fostering the spirit on which this corps was raised, and hastening succours to our Southern brethren, I own I am not prepared to give an opinion on the point and shall be very happy to be instructed by yours. Should your purposes at Petersburg be so far executed as that this should find you preparing to return to this place, I shall be so much the more pleased as the intercommunication of sentiment will be thereby facilitated.

I have the honor to be with the most perfect respect Sir Your most obedient & most humble servt., TH: JEFFERSON

RC (NHi); endorsed. Enclosure (missing): copy of a resolution of the General Assembly, 1 Dec. 1780, desiring the governor to discharge the corps of volunteer cavalry serving under Gen. Lawson "unless they shall agree to serve during the southern campaign, to be ascertained by the commanding officer in that department" (see JHD, Oct. 1780, 1827 edn., p. 33, 34).

From Steuben

SIR Petersburg Decr. 2. 1780.

I wrote Your Excellency the 30th ult. that Gen. Lawson's Corps would march Yesterday. This would Certainly have been the Case had not a report arrived that the Legislature had determined on their being discharged immediately. I should not however have suspended the march from a mere report, but Genl. Lawson himself shewed me a Copy of the Resolution of the house of Delegates on the subject.

I must confess I am not a little surprized that I have received nothing Official on this affair, and should I receive nothing this Day from Your Excellency I shall not be justified in detaining them any longer, but shall order them to march immediately.

FC (NHi). The file copy of Steuben's letter concerning LAWSON'S CORPS is dated 1 Dec., not 30 Nov., 1780, and is printed above.

To Steuben

SIR Richmond Dec. 3. 1780.

I was equally surprized and mortified to learn by your letter of yesterday that mine of the day before had not been delivered. The resolution of assembly was put into my hands at two o'clock in the afternoon of Friday. At 7. o'clock I delivered letters to an express for yourself, Genl. Lawson, and Genl. Muhlenberg, with orders to be with you at farthest by an hour by sun on Saturday. I was therefore in expectation of your answer when I received the letter informing me that you had not heard from me on this subject. Calling on the Quartermaster to know the reason of this he informs me that the express was disabled, by a fall, from proceeding and that he sent off another yesterday morning at half after six with orders to be with you in three hours. Lest any disaster should have befallen this one also I inclose a duplicate of my letter, and shall be happy to be favored with your sentiments on the subject.

I have the honour to be with great respect Sir Your most obedt.

RC (NHi); in TJ's hand, but signature has been cut away. Enclosures: see TJ to Steuben, 1 Dec. 1780.

TJ's letters of 1 Nov. to Gen. LAWSON and Gen. MUHLENBERG have not been located.

From Samuel Huntington

Philadelphia, 4 Dec. 1780. Circular letter to the state executives enclosing copy of a resolve of Congress of 30 Nov. requesting the states to furnish Commissary General Blaine or his deputy with the names of the principal agents or commissioners appointed to supply the army in each state "and to oblige them [the agents] to give Information from Time to Time to the Commissary General, or his Deputy with the southern Army, . . . of their Prospects of complying with the Requisitions made to them or the respective States." The livestock are to be delivered to the persons or places designated by Blaine or his deputy "under the Regulations of Congress of the 15th of July last."

FC (DLC: PCC, No. 15); 1 p. Enclosure (Vi): copy of a resolve of Congress of 30 Nov. endorsed: "System of the Department of the Commissary of Purchases"; printed in JCC, XVIII, 1109-11.

From Patrick Lockhart

SIR Botetourt Dec. 4. 1780.

Your Excellencys Instructions relative to my conducting the prisoners taken on Kings mountain to the place of destination did not come to hand until fourteen days after dated. I set out next day to execute your Excellencys Commands. Before I reached the Lead mines I had advice that the Tories were chiefly Inlisted but was not certified how the British were disposed of until I arrived at Surry Courthouse (No. Carolina) where I met Colo. Martin Armistrong in whose charge the prisoners had been. He informed me that the British had been ordered to Hillsborough by Genl. Gates, that some of the tories that had refused to inlist were sent to Halifax to be tried for treason. Some of those enlisted wer furloughed and that he sent one division by his brother a Major in the Continental Line to join our army. Major Armistrong also informed me that those men he took charge of was ordered by General Gates to be confined at Salisbury until exchanged, that the General and also Genl. Morgan informed him that a Carteel had been settled with Lord Cornwallis to exchange the prisoners taken on Kings Mountain for our regulars and Militia taken at Charlestown. I therefore concluded it unnecessary to proceed any further it appearing to me that the Measures adopted relative to the Destination of the prisoners were entirely changed neither could I learn where General Gates was at that time. I then returned home and hope the reasons above Assigned will prove satisfactory.

I am Yr. Excellency's hbl Servt., PAT. LOCKHART

Tr (DLC: PCC, No. 71, I); at head of text: "(Copy)"; endorsed. Enclosed, with a copy of TJ's instructions to Lockhart of 8 Nov., q.v., in TJ's letter to Huntington, 25 Dec. 1780.

HE INFORMED ME THAT THE BRITISH HAD BEEN ORDERED TO HILLSBOROUGH: Armstrong understated the case. On 16 Nov., writing from Salisbury, Gates informed Armstrong: "Your Conduct is so contrary to possitive Orders, and the Disposal of the prisoners of War committed to your care, so oposite to your Duty, that I must insist you come immediately to Salisbury to answer for the injury done this Country, in the absurd Disposal of those Prisoners of War" (copy in DLC: TJ Papers).

To Steuben

SIR In Council December 4th. 1780.

I have been just honored with your favor of Yesterday expressing your Opinion that it will be for the general good to dispense with the services of the Corps under Genl. Lawson; and take the Liberty of putting under cover to you my Letter to General Lawson desiring him to give them a discharge. The Diversion of their Services to an object different from that to which they had attached their original views seems to have had a considerable influence on their minds; as also on the Militia who were under marching orders for Carolina and stopped in like manner. Whether the same principles should lead to the same determination as to the Militia I beg leave to submit altogether to yourself. They were to serve three months from their getting to Hillsborough and we agreed that the time incurred between their rendezvousing at this place and setting out again on their Southern march should be deducted from their original term. If you think under these Circumstances that it would be better to dismiss these and to call fresh men into the field, be pleased to give the order for dismission.

I have the honor to be with the greatest respect Sir Your mo: obedt. & mo: hble Servant, TH: JEFFERSON

RC (NHi); in a clerk's hand, signed and addressed by TJ: "The honourable Majr. General Baron de Steuben Petersburg. by Express."

Steuben's FAVOR OF YESTERDAY is missing.

From John Gregory

[*Place unknown, before 5 Dec. 1780.* A minute in the Journal of the Commissioner of the Navy (Vi), under this date reads: "Letter from Capt. Jno. Gregory, referred from his Excellency the Governor, read and filed." Neither Gregory's letter nor TJ's covering letter has been located.]

From George Muter

[*Richmond, before 5 Dec. 1780.* Extract of a letter from George Muter to [Arthur?] Campbell, 5 Dec. 1781, in War Office Letter Book (Vi): "I was favoured with yours of the 2d. of November [and] that I might be fully enabled to answer it, I laid it before [the] Governor. In Mr. Smith's affair the Governor says The Board [can]not consent to advance Ensign Smith to a Captaincy on the [circ]umstances mentioned." It is impossible to ascertain whether Muter's inquiry and TJ's reply were oral or written, though matters requiring Council action were usually transmitted by letter. No exchange of letters on this subject has been found, however.]

To Benjamin Harrison

In Council December 5th. 1780.

I beg leave to lay before the General Assembly the inclosed Letter from the honourable Theoderick Bland, one of our Delegates in Congress, the subjects of which may be proper for the consideration of the Legislative Body and have the honor to be with great respect sir, Your most obedient & most humble servant,

TH: JEFFERSON

RC (Vi); in a clerk's hand, signed and addressed by TJ to Harrison as Speaker. Endorsed: "Governors Letter enclosing Colonel Blands respecting the Indiana claim & the Navigation of the Mississipi. December 5th: 1780. to lie on table." Enclosure (Vi): Bland to TJ, 22 Nov. 1780, q.v.

From Linctot

MONSIEUR fort pitt le 5. Xbre. 1780

J'ai eu l'honneur d'ecrire a votre excelence depuis mon départ de Wiliamsburg pour L'informer quelles on été mes démarche a mon arivé au fort pitt, jeusse été bien flatté que son excelence eu voulu m'honnorer de quelque reponse, jeusse parla pu sçavoir si mes démarches lui étoit agréable.

A mon arivé Monsieur le commandant de cette place m'a engagé a aller chez les loups pour sassurer deux. Je m'y suis rendu et en ai ramené peu de tems apres une party des chefs qui on donné toutes les assurances que lon pouvoit desirer comme quoi il n'iroit point en guerre. Je suis reparty peu de tems après avec les mêmes chefs pour de leurs villages me rendre chez les chawanon pour tacher d'y faire la paix, je n'ai pu reussir ayant appris dans mon voyage que le colonel Clark étoit en route avec un parti pour aller défaire leur villages. Voyant qu'il m'étoit impossible de rien faire avec cette nations je me suis déterminé à passer l'hêté avec les loups que j'ai empêché d'aller en guerre, et les ai au contraire déterminé a envoyer un parti contre nos enemis, qui vient de partir depuis mon retour au fort pitt.

Je vien d'apprendre qu'il y avoit quelque trouble aux illinois avec les nations, je part sur le champ pour tacher de les appaiser, jespere que votre excelence voudra bien me faire l'honneur de m'y envoyer ses ordres.

J'ai l'honneur d'être avec respect De votre excelence Le très humble et très obéissant serviteur, G.F. LINCTOT

RC (Vi); addressed: "A Son excelence Monsieur Gefferson gouverneur des états de virginie A richemond"; endorsed: "Majr Lintots Lr. Feby 81."

No earlier letter from Linctot to TJ has been found; see, however, TJ's Commission to Linctot as Indian agent, 17 Feb. 1780, and TJ's reply to the present letter, 13 Feb. 1781.

From John Taylor

HONOURABLE SIR Lancaster County December 5th 1780

It gives me great uneasyness that the Militia of this County By their riotous behavour have prevented my making a proper return to you. On the day appointed for the Draft they assembled in a Mob, and disarm'd the Officers as they came to the field, and took from me the papers relative to the draft which prevented my carrying it on. I had a Court Martial held according to Law, and many were condemn'd, but it has not been in my power to have them taken except a few who have since made their escape from the Guard. There were also four Desertors taken which likewise made their escape except one, which you will Observe by the inclosed was taken from John Christopher (who was ordered to Carry them to Richmond) by Capt. M. Heely. I have since endeavoured to have them retaken without effect which has prevented my making a return sooner. I have inclosed a reciept for two who enlisted Volenterily, likewise for three British prisoners taken in a Vessel by a part of the Militia of this County, Also a return of the Militia after deducting those who were deem'd rioters. I shall still endeavour to have them taken, but if your excellency should think proper to order a party of light horse they may with greater certainty be conveid to the place of Randezvous.

I am Your Excellencies Most Obt. Servt.,

JOHN TAYLOR C.L.L.

NB

I have also enclosed sixteen Tobacco certificates which is the Ballance received. JT

RC (Vi); addressed to TJ as governor; endorsed: "Jno Taylors Lr. Jany 81." Enclosures not found. The writer is not to be confused with John Taylor of Caroline. C.L.L.: County Lieutenant of Lancaster.

From the Continental Board of War

SIR War Office Decr. 6. 1780

The Board have recieved a Letter from Col. Rawlins Commissary of Prisoners at Fort Frederick in Maryland informing of the Approach of the first Division of the Convention Troops towards that Post. We have given Directions to Major Foresythe to superintend the Supplies of all these Troops as well those at their former Station as those at Fort Frederic. We propose that one half of the Supplies for the Prisoners at Fort Frederick shall be drawn from Virginia and the other half from Maryland and in Consequence requested the Government of that State to furnish to the Order of Major Foresythe their Share of the Supplies; and we are to request your Excellency and the Honorable Council, that you will be pleased to issue Orders to the Purchasers of the State of Virginia in those Parts of the State convenient for the Supply of Fort Frederick that they forthwith furnish on the Requisitions of Major Foresythe such Quantities of Provisions for the Supply of the Prisoners of War at

Fort Frederick as he shall from time to Time call for on Behalf of the United States to whom the Provisions so called for are to be charged in Part of the Quota required by Congress of the State of Virginia. As the United States have no Mode of supporting these Prisoners but from the State Supplies we entreat your Excellency to give the most pressing Directions to the Purchasers to procure an immediate Supply.

We have the H[onor] to be with the highest Respect Your very obed Servts,

R[ICHAR]D P[ETERS]
By [order]

RC (Vi); addressed: "On public Service. His Excellency Thos Jefferson Esqr Govr. of Virginia Richmond (War Office)." Endorsed: "Contl Board of War's Lr. Decr. 80."

Richard Peters was at this time the only consistently active member of the Continental Board of War. In a letter to Timothy Pickering dated 17 Sep. 1823, concerning the activities of the Board, he wrote: "After you left me [*i.e., after Pickering became quartermaster general, 5 Aug. 1780*] the *Board*, very commonly consisted of *myself*, though occasionally others attended" (Octavius Pickering, *The Life of Timothy Pickering*, Boston, 1867, I, 229). See, further, letter of Robert Forsyth to the Agent Superintending the State Supplies of Virginia, following; also TJ's letters to Huntington and others on the subject of supplying Fort Frederick, 15 Jan. 1781.

Robert Forsyth to the Agent Superintending the State Supplies

Philadelphia, 6 Dec. 1780. Announces that, by the new arrangement of the purchasing department, "there is only a Commissary General and one Deputy Commissary General continued in the service of the United States; the former for the Northern and the latter for the Sothern Army." The duties hitherto performed by the purchasing commissaries employed by Forsyth in Virginia "are in future to be performed by the Storekeepers apointed by the Deputy Quarter Master General." The Convention troops at Fort Frederick in Maryland are to be subsisted equally by Virginia and Maryland; 1,100 will be there shortly, and they will require from Virginia during the present and each following months 37,500 lb. of beef, 30,000 lb. of flour or sifted Indian meal in proportion, also a proportion of rum, salt, peas, &c. Salted beef and a supply of flour must be laid by now for the months of April-June. All provisions are to be delivered to Col. Rawlins [Moses Rawlings] at Fort Frederick. Measures must also be taken at once to provide a magazine of provisions for the Convention troops left at Charlottesville. Forsyth desires an early answer informing him "of your prospects in not only furnishing the Convention Troops; but in complying with the Requisitions of the Honorable Congress—likewise of your place of Residence." He leaves Philadelphia in eight days for Fredericksburg.

RC (Vi); 5 p.; signed "Robt. Forsyth D.C. [Deputy Commissary] Purchases Sothern Army"; addressed "To the Agent," &c., as in caption; endorsed: "Robt Forsythes Lr. Decr. 80." The endorsement is in the hand of the clerk who endorsed many of the letters received at this time, and the cover bears this further note which suggests that the letter came to TJ: "Mr. Southall is requested to forward this Lre. without delay to the principal State Agent. Should there be no such apointment he will please deliver it to His Excellency the Governor. R. Forsyth."

See Continental Board of War to TJ, preceding; also TJ to Huntington, 15 Jan. 1781.

From Nathanael Greene

SIR Charlotte, December 6, 1780.

I arrived at this place on the 2d instant, to which place General Gates had advanced with the army some days before I overtook him.

I find the troops under his command in a wretched condition, destitute of anything necessary either to the comfort or convenience of soldiers. It is impossible that men can render any service, if they are ever so well disposed, whilst they are starving with cold and hunger. Your troops may literally be said to be naked, and I shall be obliged to send a considerable number of them away into some secure place and warm quarters, until they can be furnished with clothing. It will answer no good purpose to send men here in such a condition, for they are nothing but added weight upon the army and altogether incapable of aiding in its operations. There must be either pride or principle to make a soldier. No man will think himself bound to fight the battles of a State that leaves him to perish for want of covering; nor can you inspire a soldier with the sentiment of pride whilst his situation renders him more an object of pity than envy. The life of a soldier in its best state is subject to innumerable hardships, but where they are aggravated by a want of provision and clothing his condition becomes intolerable, nor can men long contend with such complicated difficulties and distress,—deaths, desertion, and the hospital must soon swallow up an army under such circumstances, and were it possible for them to maintain such a wretched existence, they could have no spirit to face their enemies, and would inevitably disgrace themselves and him who commanded them. It is impracticable to preserve discipline when troops are in want of everything, and to attempt severity will only thin the ranks by a more hasty desertion. The article of clothing is but a small part of the expense in raising, equipping, and subsisting an army, and yet on this alone the whole benefit of their service depends. I wish the State to view this matter in its true point of light; some may think it is urged for the sake of military parade, but be assured you raise men in vain unless you clothe, arm, and equip them properly for the field. I should not dwell upon this subject did I not foresee the misfortune that must follow the neglect of it. The States may seem to derive a credit from having numbers in the field, however wretched their condition, but a general with such troops can give no protection to a country. This policy may serve to disgrace an officer, but can never promote the public interest. I see by the Charleston papers, a large reinforcement is coming from New York, and part of it has already arrived. There can be no doubt but that Lord Cornwallis will push his operations this winter, and the utmost exertion on the part of the States is necessary to counteract him. I hope your Excellency, therefore, will press the Assembly to give the most speedy and effectual support to this army. We have no magazines of provisions in this State, but depend upon daily collections for support, and the State has been so ravaged by the numerous militia that have been in the field, that it is a doubt with me whether with the greatest industry and best disposition, any considerable magazines can be formed. I have parties now exploring the rivers Dan, Yadkin, and Catawba, and am not without hopes of finding them navigable with batteaux, which will enable us to transport from the Roanoke to this place, and even within thirty miles of Charleston, with only fifty or sixty miles land transportation. If this plan succeeds, I am in great hopes of receiving very considerable supplies from Virginia, but without it little is to be expected, so great is the distance and so heavy the business of land transportation. This State, from the difficulty of subsisting the regular troops, have postponed calling out their militia until a more pressing moment. This must convince your Excellency of the necessity of sending only such troops here as are fit for actual duty, as all others will rather distress than promote the service. I inclose your Excellency an account of General Sumter's last affair with the enemy, and Colonel Washington's success, who by stratagem, took Colonel Rugely and his party. I hope these little flashes of success will not relax the exertions of the State to give us support. I have appointed Lieutenant-colonel Carrington, Deputy Quartermaster-general for the southern army, and must beg your Excellency to give him all the aid and assistance from your State which the circumstances of the service may render it necessary to call upon you for, in the different duties of his department, as fully and amply as if I was to make the requisition myself. I have heard nothing respecting the enemy under General Leslie since I left Petersburg, at which place I heard they had returned and landed again at Portsmouth.

MS not located. Text from George Washington Greene, *Life of Nathanael Greene*, N.Y., 1867-1871, III, 553-5. Enclosures not found.

Greene's appointment of Edward CARRINGTON, with his orders to him dated 4 Dec. 1780, is printed in Greene's *Greene*, III, 73-5.

To Steuben

SIR In Council Dec. 6. 1780.

I have the pleasure of inclosing to you an order for the Shoes, Shirts and Cloth you desired. Mr. Armistead the Commissary of Stores to whom it is directed and who now waits on you, sais he has not that number of Shoes, but will call on the Continental Q.M. in hopes he may have some which are of course subject to your order. He has no white cloth but will if it be possible in our circumstances procure it. I forgot the quantity you mentioned and have left it blank to be filled up by you. I also inclose the order for the waggons and a warrant for the money you desired which I have some hopes can be paid by tomorrow, but it should be presented immediately. Mr. Armistead will give you the information I mentioned as to the Issues of cloathing which have been made to our officers.

I have the honor to be with the greatest Respect Sir Yr. mo. obedt. & mo. hble Servant, TH: JEFFERSON

RC (NHi); in a clerk's hand, signed and addressed by TJ: "The honble. Majr. Genl. Baron Steuben"; endorsed. Enclosure not found.

From Meshech Weare

Hampton Falls [*N.H.*], *6 Dec. 1780.* Acknowledges TJ's letter of 27 Sep. accompanying "Copies of the Acts of the Virginia Assembly from the beginning of the year 1779. . . . I have now the Pleasure of transmitting to your Excellency Copies of the Acts passed in New Hampshire Since our first taking up of Government In the year 1776." Wishes these exchanges to be continued.

Dft (MHi: Misc.); 1 p.; unsigned; endorsed: "copy of a letter to Gov. Jefferson." Enclosures not located.

TJ's letter of 27 Sep. 1780 to Gov. Weare of New Hampshire has not been found, but see under that date for the text of a circular letter presumably sent to all the governors.

From James Maxwell

SIR — Navy Office Decr: 7th: 1780

I am to inform Your Excellency that the Lieutenant of the Jefferson thinks it will take Fourteen thousand pounds to pay her up to the present time. And there is also due the Workmen of the Ship Yard on the last of October (by Warrants on the Treasury) for Eighteen thousand six hundred and Seventy nine pounds fourteen Shillings and six pence. I am with great Respect Sir Your Excellencyes Most Obdt Servt,

JAS: MAXWELL

	£	s	d	
Brig Jefferson	14000	0	0	
Ship Yard the last day of Octr.	18679	14	10	
	£32679	14	10	Currt: Money
	544	13	0[1]	Hard Money

Clothing wanted:

26 Men	52 Shirts
	26 Jackets
	26 Breeches
	26 ℔ Stockings
55 Men being all the Sailors	55 ℔ Shoes
	55 ℔ Hats or Caps

RC (Vi); addressed and endorsed. There is a minute concerning this letter in the Journal of the Commissioner of the Navy (Vi), under this date, with the following notation: "vid. Let: Book. pag. 24." This letter book, to which reference is made throughout the Journal, is not known to be extant.

A minute in the Journal of the Commissioner under 8 Dec. orders the commissary of stores to deliver to the lieutenant of the *Jefferson* the clothing requested, but only 29 pairs of shoes and no hats or caps are included in the list. The order was signed by Maxwell and "Countersigned by the Governor." See also James Maxwell to TJ, and TJ to James Maxwell, both 11 Dec., below.

[1] This figure is in part illegible, and the reading may not be correct.

Virginia General Court: Certificates of Escheated Property

I do hereby certify that the Inquisitions taken in the County of Lunenburg against John Patterson, Andrew Johnston, John Graham, and Messrs. Cunningham & Company have been in the

Office of the Clerk of the General Court one Month without a Claim being made to any of the Estate[s] contained in the said Inquisitions. Given under my Hand this seventh Day of December 1780.

ADAM CRAIG. Dep. Clk. G.C.

MS (Vi); endorsed: "Certificate of Escheated Property in Lunenburg. For the Governor." In Vi also are two other certificates of same date, signed by Craig and identical in form but applying to inquisitions against the estates of William Campbell, Northumberland co., and Archibald Govan, King William co.

For the significance of these documents issued by the clerk of the general court, see Bill concerning Escheats and Forfeitures from British Subjects, printed above under date of 4 June 1779; also Hening, x, 67.

To Benjamin Harrison

[*Richmond, 8? Dec. 1780.* JHD, Oct. 1780, 1827 edn., p. 41 (8 Dec.): "The Speaker laid before the House, a letter from the Governor, enclosing returns of the provisions obtained under the acts of the last session of Assembly; and the same were read, and ordered to lie on the table." Neither letter nor enclosure has been found.]

George Muter to Charles Magill

SIR War Office December 8th. [1780]

I am honoured with an answer from [his] Excellency the Governor, to my letter to him wishing for [orders] with respect to the intentions of the supreme Executive concerning the troops under your command. It is as f[ollows:]

It is the opinion of the Board, that the men u[nder] Major Magill should return to their stations at which they were before the Invasion; unless it be so far as Colo. Muter may think proper to change them.

The Jail being full of Prisoners, some of them condemned Criminals to be executed shortly, I must request your affording the Jailer such a Guard as may be amply sufficient for his assistance in securing them. The Guard at the Magazeane I think insufficient for its security, as the safety of the powder is a matter of the highest importance. I must therefore request such an Addition to that Guard, as will make it proper for a Commissioned Officer to command there, and that you will order a carefull officer on that duty.

I am Sir your mo. Obt. GEO. MUTER C:

FC (Vi).

From George Slaughter

SIR Louisville 8th. Decr. 1780.

Inclosed are Copies of letters from Capt. George the Commanding officer at Fort Jefferson and Capt. Williams from the same place to Colo. Clark, also an original letter sent by Capt. Helm, by which you will learn the situation of the Officers in that Quarter. Such a number of Officers leaving their Posts, and so many of the Men Deserting, together with the Conduct of the Commertial Agent and the scarcity of Provisions (the Crews of the Boats loaded therewith having deserted and Carry'd them off) that there is too much reason to fear that the Post will be evacuated. I have therefore taken the Liberty of ordering the remains of the Country Store together with a large Cargo which is now on its way from Orleans for the use of this State to be brought hither; these reasons will I hope Justify me, but when I inform Your Excellency of the number of Complaints against Capt. Dodge both from Officers and Men of the shameful Misapplication of the Goods in his care, and of the Abuses Commited by him in his Department, you will think it prudent to prevent this, as there is too much reason to believe he did the former Cargoes. My Men have never drawn any thing from the State but Cloth and thirty Blankets at Williamsburg are all the necessaries they have drawn since their Inlistment. They now [have] no Shirts, Hats, Blankets or Breeches, not having drawn Cloth for that purpose, Shoes, Stockings [or] Mocasons, so that they are totally unfit for duty. The Indians still are Troublesome to us having Visited us Four or five times since Colo. Clark left this place, and have killed and taken 5 or 6 Men and Wounded 3 others.

I am Sir Your humb Servant, GEORGE SLAUGHTER

Tr (WHi); at foot of text: "His Excellency Thos. Jefferson Governour of Virga. Copy"; Lyman C. Draper added an abstract of contents on cover. The enclosed letters or copies of letters from Capt. Robert George, Capt. John Williams, and Capt. Leonard Helm (or Helms) to George Rogers Clark have not been located.

There is a biographical sketch of George Slaughter, Kentucky frontiersman, in Wis. Hist. Soc., *Colls.*, XXIV, 179, note.

To Steuben

SIR In Council Dec. 8. 1780.

The inclosed is a Copy of a requisition I have received this morning from Lt. Colo. Lee. With respect to cloathing for so many of his Legion as were raised in other States and consequently not credited to us in our Continental quota we do not conceive the call on us to be proper; as it is totally unprecedented for the troops of one State to be clothed by another, nor does our condition or prospect enable us to comply with it on the more enlarged principle of general good. With respect to those of the legion enlisted in this State and credited as part of its quota we consider ourselves as bound to use our best endeavors to procure them cloathing. You are so perfectly acquainted with our Condition and prospects, with the particular Corps of Continental troops belonging to this State, with the expediency of cloathing this or that Corps first, that, with your leave, we mean to submit what ever clothing we can get to your order altogether. We expect to receive the Cloathing from Winchester within about a fortnight. It is said (I know not how truly) that there is cloth enough there to cloath 500 men. The State bounty due to Colo. Lees recruits we shall pay within a few days. As to the other articles contained in his requisition, being myself not perfectly acquainted with the Continental regulations, give me leave to ask from you information whether, as you command here for the Continent, and remain for the special purpose of seeing the reinforcements equipped and sent forward, your sanction may not be proper and necessary to justify any loans or advances we may make to the Continent of Articles which we are not Specifically bound to provide. As Colo. Lee I suppose would wish all possible dispatch so far as depends on us, I ask the favor of you to honor me with your Sentiments as soon as convenient.

I have the honor to be with very great respect and esteem Sir Your most obedient & Most hble. Servant, TH: JEFFERSON

RC (NHi); in a clerk's hand, corrected, signed, and addressed by TJ; endorsed. Enclosure not located.

From Steuben

SIR Richmond 8 Decr. 1780

I am this moment favord with your Excellencys Letter of this morning inclosing a Copy of the requisition made by Lt. Colo. Lee for the Corps under his command.

I am perfectly of Opinion with your Excellency that the call on this State for the several Articles he demands is improper on any other principle than that of the general good. In the new Establishment of the Army this Corps is certainly not considered as part of the Quota of this State, whatever therefore is furnishd will be considerd as a Loan to the Continent and for which I shall on their behalf be answerable and as the service of this Corps to the southward may be important I have no doubt by [but] the state will do all in their power towards Equipping them as speedily as possible.

Our present Circumstance absolutely require that we should ask only such things as cannot be dispensd with, on this subject I wish to speak with Lt. Colo. Lee and will then have the honor of acquainting your Excellency more fully with my Sentiments on this matter.

Dft (NHi); endorsed: "Copy to Govr Jefferson 8 Decr."

From George Washington

SIR New Windsor 8th. Decr. 1780

I have the honor of introducing to your Excellency the Marq[uis] de la Fayette, Majr. General in our army and an officer of Rank in those of France. This Gentlemans character, illustrious birth and fortune, cannot be unknown to you, though you may be unacquainted with his person. I should be wanting in that justice which is due to his great merit, to his early attachment to the American Cause, and to his powerful support of it here and at the Court of Versailles; was I to permit him to depart for the Southern Army without this testimony of the sense I entertain of his worth, and recommendation of him to your attention.

He will, probably, be accompanied by his Brother in law the Viscount de Noailles, and Count Damas; Gentleman of Family, Fortune and Rank in the French Army at Rhode Island, whose Zeal to serve America has prompted them to make a Winters Campaign to the Southward if permission can be obtained from the Count de Rochambeau to be absent from their respective Commands so long.

With much esteem & respt. I have the honr. to be Yr. Excellency's Most Obedt. Hble Ser[vt], GO: WASHINGTON

RC (DLC). In DLC: Washington Papers is a draft letter in Washington's hand endorsed by him: "Substance of the Letters of introduction in favor of the Marqs. De la Fayette 8th. Decr. 1780 To sundry Gentlemen in Virginia"; this draft is printed in Washington's *Writings*, ed. Fitzpatrick, xx, 440.

This letter was not sent until 20 Mch. 1781, when Lafayette enclosed it in his letter to TJ of that date, with the explanation that "Some Month Ago, Sir, when I intended a journey to the Southward, I was Honored with A Letter of introduction to Your Excellency from General Washington." As things turned out, Lafayette did not go to Virginia until Mch. 1781, when he was sent by Washington in command of a land force that was to cooperate with a French naval squadron in an attempt to destroy the British army encamped at Portsmouth and to capture its commander, Benedict Arnold; see letters from Lafayette and from Washington to TJ, both dated 21 Feb. 1781.

To Henry Lee

SIR Richmond Dec: 9. 1780.

Baron Steuben has just favored me with a State of what is essential for your Corps. I am sincerely sorry it is in our power to comply with so little of it. I inclose you a warrant for £6000. which I fear however cannot be furnished till Thursday or Friday next, when any recruiting money *due* may be also paid. I shall be much obliged to you if you will be so good as to favor me with a return of the number of your Corps recruited in this State. The last return I have was from General Washington stating them at 52. but this was some time ago so that the number is probably reduced. As they are considered as part of our quota till the 1st of January next we will use our best endeavors to get clothing for them for this Winter: but [as] our prospects do not authorize us to say that this can be immediately done, it would be vain to give an order on our Commissary of Stores now which we know cannot be complied with. It seems properly within the line of the Continental Q.M. as we cannot furnish the other Articles from our Store, to purchase them. If you think proper to order him to do it, we will enable him to make paiment during the course of the next week. This letter will also authorize your exchanging your Swords for any we have in possession of any person which you may like better.

I have the honor to be with great respect Sir Your mo. ob. Hble Servant, TH: JEFFERSON

RC (NHi); in a clerk's hand, signed by TJ; endorsed: "Governor Jefferson Decr. 9. 1780 to Colo Lee." Enclosure not located.

From John Page

MY DEAR JEFFERSON Rosewell Decr. the 9th. 1780.

Yours in which you desire a Copy of the List of Tithe's, and of my Journal of the Weather, came through such a circuitous Chanel that it was long after the Date of it before it reached me. As to the List I gave it in to the Society without taking a Copy of it, and suppose it is now in the Hands of the Secretary. My Meteorological

Journal I took back, as I did all the Papers of my own Compositions which I had given in, finding that no one had any Inclination to attend to them. The Journal was in a mutilated State when I found it among the Society's Papers. If ever I have Leasure I will collect from it what may be worth your Acceptance. The Journals I have kept during the War are not much [to] be relied on, as I have not been able to pay that [atten]tion to many Circumstances of the Winds and Weather which [are required?] of [an ac]curate and faithful Journalist. As to the Ombrometrical [observa]tions I have relied altogether, since the Commencement of the War, on Mr. Jameson, whose Fidelity and Accuracy before the War I had experienced, and who I knew had continued his Observations from the Time I discontinued mine to the last Day we were together in Wmsburg. I therefore recommend it to you to apply to him for a Copy of his Journal. I shall be happy if you will make good your Threats, I mean of being very troublesome to me in this Way: but it gives me no small Uneasiness to find, from Reports and those confirmed by some Passages in one of Your Letters, that I am not likely to receive those agreable Tasks from you unless your Country loses the Benefit of your Services in the Office you now hold. I know your Love of Study and Retirement must strongly solicit you to leave the Hurry, Bustle, and Nonsense your station daily exposes you to. I know too the many Mortifications you must meet with, but 18 Months will s[oon] pass away. Deny yourself your darling Pleasures for th[at] Space of Time, and despise not only now, but forever, the Impertinence of the silly World. All who know y[ou] know how eminently qualified you are to fill the s[tation?] you hold, and that Circumstances may happen within the Compass of the Time above alluded to, which may requ[ire] the Exertions of greater Abilities than can be fou[nd in] any other Person within this State. I know not who besides yourself, and R. H. L.—and he I suppose is too unpopular to be thought of—we have, can possibly with tole[rable] Reputation to the State manage the important [. . .] which may occur. This I can tell you with [candor?] is the Opinion of others as well as of myself. As [for me,] if my Abilities were ever so well suited to that arduo[us . . .] the Duty I owe my large Family and the Situation of m[y] Affairs would forbid my undertaking it, especially as I [every?] Day find I can be of more service even to the publ[ic] whilst at Home than any where else. Let me D[ear] Jefferson conjure you not to think of resigning. Go on serve out the Time allowed by the Constituti[on.] Present our

Compts. and best Wishes to Mrs. Jefferson and believe me to be with Sincerity your Friend and most obedt. JOHN PAGE

RC (DLC); MS mutilated.

TJ's letter to which this is a reply is unfortunately missing; it contained requests for data which TJ doubtless wished to include in his answers to Marbois' Queries, q.v., under date of 30 Nov. 1780. THE SOCIETY: Probably the Virginia Society for Advancing Useful Knowledge, organized in 1773, of which Page was charter vice-president and David JAMESON was charter treasurer (*Va. Gaz.* [P & D], 13 May 1773). THE TIME ALLOWED BY THE CONSTITUTION: Page's reference above to "18 Months" indicates that he thought TJ's term was at mid-point and would end in June 1782, three years from his first election to office. Actually, the Constitution of 1776 provided that the governor should be elected annually and stipulated that he should "not continue in office longer than three years successively, nor be eligible until the expiration of four years after he shall have been out of that office" (Hening, IX, 115).

From Steuben,

Enclosing Instructions for Drawing the Recruiting Bill

SIR 9th. Dec. [1780]

The Frequent abuses that have happened in the Recruiting Service, and an absolute Necessity that those Men who are raised for the War in Future should be fit for the Service and the Continent and State no longer deceived, by having Old Men, Deserters, &c &c, Imposed upon them; I have made the Within Instructions and beg Your Excellency to lay them before the Legislature that when they Pass the Recruiting Bill, they may be adopted.

I am with the Greatest Respect Your Excellency's Most Obedt hbl Serv, STEUBEN Maj: Genl.

ENCLOSURE

Necessary Arrangements to be made for the Reception of the Recruits

In the Bill for the raising the recruits it Should be Ordained: That no Recruits Should be received by the County Lieutenants, who is not under 50 Years of Age, of a good Constitution, perfect in all his Limbs, and five feet four Inches high, none of the Convention Troops, nor any Deserter or Prisoner whatever to be received.

The Lieutenant of the County to deliver the recruits at the Places of RendezVous prescribed by the Officers appointed to receive them.

Whenever the County Lieutenant Sends any Recruits, he must

Send with them a List of their Names, with a Description of their Persons &c. in the following form, Viz.

Names	Age	Size	Trade	County for which they are Sent	Place of Residence	time engaged for	date of Inlistmt	whether drafted or enlisted

It would not be amiss to add another Column of the money each Recruit has received, that in Case of Desertion it may be known what to recover, if the Deserter has any Estate.

These Lists Should be uniform and for that Purpose a Number Should be printed and delivered to the County Lieutenants.

The Officers appointed to receive the Recruits will be instructed not to receive any who do not answer the above Description, and Such as are refused will be Sent back at the Expence of the County who sent them.

On the Delivery of the Recruits, the Officer appointed to receive them will Examine and measure them in the presence of the Person by whom they are Sent and will give duplicate receipts for the Number he accepts, one of these Receipts to be sent to the Governor and Council as a Voucher for the Number delivered by the County.

Colo. Davies, who is appointed to receive the Recruits at the General RendezVous, must be informed of the Number each County and District is to furnish, that he may from Time to Time inform Government of the Progress that is made in furnishing the Quotas prescribed.

When any Recruits are Sent from the different places of RendezVous to Colo. Davies or from him to the respective Regiments, Lists must be delivered with them agreeable to the above form, and in Case of desertion, the Description of the Deserter must immediately be transmitted to Colo. Davies, and from him to the Governor who will transmit it to the Lieutenant of the County to which Such Deserter belongs that the Necessary measures may be taken for apprehending him.

RC (Vi); in a clerk's hand, signed by Steuben; addressed; endorsed: "Baron Steuben's petition Decr: 11th. 1780. Referred to Commttee of whole on the Recruit Bill." Enclosure, filed with letter in Vi, and printed herewith, in a different clerk's hand. TJ transmitted Steuben's letter and enclosure to Speaker Harrison on 11 Dec., q.v.

THE RECRUITING BILL: An Act for recruiting this state's quota to serve in the Continental army was passed by the House of Delegates on 21 Dec. (JHD, Oct. 1780, 1827 edn., p. 63); the Act is printed in Hening, x, 326-37 (see p. 331-2 for Hening's highly interesting note concerning the failure of officials to observe the bounty provisions laid down in the Act).

From George Washington

Headquarters, New Windsor [*N.Y.*], 9 Dec. 1780. Acknowledges letters of 3, 10, and 19 Nov.; is most grateful for intelligence contained in them and wishes to have more concerning the enemy's movements in the South. Disposition of the American forces in the middle department, of the French fleet and army (still at Rhode Island), and of the enemy's fleet and army in and around New York. "It is happy for us, that the season will probably compel both Armies to continue in a state of inactivity," since our levies have had to be discharged before their time of service expired on account of "the present total want of flour." "A Flag Vessel has permission to go from New York to the usual place in Virginia to carry supplies and necessaries for the Troops of Convention." A postscript states that TJ's letter of 26 Nov. has just been received. "I will endeavour to obtain a *Model* for the construction of Boats, and transmit it by an early conveyance. I am this Moment informed from New York, another embarkation is taking place consisting of 1 Batt. Grenadiers, 1 Batt. Light Infantry, 1 Batt. Hessian Grenadiers, Knyphausen's Regt., 42d British; a Draft of 5 Men from each Company in the Line and 2 Troops of Light Dragoons under Genls. Knyphausen and Philips, supposed to be destined Southward."

Dft (DLC: Washington Papers); 4 p.; in the hand of David Humphreys; endorsed.

From Steuben

SIR Petersburg 10 Decr 80.

I came here Yesterday in full Expectation of sending off Colo. Greens Detachment of 400 Men this Day and it is with great pain I have to inform Your Excellency that so far from being ready to March I am even fearfull they will not be able to March at all.

Amongst the 400 Men selected for this Detachment about 60 only had Blankets. The Militia I discharged left about 20 and of 200 which I expected from Gen. Lawson 82 only have been left here and these of a very indifferent Quality so that in all the Detachment has only 160 Blankets. I have done every thing in my power to procure them here but can find only none in Town. Cloth may be had sufficient for 57 the cost of which will be 20,000 tobacco. I would have taken this but even then one half only of the Detachment would be provided.

Such is my Situation. To March the Detachment illy provided with Cloathing as this and without Blankets is improper and if your Excellency cannot point out some means of their being Supplied I see nothing left but to postpone the March and order the Men to Chesterfd. I wait your Excellency's determination & am.

FC (NHi); endorsed.

COLO. GREEN: Probably John Green, col., 6th Va. Continental Line (Gwathmey, *Hist. Reg. of Virginians in the Revolution*); see also Steuben to TJ, 15 Dec. 1780.

From the Virginia Delegates in Congress

Philadelphia, [*ca. 10*] *Dec. 1780.* Enclosing a resolution of Congress of 6 Dec. relating to the Convention troops and also "a copy of a letter from G. Anderson found among the dead letters in the post office and communicated to Congress by the Postmaster. If there should be occasion for the original of the latter it shall be transmitted on the first intimation." Imprisonment of Henry Laurens in the Tower is reported in an Irish newspaper. A letter from Jonathan Williams at Nantes, 17 Oct., "confirms an account received several days ago, of the Ariel commanded by P. Jones Esqr. and containing cloathing &c. for the Army being dismasted and obliged to return into port." Williams also reports that Portugal "has at length yielded to the solicitations of the Neutral Powers and to the remonstrances of France and Spain" by excluding English vessels of war from the privileges they formerly enjoyed in Portuguese ports. "We have received Payment of the Bill drawn by Mr. Benjn. Harrison."

RC (Vi); 2 p.; in Madison's hand and signed by him and Theodorick Bland; body of letter printed in full in Burnett, *Letters of Members*, v, No. 541. Enclosures: (1) attested copy (Vi, where there is also a duplicate, enclosed in letter from the Continental Board of War to TJ, 11 Dec.) of Congress' resolve of 6 Dec. ordering "That such of the Convention troops as are not already removed from the barracks near Charlottesville remain at that post until the further order of Congress"; (2) copy (missing) of a letter from G. Anderson to a Captain Trot (or Trott) concerning an attempt to ship corn from Virginia to Bermuda; see TJ to the Virginia Delegates in Congress, 15 Jan. 1781, answering the present letter, and the Delegates' answer in turn, 30 Jan. 1781.

TJ transmitted Congress' resolution concerning the Convention troops to Speaker Harrison, 29 Dec. 1780, q.v.

From George Washington

Headquarters, New Windsor [*N.Y.*], *10 Dec. 1780.* The places of deposit for the specific supplies required of Virginia by Congress' resolve of 4 Nov. are to be designated by Gen. Greene "or Officer commanding" in the southern department, who will be "much better enabled to judge of the proper places" than Washington.

RC (Vi); 1 p.; in Tench Tilghman's hand, signed by Washington; printed in Washington, *Writings*, ed. Fitzpatrick, xx, 450, from Dft (DLC: Washington Papers, which bears following note at foot of text: "To the Governors of Virginia & North Carolina. Information given of an embarkation getting in readiness to sail from N York."

For Congress' resolve of 4 Nov. making requisitions of supplies on the states, see Huntington to TJ, 9 Nov. 1780, and enclosure. See also Washington's circular to the states other than Virginia and North Carolina, this date (*Writings*, ed. Fitzpatrick, xx, 450-1).

From the Continental Board of War

War Office [*Philadelphia*], *11 Dec. 1780.* Enclosing a resolution of Congress of 6 Dec. respecting the Convention troops; the Board will be pleased to have TJ take order thereon.

RC (PHi); 2 p.; signed "by ord. Ben Stoddert Secy."; addressed: "(Public) His Excellency Thos. Jefferson Esqr. Govr. of Virginia (War Office)"; endorsed: "Contl. Board War Lr. Recd Feby 81." For the resolution enclosed, see Virginia Delegates in Congress to TJ, printed under 10 Dec. 1780.

To Benjamin Harrison

SIR In Council December 11. 1780

At the request of Major General Baron de Steuben, I take the liberty of transmitting to you his Letter and observations on the cautions he thinks necessary to be observed on the raising future recruits. I think it my duty also to mention to the General Assembly that I have received information from him that a very considerable proportion of the new Levies raised under an act of the last session of Assembly and now at Chesterfield are totally unfit for service, where much fatigue and hardship is to be endured, being old men, boys or decrepid: and for this reason he means to decline continuing them in Continental service and to return them to the State.

Supposing that every intelligence which may tend to discover to the General Assembly the future determination of our enemies as to the conduct of the war against us may be acceptable, I beg leave to communicate to them the inclosed extract of a Letter I have received from William Lee esquire. It will be a very happy circumstance if the force intended to oppose their armies in the south can be brought into the field in time to find them embarrassed and retarded with the difficulties of subsistance and transportation thro the inland country. Once advanced to a navigable water their communications by sea will relieve them from much incumbrance and in a great measure ensure them from capital disaster. The proposals herewith transmitted for raising a standing body of forces for the defence of this state, requiring conditions beyond the powers of the Executive I beg leave to submit them to the wisdom of the General Assembly.

I have the honor to be with the highest esteem and respect sir Your most obedient and most hble servant, TH: JEFFERSON

RC (Vi); in a clerk's hand, corrected, signed, and addressed by TJ to Harrison as Speaker; endorsed: "Governors L[ette]r December 11th: 1780. Enclosing Baron Steuben's respecting the Recruiting Service And a Letter from Mr: Wm: Lee. to lie on table." Enclosures: (1) Steuben to TJ, 9 Dec., and enclosure, printed above under date; (2) extract (filed with the present letter in Vi) of William Lee's letter to TJ, 21 July 1780, printed in full above under date.

From James Maxwell

[*Richmond, 11 Dec. 1780.* A minute in the Journal of the Commissioner of the Navy (Vi), under this date reads: "Letter to the Governor on the Subject of ordering down the Jefferson to Hampton Road, and procuring money to pay the crew." Not located, but see TJ's reply, following, and Maxwell to TJ, 7 Dec., above.]

To James Maxwell

[11 December 1780]

Money to pay off the Men of the Brig will be ready Friday Evening or Saturday Morning which may be dispatched to them by Express. In the mean time they may be informed of this, and the Brig ordered to be in readiness to proceed down as within proposed Instructions should be given to the Officer commanding on the Cruise to make particular Enquiry whether any persons he may take come within the description of Pirates, and if they do, that he make report thereof on his return into port, where the Commodore should proceed to hold a Court Martial on them, and make report to the Executive keeping the Party in the mean time securely confined.

Tr (abstract?) in Journal of the Commissioner of the Navy (Vi). The "proposed Instructions," enclosed, have not been identified.

Under date of 13 Dec. there is another minute in the Navy Commissioner's Journal: "Letter written to the Commodore informing him that the Executive have ordered the Jefferson down to Hampton Road countersigned the Governor."

From William Shannon

Louisville, 11 Dec. 1780. Desires "to know the nature of my Commission from Colo. G. Rogers Clarke on my return from Government last Spring, and must inform you that it is very difficult to execute the business I am entrusted with for want of money owing to a report prevalent that our Bills on the Treasurer have been Protested which renders the Credit of the State very Trifling." The army in this quarter is destitute; only beef, corn, and salt are to be had, and these at extravagant prices. Encloses statement of bills drawn on the treasurer during spring and summer; further money is wanting to discharge the present contracts and "to pay the expences of the late expedition." Has supplied Maj. Slaughter's troops and will continue to do so until further orders. There are reports that the destitute condition of the force at the mouth of the river [Ohio] has caused much desertion. From [New] Orleans come reports that the Spanish have not taken Pensacola because of a quarrel between Governor Galvis [Galvez] and the Spanish admiral over the command; their land forces are now at Mobile. "I expect Boats down the River dayly and intend purchasing Flour for the Troops at Fort Jefferson; Corn and Salt have sent. Shall continue to draw bills for provisions till ordered to the contrary." Urgently desires instructions.

RC (Vi); 2 p.; addressed: "His Excellency the Governor of Virginia. Favor'd by Mr John Phillips"; endorsed (in two different hands): "Wm Shannon's Letter recd Jany 81 Respecting the furnishing provisions at Louisville." Printed in *George Rogers Clark Papers, 1771-1781*, p. 473-4.

TJ had authorized Clark to commission Shannon as commissary of stores or quartermaster for the western posts early in 1780 (TJ to Clark, 29 Jan. 1780).

From the Continental Board of War

War Office [*Philadelphia*], *12 Dec. 1780.* Case of 1st Lt. Thomas Warner, formerly of the 7th Va. Continental Line, for whom no vacancy is now available in the Virginia Line, though it has been recommended and agreed that "in all Cases where the Places of Prisoners were filled by junior Officers they should retire on the Officers Exchange whose places they filled." This information is submitted to the governor so that he may "form some Rule which will comprehend this Case as well as those of many others of the Virginia Line under similar Circumstances. . . . It need not be mentioned that Lieut. Warner is exchanged and applies for his Rank, which we presume lies entirely with the State to determine."

RC (PHi); 3 p.; in Richard Peters' hand and signed by him "In Behalf of the Board." Addressed: "(On Public service) His Excellency Thomas Jefferson Esqr: Governor of Virginia. (War Office)." Endorsed.

From John Floyd

SIR Jefferson Decr. 12th 1780.

As the division of the County has put a stop to the Surveying business till the Surveyors can be again Commissioned and qualified, and as there are not a sufficient number of Magistrates in the County to hold a Court, a majority of those in the Commission of the Peace being Inhabitants of other Counties, I beg leave to recommend to your Excellency a few Persons to be put into the Commission in order to enable me to proceed upon this important business. Messrs. Richard and Wm. May have long been acting Magistrates in Kentucky, are about settling in this County and intend to continue there. Colo. George Slaughter, Mr. George May, Mr. Wm. Oldham and Mr. James Francis Moore are also settled here and would be proper Persons to be added to the Commission: With the addition of these we should be able to proceed upon Businees and cou'd then make further recommendations if Necessary.

The person appointed Major of the Militia in this County I dont expect will serve, and as the keeping the Militia compleatly Officered is a matter of consequence, I beg your Excellency to send a blank Majors Commission to be filled up upon the Courts Recommendation. And if the blank Commissions are not already sent please to order them together with those before mentioned. And a blank Escheaters Commission to be delivered to Mr. Clough Overton who waits on you for the Surveyors Commissions.

I am Sir your most obdt. hble Servt., JNO FLOYD

RC (Vi); endorsed: "May & Floyds Lr. recd Jany 81"; see Richard and William May's letter to TJ, 13 Dec. 1780.

A biographical sketch of John Floyd (ca. 1750-1783) appears in Collins, *History of Kentucky*, 1877, p. 238-9; he had been a deputy surveyor of Fincastle co. under William Preston and an agent of Richard Henderson & Co.; a companion of Boone and George Rogers Clark, he was eventually killed in an Indian ambuscade; Floyd co., Ky., was named for him, and his son John became governor of that state. THE DIVISION OF THE COUNTY: By an Act passed 30 June 1780, Kentucky co. was divided into three counties which were given the names Jefferson, Fayette, and Lincoln; Jefferson co. was the first of two counties in Virginia to be named for TJ; it is now in the state of Kentucky, and is not to be confused with present Jefferson co., Va., formed and named in honor of TJ when President, 1801 (Hening, X, 315-17; Morgan P. Robinson, "Virginia Counties," Va. State Libr., *Bull.*, IX [1916], *passim*).

From Joseph Martin

SIR Long Island the 12h Dcmer 1780

On my Return to this place I Immediately Transmitted your Excellencies Dispatches to Chiefs of the Cherokees which I Seconded with Some letters of my own and Divers private messages with the Meddles &c. but unfortunately all arrived to late. The British agents had Succeeded in their negociations, and most of their

Chiefs and Warriers of the old Towns had Determin'd To Take a Decisive part against us. The inclosed Deposition will further Explain Matters to the Executive.

Great will be the Distress of the frontier Inhabitants Soon if Something Vigorous are not Soon Set on foot to Subdue the nation.

I am sir your Excellenis most [. . .] & very humble Sert,

JOS MARTIN

RC (WHi). Addressee identified from internal evidence. Enclosure not found.

LONG ISLAND, whence this letter was sent, is in the Holston River in present Tennessee; Fort Patrick Henry had been established here, and here Martin had his headquarters as agent to the Cherokees (*Atlas of Amer. Hist.*, pl. 76, &c). TJ's DISPATCHES to the Cherokee chiefs have not been found. On the Indian MEDDLES (medals), see Robert Scot's Bill, printed under 13 Oct. 1780.

From George Muter

[Richmond, 12 December 1780]

A state of the situation of the tanyard, is left with me. It appears that things are in bad order there, but I know not how it is to be remedied. Neither do I know that I have any authority to act in it at all, farther than (perhaps) to originate orders for any articles that may be wanted, and can be furnished on such orders.

Permitt me to inform your Excellency, that several of the tradesmen in town are now idle, or nearly so, from want of materials. There is no nail rod on hand and little or no tin, in consequence of which the tinsman and all the nailers, will be unemployed, or (the nailers particularly) employed to very great disadvantage.

I must beg your Excellency's attention to the Foundery. The situation of affairs there is still very bad; far indeed! from what it ought to be. I am much at a loss to know the extent of my authority there; but at any rate, I cannot think it sufficient for the removal of a manager appointed by resolution of Assembly, or for making such alterations in the arangement there [which?] the present situation of things renders necessary

I am informed by Mr. Kemp that some militia that were lately quartered in the Capitol at Wmsburgh, have stripped the Cupola of it's lead, in consequence of which the clock stands quite exposed to the weather, and must soon be ruined. If it's preservation is wished for, Mr. Kemp wou'd be glad to receive orders concerning it.

I have the honor to be, Your Excellency's Most humble Servant,

GEORGE MUTER

RC (Vi); addressed: "His Excellency The Governour"; endorsed: "Colo. Muter Letter to the Govr. respecting the Tanyard at Warwick &c. & Govrs. answer Decr. 12th. 1780." Date supplied at head of letter is from endorsement; TJ's answer, written at foot of Muter's letter, is printed under 13 Dec. 1780.

From Richard and William May

Louisville, 13 Dec. 1780. Informing TJ that they have served as justices of the peace for Kentucky co. "almost ever since it was taken off Fincastle, but upon the late Division, [we] fall into that Part of the County which is now called Jefferson, where we have Land and intend to reside." It was therefore by mistake that the delegates for Kentucky co. put the Mays in the commission of the peace for Fayette co.; they now request that they be left out of that commission and be inserted in that for Jefferson co.

RC (Vi); 1 p.; signed by Richard May and William May; addressed and endorsed. THE LATE DIVISION: See John Floyd to TJ, 12 Dec. 1780.

To George Muter

In Council Dec. 13. 1780.

Capt. Thomas is informed by letter from me this day that he may be supplied with money the next week to put the affairs of the Tanyard into a proper state. Colo. Muter will be pleased to prepare proper requisitions on Mr. Armistead for nail rods and tin. The resolution of assembly of June 1. 80 seems to give an authority to the Executive which extends to the removal of a manager and making any necessary arrangements at the foundery, which authority they conceive (tho' the Governor and council alone are named in the resolution) to be exerciseable in the first instance by the Commissioner of the War office within whose department the foundery is. We think orders should be given to Mr. Kemp to secure the [. . .][1] clock and Cupola by stopping up the open part of the Cupola, or raising a roof over it's exposed floor, or such other measure as an intelligent workman shall think best. It must be made absolutely secure in some way or other.

TH: JEFFERSON

RC (Vi). Written at foot of Muter's letter to TJ of 12 Dec., q.v.

THE RESOLUTION OF ASSEMBLY OF JUNE 1 empowered the executive to examine the public foundry at Westham and to take such measures for regulating it as were necessary (JHD, May 1780, 1827 edn., p. 28). In the War Office Letter Book (Vi) there is a letter of 14 Dec. from Muter to James Kemp giving orders for the repairs to the cupola and adding: "I must request that you will have [the] determination of his Excellency in this matter carried [out as] quickly as possible."

[1] One word illegible; perhaps crossed out.

From the Virginia Delegates in Congress

SIR Philadelphia December 13th. 1780

The complexion of the intelligence received of late from Spain, with the manner of thinking which begins to prevail in Congress with regard to the claims to the navigation of the Mississippi, makes it our duty to apply to our constituents for their precise full and ultimate sense on this point. If Spain should make a relinquishment of the navigation of that river on the part of the United States an indispensable condition of an Alliance with them, and the State of Virginia should adhere to their former determination to insist on the right of navigation, their delegates ought to be so instructed not only for their own satisfaction, but that they may the more effectually obviate arguments drawn from a supposition that the change of circumstances which has taken place since the former instructions were given may have changed the opinion of Virginia with regard to the object of them. If on the other side any such change of opinion should have happened, and it is now the sense of the State that an Alliance with Spain ought to be purchased even at the price of such a cession if it cannot be obtained on better terms it is evidently necessary that we should be authorized to concur in it. It will also be expedient for the Legislature to instruct us in the most explicit terms whether any and what extent of territory on the East side of the Mississippi and within the limits of Virginia, is in any event to be yielded to Spain as the price of an Alliance with her. Lastly it is our earnest wish to know what steps it is the pleasure of our Constituents we should take in case we should be instructed in no event to concede the claims of Virginia either to territory or to the navigation of the abovementioned river and Congress should without their concurrence agree to such concession.

We have made use of the return of the Honble. Mr. Jones to N. Carolina to transmit this to your Excellency, and we request that you will immediately communicate it to the General Assembly.

We have the honor to be with the most perfect respect & esteem Yr. Excelly's Most obt. & humble servants,

JAMES MADISON Junr.
THEOK: BLAND

RC (CSmH); in Madison's hand, signed by both delegates. Tr (DLC: Madison Papers); certified by "Wm: Munford, Keeper of the Rolls," Richmond, 31 Aug. 1819; enclosed in cover addressed to Madison in Orange co., Va.

TJ transmitted the delegates' letter to Speaker Harrison on 25 Dec., and on 18 Jan. 1781 he replied to the delegates enclosing a resolution of the Assembly for their guidance on the subject of THE NAVIGATION OF THE MISSISSIPPI. See also Theodorick Bland to TJ, 22 Nov. 1780, and Burnett, *Letters of Members*, v, No. 543, note 2, on the problem of navigation rights and the alliance with Spain.

To George Washington

SIR Richmond December 13. 1780.

I had the honor of writing to your Excellency on the subject of an expedition contemplated by this State against the british post at Detroit and of receiving your answer of october 10th. Since the date of my Letter the face of things has so far changed as to leave it no longer optional in us to attempt or to decline the expedition, but compels us to decide in the affirmative and to begin our preparations immediately. The army the enemy at present have in the south, the reinforcements still expected there and their determination to direct their future exertions to that quarter are not unknown to you. The regular force proposed on our part to counteract those exertions is such either from the real or supposed inability of this State as by no means to allow a hope that it may be effectual. It is therefore to be expected that the scene of war will either be within our country or very nearly advanced to it; and that our principal dependance is to be on militia, for which reason it becomes incumbent to keep as great a proportion of our people as possible free to act in that quarter. In the mean time a combination is forming in the westward which if not diverted will call thither a principal and most valuable part of our militia. From intelligence received we have reason to expect that a confederacy of british and Indians to the amount of 2000 men is formed for the purpose of spreading destruction and dismay through the whole extent of our frontier in the ensuing Spring. Shoud this take place we shall certainly lose in the south all aids of militia from beyond the blue ridge besides the inhabitants who must fall a sacrifice in the course of the savage irruptions. There seems to be but one method of preventing this, which is to give the western enemy employment in their own country. The regular force Colo. Clarke already has with a proper draught from the militia beyond the Allegany and that of three or four of our most northern counties will be adequate to the reduction of fort Detroit in the opinion of Colo. Clarke, and he assigns the most probable reasons for that opinion. We have therefore determined to undertake, and to commit it to his direction. Whether the enterprize shall be at continental or State expence we will leave to be decided by Congress hereafter, in whose Justice we can confide as to the determination. In the mean time we only ask the loan of such necessaries as being already at fort Pitt will save time and an immense expence of transportation. These are

4 field peices 6 pounders
3000 balls suited to them
one Mortar
3000 shells suited to it.
2 howitzes
grape shot
necessary implements and furniture for the above.
1000 Spades
200 pick axes
1 travelling forge.
some boats ready made shoud we not have enough prepared in time.
some ship carpenters tools.

These articles shall be either identically or specifically returned. Should we prove successful it is not improbable they may be where Congress wou'd chuse to keep them. I am therefore to solicit your Excellency's order to the Commandant at Fort Pitt for the above articles which shall not be called for until every thing is in readiness, after which there can be no danger of their being wanted for the post at which they are. Inded there are few of the articles essential for the defence of the post. I hope your Excellency will think yourself justified in lending us this aid without awaiting the effect of an application elsewhere as such a delay woud render the undertaking abortive by postponing it to the breaking up of the ice in the lake. Independant of the favorable effects which a successfull enterprize against Detroit must produce to the United States in general by keeping in quiet the frontier of the northern ones, and leaving our western militia at leisure to aid those of the south, we think the like friendly office performed by us to the States whenever desired and almost to the absolute exhausture of our own magazines give well founded hopes that we may be accomodated on this occasion. The supplies of military stores which have been furnished by us to Fort Pitt itself, to the northern army, and most of all to the southern, are not altogether unknown to you. I am the more urgent for an immediate order because Colo. Clarke awaits here your Excellency's answer by the expresses, tho his presence in the western country to make preparations for the expedition, if you enable us to undertake it, is so very necessary. To the above I must add a request to you to send for us to Pittsburg persons proper to work the mortars and howitzes, as Colo. Clarke has none such, nor is there one in this state. They shall be in the pay of this State from the time they leave you. Any money necessary for their journey shall be repaid at pittsburg without fail by the 1st of march.

At the desire of the General Assembly I take the liberty of transmitting to you the inclosed resolution, and have the honor to be with the most perfect esteem & regard your Excellency's most obedient and most humble servant, TH: JEFFERSON

RC (DLC: Washington Papers); in a clerk's hand, signed by TJ; endorsed: "Richmond 13: Decemr. 1780 from Governor Jefferson. Expedition to D——— Ansd. 28." Tr (DLC). Enclosure (DLC: Washington Papers): attested copy of a resolve of the House of Delegates, 2 Dec. [misdated Nov.], agreed to by the Senate on 6 Dec., requesting the Commander in Chief "to settle the rank of the 1st: and 2d: Regiments of this State which have been attached to the Continental Army and if he shall be of Opinion that they are entitled to Continental Commissions to recommend them to Congress for that purpose ascertaining the time when such Commissions shall bear date and saying whether such officers shall take promotion in the line of this State or be confined to the said two Regiments"; Tr of this resolution is in DLC; it is printed in full in JHD, Oct. 1780, 1827 edn., p. 35; see Washington's reply, 28 Dec. 1780.

TJ's earlier letter to Washington proposing an EXPEDITION against DETROIT is dated 26 Sep.; see also Washington's reply of 10 Oct.; his reply to the present letter, 28 Dec.; TJ's instructions to the County Lieutenants, 24 Dec., and to George Rogers Clark, 25 Dec. 1780; also James, *G. R. Clark*, chap. XI, which recounts the failure of these carefully laid plans.

To Horatio Gates

[*14 Dec. 1780.* Epistolary Record: "Th: J. to Gl. Gates. merely friendly & private." Not located. Probably this letter expressed TJ's cordial feelings toward Gates at the time of the latter's quitting his command in the South.]

From Nathanael Greene

SIR Camp Charlotte Decem 14th 1780

Your Excellencys favor of the 26th I have had the honor to recieve but not till within a few days.

Lieut. Read who commands Major Nelsons corps of horse in the Majors absence; and who will have the honor to deliver this has orders to proceed to Virginia with his command: it being the opinion of Col. Washington that they are altogether unfit for further service until they are cloathed. General Smallwood is also of the same opinion, who from necessity has paid particular attention to their wants, in consequence of dayly complaints. Thirteen of them deserted in a body a day or two before I arrivd at the Army. Their sufferings and discontent is so great, that Genl. Smallwood and my self are of opinion, they had best be sent home to be cloathed, as they can be of no use here; and only serve to consume provision and forage, already grown exceeding scarce, by the amazing consumption of the numerous Militia horse, that have been in the field this Campaign. Indeed not a man unfit for actual duty for want of cloathing ought to be sent to this Army; the difficulty of obtaining subsistence is great, and the fatigue and hardships excessive. Besides the earth is so flat that it is almost under water every rain; and unless troops are well cloathed they cannot exist long in such a disagreeable situation. I wish the Corps to return as soon as they are cloathed; which I hope will be effected as soon as possible.

I have nothing new from the enemy since my former letter. And for want of hard Money I am afraid it will be exceeding difficult getting intelligence if it can be obtained at all.

Baron Stuben can give your Excellency all the information respecting the light flat boats mentioned by General Washington that may be necessary; and to him I beg leave to refer you upon the subject.

I have the honor to be with great respect Your Excellencys Most Obedient humbl serv., N GREENE

I have enclosed the return of Clothing wanted for the Corps.

Dft (MiU-C); in Greene's hand; endorsed: "To Governor Jefferson Dec. 14th. 1780. Examd. Entd." RC (Vi); in clerk's hand; endorsed with abstract of contents in an unidentified hand. Enclosure not located.

FLAT BOATS MENTIONED BY GENERAL WASHINGTON: See Washington to TJ, 8 Nov. 1780.

From Richard MacCarty

MAY IT PLEASE YOUR EXCELLENCY Cascakia 14 Decr. 1780.

Having the Honnor to be appointed by Colol. Clark, Captain of the Regular forces of the State of Virginia the 1st. of March 1779 after the Conquest of Post Vinçent, I in Consequence raised men and with my Officers had the fullest Company during a Year, and those mostly to serve for during the War, the Returns of which no Doubt have been laid before You.

In June 1779 Colol. Clark gave me Bills for their pay and my Cahôs Voluntieers for the ReConquest of Auposts, which Bills were as follows vizt.—

1st. and 2d. payable to Mr. Ls. Perault One thousand three hundred and fifty Eight Dolls. Dated 17th June 1779 for Sundries as ℔r account rendered for the Use of the Troops.

2d Sett. 1st. and 2d. payable to Mr. Ls. Perault One thousand and Ninety five Dollors One fith Dated 17th June 1779 as before and same use.

3d Sett 1st and 2d. payable to Mr. Joseph Perault Ninety five Dollors Subsistence for the Troops Under my Command dated 28th June 1779 and all Signed by Colol. Clark.

These Bills I gave in payement to Messrs. Louis and Joseph Perault as Good Money, and Mr. Joseph Perault goeing with Colol. Rogers to present the first of each Sett of Said Bills to the Treasury of Virginia for Payement was taken by the Enemy in that Unhappy Defeat and lost all he had, and Amongst the Rest the first of these three Setts of Bills of Exchange beforementioned.

Now these are in Consequence to beg that, If any One Should present the Same, to Stop payement, No One having any legal right to them but Myself, the whole being for Good Money advanced by me for the Publick Service and advancement thereof.

I am may it Please Your Excellency Your most Obedt. and Very Humle Servt., RICHARD MACCARTY

RC (Vi); addressed and endorsed. On Richard MacCarty (or McCarty), see *Ill. Hist. Colls.*, II (Cahokia Records), 2, note 3, and *passim.*

From Bennett Goode

SIR Mecklenbg. Decr. 15th. 1780.

The three months the last Guard had to serve at the Magazine at Taylors Ferry is Expired. With difficulty we have furnished a temporary guard to serve untill Your Excellency Order in what manner a standing guard be furnished. The difficulty of furnishing a guard arises from abuses committed on the soldiars by Continental Officers when at that Station; Col. Edward Carrington caned a sarjent and Ordered two of the soldiars striped and whiped which was Executed with out the formality of a trial. If such abuses is suffered to pass with impunity it will not be in the power of Your Officers to furnish a guard at that place. The guard is commanded by a Lieutenat and two Serjents which is not suffitiant to make a Court, therefore they are deprived of the advantages of the Law under which they Serve. Shall be glad Your Excellency will

Order in what manner a Court be furnished for the tryal of such of the guard as transgress.

I Received as a commissioner a Letter from Your Excellency desireing the commissioners to procure beef for the use of the army, which Requisition I should have chearfully complyed with had it been in my power, but at that time was Very indisposed and much Afflicted with Eruptions on the skin which rendered it impossable for me to Ride, therefore [could] be of Very Little assistance to the Other Commissioners which I hope Your Excellency will Excuse.

I have the Honour to be with Respect Your Excellency Most Obediant Servt.,
BENNETT GOODE

RC (Vi); addressed and endorsed. A LETTER FROM YOUR EXCELLENCY: Not clearly identifiable, though see note on TJ to William Frazer, 26 Oct. 1780.

From Timothy Pickering

Newburgh [*N.Y.*], *15 Dec. 1780.* Acknowledges a letter in which TJ stated his intention of appointing Maj. [Robert] Forsyth deputy quartermaster for Virginia. Forsyth had already requested this appointment and he is very acceptable to Pickering.

RC (PHi); 2 p.; signed: "Tim: Pickering Q.M.G."; addressed and endorsed. FC, in Pickering's hand (DNA: RG 93).

TJ's letter acknowledged by Pickering has not been found; see, however, TJ to Pickering, 6 Sep. 1780; TJ to Pickering, 15 Jan., and Pickering to TJ, 3 Feb. 1781.

From Steuben

SIR
Richmond, December 15th. 1780.

I had the honor to write some time ago to Your Excellency, enclosing a Memorial of Colo. Senf, relative to the necessary fortifications on York and James River. I have kept this Officer in this state for the sole purpose of surveying all the defensible places, and he has lately by my Order taken an Exact draught of the situation of Hood. I could wish the Assembly might come to some determination on this subject, and in case they would not approve of Colonel Senf's project, I would no longer detain him in this state, but send him immediately to the Army.

I am with the greatest respect Sir Your Excellency's Most obedient and very humble Servant,
STEUBEN Maj. General

RC (Vi); in a clerk's hand, signed by Steuben; addressed; endorsed: "Bar. Steuben abt. Hoods &c surveyed by Senf. Dec. 15 1780." FC (NHi).

On the (missing) MEMORIAL prepared by J. C. Senf, sent to TJ by Steuben in a letter also missing, see TJ to Harrison, 30 Nov. 1780; see also Steuben to TJ, 11 Feb., and TJ's reply 12 Feb. 1781.

From Steuben

[*Richmond*] *15 Dec.* [*1780*]. Col. Green's detachment marched from Petersburg on the 13th. Steuben on his return from Petersburg reviewed the troops at Chesterfield Courthouse, where there were 316 rank and file present and fit for duty, and about 200 sick; 20 of those fit for duty have been ordered to supply the places of deserters from Green's detachment; and 25 others have been assigned to Col. [Henry] Lee "as this States Quota of his Legion." Those remaining "are in the most wretched situation that can be Conceived" for want of clothing. "The Hospital in a short time will be too little to hold the sick, and the State will be sensible of the ImPolicy as well as the Inhumanity of Inlisting Men and leting them die by Inches." Urges immediate measures for their relief and enumerates the articles of clothing essential; "in three days time there may not be well men enough to do the Common duty at the Place."

FC (NHi); 2 p.; at foot of text, in a different hand, there appears this note: "His Excell. Gov. Jefferson. 15 dec." This letter, however, follows one in Steuben's letterbook which is dated 16 Dec. It is not clear from this which is the correct date.

The name GREEN appears in this letter as both "Green" and "Greene," but see note on Steuben to TJ, 10 Dec. 1780.

To James Wood

SIR Richmond December 15th. 1780.

I received your favour of the 7th instant from Annapolis and write an answer, tho I hardly know by what route to send it to you. The post at the barracks shall be duly attended to. I had a Letter from Colo. Taylor the other day when all was well and he mentions no apprehension of want. With respect to that part of the troops which are gone to Maryland we thought it right to lend all possible aid in the provision way at first as we supposed that stores coud not have been laid in, nor the business of supplies got into a regular train. We must hope however to be now acquitted as to them. When it is considered that two thirds of those troops still remain on our hands, that we have a large number of continental prisoners to support at Winchester, and that the southern army must of course (Carolina being so much exhausted) depend on us for a principal proportion of their supplies, I cannot suppose it will be thought for the common good to draw any thing from us northwardly. What ever is so drawn, will be just so much taken from the southern army. The supplies which would be drawn from us for the conventioners at Frederick town, would other wise be applied to the support of the post at Winchester. To make good these we shou'd then be obliged to draw for that post provisions from the counties southward of it, which are now called to the southern army. You seem to think we are the better enabled to contribute to the support of the British Conventioners because tho' equally destitute of money with the state of Maryland, we are armed with force to take provisions from our Citizens which they are not, but I cannot conceive but that the legislature of Maryland, if they find that their quota of specifics cannot be produced by money, will think it right to introduce force into their state also. At any rate I cannot believe it will be thought equal to impress our citizens for the deficiences of any other state. I am with great esteem Sir Your most obedt. servt,

TH: JEFFERSON

RC (MHi); in a clerk's hand, with complimentary close and signature by TJ. Endorsed precisely like TJ's earlier letters to James Wood, which confirms the deduction from the content that this letter was addressed to Wood; see TJ to Wood, 11 Nov. 1780, advising him to go to Annapolis.

Neither Wood's FAVOUR OF THE 7TH INSTANT FROM ANNAPOLIS nor the recent LETTER FROM COLO. [FRANCIS] TAYLOR to TJ has been located.

From Amable and Alexander Lory

SIR

Alexandria 16. Dec. 1780

Answering to your's Excellency's letter, concerning our advertisement of the Enciclopedie inserted in the Virginia papers We take leave to give you the following informations on the Said Work: the complet Set Consist in 28 Volumes, Whose Eight are plates, all unbounded, Second Edition, printed at Lucques in Italia by Octavian Diodati, all the Work Collected and put in Order, by Mr. Diderot member of the French academy and the Mathematical part by Mr. D'alembert, the price fifteen HHds. Tobacco or £90000 this Edition having been payed 50 guineas in Europa.

We Remain the most Respectfully Of your Excellency's The most Obedient humble servants,

AMABLE & ALEXANDER LORY

RC (Vi); addressed; endorsed (in two or three different hands): "Messr. Lory Lr. . . . Decr. 16 1780 Letter concerning Encyclopedia in course of Publication." A copy of this letter was enclosed in TJ's letter to John Fitzgerald of 27 Feb. 1781, in which TJ asked Fitzgerald to purchase the work for him; see also Fitzgerald's reply, 1 Apr. 1781, stating that he would soon forward the books.

TJ's LETTER of inquiry to the Messrs. Lory is missing, but the advertisement that evoked it is in *Va. Gaz.* (D & N), 9 Dec. 1780: "ALEXANDRIA. *Nov.* 30, 1780. To be sold, the ENCYCLOPEDY or DICTIONARY of ARTS and SCIENCES, printed in *French*, with all the cuts belonging to the said work. Cash or tobacco will be admitted in payment, by applying to the subscribers. AMABLE & ALEXANDER LORY."

From James Maxwell

[*Richmond*, *16 Dec. 1780.* A minute in the Journal of the Commissioner of the Navy (Vi) under this date reads: "Letter written to the Governor inclosing one from the Shipyard." Neither letter nor enclosure located.]

From Steuben

SIR Richmond 16 Decr. [1780]

General Green among other requisitions having mentioned the equipment of the Troops raised by the State, I have no doubt but the Legislature will be glad to know what is generally understood by the equipment of a soldier, and therefore take the Liberty of laying before your Excellency the inclosed Estimate with some remarks thereon.

I need not mention to your Excellency the necessity of measures being immediately taken to provide those Articles. The consequences resulting from the Men detained, for want of necessaries, have been too fatally experienced by this State to need mentioning.

Your &c.

FC (NHi). Enclosure missing.

From Steuben

SIR Richmond 16 Decr. 1780

I take the Liberty of laying before your Excellency, a few thoughts on the subject of raising and equiping the Troops required of this State: I should have done this before, but have been detained at Petersburg much longer than I expected, by the many Difficulties I met with in sending off a Detachment of 400 Men to re-inforce General Greene.

I was in hopes of receiving Returns from the southward, which would have enabled me to Ascertain the precise number of Men necessary to complete the quota of this State. The number required by *Congress* is for the Infantry 5448. Cavalry 844. Artillery 544. For Lee's and Armand's Legion's 50. In all 6886. From this Number very little Deduction can be made.

The far greatest part of the Troops taken at *Charles Town*, were engaged for periods which will have expired before they are exchang'd. No account can therefore be made but of those engaged for the War, and of those I am well assurd the number will be very small. With respect to the men engaged for short periods, and who are now in service, should they be reckon'd on as a part of the quota for the new establishment the Virginia Line will never be compleated. Part of those are engaged for 8 and part for 18 Months. Of those I have with great difficulty sent off about 400 including non Commissioned officers: the remainder are at Chesterfield; and by a return delivered me a few days ago, they do not amount to 600 Men. Part of the Time for which these men are engaged is already expired, and before the new establishment of the Army takes place, even the Eighteen Months men will have served one half of their Time. The Consequence that will result from reckoning on these men will be that frequent supplies of Men will be wanted to repair them as their Times expire and by being obliged to have such frequent recourse to drafting it will become much more difficult and disgusting than it is at present.

Your Excellency must have been long since convinced that the constant difficulty of men and consequently our being obliged to have such frequent recourse to drafting has been in a great measure oweing to the Errors and abuses in the Mode adopted. The most eligible means to remedy this and to keep the Regiments in the field compleate appears to me to be the following

That the Inhabitants of the State be divided into as many Classes as there are men required. The Classes being proportiond as equally as possible with respect to property, but each Class be obliged to furnish a Man for the War by a certain fixed period otherwise to be subjected to a Draft. The recruit so furnished to be considered as the representative of the Class, and in case of Death by sickness; or Desertion to be replaced by the Class in one Month after notice given in the same manner as before. With respect to those who may be killed in Action it would not be just that a particular Class, whose men may be killed should Suffer for the Bravery of their Troops. These must therefore be replaced by the Recruits who are voluntarily Inlisted by the officers left in the State for that purpose, or should these be insufficient by a General Draft from the whole.

I am confident that such a manner as this would prevent the abuses that now exist, we should no longer see children and Infirm Men put into the Field, nor men receiving enormous bounties and immediately deserting, countenanced, perhaps by the very Class that sent them. The Class by being obliged to continue their men in the field, would certainly send such as were least likely to subject them to the inconvenience of sending others in their stead. Desertion would be discountenanced, and our Regiments would be kept compleat with Men on whose integrety the Country would depend.

Your &c. &c.

FC (NHi).

From Steuben

Richmond, 16 Dec. 1780. Lt. Col. [Richard] Campbell of the 9th Va. regiment, which is now at Fort Pitt, has orders to join his regiment but is unable to do so for want of $4,000 to pay the expenses of the journey. Steuben requests that a warrant for that sum be granted to Campbell so that the public service will not suffer by his longer detention in Richmond.

FC (NHi); 1 p.

From Theodorick Bland

[*Philadelphia, 17 Dec. 1780.* Burnett, *Letters of Members*, v, No. 537, note 5, quotes from a letter of this date written by Theodorick Bland to TJ introducing "the Marquis de La Valle and the Count de Guistine," who had been introduced to Bland by La Luzerne and Lafayette. Burnett's source was a "Copy, from the original, in possession of the Carnegie Institution [of Washington]," but neither the original nor the copy has been located. See, however, La Luzerne's two letters to TJ, 18 Dec., introducing these two French officers, Laval and Custine.]

To Benjamin Harrison

[*Richmond, 18? Dec. 1780.* JHD, Oct. 1780, 1827 edn., p. 55 (18 Dec.): "The Speaker laid before the House, a letter from the Governor, enclosing several others from Major General Baron Steuben, containing requisitions for the army, which were read, and ordered to be referred to the committee of the whole House, to whom the bill 'for recruiting this State's quota of troops to serve in the continental army,' was committed." TJ's letter not located; the enclosures included those items mentioned in the first of Steuben's three letters of 16 Dec., q.v., and possibly that of 18 Dec. as well.]

From Gideon Johnston

York, 18 Dec. 1780. Acted as brigade quartermaster to the troops which marched south under Col. Porterfield last May, "and some time after was ordered to Virginia to receive and forward on the necessary Cloathing for the Regiment of State Artillery, in which I have the honour to hold a Captain's Commission." Is deeply concerned that he will not be able to serve much longer "except I can be allowed the Benefit of such Privilledges as from my Rank as an Officer, I conceive my Self to be intittled to." Being considered a Continental officer, he cannot draw forage in Virginia except where there are Continental posts, and his expenses are thereby intolerable. "Capt. [Edward?] Moody being about to visit his Family, is desirous of my taking care of the Garrison at York untill his return; upon this head I have consulted Capt. [Thomas?] Edmunds, who has no objection to my serving in the State, as we have many Officers at this time without any Command." Desires the governor's approval of this proposal.

RC (Vi); 4 p.; signed "Gn. Johnston." Addressed: "His Excellency, the Governor in Council Richmond favo. ℘ the Honble. D. Jameson." Endorsed: "Gn. Johnson respecting his being deprived of his priviledges &c. 18th. Decr. 1780."

For Johnston's military service, see Gwathmey, *Hist. Reg. of Virginians in the Revolution*, under "Johnson, Gideon."

From La Luzerne

MONSIEUR A Philadelphie, le 18. Xbre. 1780.

Cette lettre vous sera remise par M. le Marquis de Laval Montmorency, Colonel du Régiment du Bourbonnois, actuellemen à Newport. Il a voulu profiter de l'inaction de l'armée pendant l'hyver pour voir plusieurs Etats du Continent. Il se propose de passer quelques jours à Richmont et quoique les circonstances ne lui permettent pas de rendre son sejour aussi long qu'il l'auroit desiré, il a beaucoup d'empressement d'etre connu de Votre Excellence. Vos bonnes dispositions pour mes Compatriotes ne me permettent pas de douter qu'il ne recoive l'accueil le plus favorable de votre part.

J'ai l'honneur d'etre avec le plus sincere attachement Monsieur de Votre Excellence Le très humble et très obeissant serviteur,

LE CHR DE LA LUZERNE

RC (DLC); in a clerk's hand, signed by La Luzerne; at foot of text: "M. Jepherson."

Another letter (also in DLC) of very similar purport but differing in its phraseology was written to TJ by La Luzerne on the same day introducing "M. le Cte. de Gustine [Custine Sarreck], Colonel du régiment de Xaintonge [Saintonge]." The two French officers visited TJ on the 29th and wrote him a letter of thanks dated 30 Dec. 1780, q.v.; from this letter it appears that "Custine," not "Gustine," is the correct form. See *Les combattants français de la guerre américaine, 1778-1783*, Paris, 1903, p. 224, 253; also Washington to Rochambeau, 16 Nov., and to Samuel Huntington, 7 Dec. (2 letters), *Writings*, ed. Fitzpatrick, XX, 357, 435-6.

From Steuben

Richmond, 18 Dec. 1780. Encloses "some hints toward a Law to prevent illegal discharges and desertions from the Army." Has written on the same subject to Congress and the Commander in Chief.

RC (Vi); 2 p.; in a clerk's hand, signed by Steuben; addressed; endorsed, by TJ: "Baron Steuben illegal discharges." Enclosure: Probably Steuben's plan for preventing desertion, printed below at end of Dec. 1780, q.v.

From George Elliott

[*Place and date not indicated, but written after 19 Dec. 1780.*] On 19 Dec. Elliott had in his possession 64 common tents; Col. [John] Green may have taken some of these for his detachment, but Elliott is "almost Shore" that Green marched before the 19th. "If so these 64 ware Sent By Direction of Colo. Carrington to Chesterfield C. House to Care of Colo. Davis [William Davies]."

RC (DLC); 1 p.; signed: "Geo. Elliott A D Q M G."

From George Muter

War Office [*Richmond*], *19 Dec. 1780.* Capt. [Thomas] Quirk has applied to Muter to procure him a major's commission in Col. Clarke's [G. R. Clark's] regiment, but Capt. [John] Williams also claims this majority, and Muter encloses two certificates from Clark which may enable TJ to decide on Quirk's claim. Quirk must leave soon, and Clark's being here will help settle the difficulty.

Reply appears at foot of Muter's letter: "In Council Dec. 23. 1780. We cannot decide between the opinions of Colo. Clarke and of the officers to whom it was referred without knowing the principles of the dispute. Th: Jefferson."

RC (Vi); 2 p.; endorsed. TJ's reply is in his own hand.

From Edward Stevens

SIR Charlotte Decemr 19. 1780

This hands you a return of the Militia to the 16th Inst. I had them made in such a manner as would discover to you the numbers that marched from the deferent Countys, and what has become of them to the date of the Returns; Militia or indeed any new Troops, let what pains or care will be taken the more especially on such a long March, and badly supplied with necessaries, will moulter away in a most surprising manner, to those who have never experienced it. As I have no immediate command of the 18 Months Men, returns of them cannot come from me. I mentioned to Genl. Green your desire and the necessity of your being furnished with the Returns. I immagine he will order them to be made to you.

The Purport of this was intended to have been forwarded you by the last express Genl. Green sent Northward but I missed the Opportunity. Nothing of note has happened here since Washingtons affair. The Army I expect will move tomorrow from hence and I believe will take a position (near Haileys Ferry on Peadee) as much for the advantage of Supplies as any thing else; I am well Convinced the Strength of this Army is far short of what it is generally thought to be, tho' as you have had an Opportunity of seeing Genl. Gates on his return Home I presume he has given you a pretty good Idea of things here. A Body of Militia of this State is called on, and are now assembling on the South Side of the Cawtaba River to Join Sumpters [force?]. Genl. Morgan takes the Command of them; Ninety Six perhaps may be their object.

The Fleet seen off Cape Fear we have no certain Intelligence what they are or their destination, nor have we certain Accounts of the Fleet that left Virginia, since there departure from thence. It is certain the Enemy had received a Reinforcemence at Charles Town.

The Cherokee Indians will be troublesome on the back parts of this State.

On making enquiry into the cause of the lenght of time the dispaches which you mention in yours of the 19th November was on their way from Hillsborough to Richmond I received the Inclosed letter from Majr. Anderson.

I am &c.

Tr (DLC); endorsed (in part): "Copy." Enclosure not found.

From George Muter, with Reply

SIR War office Decr. 20. 1780.

A requisition is made for a hhd. of spirits to be Sent to Chesterfield Ct. house, to be issued at the reduced prices, to the officers there. I have inclosed an order on the Commissary of Stores for a hhd., tho' I am doubtfull it will not meet with your Excellency's approbation, as I understand the pay in the new money was to take place the first of August last, and also I have heard, the Assembly have a resolution now before them, to make good the depreciation 'till that time. The person who is to carry over the Spirits, if the order is countersigned by your Excellency, is now waiting.

General Muhlenberg informs me, all the hides on the south side of the James river have been brought to Petersburgh and are in Mr. Elliott's hands, well taken care of.

I have the honour to be Your Excellency's Most hl Servant,

GEORGE MUTER C.

In Council Dec. 20. 1780.

The board are of opinion that the articles directed to be furnished the army at reduced prices were intended in lieu of depreciation, and therefore ought to cease from the 1st day of Aug. last from which time depreciation is to be made up to them by advanced pay.

TH: JEFFERSON

RC (Vi); endorsed. Enclosure missing. TJ's reply, in his own hand, is on the verso of Muter's letter.

From George Muter

War Office [*Richmond*], *20 Dec. 1780.* A letter from Mr. Avery to TJ, concerning Golden Ward, was handed to Muter yesterday. Muter has no further evidence on Ward's case than "the depositions enclosed from Mr. Avery in his former letter." Avery, Capt. Maxwell, and Muter are all of opinion that it will be best to discharge Ward and allow him to return to the Eastern Shore, "provided he immediately takes the oath of Allegiance to the State." Countersigned: "In Council Dec. 20. 1780. Approved. Th: Jefferson."

RC (Vi); 2 p.; addressed; endorsed in an unidentified hand: "Letter to the Govr. respecting a Mr. Ward who was sent to me to be Examined. Decr. 20th. 1780."

MR. AVERY: Isaac Avery, lieutenant of Northampton co. on the Eastern Shore; see his letter to TJ of 16 Mch. 1781. GOLDEN WARD: The form of his first name is not certain from Muter's handwriting, and nothing further is known of his case.

From James Wood

Frederick Town [*Frederick, Md.*], *20 Dec. 1780.* Capt. [Edmund] Read of the light dragoons representing his troop to be unfit for duty for want of clothing and accouterments has been permitted to go to Richmond in order, if possible, to get them equipped. Lt. [George] Brent's resignation has been accepted, and his vacant commission must now be filled up. "I am under the Disagreeable Necessity of Reporting Cornet [William] Graves to your Excellency, who I understand has been Ordered, but has Never Joined the Troop."

RC (Vi); 2 p.; addressed and endorsed.

The officers mentioned all belonged to a state cavalry regiment; see Gwathmey, *Hist. Reg. of Virginians in the Revolution.*

From Steuben

SIR Manchester 21 Decr. 1780.

I am about writing to Majr. General Greene, and as it's of the utmost importance, he should be as exactly, as possible acquainted on what supplies he may depend, I would be glad your Excellency would let me know in writing, how far the Legislature have complied, with the requisitions, made them by General Greene.

Among the articles of that requisition, the arms are the most essential. I dont with certainty know of above 2000 Arms that are to come from the northward. Those will not be more than sufficient to supply the Troops now at the Army.

As for cartrige-boxes, I do not expect any from the northward.

As it is supposed that this State, will equip the Troops they are to raise, it is necessary that all the Arms be repair'd with the greatest expedition, and that more hands be immediately employed for that purpose.

I have a Return of a Small number of Arms that are already repaired. I shall direct Colo. Harrison of the Artillery, and one of my Aids to examine them.

As the Cartridge-boxes we are to have, are yet to be made, it will be necessary that persons should be employed, without delay.

Among those Cartridge boxes which I have seen at chesterfield Court-house and Petersburg, there is not a Single one that may be said to answer the purpose of one, which [is] to preserve the Ammunition. I would be glad the person who is to superintend the making of those may be directed to call on me for a pattern.

Your &c &c.

FC (NHi); at foot of text: "by Senf."

TJ's answer follows.

To Steuben

SIR In Council December 21. 1780

I have received authority from the Legislature, to provide cloathing and blankets for the troops by seizing the same which will be accompanied by endeavors to purchase. Agents are out procuring salted beef and others setting out to procure pork in as large quantities as they are to be had to be stored on the Roanoke and its navigable waters. Ten thousand barrels of flour will certainly be provided. The number of waggons which have been delivered to the Continental Q.M. since the date of Genl. Gates's requisition I have not yet been able to procure a return of, nor the quantities of spirit delivered to the continental commissary. Considerable deliveries of both articles have been made. Any other measures which may have been taken by the Assembly for further compliance with the requisitions of Genl. Greene are yet uncommunicated to me. As arms were never among the requisitions made by Congress on the several states, this state never supposed it woud be expected they shoud provide that article for their quota of Continental troops. They have only had in view to procure from time to time as many as might arm their militia when necessity required the calling them into service. From this stock they have furnished arms for Continental use till it is so reduced that they have not the smallest prospect of being able from the State magazines to spare as many as will Arm their new continental Levies.

I am with great respect sir, Your mo. ob: servt.,

TH: JEFFERSON

RC (NN); in a clerk's hand, signed by TJ. Tr (MiU-C); this was forwarded by Steuben to Greene.

AUTHORITY FROM THE LEGISLATURE: See the resolutions passed by the Assembly on 19 Dec. (JHD, Oct. 1780, 1827 edn., p. 57).

To Charles Wall

SIR December 21. 1780.

I laid before the Council the Revd. Mr. Fanning's Letter to Mr. Tazewell together with the Letters and other Papers found on Mr. Wickham. The general Expectations of remaining in this Country with which the Enemy (and probably) this young Gentleman came into it, the political Character of the Gentleman under whose Auspices he came, his not leaving the Enemy till they were obliged to retire, and the Complexion of his own Journals and Letters, are Circumstances which place him, in their Beleif, among the Enemies of this Country. Nothing appears which even leads to a Suspicion that a Difference in political Sentiment was among the Motives which led him from his Connections with the Enemy to seek a Union with this Country. The Manner of his effecting his Transition from the one Party to the other was not likely to produce any other than a hostile Reception. He comes, an Enemy, from an Enemy, in the midst of our Country, with Arms in their Hands, attempts to pass without Application to, or leave from, any Officer civil or Military, and to bear Letters negotiating an Interview between an Officer high in the adverse Command, and Citizens of this State. Under these unfavourable Circumstances, the Board cannot but deem him an Enemy and (being within our Power) a Prisoner of War. They are at the same Time so thoroughly satisfied of the decided Principles of Whigism which have distinguished the Character of the reverend Mr. Fanning that they shall think this young Gentleman perfectly safe under his Care, so long as he stays in this State: to him therefore they remit him until a flag, daily expected from New York into Potowmack River shall be returning to that Place when they shall expect him to take his Passage back, first calling on the Commissioner of the War Office to give a proper Parole. I am Sir with great Respect Your most obedient and humble Servant, TH. JEFFERSON

Tr (Vi); in an unidentified hand; at foot of text: "Major Wall"; endorsed: "1780 December 21. Thos. Jefferson Letter to Mr Wall." This letter (presumably the present transcript) was enclosed in a letter from Henry Tazewell to Gov. Thomas Nelson, 7 July 1781 (Vi; photostat in TJ Editorial Files); see below.

Charles Wall was presumably a militia officer, but his record is obscure. The case of John WICKHAM, on the other hand, is well documented, not only from TJ's account of it as given here but from Tazewell's letter of 7 July 1781, mentioned above and printed in full in CVSP, II, 204-7. From this it appears that young Wickham, a native of Long Island, came to Virginia from New York with his uncle, Edmund Fanning, "with a view of making this Country his place of Residence after he had qualified himself for the practice of the Law, and of living here during his minority under the direction of his uncle the Revd. William Fanning. But on his arrival at Portsmouth, he failed to observe those Precautions in coming out, which since he has found was necessary." He was apprehended near Gen. Muhlenberg's camp in Nansemond co. and examined by a court-martial; the letters and papers relative to his case were then transmitted to TJ, "who in Council came to the determination contained in the inclosed Paper" (i.e., TJ's letter to Wall, here printed). The flag vessel not arriving from New York, Wickham remained in custody of William Fanning as a prisoner on parole, and Tazewell requested that Wickham, who could scarcely study law under these circumstances, be permitted to return to New York by some other means; "Possibly on his way he may effect his exchange in Portsmouth for some of our prisoners in the Enemy's hands at that place." The *Virginia Council Journals* (II, 369), record that on 2 Aug. 1781 Wickham was granted a passport to return to Portsmouth, since he "appears to be released by the last cartel settled in the Southern Department" between Cornwallis and Greene. The Wickham, Tazewell, and Fanning families were all closely related by marriage (VMHB, XXX [1922], 65, 294-5). John Wickham later returned to Virginia and became a prominent lawyer in Richmond (DAB).

From James Arbuckle

Accomack the 22d. Decr. 1780

MAY PLEASE YOUR EXCELLENCY

Looking upon it a duty I owe to the Publick, have taken the liberty to inform your Excellency the condition that the Galleys now lie in, in our County, which were deserted by the Officers and men last summer.

A Gentleman in this County who was a Continental Officer assigned about two years ago, came home, and finish'd a vessel last fall, took the rigging of one of the Galleys as much as woud compleat *his* for the Sea, an anchor and Cable and four Guns. Our Delegates it is like may more particularly inform your Excellency as they must be well acquainted with the matter. She is scuttled in several places, so that the water ebbs and flows in her. I am inform'd also that the Hull is robed of many things Vizt. the Irons that supported the net work, and nettings, about half a cable and two other guns. The other Galley is about thirty miles distant from me, but am inform'd nothing taken away, but this in a bad and dangerous situation. I am Your Excellencies Most obedt. Servt,

JAMES ARBUCKLE

RC (Vi); endorsed: "Jas. Arbuckles Lr. Decr 22 1780."

In 1781 James Arbuckle was a commissioner for collecting taxes in Accomack co. (see the Commissioners' letter to TJ, 15 May 1781); his military record is obscure.

From Samuel Huntington

Philadelphia, 22 Dec. 1780. Encloses "the Copy of an Act of Congress of this Day, together with the Extract of a Letter from the Commander in Chief of the 15th Instant to which the Act refers"; it would be superfluous to enlarge on the necessity of compliance with the requisition called for in the enclosures. Enclosure 1, "In Congress Decr. 22d. 1780," orders that the extract from Washington's letter be sent to all the states, "And they are earnestly required by the most decided and vigorous exertions not only to urge forward the levying their respective Quotas of troops without loss of time, but to furnish the supplies of provisions and money assigned for their support with such punctuality as will put the Commander in Cheif in a condition with the Co-operation of our ally under the divine blessing to compel the Enemy to relinquish their object of subjugating these States and secure to us an honorable and permanent peace." Enclosure 2, "Extract . . . dated Head Quarters Decr. 15th. 1780," urges Congress to communicate to the states a report that British reinforcements are intended to be sent to America, making it a necessity that the states fill up their regiments in the course of the winter. Voluntary enlistments will not be effectual, nor should any system of fines be allowed to excuse men from personal service. "The Accession of Holland and Portugal to the Northern League of Neutrality" will embarrass Great Britain but it will also strengthen her determination "to revenge herself upon us."

RC (Vi); 3 p.; in a clerk's hand, signed by Huntington; endorsed. FC (DLC: PCC, No. 15). Enclosures filed with the letter in Vi; the resolution is printed in JCC, XVIII, 1182; Washington's letter is in his *Writings*, ed. Fitzpatrick, XX, 477-9.

John Clark's Invoice for Services, with Jefferson's Approval

The Commonwealth To John Clark Dr

1780 April		
	To a large table for the Council Chamber	2–15–0 old
	To alterations in the State house	0– 2–6 prices
	To Altering the table in the Council Chamber	0– 4–0
May 6		
	To Mending a press with books Pr. Mr. Beckley	0– 5–0
	To Mending a table for the Clerks Pr. Do.	0–10–0
	To 2 Days work at the Pallice Council Chamber &c	10–0
	To 100 Brads for Do.	1–0
		£4– 7–6
	To Repairing a Cabinet for His Excellency's Pallace	1– 2–6
		5–10–0

At the preisent price of provisions £350.[1]

pork 300				
Beef 144				
Corn 80				
3 | 524	174	11000	110	
	5		7	
174	870	£550	7700	

In Council Dec. 22. 1780.

The within services were performed at our requisition, except the two articles for Mr. Beckley of which we know nothing.

TH: JEFFERSON

Tabular MS (Vi); endorsed (in more than one hand): "Feb. 5th. 1781 John Clark £550. Contingent Exd." TJ's note, in his own hand, is on verso. There is a separate note accompanying this paper reading as follows: "I certify that Mr. Clarke at my request repaired a Desk containing Books & papers of the General Assembly that got injured in removing it from Williamsburg; he also repaired one and altered another table for the use of the Assembly at my instance. J Beckley. 4th: January 1781."

[1] This and the calculations below were added in the auditor's office.

From George Muter, with Reply

Sir War office Decr. 22d. 1780.

Mr. Anderson informs me that the time for which he engaged Nine lads to make nails for their victuals and clothes, for the use of the State, ends with the present Year.

As it will be of advantage to the State to engage those nailers for some time longer, on account of the heavy demand there is at present and likely to continue for nails: I beg leave to recommend to your Excellency, that Mr. Anderson shall be agreed with for them as soon as possible.

I have the honour to be Your Excellency's Most hl Servt.,

George Muter. Cr.

In Council Dec. 22. 1780.

Referred to Colo. Muter to enter into agreement, recommending to him to provide himself with an extract from the act or bill which exempts the public artificers from draughts and other militia duty.

Th: Jefferson

RC (Vi); addressed and endorsed. TJ's reply, in his own hand, is on verso of Muter's letter.

From Thomas Turpin, with Reply

Dear Sir Decr. 22d. 1780.

I have directed Horatio to wait on you with this in order to beg you will inform me by him when you think a jury will be on my land in Richmd., when you think there is a Probality of my being Paid for it, and whether in Tobo. or money. I should not have given you this trouble now but that I have some expectation of making a considerable Purchase and 'twil be highly necessary to know what payments I may be able to make, and now as I am on Enquirie shall be glad to be informed when my Right to that part of the tenement you Occupy will cease; as I don't apprehend you are to Pay the rent out of Your own Purse shall be glad to know whither, that will be in money or Tobo. As I would choose the latter, shall be glad you'd mention it in my favor. I think 8 or 10 Thousand Wt. of Tobo. or its Value will not exceed the Medium as lands and hous's now rent there: I have nothing to add but join with Your Aunt in wishing Your Self & Mrs. Jefferson Joy of a Daughter, & (waving all ceremony) am Sr. Yor. Affectionate Frd and hble Servt, Thos. Turpin

Extract from my answer Dec. 23. 1780. 'I have never expected to pay myself the rent of this tenement, but have taken for granted it would be a public charge. Nothing however has been said about it by any public body and I undoubtedly stand accountable to you for the rent, as the transaction passed between us individually. I had no right to pledge the public and therefore took it in my own name. Pursuing the same line of conduct I am willing to fix the rent at what I think a fair price, whether to be paid by myself or the public. 8000℔. of tobo. *by the year* shall be paid for it. I think it high, as in former times it ought not to have rented for more than £20. However the rent *lately* given in this town seems to entitle you to such an advance. I have to ask the favor of you, if the public should acknowlege this debt, to receive the paiment at their hands. It will not be tardy, and will relieve me from an advance which would be inconvenient.'

RC (Vi); addressed; endorsed by TJ: "Turpin Thos. senr." The "Extract" of TJ's reply, in his own hand, was copied at the foot of Turpin's letter, presumably at the time when TJ submitted all the papers relating to Turpin's claim to Gov. Benjamin Harrison, 7 Aug. 1782; see letter under that date.

HORATIO was Thomas Turpin's son (WMQ, 1st ser., XXV [1916-1917], 111). TJ's residence in Richmond from Apr. 1780 to the end of his governorship was rented from Thomas Turpin, Sr., who had married TJ's aunt, Mary Jefferson (see TJ to Thomas Turpin, 5 Feb. 1769). Its location has not been conclusively established though Mr. Dumbauld's careful researches in city, county, and state records point to a location at the southeast corner of present Broad and Governor Streets where the Memorial Hospital now stands (*Jefferson, American Tourist*, p. 45-6, 220-7). TJ had contracted privately for Turpin's "tenement" (a lot and dwelling house), and Turpin pressed for payment of what seemed to TJ a somewhat excessive rental. TJ submitted Turpin's claim to Gov. Benjamin Harrison in a letter dated 7 Aug. 1782; on 24 Sep. 1782 the Council authorized payment of 8,000 weight of tobacco to Turpin (Dumbauld, p. 45, note); and Harrison informed TJ of that fact in a letter of 3 Oct. 1782.

To Rowland Madison

SIR — Richmond decemr. 23. 1780.

It being found necessary to undertake an expedition into the country beyond the Ohio, you are desired to apply for and receive from Mr. Calloway at New London, under the order inclosed one thousd. pounds of good musket or rifle powder and to conduct the same to Montgomery court house. You are also to apply for and receive 1500℔. of lead from the manager of the lead mines, under an order likewise inclosed, and to convey it to the same place. You are moreover to act as Quarter master and commissary for the militia from Greenbrier, 137 in number who are ordered to rendezvous at montgomery court house by the 20th day of february and to proceed thence with them to the falls of Ohio. You will therefore provide subsistance for them and forage necessary for the march, and are hereby authorized to call on any commissioners of the provision law or commissaries having public provisions in their hands to furnish you. You are moreover desired to purchase three hundred pack horses, pack sadles, halters, and bells which may serve to carry the ammunition beforementioned, provisions and the baggage of the men to the falls of Ohio where the whole will be received by Colo. Clarke and your office determined. We expect you will purchase these horses for £1500 a piece. Tho aware of the necessity for purchasing them, we do not limit you absolutely in price, but rely on your discretion to get them as cheap as you can. For these several purposes you receive here five hundred thousand pounds. Take great care to obtain such authority and protection from the commanding officer of the militia that your horses may not be subject to be rode or unnecessarily burthened, and that you may be able to deliver them in good condition at the falls of Ohio. I am to warn you to use the greatest expedition in performing these several duties and to see that you be in readiness with everything required of you at Montgomery court house by the said twenty'th day of february as a failure on your part will inevitably defeat the whole design. Your accounts are to be finally settled with the board of Auditors.

I am Sir Your very humble servt, TH: JEFFERSON

RC (Vi); in a clerk's hand, with corrections, complimentary close, and signature by TJ; endorsed: "R. Madison." At foot of text appears a memorandum in Gov. Benjamin Harrison's hand: "Apr. 13. 1782. I am of opinion that the auditors ought to settle this business as it does not appear necessary to send the person employed to the Commissioners. Benj Harrison." FC (Vi); dated 24 Dec. and appearing in the sequence of letters under that date containing orders to the county lieutenants for the proposed expedition against Detroit.

From David Ross,
with a Memorandum on Improving Tobacco and Flour Inspection

SIR Richmond 23 Dcmr 1780.

As you seem to join me in opinion that an Inspection in the Upper Country would be of publick Utility and rouse a number of able bodied people inhabiting good lands to industry, I have in a hurry communicated to you a few hints on the Subject.

The wretched State of our Flower trade is such that no doubt can remain of the necessity of improving it by every possible means. I have also given you some hints upon that subject. If you have time at present to attend to these objects 'tis for many reasons a proper Season.

I have the honor to be with great respect Your Most huml Sert.,

David Ross

ENCLOSURE

An Inspection in the upper Country would have a happy effect on the Industry of the back inhabitants, enable them to pay taxes, and to live much better, as well as increasing the quantity of our Staple.

The Mouth of Autry's Creek near Oxford Iron Works would be a tolerable convenient place, and have the advantage at present of any other from the rendezvous of Canoes necessary to transport the Iron &c., which Article the Planters would often want to take home with them when they brought their Tobacco.

I think one Inspector would do, one or two Assistants to be appointed, and employ'd in case of the sickness or absence of the Inspector, Notes to be granted in the same manner as at the lower Inspections. The Inspectors at the lower Warehouses to receive it as it came down agreeable to the Manifest sent by the upper Inspector, who must take in the Notes, as he delivers the Tobacco. The Inspectors at the lower Warehouses must take in that Manifest and enter it agreeable to the Manifest, and grant a receipt for the Tobacco they receive. This Tobacco not to be subject to re-inspection, but liable to all the Expences and taxes as the other Tobacco at the Warehouses.

For the encouragement of this upper Inspection the Tobacco should be clear of expences at the upper Warehouses for the first year or two, but if this meets with any opposition it may be given up and a small impost paid at the delivery to defray the expences, Warehouse Rent, &c.

It is an object of the greatest consequence to Virginia to improve the quality of the Wheat and Flour. We have almost lost that Trade from our very bad management, and People are afraid to cultivate Wheat now, because it does not so readily command Cash. All this is owing to bad Management. What is also much to our shame, the Pensylvanians often carry away our Wheat, and find their Account in manufacturing it in their own Country. 'Tis impossible to make a Law that will lay hold of the Farmers, but 'tis easy to come at the Millers, and by obliging them to make good Flour they will soon find it necessary to be cautious in receiving of Wheat, which will oblige the Farmers to be nice and Carefull in the Management of their Crops. When this is effected we shall share the Flour Trade with the northern People. The number of good Mills are increasing and in one or two years it would be a considerable branch of our commerce. Our mild Winters which seldom obstructs our navigation gives us a very great advantage in being earlier at Market than our northern bretheren, yet we are too indolent to make use of it.

I would propose an alteration in the Law for inspecting Flour. At present 'tis inspected at the Mills, and there is no dependence on the quality, the Inspector is generally a poor man living convenient to the Mills often under the influence of the Owner who pays him, and he is seldom a judge of the Article he Inspects.

All the Flour should be inspected at the Landing or Ports from whence it is shipped, which had better be named in the Law, the Inspect[or] should receive either a Salary or so much ℔ Barrell from the Public, and be independent of the Seller and purchaser, and he ought to pay as much attention to the Cask as to the contents. The Cask ought to be of seasoned timber, well hoopt with 12 Hoops, each Barrell to contain 200℔. nett and no more which would be a very great convenience in shipping and selling it as it would then go by the Barrell. The Miller to brand his name on each Cask.

At each place appointed for the inspecting of Flour, there should be a we[igh] House, where the Inspector is to attend every day, the Waggons that bring in their Flour to unload there, have it inspected, weigh'd and marked by the Inspector, then obtain a Certificate which would enable them to sell it.

The Inspector should mark on the Cask under the name of the Miller, the name of the Town or Landing where 'tis inspected, and the quality Vizt. Superfine Fine and Seconds. By the Cask being branded as above, it would soon produce an emulation between the Millers, who should have the best Flour at the Inspection, and in a little time there would be an emulation between the different towns and Landings who should [export][1] the best Flour to Foreign Markets. Flour coming by Water may be inspected at the Landing if the weigh House is inconvenient.

To defray the expences lay a small duty of 4d. or 6d. ℔ Bbl. to be paid at Shipping. Subject the Flour to seizure if shipt without being inspected. All Flour that is found in Inspection to be false packt, to be forfeited and given to the Poor. Where the Flour is good and Casks bad, to be refused, and the owner at liberty to repack it in good Casks before 'tis removed.

RC (ViWC). Enclosure, which is a 3-page MS without date, signature, or caption, is in DLC: TJ Papers, 236: 42362-3. It does not appear to be in Ross's hand, but it is certainly the document alluded to and enclosed in the foregoing letter.

On 2 Feb. 1781 TJ appointed Ross commercial agent to the state, making the commission effective as from 23 Jan. 1781. However, Ross had been acting as a commissary officer for over a year prior to this time (see *Official Letters*, II, index). The proposals advanced by Ross for putting the inspection of flour on a more efficient basis and for establishing an inspection point in the up country were more far-reaching than the legislation on this subject reported by the Committee of Revisors (see, for example, Bills No. 44 and 50 in Report of the Committee of Revisors, 18 June 1779).

[1] This word omitted in MS.

To Steuben

SIR In Council Decr. 23. 1780

You were pleased to observe in a conversation with me some time ago that you would furnish us with a description of horses proper for the Cavalry and appoint some person to receive such as we should purchase under that description. As soon as it is convenient for you to do this we will resume the business of purchasing horses for the Continental Cavalry.

The resolution of Congress for allowing to the Officers and Soldiers a pay in their new money from the 1st. of August, has rendered that an object of importance to them. It seems therefore proper that each State should see to the paying their own line, in like manner as they heretofore were to see to the Cloathing them, the new pay being intended in lieu of cloathing. We shall be very glad if you can advise us in what manner we may advance monies and to whom to be applied solely to the paiment of the Virginia Officers and Soldiers in Continental employment.

I have the honor to be with very great esteem & respect Sir Your mo. ob. & mo. hble Servant, TH: JEFFERSON

P.S. I send you the printed Advertisements you desired.

RC (NHi); in a clerk's hand, signed and addressed by TJ to Steuben at Manchester; endorsed. Tr (MiU-C), attested by "Wm North A D Camp" and transmitted to Gen. Greene. Enclosures missing.

To the County Lieutenants of Hampshire and Berkeley

SIR Richmond December 24th. 1780

A powerful army forming by our enemies in the south and an extensive combination of savages in the west will probably render the ensuing campaign exceedingly active, and particularly call forth the exertions of this state. It is our duty to look forward in time and to make a proper division of our force between these two objects. There seems but one method of preventing the savages from spreading slaughter and desolation over our whole frontier, and that is by carrying the war into their own country: and to render even this measure effectual our movements must be so early as to be beforehand with them. Your county is allotted to the western defence. You will therefore be pleased to send of [off] your militia under proper officers by the way of pittsburg to the falls of Ohio to join under Colo. Clarke in an expedition over that river and to continue in service during the expedition as to which Colo. Clarke is instructed from hence. They must be at pittsburg precisely by the first of march. They are to be subsisted on the way by such commissary as you shall appoint who is to act as quarter master, both offices to cease when he shall have conducted the militia to Pittsburg. I send him for the purpose of fulfilling the duties of these two offices   pounds[1] which however I consider as principally to be expended in victualling the men as the baggage they take with them must be very trifling. Shoud it indeed be otherwise they will certainly lose it as the means of transportation will become less and less during their tour. Let every man go well armed, and with such arms as suit the western service. I must desire you to keep up a constant correspondence with Colo. Clarke till you shall have marched your men, and having fixed myself the number of men you are to furnish every other instruction I give you herein is submitted to any alterations he shall find necessary.

I am sir, your most obedient servant, T J.

FC (Vi). This is the "master text" of a communication sent on the same day to various other county lieutenants, each of the other communications (the four following letters) being appropriately modified in substance. The order in which they are presented here is the same as that in the Executive Letter Book for 1781 from which they derive.

This sequence of five letters to the county lieutenants of several western counties was a part of TJ's elaborate plan for an expedition against the British post at Detroit; see his letter to Washington, 13 Dec., and his instructions to G. R. Clark, 25 Dec. 1780. See the reply from the Officers of the Berkeley County Militia, 25 Jan. 1781.

[1] The following note at foot of text indicates the sum inserted at this point in each of the two letters: "Hampshire 255 Militia £25,000. Berkeley 275 [militia] £30,000."

To the County Lieutenant of Greenbrier

Sir Richmond Decr. 24th. 1780

A powerful army [as in the preceding letter to 'by the way of'][1] Montgomery court house where they will receive under their escort 1000 ℔. of powder and 1500 ℔. Lead and a large number of pack horses to be carried to the falls of Ohio. From their arrival at Montgomery court house subsistance and the means of transportation of baggage will be found by Mr. Rowland Maddison who is appointed to act as commissary and quarter master for them till they shall get to the falls of Ohio. They must be at Montgomery court house by the twentieth day of february precisely and at the falls of

Ohio by the 15th of march. They are to join under Colo. Clarke in an expedition into the country beyond the Ohio and are to continue in service during the expedition: as to which Colo. Clarke is instructed from hence. The Baggage to be taken by the men must be very trifling. Shoud it be otherwise they will certainly lose it &c. [to the end of that Letter].[2] T J.

FC (Vi).

See letter from the Officers of the Greenbrier County Militia to TJ, 29 Jan. 1781.

[1] Brackets supplied; they were intended here, as elsewhere in this sequence of letters, to enclose explanatory matter not part of the text of the (missing) recipient's copy.

[2] Brackets supplied; parentheses appear in MS.

To the County Lieutenant of Frederick

Sir Richmond Decr. 24th. 1780

A powerful army &c. [same as the letter to County Lieutenants of Hampshire and Berkeley. To the end add][1] Colo. Matthews will send you from Staunton one thousand pounds of powder and Colo. Hunter will forward to you from fredericksburg four hundred camp kettles and from this place will be sent some medicine, tents and other things for the use of the expedition to be transported by your Quarter master under the escort of the militia to Pittsburg where Colo. Clarke will have given orders for their reception. T.J.

FC (Vi).

John Smith was county lieutenant of Frederick; see his answer, 9 Feb. 1781.

[1] Brackets in MS. The following note at foot of text indicates the amount of money sent by TJ: "County Lieutenant of Frederick 285 militia £40,000."

To the County Lieutenants of Fayette, Lincoln, and Jefferson

Sir Decemr. 24th. 1780.

A powerful army &c. [as in letter to county Lieutenants Hampshire and Berkeley to 'before hand with them' then omit and add as follows][1] The counties of Fayette, Lincoln and Jefferson of course must concur in the western defence. From these three I am to desire five hundred militia under proper officers to be furnished, each county sending a quota of the five hundred proportionate to the number of its militia. I do not mean by specifying this number to restrain a greater shou'd a greater number be willing to go. They are to be at the falls of Ohio by the fifteenth of march to join under Colo. Clarke in an expedition over that river, and to continue in service during the expedition: as to which Colo. Clarke is instructed from hence. I need not observe to you that every man must go well armed for the western defence service. I must also desire you to have prepared fifty canoes proper for transporting by water both men and stores and that these be ready at the falls by the day before mentioned. I will avail myself of the first safe opportunity of sending you money to pay for them. You will be pleased to keep up a constant correspondence with Colo. Clarke who is authorized to alter any of the instructions herein given shou'd circumstances in his opinion require it.

T J.

FC (Vi). TJ's letter to the County Lieutenant of Fayette was acknowledged as received "a few days ago" by John Todd at Lexington, 15 Apr. 1781, q.v.
[1] Brackets in MS.

To the County Lieutenants of Monongalia and Ohio

SIR Richmond Decemr. 24. 1780.

A powerful army &c. [as in letter to county lieutenants Hampshire and Berkeley to 'proper officers' and leave out from thence and insert][1] to be rendezvouzed at Pittsburg precisely by the first of march to proceed by the way of the falls of Ohio for an expedition under Colo. Clarke into the country beyond that river and to continue in service during the expedition; as to which Colo. Clarke is instructed from hence. The baggage the men take with them must be very trifling. Should it &c. [to the end of the Letter].[2]

T J

FC (Vi). [1] Brackets in MS.
[2] Brackets supplied; see TJ to County Lieutenant of Greenbrier, this date, note 1.

To the Quartermasters of Frederick, Hampshire, and Berkeley Counties

SIR Richmond Decemr. 24th. 1780.

A detachment of the militia of the county of Frederick being ordered to fort Pitt on their way down the Ohio, you are desired to act as Commissary and quarter master for them till their arrival at fort pitt. The time of their rendezvousing within the county will be made known to you by the commanding officer. You will therefore provide in time subsistance for them during their march and transportation for the little baggage they will carry. You will also receive and transport with them to the same place 400 camp kettles, 1000 ℔. powder, some medicine, tents and other things, this transportation is to be effected by waggons or horses for hire, and not to be purchased. I send you for the purpose of enabling you to perform these duties £ [1] for the expenditure of which you will finally settle with the board of auditors.

[For the counties of Berkeley and Hampshire the same except omitting this sentence 'you will also receive &c. ——— tents and other things.'][2]

T J

FC (Vi).

[1] The following note at foot of text indicates the sum inserted in each of the three letters: "Q M Frederick 10,000 Hampshire 25,000 Berkeley 30,000."

[2] Brackets supplied; see TJ to County Lieutenant of Greenbrier, this date, note.

To Steuben

SIR Richmond Dec. 24. 1780.

The Southern express sets out to day. As you will probably have commands for him I will order him to call on you if you will be so good as to say at what hour. I should be exceedingly glad if by the return of the expresses (for the business which sets them in motion requires a return) I could through your means procure an accurate return of the Virginia troops in the South stating their times of service, and the particular articles of cloathing each man wants. I have the honor to be with great respect Sir Your mo. obedt. Servt,

TH: JEFFERSON

RC (NHi); addressed by TJ to Steuben at Manchester; endorsed.

To George Rogers Clark

SIR Richmond december 25th. 1780.

A powerful army forming by our enemies in the south renders it necessary for us to reserve as much of our militia as possible free to act in that quarter. At the same time we have reason to believe that a very extensive combination of British and Indian savages is preparing to invest our western frontier. To prevent the cruel murders and devastations which attend the latter species of war and at the same time to prevent it's producing a powerful diversion of our force from the southern quarter in which they mean to make their principal effort and where alone success can be decisive of their ultimate object, it becomes necessary that we aim the first stroke in the western country and throw the enemy under the embarrassments of a defensive war rather than labour under them ourselves. We have therefore determined that an expedition shall be undertaken under your command in a very early season of the approaching year into the hostile country beyond the Ohio, the principal object of which is to be the reduction of the British post at Detroit, and incidental to it the acquiring possession of Lake Erie. The force destined for this enterprize is the Ilinois battalion, Colo. Crockets battalion, Major Slaughters corps, with detachments of militia from the counties of Fayette, Lincoln, Jefferson, Ohio, Monongalia, Hampshire, Berkeley, Frederic and Greenbrier making in the whole 2000 men, necessary garrisons only to be deducted. Our desire is that the execution of this may be so timed as that you may have the advantage of that interval of time, which intervenes between the breaking up of the ice in the wabache, and in the lake so as that you may avail yourself of the navigation of the former the moment it is open for the transportation of your Men and baggage and still find the latter blocked up and the Vessels of the Enemy therein of course liable to be destroyed. That you may be fully possessed of the means which are to be in your hands for the purposes before mentioned, you are furnished with Copies of the orders given to the Lieutenants, Commissaries and Quarter Masters in the Counties before enumerated; the substance of them is as follows—Mr. Rowland Madison is employed to carry 1000℔. of Rifle powder from New-London and 1500℔. of lead from the lead mines to Montgomery Court house, to purchase 300 pack horses with pack saddles, Halters and Bells ready and to lay in subsistence for them and for 137 Militia from Greenbriar County, who, by orders given to the Lieutenant of that County are to rendezvous at Montgomery Court House by the 20th day of February, there to take under their escort the ammunition and pack-horses beforementioned and to be with them at the Falls of Ohio by the 15th. day of March. Mr. Madison is furnished with Money to purchase the horses and furniture and to lay in subsistence and forage from Montgomery Court House to the Falls of Ohio, where his duties cease.

Forty bell tents, 40 common tents, a Chest of Medicine, some

Summer Clothing will be sent from this place; 1000 ℔. of Rifle powder from Staunton, 400 Camp kettles from Fredericksburg to the County Lieutenant of Frederick who is ordered to send them with 285 of his Militia to Pittsburg at which place they are to be the first day of March.

The County Lieutenants of Berkley and Hampshire are ordered to send the former 275 and the latter 255 of their respective Militias to be at Pittsburg by the first day of March.

Proper instructions are prepared for such persons as each of the County Lieutenants of Frederick Berkley and Hampshire shall appoint to act in the joint offices of Commissary and Quarter Master to Pittsburg where their Offices determine and Money is sent to each for the purpose of subsistence and transportation.

The County Lieutenants of Monongalia and Ohio are ordered to rendezvous one fourth of their Militia at Pittsburg by the first day of March. All these Militia are ordered to go under proper Officers well armed with Arms suitable to western service and to serve during the continuance of the expedition as herein described. Colo. Crocket is ordered to be with his battalion at Pittsburg by the same day, and Money to enable him to proceed is sent to him.

An Agent is[1] sent to Baltimore and Philadelphia to purchase four tons of cannon powder and to send it to Pittsburg by the 1st. day of March.

Application is made to Genl. Washington to lend us of the Continental Stores at Pittsburg, 4 Cannon, six pounders mounted on field Carriages with ball suitable, a mortar with Shells, 2 Howitz,[2] grape shot and other necessary furnitures, 1000 Spades, 200 pick axes, 500 axes, a travelling Forge, Ship Carpenter's tools and Boats for transportation down the river should we fail in having a sufficient number in readiness and to send us skilful persons to manage the Mortars.

John Francis Moore who was sometime ago sent to purchase in the vicinities of Fort Pitt provisions for the Western Posts, is now ordered to extend his purchases to 200000. rations of Beef and Flour, and to provide 100 light Barges fit for transporting Men and Stores either down or up stream. These to be all in readiness by the 1st. of March. As we are not certain whether he may not be gone down the river, these powers were directed to himself, or in case of his absence to any Agent he should have appointed, and if he appointed none, then to Mr. William Harrison of Monongalia.

At Pittsburg we depend on orders to be given by you for the removal of Men and Stores to the Falls of Ohio by the 15 of March.

The County Lieutenants of Fayette Lincoln and Jefferson are ordered to rendezvous at the falls of Ohio by the 15 March 500 of their Militia to be furnished between those Counties in proportion to their numbers, and to have ready at the same place and by the same day 50 Canoes each: Money is sent to pay for these. In those Counties you inform us you expect 100000 rations will be provided for you. You will of course order them to the falls of Ohio.

All the preceeding orders (except as to the numbers of Men from each County) are submitted to any alterations you may think necessary, and you are authorized to supply any deficiencies in them. The Staff Officers are submitted absolutely to you, and on removal of any of them by you or their death, resignation or declining to act you are to appoint others. The County Lieutenants are desired to keep up a constant correspondence with you and the Staff Officers to inform you from time to time of their progress and to receive your orders. Thus you will perceive that we expect all to be in readiness at the Falls of Ohio by the 15. of March.

What numbers of Men and whether of Regulars or Militia you shall leave to garrison the Posts at the falls and Mouth of the Ohio, is left to yourself. As the latter however is exposed to attack from an Enemy against whom this expedition will be no diversion of force, and as it is distant from succour, it is recommended to you to leave it surely garrisoned and to take Measures for its being supported from the Spanish side of the Mississippi should it be necessary.

You will then with such part of your force as you shall not leave in garrison proceed down the Ohio and up the Wabache or along such other route as you shall think best against Detroit. By the construction of a fort or forts for retreat at such place or places as you shall think best, and by such other cautions as you find necessary, you will provide for the Ultimate safety of your Men in case of a repulse. Should you succeed in the reduction of fort Detroit, and a hopeful prospect open to you of acquiring possession of Lake Erie, or should such prospect open during the investiture of the fort you are to pursue it. As soon as you shall have accomplished both Objects of the fort and Lake, or shall have accomplished the one and find the other impracticable; or as soon as you shall find that neither is practicable, you are to consider your expedition as ended, and to withdraw your whole force if you attain neither Object, or, if you acquire one or both of them, to retain for a Garrison at Detroit so many of the Illinois and Crockets battalions as you may think necessary and to send the rest back across the Ohio; in the event indeed of declining to attempt the reduction of Detroit you are at liberty to consider whether some enterprize against the hostile Nations of Indians may not be undertaken with your force, and if you think it can, and that it will be expedient for the public good and eligible on view of all circumstances, you will undertake it and detain your force till you shall have finished it. In every event, the Militia on their return are to be marched back to their Counties under their own Officers and there to be discharged.

Should you succeed in the reduction of the Post, you are to promise protection to[3] the Persons and property of the French and American inhabitants, or of such at least as shall not on tender refuse to take the Oath of fidelity to this Commonwealth. You are to permit them to continue under the laws and form of Government under which they at present live, only substituting the authority of this Commonwealth in all instances in lieu of that of his Britannic Majesty, and exercising yourself under that authority till further order those powers which the British Commandant of the post, or his Principal in Canada hath used regularly to exercise. To the Indian Neighbours you will hold out either fear or friendship as their disposition and your actual situation may render most expedient.

Finally, our distance from the scene of action, the impossibility of foreseeing the many circumstances which may render proper a change of plan or dereliction of object, and above all our full confidence in your bravery, discretion, and abilities induce us to submit the whole of our instructions to your own Judgment, to be altered or abandoned whenever any event shall turn up which may appear to you to render such alteration or abandonment necessary: remembering that we confide to you the persons of our Troops and Citizens which we think it a duty to risque as long as and no longer than the object and prospect of attaining it may seem worthy of risque. If that Post be reduced we shall be quiet in future on our frontiers, and thereby immense Treasures of blood and Money be saved; we shall be at leizure to turn our whole force to the rescue of our eastern Country from subjugation, we shall divert through our own Country a branch of commerce which the European States have thought worthy of the most important struggles and sacrifices, and in the event of peace[4] on terms which have been contemplated by some powers we shall form to the American union a barrier against the dangerous extension of the British Province of Canada and add to the Empire of liberty an extensive and fertile

Country thereby converting dangerous Enemies into valuable friends. T. J.

FC (Vi). RC of Dupl (WHi); corrected, signed, and dated by TJ: "Jan. 19. 1781"; at head of text: "A copy of the letter dated Dec. 25th 1780." The duplicate was presumably handed to Clark on 21 Jan. 1781 (see Clark to TJ, 18 and 20 Jan.; TJ to Clark, 20 Jan.). In the text presented here of this important letter a few words have been supplied from the duplicate where the top margins of the file copy (which is in the Executive Letter Book of 1781) have been shaved off. The few differences in phraseology between the file copy and the duplicate are recorded below.

1 Dupl of 19 Jan. 1781 reads: "An Agent will be immediately sent," &c. The correction is interlined in TJ's hand.

2 Thus in FC; Dupl reads: "Howitzes."

3 Dupl: "you are to protect from injury."

4 Dupl: "a peace"; this is probably what TJ intended to say.

To Joseph Crockett

SIR Richmond December 25th. 1780

This will be handed you by Colo. George Rogers Clarke, whose orders you will be pleased to receive in future as it is become necessary that your regiment should proceed to act under him to the westward. He will settle with you the time of your marching for Pittsburg and deliver to you the necessary money for subsisting your men to that place. I am sir, Your very hble servant, T.J.

FC (Vi).

To Benjamin Harrison

SIR Dec. 25. 1780

The inclosed letter from our Delegates in Congress I beg leave at their request to transmit to the General assembly and have the honor to be with the most perfect respect Sir Your most obedt. & most humble servt., TH: JEFFERSON

RC (Vi); addressed by TJ to Harrison as Speaker. Endorsed: "Governors Letter inclosing Delegates Letter respecting the free Navigation of the River Mississippi. December 25th: 1780. Referred to Committee of whole on State of the Commonwealth." Enclosure (Vi): Delegates' letter of 13 Dec. 1780, printed above; see note there.

To Samuel Huntington

SIR Richmond Decemr. 25th. 1780.

The inclosed Instructions given by me to Capt. Lockhart for conducting on the Prisoners taken at King's Mountain, and his report, of which a Copy is also inclosed, will inform Your Excellency in what manner these Prisoners are disposed of. I have the honor to be with the highest respect Your Excellency's most obedient and most humbl Servt, TH: JEFFERSON

RC (DLC: PCC, No. 71, I); in a clerk's hand, signed by TJ; endorsed: "Letter from gov Jefferson Decr. 25. 1780. Read Jany 29." Enclosures: TJ to Patrick Lockhart, 8 Nov., and Lockhart's reply, 4 Dec., both printed above under their dates.

To Sampson Mathews

SIR Richmond Decemr. 25th. 1780.

We purchased from Capt. B. Harrison of Rockingham county one thousd. weight of powder which was to be delivered at Staunton to Colo. W. Bowyer who was to examine it. As it is more expedient for the public service that this be forwarded to the county Lieutenant of Frederic, I must beg the favor of you to have measures taken for the examining it at Capt. Harrisons and forwarding it to the county Lieutenant of Frederic. It is necessary that he receive it during the course of the ensuing month of January. T J

FC (Vi).

To James Francis Moore

SIR Richmond Decemr. 25. 1780.

The instructions given you here for the purchase of beef and flour you will now be pleased to consider as extended to the procuring 200,000 rations. I send you by Colo. Campbell £300,000 in part of what may be necessary to be paid for these and other purposes and shall avail myself of other safe opportunities as they occur to send you further sums till you shall have received a sufficiency to make good all contracts. Besides this you are desired to have built immediately one hundred light barges fit to transport men and stores either up or down stream. The whole of these provisions and boats must be in readiness at Fort Pitt by the first of march and are to be subject to the orders of Colo. Clarke. I must urge extreme punctuality as to the time of being in readiness as a body of militia and regulars are ordered to be at Fort Pitt that day to fall down immediately the river. Your accounts are to [be] finally setled with the board of Auditors. T J.

FC (Vi). The full caption reads: "Jno. Francis Moore, or such person as he shall have appointed to purchase provisions in the county and neighbourhood of Monongalia; or if he shall have made no such appointment to be then delivered to Mr. Wm. Harrison of Monongalia, who is authorized to transact the business herein pointed out."

To Benjamin Harrison

[*Richmond, 26? Dec. 1780.* JHD, Oct. 1780, 1827 edn., p. 70 (26 Dec.): "The Speaker laid before the House a letter from the Governor, enclosing one to the Executive, respecting the seizure of salt, which were read and ordered to lie on the table." Neither TJ's letter nor its enclosure has been found.]

To Nathanael Greene

SIR — Richmond Dec. 27. 1780

A Mr. Tatum of this state will have the honor of delivering you this. Being very anxious to take some station in or about the Southern army I thought it not amiss to make him known to you. He is represented to me as possessing in the fullest degree that spirit which is of the essence of a souldier. He has skill in draughts, of which you may form your own judgment on the samples he will shew you; he is particularly acquainted with the Western country of Virginia and Carolina beyond the mountains of which he has made a pretty good map; he is versed in writing and accounts and possesses understanding. He wishes no other emolument than to be fed, and would rather employ his sword than pen; but will do any thing for emploiment. If your present situation be such as that such a person will be useful to you, he will receive your commands: should you have nothing for him to do, he will return, as I have undertaken to mention him to you on this footing only. I hope you will pardon my taking the liberty of doing this when I assure you that conscious that your situation must embarrass you with applications I have stipulated that if there be no way in which you can employ his talents usefully for the public, you are to have no other trouble than barely to tell him so.

Dft (DLC).

MR. TATUM: This was William Tatham, adventurer, surveyor, geographer, inventor, agriculturist, soldier, merchant, lawyer, author, book-collector, and friend of the great, who was to be associated with TJ, at intervals, until Tatham's strange death in 1819. See article and bibliographical references in DAB; also "Letters of William Tatham," ed. Elizabeth Gregory McPherson, WMQ, 2d ser., XVI (1936), 162-91, 362-98. There is no evidence that TJ's letter of introduction was ever presented to

Greene; if it was, Greene probably found no employment for him, since it appears that Tatham remained in Virginia and served as volunteer courier for TJ during the British invasions in 1781. Indeed, in Tatham's letter to William A. Burwell of 13 June 1805 (printed below as Document IV in the series Notes and Documents Relating to the British Invasions in 1781, under date of 31 Dec. 1780 to 26 July 1816), he indicates that he was about to mount his horse "for a journey from Richmond . . . to the Southern States" (presumably on 31 Dec. 1780) when TJ asked him to place himself under Steuben's orders.

From William Livingston

Trenton, 27 Dec. 1780. Acknowledges a letter of 27 Sep. transmitting copies of the Virginia session laws of 1779 and 1780. "We have a standing Resolve in our House of Assembly for interchanging our Acts with the other States; but I believe it has not been regularly carried into Execution. The Speaker however informs me that a Set has been transmitted to the Virginia Delegates in Congress for the use of the Commonwealth."

RC (Vi); 2 p.; addressed; endorsed: "Wm Livingston New Jersey Lr. Decr. 80. Thanking the Govr for interchange of State Documents."

TJ's letter to Gov. Livingston of New Jersey, 27 Sep., is missing, but see under that date for the text of a circular sent by TJ to, presumably, all the governors.

From George Washington

DEAR SIR Head Quarters New Windsor 27. Decemr. 1780

The inclosed are the dimensions of the most convenient Flat Boats, either for transportation upon Carriages, or for transporting Men. The plan was given to me by an Officer who has made experiments with those of different kinds.

The transports, with the embarkation which I mentioned in mine of the 9th: fell down to the Hook on the 19th: instant, and as the Wind was fair, it is supposed they went to sea the same day. The British Grenadiers and Infantry had been under orders to embark, but for some reason they were countermanded, and other Corps substituted. I have little doubt of their having gone to the Southward.

I have the honor to be with great Respect and Esteem Yr Excellency's most obt. Servt.,

GO: WASHINGTON

RC (Lloyd W. Smith, Madison, N.J., 1946); in Tench Tilghman's hand, signed by Washington; endorsed: "Genl Washington Lr. inclosg a plan of flat bottomed boats. Decr 1780." FC (DLC: Washington Papers). Place and date line is missing in RC and has been supplied from FC. Enclosure missing; it was transmitted by TJ in a communication to James Maxwell, 16 Jan. 1781.

To ——— ———

[*Richmond*, *27 Dec. 1780.* Extract from Stan V. Henkels' sale catalogue, 20 May 1913 (William C. Gibson sale), lot 12 (an A.L.S., 1 p.): "Congress have determined that their troops shall be paid off from the 1st day of August in their new money of Mar. 18, consequently if for want of that you pay off in depreciated money, they have a right to receive forty times as much, that is forty times their old pay. Still I think your receipts might be better taken in new money." Not located.]

From Charles Mortimer,

with an Invoice of Medicines for the Hospital at Fredericksburg

December 28 1780.

I am persuaded your Excellency and the Honble. Council will pardon the liberty of this address, as It's intended to relieve the Distress of the Soldiery that may occasionaly be in the Hospital here.

Doctor Rickman in September last wrote to me to take Charge of the Hospital at this place and at present to find Medicine for them, Which should be repaid. *I did so*, and untill this time attended, and found Medicine for a great many of the Virginia and Maryland Line that were ordered in by the officers to be taken care of. This I carefully attended to, and sent them all away to their respective Corps except three that shall be shortly sent forward.

As It's not in my Power to find Medicine much longer out of my private Stock for Practice, I take the Liberty of sending an Invoice of such as may be absolutely necessary for the Sick and wounded, to request they may be ordered to this place, and they shall be Carefully kept for that particular purpose. As I have purchased Medicines at a very dear Rate for 12 Months past, and never received any Payment or Emolument for the Services done, I hope your Excellency will direct me and order payment in that Line, as I am unacquainted with the Mode of application. I am with profound Respect, Your most Obt Hble St, CHS. MORTIMER

ENCLOSURE

Invoice of Medicines for the Hospital at Fredericksburg

Jallap	Tartar Emetic	Mercurial Ointment
Ipeccacuhan	Glauber Salts	Quicksilver
Rhubarb	Calomel	Cream tartar

Salt peter	Oil Turpentine	Gum Arabick
Bark	Plasters	Gum Guiacum
Salt Tartar	Olive Oil	Camphire
Sperma Cœti	Spanish flies	Aloes
Laudanum	Elixir Paregoric	Tow
Opium	Bals Traumatick	Splints
Basilicon	Volatiles	

Paper and Whatever the Director general may think Proper.

CHS. MORTIMER
Fredericksburg Dcr. 28th. 1780

RC (NHi); addressed; endorsed: "Charles Mortimer to the Governor." Enclosure is filed with the letter.

Dr. Charles Mortimer practised at Fredericksburg from 1771 to 1787, where he was a prominent citizen and held various local offices. He appears afterwards to have settled in Norfolk. From Aug. 1780 he served as a volunteer medical officer in charge of the Continental hospital at Fredericksburg. By order of Congress, 26 Mch. 1783, he was at length paid for his services and expenditures. See Blanton, *Medicine in Va. in the 18th Cent.*, p. 346, 358-9; WMQ, 1st ser., XXVII (1918-1919), 80; JCC, XXIV, 158, 212.

From George Muter

War Office [*Richmond*], *28 Dec. 1780.* Encloses a letter just received from Maj. [Charles] Magill covering a return of the state garrison regiment; Magill will also furnish a statement of the blankets and clothing needed by these men if they are to be continued in service. Lack of money and workmen is the principal reason why the hospital has not been finished and huts have not been built for the regiment. "When money can be advanced, and the protection from Militia duty and draughts to the tradesmen employed in public service by law, be published, I must beg to be honoured with your Excellency's instructions, with respect to the numbers that hutts ought to be provided for, and the place where they shall be erected. If the number is considerable, 'twould probably be best that they shou'd be erected at some distance from the town." Enclosure: Magill to Muter, without place, 28 Dec. 1780, stating that "a Return of the State Garrison Regiment at present under my Command" is enclosed; 48 of these are on furlough, and "The Situation of the few at present on duty is truly Distressing Obliged to Lie in their Tents without Blankets and even without necessary Cloathing. Several are at present Sick and no Hospital for their Reception."

RC (Vi); 3 p.; addressed and endorsed. Enclosure (Vi), signed: "Cs Magill Majr Comt."

George Muter to J. P. G. Muhlenberg and Others

War Office, December 28th. [1780]

The General Assembly having Authorized the Supreme Executive, in case of an Invasion of this State, to embody and Officer as they think most adviseable a force for opposing the Enemy, the Executive think it will be essentially necessary for them, to be beforehand provided with a roll of all the resigned and supernumerary Officers in the State, wherein shall be noted their Names, places of Abode, Rank, dates of Commission and former line of Service; that if they should be obliged to ask the Services of these Gentlemen, they may be enabled to do all manner of Justice to their former Rank by giving no Commissions inconsistent with it.

His Excellency the Governor, directs me to take the most effectual measures in my power for obtaining information on the above Heads and registering it in my office. I beg leave therefore, to request of you, that you will be so obliging as to furnish me with all the information you possibly can with any degree of conveniency, that I may be (as speedily as possible) enabled to comply with his Excellency's Instructions.

I have the Honor to be, with great respect Sir Your mo. Obt.,

GEO. MUTER C.

FC (Vi); mutilated; at head of text: "[. . .] Muhlenberg, General [. . .] & General Nelson. (Copy)."

The authorization made by the General Assembly was contained in the revised Act for giving additional powers to the Governor and Council, which was passed at the Oct. 1780 session and provided that in case of invasion of the state the Governor should have power to raise and embody "any number of volunteers" and to "officer and regiment the same, as to him with advice of council shall seem best" (Hening, x, 389). Muter's letter was followed so quickly by actual invasion that the proposed roll of resigned and supernumerary officers was submerged by the chaotic conditions that prevailed during the next few weeks.

From Steuben

SIR Richmond Decr: 28th. 1780.

I am informed that the Bill which passed the House of Delegates for compleating their Regiments on the new Establishment has limited the number to 3000—by far too small a number for the end proposed—but even supposing it sufficient to compleat their Regiments in the first instance, yet from the natural casualties attending every body of Men the numbers will be constantly diminishing from the first moment they enter the Field and at the end of the Campaign, without reckoning on any Loss by Action the Regiments will be reduced one third. This is the number generally allowed when the Mens Inlistments are permanent but the Dimunition will be much greater in your Line from the short periods for which many of the Men are and will be Engaged.

Experience has sufficiently convinced us of the difficulty of raising a large number of recruits at one time. Those Men who intend entering into the service Knowing that necessity will oblige the State to engage them at any rate withold themselves till they can obtain an Enormous Bounty.

This has induced the Commander in Chief to propose and Congress to adopt the wise measure of appointing a Field Officer and an Officer of each Regiment to reside constantly in the State for the purpose of recruiting.

But that this measure may have its proper Effect it will be necessary that the Legislature should determine the sum to be given to each Recruit so Inlisted for the War, and furnish the money necessary for the payment of the Bounties—this money to be furnished to the Field Officer who is to be accountable for its expenditure.

They should also provide Cloathing necessary to Equip the Recruits immediately on their Inlisting which alone will have a great Effect in inducing Men to Engage.

There are in this as in every other State a great number of young fellows strolling about the Country, out of all manner of Employ who with proper management might be Inlisted in this manner for very moderate Sums, but who if left to the time of a general Draft will as I before observed hold themselves back till the Bounties are raised to an Enormous height. For my part I am perswaded that if the Officers are properly distributed in the State and provided with the necessary Money and Cloathing a sufficient number of Recruits may be picked up in the Course of the Year to replace the defficiencies arising in each Regiment whereby an immense expense will be saved to the State and the Inhabitants in a great measure relieved from the great inconvience of frequent Drafts.

I submit the above to Your Excellencys consideration that such measures may be adopted as the Legislature may think necessary to answer the end proposed.

I am with great respect & esteem Your Excellencys most Obed & very humble Servant,   STEUBEN Maj: Genl.

RC (Vi); in a clerk's hand, signed by Steuben; endorsed: "Letter from Baron Steuben recommending a larger Number than 3000. as necessary to complete the Regiments." FC (NHi).

THE BILL . . . FOR COMPLEATING THEIR REGIMENTS: An Act for recruiting this state's quota of troops to serve in the Continental Army, passed by the House of Delegates on 21 Dec. (JHD, Oct. 1780, 1827 edn., p. 63; printed in Hening, x, 326-37).

From George Washington

SIR Head Quarters New Windsor 28th: Decemr 1780

Your Excellency's favor of the 13th: reached me this day. I have ever been of opinion, that the reduction of the Post of Detroit would be the only certain mean of giving peace and security to the whole Western Frontier, and I have constantly kept my Eye upon that object; but such has been the reduced state of our Continental Force, and such the low ebb of our Funds, more especially of late, that I have never had it in my power to make the attempt. I shall think it a most happy circumstance, should your State, with the aid of Continental Stores which you require, be able to accomplish it. I am so well convinced of the general public utility with which the expedition, if successful, will be attended, that I do not hesitate a moment in giving directions to the Commandant at Fort Pitt, to deliver to Colo. Clarke the Articles which you request, or so many of them as he may be able to furnish. I have also directed him to form such a detachment of Continental Troops, as he can safely spare, and put them under the command of Colo. Clarke. There is a Continental Company of Artillery at Fort Pitt, which I have likewise ordered upon the Expedition, should it be prosecuted. The Officers of this Company will be competent to the management of the Mortars and Howitzers.

I dont know for what particular purpose Colo. Clarke may want the Six pound Cannon; but if he expects to derive advantage from them, in the reduction of Works of any strength, he will find himself disappointed. They are not equal to battering a common Log Blockhouse, at the shortest Range. This we have found upon experience. I would therefore advise him to consider this point, and leave them behind, except he sees a probability of wanting them in the Feild.

I have inclosed the letter for Colo. Brodhead Commanding at Fort Pitt, which Colo. Clarke may deliver whenever he sees fit. It is possible, that some advantage may arise from keeping the true destination of the Expedition a secret, as long as circumstances will admit. If so, the fewer who are intrusted the better.

Since I began this letter, I have been furnished by General Knox commanding officer of the Artillery, and by the Qr. Mr. General with Returns of the Stores, in their several departments, which are at Fort Pitt, and I find they fall very far short of your Excellency's requisition. I have therefore formed my order to Colo. Brodhead in proportion to the stock in his Hands. There is no Mortar at Fort

Pitt, but the 8 Inch Howitzer will answer the purpose, and is more convenient for transportation. The Feild peices are Sixes and Threes —two of each.

The matter which the Honble. the House of Delegates have referred to my determination stands thus. A Board of General Officers, in the year 1778, determined That Officers bearing Continental Commissions should take rank of those having State only, while their Regiments continued upon State establishment, but that when such Regiments became Continental, the Officers should be intitled to receive Continental Commissions, from the date of their State appointments. Thus you see it is not in my power to recommend them to Congress for Continental Commissions while in State Regiments, without infringing an established Rule.

As to the second point "whether such Officers shall take promotion in the line or be confined to the said two Regiments" I think they had best, for the sake of peace and harmony, be confined to the two Regiments. For, many of those officers left the Continental Line in very low Ranks, and obtained very high in that of the State. This created much uneasiness when the troops came together in service, and it was with difficulty, that many of the Continental officers could be made to brook being commanded by those, who had been their inferiors the preceding Campaign. I am therefore of opinion, that to attempt to introduce those Gentlemen, now, into the Continental Line, would create a source of infinite discontent and uneasiness, more especially, as you have a sufficient number of Officers at home and in Captivity (and Vacancies ought in justice to be reserved for such of the latter as wish to serve again) for the Quota of Continental troops assigned to the State, by the last Establishment.

I have the Honor to be with the greatest Respect and Esteem Yr. Excellency's most obt. servant, GO: WASHINGTON

PS. The number of Shot, Shells, and Intrenching Tools ordered —tho' far short of your request—is fully competent to the pieces of Ordnance and any Works Colo. Clarke may want to throw up for offence or defence.

RC (Vi); in Tench Tilghman's hand, signed and postscript added by Washington. FC (DLC: Washington Papers); lacks postscript. Enclosure (missing): Washington to Daniel Brodhead, 29 Dec. 1780; this important letter ordering the Continental commander at Fort Pitt to cooperate with the Virginia forces under George Rogers Clark in the fullest possible manner is printed in Washington, *Writings*, ed. Fitzpatrick, XXI, 33-5.

THE MATTER WHICH THE HONBLE. THE HOUSE OF DELEGATES HAVE REFERRED TO MY DETERMINATION: See TJ to Washington, 13 Dec. 1780; also TJ to George Gibson, 5 Feb. 1781, and Gibson to TJ, same date.

To Benjamin Harrison

SIR — In Council Dec. 29. 1780.

The inclosed resolution of Congress came to hand yesterday. As it is on the same subject with the resolution of Assembly of 23d. Decr. I beg leave to lay it before them. That the Assembly may be informed of the footing on which this matter stood at the time of their resolution I beg leave to inclose to them an extract from my Letter to Colo. Wood giving a general order for the removal of the whole Convention troops, and a second one which for reasons strongly urged by him suspended the removal of the Germans for a time. These Measures when taken were duly communicated to Congress and to Governor Lee and were approved of by Congress. What circumstances may have induced an alteration in their opinion I am uninformed. I conjecture however that some difficulty on the subject of provisions has arisen; for by a Letter from the board of war which came to hand with this resolution we are called on to furnish half the provisions necessary f[or] that part of the Conventioners who are gone on, and to transport this to Frederic town in Maryland. Against this I mean to remonstrate and have no doubt of satisfying Congress that this requisition has been too hastily adopted. But I should be glad to be advised by the Assembly how to conduct myself should the inclosed resolution of Congress be adhered to on their part: as our rights of jurisdiction cease at our boundary.

I have the honor to be with the greatest respect Sir Your mo: obedt. & mo: hble. Servant, TH: JEFFERSON

RC (Vi); in a clerk's hand, signed by TJ; endorsed: "Governors Letter &c. December 29th: 1780. Respecting the Convention troops. Refd: to Committee of the whole on State of the Commonwealth." Enclosures (filed with the letter in Vi): "Extract of a Letter to Colo. Wood Octr. 26. 1780" (first paragraph of TJ's letter to Wood printed above under that date); "Copy of a Letter to Colo. Wood November 3d. 1780" (also printed above under its date). A third enclosure, Congress' resolve of 6 Dec. ordering such of the Convention troops as had not been moved from Charlottesville to remain there, is not now with the letter, but is printed above in the note on the Virginia Delegates' letter to TJ, ca. 10 Dec. 1780.

THE RESOLUTION OF ASSEMBLY OF 23D. DECR., agreed to by Senate, 25 Dec. (copy attested by John Beckley and transmitted to TJ, Vi), had, directly contrary to Congress' resolve, required the Governor and Council "to remove out of this State all of the Troops of the Convention of Saratoga." On 30 Dec. the House of Delegates confirmed its earlier resolution, ordering the troops to be "forthwith removed"; and on 1 Jan. 1781 the Senate concurred (copy of resolution attested by John Beckley, in Vi).

From Custine and Laval

a richemond Ce 30 Xbre 1780.

Le Comte de Custine et le Marquis de Laval réiterent à son excellence monsieur le gouverneur tous leurs remerciemens sur sa bonté de leur avoir envoÿer des lettres pour petersbourg et york. Ils le prient de vouloir bien etre persuadé de toute leur reconnoissance, et d'agreer lassurance de leurs respects.

RC (DLC).

On these two French officers, see La Luzerne to TJ, 18 Dec. 1780. A letter from Steuben to Gen. Greene, Richmond, 31 Dec. 1780 (NHi), states that they "arrived here the day before yesterday and sat out this morning to pursue their Journey towards Portsmouth on motives of pleasure."

From Joseph Hawkins

Barracks [*Charlottesville*] *30 Dec. 1780.* Has learned from TJ's letter to Col. [Francis] Taylor that Mr. Clark [Jonathan Clarke], commissary to the Convention troops, has made a charge for 158,118℔. of meal because it was unsifted. Hawkins urges that this demand be disallowed since "their Quartermaster attended to the Issuing and no complaint ever made." Most of the meal was in fact sifted, "and that that was not ground very fine our Guard received it and I never heard the least murmer among them."

RC (Vi); 2 p.; addressed: "His Excellency Thomas Jefferson Favd. by Mr. Martin"; endorsed: "Hawkins to Govr. Dec. 30 80." Enclosed in Francis Taylor's letter to TJ, same date, q.v.

TJ's letter to Taylor, here mentioned, has not been found. See, further, Francis Taylor to TJ, this date; Jonathan Clarke to TJ, 8 Jan. and 6 Feb.; TJ to Clarke, 7 Feb. 1781.

From Linctot

MONSIEUR A la Chutte, se 30 December 1780.

J'ai eu l'honneur de prevenir votre Excelance a mon depart du fort pitt que je me rendoi aux illinois pour tacher d'y appaiser les troubles aucasioné par les nations, j'esperois en passant a la chutte rencontrer le Colonel Clark pour prendre enssemble des mesures Conforme aux instruction qu'il a de Votre excelance et faire pour le mieux, je Croÿois aussi par son moyen avoir quelques marchandises sans les quelles lon ne peut rien faire avec les nations. Je me trouve par son départ tres Embarrassé, Votre Excelance et son Conseil mayant donné des ordre pour n'en point avancer, si les Etat ne fournisse point des moyens pour prendre le détroit, ou n'en voient aucune marchandises je crains que nous n'ayons beaucoup de troubles avec les nations, cela étant les seul moyen deles arretter.

Nous espérons que nos désir seront satisfait que nous vairon une armé marcher ce primten ala quelle nous auron leplaisir de nous joindre pour tacher de prendre une place si importante a notre tranquillitée.

Jai l'honneur dêtre avec respect, De Votre Excelence le très humble et très Obeissant Serviteur, G.f. LINCTOT

RC (Vi); addressed: "To His Excellency Govenor Jeferson at Richmond Virginia"; endorsed: "Majr Lintot Lr. Feby 81 Decr 30th 1780." An English paraphrase of this letter is printed in CVSP, I, 405-6.

To Steuben

SIR In Council Dec. 30. 1780.

In answer to the letter of the 29th instant, with which you were pleased to honour me on the Subject of Artificers, we are enabled to do nothing further than to say that if you think proper to order the Continental D.Q.M. to engage the Artificers we will use our endeavours to furnish him with money debiting Congress therewith. You will be pleased to observe that the requisitions of Congress on the States are for one regiment of Artificers only, and that is required from Pennsylvania. Were not these intended for the whole service Southern as well as Northern and should not some of them be called for Southwardly?

I have the honor to be with great esteem Sir Your most obedt. servt., TH: JEFFERSON

RC (NHi); in a clerk's hand, with complimentary close and signature by TJ and addressed by him: "The honble. Majr. Genl. Baron Steuben"; endorsed.

Steuben's LETTER OF THE 29TH INSTANT has not been found.

From Steuben

SIR Cockermouth 30th. Decr. 1780

Many of our Misfortunes, to the Southward, and elsewhere, have arrisen from the Bad Arrangements of the Q.M. Department, which I hope In future will be on a better footing.

General Green has appointed Lieut. Colo. Carrington. Dy. Qr. [Deputy Quartermaster] for this Department, and directed him to make application to the Executive of this State for Money and other article[s] he may find necessary for his Department. He has already obtained a Small Sum of money, but is in immediate necessity of more. But as it is impossible for me to determine the certain Sum he may want, I beg that Colo. Carrington may be furnished with the Sum he Shall think necessary to but [put] his Department in a Situation that it ought to be.

FC (NHi); endorsed.

From Edward Stevens

Camp Hicks Creek So. Carolina East side Pee Dee
Decemr 30th: 1780

SIR

I wrote you the 19th Inst. from Charlotte by Genl. Smallwood and Inclosed you returns of the Militia under my command. I then mentioned to you I expected the Army would soon move from thence.

We arrived at this Post on the Evening of the 26th. Our Position is a secure one, And we shall be tolerable well supplyed with Provisions for some time from up and down the Pee Dee, That is if his Lordship I mean Cornwallis, does not obstruct it. Genl. Leslie is arrived and I beleive it is certain he with about Fifteen Hundred of his Party have got to Camden. The Force we have here at Present dare not show. We are about Sixty Five Miles from Camden. The Distance is too farr for to do much in the Partizan way, Tho' a few days agoe Colo. Marian with a Party of South Carolinians attacked a Party of the enemy about the high Hills of Santee, Killed Six and wounded Several And drove them.

Genl. Morgan has an exceeding Pretty command on the South Side of the Catawba. It consists of about 12 or 1500, those composed of a Picked Detachment of regular Troops and Militia and the Ballance of Desperadoes from Georgia and So. Carolina, who have lost their all and are obliged to Fly from the enemy. As Morgan will be much in the way of the Enemy I expect they will Push him hard. If the Spaniards do not make some Invasion in the Floridas or we get a Sufficient Force here to Prevent it, The Enemy will certainly advance again into North Carolina. The Troops coming from Virga. we dont hear certainly where they are.

We are all hands here much Distressed for a little money. Our Private Stock is Quite run a Ground.

The Eight months men that are here is exceeding restless and uneasy on Account of their understanding those in Virga. are cleared. If so, they certainly have Just cause to complain. I have promised them that they shall all be on a footing. Shall be glad to have some Instructions from you respecting them before the Militias time expires the greater part of which will be about the 1st February. With every sentiment of respect and esteem I have the Honour to be Sir Your most Obt. and very hum: Servt,

EDWARD STEVENS

That you may the better understand where we are, It is on the East Side of the Pee Dee, about Two miles above the Cheraws, tho' I expect Gen. Green has wrote you.

RC (PHi); addressed: "His Excellency Thomas Jefferson Esqr. Governour of Virginia By Post"; endorsed. Tr (DLC); lacks postscript.

From Francis Taylor

SIR Barracks Decr. 30. 1780

The horseman by whom I wrote to you last week on the subject of Mr. Clarke's demand about provisions is not returned. I must further observe to you that our troops drew the same kind of meal that was issued to the Convention troops without complaining, and as it was received by their Quartermasters, will their soldiers, should any allowance be made for unsifted meal, receive the money? Or have they ever paid our prisoners for any deficiency of provision whilst in captivity? I never heard of their doing it, and as we could not serve them fully with provisions from unforeseen events, have they a right to be paid for it? It is doubted whether the States will be reimbursed for Subsisting the Convention troops, doubtless these circumstances will be considered before any part of Mr. Clarkes demand will be paid.

Some time ago I wrote to Mr. David Kennedy at Winchester (who I heard had some public cloth in his possession) to know the quantity &c. but have received no answer from him. Should he have any thing suitable for soldiers I hope those of the Regiment of Guards may be supplied from thence.

The Regiment of Guards was reduced, some time in the year 1779, from nine to seven Companies: The Subalterns claim their rank respectively, as vacancies happened in those Companies and also the difference of pay, which I think they are entitled to. I shall be glad to have your determination on this subject. If they have a right, the dates of their claims shall be transmitted. They frequently complain of being treated with injustice and seem to blame me because they are not redressed. This I hope will excuse me, for having so often troubled you on the subject.

Mr. Hudson Martin intends to Richmond for money to pay the Regiment. Pray inform him what the Officers and Soldiers are entitled to receive, as I am at a loss how the Payrolls must be made.

With much respect, I am Sir Your obedient servt,

FRA TAYLOR

RC (Vi); addressed: "His Excellency Governor Jefferson Richmond Favoured by Mr Martin"; endorsed: "Colo. Taylors Lr. inclosg Mr. Hawkins Decr 30 1780." Enclosure: Hawkins to TJ, this date, q.v.

Taylor's earlier letter to TJ on the British commissary Clarke's demand is missing; but see TJ to Clarke, 7 Feb. 1781. In the case of the SUBALTERNS of the regiment of guards, see their letter to TJ, 7 Feb. 1781.

From Thomas Turpin

DEAR SIR

Decr. 30th. 1780

As you mention'd in Your Letter, that the rent of the Tenament on which you live never exceeded £20 is owing to a wrong information for I do assure you the lest that it ever rented for Since I held it, was £30 to 35£: ℔ Annm. and lest such a report may have Some weight with the Jury to my Prejudice tho't Proper to mention it to Your Excellency. I've always tho't that £30 was a very low rent. I am Dr. Sir with much respect Yor. Most hble. Servt.,

THOS. TURPIN

RC (Vi); addressed: "His Excellence the Governor"; endorsed by TJ: "Turpin Thos senr."

See Turpin's letter, 22 Dec. 1780, and extract of TJ's reply printed with it.

From Nathanael Greene

SIR

Camp on the river Pedee Decr. 31st. 1780

Since I wrote your Excellency last, I have taken an entire new position with the Army. One part is with me on this river about 80 Miles from Charlotte, and the other is with Genl. Morgan on Broad river, on the West side of the Catawba about 60 Miles from Charlotte. The State of the provisions as well as many other reasons rendered this measure necessary.

Lord Cornwallis continues in the neighbourhood of Camden, and General Lesley [Leslie] has arrived at Charles town and is on his way to join his Lordship. What they will attempt on a junction of this force it is difficult to tell, nor have I it in my power for want of hard money to get the smallest intelligence. I have given your Excellency such a full state of this department in my former letters, and of the distress and sufferings of your troops in particular, that I will not pain your humanity by a repetition.

Since my last the Cherokees have committed some depredations upon the Frontiers; and the Militia have assembled and gone against the lower towns: but with what force I am not able to say.

For the aid of the Q.M. Generals department I have found it necessary to draw on your Excellency for one hundred and three thousand eight hundred and four old continental dollars in favour of Mr. Patrick St. Lawrence which I beg you to give orders for the payment of.

I am anxious to hear what measures your assembly are taking respecting the several Matters contained in the requisition which I laid before them.

I am with great respect Your Excellency's Most Obedient & humble Servant,
NATH GREENE

RC (NN); in a clerk's hand; signed by Greene. Tr (CSmH).
THE REQUISITION WHICH I LAID BEFORE THEM: See under 20 Nov. 1780.

To Steuben

SIR
Richmond Dec. 31. 1780.

I have this moment received information that 27 sail of vessels, 18 of which were square rigged, were yesterday morning just below Willoughby's point. No other circumstance being given to conjecture their force or destination, I am only able to dispatch Genl. Nelson into the lower country to take such measures as exigencies may require for the instant, until further information is received here. Then or in the mean time your aid and counsel will be deemed valuable by Sir Your most obedt. humble servt,

TH: JEFFERSON

RC (NHi); addressed by TJ: "Majr. Genl. Baron de Steuben"; endorsed. Tr (NHi); this appears to be the actual copy enclosed by Steuben to Greene in a letter dated Richmond, 31 Dec. 1780, which was intercepted and is now (along with its enclosure) in NHi: Benedict Arnold Papers; see below.

TJ's INFORMATION respecting the British fleet was derived from a letter written by Jacob Wray, a merchant of Hampton, to Gen. Thomas Nelson and by him transmitted to TJ; this letter has not been found, but for its contents see, further, *Va. Council Jour.*, II, 269; TJ to Harrison, 1 Jan., enclosing Wray's letter; to Nelson, 2 Jan.; and to Wray, 15 Jan. 1781. Steuben, in his intercepted letter to Greene of this day transmitting a copy of the present letter, reported that Gen. Nelson had gone down "this side James River and I have dispatched Mr. Fairlie [*Maj. James Fairlie, Steuben's aide*] down the River on the other side to procure intelligence"; Col. Senf, who at this time was escorting the French officers Custine and Laval to Portsmouth, had also been ordered to gather and transmit "every possible information of the movements of the Enemy"; from Washington's letter to Steuben of 10 Dec., the latter estimated that the invading force "must amount to 2500 Men." The cover of Steuben's letter bears, among other notations now partly torn away, the following instruction: "This letter is to [*sic*] immediately as its matter [is] of great consequence. S Southall. D Q M G."

From James Wood

SIR Charlottesville 31st. December 1780.

I returned to this Post Two Days Ago from Maryland, where I left the British Troops tollerably well Accomodated. I make no Doubt you have Received before this a Requisition from the State of Maryland, for a Supply of Beef and Pork for the Troops, as the Scarcity of those Articles are so great as to Render it impossible to procure more than three weeks allowance from this time. On this Subject I wrote your Excellency from Annapolis and have hopes proper Steps have been taken to secure the Beef and Pork in the upper Counties for this Particular Purpose. The Executive of Maryland were much averse to Receiving any part of the Convention Troops, and had thought of Sending them Back, but Were Prevailed On to Receive them for a time, upon my Assuring them that the Troops were in Such a Situation for want of shoes, as to render it impossible for them to return at such an inclement Season. As to receiving the German Troops you may be Assured they will never Consent to it, as they have Neither Shelter nor Provisions for them. The Situation of Our Own Guard at Frederick Town are Really Distressing. As there is no Apartments for the Officers they are Under the Necessity of Boarding at Exorbitant Rates, are Quite Destitute of Money, and no Allowance of Spirits for either Officers or Men to be Expected, I beg leave to recommend their Situation to your Consideration, and hope that some Method will be Adopted for their Relief. In expectation from your former Letters, that the German Troops were to Remain at the Barracks this Winter, I Discharged all the impressed Teams as soon as they Arrived at Frederick Town. I shall be Glad to hear from your Excellency On those Subjects as soon as Possible. I mean to return to Maryland the first of February.

I am with Great Respect & Esteem Sir Yr. Excellencys Very Obt. Servt, JAMES WOOD

RC (Vi); addressed and endorsed.

Notes and Documents Relating to the British Invasions in 1781

[31 December 1780 to 26 July 1816]

I. DIARY OF ARNOLD'S INVASION AND NOTES ON SUBSEQUENT EVENTS IN 1781: VERSIONS OF 1796?, 1805, AND 1816

II. ARNOLD'S INVASION AS REPORTED BY JEFFERSON IN THE *VIRGINIA GAZETTE*

III. DEPOSITIONS TAKEN IN 1796 RESPECTING JEFFERSON'S CONDUCT DURING ARNOLD'S INVASION

IV. LETTER OF WILLIAM TATHAM, 1805, CONCERNING THE BRITISH INVASIONS OF 1781

V. DEPOSITION OF CHRISTOPHER HUDSON, 1805, CONCERNING TARLETON'S RAID ON CHARLOTTESVILLE

EDITORIAL NOTE

THE documents here gathered together, though covering a long span of time, are so gathered and given special annotation because of their close interrelationship and because the events they deal with had a profound effect both upon Jefferson's reputation as governor and upon his own feelings. The events they record led directly to the legislative motion of 12 June 1781 to investigate Jefferson's conduct as governor and to his spirited and successful defense before the Assembly in December of that year, which should have, but did not, close the matter. The charges proposed (but never formally preferred) against his administration in 1781 were revived for propagandist purposes in the political campaigns of 1796, 1800, and 1804; they were repeated in the histories of the Revolution written during Jefferson's later years; and they are still being analyzed and argued by historians of Virginia and biographers of Jefferson.

Nothing that happened in Jefferson's long public career wounded him so deeply as these charges of negligence, incompetence, and (though this was added long after 1781) personal cowardice in discharging the duties of his post as governor of Virginia. The scurrilities of James Callender during Jefferson's first term as President left him relatively undisturbed because he knew that only his inveterate foes would believe them. On the other hand, the demoralization of Virginia under the repeated blows of invading British forces during the last six months of Jefferson's governorship was an undeniable truth. The armies of Arnold, Phillips, and Cornwallis *had* raided and finally overrun the state, had destroyed public stores and papers, had driven the government out of the capital, and had nearly captured the governor, who had retired from office at a time of grave military crisis. Jefferson did not try to deny these facts, but he felt compelled to reply to distorted versions of them circulated by political propagandists and partisan historians. He did so in characteristic fashion. He carefully preserved his own records of the events of 1781 and added to them from the memories of other participants; and, without coming forward as a controversialist in his own name, he made his accumulated records available to historians and biographers. In the final word Jefferson had to say in vindication of his conduct as governor, set down within two months of his death, he appealed to an historical editor to look at the record, the *full* record. He invited the younger Henry Lee, who was about to reissue his father's *Memoirs of the War in the Southern Department*, to come to Monticello and study Jefferson's file of Revolutionary letters. "Many others too," Jefferson went on, "are interspersed among them which have relation to your object; many letters from Generals Gates, Greene, Stephens and others engaged in the Southern war, and in the North also. All should be laid open to you without reserve, for there is not a truth existing which I fear, or would wish unknown to the whole world. During the invasions of Arnold, Phillips and Cornwallis, until my time of office expired, I made it a point, once a week, by letters to the President of Congress, and to Genl. Washington to give them an exact narrative of the transactions of the week. These letters should still be in the office of state in Washington, and in the presses at Mount Vernon. Or, if the former were destroyed by the conflagrations of the British, the latter are surely safe, and may be appealed to in corroboration of what I have now written" (to Henry Lee, 15 May 1826).

The following series of documents is (with the exception of Document II) a part of the record that Jefferson preserved and here refers to. It includes: (I) Jefferson's own diary of Arnold's invasion, in three different autograph copies (the original having disappeared), each version containing added memoranda that vary substantially from one another; the versions of 1796? and 1816 are printed in full, and the variations and additions in that of 1805 are recorded in textual notes. (II) Jefferson's narrative of Arnold's invasion printed in the *Virginia Gazette* for 13 Jan. 1781, constituting, as Mrs. Kimball has said, a kind of official communiqué by the governor on the recent crisis (*Jefferson: War and Peace*, p. 153). (III) Depositions by Archibald Blair, Daniel Hylton, and James Currie concerning the events of January 1781, gathered by Jefferson's friends during the presidential campaign of 1796 in order to refute the old charges of 1781. (IV) A letter from William Tatham, who had served as courier to Jefferson and Gen. Nelson in 1781, to William A. Burwell, 13 June 1805, written at the request of Jefferson's private secretary in order to answer similar but more elaborate charges made by a Federalist writer named Thomas Turner. (V) Deposition of Christopher Hudson, 26 July 1805, concerning TJ's conduct at the time of Tarleton's raid on Charlottesville, 4 June 1781.

Judging from his frequent recurrence to them, it is clear that Jefferson attached much weight to this particular group of papers. Yet their importance as a vindication of his conduct as governor is dwarfed by the evidence of the mass of his papers for 1779-1781 presented in this and the succeeding volume. The larger record shows that no war governor worked more devotedly than he against odds more completely insuperable. None administered a larger or more vulnerable territory. "The real situation of Virginia," as Girardin said after studying the files of Jefferson's Revolutionary correspondence at Monticello, "is strongly depictured in the letters of the Governor" (Burk-Girardin, *Hist. of Va.*, IV, 459). In a sense, Jefferson's most grievous error in judgment as governor lay in his quitting his office at the end of two terms. The combination of strategy and good fortune that led to the victory at Yorktown in the fall of 1781 owed little to the exhausted resources of Virginia or to the abilities of Virginia's civil and military leaders, who might plan much but could execute little until Washington's army and the sea and land forces of France came to their rescue. If Jefferson had remained in office five months longer, he would have needed no vindication.

I (a). Diary of Arnold's Invasion and Notes on Subsequent Events in 1781: The 1796? Version

Sunday. Richmond. 1780. Dec. 31.[1]

At 8. A.M. the Governor [Th: J.][2] recieves the first intelligence that 27. sail of ships had entered Chesapeak bay, and were in the morning of the 29th. just below Willoughby's point, the Southern cape of James river,[3] their destination unknown.

[1]781. Jan. 2. Tuesday.

At 10. A.M. information is recieved that they had entered James river, their advance being at Warrasqueak bay. Orders were immediately given for calling in the militia, ¼ from some, and ½ from other counties. The members of the legislature, which rises this day, are the bearers of the orders to their respective counties. The Governor directs the removal of the Records into the country, and the transportation of the military stores from Richmond to Westham, there to be carried across the river.

Wed. Jan. 3.

At 8. P.M. the enemy are said to be a little below Jamestown, convenient for landing, if Williamsburg is their object.

Thursd. Jan. 4.

At 5. A.M. information is recieved that they had past Kennon's and Hood's, the evening before with a strong Easterly wind; which determines their object to be either Petersburg or Richmond. The Governor now calls in the whole militia from the adjacent counties.

At 5. P.M. information that at 2. P.M. they were landed and drawn up at Westover,[4] and consequently Richmond their destination. Orders are now given to discontinue waggoning the military stores from Richmond to Westham; and to throw them across the river directly at Richmond.

The Governor, having attended to this till an hour and a half in the night, then rode up to the Foundery, a mile below Westham,[5] ordered Capts. Boush and Irish, and Mr. Hylton to continue all night waggoning to Westham the arms and stores still at the Foundery, to be thrown across the river at Westham; then proceeded to Westham, to press the transportation there across the river, and thence went to Tuckahoe,[6] to take care of his family, which he had sent that far in the course of the day. He arrived there at 1. aclock in the night.

Frid. J[an. 5.]

Early in the morning he carried his family across the river there, and, sending them to Fine creek, 8 miles higher up,[5] went himself to Britton's, opposite to Westham.[5] Finding the arms &c. in a heap near the shore, and exposed to be destroyed by cannon from the North bank, he had them removed behind a point of land near by. He proceeded to Manchester.[7] The enemy had arrived at Richmond at 1. P.M. Having found that nearly the whole arms had been brought there from Richmond, he set out for Chetwood's to meet with Baron Steuben, who had appointed that place as a rendezvous and Head-quarters; but not finding him there, and understanding he would be at Colo. Fleming's, 6 miles above Britton's,[5] he proceeded thither. The enemy had now a detachment at Westham, and sent a deputation from the city of Richmond to the Governor, at Colo. Fleming's, to propose terms for ransoming the safety of the city; which terms he rejected.

Sat. Jan. [6.]

The Governor returned to Britton's; had measures taken more effectually to secure the books and papers there. The enemy, having burnt some houses and stores, left Richmond, after 24. hours stay there, and encamped at Fourmile creek, 10. miles below;[8] and the Governor went to look to his family at Fine creek.

Sund. Jan. [7.]

He returned to Britton's to see further to the arms there, exposed on the ground to heavy rains which had fallen the night before, and then proceeded to Manchester, where he lodged that night. The enemy encamped at Westover.

Mond. Ja[n. 8.]

At half after 7. A.M. he crossed over to Richmond, and resumed his residence there. The enemy are still retained in their encampment at Westover by an Easterly wind. Colo. John Nicholas has now 300. militia at the Forest, 6. miles above Westover,[9] General Nelson 200. at Charles city Courthouse, 8. miles below Westover,[5] Gibson 1000. and Baron Steuben 800. on the South side of James river.

Tuesd. Jan. 9.

The enemy are still encamped at Westover.

Wed. Jan. 10.

At 1. P.M. they embark; and the wind having shifted a little to the North of the West, and pretty fresh, they fall down the river. Baron Steuben marches for Hood's, where their passage may be checked. He reaches Bland's mills in the evening, within 9. miles of Hood's.

Thursd. Jan. 11.

At 8. A.M. the wind due West and strong, they make good their retreat down the river.[10]

Soon after this, General Phillips having joined Arnold with a reinforcement of 2000. men, they advanced again up to Petersburg, and about the last of April to Manchester. The Governor had remained constantly in and about Richmond, exerting his powers for collecting militia, and providing such means for the defence of the state as it's exhausted resources admitted; lodging frequently within 4. 5. and 6. miles of them, generally with only the river between him and them, and without even a centinel.

M. de la Fayette, about this time, arrived at Richmond with some continental troops, with which, and the militia collected, he continued to occupy that place, and the North bank of the river; while Phillips and Arnold held Manchester and the South bank. But Lord Cornwallis, about the Middle of May, joining them with the main Southern army, M. de la Fayette was obliged to retire. The enemy crossed the river, and advanced up into the country about 50. miles, and within 30. miles of Charlottesville, at which place the legislature being to meet on the 24th. of May, the Governor proceeded on the 16th. to Monticello near that place.[11] His office was now near expiring, the country under invasion by a powerful army, no services but military of any avail, unprepared by his line of life and education for the command of armies, he believed it right not to stand in the way of talents better fitted than his own to the circumstances under which the country was placed. He herefore himself proposed to his friends in the legislature, that Genl. Nelson, who commanded the militia of the state, should be appointed Governor, believing that the union of the civil and military power in the same hands, at this time would greatly facilitate military measures.[12]

This was the state of things when, his office having expired on the 2d June, and his successor not yet in place, Colo. Tarlton, with his regiment of horse, was detached by Ld. Cornwallis, to surprize him (supposed to be still governor) and the legislature now sitting in Charlottesville. The Speakers of the two houses, and some other members of the legislature, were lodging with him at Monticello. Tarleton, early in the morning of June 4. when within 10. miles of that place, detached a company of horse to secure him and his guests, and proceeded himself rapidly with his main body to Charlottesville, where he hoped to find the legislature unapprised of his movement.[13] Notice of it however had been brought both to Monticello and Charlottesville about sunrise, by a Mr. Jouett from Louisa, who seeing them pass his father's house in the evening of the 3d. and riding through the night along by-ways, brought the notice. The Speakers, with their Colleagues, returned to Charlottesville, and with the other members of the legislature, had barely time to get out of the way.[14]

I now sent off my family, to secure them from danger and was myself still at Monticello, making arrangements for my own departure, when Lt. Cristoph. Hudson arrived there at half speed, and informed me the enemy were ascending the hill of Monticello. I departed immediately, and knowing that I should be pursued if I followed the public road, in which too my family would be found, I took my course thro' the woods along the mountains and overtook my family at Colo. Cole's, dined there, and carried them on to Rockfish after dinner, and the next day to Colo. Hugh Rose's in Amherst. I left them there on the 7th. and returned to Monticello. Tarleton had retired after 18. hours stay in Charlottesville. I then rejoined my family at Colo. Rose's and proceeded with them to Poplar Forest in Bedford 80. miles S.W. from Monticello. On a ride into the farm about the end of the month, I was thrown from my horse, and disabled from riding on horseback some months. I returned to Monticello July 26. and learning some time after that Mr. George Nicholas, then a young man, just entered into the legislature, proposed to institute some enquiry into my conduct before the legislature, a member from my county vacated his seat, and the county elected me, in his room, that I might vindicate myself on the floor of the house. Thro' the intervention of a friend, I obtained from Mr. Nicholas a written note of the charges he proposed to bring forward, and I furnished him in return the heads of the answers I should make. On the day appointed for hearing his charges he withdrew from the house; and no other undertaking to bring them forward, I did it myself in my place, from his paper, answering them seriatim to the house. The members had been witnesses themselves to all the material facts, and passed an unanimous vote of approbation, which may be seen on their journals.[15] Mr. Nicholas was an honest and honorable man, and took a conspicuous occasion, many years after, of his own free will, and when the matter was entirely at rest, to retract publicly the erroneous opinions he had been led into on that occasion, and to make just reparation by a candid acknolegement of them.

I (b). The 1816 Version of the Diary and Notes of 1781

Extract from my diary Dec. 31. 1780. to Jany. 11. 1781.

Sat. Dec. 31. 1780. 8. aclock A.M. Received first intelligence that 27. sail were in the morning of the 29th. just below Willoughby's point. Sent off Genl. Nelson with full powers.

1781. Jan. 1. No intelligence.

Jan. 2. 10. aclock A.M. Information from N. Burwell that their advance was at Warrasqueak bay. Gave orders for militia, ¼ from some, and ½ from other counties. Assembly rose.

Wedn. Jan. 3. 8. aclock P.M. Received letter from E. Archer Swan's point that at 12. aclock that day they were at anchor a little below Jamestown. At 5 aclock P.M. of same day, I had received a letter from R. Andrews, for Genl. Nelson, that they were at Jamestown the evening of the 2d.

Thursday. 4th. 5. aclock A.M. Mr. Eppes and family &c. came and informed me from the Speaker that they had passed Kennon's and Hood's the evening before, the tide having made for them at 1. aclock P.M. of the 3d. and the wind shifted to E. strong. They had not however past Hood's; but anchored at Kennon's. Called whole militia from adjacent counties. I was then anxious to know whether they would pass Westover or not, as that would shew the side they would land.

Eod. die. 5. aclock P.M. Learnt by Capt. DePonthiere that at 2. aclock P.M. they were drawn up at Westover. Then ordered arms, and stores &c. (which till then had been carrying to Westham) to be thrown across the river at Richmond; and at half after 7. P.M. set out to the Foundery and Westham, and set Capt. Brush

[Boush], Capt. Irish, and Mr. Hylton to see every thing waggoned from the magazine and Laboratory to Westham, and there thrown over. To work all night. The enemy encamped at 4. mile creek. I went to Tuckahoe and lodged.

5. Early went over the river with my family; sent them up to Finecreek; went myself to Westham: gave orders for withdrawing ammunition and arms (which lay exposed on the bank to the effect of artillery from opposite shore) behind a point. Then went to Manchester; had a view of the enemy. My horse sunk under me with fatigue; borrowed one, went to Chetwood's, appointed by Baron Steuben as a rendezvous and head quarters, but finding him not there and understanding he would go to Colo. Fleming's, I proceeded there for quarters. The enemy arrived in Richmond at one aclock P.M. One regiment of infantry and 30. horse proceeded without stopping to the Foundery, burnt that and the magazine and Ballendine's house, and went as far as Westham. They returned that evening to Richmond. Sent me a proposition to compound for property. Refused.

6. In the morning they burnt certain houses and stores, and at 12. aclock of that day left Richmond, and encamped at 4. mile creek. I went to Westham, ordered books and papers particularly from magazine. In the evening went up to Fine creek.

7. I returned to Westham, and then came down to Manchester where I lodged. The enemy encamped at Westover and Berkley. It has rained excessively the preceding night, and continued to do so till about noon. Gibson has 1000. Steuben 800. Davis 200. Nelson 250.

8. At half after 7. A.M. I returned to Richmond. The wind gets, about this time, to N.W. A good gale in the afternoon becomes Easterly. The enemy remain in their last encampment. Genl. Nelson at Charles city C.H. Colo. J. Nicholas with 300. men at the Forest.

9. 11. aclock. The wind is S.E. but almost nothing. The enemy remain in their last encampment except embarking their horse.

10. At 1. aclock P.M. they embark infantry, and fall down the river, the wind having shifted a little North of West and pretty fresh. Baron Steuben gets to Bland's mills to night, nine miles short of Hood's.

11. 8. aclock A.M. The wind due West and strong.

Loss sustained by the public.

The papers and books of the council since the revolution.
The papers of the Auditors, but not their books.

5. brass field pieces, 4. pounders, which had been sunk in the river, but were weighed by the enemy.
About 150. arms in the Capitol loft.
About 150. in a waggon on the Brook road.
About 5. tons of powder and some made ammunition at magazine.
Some small proportion of the linens, cloths &c. in public store.
Some Q.M. stores. The principal article was 120. sides of leather.
Some of the tools in the Artificers' shops.
Foundery, magazine, 4. artificer's shops.
Public store. Q.M's store. 1. artificer's shop.
3. waggons.

The legislature was sitting when the entrance of the enemy into James river was made known. They were informed, without reserve, of the measures adopted, every suggestion from the members was welcomed and weighed, and their adjournment on the 2d. of January furnished the most immediate and confidential means of calling for the militia of their several counties. They accordingly became the bearers of those calls, and they were witnesses themselves that every preparation was making which the exhausted and harrassed state of the country admitted.

They met again at Richmond in May, and adjourned to Charlottesville, where they made a house on the 28th. My office of Governor expired on the 2d. of June, being the 5th. day of the session; and no successor had been appointed, when an enterprize on the 4th. by Tarlton's cavalry drove them thence, and they met again at Staunton on the 7th. Some members attended there who had not been at Richmond at the time of Arnold's enterprize. One of these, George Nicholas, a very honest and able man, then however young and ardent, supposing there had been some remissness in the measures of the Executive on that occasion, moved for an enquiry into them, to be made at the succeeding session. The members who had been present and privy to the transactions, courted the enquiry on behalf of the Executive. Mr. Nicholas, as a candid and honorable man, sent me, thro' a friend, a copy of the topics of enquiry he proposed to go into; and I communicated to him, with the same frankness, the justifications I should offer, that he might be prepared to refute them if not founded in fact. . . .[16]

And here it is but proper to notice the parody of these transactions which Genl. Lee has given as their history. He was in a distant state at the time, and seems to have made up a random account from the rumors which were afloat where he then was. It is a tissue of errors from beginning to end.

The nonsense which has been uttered on the coup de main of Tarlton on Charlottesville is really so ridiculous that it is almost ridiculous seriously to notice it. I will briefly however notice facts and dates. It has been said before that the legislature was driven from Charlottesville, by an incursion of the enemy's cavalry. Since the adjournment from Richmond, their force in this country had been greatly augmented by reinforcements under Ld. Cornwallis and General Phillips; and they had advanced up into the country as far as Elk island, and the Fork of James river. Learning that the legislature was in session at Charlottesville, they detached Colo. Tarleton with his legion of horse to surprise them. As he was passing through Louisa on the evening of the 3d. of June, he was observed by a Mr. Jouett, who suspecting the object, set out immediately for Charlottesville, and knowing the by-ways of the neighborhood, passed the enemy's encampment, rode all night, and before sun-rise of the 4th. called at Monticello with notice of what he had seen, and passed on to Charlottesville to notify the members of the legislature. The Speakers of the two houses, and some other members were lodging with us. I ordered a carriage to be ready to carry off my family; we breakfasted at leisure with our guests, and after breakfast they had gone to Charlottesville; when a neighbor rode up full speed to inform me that a troop of horse was then ascending the hill to the house. I instantly sent off my family, and, after a short delay for some pressing arrangements, I mounted my horse, and knowing that in the public road I should be liable to fall in with the enemy, I went thro' the woods, and joined my family at the house of a friend where we dined. Would it be believed, were it not known, that this flight from a troop of horse, whose whole legion too was within supporting distance, has been the subject, with party writers, of volumes of reproach on me, serious or sarcastic? That it has been sung in verse, and said in humble prose that, forgetting the noble example of the hero of La Mancha, and his windmills, I declined a combat, singly against a troop, in which victory would have been so glorious? Forgetting, themselves, at the same time, that I was not provided with the enchanted arms of the knight, nor even with his helmet of Mambrino. These closet heroes forsooth would have disdained the shelter of a wood, even singly and unarmed, against a legion of armed enmies.

Here too I must note another instance of the want of that correctness in writing history, without which it becomes romance. Genl.

Lee says that Tarleton, in another enterprise some time after, penetrated up the South side of James river to New London, in Bedford county. To that neighborhood precisely, where I had a possession, I had carried my family, and was confined there several weeks by the effects of a fall from my horse, and I can assure the readers of Genl. Lee's history that no enemy ever came within 40. miles of New London.

Three versions of this document survive, here designated as MS (1), MS (2), and MS (3), of which (1) and (3) are printed in full above. Each MS consists of two parts—a fair copy of TJ's (now missing) original diary of Arnold's invasion, kept from 31 Dec. 1780 to 11 Jan. 1781, together with several added paragraphs of memoranda and observations on events later in the year 1781. The texts of the Diary in MS (1) and MS (2) are virtually identical; MS (3) provides a terser version, which, however, contains some data not found elsewhere and is for that reason printed in full. The material appended to each copy of the Diary is substantially different in all three MSS; the material added to MS (2), the only MS not printed in full, is given in notes 10, 12, and 13 below. A description of the three MSS follows:

MS (1) (DLC: TJ Papers, 6: 1012-13); 4 p.; undated; entirely in TJ's hand and captioned by him: "A Diary kept by Th: J from Dec. 31. 1780 to Jan. 11. 1781. and more general notes of subsequent transactions during the British invasion." The first part of the MS (the Diary) is a copy of "memorandums . . . often written on horseback, and on scraps of paper taken out of my pocket at the moment," preserved to the end of TJ's life but not now known to be extant (TJ to the younger Henry Lee, 15 May 1826). The date when this fair copy was made has not been established, though except for one slightly later addition (see note 15) it may well have been made in 1796 when the Depositions of Blair, Hylton, and Currie (Document III) were taken down. MS (1) has apparently not been hitherto printed.

MS (2) (DLC: TJ Papers, 150: 26239-41); 6 p.; without date and without caption. This MS contains the text of the Diary without essential change (though see notes 3 to 9 below) from MS (1), but the appended matter, modified and enlarged in substance, provides conclusive evidence as to the date of this fair copy, for TJ here alludes to the slanders of a Federalist writer named Turner and mentions specifically the "lapse of four and twenty years" since the events under discussion. MS (2) was, therefore, prepared in 1805, in reply to attacks by Thomas Turner of Jefferson co., who had published a hostile and highly embroidered account of TJ's "abandonment" of Richmond in May and his flight from Monticello in June 1781 that was reprinted in New England newspapers (see Woodfin, "Contemporary Opinion in Virginia of Thomas Jefferson," p. 65-6; and Thomas Paine, "Another Callender—Thomas Turner of Virginia," *Complete Writings*, ed. Foner, II, 980-8). MS (2) has been printed in the principal editions of TJ's writings, though only Ford (VIII, 363-74) has assigned it a date, namely, Aug. 1805.

MS (3) (DLC: TJ Papers, 207: 36976-80); 10 p.; PoC in TJ's hand, with caption as printed above. This MS is part of a series of documentary enclosures in TJ's letter to Joseph Delaplaine, 26 July 1816, in reply to a request for factual details respecting Arnold's raid on Richmond and Tarleton's raid on Charlottesville. Delaplaine drew heavily on this account for the biographical sketch of TJ in his famous *Repository of the Lives and Portraits of Distinguished American Characters* (Phila., 1815-1816), but, in deference to TJ's "insuperable aversion" to being drawn into public controversy, suppressed his source of information. Girardin in his continuation of Burk's *History of Virginia*, IV (1816), xii-xv, printed the Diary of Arnold's invasion as copied out in MS (3) and also a portion of the appended matter. Girardin's work was largely written while the author lived at or near Milton in Albemarle co., 1813-1815, and was based on TJ's books and MSS. TJ himself read and corrected Girardin's chapters relat-

Encampment of the Convention Army at Charlottesville

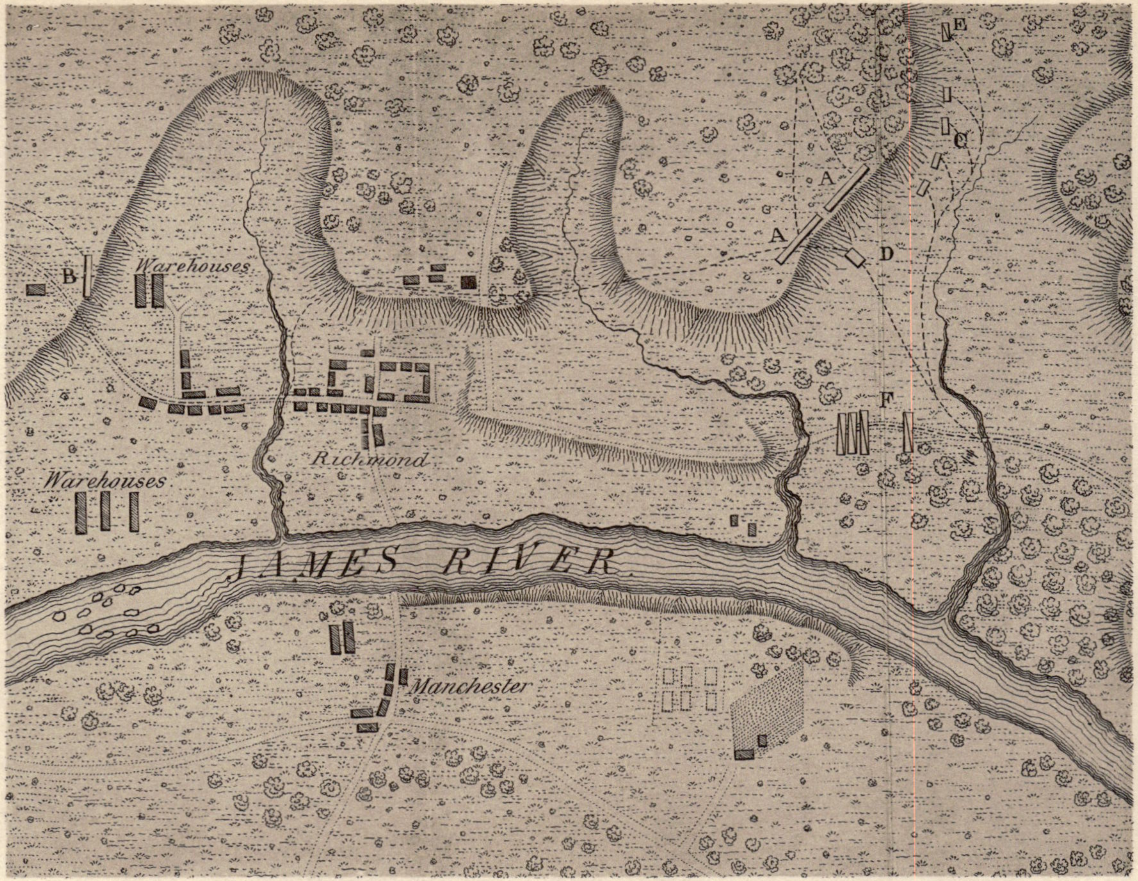

Plan of Arnold's Raid on Richmond, 5 January 1781

ing to the Revolution, and it is especially interesting to find that, in a letter of 12 May 1815 returning a draft of Chapter XVIII (dealing with the events of early 1781), TJ said that he had made important changes in the order of Girardin's narrative, though he had left "all . . . stated in your own words." He went on to say that he could now vouch for the perfect accuracy of the narrative of "the movements of the enemy, and my own, day by day as they occurred during Arnold's excursion to Richmond." These events were fairly fresh in TJ's mind in 1815 because he had evidently gone over his papers after reading Gen. Henry Lee's account of the raid on Richmond in *Memoirs of the War in the Southern Department* (Phila. and N.Y., 1812), II, 5-15. Lee's strictures on Virginia's unpreparedness for the invasion despite Washington's warning of it in December, her prostration "at the feet of a handful of men, led by a traitor and deserter," because of "the timidity and impotence" of her "rulers" (meaning TJ), were strong reasons for TJ's desire to put the facts as he knew them on record and for his later appeal to Lee's son to correct his father's account when a revised edition was in preparation (see TJ to the younger Lee, 15 May 1826; the new edition, issued in 1827, contained Lee's exchange of letters with TJ in 1826 in a long note, p. 203ff.). Comparing the text of the Diary in MS (3), that is to say, the 1816 copy, with that in MS (1) and MS (2), it is impossible to account satisfactorily for some of the differences between them. The entries in the 1816 version are much more condensed, much more truly diary-like, and this text may well be closer to the original than that of the other copies. But if we may account for the smoother style of the earlier copies by supposing that TJ was there freely expanding his original rough entries, why did he leave out certain material facts (such as the names of the persons from whom he received information of the enemy's movements on 3 Jan.) that *are* in MS (3)? A detailed comparison would reveal other variations for which there is at present no adequate explanation.

1 In MS (1) and MS (2) the dates appear as marginal glosses.

2 Brackets in MS.

3 In MS (2) this explanatory phrase is enclosed in square brackets, as are other similar ones indicated in the following notes. This suggests that in preparing MS (2) TJ was more scrupulous in distinguishing later insertions in the text of the Diary, but this supposition is incorrect if the more condensed MS (3) is actually a literal copy of the original Diary.

4 MS (2) has the following inserted in brackets after "Westover": "on the North side of the river and 25. miles below Richmond."

5 This phrase is bracketed in MS (2).

6 MS (2) has the following inserted in brackets after "Tuckahoe": "8. miles above and on the same side of the river."

7 MS (2) has the following inserted in brackets after "Manchester": "opposite to Richmond."

8 MS (2): "[8. or 10. miles below]."

9 MS (2): "[6. miles off from Westover]."

10 MS (2) continues without a break but inserts the following paragraph not in MS (1): "During this period time and place have been minutely cited, in order that those who think that there was any remissness in the movements of the Governor, may lay their finger on the point, and say when and where it was. Hereafter less detail will suffice."

11 MS (2): "Monticello, 2. or 3. miles from it."

12 In MS (2) another sentence was interlined at the end of this paragraph: "This appointment accordingly took place on the 12. day of June 1801 [*error for 1781*]."

13 From this point on, the text of MS (2) is markedly different from that of MS (1), being a reply direct to Thomas Turner's distorted account of the events in question. The remainder of the text of MS (2) reads as follows: "Notice of it however had been brought both to Monticello and Charlottesville, about sunrise. The Speakers, with their Colleagues, returned to Charlottesville, and with the other members of the legislature, had barely time, to get out of his [Tarleton's] way. Mr. Jefferson sent off his family, to secure them from danger, and was himself still at Monticello making arrangements for his own departure, when a Lieutt. Hudson arrived there at half speed, and informed him the enemy were then ascending the hill of Monticello. He departed immediately, and knowing that he would be pursued if he took the high road, he plunged into the woods of the adjoining moun-

tain, where being at once safe, he proceeded to overtake his family. This is the famous adventure of Carter's mountain which has so often resounded through the slanderous chronicles of federalism. But they have taken care never to detail the facts, lest these should shew that this favorite charge amounted to nothing more than that he did not remain in his house, and there singly fight a whole troop of horse, or suffer himself to be taken prisoner. Having accompanied his family one day's journey, he returned to Monticello. Tarleton had retired after 18. hours stay in Charlottesville. Mr. Jefferson then rejoined his family, and proceeded with them to an estate he had in Bedford, about 80. miles S.W. where, riding in his farm sometime after, he was thrown from his horse, and disabled from riding on horse back for a considerable time. But Mr. Turner finds it more convenient to give him this fall in his retreat before Tarleton, which had happened some weeks before, as a proof that he withdrew from a troop of horse with a precipitancy which Don Quixot would not have practised.

"[*Two lines and part of a third scored out beyond legibility.*] The facts here stated most particularly, with date of time and place, are taken from notes made by the writer hereof for his own satisfaction at the time. The others are from memory but so well recollected that he is satisfied there is no material fact mistated. Should any person undertake to contradict any particular on evidence which may at all merit the public respect, the writer will take the trouble (tho' not at all in the best situation for it) to produce the proofs in support of it. He finds indeed that of the persons whom he recollects to have been present on these occasions, few have survived the intermediate lapse of four and twenty years. Yet he trusts that some, as well as himself, are yet among the land of the living; and he is positively certain that no man can falsify any material fact here stated. He well remembers indeed that there were then, as there are at all times, some who blamed every thing done contrary to their own opinion, altho' their opinions were formed on a very partial knowledge of facts. The censures which have been hazarded by such men as Mr. Turner, are nothing but revivals of these half informed opinions. Mr. George Nicholas, then a very young man, but always a very honest one, was prompted by these persons to bring specific charges against Mr. Jefferson. The heads of these in writing were communicated thro' a mutual friend to Mr. Jefferson, who committed to writing also the heads of justification on each of them. I well remember this paper, and believe the original of it still exists, and tho' framed when every real fact was fresh in the knolege of every one, this fabricated flight from Richmond was not among the charges stated in this paper, nor any charge against Mr. Jefferson for not fighting singly the troop of horse. Mr. Nicholas candidly relinquished further proceeding. The House of Representatives of Virginia pronounced an honorable sentence of entire approbation of Mr. Jefferson's conduct, and so much the more honorable as themselves had been witnesses to it. And Mr. George Nicholas took a conspicuous occasion afterwards, of his own free will, and when the matter was entirely at rest, to retract publicly the erroneous opinions he had been led into on that occasion, and to make just reparation by a candid acknolegment of them."

14 The remainder of the text of MS (1) is in a smaller hand and was probably added at a slightly later date; see the following note.

15 This paragraph is written in the margin and is keyed to the text by asterisks preceding it and following the word "journals." It could not have been written before 1798, for TJ refers here, as he does at the end of MS (2) (see note 13 above) to a passage in *A Letter from George Nicholas, of Kentucky, to His Friend, in Virginia*, Lexington, 1798. "I am happy," wrote Nicholas in answering a tirade against TJ, "in having an opportunity of declaring, when it can be attributed to no improper motive, that I have long since, changed the unfavorable opinion, which, I once formed of that gentleman's political conduct, and that I consider him, as one of the most virtuous, as well as one of the ablest, of the American patriots" (reprint edn., ed. Temple Bodley, Filson Club Publications, No. 31, Louisville, 1926, p. 155). On the whole subject of the inquiry into TJ's conduct as governor, see Nicholas' Charges and Jefferson's Answers, printed below under date of 31 July 1781.

16 Here follows a copy of Nicholas' Charges and Jefferson's Answers and the Resolution of Assembly vindicating TJ in Dec. 1781; these are omitted here but are printed below under date of 31 July 1781.

II. Arnold's Invasion as Reported by Jefferson in the *Virginia Gazette*

RICHMOND, JANUARY 13.

A narrative of the late incursion made by the enemy to this place.

ON the 31st of December, a letter from a private Gentleman to General Nelson reached this place, notifying that in the morning of the preceding day, twenty seven sail of vessels had entered the Capes, and from the tenor of the letter, there was reason to expect within a few hours farther intelligence whether they were friends or foes, their force, and other circumstances. General Nelson went immediately into the lower country, with powers to call on the militia in that quarter, or to act otherwise as exigencies should require. The call of the militia from the middle and upper counties was not made till intelligence could be received that the fleet was certainly hostile. No farther intelligence came till the second instant, when the former was confirmed; it was ascertained that they were enemies, and had advanced up James river to Warrasqueak bay. All arrangements were immediately taken for calling in a sufficient body of militia for opposition. In the night of the third, advice was received that they were at anchor opposite James-town, Williamsburg was then supposed to be their object; the wind however, which had hitherto been unfavourable, shifted fair, and the tide being also in their favour, they ascended the river to Kennon's that evening, and with the next tide came up to Westover, having on their way taken possession of the battery at Hoods, by which two or three of their vessels had received some damage, but which was of necessity abandoned by the small garrison of fifty men placed there on the enemy's landing to invest the works. Intelligence of the enemy's having quitted the station at James-town, from which it was supposed they meant to [land at] Williamsburg, and that they had got in the evening to Kennon's, reached this place at five o'clock in the morning of the fourth, this was the first indication of their meaning to penetrate towards Richmond or Petersburg. As the orders for drawing the militia hither had been given but two days, no opposition was in readiness. Every effort was therefore necessary to withdraw the arms and other military stores, records, &c. from this place: Every effort was accordingly exerted to convey them to the foundery and labaratory, till about sunset of that day, when intelligence was received that the enemy had landed at Westover: From this it appeared that Richmond, and not Petersburg, was their object; it became necessary to remove every thing which remained here, across the river, as well as what had been carried to the foundery and labaratory; which operation was continued till the enemy approached very near. They marched from Westover at 2 o'clock in the afternoon of the 4th, and entered Richmond at one o'clock in the afternoon of the 5th. A regiment of infantry and about fifty horse continued on without halting to the foundery, they burnt that, the boring mill, the magazine, and two other houses, and proceeded to Westham, but nothing being in their power there, they retired to Richmond. The next morning they burnt some buildings of publick and some of private property, with what stores remained in them; destroyed a great quantity of private stores and about 12 o'clock retired towards Westover, where they encamped within the neck the next day. The loss sustained is not yet accurately known. At this place about 300 muskets, some soldiers clothing to a small amount, sulphur, some quarter masters stores, of which 120 sides of leather was the principal article, part of the artificers tools, and 3 waggons; besides which five brass 4 pounders, which had been sunk in the river, were discovered to them, raised and carried off. At the foundery about 5 tons of powder was thrown into the canal, of which there will be a considerable saving by remanufactoring it. Part of the papers belonging [to] the Auditors office, and the books and papers of the Council office, which were ordered to Westham, but in the confusion carried by mistake to the foundery, were also destroyed. The roof of the foundery was burnt, but the stacks of chimnies and furnaces not at all injured. Within less than 48 hours from the time of their landing and 19 from our knowing their destination they had penetrated 33 miles, done the whole injury, and retired. Our militia, dispersed over a large tract of country can be called in but slowly. On the day the enemy [march]ed to this place, two hundred only were [embodi]ed, they were of this town and neighbour[hood] and were too few to do any thing effectual. The enemy's forces are commanded by the parricide Arnold.[1]

Printed from *Virginia Gazette* (Dixon & Nicolson), 13 Jan. 1781. Only one copy of this issue is known to have survived (in Vi); it is mutilated slightly.

The authorship of this narrative may be attributed with entire confidence to TJ despite the absence of documentary evidence to that effect. TJ was the only person at this time in possession of all the facts related here, and some of the language in the narrative is identical with that in his letters to Huntington and Washington dated 10 Jan. 1781 as well as other letters and memoranda written by him at this time. On 16 Jan. 1781 TJ sent a copy of the newspaper to Gen. Greene, remarking that it contained "a pretty exact narrative" of Arnold's raid.

[1] To this account the printers added the following paragraph, marked by a typographical fist: "The Gentlemen who furnished us with advertisements, &c. just before the incursion of the enemy at this place, are desired to furnish us with another copy, as they were destroyed together with the best part of the materials of this office."

III. Depositions Taken in 1796 respecting Jefferson's Conduct during Arnold's Invasion

Archibald Blair's Deposition

Being requested to state what I recollect of the circumstances which occasioned the loss of the public records in the year 1781, and the time Mr. Jefferson, the then Governor of Virginia, quitted Richmond upon the approach of the enemy,—I do well remember that Mr. Jefferson was extremely active in removing all public records from Richmond, and I have reason to believe that the Chief of their loss was owing to a mistake of the Waggoners conveying them to the foundery, instead of Westham where they were to have been thrown over the river, if pursued by the enemy. Mr. Jefferson desired me, as Clerk to the Council, to continue with him, and to take with me the public Seal and such papers as might be immediately wanted. I accordingly procured a Servant and horse to carry a small Trunk containing the papers, and, on the afternoon preceding Arnolds taking possession of Richmond, Mr. Jefferson desired me to proceed to Tuckahoe where he wou'd come to me. I sat out about sun-set, and left Mr. Jefferson busy in getting off the records.

A Blair
Oct. 12. 1796

Daniel Hylton's Deposition

I the subscriber an Inhabitant of the County of Henrico do hereby certifie that in January 1781 when Arnold invaded this Place, I was living very near the Foundery at West-Ham; That I was going out to Join the Militia to oppose the said Arnold, when I was stopt by Mr. Jefferson, then Governor of the state, and requested by him to attend to the removal of the Powder, ammunition, arms, and other Property belonging to the Public then in the magazine near West-Ham; That his orders were, to have every thing removed with all possible expedition across the River; That on the night preceeding the day of Arnolds arrival at the Foundery, Mr. Jefferson was at the subscribers House, as late as Eleven or twelve OClock at night, attending and giving directions about the Public Property; That he then said he should go up the River about 8 or 10 miles, cross the next morning and come down to Brittains Opposite west-Ham and that Carriages &ca, should be provided to take off the said Property; that this was done; that a very considerable quantity (I suppose about fifteen Tons) of Gun-Powder, and amunition with a number of arms, stores, &ca were transported as directed and thereby saved to the public; that the Enemy were so

Close upon us that I was obliged to have about three Hundred stand of arms thrown into the River, the greater part of which were afterwards recovered; that in the night preceeding the day of Invasion, the waggons (driven by white men) employed to bring the Records, &ca, from Richmond, by mistake attempted to get to the magazine, instead of the Landing on the River, and near the magazine overset and broke some arms &ca, that in Consequence of this accident, the Packages, which I found afterwards contained Records, were Lodged at the magazine and carriages could not be procured in time for the Removal, as the alarm was so great and sudden, that almost every person in the neighbourhood was endeavouring to put some of his Property in a state of safety by removing it; That it then and ever since, has appeared to the subscriber, that the said Mr. Jefferson did every thing which the nature of the case and his situation would admit, for the Public Interest.

Henrico County — DANL L. HYLTON
12th. October 1796.

Henrico Sc.

The foregoing certificate was subscribed and sworn to, in due form, before me, a magistrate for the County aforesaid.

Given under my Hand this 12th. day of October 17[96].

W: FOUSHEE

James Currie's Deposition

On application made to me, if I recollect any thing, in regard to the circumstances which led to the loss of the Publick records and other valuable papers in the year 1781 during the invasion of the British Army, when Mr. Jefferson was Governor, do well remember, that he appeard extremely anxious and very active, in having them removd from Richmond and deposited in a place of safety: and if possible entirely out of the reach of the enemy and for that and other duties of his office as chief magistrate did remain in Town fully as long as was either proper or prudent for him so to do; without manifest danger of becoming the prisoner of the invading Army, who were fast approaching the Seat of Government, without any efficient force that could at that time be brought against them, to stop their March, and that his conduct was then perfectly proper and that of a real patriot and friend of his country will be very fully evincd, by the concurrent voice of the Gentlemen who then acted with him in Council as well as the unanimous approving voice of the Virginia Legislature at the Subsequent meeting of the assembly of the State. JAMES CURRIE

MSS (DLC); all three documents are presumably, but not certainly, in the hands of their respective signers. Currie's deposition lacks a date but without doubt was taken down at about the same time with the others.

Though the precise circumstances evoking these statements in vindication of TJ's conduct during Arnold's raid have not been determined, it is clear that they were intended for publication as counterpropaganda to Federalist attacks on TJ during the presidential campaign of 1796. TJ's personal responsibility for the loss of many of Virginia's public records was a favorite charge of anti-Jeffersonian writers, and this was not the last time it was raised. For one so scrupulous as he was in preserving and disseminating public records, this must have been as peculiarly painful a charge as it was a false one.

To these depositions might well be added a communication to Fenno's *Gazette of the United States*, 29 Oct. 1796, signed by "A Subscriber," who was John Beckley, clerk of the Virginia House of Delegates. Beckley's statement was in reply to "Phocion" (William Loughton Smith and Oliver Wolcott, Jr.), who had in the same paper accused TJ of having "abandoned his trust at the moment of invasion" and had raked up other well-worn charges against TJ's conduct as governor. Beckley pointed out that TJ had not resigned until his term of office had expired, that his official conduct had been unanimously approved by the Delegates' resolution of 12 Dec. 1781, that he had personally superintended the removal of records and stores from Richmond before Arnold's attack on that town, that he had returned to the capital the moment the enemy evacuated it, and that Tarleton's force during his raid into Albemarle was "about 500 cavalry," not (as "Phocion" alleged) "a few light horsemen." To most of these events Beckley asserted that he was himself an eye-witness, as no doubt he was because of his official duties. Philip Marsh, in "Jefferson and the Invasion of Virginia," VMHB, LVII (1949), 322-6, prints Beckley's communication in full, with a commentary; Beckley's acknowledgment of his authorship is in a letter, not noted by Marsh, to William Burwell, 28 June 1805 (DLC: TJ Papers).

IV. William Tatham to William Armistead Burwell

SIR George Town, Columbia, June 13th. 1805

In compliance with your request, I have endeavoured to charge my recollection more minutely, concerning the particulars of my intercourse with Mr. Jefferson (at present the President of the United States) at several times while the British Army were in Virginia, in and about the year 1781.

At the time General Arnold arrived within the Capes, I was preparing for a journey from Richmond, on James River, to the Southern States: I had my horses Portmanteau &c. ready fixed at the door (and perhaps my foot actually in the stirrup) when an express was said to have that moment arrived at the Governor's with intelligence of the approach of an invading Enemy. I immediately rode to his house, and met Governor Jefferson walking out on the hill, by the side of his Garden, (now, or since that time, the Property of John Mayo Esqr).

He told me he had recieved such an express, but that, as other intelligence led him to suppose they were nothing more than a foraging Party, unless he had farther information to justify the measure, he should not disturb the Country by calling out the Militia: he would thank me, nevertheless, if I would go down to the late Major General Baron Steuben, who was at Wilton, (then the Estate of Peyton Randolph Esqr.) and recieve his orders if needful. I rode immediately to Wilton, and was dispatched by General Steuben to General Nelson at Williamsburgh; but, on my arrival there, I found the Town in confusion, and the inhabitants alarmed by the expectation of an immediate engagement at Kings Mills, near that Place, (an Estate then belonging, I believe, to Lewis Burwell Esqr.) whither I directly hastened.

On my arrival I found the late General Nelson, and the late Colol. James Innis at the head of about fifty five men, under the more immediate command of a Major Harrod, waiting to give the Enemy battle as they landed; and most of the Enemy's Ships were come to an anchor off the Place, a small boat taking the Soundings towards the Shore, and larger boats filled with men were manœuvering towards the land in readiness for debarkation. I delivered Baron Steubens orders to General Nelson, and was invited to join his suite.

I believe the Enemy were deterred from effecting their purpose on this occasion, partly by Colol. Innis's good management, and partly by an accidental occurrence, which happened, much to the soldierly credit of old Chancellor Wythe, and one or two other old Gentlemen who "*took a pop at them*" while Partridge shooting near the mouth of Archers Hope Creek.

From this time forward, a considerable share of active duty fell to my lot; and I was alternately in view of the Enemy and in personal communication with the commanding officer, many miles apart, sometimes repeatedly in the twenty four hours; so that I had speedily ridden down several very fine horses. While we lay at Holts Forge, on Chickahominy, shortly after the taking of the Works at Hoods and surprize at Charles City Court house, General Nelson desired me to have the best horse procured which could be found, in Camp or out of Camp, and to hold myself ready, at a Moment, for a very particular service. I ran to the Parade, where (almost at the same instant) a noted four mile running horse made his appearance, (*well known by the Name Epperson's Sorrel*) with the owner upon his back. He was impressed, and in a few minutes equipped with my saddle and Accoutrements and, I think, he was valued to three thousand Pounds, and, I believe, laid the basis of some popular maneuvrings, which produced ultimately an act of indemnity in favor of the General.

General Nelson then informed me that there were various reports about the Governor; that I must find him be he wheresoever he might; but, that as the dispatches I was to carry were of the utmost importance, I must (so far as the same was practical in effecting my purpose) avoid all risks of being taken—passing up the Country by way of Newcastle, and venturing no nearer to Richmond than that neighbourhood (*about twenty Miles off*) unless on good information that I could pass their Light Troops in safety. As I knew the Country well, I however ventured in among the Plantations till I got to that of Daniel Trueheart, Esqr. near the Meadow Bridges: here I learnt that the Enemy's Picquet was just called in, and retired from the Bridges towards the main body, at Richmond. I followed the Picquet carefully, entered Mr. Du'Vals House at Mount Comfort while the floor was flowing with the Liquors spilt by the British Soldiers and pushed into Richmond, from whence the army had just retreated. Here, one of our well affected Citizens (*I think old Richd. Crouch*) referred me to Moses Treadway, in Manchester, who conducted me to Mr. Jefferson, at a small Batcheler's House in Town then occupied by Doctr. Evans; and here I delivered my dispatches and spent part of the Evening. I understood the Enemy encamped that night about four mile Creek; perhaps about ten or twelve miles in a direct course, and were then on their retreat.

On another occasion, when the British Army marched from Petersburgh up to Manchester, I had been all Night with Baron Steuben who lay encamped at Chesterfield Court House, on business from General Nelson. In the morning, I went down to the Church near Osbornes, where I found an advanced Post commanded by Colol. Robert Goode, and his Videts coming in successively with intelligence that the enemy were advancing in force. As Colol. Goode doubted whether we had not mistaken a party of our own Men for the Enemy, I rode up to their advance, spoke to them, and recieved a rifle shot which settled the question. I covered Colol. Goode's retreat, on this occasion, with a small party of Volunteer Cavalry; availing ourselves of a dusty road, and our own impudence, in lieu of charging the Enemy when we were incompetent. I came off slowly before them till I gained the heights above Osbornes, and after alarming the intermediate route, along the road, was with Mr. Jefferson several times in the course of the night; when I conversed with him in his bed, without his shewing any kind of apprehension. I believe the Enemy encamped this Night about Ampthill and Warwick, distance from Mr. Jefferson about four to seven miles. The following morning, I joined Baron Steuben near the Coal Pits (ten or twelve Miles above Manchester) and, by his order, passed in between the Enemys main Body and Flanking Parties; being so near the Flare of their Drums that my Horse erected his Ears at them in getting off through a thicket. This was less than two Miles from where Mr. Jefferson slept; and I afterwards delivered Baron Steubens orders to Major Call who commanded the Cavalry hanging on their Rear.

After escaping from the defeat at Sedbarys near Chesterfield Court-House, on another occasion, I was bitten by a Dog which laid me up; and when Lord Cornwallis marched up the Country I was carried off by a trusty Negroe, in a cart laden with muskets and Bayonetts, which I understood were part of the Governors savings from the arms abandoned by the militia. We took a private way to Tuckahoe, *then the hospitable mansion of the late worthy T. M. Randolph Esq.*; This faithful old fellow I remember, was determined that no small party of the Enemy should take his charge from him as long as we were able to use the metal we were possessed off.

Shortly after this I recieved a hurt in Amelia County, by falling in with about three hundred of the present Major Genl. Tarlton's Mounted Legion, alone; though, by ten days hard struggle I had the good fortune to get clear of them. This circumstance rendered me unfit for service, till I joined the Army at Williamsburgh, before Genl. Washington took command on our way to the siege of York.

I understood, in the interim, the whole Government had become Itinerant, like that of Carolina; and had probably found safety both at Charlottesville, and Stanton. I frequently heard of Mr. Jefferson's exertions, *individually when the Militia left him to shift for himself*; And I am persuaded that if it had been as easy to raise Recruits at that day as it was stock jobbers, peculators, and Land Mongers afterwards, Mr. Jefferson (though left alone by many Coadjuters who should be ashamed of themselves) would never have had occasion to retreat far from the falls of James River. I have been thus particular to refresh the recollection of others;—& am Sir Your H Servt,

Wm Tatham

RC (DLC); at foot of text: "William Burwell Esqr."; endorsed by TJ: "Tatham Wm. to mr. Burwell." In DLC are two identical transcripts in TJ's hand of those portions of Tatham's letter that particularly refer to TJ himself; one of the transcripts was sent to Joseph Delaplaine as part of the series of enclosures in TJ's letter of 26 July 1816; see Document I, note on MS (3), above. The transcripts were probably made, however, soon after the receipt of the original letter by Burwell, who was at this time TJ's private secretary.

It is scarcely necessary to put the reader on guard against some of Tatham's more romantic memories; the circumstances of this interesting adventurer at the time the present letter was written will induce a necessary caution in using his testimony. He had just returned in 1805 from a decade of more or less frustrating travels in Spain and England, and he was about to try to sell to the federal government the remarkable collection of books, manuscripts, maps, enginering data, &c. that he had assembled—a collection that he hoped would become the basis for a department of public works (with, no doubt, Tatham at its head); he was, therefore, most willing in 1805 to oblige TJ by recalling these events and, while the essential facts here recalled are no doubt reliable, both the circumstances in which he found himself and Tatham's rather romantic and eccentric nature would naturally cause him to magnify and embroider his own exploits (see DAB and references there, especially *Am. State Papers*, *Misc.*, I, 1834, p. 457 ff.). In view of the Virginians' hostility to the impressment of any of their blooded horses, as reflected in the correspondence between TJ and Gen. Greene, it is quite unlikely that Tatham always found himself mounted on, and riding to earth, such fine animals as he describes; it is extremely unlikely that he encountered very dusty roads in Virginia in January.

V. Deposition of Christopher Hudson respecting Tarleton's Raid in June 1781

July 26 1805.

In the Month of June 1781, near Milton on my way to Join the Marquis La Fayette's Army I met with a Mr. Long, who informed Me that Duvit [Jouett] had arrived the preceeding evening at Charlottesville, and brought information of the approach of the English to that place under Tarleton. Upon inquiring from Long whether Mr. Jefferson had receiv'd information he was ignorant; I immediately proceeded to Monticello, where I found Mr. Jefferson, perfectly tranquil, and undisturbed. At my earnest request he left his house; which was Surrounded in Ten Minutes at farthest by a troop of Light-horse. I was convinced his Situation was truly critical since there was only one Man (his gardener) upon the Spot. I well remember he was not governor at that time his term of Service having expired and General Nelson appointed his Successor.

I was also attach'd to Captn. Call's Troop of horse, when Philips and Arnold, in their Second invasion of Virginia, reach'd Manchester; I was constantly on duty, where, Mr. Jefferson (then Governor) always appear'd, and by his presence, activity and perfect composure, inspired the Troops with the utmost confidence; he remain'd in Richmond until the retreat of the English to Warwick and down James River. CHRISTOPHER HUDSON

MS (DLC); endorsed: "Sign'd by Captn Hudson in presence of Isaac Coles & myself Wm A. Burwell Augst 4th 1805. [*In another hand*:] Statement of Captn Hudson."

This Deposition, like Tatham's letter (Document IV), was obtained by W. A. Burwell, undoubtedly at TJ's request, in order to refute the charge of cowardice on TJ's part circulated by Thomas Turner in 1805; see note on Document I. The relative rank of John Jouett and Christopher Hudson, both of whom brought warnings to Monticello of the approach of Tarleton's horsemen, in the annals of Virginia heroism has been much debated by antiquarians; see *Tyler's Quart.*, XXII-XXIV (1940-1948). TJ's Account Book has a characteristically laconic entry for that momentous day: "June 4. British horse came to Monticello." In Randall's *Life* (I, 335-9), however, is a very circumstantial narrative of TJ's movements on 4 June, based largely on "the statements, oral and written, of several members of Mr. Jefferson's family, who repeatedly heard all the particulars from his lips, and from those of other actors in the scene." Lt. Col. Banastre Tarleton's narrative of his foray on Charlottesville has this sarcastic sentence, which no doubt influenced later, unfriendly American historians: "The attempt to secure Mr. Jefferson was ineffectual; he discovered the British dragoons from his house, which stands on the point of a mountain, before they could approach him, and he provided for his personal liberty by a precipitate retreat" (*History of the Campaigns of 1780 and 1781, in the Southern Provinces of North America*, London, 1787, p. 297). ISAAC COLES was TJ's secretary in 1805.

From Charles Scott

SIR
Hadrels Point Decr 80

I am unhappy to inform Your Excellency of the Distressed Situation of our troop prisoners at this place, for want of Clothing and Necessaries. The Very long delay I have no doubt has been occasioned by Some unforeseen Circumstances, perhaps the probability of a General Exchange of prisoners. However I hope the latter is not the reason why the Supplies are not Sent on, for Wear we Exchangd tomorrow we Could not Move without Much Injury to the Troops which might Probabily be Charged to Some other Cause unjustly. I have not time to write Your Excellency so fully on this Subject as I wish. This will be handed You by Colo. [Burgess] Ball who will Point out to You our Situation more Clearly.

I have the Honor to be Sir Your obt. Servt., CHS. SCOTT

RC (Vi); addressed twice, once in Scott's hand and again in a bold calligraphic hand; also endorsed twice, one endorsement reading: "Genl Scotts Lr. recd Feby 81." Cover also bears notation: "Examined by Geo B Gibbs D.C. P."

Steuben's Plan for Preventing Desertion

[*Without place or date*] In a long war the difficulty and expense of raising men increases, and "every possible means should be employed for the preservation of the Men after they are raised." The incomplete state of the regiments obliges one regiment to be shifted into another, destroying the attachment between officers and men "which is necessary for their preservation." The officers, "disgusted at the instability and smallness of their Commands," become careless of the welfare of their men and allow them to absent themselves when well and take no pains for their recovery when sick. Discharges from the army have no prescribed form and are not printed. "It is more than probable that many have been Counterfeited by Deserters." To prevent abuses the following suggestions are submitted: "That the County Lieutenants be Charged to make the Strictest Enquiry" concerning all men who return home before the expiration of their term of draft and to have deserters punished—but not by serving in the army, it being "disgraceful to the service to have Malefactors sent to Serve in the Ranks with those who defend their Country"; that those who have written discharges be required to produce them to the county lieutenant, who, if the draftee has no infirmity, will send the discharge to the Governor who will send it to the officer responsible, in order that the person may be punished; that forms of discharge and furlough be printed and no officer "under a Certain Rank should be authorized to grant them"; that a returned soldier be required to report to the county lieutenant in 8 days, otherwise taken up as a deserter; that the county lieutenant make regular reports to the Governor of all persons returned from service.

MS (NHi); 3 p.

This document certainly belongs in the sequence of Steuben's letters to TJ advising reforms in the organization of the army and was probably enclosed in his letter of 18 Dec., q.v.; see also Steuben's letters of 9, 16, and 28 Dec. On 13 Jan. 1781 Greene wrote to Steuben: "I intirely approve of your forms for furloughs and discharges; but wish you to consult with Colonel Davis upon the subject, who is a man of great observation and has had long experience respecting the abuses prevailing in the Army and State, in this matter, after which you will follow your own judgment and get some blanks printed as soon as possible" (NHi).

From Francis Kinloch

SIR Wednesday Evening [1780?]

I have to [entreat?] that your Excellency would be so kind as to forward the letters that accompany this; that addressed to [Gen.?] Huger to Charles Town You will be pleased to send southwardly, and I could wish that your Excellency would so far indulge me, as to enclose it with any occasional dispatches, either to Genl. Greene or to Governor Nash.

I have already, If I am not mistaken, Mentioned to You, Sir, the name of a Capn: Miller, a prisoner on parole in this neighborhood, and have now to solicit a favour in his behalf, which is, that Your Excellency would permit him to remain in his present situation for a week or two by which time I am in hopes, that I shall obtain an answer from Gen: Greene, to whom also Baron de Steuben has written on the same subject, relative to the enlargement of his parole. My wish is that this Gentleman may be allowed to return to Charles town, as it would be an excellent opportunity of writing to my Mother, and Sister, and as he could render them many services in their present helpless situation. On my representation to Col: Coles, that Gentleman consented to Capn: Millers remaining where he is, 'till Your Excellency's further orders could be obtaind. I have therefore to solicit, Sir, that You would be so kind as to convey them by return of the bearer: Enclosed is the answer I received from Col: Coles.

The Ladies of this place present their best respects to Yourself, and Mrs. Jefferson. I beg leave to add mine & am, with every sentiment of respect & esteem, Sir, Your Excellency's Most Obedt. Servant,

F: KINLOCH

RC (DLC); addressed; endorsed by TJ: "Kinloch." Without date or place, but doubtless written late in 1780 or early in 1781 from Albemarle co.

Francis Kinloch of South Carolina, who had had a European education, returned to America in 1778, served in several southern campaigns and was captured at Charleston, May 1780; he was paroled and came to Virginia, where, in Feb. 1781, he married Mildred, daughter of TJ's friend and neighbor John Walker (H. D. Bull, "Kinloch of South Carolina," *S.C. Hist. & Geneal. Mag.*, XLVI [1945], 65-7). Hence COL: COLES must be John Coles, at this time county lieutenant of Albemarle (*Official Letters*, II, 479-80); and THE LADIES OF THIS PLACE were no doubt those of the Walker families of Albemarle co.

To George Muter

[1780?]

Colo. Muter will be pleased to enquire into the particular arms and accoutrements delivered by deserters into hands responsible to the state, and to settle a price on them at about 80 for one of what they used to cost in the state. I will send the individuals to Colo. Muter.

RC (PHi); unsigned; addressed by TJ: "Colo. Muter"; endorsed: "Govr. respecting those people who have recd. Arms from Deserters & pointing out a mode of payment for them." Without place or date, but doubtless written in late 1780 or early 1781.

Pass for Charles? Torriano

VIRGINIA TO WIT [1780?]

Mr. Torriano has permission to visit Colo. Wilson Miles Cary at his residence either in Fluvanna or Hanover, he there considering himself as under all the obligations of his parole other than that which is meant to be hereby dispensed with as is necessary to give him the benefit of this permission.

Dft (DLC).

There were two Torrianos who were British officers serving in America: Charles, lt. and quartermaster of the 20th regt.; and George, lt., 64th regt. (W. C. Ford, *British Officers Serving in the American Revolution*, Brooklyn, 1897); the 20th was one of Burgoyne's regiments surrendered on convention. See also Geismar to TJ, Nov.? 1780.

Form of Pass for British Deserters

VIRGINIA TO WIT Richmond [1780?]

The bearer hereof a deserter from the British army has permission to cross James river at Goochland Courthouse and to remain on the South side of the river above Chesterfeild county, conducting himself with fidelity to this commonwealth.

Dft (Vi); endorsed: "Pass to the Deserters." At foot of text, in a hand other than TJ's: "*15 Copies*." There is no good clue as to the date of this paper.

Notes concerning the Right of Removal from Office

[1780]

Whether the Executive may remove officers of the line or staff.

There may be a difference as to the Chaplains and such others as are not appointed by the Executive. But qu?

Again as to officers of the line, it is highly probable that no such would ever be removed but on regular trial by a court martial: unless indeed the occasion was very great, as in the case of Genl. Lee where the sentence given by the court martial was against the universal sense of mankind.

The question principally affects the Staff, whose rapacity, inattention and means of evasion require energetic superintendance.

The power of appointing and removing executive officers inherent in Executive.

Executive inadequate to every thing. Appoint deputies—qui agit per alterum &c. Ministerial office may be executed by deputy but not judicial. He who appoints may remove.

Difference between an office and estate.

An indefinite conveyance of an estate is for life—not to be accounted for ex vi termini, but historically from known progress of feuds. In their early state was not so.

An indefinite appointment to office is during pleasure. Escheat—clerks of parliament—clerks of council &c. Otherwise if I employ a steward indefinitely he would have freehold.

Ld. Coke's opinion as to privy counsellor condemned by practice and general opinion.

Law has so considered it. And where the officers of government should have freehold has declared they shall hold during good behavior. Judges—Register Clerks—Attorney General. Where not removable by Executive, reserved expressly to legislature or others. Aud. B. W. & T. [Boards of War and Trade] Treasurer.

All the principles of law which may be retailed on this subject restrained to civil government.[1]

The freest governments in the world, have their army under absolute government.

Republican form and principles not to be introduced into government of an army.

Congress exercise powers of dismission—Genl. Lee.

Consequences. Cannot dismiss nor suspend the most pettifogging and rascally officer. Forage masters—waggon masters—gardeners—purveyors—nurses—expresses—waggoners—smiths—carpenters—mercantile agents—ambassadors—Directors general—surgeons—surgeons mates—chaplains—Commissaries—Quartermasters—

Indolence, rapacity and means of evasion of Staff may account for the ordinary exercise of the powers of dismission on them, while those of the line, over whom the powers have been equal, have been submitting to the regular but more dilatory forms of trial by a military court.

N (DLC); entirely in TJ's hand. Undated, but after Gen. Lee's dismissal by Congress 10 Jan. 1781 (JCC, XVI, 33) and before the Boards of War and Trade were abolished in June 1780. TJ became familiar with the "rapacity, inattention and means of evasion" practised by forage masters, purveyors, &c., soon after becoming governor.

[1] Following this is a deleted line reading: "The army, as such, not comprehended within civil constitution."

To William Armistead

SIR In Council January 1. 1781

There is an account of very considerable amount between us and Mr. S. Nathan a merchant from the Havannah which we are to desire you to settle with Mr. Smith who acts for him. The debts against us may be arraigned under three heads. First, advances on a purchase of goods made at Baltimore and Philadelphia for us by Mr. Nathan; this is to be settled according to the price of tobacco at the time. The money was advanced. Second, a set of bills drawn at St. Vincennes, Kaskaskeas and the falls of Ohio on Colo. Clarke the Governour and Treasurer of Virga. These Bills have no acceptances on them, but we agreed to pay them according to the rate of depreciation which shoud be certified by Colo. Todd and Colo. Clarke. I inclose you a table of depreciation certified by them and on another paper a settlement of the true worth of the bills in hard money according to that table which you can readily convert into currency by the medium of tobacco. 3rd a set of bills drawn at the same places on the same persons and on Mr. Oliver Pollock of new Orleans. These bills Mr. Nathan brought with him and presented to the executive, informing them that he had taken them up at new Orleans or the Havanna and paid hard money for them, dollar for dollar; the executive being then uninformed in what manner these bills had been negociated and having no particular reasons to doubt but that they had been disposed of by Colo. Clarke and Colo. Todd as hard money assumed on every Bill that they would pay it in Tobacco at twenty five Shillings the hundred. Since this it has appeared from Colo. Clarkes Information that these Bills except the one drawn on New Orleans were drawn and negotiated precisely on the same Footing with the others, that is that they were drawn to pay for Articles purchased at the depreciated Prices and were not expected by the Person in whose Favour they were drawn to be paid for otherwise than in depreciated Money. The Difference which this makes to the State is immense and as our Assumpsit was on Mr. Nathans own Word we do not think that any Error into which we have been led by want of Information or Misinformation can in Equity be irrevocable. We do therefore insist on settling this set of Bills on the same Principle of Depreciation on which the other is settled and cannot but believe Mr. Nathan will be sensible of the Justice of this and will concur in it. I am Sir your very humble Servant,

T.J.

P.S. Monies have been advanced to Mr. Nathan, Colo. Legras and Majr. Lintot in Part of the above Accounts. These will appear on the Auditors Books and in Mr. Days Book.

FC (Vi). Enclosures not located.

For the accounts of Simon NATHAN, see TJ to the Board of Trade, 18 Mch. 1780, and notes there. On 1 Jan. the Council ordered a warrant for £50,000 to William Armistead "on account of

Mr. Simon Nathan" (*Va. Council Jour.*, II, 269); and on 30 Jan. another order (Vi: Contingent Fund Vouchers), signed by TJ, was issued to Nathan for £10,-000 for the same purpose. See also TJ to Va. Delegates in Congress, 15 Mch. 1781 and references there.

To William Armistead

SIR In Council January 1st. 1781

I desired you some time ago to provide cloathing for five hundred and odd Men according to a List from Baron Steuben which I put into your hands: be pleased now to deliver the Materials to the Person attending from Colo. Davies to receive them out of the Stock you purchased or what came from Winchester or from any other Stock you have.

I am Sir your humble Servant, T.J.

FC (Vi).

To John Browne

SIR In Council January 1st 1781

The inclosed Letter will inform you what measures have been taken for procuring a proper Stock of Flower for the ensuing Year. It contains a List of the Counties on which we called for Flower and the Quantity from each County. You will be pleased to take measures for raising it [for] use to fifteen thousand Barrels by calling on the Commissioners of such other Counties as you think proper or any other more eligible Means. Mr. Benjamin Harrison lent some bread and Flower to the State. Be pleased to inform of the Quantity and repay it immediately. I am &c, T.J.

FC (Vi). The enclosed letter has not been identified.

John Browne (this is the form of his name he invariably used in signing letters, though other records indiscriminately give "Brown" and "Browne") was appointed a commissary of purchases and issues for Virginia 29 Oct. 1778 (*Va. Council Jour.*, II, 206; *Official Letters*, II, 537); on 3 Jan. 1781 he was appointed commissioner under the Act for procuring a supply of provisions and other necessaries for the use of the army (same, p. 270); thereafter he is sometimes referred to as state commissary general.

Edward Carrington and Richard Claiborne: Plan for the Quartermaster's Department in Virginia

1st. January 1781

Whereas the irregular manner in which the Quarter Masters Department for the State of Virginia has hitherto been conducted, has been attended with many delays and inconveniencies both to the people and to the public service; and it being expedient that a new disposition should be made to remove those difficulties agreable to the late System for the Quarter Masters department, established by Congress; and the duties of the Officers to be employed and their districts and posts be more clearly understood, it is therefore proposed.

That, there be nine Assistant deputy Quarter Master's, who shall have charge of the principle posts to be established in the State, as the governing places to which the Stores and supplies are to be drawn, and that a certain District be given to each.

That as the great line of communication from Philadelphia to the Southern Army through this State will be from Alexandria to some part of Staunton, or Dan rivers, there be one principle post at Alexandria, one at Fredericksburg, one at Carters ferry on James river, and one at some convenient place on Dan, or Staunton which will be governed by the navigation up the river Dan.

That, as Richmond is the seat of Government and a place where the principle Factories for the Southern department are established, it be a principle post.

Williamsburg being a place where the supplies from the lower Counties should be collected it is necessary to establish it as a principle post for that purpose.

That Charlottesville be continued as a principle post for the accommodation of the Convention Troops.

Winchester being a place where good Wagons and Horses may be procured with great ease, that it be a principle post for that purpose, and to comprehend as much of that Country as supplies can be drawn from with convenience.

That as Petersburg is allways a post of convenience in case of invasions in the lower parts of the State, and a place to which the supplies from the Counties below the falls of Ronoke, and others convenient for the navigation of the Appomattox River, should be collected that it be held a principle post.

That the District of Alexandria comprehend the Counties of Fairfax, Prince William, Loudon.

The District of Fredericksburg the Counties of Northumberland, Lancaster, Richmond, Westmoreland, King George, Stafford, Fauquier, Spotsylvania, Caroline, King & Queen, Essex, Middlesex.

The District of Carters ferry the Counties of Louisa, Goochland, Powhatan, Cumberland, Buckingham, Prince Edward.

The District of the Rivers, Dan and Stanton the Counties of Mecklinburg, Lunenburg, Charlotte, Bedford, Hallifax, Pittsylvania, Henry.

The District of Richmond the Counties of Hanover, Henrico, King William, New Kent, Charles City, Chesterfield.

The District of Williamsburg the Counties of James City, Warwick, Elizabeth City, York, Gloucester, Princes ann, Norfolk, Nansemond, Isle of White, Northampton, Accomack.

The District of Charlottesville, the Counties of Culpeper, Orange, Albemarle, Fluvannah, Amherst, Augusta.

The District of Petersburg, the Counties of Surry, Prince George, Dinwiddie, Southampton, Sussex, Brunswick, Greenesville, Amelia.

That there be so many depending posts within the different Districts, as shall be found necessary for the purpose of collecting supplies and that the direction be given to a Storekeeper.

That it is expected the supplies beyond the blue Ridge, to the Southward of the Winchester District are used for the support of the Troops in that Quarter, and are under the direction of proper persons, they are omitted in this arrangement. But should it be found necessary hereafter to comprehend them, they will be added to one, or more of districts already pointed out or formed into other districts as may be convenient.

That as the supplies within the districts are to come from the Counties, forming them in proper proportions, it is proposed that the assistant Deputy Quarter Masters for the district shall be authorised by the Executive to call on the Civil authority to furnish them from time to time with the necessary means of transportation for the supplies coming from each respective County so that each County will regularly do its own separate duty.

That the transportation from one post to another shall be made by public Wagons, or Boats, as far as we shall have them to answer the purpose, and that where we shall want the aid of private property the Quarter Master from whose district the stores are to go, in the first instance shall have power to call on the civil authority within the district for such aid; and that the private Wagons, or Boats so furnished shall be discharged at the next post from whence the stores are to be forwarded by the same means from that district, timely information being given from post to post by the Quarter Masters of the coming of such a number of Boats, or Wagons.

This is a system proposed in consequence of our having experienced the good effects of similar ones to the northward both in public and private points of view.

EDWARD CARRINGTON D.Q.M. Genl. for the S. Army
RICHARD CLAIBORNE D.Q.Mr. S.V.

Tr (Vi); endorsed twice—at the end of the communication of 1 Jan., and on the final page of the additional memoranda; see below. Another Tr (DNA: RG 93); endorsed: "No. 1. Plan for conducting the business of the Quarter Masters department in Virginia." Both transcripts addressed at foot of text: "His Excellency Governor Jefferson & Council."

There is no indication in the extant Council Journals that this plan was considered at this time, but see Richard Claiborne to TJ, 29 Jan. 1781, with which a copy of the plan was enclosed.

Below the text in Tr (Vi) there are the following entries, in the same hand, under the dates indicated:

"February 15th 1781.

"An order from Colo: Carrington advising the approach of the Army under the Command of Lord Cornwallace to Boyds ferry and the necessity of sending all the heavy Baggage of General Greenes Army to Prince Edward Court house rendered an alteration in the arrangement indispensable. Capt. Charles Russell is therefore to retire to Prince Edward Court house and take charge of the Stores. To the post of Prince Edward Court house are given the Counties of Prince Edward, Charlotte, Lunenburg, Mecklenburg, Bedford, which are to be taken from the Districts of Carters ferry and Boyds ferry.

"March 11th 1781.

"The Enemy having retired from Dan river, Mr. William McCraw is appointed to that Station and to keep his principal post at Winbishes Stores in Peytonsburg.

"April 2d. 1781

"The prisoners having marched to Winchester from Charlottesville, that place is to be discontinued as a principal post; the Counties of Orange, Albemarle, Fluvannah, Amherst, and Augusta to be given to Carters ferry; and the County of Culpeper, to Fredericksburg district. Capt. Rice to settle his accounts as soon as possible.

"May 10th 1781.

"The honorable Major General Baron Stuben having directed that Charlottesville be the place of General rendezvous for the equipment of the Troops now raising in this State for the Continental service, and as a large number of Wagons, horses and drivers are to be procured for the Army under the Command of the Marquis de la Fayette makes it necessary that it be again established a principal post; Capt. Rice is restored to the full possession of his former District and to be Stationed at that place as Assistant Deputy Quarter Master.

"Captain Charles Russell being appointed to superintend the receiving and delivery of the Stores which are to be collected at Albemarle old Court house as a place of security from the incursions of the Enemy, the post of Prince Edward Court-house which was under his direction is discontinued and the Counties comprehended with it are annexed to their orriginal districts of the Rivers Dan and Stanton, and Carters ferry on James River.

"The Enemy having taken possession of the post of Petersburg, and made prisoner Capt. Holmes, who was Assistant Deputy Quarter Master at that place, the district is discontinued, and the Counties are to be annexed to the adjoining districts as may hereafter be found convenient. Mr. Daniel Teasdale, Clerk to Capt. Holme's is to settle the accounts as soon as possible.

"14th June 1781

"The Enemy having got possession of the lower parts of the State and the public Stores being directed to be sent beyond the Mountains that Staunton in

Augusta be a principal post for that purpose, and to influence the Counties of Augusta, Rockingham, Rockbridge and Greenbrier, and the direction of it be given to Capt. Thomas Hamilton. This alteration is agreable to an order from Colo. Edward Carrington Deputy Quarter Master General for the Southern Army, dated 23d May 1781."

To William Davies

SIR In Council January 1st 1781

Baron Steuben having desired that all Issues and Furnitures from us to the Continent might be on his Order while here, I immediately on Receipt of your Letter sent it down to the Baron; he was just set out to Hoods. I therefore have given an Order to Mr. Armistead to deliver the Materials to the Person attending for you that they may be making up and paying due Attention to the Barons Request. Am to ask the Favour of you to let not a Shred be issued till the Baron shall give orders on the Subject. Before that Time I hope some Arrangement will be taken for debiting the Souldiers with them at proper Prices as that is to be done as to all Issues after the first of August last which were not due. On the Order of Baron Steuben a Person is gone to Petersburg to select a Number of the best Arms there and have them brought on to your Post which I suppose will answer your request of [one] hundred Stand. I am &c.,

T.J.

FC (Vi).

From Nathanael Greene

SIR Camp on Pedee January 1st 1781

This will be handed your Excellency by Capt. Watts who is ordered to Virginia to recruit for the first Regiment of Light Dragoons. Cavalry is of great importance to the service in this department and I must beg your Excellency to give every aid in your power to fill the Regiment as soon as possible and that immediate measures may be taken for compleating the compliment of horse required of your State for the first and third Regiments. It will promote the service and give great security to the Army, if all the Dragoons are picked men, and natives of America; as foreigners frequently desert, and give intelligence to the Enemy in an unfavourable moment and generally carry off with them a very valuable horse with all the accoutrements. For these and many other reasons which might be mentioned I am clearly of opinion that none but natives ought to be in the Cavalry and even then ought to be of the better order of men, as so much frequently depends upon the information of a single dragoon.

I pursuade myself this business is of such importance as this Army is very weak in Cavalry and the enemy greatly reinforced, that your Excellency will give the business all the dispatch that the nature of it will admit.

Your Col. White will furnish your Excellency with a return of the strength of the Regiment. [I] am with great respect Your Excellency's Most obedt Humble Servt, NATH GREENE

MS not located. Text from *Pennsylvania Magazine of History and Biography*, XXVIII (1904), 241-2, where the letter is printed from an unnamed source.

To Benjamin Harrison

SIR In Council Jan. 1. 1781.

The inclosed letter conveying intelligence of a fleet appearing in our bay, came to hand yesterday. It's size has given suspicions that it may be hostile, more especially as we have been lately informed that an embarkation was taking place at New York. I have thought it my duty to communicate it to the General assembly before their rising, as they might perhaps wish to give some advice to the Executive on this subject. I have the honor to be with the greatest esteem & respect Sir Your most obedt. servt., TH: JEFFERSON

RC (Andre deCoppet, New York City, 1949). Addressed in TJ's hand: "The honble Benjamin Harrison Speaker of the House of Delegates." Endorsed: "Governor's Letter January 1st: 1781. Respecting an Invasion. to lie on table." FC (Vi).

THE INCLOSED LETTER: No doubt the (missing) letter of Jacob Wray to Thomas Nelson which arrived in Richmond on 31 Dec., giving the first news of the impending invasion (see TJ to Steuben, 31 Dec. 1780; James Maxwell to TJ, following; TJ to Thomas Nelson, 2 Jan. 1781). There is no evidence in the proceedings of the House that further consideration was given to TJ's letter. A message from the Senate, stating that it adhered to its amendments to the bill to revive and amend the Act for regulating and disciplining the militia, was considered by the House and a reply returned that the House adhered to its disagreement to the amendment. No further action was taken on the bill. The House then agreed to the following resolution (MS, Vi), to which the Senate agreed the same day: "Whereas the regiments on State Establishment are greatly reduced in their Numbers of Men insomuch that most of the Officers belonging to them are without Employment, the General Assembly taking the same into their Consideration, and sensible of the merit of the said Officers of whose Services they cannot now be availed for want of Men, induced by the exigencies of the State, have Resolved that the Governor with advice of Council be desired to discontinue for the present from actual service such of the said Officers who are supernumerary to the Men composing at present the several Regiments or Corps on State Establishment." The only apparent recognition taken of the impending danger was a resolution of the following day (2 Jan.): "That in case the next meeting of the General Assembly at this place, be rendered inconvenient by the operations of an invading enemy; that the next meeting of the Assembly be at such proper place, as the Governor with the advice of the Council, shall appoint by proclamation" (JHD, Oct. 1780, 1827 edn., p. 78-9).

From James Maxwell

SIR State Ship Yard Jany: 1st: 1781

Yours of Yesterdays date I received this Morning by Mr: Webb and am to inform Your Excellency that in consequence of the News I herd of the Enemy's Arivial have fited out the Lewis Gally and sent her down the river under the command of the Lieutenant of the Jefferson with twenty Volunteer[s] from the same Vessell who have Agreed to serve for the present Invation. The Brig has been totally dismantled of evry thing she had on board, for heaving down, having been Aground and in want of Repair. But from the Above News have got her Guns on board, and are puting in the best posture of defence we are able. I have also sent of [off] the letter you were pleased to send me for the Aid of the Malitia which am Afeard we shall want much as all the peoples times belonging to the brig is expired and cannot get any of them to agree to continue any longer in the service. Shall therefore be under the disagreeable Necessity of detaining them Against their Will. I can only inform Your Excellency that I shall do all in my power towards the saveing and defending the publick property at this place. I have the Honour to be verry Respectfully Sir Your Excellency's Most humble Servt:, JAS MAXWELL

RC (Vi); addressed and endorsed.

TJ's letter OF YESTERDAYS DATE and the LETTER . . . FOR THE AID OF THE MILITIA: When the Council met on 1 Jan., "The Governor reported that being informed yesterday by a Letter from Mr Jacob Wray to General Nelson, of a British Fleet of 27 Sail arriving in our bay, he had written to General Nelson, Captain Maxwell, Lieutenant Reid and the County Lieutenant of Charles City requiring several necessary measures to be taken, and had given orders for stationing expresses for obtaining proper intelligence: Of which the board expressed their approbation" (*Va. Council Jour.*, II, 269). The letters to Maxwell and others have not been located. The LIEUTENANT OF THE JEFFERSON was Richard O'Bryan (see O'Bryan to TJ, 25 Sep. 1787).

Draft of a Letter to Officers Retired from Service, enclosed to Baron Steuben

SIR Richmond [ca. 1] Jany. 1781.

The readiness with which the gentlemen who had formerly borne commissions in the regular line made a tender of their services on the late invasion of their Country, induce me to rely on their aid in repelling the present enemy headed by the blackest traitor who has ever disgraced the American history. With those gentlemen who have continued in service it is not within my powers to give you the priority of rank which you may have formerly held. I must therefore only undertake to preserve it with respect to those, who having been out of commission, shall again come into service on the present occasion. A large body of Militia being called into the field, and likely to be all in by the 20th. instant, I take the liberty of asking the favor of you to accept of a command over them in the rank you formerly held, and that for this purpose you will be pleased to repair within that space of time to Major General Baron Steuben's headquarters who undertakes to arrange the commands on the principle before laid down.

I have the honor to be with great respect Sir yr very hble Servt.,

The above is a copy of the letter I mean to send to the officers to be called into service. I take the liberty of sending it to Baron Steuben as an explanation of our idea of arranging them.

TH: JEFFERSON

RC (NHi); endorsed: "Governor Jefferson January"; the note to Steuben and the signature are in TJ's hand; the copy of the proposed letter to the officers to be called into service is in a clerk's hand.

The date when TJ sent Steuben a copy of this letter cannot be determined. However, it seems possible that it was sent on 1 or 2 Jan. and that, in the pressure of events in the days following, no further action was taken on it. See Kimball, *Jefferson: War and Peace*, p. 129-30.

From Steuben

SIR Jany. 1st 1781

Your Excellencys Observation with respect to the artificers is just. A proportion of the Regiment furnished by Pennsylvania should certainly be destined for the Southward. I shall write the Board of War immediately on the Subject and have no doubt they will be sent on.

The situation of our affairs are such that Necessity obliged Gen. Greene to require many things from the southern States which were not Alloted them in the general requisitions of Congress but which it was necessary they should furnish, tho' at the Expence of the Continent. Such were the Horses for Lees Corps from Maryland, arms and Equipment of the new recruits from this State, and many other Articles. The call for artificers must be considered in the same light. It must be a considerable time before those from

Pennsylvania can be raised and sent on, and therefore without we can procure a temporary supply from hence, the service must suffer—and that at a time when our greatest efforts are necessary to stop the progress of the Enemy.

To employ the Quarter Master to engage the Artificers, with the few means in his power of finding them, would be a loss of time, which in the present moment might prove dangerous, whilst Government, from the variety of agents they could employ in the business, would be able to procure them in a short time. These considerations urge me to repeat my request that the State would furnish the Artificers called for. I am &c.

FC (NHi).

THE PRESENT MOMENT: Steuben was aware of the report of an enemy fleet. On this same day he wrote a letter (Vi) to Muter, dated "Cockermouth, 1st Jany. 81," informing him that "The present alarm has occasioned my ordering four hundred of the [Continental] troops at Chesterfield to hold themselves in readiness for marching." Steuben further stated that the distressed situation of the troops and the depleted magazines made it necessary for him to call upon the state for such supplies as Col. Davies might need—particularly "some chords to make loops for the tents . . . which without them are entirely useless."

From the Virginia Delegates in Congress

SIR Philadelphia Jany. 1st. 1781

We have been Honored with Your Excellencys favor in answer to ours concerning the Safest and best Harbor &c. &c. which has been duely communicated, through the proper Channel, and we beg leave to inform you that we have endeavord to improve the intended design into a mode for obtaining a more speedy and safe Conveyance of the Cargoe of the Comite to Virginia (should it take place,) than a land Carriage would be and hope it will meet with Your approbation; as it appeard to us the most eligible method, we have venturd to adopt it without particular Instructions for so doing. Monsr. L——— [La Luzerne] has promised to use his endeavors to have our request complied with. We have the Honor of transmiting to Your Excellency a Proposal from a Baron D'Arendt. He Speaks of a Commission with which he is charged but we have not as yet seen his Commission or powers, we have seen Mr. Wm. Lees written request to him to endeavor to negotiate the Sending of Arms, Linen, &c. with Mr. Wm. Lee's promise to him in writing that if he Succeeded he should be handsomely rewarded by the State of Virginia, but if not he should be Entitled to receive from that State twenty five Louis D'ors for his trouble; all these things we offer to Your Excellency at his request (being ourselves Ignorant of the whole transaction except as stated above) and wait your orders thereon.

In a letter from his Excy. Genl. Washington dated New Windsor Decr. 27th. 1780 we have the following Intelligence—"Another embarkation has taken place at New York supposed to consist of two thousand five Hundred land forces, whose destination is not yet known. The fleet fell down to the Hooke on Wednesday last." *Our* Conjecture is that they are destined to the Southward, and indeed all the Enemy's political and military manœuvres seem to indicate their Intention of making a Vigorous effort against the Southern States, this Winter. We are Sorry to inform your Excellency that we receive very little Authentic Intelligence of the Steps which are takeing to counteract those vigorous operations, that we are in a great measure uninformed of the progress that has been made in raising the new army, and on what terms, of what has been, and will be, done in establishing Magazines for its Support, and above all, of the measures persuing to cancell the old money and give an effectual Support to the new, by providing for its punctual and final redemption with Specie. This is a crisis at which we concieve a most assiduous application to these great objects to be necessary, and (next to the completion of the Confederacy which is perhaps the Basis of the whole) of the first importance to America therefore highly importing us to know, as the measures of so large a state as ours cannot but have considerable effects on the other states in the Union.

We have the honor to be with the greatest respect Yr obt & Humble servants,

JAMES MADISON Junr.
THEOK. BLAND

RC (Vi); in hand of Madison, signed by Madison and Bland. Endorsed, in a clerk's hand: "Col Blands Lr. inclosg Baron de arendts." The enclosed proposal: "A L'Assemblée du L'Etat de Virginie," caption supplied from Burnett, *Letters of Members*, v, No. 568, note 2, where it is stated that the proposal is in Vi, but it has not been located.

YOUR EXCELLENCYS FAVOR: TJ's letter to the Virginia Delegates with instructions concerning the cargo of the French vessel *Le Comité* has not been located. The negotiations concerning the disposal of the cargo were placed in the hands of Benjamin Harrison when he subsequently went to Philadelphia (see TJ to Harrison, 29 Jan. 1781). BARON D'ARENDT: Henry Leonard Philip, Baron d'Arendt was appointed a colonel of the German battalion of the Continental army in 1777; while in Prussia on furlough, he received letters from William Lee, dated 3 and 5 July 1779, requesting him to solicit arms and military stores for Virginia (JCC, XIX, 143-4).

From Nathaniel Burwell

Burwell's Ferry Tuesday 2d: Jany
SIR Ten o'Clock a:m

The Enemy's Fleet have just now come to off this Place; they consist of 23 Sail, including two Men of war; a number of Flat-bottom'd Boats are a-Stern of the Ships full of men. We have near 200 men under the Command of Colo: Innis and myself a number very insufficient for the present Purpose: however nothing shall be wanting as far as we're able to oppose the Enemy if they attempt to land. A Small Party of Foot and Horse are now engag'd with a Boat detachd from the Fleet.

I am Sir your humble Servt., NATH BURWELL C.L: J.C.

RC (NHi); endorsed.

Burwell was lieutenant of James City co. The presence of his letter in the Steuben Papers indicates that TJ may have forwarded it in his letter to Steuben of 2 Jan.

To the County Lieutenants of Charlotte and Certain Other Counties

SIR Richmond Jany. 2d. 1781.

The Arrival of a hostile force within our State being confirmed, and their movements indicating an intention to come immediately into the heart of the Country, renders it necessary, to call for one fourth[1] of your Militia under proper Captains and Subaltern officers to rendezvous at Petersburg.[2] That there may not be a moments delay, let them come in detached parcels as they can be collected, every man who has arms bringing them. The good of the service requires that the field officers at least should be experienced in the Service. For this reason these will be provided at the rendezvous. I beg that this may not be consider'd by the Militia field officers as proceeding from a want of respect to them. We know and confide in their zeal: but it cannot be disreputable to them to be supposed less knowing in the art of War, than those who have had greater experience in it, and being less knowing, I am sure that, that true spirit of patriotism with which they are animated will lead them to wish that measure to be adopted which will most promote the public safety, however it may tend to keep them from the post in which they would wish to appear in defence of their Country. The Militia must be subsisted to their rendezvous under the rules of the

Invasion law; a list of all certificates given being kept and returnd to the Auditors.

I am Sir with respect, your mo. Obt. Servt., TH: JEFFERSON

RC (O. O. Fisher, Detroit, 1950); in a clerk's hand with the exceptions noted below; signed and addressed by TJ: "County Lieutenant of Charlotte." Endorsed: "The Governor to Tho. Read. Ordering ¼ of the Charlotte Militia to Petersburgh. 2 Jan 1781 Recvd. 4th. of Jan. 9. O'Clock at Night." FC (Vi); at the head of text: "A Circular Letter to the County Lieutenants of Henrico, Hanover, Goochland, Fluvanna, Albemarle, Amherst, Chesterfield, Powhatan, Cumberland, Dinwiddie, Amelia, Buckingham, Bedford, Halifax, Charlotte, Prince Edward, Lunenburg, Mecklenburg, Sussex, Southampton, Brunswick."

On 8 Jan., Hugh Rose wrote to George Muter (RC in Vi): "Being entrusted by his Excellency with Dispatches for the upland Counties, I was constrain'd to leave Richmond in such Haste as to bring not one Article of my Baggage along with me. . . . Our Militia turn out with great Alacrity, I never got up 'till late on Saturday Night, and hope to have one compleat Company with you by Friday next and the Ballance in a few Days after." See also Hugh Rose to TJ, 26 Sep. 1781, and enclosures. One of the letters, which was probably carried by Rose, was delivered to Reuben Lindsay, Albemarle co. militia officer, who wrote to Capt. Michael Wallace, of the Albemarle militia, on 7 Jan. (RC in Vi): "I have received a letter from the Governor directing such a number of the Militia of this County to march immediately to Richmond. As the Near approch of the Enemy makes it Necessary that not one Moment be lost, you are hereby directed immediately on the receipt of this to send down Twenty men of Your Company, armed in the best manner, under the Command of Lieut. James Read. He will be Joined by the rest of the Militia of this County on his way, or, at Richmond. Lieut. Read is hereby authorized to seize provision on his march, and to grant receipts for the same; He must keep a list of all such receipts so granted, which He must deliver to the auditors. I am inform[ed] that on Wednesday last the Enemy were landing within Twenty Miles of Richmond, which I am sure will be a sufficient spur to you and every good man to loose no time in hurring the Militia down." (For Lindsay and Wallace, see Gwathmey, *Hist. Reg. of Virginians in the Revolution.*)

1 "one fourth" inserted by TJ. FC has a blank here.

2 This word substituted by TJ for "this place." FC has a blank here.

To the County Lieutenants of Shenandoah and Certain Other Counties

SIR In Council January 2d 1781

The Enemy having again thought proper to invade our Country and being now on their Way up James River I have thought proper with Advice of the Council of State to require [1] of your Militia under proper Officers to repair immediately to Richmond armed with good Rifles and Accoutrements suitable as far they have them; such of them as have not Rifles will be armed here with Musquets and joined to the Battalions of Musquetry. Those who bring Rifles will be formed into a separate Corps. Much will depend on the proper Choice of Officers. They are to be furnished with Provisions by impressing it as directed by the Invasion Law, the Person procuring it for them keeping and returning to the Auditors a List of the Certificates they grant and stating the Name, Article, Price and Purpose. As the enemy shew by their movements an Intention to take Post in the Heart of our Country at once I beseech you to lose not a moment in sending off your men. I am with great Respect Sir your mo. hble Servt.,

T.J.

FC (Vi). At head of text: "A Circular Letter to the County Lieutenants of Shenandoah, Rockingham, Augusta, & Rockbridge."

[1] At foot of text the names of the counties and the number of militia required of each are listed, as follows: Shenandoah 216, Rockingham 219, Augusta 344, Rockbridge 146.

To Benjamin Harrison

SIR

Jan. 2. 1781.

I have this moment received a confirmation of the arrival of a hostile fleet consisting of 19. ships, 2 brigs and 10 sloops and schooners. The advance of the fleet were yesterday morning in Warrasqueak bay, and just getting into motion up the river with a favorable wind and tide. Their destination from the intelligence of deserters and some captured mariners whom they put on shore is up James river. I beg the favor of you to communicate this intelligence to the General assembly and have the honor to be with the most perfect respect Sir your most obedt. servt.,

TH: JEFFERSON

RC (DeHi); addressed and docketed: "Governors Letter January 2d. 1781. respecting the Enemys advance up Jas: river. to lie on table." FC (Vi).

George Muter to William Davies

SIR

War office Richmond Jany 2d 1781.

The enemy's approach rendering the removal of the arms and stores belonging to the state at Petersburgh, immedeatly necessary; Capt. Spiller (State Commissary of Military stores) goes directly from hence towards Petersburgh for that purpose, and will call on you. I must request the favour of you to render Capt. Spiller what assistance you can in the execution of the duty he goes on. The powder at the powder mills and at Manchester is also an object of Capt. Spiller's present attention, in which it is probable he will also stand in need of your assistance. I am with respect Sir Your most humble servant,

GEORGE MUTER. C

TH: JEFFERSON

RC (Vi); countersigned by TJ.

A letter from Edward Carrington to Davies (Vi), dated "Petersburgh Jan. 3d. 1. o.Clock in the Morning," reported that "Mr. Patten W.C. comes with the last of the Arms and fixed Ammunition, to wit 11 Waggons with 1270 Stands of Arms with Accoutrements compleat, and 27 Boxes of Cartridges. There are still at this place a Very large quantity of powder and Lead, and other Valuable Military Stores, besides large quantities of provisions and Spirits, which it will be impossible to get Waggons to get off." In another letter to Davies, dated 4 Jan. (Vi), Carrington requests the return of cartridges for the militia and 40 or 50 swords "which went from here yesterday." See also George Muter to TJ, 19 Jan. 1781.

To Thomas Nelson

SIR Richmond January 2d 1781.

It happened unfortunately that from the Tenor of Mr. Wrays Lett[er] which gave us the first Intelligence of the Appearance of an Enemy we had reason to expect more precise Information within a few Hours. None such having come within fifty Hours, the first Intelligence had become totally disbelieved. At 10 o'Clock this morning I first received Confirmation of it. Orders go out by the members of Assembly to call together Half the Militia of the most convenient Counties for present Opposition and one fourth from more distant Counties. We mean to have four thousand six hundred Militia in the Field. In this Number is not included any below this County. Hanover, Chesterfield, Dinwiddie, Sussex and Southampton, all below these Counties we have left uncalled on to be drawn by you (or such of them as you think proper) into such Parts of the lower Country as you shall think best. Mr. Brown the Commissary has Orders to send a Deputy to furnish you with Provisions. I do myself the Pleasure of sending you a Commission. I pray you to send us as frequent Intelligence as possible, Expresses being in readiness for this Purpose at Williamsburg and New Kent Courthouse. Be pleased to give the same Notice to the Militia as formerly that no Man will be ever discharged till he shall have returned whatever Public Arms or Accoutrements he shall have received; be also particular in noting what is delivered to every Man. We mean to appoint the Field Officers on the same Plan as in the former Invasion from the resigned and supernumerary, preserving the Ranks of those Gentlemen accurately as among themselves. I am with great Respect, Sir, your mo. obt. Servant, T.J.

FC (Vi).

To ——— Reid

SIR January 2d 1781

The arrival of a Hostile Army here being confirmed and there being Reason to believe they mean immediately to push into the Heart of the Country, you will be pleased in the instant of receiving this to put your Troops in motion for Petersburg leaving Orders for the Cloathing which will come to Brunswick to follow you.

I am Sir Your very humble Servant, T.J.

FC (Vi); at head of text: "To Lieutenant Reid or the commanding Officer of Major Nelson's Cavalry at Brunswick Courthouse."

The first name of the recipient of this letter has not been determined because of the various forms of spelling his surname. Reid (Read) held a lieutenancy in the third troop of Nelson's cavalry; served in the Carolinas; and in Dec. 1780 returned to Virginia in command of the troop (Board of War to TJ, 20 Jan. 1780, and TJ's reply thereto, 25 Jan.; Nathanael Greene to TJ, 14 Dec. 1780). This officer has been frequently confused with Capt. Edmund Read, in command of another troop of Nelson's cavalry, serving as a guard to the Convention troops and at this time in Maryland (see George Muter to the Auditors, 18 Jan. 1781 and note there).

To Steuben

SIR Jan. 2. 1781.

I have this moment received a confirmation of the arrival of a hostile fleet consisting of 19 ships, 2 brigs, and 10 sloops and schooners. The advance of the fleet were yesterday morning in Warrasqueak bay, and just getting into motion up the river with a favorable wind and tide. Their destination from the intelligence of deserters and some captured mariners whom they put on shore is some where up the river, supposed to be Petersburg. We shall be very glad of the aid of your counsel in determining on the force to be collected and other circumstances necessary to be attended to for the purpose of opposition, if it be convenient for you to call on the council immediately. I have the honor to be with the greatest respect Sir your most obedt. servt., TH: JEFFERSON

RC (NHi). Addressed: "The honble Majr. Genl. Baron Steuben Cockermouth." Endorsed. Nathaniel Burwell to TJ, same date, was probably enclosed with this letter.

From Steuben

SIR 2nd. Jany 1780 [i.e., 1781]

In case of the calling out a Body of Militia it will be highly necessary to adopt some measures to prevent the numerous abuses and terrible distruction of the Country which generally prevails. For want of having the Quarter Masters and Commissary Generals Departments under the direction of persons of Credit and influence the Inhabitants are wantonly distressed and thrice the quantity of Provision and Forage consumed as would be necessary with proper regulations to prevent this. I would wish your Excellency to appoint two Gentlemen to act during the Invasion as Quarter Master and Commissary General for the State to recieve their Instructions from me.

It will however be necessary that the persons appointed to these Offices should be Gentlemen of Credit and influence in the State who would undertake the Office from no other motives but those of serving their Country in a time of distress. With such assistance I think I could answer that every Species of wanton destruction should be punished and yet the troops be better supplied than they have always been.

I am &c.

FC (NHi). See TJ to Meade, 4 Jan. 1781.

To Francis Taylor

SIR Richmond January 2d 1781

Another powerful Army of the Enemy having invaded us and seeming to be pushing directly up we have determined that the residue of the Convention Troops be removed immediately. You will therefore take measures instantly for their Removal to Fort Frederic in Maryland or Frederic Town as shall be ordered. You are hereby authorized to impress Waggons, Teams, Drivers for transporting Provisions and Forage for subsisting them on the Road for which Purpose you had better send forward proper Persons to lay in the necessaries at proper Stages on the Road. Beef will be the best animal Food because it will move itself. T.J.

FC (Vi).

From George Washington

DEAR SIR Head Quarters New Windsor Janry. 2nd. 1781.

Since I had last the honor of addressing Your Excellency, the Embarkation which had been some time preparing and which had undergone several changes has sailed from New York. The fleet, including the Convoys consisted of 32 Sail, and left the Hook the 22 Ulto. By the best information I have been able to obtain The Light Infantry and Grenadiers with some other Corps, which were at first under embarking Orders, were afterwards countermainded and the Detachment finally amounted to about 1600 Men, of which Simcoe's is the only entire Corps, that we know with certainty has embarked; the remainder is said to be principally composed of Drafts from the Line—The whole under the command of Arnold, and still conjectured to be destined to the Southward.

I have the honor to be.

Dft (DLC: Washington Papers); in the hand of David Humphreys with an interlineation by Washington.

From Edward? Archer

[*Swan's Point, 3 Jan. 1781.* The 1816 version of TJ's Diary of Arnold's Invasion (Document I in Notes and Documents Relating to the British Invasions in 1781, printed under 31 Dec. 1780) contains the following entry under 3 Jan.: "8. aclock P.M. Received letter from E. Archer Swan's point that at 12. aclock that day they [the British fleet] were at anchor a little below Jamestown." Archer's letter has not been located.]

William Armistead to William Davies

Richmond, 3 Jan. 1781. Has been directed by the governor to order the tailor and shoemaker at Warwick to go to Chesterfield Courthouse immediately; but fears that without an officer to attend them they will desert; suggests that they be sent for, with a wagon or two to remove the leather and cloth on hand.

RC (Vi); 2 p.; addressed: "Colo. William Davies Chesterfield Court House"; endorsed; summarized more fully in CVSP, I, 414.

From Samuel Huntington

Philadelphia, 3 Jan. 1781. Encloses extract of a letter from General Washington of 27 Dec. concerning the embarkation of the British from New York.

RC (PHi); docketed: "Pr. Congress enclosg. extract of Genl Washington recd Jany 13. 81." Tr (DLC: PCC, No. 15); addressed to the governor of Maryland; at foot of text: "N. B. The like verbatim to the governors of Virginia & North Carolina." The enclosed extract has not been located. The letter from which it was taken is printed in Washington, *Writings*, ed. Fitzpatrick, XXI, 22.

From Abner Nash

Newbern, 3 Jan. 1781. Acknowledges TJ's letter requesting permission to purchase pork in North Carolina for the southern army; has sent "Mr. Brown a proper Commission for the purpose."

RC (NN); addressed and endorsed; 2 p.

TJ's letter to which this is a reply has not been located. MR. BROWN: John Browne, commissary of purchases and issues for Va. (*Va. Council Jour.*, II, 206; *Official Letters*, II, 537).

To George Skillern

SIR Richmond January 3d 1781.

I am pleased to hear that two Companies of Volunteers have gone from your County to the aid of the Southern Army. That is the Direction in which it seems most convenient to point your Efforts to aid the Public Cause. We are at present invaded in this quarter, the Force not yet precisely known. We shall not however suffer it to divert your Aids from the Southern Army. The Company in your County which is incomplete cannot be made up by draughting. As to the light Horse you wish to raise we have it not in our Power to arm them; the applications to our Magazine from the Continental Horse and the Losses sustained during the late Invasion have left us unfurnished with Swords and Pistols. The Deserters whom you have taken up may either be sent to the Southern Army or to Chesterfield Courthouse wherever you should first meet with an Escort. The Bedford Militia are called here; perhaps you might send the Deserters to the County Lieutenant of Bedford to be forwarded under Guard of his Militia. If the Intelligence be certain that the Cherokees are taking up the Hatchet I hope your County Washington and Montgomery will crush it at once by a vigorous effort, but if it be not certain it would be imprudent while we have an Enemy to combat in the North, South and East to draw on one in the West also. I have purposely avoided giving particular Instructions as to this Matter, having repeatedly [observed] that from the Circumstance of Distance before my Letters can get out a Change of Appearances renders their Contents improper or ineffectual. The only Requisition therefore which I have to make is that on such Occasions you will lend to the Counties exposed that ready and effectual Aid which you have ever done. I am with great Respect Sir your mo. obt. hble Servant, T.J.

FC (Vi). See entry for TJ to Skillern, 18 Oct. 1780.

From Leighton Wood

SIR Richmond 3rd January 1781.

This Morning to my mortification I received the inclosed Letter from Mr. Everard which I beg leave to lay before your Excellency and Council. From the nature that I conceive of my late appointment I cannot be too early in applying myself to the duties of that Office and wished to qualifie therefor on Monday next tho' should it appear necessary that I should continue to act as an Auditor on account of the present Invasion will defer it for a few days.

I have to request from your Excellency and Council a direction where to keep an Office and doubt not but that reasons will readily occur to point out the necessity of being near the Auditors.

I am with the greatest respect Sir Your most Obt. & very hble Servt:, L. WOOD JR.

RC (Vi); addressed and endorsed. Enclosure: Thomas Everard to Leighton Wood, 2 Jan. 1781 (Vi), declining to serve as an auditor of public accounts.

On 30 Dec. 1780 the Assembly had appointed Wood to the post of solicitor general, and on 1 Jan. appointed Everard to serve as an auditor of public accounts in the place of Wood, who had been serving in that capacity (JHD, Oct. 1780, 1827 ed., p. 76, 78). On 31 Jan. the Council appointed Bolling Starke to replace Everard until the next session of the legislature (*Va. Council Jour.*, II, 282).

To John Banister

SIR In Council January 4th 1781

My former Order required only half of your Militia to be embodied. The rapid Approach of the enemy renders it necessary that for instant Opposition you embody the whole able to bear arms. Should they not be armed, there are Waggons loaded with Arms at Chesterfield Courthouse under orders to proceed to Powhatan Courthouse. By an Application to Colo. Carrington or other Commanding Officer, you can stop a sufficient number of these Arms. Should events make it necessary I hope you will call on the neighbouring Counties for the whole of their Militia. As you may have earlier Intelligence than myself I cannot do better than repose this Trust with you. I am with great Respect Sir Your mo. obt. hble Servt., T.J.

FC (Vi); at head of text: "Colo Banister." There are several variant checkmarks on FC opposite the salutation; these may possibly indicate that similar orders were sent to other county lieutenants of those counties that had been previously ordered to call out only half of the militia.

From Edward Carrington

SIR Petersbg. 4. O Clock Jan 4th. [1781] P.M

Col: David Meade just from logans point informs us that he saw the Enemy land in Force at Westover about 3 or 4 Hours ago, and take up their March towards Richmond.

I am with respect Yr. Excellencies Mo Obt ED. CARRINGTON

RC (NHi); addressed.

To the County Lieutenants of Henrico and Certain Other Counties

SIR Richmond January 4 1781

The Enemy having last Night past far up James River and seeming to point immediately to this Place or Petersburg, I must desire you without a moments Delay to send every man of your County able to bear Arms to rendezvous at Westham. Let them come in small Detachments as they can be collected and not wait to be formed into Companies.

I am Sir your mo obt. hble. Servt., T.J.

FC (Vi). At head of text: "A Circular Letter to the County Lieutenants of Henrico, Hanover, Goochland, Powhatan & Chesterfield."

From Joseph Crockett

SIR Frederick Town Maryland 4th Jany. 1781

When ordered as a guard for the Convention troops to this place haveing on hand eight Hundred weight of powder and nine Hundred fathom of rope for which we had no use, I stored it in the Magazine at Alb: Barracks, for which the Quarter master of the Regiment of Guards passed his receipt.

The other stores that was laid in for the use of the western Battalion are now here. I am sorry to trouble your Excellency in seting forth the difficulties the officers labour under in this part of the world, being debar'd of many emoluments that officers in Virginia are priviledged to. We draw but one pound of beef one of Flower and one gill of liquor per day, no sugar, Coffee or Tea, nor Barrack rooms found by the public, are obliged to get lodgings on the best terms we can. I have sent the due bill by Majr. Read for the deficiencey of the half years Cloathing drawn by Majr. Walls, for the officers of the western Battalion. And hope the Executive power will think it reasonable to let us draw as much cloathing as will make up one years allowance including what we have already drawn with such other allowances as the laws of our Country intitles us to, or you in your wisdom shall think Necessary.

I Have the Honour to be your Excellencys most Obedt. and very Hble Servt.,
JOSEPH CROCKETT

RC (Vi).

From Charles Dick

SIR
Fredg. Jany. 4th. 1781

I have just time to acquaint You That the Gentlemen of this Town and even the Ladys have very spiritedly attended at the Gunnery and assisted to make up already above 20000 Cartridges with Bullets, from which the Spotsa. [Spotsylvania] Militia and [those] of Caroline have been supplied, as also above 100 Good Guns from this Factory; As I propose to do all the good in my power in these troublesome times I shall continue to direct the Factory and keep the Workmen together if possible, which I find pretty difficult to do without Money and Provisions. I shall wait on your Excellency as soon as I hear the Offices begin to do Business, and have the Honour to be with the greatest Respect Your Excellencys Most Obedt Hbl. Servt.,
CHAS DICK

RC (Vi); addressed: "His Excellency Thomas Jefferson Esqr. Governour &c. Virginia. favour Mr. Strachan."

From Benjamin Harrison

3 O:clock thursday evening [4 January 1781]
SIR
Terrils about 2. miles from the Bridge

I am inform'd by Colo. Munford from the Upper Church [that] the Enemy are landed at Westover from which [I] think it plain their object is Richmond. [He saw] about fifty light horse and about seven hundred infantry [at] the [Westover]—landing fast. I gave orders for raising the militia of this county late yesterday. They are assembling fast and I expect all that remain fit for duty will be out to-day. But many of them are quite without arms of any kind, what they have are mostly unfit for service, to add to this dismal account I must inform you that we have no amunition of any kind, or so small a quantity that it is scarcely worth naming; I have powder at Osbornes and this morning order'd over 190 ℔ of it but I much fear it will fall into the hands of the enemy as the orders were given before we had an Idea of their landing so near us. I have also furnish'd them with about 160 of lead but this is to run into bullets a work of some difficulty; From this state of our situation you will easily see it is necessary we should have an immediate supply of all the above articles if any service is expected. I shall order the militia into this part of the county in hopes of their being supply'd thro' N. Kent in which case I think I can pick out a hundred m[en] that will give them some trouble. I am your most obedt Hble Svt,

Benj Harrison

RC (NHi); addressed: "His Excellency The Governor Express"; endorsed: "Benja Harrison 5 Jany. 1781." Undated; moreover the endorsement is in error, since Thursday was 4 Jan., in the early afternoon of which the British disembarked at Westover (TJ's Diary of Arnold's Invasion, Document I in Notes and Documents Relating to the British Invasions in 1781, printed under date of 31 Dec. 1780).

To Richard Meade

Sir

In Council January 4th 1781.

The present invasion having rendered it necessary to call into the Field a large Body of Militia, the providing them with Subsistence and the means of transportation becomes an arduous Task in the unorganized State of our military System. To effect this we are obliged to vest the Heads of the Commissary's and Quarter Master's Departments with such Powers as if abused will be most afflicting to the People. Major General Baron Steuben taught by experience on similar Occasions has pressed on us the necessity of calling to the Superintendance of these two Offices some Gentleman of distinguished Character and Abilities, who, while he prescribes to them such Rules as will effectually produce the object of their appointment will yet stand between them and the People as a Guard from Oppression.

Such a Gentleman he would propose to consider as of his Family. Under this exigency we have taken the Liberty of casting our eyes on yourself as most likely to fulfill our wishes and therefore sollicit your undertaking this charge; in doing this merely on the impulse of purer motives than those which would spring from any pecuniary reward it is in our Power to offer. At the same Time we cannot with justice permit that any expences incurred in such a station should be borne by yourself. I shall hope to receive your answer by the return of the Bearer and am with great esteem, Sir, your mo: obt. hble Servt., T.J.

FC (Vi). See Steuben to TJ, 2 Jan. 1781.

To George Muter?

[4 January 1781]

Be pleased to send some trusty person to gather waggons at Hanover town and remove the powder there across the river and so up into the country thirty or forty miles to some church or other place it may be stored.

MS not located. Extract printed from American Art Association sale catalogue, 6-7 Dec. 1921 (Edward Tuckerman Sale), lot 380, a 1-page A.L.S. without designation of addressee.

The recipient's name has been assigned on the basis of a letter signed by David Lambert for George Anderson to Muter (Vi): "Hanover 6th Jany. 1781. . . . I have sent the powder according to your directions to the Commanding Officer of Chesterfield in Caroline County." Another letter from Anderson, dated Richmond, 4 Jan. 1781, and addressed to the Commanding Officer of the Militia near Chesterfield (Vi), states: "I am properly empowered to require you to take charge of the powder . . . and have same put under a proper Guard, . . . stored in some Church or other place of Security . . . untill further orders from the Executive. . . . This will be delivered to you by Mr. Cary who has charge of the powder." See also TJ to an unidentified correspondent, following, and George Muter to TJ, 7 Jan.

To ——— ———

Sir Jan. 4. 1781.

Baron Steuben asks the favor of you to appoint some confidential officer or gentleman to go immediately to Chesterfeild court house to take charge of the waggons which are there loaded with arms, conduct them up into the country under such orders as the Baron will give him, for which reason he must call on the baron immediately. I think some such person necessary at Westham. I am, Sir, your most obedt. servt., Th: Jefferson

RC (PHi); endorsed: "Govr. respecting some person to be appointed to take charge of Waggons with Arms at Chesterfield. Jany. 4th. 1781. [*In another hand*] Baron Steubens request. Miscellanies. Taken from War Office. A.D. 1781."

The addressee of this letter cannot be precisely identified. It may have been written to George Muter after the preceding letter, q.v.

From Thomas Nelson

Pierres 12 Miles above Wmsburg Jany 4th 1781

SIR 3 o clock p: m:

I have just receiv'd the inclos'd Letter from Wmsburg which gives the best account of the Enemy's force that I have yet obtain'd. Their intentions are higher up the River, either to Petersburg or Richmond, which they will make a bold push for, if not check'd on their landing. If they discover a determination in the Inhabitants to oppose them, they will [m]ove with caution, and perhaps return to Hampton with disgrace. They will proceed as high up the River as they can for fear of desertion among their Troops, to which they are much dispos'd.

I remain still very weak having receiv'd no reinforcements from the Neighbouring Counties yet. Our Expresses behave most infamously and in what manner to act with them I know not. Unless some rigorous measures are taken with them we shall have no regularity.

I am with much esteem Your Obed servt, THOS NELSON JR

RC (NHi). Enclosure not identified. There is no indication of the name of the addressee of this letter. It is probable that it was sent to TJ, who in turn forwarded it to Steuben; see Marie Kimball, *Jefferson: War and Peace*, p. 132-3; also Nelson to TJ, following.

From Thomas Nelson

Byrds Tavern Jany 4th 1781

SIR 8 o'Clock PM

On my Way here this Evening I received Information that the Enemy had landed their whole Force at Westover, and were marching for Richmond. I have ordered the whole Strength of King Wm., King & Queen, and Gloucester, to rendezvous at Bacon's Ordinary 6 Miles above New Kent Court House, whence I shall march them as will appear best for the Service. The whole Militia of New Kent are now turning out. I am with the greatest Respect, Sir, Your Mo: Obedt. & hble Servt., THOS NELSON JR

Col. Innes is with me, and is without a Commission. Col. Griffin is also in this Neighbourhood. His Colonels Commission from Congress was dated the 26. June 1776.

RC (NHi).

Although this letter is without name or address, it was probably sent to TJ, who forwarded it to Steuben (see Nelson to TJ, preceding). Another letter in the Steuben Papers (NHi), written by Nelson at the same time and conveying the same intelligence, was sent directly to Steuben. It omits the postscript in the present letter but has the following additional passage: "I shall to Morrow march what Force I can collect by the Route of Holt's Forge, and thence as the Movements of the Enemy shall direct. I expect my Force will by to Morrow Noon be about 350. It will give me Pleasure to receive from you as frequently as possible such Advice as you shall think proper to communicate."

To Steuben

SIR Jan. 4. 1781.

Majr. Dick calls on me for an order for the militia of this place to march. I beg you will be so good as to consider the militia of every place as under your command from the moment of their being embodied, and to direct their motions and stations as you please.

I have the honor to be with great respect Sir your most obedt. servt., TH: JEFFERSON

RC (NHi); addressed and endorsed.

To Francis Taylor

SIR In Council January 4 1781

The enemy now appear to be pushing to this Place and we know not how much further they may attempt to penetrate. A Suspicion that the Conventioners might be induced to attempt a Cooperation and by that means distract the efforts of our People renders it necessary that in the instant of your receiving this you put those Troops into Motion without waiting for their Baggage or any thing else. Within a verry few Hours we expect you may throw the whole across the blue ridge and it may be well for you to call on the counties of Augusta, Amherst and Albemarle to collect a Force at Rockfish gap to oppose any pursuit. I would not have those Counties on account of such a Call withold the Militia required to come here. They must furnish so many additional as you call for. A Multiplicity of Business puts it out of my power to send you written Powers of impress. But you must exercise that Power for every Purpose only requiring your agents to keep exact Lists of their Certificates to be returned to the Auditors as directed on a former Occasion.

I am Sir your very humble Servant, T.J.

FC (Vi).

From Thomas Sim Lee

Annapolis, 5 Jan. 1781. Joseph Shoemaker, said to be a subject of Virginia and a former resident of Yorktown, was taken in Chesapeake Bay; he has a captain's commission from the enemy and is confined in the Baltimore co. jail as a prisoner of war. If upon inquiry it is thought "proper to claim him" as a "subject" of Virginia, he will be delivered under guard to Alexandria and delivered to any person directed to receive him. In the meantime he will remain in custody.

RC (PHi); 2 p.; addressed and endorsed. FC in Governor's Letter Book (MdAA); printed in *Md. Archives*, XLV, 264. See TJ's reply, 1 Feb. 1781.

From the Maryland General Assembly

Annapolis, 5 Jan. 1781. The situation in the south indicates that the enemy will establish a post at or in the vicinity of Portsmouth in the summer, "if such a Post is not established against them. The French without whose assistance it cannot be done may probably not make any movement for that end under an apprehension it would give umbrage unless your State should desire it." Because of the importance to the trade and security of the inhabitants of both states and the subsistence of the southern army, it is hoped that Virginia will join in a request that the French may establish a post at the most convenient place in the Bay. Maryland can furnish "20—18 and 16—9 Pounders." A copy of a letter to the French minister requesting that a marine force be stationed in the Bay is enclosed. "We are so drained of Men, especially seamen, that very little towards the defence of the Bay remains in our power, yet have we resolved to exert ourselves in fitting out one Galley, a Sloop of 10 Guns and a few Barges." It is requested that the matter be submitted to the legislature and the result communicated to the executive. Signed by Daniel of St. Thomas Jenifer, President [of the Senate], and W. Bruff, Speaker of the House of Delegates.

RC (Vi); 2 p. Enclosure missing.

From Philip Mazzei

SIR Florence, January 5th. 1781.

Being still deprived of the honour of an answer from you, I think it a duty to inform you of it. You may probably have sent me before now, either new Commissions and Instructions, or the duplicates of my first, and expect that I have received them. Untill I do, I shall trouble you every now and then to remind you, that to my great sorrow I am, and must continue to be a useless servant of the

State. I shall be very short, having nothing material to add to the contents of my preceding 22 letters. Permit me, Sir, to intreat you to send me a sufficient number of duplicates of your commands, directed to Mr. Mark Lynch Merchant in Nantes, Mr. John Adams, or Mr. Favi Agent for the Grand-Duke of Tuscany in Paris, that I may have a better chance of being relieved from the present most disagreable State of inactivity, and uncertainty.

I am most respectfully, Sir, your Excellency's most Humble & most Obedt. Servt., PHILIP MAZZEI

P.S. I inclose the continuation of the account sent the 26th. June in letter 20; concerning the distpach of my letters. In the former account it appears, that one copy of 7 and 8 went by the Lauzun Capn. Bell, which sailed from Lorient; and as the Luzerne Capn. Bell sailed likewise from thence, I apprehend that it may be the same vessel, and that my corrispondent may have written at first Lauzun instead of Luzerne by mistake. I shall inquire, and rectify the error if it should be so. I have had from time to time the following accounts, viz:, that the Betsey Capn. Boardman, the Committé Capn. Brisson, and the Luke Capn. Clarke were taken; and that the Cecile Capn. Fridin, the Isabella Capn. Trippe, the Independence Capn. Kirk, the Tom Johnson Capn. Martin, the Sally Capn. Coggshall, the Alliance Fregate, the Dove Capn. McKerdy, the Luzerne Capn. Bell, and the George Capn. Montgommery got safe over. Therefore have the satisfaction to find, that you must have received all the 4 copies of Letters 14 and 15; three of 1, 3, 4, 8, 9, 10, 11, 12, and 13; and no less than two of 2, 5, 6, 7, 16, and 17, as one of the 7 went by Marquis de la Fayette. I must observe however, that on account of the brave Jones having lost the command of the Alliance, some of the Letters noted as sent ℔ the Alliance may be in the Ariel; which I have not been able to know, although Mr. Adams promised me to make some inquiries about it.

RC (CtY); at head of text: "23 [i.e., dispatch 23]"; endorsed. The "2d. Copy" of this dispatch, in a clerk's hand with complimentary close and signature in Mazzei's hand, is in NN. Enclosure: 2-page list (CtY) of dispatches 9-22 and their means of conveyance, with caption: "Continuation of the account sent you the 26th. June in letter 20., concerning the dispatch of my letters." See also list enclosed in Mazzei's letter to TJ, 22 June 1780.

From Charles Fleming

SIR Tuckahoe Jany. 6th. 1780 [i.e., 1781].

I left the enemies lines at West Ham yesterday evening a little before sun set, their proceedings there you no doubt are well acquainted with. There will be a very considerable body of Malitia will be[1] collected between this and Westham in the course of the day. It appears to be [the] wish of all parties that Colo. Nicholas and myself shall take command of them as field officers, and as I am informd by Mr. Webb, it is your determination with advice of Council that the Malitia on the present alarming occasion will be officered as before with respect to the field officers.

I am ready, and will at all times Sir, to render any and every service to my Country in my power. As I have no Commission of any sort don't [doubt] but you will think with me that it is necessary, I should have a commission or some writing under your Signature for my taking command with propriety. I am Sir Your most Obedt. Humbl. Servt. CHAS. FLEMING

RC (Vi); addressed and endorsed.

1 Thus in MS.

From Matthew Godfrey

SIR Norfolk January 6th. 1781.

In Consequence of William Godfrey, Henry Whiting, John Livingston, Richard Lee, and John Cook, falling into the hands of Comodore Symonds, of the Brittish fleet off Newport News I sent down Colo. Mathews with a flagg in order to get off the prisoners, or if that could not be obtain'd, to Supply them with some Specia.

In Consequence the Comodore releas'd on parole Henry Whiting and wrote the inclosed. Having no Chance of Collecting any of his brittannick Majesties Subjects, unless some of their present party should fortunately fall into our hands here, having none at present, hope your Excellency will order an exchange of the above mentioned Young men as early as your Excellency pleases. I am Sir Your Mo Obedt. Hble Servt., MATTHEW GODFREY

RC (Vi); addressed and endorsed. Enclosure; see below.

THE INCLOSED letter: Thomas Symonds to Matthew Godfrey, "Charon off Newporte Nuse," 4 Jan. 1781 (Vi), stating that he has granted a parole to Henry Whiting and that he has no wish to keep the prisoners on the Charon except for exchange; "if that cannot be Complyed with soon, shall have no Objection to send them on parole also" (printed in CVSP, I, 417-18). Matthew (or Mathew) Godfrey was county lieutenant of Norfolk (Gwathmey, *Hist. Reg. of Virginians in the Revolution*); see further, Thomas Newton to TJ, 21 Jan. 1781.

From Steuben

SIR Warwick Jany. 6. 1781

I have the pleasure to acquaint your Excellency that the Enemy left Richmond this Afternoon about one o'Clock and proceeded towards their Vessells in consequence of which I immediately ordered a Battalion of Continental Troops and a Battalion of Militia to March to this place, and came myself as well to oppose any attempts to Land here as to be so far on the way to Petersburg where it is supposed the Enemy intend to proceed. Colo. Gibson informs me they have near 1000 Militia together tho' only 400 of them were then armed. It is said the Vessells have already got up as far as Broadway. Should this prove true I shall proceed early tomorrow morning with the Troops here, to Petersburg and make every possible Opposition. I have not heard of a Single Gun being fired at them either on their March from Westover or during their Stay at Richmond nor have I had the least intelligence from Genl. Nelson since the inclosed Letters.

As the Militia will be still arriving at Petersburg and as there are already 600 unarmed I must beg your Excellency to give immediate Orders to have 1000 stand of Arms Sent down there with Ammunition.

I am with respect Your Excellency's most Obed Servt.,

STEUBEN Maj: General

RC (Vi); addressed and endorsed. Enclosures not identified.

From William Davies

SIR Briton's Jany. 7. 1781. 6 o'clock P. M.

I am informed a considerable number of public papers, brimstone and other articles are lying round the works at Westham, many of them very little damaged. I cannot well spare any body from this side to collect them, but think it my duty to give your Excellency the information.

The number of Hanover militia on the other side the river, is so considerable as to take the whole of the good arms. I have had them all selected this afternoon and shall early in the morning send the lead up the river. I think there seems to be a greater call for ammunition on the other side than on this. I shall therefore send over a quantity of powder to them, to be under the care of Capt. Grier.

I am the more disposed to take this step, as I am informed the enemy have crossed opposite fourmile creek and are on their march into the country, tho' from the silence of your Excellency on that subject, and having received no information from Baron Steuben I am beginning to be doubtful of the truth of the report. Captain Irish has come over to me, and I am persuaded will soon arrange the military stores into more order so that we may know what may be had and where it may be had.

The waggons impressed by Capt. Harris are come almost too late for any purpose here, except that of bringing up flour from Manchester and removing the Commissary's stores from Col. Friend's higher up. The bad arms can be easily sent away in the boats, and the good will be almost entirely applied to the Hanover men, as I mentioned before.

There is one *Cunningham* not far from the falling creek church that, I am told, is a very good gunsmith, and has every thing in order for that business; perhaps he might be useful.

I have the honor to be, sir, your Excellency's most obedt servt.,

William Davies

I wrote the above before I received your Excellency's favor of last night. I had taken the proper steps for the immediate removal of the stores, upon hearing the same report in the afternoon. I am applied to on all quarters for military stores. It will therefore be absolutely necessary that I should have every information from the state officers where they have lodged them. Inclosed I send you a commission offered to me this morning. I have promised to lay it before your Excellency, and to inform him whether he has leave to resign or not. He is recommended to me by Capt. Markham and Capt. Patterson as a very proper person for a resignation, as he takes sick whenever he is ordered on duty. I beg to have the earliest intelligence of any movements of the enemy towards the stores.

I am your Excellency's most obedt servt., William Davies

RC (Vi). Addressed: "His Excellency Governor Jefferson Manchester Express"; endorsed. Enclosure missing.

YOUR EXCELLENCY'S FAVOR OF LAST NIGHT has not been located.

To George Muter

Sir Manchester Jan. 7. 1781. half after 9. P. M.

By a letter from Genl. Nelson received this evening he informs me has by no means a sufficient stock of ammunition, having received none since this invasion, and he desires an immediate supply. I thought you had sent him a waggon load. Be pleased to take measures for his supply, and in the mean time to let me know what he may expect that I may write him accordingly. He also desires two feild-peices. Are there not some gone towards Goochland courthouse or what other place, or are there any more convenient on the North side? On this head I wish also that measures should be taking to furnish him, and that I might know what to write him.

Baron Steuben insists that we shall appoint some person to find out where the arms have been sent to, and to deliver them to the militia as they arrive. You will therefore be so good as to appoint some person to set out on the execution of this business immediately. I apprehend Colo. Davies can best inform the person to what places the arms have been sent and in what numbers, and also what particular militia have been ordered to call for them at these places. This I readily apprehend will be a puzzling business, but it is necessary. There are 1000 arms now wanting at the Baron's head quarters and at Petersburg. It will be well to know the whole extent of our stock capable of use as I fear there will shortly be more men than arms.

I must beg the favor of an answer very early tomorrow morning as Mr. Tatum waits my answer to Genl. Nelson. I am Sir with great esteem Your most obedt. servt., TH: JEFFERSON

RC (PHi). Addressed by TJ: "Colo. Muter. Richmond." Endorsed: "Govr. respecting some Ammunition for Genl. Nelson &c. Jany. 7th. 1781."

The LETTER FROM GENL. NELSON has not been located. MR. TATUM: See Tatham's account of this meeting with TJ, Notes and Documents Relating to the British Invasions, Document IV, under 31 Dec. 1780.

From George Muter

SIR Richmond Jany. 7. 1780 [i.e., 1781].

I am this moment honoured with your Excellency's note.

The moment it is in my power, I will send the gentlemen you wish for to you; but I am alone, and unable to act for want of the necessary assistants, except in a very limited degree.

Capt. Spiller (you may recollect) was ordered below, to secure the arms in the Isle of Wight and Southampton. I have appointed Mr. Bourk to the particular care of the arms at Westham; but little can be done at present towards selecting, or putting in order.

I have heard nothing of Mr. Anderson, nor indeed do I know where any of the gentlemen you wish to see are.

This place is in the utmost confusion. Plunderers of our own have been very mischievous; perhaps more so than the enemy. Considerable public stores will be recovered; some are, but it is difficult indeed to secure them. I will exert myself to the utmost, but fear I can't produce that degree of benefit for the state, that will give me satisfaction.

Expresses I will want, and be unable fully to procure. Perhaps your Excellency's presence here, will be of signal service if in your power to come.

I have the honour to be your Excellency's most Ob Sert.,

GEORGE MUTER

RC (Vi); addressed and endorsed.

From George Muter

SIR Sunday evening [7 January 1781]

Colo. Syme is here, and his militia are mostly at Westham. From some difficultys that arise in consequence of the orders he has received, he is induced to send his son to wait on your Excellency for orders. I beg leave to refer to him for particulars.

I have a letter from Mr. Rose: Majr. Peirce (he informs) with two pieces of artillery, and stores to a considerable amount are at Goochland Court house. He intends to wait your Excellency as soon as he can.

Majr. Claiborne has orders from Barron Steuben to send 20.000 cartridges to Genl. Neilson. That (or rather a larger) quantity is on this side the river somewhere above but the Majr. and myself, will find it difficult to get an express to send to order it down. He is now gone in search of one.

Mr. Anderson has saved some of his tools: his bellows are all gone. Mr. Moody's tools are some part lost, but still he has a considerable part remaining.

The damage at the Palace is very triffling; hardly worth speaking of.

It seems most probable, from what I have heard, that the British are gone to Westover again: tho' I can learn nothing certain.

I have the honour to be Your Excellency's most hl servt,

GEORGE MUT[ER]

The brass cannon that cou'd not be carried off, and were put in the river, are lost. The Enemy had intelligence where they were, and got them up and carried them off.

RC (Vi).

This letter, without place or date, was obviously written at Richmond on 7 Jan., since that day was a Sunday. The preceding letter must have been written earlier the same day. See also Steuben to TJ, same day, below, concerning his order to send cartridges to Gen. Nelson. LETTER FROM MR. ROSE: William Rose to George Muter (Vi), dated. "Anderson Peers Tavern Goochland 6th Jany 1781," stating that he had "this moment sent on from this place seven waggons with the Laboratory and Military Stores and Tools from the Works at Westham to Goochland Court House where Major Pierce is, and two field Pieces"; that "Two Waggon Loads of Powder was safely conveyed from Hanover Town to a brick Church 8 miles below Chesterfield in Caroline County and a guard placed over it"; that "The Foundery and public buildings at Westham are destroyed"; and that, as soon as the scattered Stores are safe, he would inform Muter and "wait on his Excellency the Governor for his Commands when I am certain where he is" (printed in CVSP, I, 418-19).

From John Nicholas

MAY IT PLEAS YOUR EXCLLY: The Forrest Jany 7th: [1781]

I have just received an express from Charles City Court-house who proves my mistake last night of Genl: Nelsons being there and informs me of a small party of this Countys militia being surprised there last night. Neighther good intelligence or any manœuver of consequence can take place untill we have more Horse. I just received [word that] the Enemy are in motion on Berkley plains and for want of fresh horse I shall be under the necessity of retreating to Mawben [Malvern] hill where I shall endeavour to stand.

In haste, J. NICHOLAS

RC (Vi).

To Steuben

SIR Manchester Jan. 7. 1781. 2. o'clock P.M.

I have thought myself very unfortunate in missing of you for two days tho' riding over the same ground on which you were. On my arrival here I was informed you were at Ampthill and was setting out there when a gentleman came who assured me you were at Ozborne's, and having rode thirty miles thro' the rain have not resolution enough to undertake to go to Ozborne's, this evening.

I received your letter of yesterday at Westham today at noon. I fear it will be impossible to furnish the thousand stand of arms you desire. Colo. Davies has sent some hundreds from Westham to different places to be put into the hands of the militia coming in. He has undertaken to have those remaining there separated, in order that such as are capable of being used may be sent you, and I have engaged persons who are gone out to impress waggons to transport them to you. Colo. Davies seemed doubtful to what place they should be ordered. I mean to continue here or at Richmond to see whether I can collect the several staff officers of the state, and have the benefit of their services on the present occasion. I shall be very happy to aid those of the Continent with every power I am invested with. While at either of these places I shall be able to communicate both with yourself and General Nelson, and to do everything you will be pleased to suggest for the service. I fear the want of arms fit for service will be a most distressing circumstance. Are there no Continental arms which can be used on the present occasion? I mean to endeavor to collect hands and tools immediately to repair arms. Tools will be the most difficult to be procured.

I have the honor to be with great esteem Sir your most obedt. humble servt., TH: JEFFERSON

RC (NHi).

From Steuben

SIR Osborns 7 Jany 81. 7 o'Clock PM

I have this moment the honor of your Excellencys Letter of this day. The thousand Stand of Arms I desired Colo. Davis to send to Colo. Gibson at Petersburg on being advised there were then 400 Militia there unarmed and more arriving and I must again request that no time may be lost in Sending as many there as can be collected. The Continental Arms were in the hands of Capt. Irish. I am ignorant were [where] they were removed to, but they must undoubtedly be deliverd out on the present occasion and I will be obliged to your Excellency to give orders accordingly. Fearful lest all we can get will not be sufficient I have sent orders to recall the Arms which passed thro' Richmond some days since for the Southern Army.

I am exceedingly happy to understand that your Excellency intends collecting the several Staff Officers of the State. I cannot but say that hitherto I have received little or no Assistance from them. On the Contrary I have been obliged to employ Continental Officers to do their Business.

I am much distressed to provide for the troops having not a single Quarter Master or Commissary. Let me beg your Excellency to send me some persons to act in these capacities. The method of suffering Corps to provide themselves is exceeding distressing to Individuals and ruinous to the State some person must also superintend the forage Department for the same reasons. Capt. Fairlie who returnd this Evening informs me that Genl. Nelson is in want of Ammunition. I sent off an Express immediately to Maj. Claiborne, not knowing where else to apply, to endeavour to procure 20,000 Cartridges and send them down with an Escort. If he meets with any difficulty you will be so obliging as to assist him.

Ammunition will also be wanting on this side. Desire Col. Muter to send all he can collect to Petersburg.

I have orderd the Militia of Chesterfield Powhattan and Amelia to march with all possible expedition to Petersburg tomorrow. I march there myself with 400 Men I have here. My intention is, at the same time that I come to Petersburg, to endeavour something at Hoods. If any Cannon can be got and a force sufficient collected to prevent Their Landing I think we may give them some trouble. Genl. Smallwood is arrived at Petersburg and will give me his Assistance.

With great esteem & respect I am Your Excellency Most Obed Servt., STEUBEN Majr. General

RC (Vi); addressed and docketed in an unidentified hand.

To Steuben

SIR Manchester Jan. 7. 1781. half after 9. P.M.

Your letter of this morning on the subject of finding where the arms have been sent and having them put into the hands of the militia I have this moment received. I think most of these arms have been sent off in different directions by the orders of Colo. Davies who I beleive therefore to be best acquainted with their situation. If I did not misunderstand him to-day he has accordingly directed particular bodies of militia to go to particular places to receive arms. However (if I do not go to Richmond to-night which I have some thought of doing) I will write to Colo. Muter to appoint some proper person to undertake and execute this business immediately as you desire, as I wish exceedingly to relieve you from every unnecessary embarrasment when I know you are exposed to but too many which are unavoidable.

I have the honor to be with great esteem Sir Your most obedt. servt., TH: JEFFERSON

RC (NHi); addressed and endorsed.
Steuben's LETTER OF THIS MORNING has not been located.

From Jonathan Clarke

SIR Albermarle Barracks Jany: 8th: 1781

I was yesterday favor'd with your Excellency's Letter of 27th: Decr: in answer to one I had the honor to write you of 22d: Novr: relative to the Provisions due to the Convention Army; I take the earliest opportunity to acquaint you, Sir, that agreeable to your desire I have ascertain'd the quantity due, to the satisfaction of the Issuing Commissary, and he has certify'd it to Mr. Hawkins the purchasing Commissary, who acquaints me he goes off t[o]morrow for the money; he expects to have it in his power to settle with me in the course of next week, after which, I shall be ready to join the Convention Troops; I have Colo: Woods permission to remain for the present.

I have the honor to be very respectfully Sir Your Excellency's most obedient Hum: Servt:, JONA: CLARKE

Senior Commissy: of the Convention Troops

RC (CtY). Clarke's former letter of 22 Nov. and TJ's reply of 27 Dec. 1780 have not been located; see Clarke to TJ, 6 Feb., and TJ to Clarke, 7 Feb. 1781.

From Charles Fleming

Manchester Town Ferry, 8 Jan. 1781. In accordance with TJ's order "of this morning," a wagon load of ammunition has been sent "from this place"; another, from the other side of the river, ordered for Gen. Steuben, will be forwarded by Col. Davies.

RC (Vi); 2 p. Addressed: "His Excellency The Governor Richmond." Endorsed.

TJ's orders to Fleming have not been located. There is also in Vi a letter from Charles Fleming to William Davies, at "Briton's Ferry," same date, stating that he is enclosing a letter from TJ to Steuben (not identified), "with a Waggon load of amunition from the other side there being imediately convenient here than [*sic*] a Waggon load I have also just dispatched to Richmond for Genl. Nelson agreeable to the Governors order just now received"; Fleming added that the men there, about 250 in number, "are arming by companies and will march to Westham immediately in that order as fast as they are ready."

From John Montgomery

SIR New Orleans January 8th. 1781.

This is to Represent the distressed situation of Fort Jefferson and the impossibility of mentaining said Post without some Speedy relief.

First the Inhabitants in General are leaving the Settlement for want of Subsistance, and continually Harrassed by an Unmerciful Enemy, the Loss of their Corn and Stock and we not being able to support those Adventurers by Reason of our Credit being so far Reduced for want of Funds.

Secondly the certainty of our Soldiers deserting as numbers has already for want of provisions. &c. &c.

Thirdly Experience fully Shews me that if the late Attack had held a few days longer, all our Stores and Amunition must fall into the hands of the Enemy. By reason we had nothing but Corn in the Garrison and no more then what would support Us for Six days longer, it was impossible for us to Repulse the Enemy, their Force being Superior to Ours if they w[ere] certain of our Situation. We being above half a mile from the Missisippi and that thorough a Thick Wood Except where the Channel Run when the Missisippi was high, it's well known the impossibility of Transporting Provisions that way to the Fort in time of an Invasion. All these Reasons are Evident to every Person. The different advices Received of this place Minaced with Attacks from different Quarters and Nations and the long time we have had no advice from Government makes me represent to You the inavoidable Loss that must happen to this place if continued as it now is and the great loss to Government not only of this place with the Stores but all the Illinois Country was this Post to Fall. I further think it highly necessary that this Post may be removed to Some place where an Open Communication may be kept up with the Missisippi or to remove all the State Stores Amunition &c. with the Troops where they can be provided for, They Establishing a Settlement agreeable to their intention, as the Situation of this can no ways answer having no Communication with the Missisippi for better then half a Mile for one half the Year. The Bearer hereof Capt. Robison can inform You the Particulars, and had it not been for the Assistance of Mr. Oliver Pollock with whom I am now present, we must undoubtedly evacuate that Post. He well knowing that Government having to heart the Setling a place of so much Consequence and from those good principles he hath always Shewn, Sent us Relief from time to time both Amunition and Goods in our Greatest distresses until he has Sent his All, and is Still Striving to send Us further Supplies. I am fully Convinced it will not be in his Power to send further Supplies without further Relief. I am in hopes You will take the Speediest Method of sending him Remittances or Providing a Fund for our future Relief, as I can See No other Method for the Preservation of the Illinois Country. Pray Excuse me for takeing Such Libertys, it being the true State of our Situation and in Colonel Clarks absence I think it my duty. I am Sir With Respect Your Excellencies most obt Humble Servant,

JNO. MONTGOMERY

RC (Vi); addressed and endorsed.

FORT JEFFERSON, at the mouth of the Ohio, was evacuated on 8 June 1781, "for want of Provisions"; see John Montgomery to Gov. Nelson, 10 Aug. 1781 (*George Rogers Clark Papers, 1771-1781*, p. 585).

From Thomas Nelson

DEAR SIR Holt's Forge Jany. 8. 1781. 7 o'Clock P.M.

I am pained to the very Soul that we have not been able to prevent the Return of the Enemy, but even the Elements have conspired to favour them. On Saturday Night I intended a Blow at their Rear, when the Gates of Heaven were opened, and such a Flood of Rain poured down as rendered my Plan abortive by almost drowning the Troops, who were in Bush Tents, and by injuring their Arms and Ammunition so much that they were quite unfit for Service. That they may not go off without some Injury, I have ordered two Pieces of Cannon to be planted at Kennon's, where I am told we may do them Mischief. These Cannon I propose to defend by Infantry as long as I can. Should they overpower us, it is better to lose the Guns than not to attack them somewhere. Mr. Smith staid with me at my most earnest Request, but will set out to Morrow. Mr. Brown is not here. I am, Dear Sir, with the greatest Respect, Your mo: Obedt. & hble Servt.,

THOS NELSON jr B. G.

Both your Letters dated Yesterday I have received.

RC (PHi); addressed and endorsed.

BOTH YOUR LETTERS: TJ's two letters to Nelson of 7 Jan. have not been located, but see Charles Fleming to TJ, 8 Jan. There is also a letter from Nelson to Major Charles Dick (Vi), dated 8 Jan. "after six. P M," instructing Dick "to keep as near them [the enemy] as you prudently can. In Case of their Embarkation, and going down the River, you will march your Troops by the most direct Route towards Williamsburg"; and informing Dick that if the enemy do not embark, "I shall to Morrow draw closer to them by the Way of Charles City Court House."

From John Nicholas

The Forrest Jany: 8. 12 oclock at Night

Your Excellency I doubt not is anxious to hear of the enemy's situation; they are from every account at Westover with some Corps advanced on the road leading to this place who appear to be under arms as I am. I have about 300 men tolerably well appointed about 40 the best of which are advanced under the command of Cap. Selden within sight of their advanced posts. Genl. Nelson I suppose you have late accounts from. He is at C. City Court-house his Videts and mine were together today at the Church near J Byrd's. I should be glad of a few good horsemen.

Excuse the want of wafers and command as you think best.

Your devoated J. NICHOLAS

[*On verso*:] A list of Capt. Selden's Company.

Wm. Blackburn	Elisha Owen	Wm. Bullington
Michaja Bottom	George Milton	Jacob Carter
John Gunn	John Mcquilque	Absalam Browning
Richd. Cock	Richd. Barley	Symon Sholts

RC (Vi); addressed and endorsed.

From the North Carolina Board of War

War Office, Halifax [*N.C.*], *8 Jan. 1781*. A report having been received that British troops have landed in Virginia, information is requested concerning "their Numbers, Movements, and Intentions, that if necessary our Militia . . . [may] act in concert . . . to repel them." Doubtless their principal object is the reduction of North Carolina, and their landing in Virginia may be either to plunder or "a Finesse to stop Succours from joining the Southern Army." Should there be a serious attempt to form posts in Virginia, the British will attempt to extend the line southward. All intelligence "which not only concerns the mutual Interests, but very Being of both States" should be sent to the Governor or the Board of War who in turn will communicate any important information received. Signed by Alexander Martin.

RC (Vi); addressed and endorsed; 3 p.; printed in CVSP, I, 423-4.

From Edward Stevens

SIR South Carolina Camp Hick's Creek. Jany. 8th. 1781.

I wrote you the 30th. of last Month, Giving you some Account of our Movements. It gives me much pleasure that I have it now in my Power to inform you a Detachment of Horse (from Genl. Morgans Party) Consisting of Baylors Regiment of Dragoons and Two Hundred Militia Horse Commanded by Colo. Washington, has Totally defeated a party of Tories of about Two Hundred and

Fifty commanded by a Colo. Verner. This happened about Twenty Miles from Ninety Six. Colo. Washingtons party Killed and Mortally Wounded a hundred and Sixty Four and made Forty Prisoners, without having a Single man of his party Killed or Wounded.

The Misfortunes the Tories has latterly met with, I hope will Sicking them of their Cause.

Our Accounts Here say that the British are making every preparation for a move. Some thinks that this part of the Army is their object. But I rather incline to believe Morgans party will be thier first Object. If it should I am in hopes they'll not be able to make any thing of them as they are a light party without any incumbrance, And Morgan will take care to Keep himself in such a Situation as not to be Surprized and to fight or not as he may think best, and may have Strong Ground to retreat to. Should their designs be against the Force here, I expect we shall be obliged to retire, as their Strength will be formidable when compared with ours.

I do not assert it from any authority, but entirely from my own conjecture, that when Colo. Green gets up we could not raise more than Fifteen Hundred of every Kind for Action. Colo. Lea [Henry Lee] with his Legion, arrived a day or Two agoe and Colo. Green is expected to Join every day.

The Enemy imediately after our move to this place, reinforced their post at George Town with Three Hundred men from Charles Town. At first our Movements hence I apprehended surprized them, but by this, they will be sensible of the cause.

I understand Morgan begins to meet with difficulties in supporting his party with Provision. That part of the Country has been much Eaten up by the great numbers of Militia horse that has been in that Quarter. Indeed the Country throughout here has been much distroyed (I mean the Provisions) by them Kind of Troops. Provisions for the Support of such an Army as we ought to have in this country through the Course of next Summer ought in my Opinion be paid the greatest attention to. From what has already appeared to me I think the State of North Carolina do not attend so particularly to that, as the necessities of our Troops will point out to them next Summer. That State at this Time has not, of any Kind, Five Hundred men in the Field. Their is about Eighty or a Hundred of them with this part of the Army.

As the Information of these Matters, that you get from Genl. Greene must be so much more particular, and more to be depended on, I shall now decline taking up any further of your time.

As soon as the Month expires from the date of the last returns sent you, I shall send you a monthly return of the Militia. With Respect & Esteem I have the Honor to be Sir Your most obedt. & very hum. Servt., EDWARD STEVENS

RC (NN); without indication of name of addressee; Tr (DLC); endorsed: "Copy of a Letter from Edward Stevens to Governor Jefferson dated January 8. 1781."

From John Browne

SIR Petersburg Jany. 9th. 1781

I arrived here this evening after a fatigueing journey being obliged to walk the greater part of the Way. The Baron being out of Town prevents my waiting on him untill the morning. I find provisions sufficient for five days, and expect hourly two hundred and fifty beeves from Mr. James Mason of Brunswick. I have agreed for upwards of a hundred hogs which will be deliverd in a few days, which I hope your excellency will enable me to make payment for. I can get five hundred barrels of flower if wanted. I am Your excellencys very Hbl Servt., JOHN BROWNE

RC (Vi); addressed and endorsed.

From Samuel Huntington

[*Philadelphia, 9 Jan. 1781.*] Encloses copies of resolutions of Congress of 5 and 8 Jan. The former relates to "the unwarrantable and cruel Treatment which . . . Prisoners with the Enemy have of late received," necessitating the "Exercise of the Law of retaliation"; recommends that measures be taken for carrying into execution the resolves of Congress of 13 Jan. 1780 respecting prisoners taken by the citizens or forces of the states. The second resolution recommends to the states from New Hampshire to North Carolina, inclusive, the procuring and forwarding their quotas of money for use of the officers in captivity at New York and on Long Island. Postscript acknowledges receipt of TJ's letter of 25 Nov. 1780.

RC (Vi); 3 p.; undated; endorsed: "Pr. of Congress Lr. Feby 12. 81." Enclosures: (1) resolution of Congress, 5 Jan. 1781 (Vi), endorsed: "Congress resolves Virginia for retaliation Feby 81."; (2) resolutions of 8 Jan. 1781 (Vi), endorsed: "Congress requisition Virginia of money Feby 81." FC (DLC: PCC, No. 15); dated 9 Jan. 1781.

The resolutions of 5 and 8 Jan. 1781 are printed in JCC, XIX, 27-8, 38; those of 13 Jan. 1780 in same, XVI, 48-52. TJ's letter of 25 Nov. has not been located, but see TJ to George Washington, 26 Nov. 1780, which is probably the same in substance.

From James Madison

SIR Philada. Jany 9th. 1781

The inclosed extract of a letter from General Washington No. 1 will give your Excellency a more particular account of the late embarkation from N. York than has been before obtained.

On Thursday last Congress were informed by General Potter and Col. Johnston who came expresses for the purpose that a general mutiny of the Pennsylvania line stationed near Morris Town apart from the rest of the Army had broken out on the morning of New Year's day. Every effort was used by the officers to stifle it on its first appearance but with out effect. Several of them fell victims to the fury of the Mutineers. The next information came from Genl. Wayne who wrote from Princeton whither the troops had marched in regular order on their way to Philada. as they gave out, with a determination not to lay down their arms nor return to their obedience till their grievances should be redressed. They did not suffer any of their officers to remain with them except Genl. Wayne and Colos. Stewart and Butler and these they kept under a close guard, but in every other respect treated with the utmost decorum. The grievances complained of were principally a detention of many in service beyond the term of enlistment and the sufferings of all from a deficient supply of cloathing and subsistance and long arrearage of pay. Several propositions and replies on the subject of redress passed between a deputation of Sergeants on the part of the Troops and General Wayne, but without any certain tendency to a favorable issue. The Affair at length took a very serious aspect and as a great proportion of that line are foreigners and not a few deserters from the British Army, and as they shewed a disposition to continue at Princeton from whence a refuge with the Enemy, who it was said were coming out in force to avail themselves of the situation of things, was very practicable, it was thought necessary to depute a Committee of Congress with powers to employ every expedient for putting a speedy end to it. The President of the State with a number of Gentlemen from this place also went up to interpose their influence. The inclosed copy of a Letter from the Committee No. 2 with the paper No. 3 referred to in it are the last accounts received of the matter. The manner in which the offers and emissary of Clinton were received and treated is a very auspicious circumstance and will probably in its impression on the enemy fully balance the joy and encouragement which this event tended to give them.

Col. Bland being one of the Committee does not join me in this.

I have the honor to be with great respect & esteem Yr. Excelly's Obt. & hum servt, JAMES MADISON JR.

RC (Vi). Enclosures: see below. LETTER FROM GENERAL WASHINGTON NO. 1: Extract from George Washington to Samuel Huntington (see Huntington to TJ, 3 Jan. 1781); LETTER FROM THE COMMITTEE NO. 2: John Witherspoon to Samuel Huntington, Trenton, 7 Jan. 1781; THE PAPER NO. 3: Proposals of General Clinton "To the Person appointed by the Pennsylvania Troops to lead them in the present struggle for their liberties and Rights" (all the enclosures are printed in full in CVSP, II, 149-50, after the above letter, which has been erroneously dated 9 June); see also Burnett, *Letters of Members*, V, Nos. 577-84, 589-93, for accounts of and negotiations concerning the mutiny of the Pennsylvania Line. The definitive study is Carl Van Doren's *Mutiny in January*, N.Y., 1943.

To Steuben

SIR Richmond Jan. 9. 1781. 11 o'clock A.M.

The State commissary having come to me yesterday I sent him on to your Headquarters to provide subsistence for the troops and observe your orders in every thing. A waggon load of fixed ammunition and two feild peices have past this place for General Nelson. The residue (I beleive about two waggon loads) was ordered on to you yesterday. I am very happy to hear you have General Smallwood's assistance, tho' the means with which you are furnished are not likely to add to your reputation, except that by undertaking to make the most of them your zeal will be still more fully displayed. A battalion of Hanover militia which were at Westham were ordered to you.

Your favor of yesterday was put into my hands this morning. The enemy encamped at Westover the night before last, and had not moved at midnight last night. They keep very close. Genl. Nelson was last night at Charles city Court house. Colo. Nicholas with 300 militia were at the Forest six miles above Westover. Colo. Harrison is exerting every endeavor to get a couple of 18. pounders over to you. Those who sunk the boats here did them such injury that it is difficult to repair them. I really fear they will be much too late for you. However a possibility of their getting to you in time is worth every exertion we can use. I have desired Colo. Nicholas to communicate to me every movement of the enemy which I will forward on to you immediately.

I have the honor to be with great esteem Sir Your most obedt. servt., TH: JEFFERSON

P.S. Colo. Clarke of Kaskaskia having heard of the situation of things, has come to me this morning. I send him to you, supposing you must be in want of officers.

RC (NHi); endorsed. YOUR FAVOR OF YESTERDAY has not been located.

To Steuben

SIR Richmond Jan. 9. 1781.

Mr. Granville Smith a State Quarter-master now waits on you. As I am not thoroughly acquainted with the Continental regulations I shall just mention to you my ideas on this particular matter without laying any stress on them and leave to your determination the propriety of using Mr. Smith. I have ever understood that the rule of Congress was to admit no expences to be Continental which were incurred by any state merely under an *apprehension* of an invasion, but that whenever a state was *actually invaded* all expences became Continental. This I know was the rule while I was a member of Congress, but as it is four years since I left it, I cannot affirm of my own knowlege tho' I have ever understood that it still is the rule. The practice here has accordingly been for the Continental Quartermaster to come into duty as soon as the state has been invaded. He being appointed under the authority of Congress it has been supposed that he could best regulate all expences according to the Continental rules. The state quartermaster, not being appointed under Congress, nor possessing their confidence, nor subject to their removal or punishment, seems for these reasons an improper person to dispense their monies. I submit these matters however altogether to yourself. Should you think it proper that the State quartermaster should act, Mr. Smith is instructed to receive your orders. He is a discreet and sensible officer.

I have the honor to be with great esteem Sir your most obedt. humble servt., TH: JEFFERSON

RC (NHi); endorsed. FC (Vi).

From Steuben

SIR Petersburgh. 9th. Jany. 1781

I would suggest to you the Defenceless condition of Hunter's Works at Fredericksburg full as great or greater an object than any were at Richmond. The people in that part of the Country as destitute of arms, as they are in this. The Distance to the Works from Potomack River about half as far as from Westover to Richmond.

I would recommend it to your Excellency to order some fortification erected to protect those works and some Militia from the neighboring Counties Sent there to defend them.

I have the honor to be Your Excellencys Most Obed Servant.

Dft (NHi).

From Edward Carrington

SIR Petersburgh Jan. 10. 1781

The Baron Steuben directs that I shall apply to your Excellency for one Hundred and fifty Tents, and two hundred Camp kettles, for the use of the Militia, to be sent to this place immediately. Should your Excellency find it difficult for the State Quarter Masters to dispatch them, those of the Continental Service at Richmond will be ready to lend their Aid. Your Excellency has wrote the Baron, that a Commissary of provisions, has been sent to him, but he has never yet made his appearance. He is really much wanted. The Baron has just now moved to Prince George Court House, where our principal force is.

I have the Honor to be with Esteem & respect Yr. Mo Obt.

ED. CARRINGTON
DQMGSA

Since Writing the above Mr. Brown Commissary has Arrived.

RC (Vi); addressed and endorsed.

From William Davies

SIR Briton's Jany. 10. 81.

I thank your Excellency for your information of yesterday. It is improbable Cunningham would be willing to work, and the shortest method in such times of emergency, is to impress the shop and tools for a while. I am surprized your Excellency could conceive I should know where the military stores of this state were dispersed having had no kind of connexion with them, either in point of authority or information. I have, it is true, done every thing to gain intelligence where they have been hid, and am endeavoring to get them together as well as I can. I was fearful, when I attempted to furnish the militia with the necessary equipments for the field, that I might be blamed by them for their very insufficient state, but I always thought I should stand acquitted before the Executive; who must, I think, by this time, be fully sensible that the former management of the military stores of this country was never adapted to the defence of it. Should it, however, be desired I would not hesitate with the necessary tools to attempt to put the public arms into a condition, that would not again expose this country to such disgraces, as it has lately suffered.

I have the honor to be most respectfully your Excellency's most obedt servt., WILLIAM DAVIES

RC (Vi); addressed and endorsed.

TJ's INFORMATION OF YESTERDAY has not been located. The following letters in Vi give evidence of Davies' attempts to supply the militia and to gather together the arms and supplies which had been widely scattered during the invasion: Davies to Steuben, 6 Jan., suggesting that the militia "cross the river and getting arms where they have been lodged by me"; A. Kirkpatrick to Davies, 7 Jan., concerning moving military supplies up the James (CVSP, I, 421); J. Robertson to Davies, 9 Jan., concerning supplies for Steuben's men (same, p. 426); A. Kirkpatrick to Davies, 12 Jan., in reply to Davies' letter "of yesterday" forwarding camp kettles and enclosing an inventory of supplies at "Friends" (same, p. 431).

Charles Fleming to William Davies

Manchester, 10 Jan. 1781. Arrived at this place the previous evening; the men "had a very disagreeable night, seven of them taken sick"; will proceed as soon "as they get comfortably dried and get their breakfast"; requests supplies. "The Governor lodged on this side last [night], whom I have seen. He informs me the enemy were yesterday morning lying still at and about Colo. Harrissons mills: that they surprised and routed about 100 foot and 25 horse at Charles City the night before. He hadn't heard what loss they sustained. There is a report that they [are] intrenching, but by no means authentick."

RC (Vi); 2 p.; endorsed: "Col. Charles Fleming Jany. 10. 1781"; printed in CVSP, I, 426-7.

The recipient's name has been assigned from internal evidence. See also Charles Fleming to TJ, 8 Jan. and references there.

To James Hunter

SIR Richmond Jany 10. 1781

The importance of your Works to the operations of War will doubtless point them out as a proper object of destruction to the desolating Enemy now in the Country. They are at this time at

Westover and will possibly embark there. Their next expedition we cannot foresee; lest it should be to demolish your Works, I write to Genl. Weedon to take measures for protecting them: In the mean time I would advise you to move directly off into the Country every thing movable. Should you not be able to effect this by your own and hired Waggons, I hereby authorize you to impress Waggons, teams and drivers for that purpose, only placing yourself instead of the public in point of responsibility to the Owners.

I am Sir Your most obt Servt, T.J.

FC (Vi).

Hunter's WORKS were located in Fredericksburg. The immediate measures taken by TJ to protect these works were in response to Steuben's letter of 9 Jan., q.v.; see TJ to Steuben and to Weedon, both of the present date.

To Samuel Huntington

Richmond, 10 Jan. 1781. This letter is almost identical with TJ's letter to George Washington of this date, q.v.

RC (DLC: PCC, No. 71, II); 4 p.; in a clerk's hand, signed by TJ; endorsed: "Letter from Govr. Jefferson Jany 10. 1781 Read 18. Referred to board of war"; MS mutilated. Tr (DLC); in an unidentified hand, with signature and the following caption in TJ's hand: "Letters from Th: Jefferson Governor of Virginia to the President of Congress." FC (Vi). Tr (PPAP).

From John Nicholas

Malvern hills January 10. 1781

MAY IT PLEAS YOUR EXCELLENCY

We have been under arms a great part of the night from repeated firing of the out centinals. Our patrols report the fire was returned by some scattering parties of horse on the back of this place. I have to inform you that from the repeated solicitations of many good and well affected people of this neighbourhood together with Majr. Dick's advice I permitted a Flag to pass to the Lines directed to the Commander in chief of the British Army at Westover who returnd for answer the following Letter.

Sir I have this minute received the letters delivered to Colo. Dundas this morning. You have my permission to come down to Westover with your Flag as I wish to give every possible satisfaction in my power to the peaceable and innocent inhabitants of this unhappy Country; such

Negroes, Horses &c. as can be given up consistand with my duty shall be delivered to you if my conditions are agreable. I am Sir Your hbl Svt.,

B Arnold B G

As it plainly appears in this Letter that this Vilian agreeable to his passed actions actuated by motives of gain and rascaly pursuits is determined to discriminate in what he may think a favour, Majr: Dick will descend in no degree below the spirit of a true American Son; or do anything derogatory to the interest of his patriotick Countrymen and may by Arnold's darring confidence of his own power and great contempt of ours be permitted to such familiar lengths as to put it in his power to give you some certain and trusting accounts. My advice to the Major is that he shall receive no property without an indiscriminate return of property shall take place as anything the reverse might tend not only to encourage our internal enemies but to shock and render doubtful the feelings of our friends who may in future come within their power.

Necessaries for cooking &c: would be very necessary if to be had. I expect to hear from Genl. Nelson every minute. Shall depend on your Correspondence with the Barron.

I am Sir with the greatest respect Yr: Mst: Obt Svt,.

J Nicholas

RC (Vi); addressed and endorsed.

To John Nicholas

Sir January 10. 1781.

I am not fond of encouraging an intercourse with the Enemy for the recovery of property; however, I shall not forbid it while conducted on principles which are fair and general. If the British Commander chuses to discriminate between the several species of property taken from the People, if he chuses to say he will restore all of one kind, and retain all of another, I am contented that Individuals shall avail themselves of this discrimination; but no distinction of persons must be admitted. The moment it is proposed that the same species of property shall be restored to one which is refused to another, let every application to him for restriction be prohibited. The principles by which his discrimination would be governed are but too obvious and they are the reverse of what we should approve.

I am Sir Your most obt. Servt., T.J.

FC (Vi).

From George Slaughter

Louisville, 10 Jan. 1781. Last May on the Monongahela, Slaughter purchased, for the building of boats, $396 worth of timber from William Bruce and £968.8 worth of plank from Benjamin Kuykendall, for which receipts were given on 15 and 17 May last, respectively. Is informed that these receipts were refused by the Council for want of authorization, but the claims are just and should be paid.

RC (Vi); addressed: "To His Excellency Thomas Jefferson, Esqr. at Richmond. favd. by Mr. Kuykendall"; endorsed.

To Steuben

SIR Richmond Jan. 10. 1781.

I received last night your favor of yesterday; and shall immediately dispatch an express to Genl. Weedon and recommend to him to attend to the measures necessary for the preservation of Mr. Hunter's works. I have heard that he has with difficulty armed some four or five hundred men and means with them to join Genl. Nelson. I am really at a loss what to advise him. If he comes away with that force it may leave the neighborhood unable to protect Hunter's works; and if he does not come, Genl. Nelson will not have a force sufficient to cover the country below him. I think therefore to leave him to act according to his discretion, recommending to him to send on his force if from a knowlege of circumstances he thinks a sufficient number can be armed and embodied to protect Hunter's works; otherwise to remain there. Will it be in your power, if the enemy should point towards Williamsburg to have boats enough to throw hastily over a body of men to support Genl. Nelson? If you think of any thing better than what I have above proposed to write to Genl. Weedon be so good as to communicate it and I will by another express correct what is amiss.

I was misinformed as to the situation of Genl. Nelson. Colo. Nicholas, who had given me the information corrected it in his next letter. Genl. Nelson had been stationary at Holt's forge on Chickahominy, but proposed to move yesterday to the Shipyard. I am not certainly informed of his force. Colo. Nicholas is with 300 militia at Malvorne hills. A party of 140 militia at Charles City court house were surprised by the enemy's horse the night of the 8th. one killed, three or four badly wounded and some (I know not how many) taken. Colo. Fleming with 560. militia of Hanover and Goochland leave Manchester this morning to join you. They are armed. I saw one 18. pounder set out from there at sunrise this morning. The carry-log for the other is not quite ready. The enemy remained at three o'clock P.M. yesterday at Westover and Barclay their former encampment. I cannot conceive what has kept them there so long.

I am with great esteem Sir your most obedt. servt.,

TH: JEFFERSON

RC (NHi); endorsed.

To George Washington

SIR Richmond Jany 10. 1781.

It may seem odd considering the important events which have taken place in this State within the course of ten days past, that I should not have transmitted an account of them to your Excellency, but such has been their extraordinary rapidity and such the unremitted exertions they have required from all concerned in Government that I do not recollect the portion of time which I could have taken to commit them to paper.

On the 31st. of December a Letter from a private Gentleman to General Nelson came to my hands, notifying that in the morning of the preceding day 27 Sail of vessels had entered the capes and from the tenor of the letter we had reason to expect within a few hours further intelligence whether they were friends or foes, their force, and other circumstances. We immediately dispatched General Nelson to the lower Country with powers to call on the Militia in that quarter or to act otherwise as exigences should require, but waited further intelligence before we would call for Militia from the middle or upper Country. No further intelligence came till the 2d inst. when the former was confirmed, it was ascertained that they were enemies and had advanced up James river to Warrasqueak bay. All arrangements were immediately taken for calling in a sufficient body of Militia for opposition. In the night of 3d we received advice that they were at anchor opposite James Town. We then supposed Wmsburg. to be their object. The wind however, which had hitherto been unfavorable, shifted fair, and the tide being also in their favor they ascended the river to Kennon's that evening and with the next tide came up to Westover, having on their way taken possession of some works we had at Hoods by which two or three of their vessels had received some damage, but which were of necessity abandoned by the small garrison of 50 men placed there on the enemy's landing to invest the works. Intelligence of their having quitted the station at Jas. town from which we supposed they meant to land for Wmsburg. and that they had got in the evening to Kennon's reached us the next morning at 5. o Clock and was the first indication of their meaning to penetrate towards this place or Petersburgh. As the orders for drawing Militia hither had been given but two days no opposition was in readiness. Every Effort was therefore necessary to withdraw the arms and other Military Stores records &c. from this place. Every Effort was accordingly exerted to convey them to the Foundery five miles and to the laboratory six miles above this till about sunset of that day when we learnt that the enemy had come to an anchor at Westover that morning. We then knew that this and not Petersburgh was their object and began to carry cross the river every thing remaining here, and to remove what had been transported to the Foundery and Laboritory to Westham the nearest crossing seven miles above this place, which operation was continued till they had approached very near. They marched from Westover at 2 o Clock in the afternoon of the 4th. and entered Richmond at 1 o Clock in the afternoon of the 5th. A regiment of infantry and about 30 horse continued on without halting to the Foundery. They burnt that, the boring mill the magazine and two other houses, and proceeded to Westham, but nothing being in their power there they retired to Richmond. The next morning they burnt some buildings of public and some of private property, with what Stores remained in them, destroyed a great quantity of private Stores and about 12 o Clock retired towards Westover where they encamped within the neck the next day. The loss sustained is not yet accurately known. As far as I have been able to discover it consisted at this place in about 300 musquets, some soldiers clothing to a small amount some quarter masters Stores of which 120 sides of leather was the principal article, part of the artificers tools and 3 waggons, besides which 5 brass 4 ℔rs. which we had sunk in the river were discovered to them, raised and carried off. At the Foundery we lost the greater part of the papers belonging to the auditors office, and of the books and papers of the Council office. About 5 or 6 tons as we conjecture of powder was thrown into the canal of which there will be a considerable saving by remanufacturing it. The roof of the foundery was burnt but the Stacks of Chimnies and furnaces not at all injured. The boring mill was consumed. Within less than 48 hours from the time of their landing and 19 from our knowing their destination they had penetrated 33 miles, done the whole injury and retired. Their numbers from the best intelligence I have had are about 1500 infantry and as to their cavalry accounts vary from 50 to 120. the whole commanded by the parricide Arnold. Our Militia dispersed over a large tract of Country can be called in but slowly. On the day the enemy advanced to this place 200 only were embodied. They were of the town and its neighbourhood, and were too few to do any thing. At this time they are assembled in pretty considerable numbers on the South side James river but are not all yet brought to a point. On the north side are two or three small bodies amounting in the whole to about 900 men. The enemy were at 4 o Clock yesterday evening still remaining in their encampment at Westover and Berkeley neck. In the mean while Baron Steuben a zealous friend has descended from the dignity of his proper command to direct our smallest movements. His vigilance has in a great measure supplied the want of force in preventing the enemy from crossing the river, which might have been very fatal. He has been assiduously employed in preparing equipment for the Militia as they should assemble pointing them to a proper object and other offices of a good commander. Should they loiter a little longer and he be able to have a sufficient force I shall flatter myself they will not escape with total impunity. To what place they will point their next exertions we cannot even conjecture. The whole Country in the tide waters and some distance from them is equally open to similar insult.

I have the honor to be with every sentiment of respect Your Excellency's mo. ob. & mo. hble Servt., TH: JEFFERSON

RC (DLC: Washington Papers); in a clerk's hand, signed by TJ; endorsed: "No. 23 January 10h: 1781 from Govr. Jefferson Ansd. 6h Feby." PrC (DLC: TJ Papers). FC (Vi); at head of text: "President of Congress & General Washington." TJ sent the same letter on this day to Samuel Huntington. The texts vary only slightly in spelling and punctuation.

To George Weedon

SIR Richmond Jan. 10. 1781.

I inclose you a copy of a letter I have received from Baron Steuben and must rest on you the taking such measures as you may think most likely to effect his recommendation, for which purpose you will be pleased to call on any militia you think proper and for any public arms or other stores which may be at hand. I have heard you have embodied a number of men to join Genl. Nelson. Under this situation I am really at a loss what to direct, and must leave you to act according to your discretion. You know the situation of Hunter's works, and the militia and arms which may be collected for their defence. If you think them adequate to the purpose after those embodied by you shall have come away, I would wish you to come by all means as Genl. Nelson's force neither is, nor is like to be sufficient to cover Wmsburg and the lower country. If you think those works cannot be protected without your force, it seems to be the Baron's opinion that the works should be saved. I have written him that I should recommend to you to govern yourself by this circumstance and desired him to communicate any better plan he can suggest and promised to forward it to you.

The enemy consisting of 1500 infantry and from 50. to 100 horse commanded by Arnold landed at Westover on the 4th. marched from there at 2. o'clock in the afternoon and arrived here at one in the afternoon of the 5th. A regiment of infantry and thirty cavalry immediately proceeded to the foundery. They burnt the roof of that but did not injure the works, burnt the magazine and boring mill. We had withdrawn every arm from there and almost the whole powder. What powder remained they threw into the canal but there will be a considerable saving by remanufacturing it. At this place we lost 5. brass feild peices 4. pounders which had been sunk in the river, about 300 muskets, some goods of the public store, some Quartermaster's stores, of which 120 sides of leather was the principal article, some of the artificers tools and three waggons. The books and papers of the Council for the years 1779. 1780, and most of the Auditors papers, but not their books are lost. This is the sum total. In truth we have escaped to a miracle. The militia come in very slowly.

I am with great respect Sir your most obedt. servt.,

TH: JEFFERSON

P.S. I omitted to mention that 23. hours after they entered this town, they left it and got to their former encampment at Westover and Barclay the next day, where they still were yesterday afternoon. The people who remained here say they were most visibly disappointed in finding we had removed almost every thing out of their reach, which had been effected in 19. hours the whole space of time between their destination being certainly known and their arrival in this town. They have done very great injury to some individuals. They only burnt the artificers shops, here of public property and 3 or 4. houses of private property.

RC (A Midwestern Collector, 1945); without indication of name of addressee. FC (Vi), of first paragraph only; at head of text: "Brig. Genl. Weedon." Enclosure: doubtless a copy of Steuben to TJ, 9 Jan. 1781.

From William Davies

SIR Briton's Jany. 11. 1781.

In answer to your Excellency's favor of yesterday, I would observe that it is necessary the good arms and prepared ammunition should continue here to be issued to the militia, as they arrive. If there should be danger, which I do not conceive there is at present, the arms &c. may be removed in boats, of which I have a number collected. There is a considerable quantity of loose ammunition lodged in a barn of Mr. Ob. Smith's, which ought undoubtedly to be sent off; but there is no Commissary of military stores here, nor any body to do his duty. By a letter from Baron Steuben of the day before yesterday, received late last night, I am ordered to Richmond; and therefore cannot give any further attention to these matters, which really require the presence of the proper officers to conduct them. As for camp kettles I am entirely a stranger to the places where they have been hid, nor do I know of any but those sent from the court house, a great part of which have already been issued, and the remainder I shall instantly send for. At present I have not more than 10 here. As soon as I can put matters in a safe way, I shall leave this place. I shall be glad of any intelligence you may have received, particularly where General Nelson is, with whom I am ordered to cooperate. I have the honor most respectfully to be your Excellency's most obedt servt.,

WILLIAM DAVIES

[*On address-leaf:*] Since writing the within Mr. Scott has come to take charge of the military stores.

RC (Vi); addressed: "His Excellency Governor Jefferson Manchester." TJ's FAVOR OF YESTERDAY has not been located.

From Steuben

SIR [11 January 1781]

I am favored with your Excellencys Letter of the 9th.

Upon the principles of a united opposition against the invaders of the United States, it certainly must be agreed, that when one of those States are actually invaded by the Common Enemy, the expences incurred by such invasion, must be common also. This Naturally throws the provision for such Troops as shall be employed on such particular occasion, into the hands of Continental Officers upon the great scale, but, as it would be impracticable for those Officers to take up the business before it is brought within the view of those under whom they are Acting, and whose orders they are bound to obey, it certainly must of Necessity be incumbent on the State officers to bring it to that point, from which it will regularly be taken up by the Continental officers. I think that this might take place from the time the Troops are Armed, fitted for the Feild, and brought to the place of rendezvous then the General Commanding has cognizance of them as a part of his Force, and, at the same time, all his Subordinate officers, both Military, and staff, have them under their view. I do not see how it would be possible to Charge them with them before this period. The provisions for the Troops from their first assembling in the different Counties, to the aforesaid period, must be attended to by the State agents even though it should be Ultimately a Continental Charge.

This is the light in which it appears to me on duly considering your Excellencys Letter and I have accordingly made application to the D Q M G. to appoint an assistant for this occasion. Mr. Smith may therefore return. I am however exceedingly obliged to you for your readiness to assist me on this occasion.

With respect to the Commissary Department I am not so happy. Mr. Forsyth who is at the head of that Branch is absent and not knowing to whom to apply, I take the liberty to detain Mr. Brown the Gentleman you so obliging Sent me.

Dft (NHi); endorsed: "Copy to the Governor Jany. 11th."

To Steuben

Sir Richmond Jan. 11. 3. o'clock P.M.

I am favored with your letters of yesterday and this day. The peices of artillery at Cumberland were ordered on the first news of this invasion to be carried up the river to Newcastle and on hearing of their arrival there I ordered them to the forks of James river 50 miles above this but very convenient to be brought down by water whenever wanting. Indeed I think in future to divide our stores between that place and Westham. On receipt of information from Colo. Nicholas that the enemy had embarked I wrote to Genl. Nelson to desire if they should pass Burwell's ferry (which would prove they meant nothing against Wmsburg or York) to send off, in that point of time, notice to Genl. Weedon that he might consider his whole attention as drawn to Hunter's works. I omitted to mention to you that I had desired Mr. Hunter to move off every thing moveable. But a small proportion of the militia were ordered to rendezvous at Richmond, most of them having been called from the counties South of James river. From the nature of the orders explained in your letter of to-day I apprehend you would chuse the upper militia generally to be sent down the North side of the river tho' they may have been directed to rendezvous at Petersburg in the first orders. I shall therefore as far as their approach comes within my knolege endeavor to turn them over to the North side, which, should it be contrary to your plan, be pleased to notify me.

I am with the greatest esteem Sir Your most obedt. servt.,

TH: JEFFERSON

RC (NHi); endorsed.

YOUR LETTERS OF YESTERDAY AND THIS DAY (the latter is not the preceding letter, which was acknowledged by TJ on 13 Jan.) have not been located. INFORMATION FROM COLO. NICHOLAS . . . I WROTE TO GENL. NELSON: the letter from John Nicholas informing TJ that the enemy had embarked (probably dated 10 Jan.) and TJ's letter to Nelson (probably dated 11 Jan.) have also not been located.

To George Weedon

SIR Richmond Jan. 11. 1781. 4. o'clock P.M.

The enemy moved down the river from Westover yesterday. I wrote by express to Genl. Nelson this morning to desire that if they should pass Burwell's ferry (which would prove that they mean nothing against Wmsburg or York) he would in that point of time send off an express to you that you might thereby know that your whole attention should be pointed to Fredsbg. They have had the winds at their command and I am persuaded are at this moment either past Burwell's ferry or in Williamsburg. If the former I expect you will receive notice by tomorrow night. Should you not I suppose you may presume the enemy have not passed that point but on the contrary have invaded Williamsburg and that you should move that way. By halting a day you will refresh your men, and perhaps increase your numbers so as to render your approach to Williamsburg more safe and more effectually relieving. So that perhaps under this incertainty which way you should point it may be better for you to halt a day. I communicated to Baron Steuben my having referred your movements to your own discretion and in a letter from him to-day he perfectly approves of it. I cannot do better now than leave you master of your own actions, as events may become known to you sooner than to me which might render any thing positive not only improper but mischeivous.

I am with great respect Sir your most obedt. servt.,

TH: JEFFERSON

RC (A Midwestern Collector, 1945); addressed: "Brigr. Genl. Weedon Hanover Court house" and bearing TJ's signature on the cover; endorsed: "Governor Jefferson dated [received?] 12th."

LETTER FROM HIM [Steuben]: not the letter printed above under this date, but the missing one referred to in the appended note to TJ to Steuben, 11 Jan., q.v. I WROTE BY EXPRESS TO GENL. NELSON: No letter from TJ to Nelson of 11 Jan. has been found; but Nelson apparently wrote TJ on 10 Jan. that the enemy had left Westover (see TJ to Nelson, 15 Jan.).

From Richard Claiborne

SIR Richmond. 12th. January 1781.

Since the time your Excellency and Council did me the honor to approve of my being appointed Deputy Quarter Master for the State of Virginia, I have acted as such under an appointment from the Quarter Master General, and approved of by the Deputy Quarter Master General for the Southern Department.

I sensibly feel the difficulties which are thrown in my way by the late excursion of the Enemy to this place, and sincerely lament, that the consequences fall so heavily upon your Excellency. I shall ever avoid giving you trouble except when the public service obliges me, which I make no doubt, will be a sufficient apology.

The irregular manner in which the business of the Quarter Masters Department in the Continental Line for this State has been done heretofore, clearly proves the many disadvantages which have arose to the public and to individuals for the want of system. To recover from this deplorable situation by giving life to the business, and to discover to the people that we mean to do them justice in the execution of our duty, a plan has been laid before the Council by Colonel Carrington and myself, calculated for this purpose. It cannot be decided on too soon; and I am persuaded your Excellency will see the good effects of it, if it is carried into execution, and properly assisted by the civil authority. The impositions upon the public, of which I see instances daily, are likewise reasons which urge me to beg your Excellency to aid me in arranging my business under the new system established by Congress, that I may prevent such abuses as come within the Line of my Department.

Your Excellency cannot be a stranger to the jealousies which have prevailed against the staff Departments; and I am sorry to say that the conduct of some was a sufficient foundation for the suspicion. It is impossible to prevent abuses totally, but I have guarded against any thing that might have a tendency that way in future, by appointing none to office, but Gentlemen of undoubted varacity, and capable of transacting the business. Upon this principle I shall continually act, and hope that my attention to the public good will be followed by all the Agents; if it is not, I shall take care to displace the agressor, by putting in his stead, a more proper person.

With respect to the emoluments which will arise from the office, I see of none; neither was it with any pecuniary view that I entered the Department. The appointment was proposed when the idea had never occured to me before, and nothing superior to a desire to serve my Country, prevailed on me to accept the commission. Human nature is such, that it will not sacrifice time and private interest to the public altogether; but I only expect a bare compensation for my services, and shall not withdraw my assistance while I can be useful. I am too well acquainted with the low state of our finance to make any demands for money, except where absolute necessity obliges me for the good of the public service; and shall be careful in the issues, that none be paid but where it is indispensably necessary. I am at a great distance from the Continental Treasury, which I am afraid is very bare, and expect to be obliged to call on the Treasury of this state for such sums of money as shall be wanted for the purpose of defraying contingent expences. As to the pay of the persons to be employed, I hope to get money for them from the Quarter Master General, and the manner of obtaining supplies from the state, will require no money from me for that purpose. I have to beg therefore, that your Excellency will direct the Treasurer to reserve a sum of money, to be apropriated particularly to the use of the Quarter Master's Department in the Continental Line of this state, to be ready whenever I may call for it.

I shall be happy at all times to receive any information from your Excellency that may enable me to answer the purpose of my appointment. The department is very naked at present; but I shall spare no pains to get the business into a proper channel as soon as possible.

I have the honor to be with sincere respect and regard Your Excellency's Most obedient Humble servant,

Rd. Claiborne DQ Mr. S. Virga.

RC (Vi).

The plan . . . laid before the council is printed above under date of 1 Jan. 1781. For the circumstances of Claiborne's appointment as deputy quartermaster for Virginia, see TJ to Timothy Pickering, 15 Jan. 1781. On 7 Jan. Claiborne wrote to William Davies: "The irregularity of public measures, and the destruction of public property, are things which keep me in constant pain. . . . Since this invasion I have acted in a capacity to which I am not appointed, and am sorry to say, that the little assistance which has been given me, has rendered my endeavors almost ineffectual" (Vi; printed in full in CVSP, I, 419-20).

From William Davies

SIR Richmond Jany. 12. 1781.

I have taken my quarters in the Senate house, and find in one of the rooms below, a great variety of public papers scattered about and open to every body. This I am told is the case with the papers of the General court at the lower end of the town. As I am not acquainted who are the proper officers, and as I suppose these papers must be of some value, I have taken the liberty to inform your Excellency of it, and should it be agreeable to you, will order my men to collect them and deliver them to such person as you may appoint.

As soon as I came to town I made enquiry about camp kettles, and to my surprize found there were above 80 in this town in the possession of Mr. Southall.

I find there is a very drunken man here of the name of Triplet, that is acting as commissary. I would be glad to know whether he acts by any authority from the state. If he does not, I will dismiss him.

I have the honor to be, sir, with the highest respect and esteem, your Excellency's most obedt servt, WILLIAM DAVIES

RC (Vi); addressed and endorsed.

From George Elliott

MAY IT PLEASE YOUR EXELENCY Petersburg 12th Jany 81

The provision for the army on there March from this place Down the Country is Chiefly My Business, Being directed by the Barron and requested By Mr. Brown to undertake the Business. The troops Are Marching, and Some distance from here. My Athority, Which I receivd from you Before for the other invation Having Expird, and provissions for the men being very Scarce and None at all provided for the Horses, I know Not by what Means I am to proceed. It is reported that the last assembly fixt a price for Corn &c. which prevents the people from leting Me have it as the inclosd will Explain. I hope Your Exelency will furnish Some assistance Eighther by Athority as before to Impress or purchase Corn fodder &c. I am Sr. with Much respect Your Exelencys Most Obt. Humle. Servt., GEO: ELLIOTT D Q M G

RC (Vi); addressed and endorsed. Enclosure: David Ross to George Elliott, "Arrowfield," 12 Jan. 1781 (Vi), stating that he has loaded three wagons with corn and fodder and "can spare more of both, provided the Country allows an adequate price, if they have fixt an under price, it then becomes a kind of tax which ought to fall equally upon all."

George Elliott was appointed agent for collecting the specific tax at Petersburg on 3 July 1780 (*Va. Council Jour.*, II, 265). The act of the LAST ASSEMBLY which fixed a PRICE FOR CORN &C.: "An Act to revive and amend the act . . . for procuring a supply of provisions and other necessaries for the use of the army" (Hening, X, 344-6).

To Sampson Mathews

Richmond Jany 12. 1781.

The Enemy have retired from this place and fallen down James River. We have reason to apprehend their next stroke is at Fredericksburg where Mr. Hunter's Works and some public Works are of such importance as to require protection. Having heard of your being on the road with the Militia from beyond the Ridge I am to desire you to turn off immediately to Fredericksburg, and to proceed with all possible dispatch. There Genl. Weedon will be ready to direct your operations. It is apprehended the Enemy (if they aim at that place) will land on Potowmack, from which they will have seven Miles to march through Woods and defiles. The distance is short, but the ground very favorable for the Rifle service.

T.J.

FC (Vi).

To George Muter

Richmond Jany. 12. 1781.

Colo. Muter is desired to make enquiry where any equipments for Cavalry are, and originate an order for furnishing Mr. Eppes, Dr. Griffin, Dr. Foushee, Mr. Hylton, Mr. Selden and others who are willing to enter into the service, with such as may be necessary and I will countersign it. TH: JEFFERSON

RC (Vi); in a clerk's hand, signed by TJ; endorsed.

To Thomas Nelson

SIR Richmond Jany. 12. 1781.

Mr. Eppes, Doct. Griffin, Doct. Foushee, Mr. Hylton, Mr. Selden and others wish to serve in the Cavalry during the Invasion. We give orders to furnish them with such accoutrements as we have, and will be oblig[ed] to you to form them and others into a proper troop or troops, settling the commands as shall be most agreeable to themselves.

I am With great respect, Sir, your most obed. Servt., T.J.

FC (Vi).

To Thomas Nelson

Richmond Jany. 12. 1781.

The Enemy left a number of Horses at Westover which they had taken during their late incursion. Colo. Nicholas very properly ordered a party to take charge of them and bring them to the Quarter Master where they might be kept for the Owners to come and claim them; but I am well informed that in the [mean] time several Men of Capt. Hockaday's Command of Charles City have plundered and carried them off. These Men being under your Command I beg you to take the most coercive measures for compelling a restitution and letting them know that the most vigorous and exemplary punishment will be inflicted on every Man who shall be known to have one of them and not to deliver him up. Such as are recovered be so good as to have brought up. The mischeif done us by our Citizens, plundering one another has far exceeded what the Enemy did. T.J.

FC (Vi).

To Steuben

SIR Richmond Jany 12. 1781.

I was honored with yours of yesterday by Colo. Loyauté. General Weedon to whom the care of the works at Fredericksburg had been committed being now at Hanover Court-house I have referred Colo. Loyauté to him, and given them authority to make use of the brass canon Howitzers or Mortars at New Castle if they can use them, for they are unmounted.

I heard in the same instant that 744 riflemen under Colo. Mathews were as far as Albemarle on their way down. Being then within 60 miles of Fredericksburg I have ordered them to proceed immediately to that place.

I have the honor to be with great esteem, Sir your mo: ob: Servant,

TH: JEFFERSON

RC (NHi); in a clerk's hand, signed and addressed by TJ: "The honble Majr. Genl. Baron Steuben Petersburg"; endorsed. FC (Vi).

YOURS OF YESTERDAY: Steuben's letter of 11 Jan. to which this is a reply has not been located.

From Steuben

SIR

Petersburg Jan. 12th. 1781

Towards forming a force for the defence of the Country upon the present invasion, I have made such dispositions for arranging the Militia as regularly throws them into actual service as they arrive within my power.

As the Arms to be put into the hands of the Militia are the property of the State, and Subject to the direction of Officers not under my Command, I do not conceive those Troops connected with me or subject to my orders before they are Armd and [equip]ped for the Feild. Such as [have] been put in that situation I have now on duty, to which I [now] wish more could be added.

Large Numbers of Men are hourly Crowding to this place destitute of Arms, applying to me for Orders, but I think it would be highly improper for me to interfere with them. Col. Muter, I apprehend, is the proper person to provide for the equipping of the Militia, as having the general Care of the Means by which this business is to be done. Should the Stores be exhausted, and it become necessary to discharge such Men as Cannot be Armed, it must be evident to Your Excellency that orders giving such discharge should come from the Executive. To Your Excellency's Orders, therefore, I shall leave those bodies of Militia who are not equipped for the Feild. When I have such a Force as I think adequate to the defence of the Country, I shall do myself the ho[nor] to Notify Your Excellency of it.

What situation Col. Muter is in with respect to Arms, I cannot possibly have the least knowledge, as I have had no communication with him since the Enemy left Richmond.

I just beg leave to suggest to your Excellency that Men without arms can Answer no purpose but the Consumption of Provisions.

The Militia already embodied are without Camp Kettles, and Entirely destitute of Tents. As we may expect Snow and Severe weather in a Day or two, I beg your Excellency would appoint an Officer whose business it may be to Collect the Tents belonging to the State as soon as possible.

FC (NHi).

To George Washington

[*Richmond, 12 Jan. 1781.* The proceedings of the Council for 19 Jan. 1781, the first meeting after the invasion, state that TJ "communicated his proceedings during the recess together with Copies of the Letters which have passed between him and certain persons which being read and approved the board directs to be registered to wit: . . . to His Excellency General Washington of the 10th and 12th" (*Va. Council Jour.*, II, 273). The letter to Washington of 12 Jan. has not been located.]

To George Weedon

SIR Richmond Jany. 12. 1781

Hearing of 744 Militia from Rockbridge and Augusta and Rockingham on the road through Albemarle, I have sent orders to meet and turn them down to Fredericksburg, where they will expect your orders: They are commanded by Colo. Sampson Mathews. You will please to observe that as all these were to be rifle Men they were to bring their own field Officers.

Baron Steuben has sent Colo. Loyauté the bearer of this to me, and proposed that we should avail ourselves of his Services as an Artillerist for the protection of Fredericksburg. As this matter is entirely in your hands, I beg leave to refer him to you altogether. He is desirous of carrying thither some brass 24. ℔ers from New Castle. They are without Carriages and of course if mounted on batteries would be in extreme danger of being taken. I had moreover ordered them to the forks of James River as a place of safety. Nevertheless should they be absolutely necessary for you, you will take them, for which this will be your Warrant. T.J.

FC (Vi).

From George Weedon

Dear Sir Hanover Court House Janry 12th 1781

I am honored with your Excellencies letter of Yesterday, and should have stood fast to day had I not heard from Genl. Nelson. That Gentleman recommends our return immediately, and thinks the Enemy will make only Sudden Descents on the lower Counties if they disembark again at all. I have in Consequence set the Troops in motion this morning and shall proceed up to Fredericksburg with all dispatch keeping them embodied till the further designs of Mr. Arnold is known, or till I hear from your Excellency.

I have Sent of an Express to the lower Counties in the Northward Neck warning them of what may happen, and shall have the Earliest Intelligence should the Enemy Approach Potowmack.

I am Sincearly Yr. Excenlency's Most Obt st., G Weedon

RC (PHi); addressed and endorsed.

To James Wood

Sir Richmond Jany. 12. 1781.

The Enemy having returned from this place and fallen down James River, and the German Prisoners being represented by you to be in a distressed situation for want of covering and food, you will be pleased to march them back again to the barracks in Albemarle.

I am Sir Your very humbl. Servt., T.J.

FC (Vi).

From Edward Carrington,

with Jefferson's Instructions to George Muter

Sir Petersbg Jan: 13th. 1781

I do myself the Honor to inclose you a return from Colo. Gibson for a Number of Articles wanted for the Accommodation of the Militia under his Command. Those are Articles of equipment which these Troops should have been furnished with before they were put into the Feild, which plainly determines that the Continental Staff are not the proper Officers for furnishing them. If your Excellency can have them sent down now I will direct my Officers to see them delivered. I beg leave to observe to your Excellency, that the persons employed to provide Magazines of provisions for the Southern Army, according to General Greenes requisition, are now Committing these very provisions to the Consumption of the Militia now in Service here. I am sure I need not point out to your Excellency, the fatal consequences that must result from such a diversion. Our Army must really starve next Summer if those Magazines are not laid in. Even the Hoggs intended for Bacon are now to be killed and issued fresh. This would in any case be a Misapplication, as Pork ought never to be issued to Troops in that State. The Gentlemen concerned in this business Alledge that they cannot supply the Militia by any other Means. However I conceive Beef could certainly be got in sufficient quantities to Answer this purpose.

I shall be much obligd to your Excellency to acquaint me when the Executive will be convened for business, as I wish to Compleat my business in the State so as to repair to the Army.

I have the Honor to be with much respect & Esteem Yr. Mo obt.

Ed. Carrington

Jan. 15. 1781.

The within articles required by Colo. Carrington Continental D.Q.M. Colo. Muter will be pleased to order such of them as we have to be delivered to the Continental Q.M. here.

Th: Jefferson

RC (Vi); addressed in part, "Favoured by Mr. Brown"; endorsed. The instructions to George Muter are written in TJ's hand on the verso of the enclosure. Enclosure: Copy of a "Return of Camp Equipage wanting for the Militia Commanded by Colo. George Gibson Jany 12th. 1781" (Vi).

The "Return of Camp Equipage" listed a total of 3 "Marques," 17 "Horsemens tents," 149 "Com Tents," 94 "C Huttels [?]," 61 axes, 847 canteens, 3 padlocks, and 15 "Spades & Shovils."

To George Rogers Clark

Sir

Richmond Jan. 13. 1781.

I received last night from General Washington a letter on your subject in which he has complied with my request. As every movement will depend so much on yourself in the Western quarter I leave to yourself to determine whether you should not as soon as possible repair hither and take the ultimate measures which are necessary.

I am Sir your most obedt. servt.,

Th: Jefferson

RC (WHi); addressed, in TJ's hand; "Colo. George Rogers Clarke on command under Baron Steuben"; endorsed: "Govr. Jefferson 13th 1781. Detroit Expedition Gen. Washington's consent." FC (Vi).

See George Washington to TJ, 28 Dec. 1780.

To William? Graves

Richmond Jany. 13. 1781.

As you have been very long appointed Cornet to a Troop of Dragoons, and have never repaired to duty; I am to desire that you will immediately assign to me the reasons which have kept you from duty. Should they not be satisfactory, a report of your conduct having been regularly made by Colo. Wood, an arrest must of course follow.

Th: J.

FC (Vi); at head of text: "Cornet Graves."

The first name of the addressee is uncertain; it was, however, probably William. A William Graves was cornet and quartermaster (Gwathmey, *Hist. Reg. of Virginians in the Revolution*, p. 322). See James Wood to TJ, 20 Dec. 1780.

From Henry Heth

Sir

Fort Pitt January 13th. 1781

On the 3rd and 24th of October last the following Resolve of Congress was passed, Viz. That such of the Sixteen additional Regiments as have not been annexed to the Line of some particular State and all the seperate light Corps of the Army &c. be reduced on first day of January next that the non Commissioned Officers and privates in those several Corps be incorporated with the Troops of their respective States &c. Whether my Company comes under that Resolve or not Your Excellency is a better Judge than myself but according to the nature of their Enlistment I am led to believe they do not as they were Enlisted for the defence of this Garrison and not to be removed without their own consents which you will see by the enclosed Resolves of Congress. But contrary to the Resolves and common Justice they are taken from under my Command and myself and Lieutenat ordered home and the Men put under the Command of an Officer of the late 8th. Pensylvania Regiment by order of Colo. Brodhead (who is Commanding Officer of the western District and Colonel of Said Regiment) and it appears very evident that it is his intention to annex them to his own Regiment notwithstanding they are Virginia Troops. As to my own part I am well satisfied to retire on half pay but as I did (when recruiting) give my Men full assurance that they should not be called from this Garrison without their own consents I think it a duty incumbent on me to do what I can in their behalf. For further particulars I refer Your Excellency to Colo. Gibson.

I am With Respect Your Excellencys Most obedient and Very Hble Servant, HENRY HETH

RC (Vi); addressed, in part: "favord by Col. John Gibson." Enclosures: Resolutions of Congress of 8 Jan. and 9 Apr. 1777, organizing two Virginia companies for the defense of Forts Pitt and Randolph, and declaring that these companies "shall not be called to any other service, without their consent" (JCC, VII, 21, 247); these resolutions were in turn transmitted by TJ to Steuben in a letter of 13 Feb. 1781, stating Heth's case.

THE FOLLOWING RESOLVE OF CONGRESS: Printed in full under date of 3 Oct. 1780 in JCC, XVIII, 893-4, as part of a long series of resolves reorganizing the army.

From Samuel Huntington

Philadelphia, 13 Jan. 1781. Encloses copy of resolution of Congress regulating the additional pay of various officers of the army, part to be paid in specie and part in "Bills of the New Emissions."

RC (Vi); 2 p.; in clerk's hand, signed by Huntington; endorsed. FC (DLC: PCC, No. 15); at head of text: "Circular." Enclosure (Vi): Resolution of Congress of 12 Jan. 1781; printed in JCC, XIX, 51.

From Sampson Mathews

SIR Byrd ordenary 13th. Janry 1781

I Received your favour of the 12th. Inst. and Shall Proced Early tomorrow morning to Fredricksburg with about 250 Militia from augusta which is all that is Come this Length. Those of the 2d. Battallion which are on the way as also the Militia from Rockbridge and Rocking [Rockingham] I Shall send by Express to order their March to Fredricksburg, which Place I hope to Reach by Monday Night.

I have Prevailed with Major Posey to go with me who will be of great Service. His Letter accompanys this which he Requests may be Immediately Forwarded to the Barron. I have ordered Some beef Cattle which are to be Brought by the Militia Left behind from augusta. I have the Honour to be with Due Respect & Esteem your Excellencys obedt. Huml. Servt, SAMP. MATHEWS

RC (Vi); addressed in part: "Pr Bena. Clemens Express"; endorsed.

MAJOR POSEY: Thomas Posey, of Botetourt co.; maj., 7th Va. Line (Gwathmey, *Hist. Reg. of Virginians in the Revolution*); his LETTER accompanying that of Mathews has not been located.

From Thomas Nelson

Williamsburg, Jan. 13, 1781.

This Day the Enemy's Ships passed Burwell's Ferry and have fallen so far down the River that I think they intend nothing further on the North Side of James River at present. They yesterday landed some Troops at Cobham, in Surrey, and it is said that Arnold himself was with them. If this be so, it is probable they intend marching by the Route of Smithfield and Suffolk to Portsmouth. I write to Genl. Weedon informing him of this movement of the Enemy, that he may stop the Militia who were coming down under his Command, and who possibly may be necessary for the Defense of Hunter's Works. I shall order Part of the Troops under me to attend the motions of the Enemy down the River and give Protection to the Country.

MS not located. Text from Samuel T. Freeman & Co. sale catalogue, 18 Nov. 1924 (George C. Thomas Sale), part of lot 168, a 1-page A.L.S.

From John Robertson

Chesterfield Court House, 13 Jan. 1781. Prevented by urgency of business from coming himself, has sent James Ball to obtain a warrant in the amount of £20,000 or £30,000 to be charged to Robertson for the use of Major Forsyth in provisioning the troops and the hospital. "The Hospital at present is in want of Wine, Tea, Sugar, Coffee, Rice and Molasses, besides the daily quantitys of fresh meat. . . . It is impossible . . . to Act without money"; has already purchased more than the warrant requested will discharge; accounts of purchases and issues "to the end of last year" will be submitted to Major Forsyth "as soon as the Invasion is over."

RC (Vi); 2 p.; addressed and endorsed. At the first meeting of the Council after the invasion, 19 Jan., the auditors were ordered to issue a warrant for £30,000 to Robertson in accordance with his request (*Va. Council Jour.*, II, 275).

To Steuben

SIR — Richmond Jany. 13. 1781.

I received your favor of the 11th. by Mr. Smith. I cannot say at what point of time the Expences attending an Invasion become Continental. I suppose Congress have some fixed rule on that Subject which, whatever it be, when applied to all the States, will be equal.

From the time at which they called for specific Quotas of Provisions from the several States they seem to have considered their purchasing Commissaries as useless and therefore desired us whenever we should have appointed a Person to furnish these Specifics, we would discontinue their purchasing Commissaries. We appointed Mr. Brown to procure the Specifics, which he is either to deliver to certain Store keepers appointed by the Continental Quarter Master or to the Continental issuing Commissaries. I think therefore Mr. Brown may continue to act with you with propriety and I hope he will with effect. We did not discontinue the Continental Deputy Commissary of purchases here (Majr. Forsyth) but his acceptance of a similar Office in another Quarter seems to have determined his former Commission.

I have heard nothing of the Enemy since their reaching Sandy-Point. This leaves me very anxious for our Shipyard up Chickahomminy.

I have lately received some dispatches which render it necessary for Colo. Clarke to proceed immediately to the Western Country. I have written to him on this Subject and hope he will obtain your permission to return. I did not expect at the time he went to you that his stay would have been rendered so short.

If this incursion of the Enemy should much longer postpone the execution of the late law for raising new Levies it will be among it's worst effects. Yet this Law cannot be carried into execution in those Counties from which Militia are sent. Foreseeing this, when you had favored us with your advice as to the numbers which should be called into the feild we confined the call to the following Counties and requiring from each a fourth we expected the following Numbers

Halifax	247	Goochland	145	Chesterfield	164
Charlotte	156	Cumberland	102	Henrico	155
Prin. Edwd	142	Powhatan	71	Southampton	218
Bedford	325	Amelia	275	Rockbridge	146
Buckingham	162	Lunenburg	169	Augusta	344
Amherst	224	Mecklenberg	212	Rockingham	219
Albemarle	218	Brunswick	325	Shenandoah	216
Fluvanna	65	Dinwiddie	175	Sussex	175
					4650

The whole amount is something larger than you desired, but we of course expected deficiencies. Some of the adjacent counties were called on at first for one half and afterwards the whole of their Militia for present defence. In like manner Genl. Nelson was authorised to call on certain other Counties for present defence; but it was meant that as soon as the proportions above mentioned from the Counties particularly named were come in, all others should be dismissed. I state this matter to you supposing you will think with me that the sooner you can begin the Business of arranging your force on the plan originally intended, the better it will be. As soon as the whole Militia of the Counties not meant to be kept in the field can be discharged we will send the act into those Counties and have it carried into Execution.

I have the honor to be with great esteem Sir your most obedt humbl Servt., TH: JEFFERSON

RC (NHi); in a clerk's hand, signed by TJ. FC (Vi).

From James Wood

SIR [Richmond] 13th. Jany. 1781

I forgot to Ask your Opinion whether the Soldiers of the Regiment of Guards might with Propriety be enlisted into the Continental Service. If so, and Money cou'd be Advanced I make no Doubt but a Considerable part of them wou'd enlist. I am Sir Yr. Excellency's Very Obt. Servt., J WOOD

RC (Vi); addressed. Place of writing assigned on basis of internal evidence.

To James Wood

Richmond Jany. 13. 1781

We have no board: the three Members present concur with me in opinion that it would be well to enlist as many of the Regiment of Guards as will engage for the War. The bounty is 2000 dollars. I cannot say whether the Money can shortly be furnished. T.J.

FC (Vi).

Pledge of Volunteers for Cavalry Service, with Jefferson's Approval

[*13 Jan. 1781.*] Subscribers pledge their honor to "serve our Country as Cavalry during the present invasion," though for not more than six months. Equipment, forage, and rations to be furnished by the state. Signed by Jno. Pleasants, Sam. Pleasants jr., Isaac Pleasants, Robt.

Crew, Sam. Woodson, Matt. Pleasant, Jno. Cheadle, Phill. Pleasant, Isham Woodson, Pleasants Younghusband, Wm. Hay, Wm. Mosby. [*On verso*:] "Jan. 17. 1781. The within proposition is approved, and we will furnish every accoutrement which we have or can produce. Horses cannot be found[1] by the public. Some of the Gentlemen will be pleased to apply to Colo. Muter to be informed what accoutrements we have. Th: Jefferson."

Tr (Vi); the pledge, approval, and all signatures are in a clerk's hand. Endorsed: "Volunteer Proposition Jany. 13. 1781. Approved." Printed in full in CVSP, I, 431-2.

[1] The word is here used, of course, in the sense of "provided."

From George Muter

SIR Jany 14. 1781.

I am honoured with your Excellency's letter and note.

What is required in the letter, shall be instantly (as far as possible) sett about.

'Twill be very proper to engage some barr iron of Mr. Ross; tho' I don't think it will be necessary to have any brought down immedeatly. There is a sufficient quantity of his pig iron to work up into cannon now at and near the foundery; but it is impossible to cast cannon (I think) 'till a house for moulding in is built. If Mr. Ross can cast cannon; I think it wou'd be very advantageous to get him to cast some for the Thetis and on the plan of the field piece cast at the foundery; but from some conversation I had with him, I am doubtfull whether he is either prepared or inclined to cast cannon.

I have the honour to be Your Excellency's most hl servant,

GEORGE MUTER

RC (Vi); address lacking.

TJ's LETTER AND NOTE have not been located.

From David Ross

SIR Sunday Evening [14? January 1781]

Since I had the pleasure of seeing you have mentioned to several of my acquaintances the necessity of rebuilding the publick Work houses &c. They mention some excellent workmen at present in the Militia that would gladly engage and carry with them many workmen black and white. I recommend your Excellency to Mr. Thos. Pleasants and Capt. John Pleasants who can inform you of a considerable number of hands necessary at present.

I am with great regard Your huml Servt., DAVID ROSS

RC (Vi); addressed: "His Excellency the Governor"; endorsed: "David Ross's Letter recd Jany 81." This letter was probably written on Sunday 14 Jan. See TJ's letter to the Person Employed to Collect Workmen, 15 Jan. 1781.

From George Slaughter

SIR Louisville Janry. 14th. 1781.

I have the Honour to inclose to your Excellency letters from two Gentlemen at Auposte and copys of several others from Kaskaskias directed to Colo. Clark and Colo. Todd. I have taken the Depositions of three persons which coroborates with the contents of these letters and have enclosed them also, for the consideration of your Board.

The Contents of the letters from the two French Gentlemen being a request for ammunition and understanding they apprehended an attack'd upon that post, I gave orders for Capn. George to send to Kaskaskias one hundred weight of powder and four hundred wt. of Lead, with directions for Capn. Rogers to lend what aid he can in getting across the country to Auposte and shall endeavour to [send] a small supply to that place immediately from here. This [I] thought it necessary to do as I consider it of very great importance to this place the keeping the Auposte in our favour.

With respect to Capn. Dodge the complaints against him are so general and I have so good authority for his having misapp[lied] the publick goods, and apprehending that he may possibly be collecting a cargoe of Peltry for the New Orleans mar[ket] that I have given Capn. George Orders to make enquiry into his conduct and if any thing of this sort appears, to Seize upon his person and what goods he may be Possessed of and secure them till further Orders.

The letters now inclosed with those sent some time ago will so fully inform you of the State of Affairs in the Illinois that I shall not enlarge on the disagreeable subject.

I must beg leave to mention the mismanagement of the person appointed to Superintend the making Salt with the Country's Kettles. Somewhere about 50 or 60 bushels is all that has been received from the persons who has work'd them, when private adventurers has been making near 10 times the Quantity with Kettles not boiling more than one fourth as much Water, owing principally to the indolence of the man who is appointed to carry on the business.

If, Sir, Your Board should think proper to appoint Colo. Floyd or myself to take the directions of the Kettles I am persuaded a sufficiency would be made for the Troops in this department. I am with much respect Your Excellencys Most obt. & very Hble Servt.,

George Slaughter

The two Letters from the French Gentlemen of the Auposte was by a mistake inclosed to Colo. Clark who will no doubt lay them before you.

I cannot Omit mentioning two you three Bills which I drew late in October last, in favor of John Williams Province,[1] one for 220½ Dollars, one other for 286 Dollars and another for £2120. which I hope will be paid. Yrs. as before, G.S.

RC (WHi); addressed and endorsed. Enclosures missing.

AUPOSTE: Vincennes.

1 The word appears to be "Province," but it may be "Provisioner" in abbreviated form.

To Steuben

Sir

Richmond Jan. 14. 1781.

Your letters of the 12th. and 13th. are now before me. They are in some measure answered by some marginal notes on the several articles in a paper delivered me by Majr. Walker. If there be any state arms, fit for use, and still undelivered they are so few, that we may consider them as nothing. I should therefore think it proper to discharge so many militia as cannot be furnished with arms. My letter of yesterday will point out what particular militia should be discharged. Should it happen that there are already more militia with you from the Counties enumerated in my yesterday's letter than you have arms for, would it not be proper to send the surplus of such militia over to Genl. Nelson to take the place and arms of so many of his who were not meant to be detained?

The public have not a pound of powder or other article of military stores at South Quay, except some twenty four and eighteen pound iron cannon. They are most unusually heavy for their bore and tho' a Quartermaster has been especially sent and employed there during the last summer in bringing them over to Suffolk or Smithfeild they have so far baffled his attempts as that he has got over but one of them: another broke down a bridge on it's passage which suspended his further endeavors. I have the honor to be with great esteem Sir your most obedt. humble servt.,

Th: Jefferson

P.S. If it be possible for you to spare Colo. Senf to plan the reedification of our works at Westham we shall be exceedingly glad of his assistance.

RC (NHi); addressed. FC (Vi). Steuben's letter of the 13th has not been located. For the PAPER DELIVERED ME BY MAJR. WALKER, see Steuben's Queries, following. MAJOR WALKER: Benjamin Walker, aide-de-camp to Steuben (Heitman).

Steuben's Queries concerning Military Supplies, with Jefferson's Answers

[Before 14 January 1781]

All are delivered	1 To know if all the State Arms are already distributed. If not where are the remainder?
Richmond and Westham. They shall be delivered to Capt. Pryor.	2 To fix on a place where all the Arms Ammunition and Camp Equipage may be collected and appoint some Officer to collect and distribute them. If the Governor thinks proper, Capt. Prior may be appointed to distribute them after they are collected.
We are endeavoring to do this.	3 The Arms out of repair should immediately be put in order and as fast as they are repaired delivered to the Person appointed to distribute them.
Colo. Harrison sais he will see to this.	4 The Ammunition already made up should be delivered to the same person at least 60,000 must be immediately prepared.
There are no tents. All the camp kettles we had have been delivered and we shall send to Fredericksburg immediately for more.	5 Tents and Camp kettles sufficient for the troops now in the Field must be immediately sent on to them, besides which a sufficiency of these Articles must be collected for the Troops coming in always reckoning on the 4000 Orderd out.
	The 2d Article must be determined immediately that I may acquaint Gen. Weedon and Nelson to whom to apply.
If I can find such a person who will be of real utility I will send him to the baron.	If it would not be proper to have with me some Officer of Government who being better acquainted with the resources of the State, I could confer with him on any Emergency. This Officer to keep a constant correspondence with the Executive power.
Col. Harrison has an officer engaged in this business.	I ordered Colo. Harrison to secure 200 pair boots which were at Williamsburg. What is become of them. They are wanted for Armand and Nelsons Corps.

This shall be done within a few days, as soon as we can get The Treasury brought back.	To pay 200,000 Dollars to Mr. Harrison on account of the United States that I may draw on him, when necessary.
This shall be done: it is proper to inform Baron Steuben that among the Cannon at South Quay there are 10 twenty four pounders Swedish, and there were two at Suffolk some time ago. Whether destroyed or carried away by the enemy at the former invasion I know not.	To put in order immediately 6 or 8 of the 10 pounders at Richmond and a Block-house and Battery to be immediately built at Hoods to defend the River. This I insist on in the Name of the United States. Colo. Senf is already making the Plans of the Work I wish to have made there.
An order has been given for procuring a number of canoes.	As the last incursion will rather induce the Enemy to return I desire the necessary arrangements may be made to have as many Boats and Scows built and assembled at Westham to preserve a Communication at that place.
I shall immediately know whether any linen for shirts has been saved, and order it. Hats we had not.	50 or 60 shirts and overhalls to be furnishd for Armands Corps.
Colo. Brooking is triable by a court martial according to[1] the Continental articles of war, only that his court must be of militia officers only. Our invasion law directs the manner of constituting the court.	Colo. Booker Arrested.

About 100 Blankets and 400 pr. Stockings will be Delivered to the Barons Order by Mr. Ross at Swift Creek near Petersburg.

MS (NHi); the queries are written in an unidentified hand; the marginal replies are all in TJ's hand. Endorsed: "Questions asked the Governor."

This document has been dated from the text of the letter preceding, with which it was probably sent.

COLO. BOOKER, COLO. BROOKING: The name was not clearly written and TJ misunderstood. Steuben was referring to the arrest of Lt. Col. Edmund Booker of the Amelia militia (Captain William Finney of the same militia was arrested at the same time); TJ thought Steuben meant Col. Vivian Brooking, county lieutenant of Amelia. See Brooking to TJ, 2 Feb. 1781. The date of the arrest, 12 Jan., proves that the present document was written between 12 and 14 Jan.

[1] TJ deleted "under" and interlined "according to."

From Edward Stevens

SIR So Carolina Camp Hickes Creek Jany 14th. 1781

I wrote you the 8th Inst. from this place by Lieut. Fraser of the Militia. This Covers a monthly Return of the Militia through the course of Yestreday. Genl. Green received several dispatches from Virginia and the Northward. These with the reports we have hear with respect to the Enemy in your Quarter, at first is rather alarming to young Soldiers, But I hope my Countrymen will not get into any State of Dispondencey, but will rather be roused in such a manner that their Enemies Present manuvers will turn to our advantage. I believe it is beyond a doubt that the Enemy in this Quarter is making every preparation for a move. I expect their movements here and those in Virginia are to Cooperate. This sudden and rapid move of the Enemy will show us the necessity of always keeping a Proper Posture for making a sudden Defence.

About Six or seven Hundred Militia of this State under the Command of Genl. Lillington I believe is now in motion to Join this Part of our Army. I have the Honour to be with every Sentiment of Respect Your Excellencys Most Obt & very hum: Servt.

Tr (DLC). Endorsed (in part): "Copy." Enclosure missing.

From Arthur Campbell

SIR Washington County Janr. 15. 1781

The Militia of this, and the two Western No. Carolina Counties, have been fortunate enough to frustrate the designs of the Cherokees. On my reaching the frontier, I found the Indians meant to annoy us by small parties and carry off Horses. To resist them effectually, the apparently best measure was to transfer the War without delay to their own border. To raise a force sufficient and provide them with Provisions and other necessaries, seem'd to be a work of time, that would be accompanied with uncommon difficulties, especially in the Winter season; our situation was critical, and nothing but an extraordinary effort could save us, and disappoint the views of the enemy: all the miseries of 1776 came fresh in remembrance, and to avoid a like scene, men flew to their arms, and went to the field. The Wattago [Watauga] Men under Lieut. Col. Seveir first marched, to the amount of about 300, the Militia of this, with that of Sullivan County, made 400 more, the place of rendezvous was to be on this side the French-River, call'd also

French-Broad or the Equoam properly the main branch of the Cherokee River.[1] Colo. Seveir with his men got on the path before the others, and by means of some discoveries made by his Scouts, he was induced to cross the River in pursuit of a party of Indians, that had been coming towards our settlements. On the 16th of December, he fell in with the party, since found to consist of 70 Indians, mostly from the Town of Chote, out of which was killed 13, and he took all their Baggage &c. in which were some of Clintons Proclamations and other documents expressive of their hostile designs against us.

After this action the Wattago Corps thot proper to retreat into an Island of the River. The 22d. I cross'd the French-River, and found the Wattago Men in great want of Provisions; we gave them a supply from our small stock; and the next day made a forced march towards the Tenasee. The success of the enterprize seemed to rest on our safely reaching the further bank of that River; as we had information the Indians had obstructed the common fording places, and had a force ready there to oppose our crossing. The morning of the 24th. I made a feint towards the Island Town, or Dragging-Canoes Town the lowermost on the River, and with the main Body pass'd the River without resistance at Timotlee. We were now discovered, such of the Indians we saw, seemed to be flying in consternation. Here I divided my force, sending a part to attack the Towns below, and with the other, I proceeded towards their principal Town Chote. Just as I passed a defile above Toque, I observed the Indians in force, stretching along the Hills below Chote, with an apparent design to attack our Van then within their view; but the main body too soon came in sight, for me to succeed in decoying them off the Hills; so they quietly let us pass on in order, without firing a Gun, except a few scattering shot at our Rear, at a great distance from the Clefts. We soon were in possession of their beloved Town, in which we found a welcome supply of Provisions. The 25th. Major Martin went with a Detachment, to discover the rout the enemy were flying off by; he surprized a party of Indians, took one Scalp, and seventeen Horses loaded with Cloathing, Skins, and House furniture; he discovered that most of the fugitives were making towards Telico, and the Hiwasee. The same day Capt. Crabtree of the Virginia Regiment was detached with 60 Men to burn the Town of Chilhowee; he succeeded in seting fire to that part of it situated on the South side the river, altho in the time, he was attacked by a superior force. He made his retreat good. The 26th. Major Tipton of the Carolina Corps were detached with 150 mounted Infantry, with orders to cross the River, dislodge the enemy on that side, and destroy the Town of Telassee; at the same time, Major Gilbert Christian with 150 foot who were to patrol the Hills on the South side Chilhowee, and burn the remaining part of that Town. This party did their duty well; killed three Indians and took nine Prisoners: the Officer of the Horse, by an unmilitary behaviour, failed in crossing the River. This trip took two days, in the time, the famous Indian Woman Nancy Ward came to Camp, she gave us various intelligence, and made an overture in behalf of some of the Cheifs for Peace; to which I then evaded giving an explicit answer, as I wished first to visit the vindictive part of the nation, mostly settled at Hiwasee, and Chistowee; and to distress the whole, as much as possible, by destroying their habitations and Provisions. The 28th. we set fire to Chote, Scitigo, and little-Tuskeego, and moved our whole force to a Town on Telico River called Kai-a-tee, where I intended a Post, for to secure a Retreat, and to lay up Provisions in. This evening Major Martin on returning from a patrol, attacked a party of Indians, killed two, and drove several into the River. The same evening in another skirmish, we lost Capt. James Elliott, a gallant young Officer, being the first, and only Man the enemy had power to hurt on the Expedition. The Indians lost three men on the occasion. The 29th. I set out for Hiwasee, distant about forty Miles, leaving at Kai-a-tee, under Major Christian a Garrison of 150 Men. The 30th. we arrived at the Hiwasee, and found the Town of the same name abandoned; in patroling the environs, we took a sensible young warrior, who informed us that a Body of Indians with M'Donald the British Agent, and some Tories were at Chistowee, twelve miles distant, waiting to receive us. I had reason to believe the enemy had viewed us from the Hills above Hiwasee; for which reason, I ordered our Camp to be laid off, fires kindled and other shews made as if we intended to stay all night. At dark we set out with about 300 Men (the Wattago Men refusing to go farther) crossing the River at an unexpected Ford, and that night got near the Town. Early in the morning of the 31st. we found that the enemy had fled in haste the evening before, leaving behind them, as they had done at the other Towns, almost all their Corn and [ot]her Provisions, together with many of their utensils for agriculture, and all their heavy houshold furniture with part of their stocks of Horses, Cattle, and Hogs. These Towns I expected would have been contended for with obstinacy; as most of the Chickamogga People had removed hence, after their visitation in

1779. Our Troops becoming impatient, and no other object of importance being in view, it was resolved to return homewards. Major Martin with a detachment were ordered by Sattoga, and the other Towns on Telico-River. In his rout, he took four prisoners, from whom he learnt, that several of the Cheifs, had met a few days before in order to consult on means to propose a Treaty for Peace. As I found the enemy were humbled, and to gain time, I took the liberty to send the Cheifs a message, a Copy of which I send herewith, as the fulfilment thereof will require your Excellencies further Instructions; and in which I expect N. Carolinia will assist, or that Congress will take upon themselves the whole. I believe advantageous promises of Peace may easily be obtained, with a surrender of such an extent of Country that will defray the Expences of the War; but such terms will be best ensured by placing a Garrison of two hundred Men, under an active Officer, on the banks of the Tenasee.

Our whole loss on this Expedition was one Man killed by the Indians, and two wounded by accident. It would have been very pleasing to the Troops to have met the whole force of the nation at once, on equal grounds; but so great was the panic that seized them, after seeing us in order over the Tenasee, that they never ventured themselves in sight of the Army, but on rocky clefts, or other inaccessable ground to our Mounted Infantry. By the Returns of the Officers of different detachments we killed 29 Men, and took 17 Prisoners, mostly Women and Children. The number of wounded is uncertain. Besides these we brought in the Family of Nancy Ward, who for their good offices, we considered in another light. The whole are in Major Martins care at the Great-Island, until the sense of Government is known how they are to be disposed of. The Towns of Chote, Scittigo, [,] Chilhowee, Toque, Mieliqua, Kai-a-tee, Sattoogo, Telico, Hiwasee and Chistowee all principal Towns, besides some small ones, and several scattering settlements, in which were upwards of One thousand Houses, and not less than fifty thousand Bushels of Corn, and large quantities of other kinds of Provisions, all of which, after taking sufficient subsistance for the army, whilst in the Country and on its return, were committed to [the] flames, or otherwise destroyed. No place in the Over H[ill?] Country remained unvisited, except the small Town of Telassee, a scattering settlement, in the neighbourhood of Chickamogga, and the Town of Caloogee situated on the sources of the Mobile. We found in Okana-Stote's Baggage, which he left behind in his fright, various manuscripts, copies of

Treaties, Commissions, Letters, and other Archives of the nation, some of which shews the double game that People have been carrying on, during the present War. There seem'd to be not a man of honor among the Cheifs, except him of Kai-a-tee, whom I would willingly have discriminated had it been in my power. Never did a people so happily situated, act more foolishly in loosing their livings, and their Country, at a time an advantageous neutrality was held out to them, but such is the consequences of British seduction.

The enemy in my absence did some mischief in Pow[ell's] Valley and on the Kentucky path near Cumberland Gap; besides three Children that they Scalped on Holstein; one of the perpetrators of which, we knock'd up on our return, and retook a number of Horses. The Botetourt and Montgomery Militia were too slow in their movments to do any service.

The Virginia Militia that served with me on this Expedition, expects to be paid in the same manner with those that served last year in Carolinia.

What Provisions were needed on our seting out, were purchased on short credit, which I trust will be punctually paid on the first application.

Your Excellency will please to excuse the length of this narration. I thought it my duty to give a circumstantial detail of Facts, as the undertaking had something singular in [it] and may lead to important consequences.

I am Sir Your most Obedient & very Humble Servant,

ARTHUR CAMPBELL

RC (Vi); addressed and endorsed; MS mutilated. Enclosure: Copy of address to the Indians, dated Kai-a-tee, 4 Jan. 1781 and signed by Arthur Campbell, John Sevier, and Joseph Martin; printed in CVSP, I, 414-15.

The victory of COLO. SEVEIR (John Sevier) on 16 Dec. 1780 is known as the battle of Boyd's Creek; see Samuel Cole Williams, *Tennessee during the Revolutionary War*, Nashville, 1944, p. 187. THE FAMOUS INDIAN WOMAN NANCY WARD: She was Maj. Joseph Martin's mother-in-law, his wife being Betsy Ward, grandniece of the Cherokee chief Attakullakulla (same, p. 188, note). WE FOUND IN OKANASTOTE'S [Oconostota's] BAGGAGE . . . VARIOUS MANUSCRIPTS: These "Archives" of the Cherokee nation were sent to TJ at his request by Campbell on 20 June 1781, and were forwarded by TJ to Thomas McKean, president of Congress, 20 Dec. 1781; they are filed in DLC: PCC, No. 71, II, 143-221. The reference to the "Archives" of the Cherokee nation did not escape the keen eye of Ebenezer Hazard, who, under the patronage of the Continental Congress, was already engaged in collecting American state papers (see Huntington to TJ, 27 Apr. and its enclosure).

1 The words "call'd also . . . Cherokee River" were written at the bottom of the page.

From William Davies

SIR Richmond Jany. 15. 1781.

As considerable numbers of militia are daily arriving at this place, very many of whom are not armed, and as I know of no public stores from whence they can be supplied, I beg to know your Excellency's sentiments with respect to the propriety of discharging such as cannot be equipped, or whether it would be your wish that they should be detained here, till a sufficient number of arms can be repaired to put into their hands.

I have the honor to be, Sir, your Excellency's very obedt servt,

WILLIAM DAVIES

RC (Vi); addressed and endorsed.

To Charles Dick

SIR Richmond Jany 15. 1781.

I am exceedingly pleased at the spirited exertions of your town and its Neighbourhood, which with the aid Gen. Weedon carries back, and the Militia called from the Counties of Rockbridge, Augusta, Rockingham and Shenandoah (supposed about 900) and directed to proceed to Fredericksburg will I hope secure you. I meant this day to have begged the continuance of your attention to the Gun factory till a restoration of quiet and leisure will permit us to look out another. We mean to send off from this place immediately a number of Muskets to be repaired at the factory and Mr. Hunter's Works. Should danger appear in the mean time be so good as to lodge an order some where on the road for stopping and storing them at a proper distance, or at least so many of them as cannot be repaired in a short time. The Offices have not yet resumed Business. T.J

FC (Vi).

From John Floyd

SIR Jefferson January 15th 1781.

My want of knowledge and experiance in the military department will I fear cause me to be more troublesome to your Excellency than is necessary, or than I would wish to be. And as the

County Lieutenant may probably not come out for some time to take the Command, and numbers of People are daily removing them[selves] into the interior parts of the County for safety; it will be high[ly] necessary to adopt some measure early in the spring for the protection of our frontier. I would therefore beg your Excellency to give me a few general instructions by which I may regulate my conduct till Colo. Christian comes out. The inhabited frontier part of this County is about seventy miles in length on the Ohio on which if a few small posts were kept up during the spring and Summer seasons it would be a great means of preventing the Enemy Indians from many of their mischievous practices, in which they have hitherto been so successfull as always to escape with impunity. We have had no Court as yet and of course no regularity with the Militia so that I can't give you the exact number, but I imagine we have in this County about four hundred Men able to bear Arms.

The inhabitants in general seem to have much more dependance on the militia if they can be legally called upon and posted along the Ohio, then upon any number of regular Troops they have a right to look for here, unless Colo. Clarke cou'd be enabled to carry on an Expedition early in the spring. If this can't be done, nor the militia Stationed along the River I really believe the County will be nearly depopulated next Summer.

There will in this County I think be upwards of 100000 ℔. of Beef saved this Winter for publick uses, indeed I don't know but what there is that quantity already saved. And Corn and Flour is far from being scarce.

The bearer Capt. Sullivan is well acquainted with the Situation of County in general and I cou'd wish your Excellency to ask him a few Questions relative thereto.

I am your Excellencys most Obdt. & very hble servt.,

JNO. FLOYD

RC (Vi).

THE COUNTY LIEUTENANT: John Floyd was himself appointed county lieutenant of Jefferson co. on 22 Jan. 1781 (George Rogers Clark to TJ, 21 Jan. 1781).

From Nathanael Greene

Camp on the Pedee, 15 Jan. 1781. Requests credit in the amount of £2,000 for Dr. Brownson, newly appointed purveyor general to the hospital of the southern department, who is on his way to Virginia.

RC (MiU-C); 1 p.; endorsed. Tr (CSmH).

DR. BROWNSON: Nathan Brownson, M.D., formerly a Georgia delegate to Congress; governor of Georgia, 1782 (*Biog. Dir. Cong.*); see further, TJ to Greene, 10 Feb. 1781.

To Samuel Huntington

SIR Richmond Jan: 15th. 1781

As the dangers which threaten our Western frontiers the ensuing spring render it necessary that we should send thither Col. Crocket's Battalion, at present on guard at Frederick Town, but raised for the Western service, I thought it necessary to give your Excellency previous information thereof that other forces may be provided in time to succeed to their duties. Cap. Read's troop of Horse if necessary, may be continued a while longer on guard.

I have the honor to be with the greatest respect Your Excellency's Most obedient & most hum. Servt., TH: JEFFERSON

RC (DLC: PCC, No. 71, II); in a clerk's hand, signed and addressed by TJ; endorsed, in part: "Read Jany. 29." Tr (DLC), signed by TJ. FC (Vi).

From Samuel Huntington

SIR In Congress Jany. 15. 1781

A circular Letter addressed to the respective States of the 9th Day of November last communicated a requisition of Congress for Service of the current Year. This Act, and the System of the 18th of March respecting our Finnances included the principal Means which their present Powers have enabled Congress to adopt for prosecuting the War. Measures so deeply interesting not only demand the unremitted Attention and vigorous Support of the Legislatures: but Congress ought to be informed of their Progress with the utmost Precision. Both are necessary to public Credit, to the Success of our military Operations, to the very Existence of our Armies. By our Act of the 21st of October the State Agents are directed to transmit to the Commander in Chief, and to the Commissary General respectively, monthly returns of all Supplies which shall be drawn into their Hands, specifying the Articles and the Magazines where they shall be deposited. It is equally incumbent on the State Treasurers to make similar returns to the Board of Treasury of all the Taxes which shall be brought into their respective Offices, and of the Issues of the new Emissions.

These are regulations which cannot be dispensed with, and it is recommended to the Legislatures to enjoin them under such Penalties as will enforce a prompt and punctual Obedience.

Besides those Supplies for the current Year which cannot be anticipated without the utmost Danger the Pay in Arrears to the Army demands your most serious Consideration. The Honor of Government, and military Order and Discipline depend on its regular Discharge: nor was a Fund sufficient for this and other Purposes neglected; for had the requisition for Taxes prior to the Act of the 18th of March been productive: had the Warrants on the State Treasurers for the Balances of those Taxes drawn so long ago as the first of July, been satisfied, a Complaint of this Nature could not have existed.

We are not unapp[r]ized of the Embarrassments attending the Collection of Taxes from the Credit given on Commissary and Quarter Masters Certificates for the Support of the Army: but it is manifest that Congress could not provide a remedy. It was found expedient to discontinue the Emission of Paper Money, and from various Causes the public Necessities were not relieved by Loans: at the same Time that the Measure was embraced of extinguishing those Certificates in the Taxes. Hence the Treasury has been destitute of Supply, almost every resource being cut off at the same Instant. In vain have we endeavoured to obtain a Knowledge of the Amount of those Certificates, or how far they have been reduced; and they continue to obstruct every Plan which hath been devised for restoring public Credit and supporting the War.

This is a Subject to which Authority of the Legislatures alone is competent and it will become their Wisdom and their Zeal for the public Service to give it the fullest Investigation. In the mean Time an immediate Provision for the Pay of the Army is indispensably necessary. We need not dwell upon the Injustice or the probable Effects of a Delay. They are obvious and alarming; and we earnestly call upon the several States to devise prompt and efficient Means for remitting to the Paymaster General on Warrants to be issued in his Favour the respective Quotas assigned to them by the enclosed Estimate. The Necessity of great and spirited Exertions becomes every Day more evident, while the cruel Policy of our Enemy raises universal Indignation and Abhorrence it admonishes us that no Time is to be lost in rescuing our bleeding Country from Desolation, and establishing its Independence on the Basis of an honorable and permanent Peace. However great may be the Burthens which we are called upon to sustain let us remember that they are the Price of Liberty; and that they have been common to every People who have dared to struggle for social Happiness against Violence and Oppression. Let us reflect on our solemn Engagements to devote our Lives and Fortunes to the best of Causes; and we shall find that we cannot be destitute of resources. Let us view the past Miseries of a lingering War and the Danger of its further Protection and we shall seize the golden Opportunity of cooperating with our generous Ally by every possible Effort to render the approaching Campaign glorious and decisive. If we are unable in this Stage of the Controversy to defend ourselves by annual Taxes; can we hesitate to interpose our responsibility or to contribute a Portion of our Capitals? Will a People whose Fortitude and Patriotism have excited the Admiration of Europe, languish at the bright Dawn of Triumph, and endanger the public Happiness by a selfish Parsimony? While Congress entertain just Sentiments of their Constituents there can be no Place for such humiliating Apprehensions. On the contrary we shall ask with Confidence for a liberal Compliance with every requisition which the public Exigences dictate. Experience has pointed out the Danger to which we have been exposed by a Want of Punctuality in former Supplies: and we are persuaded that those Dangers will for the future be carefully prevented.

For our own Part we have left nothing unessayed to render the Operations of the War more vigorous and successful. We have applied for naval Succours from abroad. If we no longer continue unfortunate in the Importation, we shall not want a competent Supply of Clothing, Arms and Amunition. We are once more attempting a foreign Loan of Specie. We have pointed out and required the Aids of Men, Provisions and Money which in every Event must be produced from our own internal resources. We have strenuously urged upon the States a punctual Compliance on their Part with those requisitions. With the States who alone have Authority to execute, With an enlightened People who know how to estimate the Blessings for which we contend it remains to give the Measures which we have recommended their ful and seasonable Effect.

By Order of Congress. SAM. HUNTINGTON President

Estimate of the Sums necessary to be forwarded by the respective States from Pennsylvania to New Hampshire inclusive for the immediate Pay of the Army composed of the Lines of those States

Total 879.342 Dollars

Apportioned by Congress as follows

New Hampshire	51,726
Massachusetts	284,493
Rhode Island	25,863
Connecticutt	155,178
New York	77,589
New Jersey	51,726
Pennsylvania	232,767
	879,342

The above is calculated on six Months Pay in Specie Value, one half of which should be advanced without the least Delay and the remainder by the first of April.

FC (DLC: PCC. No. 15); at head of text: "Circular."

This circular to the states was drawn up by a committee of Congress which reported on 15 Jan. The draft report, in the hand of James Duane, is in DLC: PCC, No. 24, and is printed in JCC, XIX, 58-61. See also Samuel Huntington to TJ, 20 Mch., 26 Oct. (second letter), and 9 Nov. 1780.

To Samuel Huntington

SIR Richmond Jany 15. 1781

I received some time ago from Major Forsythe, and afterwards from you a requisition to furnish one half the supplies of provision for the Convention troops removed into Maryland. I should sooner have done myself the honour of writing to you on this subject but that I hoped to have had it laid before you more fully than could be done in writing by a Gentleman who was to have passed on other public business to Philadelphia. The late events in this State having retarded his setting out I think it my duty no longer to postpone explanation on this head.

You cannot be unapprized of the powerful armies of our enemies at this time in this and the Southern States, and that their future plan is to push their successes in the same quarter by still larger reinforcements. The forces to be opposed to these must be proportionably great, and these forces must be fed. By whom are they to be fed? Georgia and South Carolina are annihilated, at least as to us. By the requisition to us to send provisions into Maryland it is to be supposed that none are to come to the Southern army from any State north of this; for it would seem inconsistent that while we should be sending North, Maryland and other states beyond that should be sending their provisions South. Upon N. Carolina then, already exhausted by the ravages of two armies, and on this State are to depend for subsistence those bodies of men who are to oppose the greater part of the enemy's force in the United States, the subsistence of the German and of half the British Conventioners. To take a view of this matter on the Continental requisitions of Nov. 4. 1780 for specific quotas of provision it is observable that N. Carolina and Virginia are to furnish 10,475,740℔ of animal food and 13,529 barrels of flour while the States north of these will yield 25,293,810℔ of animal food and 106,471 barrels of flour. If the greater part of the British armies be employed in the South it is to be supposed that the greater part of the American force will be sent there to oppose them. But should this be the case, while the distribution of the provisions is so very unequal would it be proper to render it still more so by withdrawing a part of our contributions to the support of posts northward of us? It would certainly be a great convenience to us to deliver a portion of our specifics at Frederic town rather than in Carolina: but I leave it to you to judge whether this would be consistent with the general good or safety. Instead of sending aids of any kind to the northward it seems but too certain that unless very substantial and timely assistance is received from thence our enemies are yet far short of the ultimate term of their successes. I beg leave therefore to refer to you whether the Specifics of Maryland, as far as shall be necessary had not better be applied to the support of the posts within it, for which it's quota is much more than sufficient, or were it otherwise, whether those of the States north of Maryland had not better be called on, than to detract any thing from the resources of the southern opposition already much too small for the encounter to which it is left. I am far from wishing to count or measure our contributions by the requisitions of Congress. Were they ever so much beyond these, I should readily strain them in aid of any one of our Sister States. But while they are so far short of those calls to which they must be pointed in the first instance, it would be great misapplication to divert them to any other purpose: and I am persuaded you will think me perfectly within the line of duty when I ask a revisal of this requisition.

I have the honor to be with the greatest respect Sir Your Mo. ob. & Most hble. Servant, TH: JEFFERSON

RC (DLC: PCC, No. 71, II); in a clerk's hand, corrected and signed by TJ; endorsed, in part: "Read 29 Referred to Mr. Burke Mr Montgomery

Mr Bland who are to confer with the board of war"; Tr (DLC), signed by TJ. On this same date TJ wrote letters almost identical with this to Thomas Sim Lee and to the president of the Continental Board of War, having only such variations as were made necessary by the change in addressee.

On the REQUISITION from Maj. Forsyth, see Forsyth to the Agent Superintending State Supplies, 6 Dec. 1780, and Continental Board of War to TJ, same date. For Congress' further action on TJ's appeal, see report of Board of War, read 2 Feb. (JCC, XIX, 106), and report of the committee, read 15 Feb. (same, p. 147-8). Congress on the latter date ordered that the whole subject "be referred to the committee appointed to confer with Colonel B. Harrison," who was the GENTLEMAN mentioned by TJ as about to come to Philadelphia; see TJ to Harrison, 29 Jan. 1781.

To Thomas Sim Lee

Richmond, 15 Jan. 1781. This letter is virtually identical in substance with the preceding letter to Samuel Huntington, q.v.

FC (Vi); 2 p.; at head of text: "Governor Lee and President of the Board of War"; the letter sent to Lee is printed in *Md. Archives*, XLVII, 17-19. A copy was enclosed in TJ's letter to Benjamin Harrison, 29 Jan. 1781, q.v.

To Thomas Nelson

DEAR GENERAL Richmond January 15. 1781.

As I suppose by this time you may have more Men than Arms, and there are no more Arms fit for use remaining in the public Stock, œconomy will require that the surplus Militia be discharged. This measure is the more necessary, as the law for raising new levies remains unexecuted while the Militia are from their Counties. I shall therefore take the liberty of pointing out to you, as I have done to Baron Steuben, what particular Militia should be first discharged. On confirmation of the intelligence that a hostile fleet had arrived we asked the advice of Baron Steuben as to the numbers which should be brought into the feild: He advised 4000. We therefore called on the following Counties for one fourth of their Militia which we expected would produce the numbers as annexed to them viz.

Halifax .....247.	Cumberland ..102.	Sussex ......175.
Buckingham .162.	Mecklenburg .212.	Rockingham .219.
Goochland ...145.	Henrico .....155.	Bedford .....325.
Lunenburg ...169.	Augusta ....344.	Fluvanna .... 65.
Chesterfield ..164.	Prince Edward 142.	Amelia .....275.
Rockbridge ..146.	Albemarle ...218.	Dinwiddie ...175.
Charlotte ....156.	Powhatan ... 71.	Southampton .218
Amherst ....224.	Brunswick ...325.	Shenandoah ..216.

The amount (4650) was greater than the Baron's requisition because we of course expected deficiencies. The above were intended to be kept in the feild for some time: but as some of these Counties were distant, we called on those in the neighbourhood of this place at first for one half and afterwards for all their fighting Men for present defen[ce] meaning that as soon as those before enumerated should be in the feild those called for present defence should be discharged. In like manner you are authorized for the purpose of hasty opposition to call on certain Counties, which it was likewise our idea to discharge on receiving the force which was to remain. Whenever, therefore, all your Arms shall be taken up, should more Militia come in we would chuse that you discharge so many of those Counties not originally called on, or of those which tho' originally called on have yet more than one fourth in the feild. By these means we shall in time have in the feild the Militia of those particular Counties only which were first called on, and the other Counties being all at home we may proceed to send to them the law for raising levies in order to its execution. T.J.

FC (Vi).

To Thomas Nelson

DEAR GENERAL Richmond Jany 15, 1781

I have never heard a tittle of the Enemy since your information that they were at Sandy Point the day after they left Westover; nor is any thing known at this place as to their subsequent Movements. As this want of intelligence might eventually be fatal, I have ordered an Express to be stationed at Bottom's Bridge, another at New Kent Court House, a third at Bird's tavern, a fourth at Williamsburg, a fifth half way between that and Hampton and a sixth at Hampton. It will be easy for Mr. Kemp to throw letters from you wherever situated into this line, and as each Rider will have but 15. Miles out and the same back they may if necessary be put into motion every day. By the same means you may have communications with Hampton. Your Business may probably put it out of your power to write so often, but hope that some of the Gentlemen about you may be able to give us intelligence every day or two. T.J.

FC (Vi). YOUR INFORMATION: No letter has been found from Nelson to TJ indicating that the enemy "were at Sandy Point the day after they left Westover." Since they left Westover on 10 Jan. (see TJ to Weedon, 11 Jan.), it seems clear that Nelson must have written to TJ on that day, to which TJ replied in a (missing) letter of 11 Jan.

From Thomas Nelson

DEAR SIR Wmsburg Janry. 15. 1781

Since my last, informing you that the Enemy's Fleet had passed Burwell's Ferry, it has only fallen down the River as low as Hardy's Ferry. They land on the South Side wherever they have a Prospect of getting any valuable Plunder. I am concerned to hear of the bad Conduct of the Men commanded by Capt. Hockaday, and shall, as soon as they join me again, make the strictest Enquiry into it. I am, Dear Sir, with great Respect, Your mo: Obedt. Servt.,

THOS NELSON JR. B.G.

RC (PHi); addressed and endorsed.

To the Person Employed to Collect Workmen

SIR Jan. 15, 1781

The destruction of the public Storehouses, Magazines, Laboratory, Shops and other Works at this place and Westham by the Enemy having left our Arms, Powder and other Stores exposed in open Houses to plunder and our Artificers unfurnished with Houses to proceed in the repair of Arms and other necessary Works, obliges me, as the only resource for a hasty collection of Sawyers, Carpenters and Wheel-Wrights, to apply to the public spirit of the Gentlemen of this Country who possess Workmen of that kind. You will therefore go out for this purpose and address yourself to them apprising them fully of the necessity for throwing up hasty Works for these purposes. Whatever Workmen they have we hope they will spare and send in immediately with their Saws and Tools. They will not be long wanted, and their hire shall be fixed by some impartial and judicious person according to the rates in hard money formerly allowed with a proper attention to the late advance of Wages, which shall be paid in Tobacco at 20/ ₱ hundred or its worth in paper Money. If Gentlemen who have timber on James River above the Falls chuse rather to employ their Sawyers under their own eye, and will cut and send to Westham or the fork of the River as they shall be advised Quantities of Plank fit for Building it will answer the public purpose as well as if they sent their Sawyers to us. In this case they must fix the quantity and time within which it shall be delivered. The worth of this shall be fixed on the principles before explained. T.J.

FC (Vi).

To Timothy Pickering

SIR Richmond Jan. 15. 1781

I wrote you in a former letter that on the recommendation of Gen. Greene we had proposed to Maj. Forsythe the accepting the appointment of Deputy Quartermaster here which you had been pleased to refer to us. This appointment was kept open I think a Month, during which time (and indeed at any time since) we never received any answer from Maj. Forsythe, or intimation through any other channel that he would undertake it. On the contrary it appeared by letters from him that he had accepted the office of Deputy Commissary of Purchases for the Southern department. In the mean time Col. Carrington, appointed by Gen. Green Deputy Quartermaster to the Southern Army, arrived here, claimed the right of nomination, and nominated a Maj. Claiborne. Tho' we doubted the propriety of his claim, yet it was a want of acquaintance with Maj. Claiborne, and a real inability (after the refusal of Mr. Divers and Major Forsythe) to find another whom we could recommend in all points, which induced us to refer the nomination altogether to Baron Steuben who was here. He approved of Maj. Claiborne as having formerly known him while of Gen. Green's family and assured us the appointment would be particularly agreeable to Gen. Greene, and that he would undertake to satisfy you also of it's propriety. I thought it my duty to inform you of this matter, and have no doubt from any thing which I have yet seen but that Maj. Claiborne will do justice to the Baron's expectations.

I have the honor to be with the greatest esteem & respect Sir Your mo. obt. hb Servt., TH: JEFFERSON

RC (J. M. Fox, Philadelphia, 1946); in a clerk's hand, signed and addressed by TJ: "Colo Timothy Pickering at Genl. Washington's Head-Quarters"; endorsed: "Govr. Jefferson Jany. 15, 1781. Major Claiborne appointed D. Q. M. for Virginia." FC (Vi).

TJ's FORMER LETTER has not been located, but see Pickering's answer to the present letter, 3 Feb. 1781.

To the President of the Continental Board of War

Richmond, 15 Jan. 1781. This letter is virtually identical in substance with the letters to Samuel Huntington and to Thomas Sims Lee of the same date, qq.v.

FC (Vi); 2 p.; at head of text: "Governor Lee and President of the Board of War."

To John Christian Senf

SIR Richmond [15 January 1781]

As it is necessary for us instantly to build pro[per] Shops and Magazines at Westham, and first of all things a plan is to be laid, I will beg the favor of you to come to this place and lend us your Assistance in forming the plans. Magazines, Laboratories, and artificers Shops both for the State and Continent, on a tolerably large Plan are to be so brought together as that they may be covered by some small Works for the present and in future included within a fortification, when we shall be able to build one. T.J.

FC (Vi); date largely shaved off at top of page.

This letter is printed in *Official Letters* under date of 13 Jan. However, in the proceedings of the Council of 19 Jan. TJ reported only one letter written to Senf, of 15 Jan., during the time the Council was not in session (*Va. Council Jour.*, II, 273). Moreover, in his letter to Steuben of 14 Jan., q.v., TJ first requested Senf's assistance. This letter has therefore been assigned the date of 15 Jan.

From George Slaughter

Louisville, 15 Jan. 1781. Having appointed an assistant to complete purchases to be made on the Monongahela, Slaughter proceeded to Louisville and, on arrival, began purchasing beef and salt, the supply of which is sufficient; has drawn bills in favor of James Sullivan and David Standford for the purchase and delivery of provisions "from Hunters that would not credit the state," and hopes they may be paid; encloses list of bills drawn last summer, part of which are still unpaid; was directed to draw bills when appointed by Clark (encloses copy of appointment) and having done so, hopes the "Board will take them in"; needs at least £250,000 to comply with contracts; wrote "from Monongahalia" that Nathaniel Randolph had been appointed to complete purchases there and provide for their transportation to Louisville with orders to draw on the government when necessary.

RC (Vi); 3 p.; signature omitted; addressed, in part: "favd. by Capn. Jas. Sullivan." Enclosures missing.

Slaughter's letter of uncertain date "from Monongahalia" has not been located.

From George Slaughter

Louisville, 15 Jan. 1781. Has been obliged to purchase a quantity of shoe leather, whiskey, tobacco, flour, and a boat; drew a bill in favor of Simon Triplett for £11,874 which he hopes will be paid, "Particularly as these articles were furnished me at the same price he was selling them at for ready money." Also drew bill on the 13th instant in favor of Sandford Edwards for £21,320 for beef. Has been informed that several bills drawn were protested "for want of advice"; did not know this was necessary. Some bills, having been returned, will be presented again, accompanied by letters. Hopes other bills, which "will not amount to any thing considerable," will be paid.

RC (Vi); 2 p.; signed: "George Slaughter Commt"; addressed, in part: "favd. by Capn. Sullivan"; endorsed.

To the Virginia Delegates in Congress

GENTLEMEN Richmond Jany. 15. 1781.

I called on Mr. Anderson the Writer of the letter to Capt. Trot which you were pleased to inclose to me and desired he would explain the foundation on which he had written that letter. His explanation I now inclose you, from which you will be able to collect only thus much, that his application on behalf of Mr. Trot was utterly rejected and nothing said which could authorize him to suppose we should wink at his loading his Vessel with Corn. He has trimmed up an Answer for me of which I only wish to be acquitted till it can be understood.

I must at the same time acknowledge to you with candor that considering the neutral light in which Congress have placed the Bermudians and the extreme want of Salt here we have at various times permitted them to bring in Salt and exchange it with Government at the rate of one Bushel of Salt for two at first and afterwards three of Corn: and sometimes for Tobacco. We have been rigorous in allowing no more to be carried out than was procured by exchange in this way. You cannot be made more sensible of the necessity which forces us to this Barter, than by being assured that no further back than the Counties adjoining the Blue-ridge Salt has sold lately for from 4 to 500£ the Bushell. T.J.

FC (Vi). Enclosure not located. THE LETTER YOU WERE PLEASED TO INCLOSE TO ME: See Virginia Delegates to TJ, 10 Dec. 1780; also same to same, 30 Jan. 1781. THE BERMUDIANS: See TJ to Benjamin Harrison, 29 Jan. 1781.

From George Weedon

DR SIR Fredericksburg 15 Jany 1781

Since the receipt of yours of 11th Inst: I have taken every measure in my power to fulfil your request; the County Lieutenants of Northumberland, Richmond, Lancaster, Westmoreland, King

George, Stafford, P. William, Fairfax, Loudon, Fauquier, Orange, Culpepper and Spotsylvania are apprized of the danger and requested to have every Man they can Arm and equip arranged and ready to march at a moments Warning. I have between 6 and 700 Men ready embodied and posted at different parts between this and Potowmac; out of this Number 150 are Rifle Men and from the Information of Col. Matthews I may expect in the Course of next Weeks 500 more so that I hope I shall be able to give your Excellency a favorable account from this Quarter should the Enemy make any attempts. I have had all the Lead at this Post run in to Ball and find upon a very moderate Calculation that we shall be very deficient in that Article. There is a constant Fatigue Party making up Cartridges, which must shortly be stopped unless your Excellency can send me an immediate Reinforcement of Lead.

You may depend that no exertions of mine shall be wanting for the Service of my Country and every intelligence of consequence from this Post you may be assured shall be forwarded to your Excellency without delay. I am Dr Sir With high Esteem & Regard Your most Obt Servt.,

G Weedon

RC (NN); addressed.

To Jacob Wray

Richmond Jany. 15. 1781.

To want of intelligence may be ascribed a great part, if not the whole of the Enemy's late successful incursions to this place. Tho they appeared in the Bay on the Saturday, no notification of it addressed to the Executive came to hand till 10 o'Clock A.M. on tuesday: There did indeed on Sunday Morning come to my hands a letter which you were so kind to write to Genl. Nelson informing him that 27. Sail had been seen in the Bay, and that Commo. Barron had gone to reconnoitre there more closely: But as it was not known whether they were Friends or foes, and we hoped more particular intelligence on the return of Commo. Barron, none but the lower Militia were called out, till the Tuesday following, by which two days were completely lost, which would have added so much to the collection of Militia in this quarter as to have rendered doubtful at least, whether the Enemy could have got here.

I mention these circumstances to shew you the necessity of our being better furnished with intelligence of the Enemy's Movements, and to apologize for my troubling you with the task of communicating every thing interesting through the line of Expresses stationed at every 15 Miles from hence to Hampton. One is to be fixed by Mr. Kemp at Hampton, who will set out on yours, or Commo: Barron's order and deliver his dispatches to the next who is ordered to be stationed halfway between Hampton and Williamsburg: the particular place I cannot inform you, but the Express may do it. I hope you will be so good as to undertake this trouble and to continue it so long as it may be necessary to keep up the line. T.J.

FC (Vi).

Wray's LETTER to Nelson: Not found, but see TJ to Steuben, 31 Dec. 1780.

To Edward Carrington

SIR Richmond Jany. 16. 1781.

I have desired Colo. Muter to have delivered to Majr. Claiborne such of the Articles applied for in your Letter of the 10th. inst. as we have. We have no tents of any kind. Axes, Spades, Shov[els] and Padlocks can probably be furnished. We have sent to Fredericksburg for Camp-kettles, which shall be forwarded as soon as they come.

I think a few days will probably determine the Enemy's ultimate designs as to us: in the mean time I do not wish to give any decisive orders as to the place of slaughtering the Provisions. The expenditure of Pork indeed at this Season must be forbidden. It shall be my endeavor to suffer this invasion to divert as little as possible of our Supplies for the Southern Army. T.J.

FC (Vi).

From Archibald Cary

DEAR SIR Tuckahoe Tuesday Morn. [16 January 1781]

I have Continued As ill as any Person could well be with a Cold, for upwards of 3 Weeks, it has reduced me so that I can with difficulty walke up and Down Stairs. I thank God it has Mended greatly for 3 days past, and I have gatherd a little strength.

I have heard nothing of the Enemy Since their Stop at Sandy Point, untill this Morn. A Man Came to press a Waggon who Says they have landed at Hampton, are Fortifiing and have received a reinforcement. I pray Sir, that you Give what News Can be depended on. I hope to be at Ampthill the last of the Week. Pray Sir, How Can the people furnish a Beef for Each Souldier from a County, if the Commissioners as fast as we put them up for that purpose take them away. This is the Case with Many. Yr Afft. and obedt. Servt.,

ARCHIBALD CARY

RC (Vi); on verso: Dft of TJ's Proclamation on Paroles, 19 Jan. 1781, q.v.

The only Tuesday between the time the enemy were at Sandy Point (see TJ to Thomas Nelson, 15 Jan.) and 19 Jan., when TJ presented his Proclamation on Paroles was 16 Jan. This letter has therefore been assigned to that date.

From William Davies

Richmond, 16 Jan. 1781. There are about 100 Chesterfield militia now at Manchester, consisting of old men and boys. No purpose can be served by continuing them. Since some militia are to be dismissed, "at least such whose turn has been already taken, previous to the present invasion," and Col. Haskins says he has "sent all the able men to the army without regard to classes," orders are requested.

RC (Vi); 2 p.; addressed and endorsed.

To Nathanael Greene

SIR

Richmond Jany 16. 1781.

Your favors of the 14th. and 31st. of December remain unanswered. I have been less attentive to the communication of our progress in preparing for the Southern war as Baron Steuben who knows all our movements, gives you no doubt full information from time to time. The present invasion of this State you have before been apprized of by the Baron. The very extraordinary and successful attempt of the enemy on this place you will also have heard of. The inclosed paper containing a pretty exact narrative of it, I take the liberty of transmitting you. The enemy, on Baron Steuben's approaching towards Hood's hoisted sail, and with the assistance of a very fine gale which sprung up in the instant (for they seem to have had the elements perfectly at their command thro' the whole) they fell down the river in a very short time. When they came we were getting into a fair way of providing both subsistence and men. They have amazingly interrupted both operations. The latter indeed has been totally suspended. I have just written to Baron Steuben so to arrange his force of Militia, as by permitting those from the greater number of Counties to return home, to put into our power to have the law for raising regulars carried into execution. This his anxiety for regular force will lead him to do with all practicable expedition.

Your bill in favor of Mr. St. Lawrence has been accepted, and will be paid as soon as the several boards resume business.

When the departure of the enemy, or indication of their fixed plan as to this Country shall have enabled me to judge how far they will interrupt our succours to you, I will take the earliest opportunity of stating to you under every head of your requisitions from us what we shall have a prospect of doing.

I have the honor to be with very great esteem & respect Sir, your mo: ob. & mo: hble Servant, TH: JEFFERSON

RC (NHi); in a clerk's hand, signed by TJ; without indication of name of addressee; FC (Vi); at head of text: "Genl. Greene."

THE INCLOSED PAPER: *Va. Gaz.* (D & N), 13 Jan. 1781, containing an account of Arnold's invasion printed above, 31 Dec. 1780, Notes and Documents Relating to the British Invasions, Document II. YOUR BILL . . . MR. ST. LAWRENCE: On 18 Jan., at the first meeting after the invasion, the Council approved a "Warrant drawn by General Greene in favor of Patrick St. Lawrence for a hundred and three thousand eight hundred and four Dollars accepted the 15th instant, to be charged to the United States" (*Va. Council Jour.*, II, 273).

To James Maxwell

Jaunary 16. 1781

I inclose you a plan for building portable Boats recommended from General Washington and shall be glad that you will take measures for having about twenty of them made without delay. I suppose it will be necessary for you to send out in quest of Workmen. Any such which can be engaged shall receive a hire according to the former hard money prices having reasonable attention to the late advances of Wages, to be paid in Tobacco at 20/ ℔ hundred or its value in paper. It would be more agreeable to have them built at this place unless you think convenience very considerably in favor of the Ship Yard. We have doubts whether this plan will suit for our broad rough Waters, or for transporting Waggons at all: if you think it may be improved, or a better suggested we shall be glad to confer with you on the subject. T.J.

FC (Vi). The enclosed plan for building portable boats is missing; it was originally sent by Washington to TJ in a letter of 27 Dec. 1780, q.v.

To Abner Nash

Sir Richmond Jany. 16. '81

I am honored with your Excellency's favor of the 3d inst, and am to thank you for your permission and countenance to our Pork purchases.

The late invasion of this State by the Enemy should not have been so long uncommunicated to you by me, but that the very extraordinary movement they made was such in its nature as to allow little time to those concerned in Goverment to think of any thing but the providing means of opposition and in the meantime withdrawing everything from their power. From a fatal inattention to the giving us due notice of the arrival of a hostile force two days were completely lost in calling together the Militia—a time which events proved would have added so much of our collection of Militia as to have rendered doubtful their getting from this place. The Winds favoring them in a remarkable degree they almost brought the first news themselves of their movements. They were landed within twenty six miles of this place before we had reason even to suspect they would aim at it: The little interval of twenty three hours between that and their actual arrival here was assiduously and successfully employed in withdrawing the public Stores from hence and from Westham, seven miles above this. This was so far done that our loss did not exceed 300 muskets, about 5 Tons of Powder, some Sulphur, 5 feild peices, four pounders, and some inferior articles of no great account. The letters and records of the Executive were the greater part lost. They retired hastily to their shipping after 23 hours possession of this place. The interruption which they have given to raising men and providing subsistance is likely to be very injurious. We are endeavoring to get over this difficulty also as well as we can. Should any movements take place interesting to your State I shall communicate them to your Excellency as soon as known to me, tho the communication will be circuitous. Perhaps, should they take Post at Portsmouth, you might think it expedient to establish a line of Expresses to the neighbourhood of that place. T.J.

FC (Vi); at head of text: "Governor Nash & in part to the Prest of the Board of War. N Caro."

To Thomas Nelson

SIR Richmond Jany 16. 1781

The Bearer hereof Capt. Joel proposes to engage two others to undertake with himself an enterprize on the Enemy's fleet wherever it shall be collected in Harbour. As he requires only an old Vessell of the most worthless kind, and proper preparations for her, I think the object will justify the risk. So many Orders and Measures may be necessary in the detail of executing this Business that I cannot do better than to give a general sanction to it and ask the favor of yourself to have everything provided which he may think necessary to ensure Success. Rewards are expected on desperate undertakings of this kind, and tho not necessary to stimulate him may be necessary for his associates. I will therefore leave it to yourself to fix them previously, or to agree with the Gentlemen that they shall be referred to the Executive after the Service shall have been performed.

T.J.

FC (Vi).

CAPT. JOEL: Beesly Edgar Joel, an adventurer who had represented himself to the Pennsylvania authorities as a deserted British officer. He was imprisoned from June to Aug. 1780, when he was liberated at the direction of Washington, but "with positive injunctions not to come near the Army" (Joel's deposition before Penna. Executive Council, 23 Nov. 1780, MS in PHMC; Washington, *Writings*, ed. Fitzpatrick, XIX, 11, 375-6, 379; XX, 256; see also, *Penna. Colonial Records*, XII, 495; *Penna. Archives*, 1st ser., VIII, 576). For the abortive result of Joel's ENTERPRIZE, see Nelson to TJ, 7 Feb.; TJ to Nelson, 13 Feb.; Joel to TJ, 9 Feb.; TJ to Joel, 14 Feb. 1781. Joel's proposal to conduct a fire ship against the enemy fleet was probably the subject of the following letter from the Rev. Robert Andrews, who at this time was serving as secretary to Gen. Nelson: "Genl Nelson has something of Consequence to communicate to you and consult you upon. As it cannot be done with so much Propriety by writing, he wishes to see you as soon as possible." This letter is dated at Williamsburg, 18 Jan. and is addressed: "James Maxwell Esqr. Commissioner of the Navy Chicahominy" (RC in Vi).

From Thomas Nelson

DEAR SIR Williamsburg Jany. 16. 1781

In my Letter of Yesterday I informed your Excellency that the Enemy's Fleet had fallen down to Hardy's Ferry. This afternoon I have Intelligence that it was on its Way again, and standing for Newport-news. Yesterday about twelve o'Clock, the Enemy were seen from this Shore to land a Number of Men on a Point below the Mouth of Pagan Creek, and soon afterwards a heavy firing commenced, the Issue of which has not yet reached me. Very few Men have joined me from those Counties, whose Militias, according to your's of the 15th., were to compose the Armament for our Defence on this Occasion; for which Reason it will not be immediately in my Power to comply with your Instructions. So soon as it can be done, I shall pay them due Attention. The Louisa Militia I have ordered to file off for the Defence of Fredericksburg. The Number of effective Men now at this Post and York is about one thousand, some of whom are not yet armed; and as it appears to be impracticable, such shall be discharged. I shall be careful to have communicated to you every thing of Moment; & am Dear Sir, with the greatest Respect Your mo: Obedt. & hble Servt.,

THOS NELSON JR. B.G.

RC (PHi); addressed and endorsed.

To the President of the North Carolina Board of War

Richmond, 16 Jan. 1781. This letter is virtually the same as that to Abner Nash of the same date, q.v.

FC (Vi); at head of text: "Governor Nash & in part to the Prest of the Board of War N Caro."

From Duncan Rose

Col. Banister's, 16 Jan. 1781. Has obtained material for shirts requested by Steuben and is having them made up; will pay for them out of a balance due him from the auditors; payment may be delayed until convenient. Has been informed that "the Present Emission of our Currency has been destroy'd by the Enemy on their late excursion to Richmond"; should the report be false, requests that the treasurer give the auditors a warrant for £8,000 in payment for the shirts.

RC (Vi); 2 p.; addressed and endorsed. In the Contingent Fund Vouchers (Vi) there is an order of 25 Jan. 1781, in a clerk's hand and signed by TJ, directing the auditors to issue the warrant requested by Rose.

From Steuben

SIR Cabbin point 16 Jany 1781

From every intelligence it appears evident that the Enemy mean to take post in the lower Counties. The last I heard of them was that they were marching their whole force towards smithfield. In consequence of this I have ordered Genls. Muhlenburg and Weedon to march with what Militia they may have together to Williamsburg from whence I shall be able to order them as circumstances may require.

It now becomes of the utmost consequence to open a Communication with the other side of the River from some place near this. I have orderd Genl. Nelson and Colo. Carrington to do all they can to procure Boats and I must request your Excellency to give orders that all the boats that can be got may be sent down to Hoods.

The Enemy Landed at Mr. Hardey's near Lyon Creek.

I am &c.

FC (NHi).

From Anthony Thornton

Hanover Town, 16 Jan. 1781. Has received orders from Gen. Nelson to "March back to Caroline" and keep troops embodied for further orders; thinks they will be sent to Potomac; is sending Capt. Coleman with a request for 250 stand of arms, without which the troops can be of no service.

RC (Vi); 2 p.; addressed and endorsed.

To George Weedon

Sir [ca. 16 January 1781]

The Executive will undertake to impress any boats which may be necessary in the opinion of the military officers. We are endeavoring here to build some light boats for transporting troops across the river. But they are not to be waited for or depended on. I am with esteem Your most obedt. servt., Th: Jefferson

RC (PPAP); addressed and endorsed.

This undated letter was probably written about this time because Weedon was in the process of moving his troops, and on this day TJ ordered the manufacture of small boats (TJ to James Maxwell, 16 Jan.). Furthermore, in the Contingent Fund Vouchers (Vi) there is an order to the auditors, dated 15 Jan. 1781, directing that a warrant for £6,000 be paid to Granville Smith "for the purpose of procuring a number of Canoes for public use"; the order to the auditors is in a clerk's hand, signed and with the following annotation by TJ at foot of text: "The treasurer will be so good as to pay the above as it is for an immediate purpose and the Auditors not here"; see also TJ to Richard Claiborne, 18 Jan. 1781. On 21 Jan. Joseph Thomas reported lack of success in impressing canoes: "Agreable to instructions, I have proceeded as far up James River as this County and am sorry to inform you that I fear it will be out of my power to compleat my purchase of the number of Canoes wanted, at least of such as you Mention, new sound Tobo. Canoes"; Thomas added that there were few new canoes on the river, but that he had purchased four which he had dispatched to Westham by Joseph Childress, bearer of the letter (RC in Vi, dated at Albemarle). These canoes were vessels capable of carrying from eight to ten hogsheads of tobacco.

From Daniel Brodhead

Fort Pitt, 17 Jan. 1781. Acknowledges receipt of letter of 12 Oct. 1780. Has information from Detroit that the Indians are in council there and expects "they are meditating with the British to attack these frontier posts, as soon as the season will permit." The orders to James Francis Moore to purchase rations "on this side the Mountain" will distress the troops there "and probably greatly disappoint . . . the Commander in chief, if he has not been consulted respecting the measure." Despite his great respect for TJ, Brodhead cannot "be justified in suffering the Provisions which are designed for the Troops . . . to be transported down the River" unless ordered to do so by the Commander in chief. Col. Gibson will present this letter and can give particular information concerning the western district.

RC (Vi); 3 p.; addressed and endorsed; printed in *George Rogers Clark Papers, 1771-1781*, p. 494-5.

For the purchase of provisions by Virginia in the West, see James Francis Moore to TJ, 20 Nov. 1780. On 23 Jan. 1781 Brodhead wrote to George Washington (DLC: Washington Papers) concerning the purchase of grain by Virginia, stating that "this purchase, together with the Consumption of multitudes of emigrants, arrived and expected within this District (chiefly to avoid Militia Duty and Taxes) will scarcely leave a pound of Flour for the Regular or the other Troops, which your Excellency may judge it expedient to employ against the Enemy." See TJ's reply to the present letter, 13 Feb. 1781.

From Charles Fleming

SIR Camp, Holts forge, 17h. Jany. 1781

I am now, with the Troops under my command, at this place by Order of Genl. Nelson. I have to inform your Excellency, that there is not a fourth part of the Regiment supplied with Amunition, and as I am Ordered by the General to join the Baron, and begin my March early tomorrow, unless Amunition is sent on, or ordered to follow me I shall find myself in rather an awkward situation. Your Excellency will no doubt consider this matter and inform me by Mr. Bates, who I have dispatched with [this] and who will join me on my March.

The situation of the Regiment being composed of Goochland [and] Hanover Militia, it may not be amiss to acquaint you with. The murmurs, and applications for leave of absence are not uncommon, but when I reflect that there is scarce a man left in those counties, that a considerable number have but just returned from their tour of duty, and many have now substitutes in actual service, that not more than half having been first called out, the rest were hurried precipitately from home, totally unprovided for a campaign of any continuance, I cannot think their complaints entirely groundless. Your Excellency may rest assured, I do my utmost endeavours to silence their murmurs, and to impress them with a sense of the necessity of their continuing in service, but still I can by no means continue a stranger to their complaints. Might I have liberty to observe upon this occasion, it should be that I fear the Militia of those two counties will on any future emergency be, with infinite difficulty drawn out, unless (as they wish for) those who did their tour of duty in the last invasion, might be discharged, so soon as the situation of affairs will admit. And from what I can gather in WmsBurgh, there are nearly Militia enough to oppose the Enemies designs, already in service, and more expected from the back counties.

Your Excellency will consider if it may not be necessary to give them some kind of promise on this head. Every exertion on my part shall be used to quiet their minds, and I hope I may stand excused in making you acquainted with these circumstances.

I have the honour to be with very great respect Your Excellencys mo. obed. Svt., CHAS. FLEMING
Lt. Colo. commdg.

RC (Vi); addressed and endorsed.

To Samuel Huntington

SIR Richmond Jany. 17th. 1781.

I do myself the honor of transmitting to your Excellency a resolution of the General assembly of this Commonwealth entered into in consequence of the resolution of Congress of September 6th. 1780.[1] on the subject of the confederation. I shall be rendered very happy if the other States of the Union, equally impressed with the necessity of that important convention, shall be willing to sacrifice equally[2] to it's completion. This single event, could it take place shortly, would overweigh every success which the enemy have hitherto obtained and render desperate the hopes to which those successes have given birth.

I have the honor to be with the most real esteem & respect your Excellency's Mo. ob. & mo. hble Servt., TH: JEFFERSON

ENCLOSURE

In the House of Delegates
Tuesday the 2d *of January* 1781

The General Assembly of Virginia being well satisfied that the Happiness, Strength and safety of the United States depend under providence upon the ratification of the Articles for a federal Union between the United States heretofore proposed by Congress for the Consideration of the said States,[3] and preferring the Good of their Country to every Object of smaller Importance do Resolve that this Commonwealth will yeild to the Congress of the United States for the Benefit of the said United States All Right Title and Claim that the said Commonwealth hath to the Lands North West of the River Ohio, upon the following Conditions to wit That the Territory so ceded shall be laid out and formed into States containing a suitable Extent of Territory and shall not be less than One hundred nor more than one hundred and fifty Miles Square, or as near thereto as Circumstances will admit.

That the States so formed shall be distinct Republican States and be admitted Members of the Federal Union having the same Rights of Sovereignty Freedom and Independence as the other States.

That Virginia shall be allowed and fully reimbursed by the United States her actual Expences in reducing the British Posts at the Kaskaskies and St. Vincents the Expence of maintaining Garrisons and supporting Civil Government there since the Reduction of the said Posts and in general all the Charges she has incurred on account of the Country on the North West Side of the Ohio River since the Commencement of the present War.

That the French and Canadian Inhabitants and other Settlers at the Kaskaskies St. Vincents and the Neighbouring Villages Who have professed themselves Citizens of Virginia shall have their Possessions and Titles confirmed to them and shall be protected in the Enjoyment of their Rights and Liberty for which purpose Troops shall be stationed there at the Charge of the United States to protect them from the Encroachments of the British Forces at Detroit or elsewhere unless the Events of War shall render it impracticable.

As Colo. George Rogers Clarke planned and executed the secret expedition by which the British posts were reduced and was promised if the Enterprize succeeded a liberal Gratuity in Lands in that Country for the Officers and Soldiers who first marched thither with him, That a Quantity of Land not exceeding one hundred and fifty thousand Acres be allowed and granted to the said Officers and Soldiers and the other Officers and Soldiers that have been since incorporated into the said Regiment to be laid off in one Tract the Length of which not to exceed double the Breadth in such place on the North West Side of the Ohio as the majority of the Officers shall choose and to be afterwards divided among the said Officers and Soldiers in due proportion according to the Laws of Virginia.

That in Case the Quantity of good Lands of the South East Side of the Ohio upon the Waters of Cumberland River and between the Green River and the Tenessee River which have been reserved by Law for the Virginia Troops upon Continental Establishment[4] should from the North Carolina Line bearing in further upon the Cumberland Lands than was expected prove insufficient for their legal Bounties the Deficiency shall be made up to the said Troops in Good Lands to be laid off between the Rivers Scioto and Little Miamis on the North West Side of the River Ohio in such proportions as have been engaged to them by the Laws of Virginia.

That all the Lands within the Territory so ceded to the United States and not reserved for or appropriated to any of the herein before mentioned purposes or disposed of in Bounties to the Officers and Soldiers of the American Army shall be considered as a common Fund for the use and benefit of such of the United American States as have become or shall become Members of the Confederation or Federal Alliance of the said States (Virginia inclusive) according to their usual respective proportions in the general Charge and Expenditure and shall be faithfully and bona fide disposed of for that purpose and for no other use or purpose whatsoever. And therefore that all purchases and Deeds from any Indian or Indians or from any Indian Nation or Nations for any Lands within any part of the said Territory which have been or shall be made for the Use and Benefit of any private Person or persons whatsoever, And Royal Grants within the ceded Territory inconsistent with the Chartered Rights Laws and Customs of Virginia, shall be deemed and declared absolutely void and of no Effect in the same Manner as if the said Territory had still remained subject to and part of the Commonwealth of Virginia.

That all the remaining Territory of Virginia included between the Atlantic Ocean and the South East Side of the River Ohio and the Maryland Pensylvania and North Carolina Boundaries shall be guaranteed to the Commonwealth of Virginia by the said United States.

That the above Cession of Territory by Virginia to the United States shall be void and of none effect unless all the States in the American Union shall ratify the Articles of Confederation heretofore transmitted by Congress for the Consideration of the said States.

Virginia having thus for the Sake of the general Good proposed to cede a great Extent of valuable Territory to the Continent it is expected in Return that every other State in the Union under similar Circumstances as to vacant Territory will make similar Cessions of the same to the United States for the General Emolument.

Teste

JOHN BECKLEY C.H.D.

1781. January 2d.
Agreed to by the Senate
Will: Drew C.S.

A Copy Teste John Beckley C.H.D.

RC (DLC: PCC, No. 71, II, 13-16); endorsed: "Richmond January 17th 1781. Letter from Govr. Jefferson of Virginia enclosing a resolution of the Genl. Assembly of that State passed in consequence of resolution of Congress of Septr. 6th. 1780 on the subject of the confederation. Read Jany. 29th. 1781"; in a clerk's hand, signed by TJ. Tr (DLC); signed by TJ. FC (Vi). Enclosure: Resolution of the General Assembly of 2 Jan. as printed above. There are two copies of this resolution which are here, for the sake of clarity, referred to as Tr (1) and Tr (2). Tr (1) is in PCC, No. 71, II, 17-20. It is endorsed: "A Copy of the Resolutions for a cession of the Lands on the No. West Side of the Ohio River to the United States. Virginia—January 2d 1781"; in an unidentified clerk's hand; being an attested copy of an attested copy, only the second of the signatures of John Beckley is in his hand. Tr (2) is in PCC, No. 75, 355-8. It is endorsed: "Copy. Resolution of the Genl. Assembly of the Commonwealth of Virginia for a Cession of Western Territory 2d. Jany. 1781"; in the hand of Charles Morse, who transcribed all of the signatures. For reasons indicated below in note 4 concerning the error in transcription of Tr (1), it is clear that Tr (1) was the copy enclosed in TJ's letter. Tr (2) was probably made in 1781 when Morse was employed as a clerk in Congress. He may have copied it from a copy that was sent to one of the Virginia delegates in Congress. It could have been copied from Tr (1), but only if the error in that copy described in note 4 below had been called to the attention of the copying clerk by someone in Congress. The Resolution of 2 Jan. 1781 is printed in JHD, Oct. 1780, 1827 edn., p. 80.

It seems ironic that the transmittal of the General Assembly's resolution upon which the "Happiness, Strength and safety of the United States" depended should have been delayed a fortnight because the enemy had entered the capital of Virginia and had put the government to flight. Indeed, it appeared to be almost by chance that this crucial resolution was drafted and adopted before Arnold's dragoons arrived in Richmond. The resolution of Congress of 6 Sep., transmitted to TJ by Samuel Huntington in his letter of 10 Sep. (q.v., with references and notes there), was presumably included in the letters and documents sent by TJ to Benjamin Harrison, speaker of the House of Delegates, early in November (see TJ to Harrison under date of 7 Nov. 1780). Not much legislation engaged the attention of that body during November and December, some of it of great importance and some fairly trivial. The House had been delayed several days at the opening of the session because of lack of a quorum, and toward the end of December absences threatened to disrupt legislative business. On Saturday, 23 Dec., the sergeant-at-arms was ordered to take into custody no fewer than forty-five members and at the same time the House resolved that it would "with all the severity of censure, publish the names of members who shall absent themselves in future, from their duty in the House at this critical juncture, without leave; that the calamities which will probably ensue upon leaving our affairs deranged, may be attributed to the authors of them." However, it was not until 1 Jan. that the House finally resolved itself into a committee of the whole to discuss the subject brought up in Congress' resolution. The next day, in the midst of alarms about the approach of an enemy fleet in Virginia waters, the resolution printed above was hastily approved. The Senate concurred immediately and both houses adjourned forthwith (JHD, Oct. 1780, 1827 edn., p. 10, 67, 79, 80, 81). Since, from this brief outline, it appears that no special committee was directed to draft the resolution, some member must have had a draft ready to present in the closing hours of the session. TJ had been much concerned with the northwest in the preceding days (see his letter to George Rogers Clark of 25 Dec. 1780). These facts, together with TJ's work in Congress in 1783-1784 on the same subject, seem to reinforce the conjecture stated below that TJ may have had a hand in drafting the resolution.

While the conditions stated in the resolution were, as the Virginia delegates affirmed, "not precisely conformable to the recommendations of Congress on the subject" (see their letter to TJ, 30 Jan. 1781), Congress did not hesitate to put the Articles of Confederation into force early in 1781. Virginia had already ratified the Articles in 1777 and her delegates had subscribed their names to the engrossed parchment (see above, Vol. 1: 111-12; JHD, Oct. 1777, 1827 edn., p. 80-1; JCC, XIX, 223). Maryland on 2 Feb. 1781 authorized her delegates to sign. The Act of authorization was read in Congress 12 Feb. On 1 Mch., when John Hanson and Daniel Carroll signed for Maryland, this was regarded by Congress as the act "by which . . . the Confederation of the United States of America was completed" (JCC, XIX, p. 96, 186, 138, 191, 214). Yet, three years later, there was doubt as to whether Congress would accept the terms on which Virginia had predicated her cession of lands northwest of the Ohio. On 13 Sep. 1783 Congress stipulated the terms on which Virginia's conditional cession of 2 Jan. 1781 would be accepted; the General Assembly at its session of Oct. 1783 authorized the Virginia delegates in Congress to execute a deed of cession accordingly; TJ himself, as a member of Congress, drafted the deed of cession of 1 Mch. 1784. TJ's letter of 3 Mch. 1784 to Benjamin Harrison is a cogent analysis of the tactics required of the Virginia delegates even at that date to obtain acceptance by Congress (see Hening, XI, 326-8; 567-70; Virginia Delegates to Benjamin Harrison, 22 Mch. 1784, covering the deed of cession executed 1 Mch.; both are printed in Hening, XI, 571-5).

THE STATES SHALL BE DISTINCT REPUBLICAN STATES: This significant condition guaranteeing admission of new states on a basis of full equality, points both to the Northwest Ordinance of 1784 and to TJ's draft of a Constitution for Virginia in 1776. The latter, however, had in view the establishment of new governments "free and independent of this colony and of all the world" (see above, Vol. 1: 385, note 19), whereas the former sought to guarantee equality of sovereignty, freedom, and independence within the "Federal Alliance." Whether or not this indicates that TJ had any influence in drafting the resolution, there are the following facts to be noted. First, in respect to the requirement that Virginia should be reimbursed for EXPENCES IN REDUCING THE BRITISH POSTS, there is a document in DLC: TJ Papers in TJ's hand that may possibly relate to, or have been drawn up to be inserted in, some document concerning Virginia's claim to western lands, possibly even the present resolution. It reads as follows: " 'A judicious state of our right to the lands we claim, comprehending the progression of grants and settlements under the government of Virginia from at least the period or some time before the Lancaster treaty [1744] shewing the expence we have been at from time to time in treaties with the Indians and protecting the Frontier and the extent of our exercising jurisdiction in that country down to the time of the revolution when Independance was declared, will serve' &ca." Since this fragment is embraced by quotation marks, TJ may, of course, have copied it from some other document. Second, the requirement that the French and Canadian settlers of the Northwest should be confirmed in their possessions and title and "protected in the Enjoyment of their Rights and Liberty" closely parallels the final part of the instructions given by TJ to George Rogers Clark (see TJ to Clark, 25 Dec. 1780).

1 The full date is in TJ's hand.

2 The word "equally" does not appear in FC (Vi).

3 The resolution as printed in JHD adds the word "respectively."

4 At this point Tr (2) adds the following: "and upon their own State Establishment"; so does the text in JHD, Oct. 1780, 1827 edn., p. 80. Hening notes this omission in one of the texts subsequently derived from Tr (1) and, in printing the text of the resolution described as "Copy sent the Governor 15th January," makes the following comment: "It is most obvious that, in transcribing the resolution, or in some copy of the subsequent proceedings founded on it, the words 'and upon their own state establishment,' were inadvertently omitted by the clerk. For it cannot be presumed that the state of Virginia, who had by several solemn acts of the legislature, declared that the bounties in land given to the officers and soldiers of the Virginia line on continental establishment, should be extended to those on state establishment, would make provision for the one class, in ceded territory, and omit the other. Nor is it within the bounds of probability that, while Virginia was *giving* away such an extensive territory to the United States she should not so have *disposed of the gift*, as to do complete justice to her own citizens" (X, 565). In his next volume, Hening modified this opinion. From a line by line printing of the pertinent passage in the "original manuscript" (presumably the engrossed copy), he proved that the omission was made in the "first copy" sent to the governor and not in some "subsequent proceedings founded on it" (same, XI, 566-7). This, of course, is correct, but it is an explanation that invites comment. For the text that TJ transmitted to Congress set in motion an error that could not be reversed. When, a year and a half later, Congress adopted its resolve of 13 Sep. 1783 and embodied in it the text of the resolution of 2 Jan. 1781, that body was legally bound to employ the officially attested text that TJ had sent, not the correct text that, for some reason or other, was at that time in Congress' records. Similarly, when Congress' resolve of 13 Sep. 1783 was laid before the Virginia General Assembly, the Assembly in turn was legally obligated to recite, in its Act passed at the Oct. 1783 session, the inaccurate version that Congress had employed. But this was not the completion of the circle. When TJ, then a member of Congress, received Virginia's Act of 1783 authorizing the delegates in Congress to execute a deed of cession, the two drafts of a form of deed that he drew up specified that the Virginia Act should be copied verbatim—as, indeed, he was bound to do. Once TJ had transmitted the erroneous but officially attested copy to Huntington on 17 Jan. 1781, the error could not be overtaken even if noticed. On Monday, 1 Mch. 1784, the Virginia delegates signed, sealed, and delivered the deed of cession in which was imbedded the defective text and Congress directed that "the same be recorded and enrolled among the acts of the United States." Thus John Beckley's error was made perpetual. It still stands, protected in

its unassailable legal position and enshrined in one of the most important series of Acts that the Virginia General Assembly or the Continental Congress adopted at that period (Hening, x, 565; xi, 326, 568, 573; JCC, xxvi, 115, 117; Virginia Delegates to Benjamin Harrison, 22 Mch. 1784, enclosing an exemplification of the deed of cession as executed).

From George Slaughter

SIR — Louisville Janry. 17th. 1781.

Yesterday Capt. Shannon who is a Commissary of Purchases for this department apply'd to me to Countersign Sundry Bills which he had drawn for Purchases that he had made here. Colo. Clark under whose appointment he Acts being absent was the cause of this Application. It being the first of the kind and my knowing very little about the Purchases together with the several sums amounting to something considerable, occasioned me to hesitate some time before I would countersign them, however after considering that the service might be considerably injured without somebody would give Sanction to Bills from this Country and that a refusal would probably prevent any more Purchases being made, I was prevailed upon to countersign them.

Since this was done I have made some little enquiry into the Conduct of the Several Commissarys at this Post, and it appearing to me that there is a Combination very Pernicious to the State carrying on between a certain Capt. James Sullivan and this set of Gentlemen, I think it my duty to give you information. I am told it can be proved that Capt. Shannon refused Corn at forty Dollars ℔ bushel when Bills on the Treasury was offered to be taken in payment, and Contracted with Capt. Sullivan for all the corn he could purchase at 60 Dollars ℔ bushl. and the rising price to the first of May Next, and among the rest of Capt Sullivans Purchases was this very corn that Capt. Shannon had refused. I [am] also told it can be proved that these Gentlemen refused to purchase whiskey which was offered to them in this Town at £45 ℔ Gall. and gave Capt. Sullivan £60 for the same Whiskey which he bought at that price and took it the same day Sullivan bought it.

I am further told that it can be proved that Capt. Moore last Spring Purchased some Articles of Commerce in partnership with Capt. Sullivan and for payment, passed a Bill which he drew payable to Capt. James Sullivan in which he set fourth that it was for a Quantity of corn furnished by the said Sullivan. If these things cannot be proved I am much misinform'd. My Authority is however so good that I have no doubt of it's truth, and I am warranted to say that this Capt. Sullivan and Capt. Moore is in partnership and a Number of circumstances induces me to believe that Capt. Shannon is in the same business. Being made acquainted with these Circumstances and understanding there are other drafts to a very considerable amount now on their way down, I thought it my duty to Mention them of which you will make what use you Please.

I am just now inform'd that a prisoner from the Shawanese has lately come in. He came with a Party of seven Indians for the Purpose of Stealing Horses of which they got a good Booty at Bryants Station where he left them. He says the Indians are still in the Neighbourhood of the Towns [th]at were destroy'd last summer, that they mean to continue there next year, and make an Early Attackd on this Country in the Spring and have expectation [of] driving the People out of it. I am with much respect Yr. Excellencys Obt Hble Servt.,

George Slaughter
Commandant at Falls Ohio

RC (Vi); addressed and endorsed.

This letter was probably enclosed in a letter from TJ to George Rogers Clark, 19 Feb. 1781, q.v.; see also George Slaughter to TJ, 13 Apr. 1781, with an enclosed report of the commissioners appointed to investigate Slaughter's charges.

From Steuben

Sir

17 Jany. 81

This will be delivered your Excellency by an Officer of Colo. Armand's Corps who will also present a List of some few articles necessary to render that Corps fit for Service.

The absolute necessity of employing this Corps induces me to request your Excellency's assistance in procuring these Articles for the expence of which I will answer for the Continent.

The advantages of a Superiority in Cavalry are evident. The Enemy have now near 100 Mounted. This makes me urgent with your Excellency to afford me your Assistance in putting this Corps in a state to render service to the Country. I am &c.

FC (NHi).

colo. armand: Armand-Charles Tuffin, Marquis de La Rouërie, a French cavalry officer who was commonly known while serving in America as Armand; he received a colonel's commission from Congress on 10 May 1777 and served throughout the war with varying success (Lasseray, *Les français sous les treize étoiles*, p. 454-62; Washington, *Writings*, ed. Fitzpatrick, xxvii, 274-6, and *passim*; jcc, vii, 346).

From Steuben

SIR 17 Jany. 81

I must request your Excellency to order 200,000 Dollars to be paid to Mr. Benj. Harrison Subject to my orders for which the United States is to be accountable. I am &c.

FC (NHi). RC (not found) was enclosed in a letter from Steuben to Benjamin Harrison of the same date, FC of which is also in NHi.

To Richard Claiborne

SIR Richmond January 18. 1781.

It being necessary to collect at Hoods as large a number of boats as possible to transport men and horses across the river as occasion may require, you are hereby authorized to impress all the boats on this and Chickahominy river except only one to be left at each ferry and except also such boats as from particular circumstances of which you are to Judge in your discretion it woud be attended with very peculiar distress to take. Care shoud be taken to distinguish every man's boat oars &c. and when no longer wanted for the public you will see that they be returned, taking receipts for them. I am, sir, Your very humble servant, T.J.

FC (Vi); at head of text: "Major Claiborne Continental Q M G or any person acting by authority from him."

From Richard Claiborne

SIR Richmond. 18th. January. 1781.

I have received your Excellency's Warrant for impressing a number of Boats to be sent to Hoods, for the purpose of transporting of men and horses across James River. I shall put this matter into execution immediately, and give such directions to the person who will be employed upon the occasion, as may best answer the end, and not distress the proprietors.

I am truely sensible how liable the public is to be burthened with expence, especially where one person's property is taken and put under the direction of another who is not interested in it, to answer the demand, but I cannot be accountable for any loss, in this matter, should any happen, nor to return the Boats to the Owners.

I shall put the business under the direction of an officer, with a party of men, to serve with the Boats as long as occasion may require, and direct him to act with great care, and to have them returned safe. I shall leave him no other alternative; but when the boats are collected, should the Baron, or any officer he may appoint, direct them contrary to my instructions, they consequently become void.

I am with great Respect Your Excellency's Most obedient Humble Servant.,

Rd. Claiborne
DQM. S. Virga.

RC (Vi); addressed and endorsed.

From George Rogers Clark

Dr Sr Richmond Jany 18th. 81.

I have examined your proposed Instructions. I dont Recollect of anything more that is Necessary Except the Mode of paying the Expences of the Garison of Du Troit, in Case of Success, as supporting our Credit among strangers may be attended with great and good Consequences and my former Experience Induce me to wish it to be the Case whare I have the Honour to Command. I would also observe to your Excellency that I could wish to set out on this Expedition free from any Reluctance which I doubt I cannot do without a Satisfactory Explination of the treatment of the Virginia Delegates in Congress to me in objecting to an appointment designed for me, which your Excellency Cannot be a Stranger to. I could wish not to be thought to Solicit promotion and that my Duty to my Self did not oblige me to transmit these Sentiments to you. The Treatment I have Generaly met with from this State hath prejudicd me as far as Consistant in her Interest and wish not to be disturbed in the Execution of her orders by any Continental Colonel that may be in the Cuntries that I have Business in, which I doubt will be the Case although the Orders of the Commander in Chef is very possitive. I am Sir with the Greatest Esteem yr. Excellencies Very Hbl Servt,

G R Clark

PS I hope to be Honoured by a line from your Excellencie as before. G R C

RC (Vi); addressed and endorsed.

YOUR PROPOSED INSTRUCTIONS: TJ to George Rogers Clark, 25 Dec. 1780, q.v.

James Cocke to George Muter

SIR Bon Accord Jany. 18 1781

My having an oppertunity Yesterday of perusing the Newspaper I observed in the Account of the rapid progress of the Enemy up the River, that in respect to their passing the post at Hoods is different from what it is their represented. On the Morning of the 3rd. Inst. I ordered an Officer and two Men to Brandon to give us Intelegence of the Enemy should they land at that Place, and if after landing form into a Line to March, or if passing by without landing. At Six O Clock the Signal was made that the whole Fleat had past. At 8 O Clock a Schooner was abrest of the Fort. She was often haild, the Wind and tide being in her favour. She soon past and gave us a shot, on which we gave her another but was under the Necessity to change our Ambrazier [embrasure] which [gave] her time to get a considerable distance from us, but I am informd did them some Damage. On her geting out of Danger from the Fort she made a Signal, on which the whole Fleat brought to an Anchor. It being very Hazey I Judged by their Lights that they must be to[o] far from us for us to do any Execeution by Firing on them; At 10 O Clock the Haze clear'd away, we could see their Hulls very plain at which time we began a Fire of Twice every half Hour from [. . .] of the three Guns that we could make Bear on them which Fire I intended to keep up during [all] of the Night, as I had not the least thought of their attempting to Land till near the Morning, as the Wind Blew very fresh and made a large Sea which must make it very troublesome for them to Land. I must belive that their shiping must have suffered from our Fire; as I have reason to beleve we fired but few shot but what did some execeution as we fired very deliberatly. On the Signal being made that the Enemy had past Brandon I orderd a Captain and Twenty Five Men down on the Mouth of Wards Creek and to keep a look out should the Enemy attempt to Land. At Twelve o Clock to our great disappointment they brought us Intelegence, that between Twenty and Thirty Boats were landing about Six Hundred Yards up the Creek. By their place of landing, I was confident that their Intention was [to] come round on our Backs and cut of[f] our retreat. As we then had but about 40 Men in the Fort we thought it was in Vain for us to continue as we had not the least hopes of defending ourselves. Therefor I gave orders for every Man to take his Arms and March out of the Fort which was Accordingly done. I believe the above a true state of the Case. As this will be handed you by Capt. Allen, he will give you information of many things which I may not have recolected. I am Sir Your mo obt. hhble Servant, JAMES COCKE

RC (Vi); addressed: "Colo. George Muter Richmond ℘ Capt Allen"; endorsed.

This letter was enclosed in Muter's letter to TJ of 20 Jan. 1781 (third letter). The following minute appears in the War Office Journal (Vi) under 20 Jan.: "Letter to the Governor informing of the impossibility of the Q. Mrs. furnishing the necessaries for Capt. Read's Troop. . . . Also inclosing Major Cocke's Letter to me, for his Excellencies perusal." The NEWSPAPER account mentioned by Cocke must be that of 13 Jan., printed above as Document II in Notes and Documents Relating to the British Invasions in 1781, 31 Dec. 1780.

From George Elliott

Petersburg, 18 Jan. 1781. Last August Elliott purchased, at Gen. Muhlenberg's request, a quantity of saddles and bridles from Josiah Moffitt which cost £22,945, paying £2,000 from money on hand. The Council has refused payment of the balance for want of a printed certificate. Although instructed not to issue certificates after a date which was prior to the purchase, encloses one, which, if proper, should be given to Mr. Moffitt, who has "render'd a singular Service"; it is a "Great Pitty he Should Suffer or be Discourag'd."

RC (Vi); 3 p.; addressed and endorsed.

On 20 Jan., the Council ordered payment of the balance due Moffitt "to be charged to the United States" (*Va. Council Jour.*, II, 277).

From James Hayes

SIR Richmond, Jany. 18th. 1781

When I inform'd your Excellency, that I intended for Philadelphia this week, in order to forward the Printing Apparatus for the use of this State, I had not the presence of mind to mention, that a Horse to carry me there, and a sum of Money would be requisite to purchase Paper and other articles absolutely necessary for the Public use. That alone will now detain me, and as I would wish not to delay time any longer, I hope your Excellency will consider of the matter, that I may immediately set off.

I am, Sir, With great respect, Your very humble Servant,

JAMES HAYES

RC (Vi); addressed and endorsed.

For the earlier negotiations concerning Hayes' establishment of a printing press in Virginia, see TJ to the Virginia Delegates in Congress, 31 Aug. 1780. See also James Hayes to TJ, 23 Jan., and Joseph Jones to TJ, 6 Feb. 1781.

George Muter to the Auditors

[*Richmond*] *18 Jan. 1781.* Order to issue to Capt. Edmund Read a warrant for $35,000, to purchase "Three pair of officer's boots and thirty two pair of boots for non commissioned officers and soldiers of his troop." Countersigned: "Th: Jefferson. This is not to be paid till the warrants of this day in favor of Mr. Harrison and Colo. Clarke shall be paid."

RC in Contingent Fund Vouchers (Vi); countersignature and instructions in TJ's hand.

EDMUND READ, captain of the light dragoons sent to Maryland with the Convention troops (James Wood to TJ, 20 Dec. 1780). There is a file copy of a letter from George Muter to Edmund Read of the present date in the War Office Letter Book (Vi), instructing Read to purchase the boots in Maryland because they are not available in Virginia. A minute in the War Office Journal (Vi) states that this letter was also countersigned by TJ.

To William Smith

SIR Richmond January 18. 1781

You will be pleased to proceed into the Country and engage eight good Gun-smiths and one good Blacksmith (a white man) to come immediately to work with Mr. Anderson in the repairs of Arms. Should you be able to find any good and faithful hands, who tho' unwilling to come here would undertake to repair such Arms as should be sent to them, you will be pleased to engage them and to know what number of Arms we may send for the first Month, at the end of which they shall be sent for and others carried. In this case I think it necessary that some good Gentleman in the Neighbourhood be applied to to superintend their proceedings, to keep them to the public Work, and to report to us from time to time what progress they make; whether they do their Work faithfully, and whether they do so much as to render it worth our while to continue to employ them. Those who come here shall receive a liberal hard Money pay by the day. Those who undertake to repair at their own Shops shall be paid by the piece at the old hard Money prices, according to the rate of Exchange. It will be best for you to proceed first to Colo. Wood at the Barracks, and get those he expected to furnish. T.J.

FC (Vi).

To Steuben

SIR Richmond Jan. 18. 1781.

I inclose you a letter from Genl. Weedon which I suppose will inform you, as he did me, that he has between 6 and 700 men embodied, and expects 500 more in the course of this week from the Western side of the Blue ridge. By a letter of the 16th from Genl. Nelson he informs me he has ordered the Louisa militia (about 150) to turn off to Fredericksburg. They were not called on at all, so that they may either be discharged at Fredericksburg or brought on to Williamsburg as you think best. Orders shall be immediately given for sending to Hood's all the boats from this river which can be found fit for that place.

I have the honor to be with great respect & esteem Sir your most obedt. & most humble sevt., TH: JEFFERSON

P.S. In discharging the militia I must beg the favor of you to let none be discharged who do not produce proper vouchers for the delivery of whatever public arms or accoutrements shall have been put into their hands.

RC (NHi); addressed and endorsed. Enclosure not found, but see Weedon to TJ, 15 Jan. 1781.

To the Virginia Delegates in Congress

GENTLEMEN Richmond Jan. 18. 1781.

I inclose you a resolution of Assembly directing your Conduct as to the navigation of the Missisippi.

The loss of powder lately sustained by us (about 5 tons) together with the quantities sent on to the Southward have reduced our stock very low indeed. We lent to Congress in the course of the last year (previous to our issues for the Southern army) about ten tons of powder. I shall be obliged to you to procure an order from the board of war for any quantity from five to ten tons to be sent us immediately from Philadelphia or Baltimore, and to enquire into and hasten from time to time the execution of it. The Stock of Cartridge paper is nearly exhausted. I do not know whether Capt. Irish or what other officer should apply for this. It is essential that a good stock should be forwarded and without a moments delay. If there be a rock on which we are to split, it is the want of Muskets, bayonets and cartouch boxes.

The occurrences since my last to the President are not of any magnitude. Three little rencounters have happened with the enemy. In the first General Smallwood led on a party of two or three hundred Militia and obliged some armed vessels of the enemy to retire from a prize they had taken at Broadway's, and renewing his attack the next day with a 4 ℔r. or two (for in the first day he had only muskets) he obliged some of their vessels to fall down from City point to their main fleet at Westover. The enemy's loss is not known. Ours was 4 men wounded. One of the evenings during their encampment at Westover and Berkeley their Light horse surprized a party of about 100 or 150 Militia at Charles City Courthouse killed and wounded 4 and took as has been generally said about 7 or 8. On Baron Steuben's approach towards Hood's they embarked at Westover; the wind which till then had set directly up the river from the time of their leaving James Town, shifted in the moment to the opposite point. Baron Steuben had not reached Hood's by 8 or ten miles when they arrived there. They landed their whole army there in the night Arnold attending in person. Colo. Clarke (of Kaskaskias) had been sent on with 240 men by Baron Steuben, and having properly disposed of them in ambuscade gave them a deliberate fire which killed 17 on the spot and wounded 13. They returned it in confusion by which we had 3 or 4 wounded, and our party being so small and without bayonets, were obliged to retire on the enemy's charging with bayonets. They fell down to Cobham, from whence they carried all the tobacco there (about 60 hhds.) and the last intelligence was that on the 16th they were standing for Newports news. Baron Steuben is of opinion they are proceeding to fix a post in some of the lower Counties. Later information has given us reason to believe their force more considerable than we at first supposed. I think since the arrival of the three transports which had been separated in a storm, they may be considered as about 2000 strong. Their naval force according to the best intelligence is the Charon of 44 guns, Commodore Symmonds; the Amphitrite, Iris, Thames and Charles town Frigates, the Fowey of 20 guns, 2 sloops of war, a privateer Ship and 2 brigs. We have about 3700 militia embodied, but at present they are divided into three distant encampments: one under General Weedon at Fredericksburg for the protection of the important works there; another under General Nelson at and near Wmsburg; and a third under Baron Steuben at Cabbin point. As soon as the enemy fix themselves these will be brought to a point.

I have the honor to be with very great respect, Gentlemen your most obedt. servt., TH: JEFFERSON

RC (DLC: PCC, No. 71, II); in a clerk's hand, with corrections, complimentary close, and signature in TJ's hand; endorsed (in part): "so much as relates to a supply of ammunition & military stores Referred to the Board of War." FC (Vi); Tr (DLC), in an unidentified hand, signed by TJ. Enclosure (missing): resolution of the Virginia Assembly of 2 Jan. 1781 respecting the free navigation of the Mississippi; printed in Hening, X, 538.

For the delegates' request for instructions respecting the navigation of the Mississippi, see Virginia Delegates to TJ, 13 Dec. and TJ to Benjamin Harrison, 25 Dec. 1780; see also JHD, Oct. 1780, 1827 edn., p. 68, 79, 80-1.

To John Walker

SIR Jan. 18 [1781]

Baron Steuben who commands the military force in this state on the present invasion, being very much unacquainted with its laws, customs, resources, and organization while he has hourly cause to apply to them has desired we will prevail on some gentlemen acquainted with these to be of his family to point his applications to the proper persons and places and to enable him to avail himself of our strength and resources. Searching about for such a person we cast our eyes on you, and hope you will undertake the office. Whatever expences may be incurred by you on this occasion must be public and a proper compensation moreover [will] be paid for time and trouble. These matters may be settled either before or after the service performed as you chuse. Your answer by the bearer and immediate attendance if possible will oblige sir, your most obedient and most hble servant, T.J.

FC (Vi).

To the County Lieutenants

SIR IN COUNCIL January 19, 1781.

THE invasion of our country by the enemy at the Close of the last Session of Assembly, their pushing immediately to this place, the dispersion of the publick papers, which for the purpose of saving them necessarily took place, and the injury done at the printing office, have been so many causes operating unfortunately to the delay of transmitting you those acts of Assembly which required immediate execution. The principal of these, the law for recruiting the army, having been framed on the idea that the militia of the several counties would be in quiet at home, has been peculiarly retarded by the necessity we were under of calling militia from almost every county. We have seized the earliest moment possible for discharging those of as many counties as could be, in order that this important law may be put into a course of execution. It is now enclosed to you. Your duty till the new levies shall be ready to march from the county being precisely pointed out by the act, I shall take up the subject from that period only. New London, Staunton, Winchester, Fredericksburg, and Chesterfield courthouse, are appointed for the rendezvous of the levies. You are at liberty to send them to any of these places, but as they are ultimately to proceed to Chesterfield court house, I would recommend to you to consider this in your choice of rendezvous. At each of these places an officer will attend from the 10th day of March next for the purpose of receiving them. You will send them under the charge of an officer, who being enabled by the act itself to provide means of transportation, is hereby authorized to apply for subsistence to any commissary, commissioner, or other person, principal or subordinate, having publick provisions in their possession, and on failure to obtain a sufficiency in that way, he is to impress it, giving certificates to the persons from whom he shall impress, and returning to the Auditors a list of such certificates, specifying the party's name, article, price, and date. Let this officer be furnished with a proper certificate from you that he is appointed to this duty, which he is to send to the Auditors together with his list, that they may be satisfied of his authority.

I inclose you two blank calendars, in which you will insert the names and descriptions of your levies delivered to the officer who will be appointed by us to receive them as directed by the act of Assembly; the one of these he will sign and leave as a voucher to you, the other should be signed by yourself or the officer delivering the men for you, and left in the hands of the receiving officer.

On the close of your draught I must desire a return of your militia, and as the law obliges the Captains to make exact returns to you at every general muster, I am to require that from these you make always an exact return to the Executive, so that[1] we may have a constant knowledge of the actual strength of your militia. Notwithstanding the requisition I made you six months ago for a return of your militia, you have not been pleased to comply with it, an inattention which cannot be justified on any principle of military subordination, and which cannot again pass unnoticed.[2]

A very dangerous practice having been introduced by the enemy of laying under paroles the whole country, through which they are at any time able to march, and thereby attempting to disarm its future opposition, has rendered it necessary for government to take up and reprobate the idea, that any citizen may thus cancel his duties to his country. I inclose you a number of proclamations on this subject, and desire that you will put one into the hands of every Captain in your county, with orders to read it at the head of his company at every private muster during the present year.

Such is the present aspect of the enemy towards this country, that no foresight can predict the moment at which your militia will be called into active duty. Let me exhort you therefore, and through you, your officers and men, to consider that moment as if now come, that every man, who has or can procure a gun, have it instantly put into the best order, a bayonet fitted to it, a bayonet belt,[3] cartouch box,[4] canteen with its strap, tomahawk, blanket, and knapsack. Some of these articles are necessary for his own safety, and some for his health and comfort. The constant exhausture of the publick stock of these articles, by calls from all quarters, renders it vain for the militia to expect to be supplied from thence, when they come into the feild, and nothing is so easy as for every man to have them prepared while quiet and at home. The cartouch box with a leathern flap, a wooden canteen with its strap, and a knapsack of thick linen (the better if painted) are what may be made in almost any mans family, and there are few neighbourhoods which do not afford artificers equal to the repair of a firelock, and furnishing it with a bayonet. Let me then again entreat you Sir, not only to give out in general orders to your Captains, that these preparations be instantly made, but to see yourself as far as possible that your orders be carried into execution. The soldiers themselves will thank you when, separated from domestick accommodation, they find themselves, through your attention to their happiness, provided with conveniencies which will administer to their first wants. When you order them into service, it will be proper that you order them to bring these things with them. Consider also the sending a waggon with every seventy five men as a standing rule, and that the officer who attends to lay in provisions for the men on their road, always return to the Auditors a list of the certificates he gives, stating the name, article, price, and date, in separate columns. These are circumstances always necessary, and as in the first hurry of an invasion, when it is necessary to write an infinity of letters and give a multiplicity of orders, it is not practicable then to enter into these details, I wish now to lay them down to you as standing rules, which may save the necessity of repeating them in future on every special occasion.

I must request you to make diligent enquiry and search through your county for any publick arms or accoutrements in the hands of individuals, to collect them together, and make report of them to me.[5] I am with great respect, Sir, Your most obedient And most humble servant,

Th: Jefferson

Broadside (DLC: Broadside Collection); signed by TJ and with MS insertions by Archibald Blair (see below); Sabin 100197; Swem, "Va. Bibliog.," 7268. FC (Vi); captioned: "A Circular Letter to the County Lieutenants." Enclosures: (1) Copy of "An act for recruiting this state's quota of troops to serve in the continental army," printed in Hening, X, 326-37; (2) two blank calendars for reporting the troops raised, not found; (3) Proclamation concerning Paroles, 19 Jan., q.v., following.

The Executive Council met for the first time after the invasion on 19 Jan. It is evident from their proceedings (*Va. Council Jour.*, II, 273-6) and from the three following documents that TJ had carefully prepared the agenda and had ready for the Council's approval measures of defense intended to obviate the costly mistakes that had become evident during the invasion. TWO BLANK CALENDARS: Here the word calendar is used in the now obsolete sense of *guide* or *pattern*.

1 Both texts read: "that so," an obvious error.

2 At this point Blair drew a line into the margin, and at the foot of the text he wrote: "6 copies to the word unnoticed." No copies of the shorter text have been found.

3 Blair here inserted "&."

4 Blair here inserted "or instead of these a rifle, a."

5 Text of FC ends at this point and is signed "T.J." in a clerk's hand.

Proclamation concerning Paroles

By his Excellency Thomas Jefferson, esqr; Governor of the Commonwealth of Virginia:

A Proclamation.

Whereas during the incursions which have been made into this and others of the United States by the forces of his Britannic Majesty, a practice hath been introduced by them unauthorized by the law of nations and unattempted in any other age or by any other enemy of seizing peaceable citizens while in their beds or employed in domestic occupations, and extorting from them paroles[1] that they will not on pain[2] of life and fortune be aiding or assisting in any respect to the enemies of great Britain which paroles such citizens have given sometimes through ignorance and at other times, with the wicked designs while they enjoy all the benefits of Government to shift from themselves their just share of its burthens, and it is even believed that instances have not been wanting where they have voluntarily gone in to the enemy and tendered such paroles. And the Laws of this Commonwealth not permitting any citizen thereof taken under such circumstances, or otherwise than when in arms by order of a proper officer to enter into any engagements with the public enemy which may withdraw from his Country those duties he owes to it: To the end therefore that none may be induced to the like act hereafter through ignorance of the law either real or pretended, and that all others whom it may concern, whether friends or foes, may be apprized of their nullity at the time of giving or taking such paroles or engagements: I have thought fit with the advice of the Council of State to issue this my Proclamation hereby declaring and making known that citizens taken or yeilding themselves in the manner before described are incapable by law of contracting engagements which may cancel or supercede the duties they owe to their country while remaining in it, and that notwithstanding such paroles or engagements they will be held to the performance of every service required by the Laws in like manner as if no such parole or engagement had been entered into. And whereas some citizens who may already have entered into such engagements may expect to withold their duties under pretence of being bound in conscience notwithstanding their legal disabilities to contract them, and it is inconsistent with the spirit of our Laws and constitution to force tender consciences, I do therefore further publish and declare that all Citizens taken or yeilding themselves in the manner before described who conceive themselves under such conscientious obligation to refuse obedience to the laws of their Country are hereby authorized and required taking passports as hereafter provided forthwith to repair to some of the posts, encampments or vessels of the forces of his Britannic Majesty, and by surrender of their persons to cancel such their engagements and thereafter to do as to themselves and those in whose power they shall be shall seem good save only that they shall not rejoin this Commonwealth but in a State of perfect emancipation from its enemies and of freedom to act as becomes good and Zealous citizens and saving also their fidelity to the Commonwealth. And all officers commanding forces either of this State or of the United States, who shall be nearest in their position to the said posts encampments or vessels of the enemy are hereby authorized and required paying necessary attention to times, situations and circumstances to grant passports to all such Citizens for the purposes before mentioned.

Given under my hand and the Seal of the Commonwealth at

Richmond this 19th Day of January in the year of our Lord 1781 and of the Commonwealth the fifth. TH: JEFFERSON

Engrossed copy (Vi); in a clerk's hand, signed by TJ, with seal attached. Dft (Vi); written on verso of letter from Archibald Cary to TJ, 16 Jan. 1781; entirely in TJ's hand and heavily scored out and corrected; endorsed: "Proclamation Jany 19th 1781." Broadside (DLC: Broadside Collection); Sabin 100198. Another broadside (NHi); this is a separate printing, no doubt by a different printer.

For the circumstances which occasioned this Proclamation, see TJ to the County Lieutenants, preceding, with which it was enclosed; see also TJ to Nelson, 25 Jan. 1781, and Kimball, *Jefferson: War and Peace*, 176-9. The numerous deletions and revisions of the draft indicate that TJ spent considerable time in its composition and undoubtedly had it ready to present to the Council on 19 Jan., when it was approved.

1 The following is deleted in Dft: "that they will not . . . say or do anything to the prejudice of his Britannic majesty." By deleting this and substituting the phraseology that occurs in the Proclamation, TJ caused its final form to be more accurate. A copy of one of the paroles (Vi) has the following form: "I David Jones of the County of Henrico by trade a Taylor aged thirty one years, do acknowledge myself to be a Prisoner on Parole to his Majesty the King of Great Britain; and I do hereby engage to remain as such until properly exchanged, or this Parole is altered. And I do solemnly promise not to be aiding or assisting in any respect to the Enemies of Great Britain while I continue under this obligation, under the penalty of forfeiting life and fortune; and I do further acknowledge that I have voluntarily signed this Parole. Given under my hand at Richmond this 5th day of Jany. 1781. Signed David Jones. Thomas Dundas Lt. Colo. 80th Regt."

2 In both Dft and engrossed copy, "penalty" was deleted and "pain" inserted by TJ.

Order in Council to Regularize Impressment of Wagons, Teams, &c.

In Council, Jan. 19, 1781.

THE board advise that Mr. Browne, commissioner of the provision law, be instructed to give orders to his deputies in the different Senatorial districts[1] to call on the owners of all waggons, teams and drivers, and of all vessels for river transportation, with their navigators, within the same, to register with them the said waggons, teams, drivers, vessels, and crews, to divide the said waggons into brigades of ten each, and the vessels as may be most expedient, appointing some trusty person to act as master of the brigade when called into actual service; that whenever it shall be necessary to impress within their district any waggons, teams, and drivers, vessels and navigators, they call forth the said brigade in regular rotation, and assure the people that so long as they continue to bring in their waggons or vessels into service when required, they shall not be required but in regular rotation; that if any owner shall fail to send his waggon or vessel when called on, it shall be subject to perform a double tour of duty; that the value of every waggon, team, and geer, and of every vessel, be ascertained by appraisement as directed by law, and a hire of fifty pounds of tobacco per day be allowed for the waggon, team, and driver, besides their being found forage and provisions; and a reasonable hire for the vessel and navigators; that regular accounts be kept by each deputy, of the debts to be contracted, and that he apply for the same to the executive once in every six months; that persons who shall conceal or fail to register their waggons and vessels within a reasonable time, to be fixed and published by the deputy, shall not have the benefit of the publick protection from impresses which will accrue to those registered, and that particularly all distant services be thrown on such waggons and vessels without regard to turn or proportion; that Mr. Browne further instruct his deputies to deliver to the continental store-keeper within his district, the articles of provision and forage which he shall be directed to procure, using the waggons and vessels of his district for transporting them to the stores; and that whenever the deputies of the continental Quarter Master shall be unable otherwise to transport the said articles from post to post, he aid them with the waggons and vessels of his district, as before directed:

(A Copy) ARCHIBALD BLAIR, C. C.

Broadside (Vi); not listed in Sabin or in Swem, "Va. Bibliog."

1 Preceding two words crossed out in text, and at foot appears this notation in Archibald Blair's hand: "instead of Senatorial districts in the Second line read Counties."

Proclamation of Embargo

[*Richmond*] *19 Jan. 1781.* A reissue of the Proclamation of 30 Nov. 1779, q.v., extending the embargo "until the end of the next session of Assembly."

Engrossed copy (Vi); 2 p.; in a clerk's hand, signed by TJ, with seal attached; endorsed: "a proclamation for laying an embargo. Jany 19. 81." Printed in *Va. Gaz.* (D & N) 17 Feb. 1781; renewed 26 Mch. 1781 and printed in same, 31 Mch., 7, 14 Apr.

From William Davies

SIR Richmond Jany. 19. 1781.

The militia from the counties your Excellency mentions have all arrived. Those from Amherst, who came in the last, marched today.

All the military stores, I have directed to be issued since my arrival at this place, have been issued by Captain Spiller and Captain Irish. A number were previously delivered by a Waggon master Patten at Manikin town and Judes ferry. He lives at Petersburg. I shall make every enquiry within my power, and shall chearfully give every information I can, towards the recovery of the public arms and accoutrements.

I have the honor to be, sir, your Excellency's most obedt hble servt., WILLIAM DAVIES

P.S. As I shall leave town tomorrow, I beg to mention that a number of valuable books are lying open in the Senate house and may be carried off by any body that chuses. Major Claiborne has a few of them.

RC (Vi); addressed and endorsed.

From Dudley Digges

SIR Ruffin's Ferry Janry 19. 1781.

I have, this Moment received Your Letter requiring my Attendance at Richmond. It gives me pain that some days must elapse before I shall be able to attend where my duty and Inclination would certainly induce me to go. I am thus far on my Way to Williamsburgh to collect the scattered remains of my property, which was hastily distributed in such places as were deemed the most secure. When this business is effected I shall, without delay, wait upon You at Richmond, and in the mean time I have to hope, that a sufficient Number of Members may be found to prevent any ill consequences.

With great Respect & esteem I am Your Excellency's Most hble & Obt. Servt., DUDLEY DIGGES

RC (Vi). TJ's letter to Digges has not been located.

From Col. William Fleming

SIR Botetourt Jany. 19. 1781

I wrote Your Excellence from Colo. Mosebys intimating my desire to visit my Family, during the recess of Council. On my way home I met by accident with the Inclosed, from Martin. Colo. Arthur Campbels progress in the Cherokee Nation, Your Excellency will have an Account of before this reaches you. I wish it may be attended with a good effect. The burning of their huts, and destruction of their corn, will I fear make the whole Nation Our irreconciliable Enemies, and force them for Sustenance to live altogether by depredation on our frontiers, or make an open Junction with our Foes, as the loss they have sustained in Men is little or nothing. The Waggoner who took up the Salt to Washington County brings down a Chest of Arms, containing thirty four Firelocks that want repairing, with Six that are in order, retained for the use of the Militia makes up the compliment of Arms committed to my care. I have the Honr to be Your Excellencys, Most Obt. Humble Servt,

WILLM. FLEMING

RC (Vi); addressed and endorsed. Enclosure (Vi): Deposition of William Springstone, "formerly a Trader in the Cherokee Town called Scitigo and occasional Interpreter to the Virginia agent for Indian affairs," stating that the Raven, chief of the Cherokees, had "returned from a Treaty with the British Agent in Georgia" on 22 Nov., last, and that the Indians had agreed to go to war against the inhabitants of Virginia and Carolina in the west; that John Martin and others were to be put to death, but had escaped. Deposition certified by John Martin, Francis Budwine, and John Hawkins (printed in CVSP, I, 446-7).

Fleming's former letter, FROM COLO. MOSEBYS (i.e., Littleberry Mosby, county lieutenant of Powhatan), has not been found.

To the Manager of the Lead Mines

SIR Richmond January 19th 1781

The Invasion of this State calling for an immediate and large Supply of Lead, be pleased to send us immediately all the Lead you have on Hand, notwithstanding my former Direction to let one half go to the Southward Army with which on the present Occasion we must dispense. The Bearer Mr. Tate is sent to see this Service performed. The Money for paying the Waggonage not being ready at this moment and it being improper to detain him, that shall follow before the Services are compleated. I am Sir Your mo: obt. Servt.,

T.J.

FC (Vi); at head of text: caption as printed above.

This letter is printed in *Official Letters* (II, 294) as directed to James Callaway; but on 5 Dec. 1777 Callaway was replaced as manager of the lead mines by Charles Lynch, who was still in that post in Mch. 1781 (see TJ to Charles Lynch, 27 Mch. 1781).

From George Muter, enclosing an Exchange of Letters with William Spiller

[*Richmond*] *19 Jan. 1781.* Encloses: (1) letter written to William Spiller, commissary of military stores, 18 Jan.; (2) Spiller's reply of 19 Jan.

ENCLOSURES

1. Muter to Spiller

[*Richmond*] *19 Jan. 1781.* The Executive Council have received information that although Spiller received orders [2 January] to go to Petersburg "between 10 and 11 o Clock in the forenoon" to remove the stores there, and Col. Carrington did not leave Richmond until after 2 o'clock, yet Col. Carrington arrived first and "actually got all or most of the Arms removed out of Town" before Spiller arrived. "Delay in such cases when the utmost expedition is most essentially necessary, being frequently attended with the worst consequences," an explanation in writing is requested.

2. Spiller to Muter

SIR Richmond January 19th. 1781

I have recieved your letter, informing me of the information the supreme executive have recieved, concerning the time of geting to Petersburg and removing the stores &c. from that place and I shall indeavor to relate it as minutly as I can recollect. I set out from this place about twelve Oclock or after, my orders was to proceed to Chesterfield Courthouse, to call on Colo. Davies for his assistance, and from thence to Petersburg. It was after dark before I arrived at Petersburg. I went immediately to the Quarter Masters Office (he having previous notice from Colo. Muter to prepare waggons for the removal of the stores) and inquired for him, was told by his assistant, that he was gorn home; I then inquired if he had left no orders, to prepare waggons for the removing of the Stores. The man informd he had ordered him to impress all the waggons that he could find, he had accordingly; as he said, impresst several, but having no Guard, they had gorn off, that he had sent several men differrent ways to stop the said waggons, that he expected them brought. I desired him to send for Mr. Elliott the Q. Master at that station, informing him that I was waiting for waggons to remove the stores. He immediately sent off a servant to Mr. Elliott. I then told him I should go to a Tavern near, and desired him to send for me when the Q. Master or the waggons, come to the Office. Having rode a horse that nearly gave out, before I got to Petersburg I was greatly fortug'd, when I got to the above mentioned tavern, I went to a bed and lay down, and fell a Sleep, and proberly Sleep two or three hours: when I awoke I went to the Office. Colo. Carrington was their, and had sent off several waggons loaded with stores. I met the said waggons as I went to the Office. Colo. Carrington told me he should inform against me. I told him he was very welcom to do so. He then gave me orders that he had recieved from you, to proceed to the Countys of Islewhite and South Hamton; which I did and rode the whole night. Thus Sir you have all the circumstances relative to that business that I can remember. The informer (which I suppose to be Colo. Carrington) is much mistaken, about the time of my geting to Petersburg. I was their before him, and do declare I lost no time, on the road, nor stopt at no place except Chesterfield Courthouse. The post I now hold as Commisary of Military Stores, seems to have many directers, more than one man can possible please.

I therefore from this moment resign the said post. I should be exceeding glad the supreme executive would determine what pay to allow me for the time I have served, which will inable me to pay my board &c. which has been very high.

I am with much Essteem Sir your most Obdt. & very huml. Sevt.,

Wm Spiller

RC (Vi); 1 p. Enclosures: (1) Copy, written below Muter's letter to TJ; printed in CVSP, I, 442. (2) RC (Vi); addressed: "Colo. Muter"; endorsed.

From Matthew Pope

[*Richmond*] *19 Jan. 1781.* Encloses a list of medicines "necessary to be imported for the use of the State"; has confined them to "such only as are common and useful"; the cost of the medicines and instruments will be about £600 sterling.

RC (Vi); 2 p.; addressed and endorsed. Enclosure not located.

From George Slaughter

Sir — Falls of Ohio January 19th 1781

By information by Letters from North side Kentucky and every coroborating circumstance, I have the greatest reason to believe that there has a young Man by the Name of Whitsyl, who has been a Captive for two or three years past among the Shawnese Indians, made his escape from a detach'd party come over from the main body, who were hunting on the Ohio, in order to lay in provisions for the Indians and English who in conjunction intended to carry on [an] expedition against this Country very early in the Spring, and that the party came over to get a prisoner to give them intelligence of the State of the Country and to take Horses for the purpose, which they did to the amount of 14. This Account I have the greatest reason to think true from the well known varicity of the informant and some mischief done by the Indians yesterday about 10 Miles above this place where they captured one Man and am afraid have kill'd 2 More out of a hunting party of 4. which were out on my Account for the State.

I cannot say but I am uneasy at the present Situation of the Country, the Militia being under no kind of subordination for want [of] officers regularly quallified in this County to command them and every man seems to do that which he thinks best. And I have some doubt from information of Colo. Simon Triplett, that Colo.

Broadhead will not allow provisions brought down the River, saying that he has orders to stop them for the use of that department. But as to that your Excellency can be a better judge of than it is in my power to inform you. Shall therefore only add that I am Yr. Excellency's Yr Mo Obt Huml Servant, GEORGE SLAUGHTER

RC (PHi); addressed and endorsed.
WHITSYL: Martin Wetzel, one of the five sons of Captain John Wetzel who became noted frontiersmen. Martin Wetzel was captured in April 1778, and remained in the hands of the Shawnee almost two and a half years (R. G. Thwaites and L. P. Kellogg, *Frontier Defense on the Upper Ohio, 1777-1778*, Madison, 1912, p. 296). See John Todd to TJ, 24 Jan. 1781.

To Steuben

SIR Richmond Jan. 19. 1781

Shirts had been ordered for Colo. Armand's Corps on your former requisition. These I believe are ready. They are ordered to be delivered to Majr. Lomagn's order. We have not a single article of the others enumerated in his list of necessaries wanted. We could therefore only undertake to him to furnish money to the Continental Quarter Master or any other proper person to procure them if this mode should be approved. This or any other assistance we can give shall be afforded.

The practice introduced by the enemy of laying the country through which they pass under parole is so mischeivous that I have thought it necessary to issue the proclamation of which I inclose you a copy.

I have the Honour to be with the greatest esteem, Sir, your most obedt. & most humble servt, TH: JEFFERSON

RC (NHi); addressed and endorsed; FC (Vi).
MAJR. LOMAGN: Viscount de Lomagne (Laumagne), a major in Col. Armand's corps (Lasseray, *Les français sous les treize étoiles*, p. 268-9; see Steuben to TJ, 17 Jan. 1781).

To Steuben

SIR Richmond January 19th 1781

A warrant was yesterday made out for Mr. Harrison for two hundred thousand Dollars and I shall take the first opportun[ity] of informing him that the money is in readiness. This is in consequence of your requisition communicated by Major Walker. Dr. Evans the Bearer of your Letter will receive from the Gentleman who has the care of our Medicine whatever articles can be furnished from that Stock. It is a very imperfect Collection. Immediately on receiving the communication from you by Major Walker that you would wish such a Person as you therein described to be with you, I laid it before the Council. We concluded to propose to Mr. Walker (late one of our Delegates) to accept of this Office. Having once been a member of the Council he is not unacquainted with our Arrangements. I sent to him by express and shall hope an answer very shortly. I sincerely wish he may consent to undertake it as I am satisfied he can save you much Trouble. Should he decline it I apprehend it not easy to find another who will be of real use to you. None of the militia with Genl. Weedon (except from the Counties of Rockbridge, Augusta, Rockingham, and Shenandoah) were of the Counties intended to be kept in the Field. I thought it necessary to mention this Circumstance to you as you might perhaps think proper to discharge them before they join Genl. Nelson. I have the Honour to be with great Respect and esteem, Sir, Your mo: obt. & mo: hble Sevt.,

T.J.

FC (Vi).

COMMUNICATION . . . BY MAJOR WALKER: See Steuben's Queries, under 14 Jan. 1781. The proposal to MR. WALKER: See TJ to John Walker, 18 Jan. 1781.

From John Syme

SIR New Castle 19th. Jany 1781.

Our Waggons and Men being Chiefly Out With the Militia, I Have met with Great Difficulty in procuring them both with that Dispatch with Which I would be Glad to Execute any thing Committed to my Care by Your Excellency; However, the Business is now in Some forwardness. You Have Half a Dozen Waggons Loaded with Spirits, with Directions to Wait on You, as You Desir'd, and Riders Out to get more.

Will it not be Necessary to appoint a Waggon Master, a Receiver and Deliverer of Stores Here, or Would you Call Him Commissary. I Know not the Several Appellations, proper, for the Men Necessary in this Department, But you'll be Assur'd, it is Exceeding Troublesome and Expensive. You Will be Pleas'd to Direct me, in the Delivery of these Articles. I Have had a Number of Applications, But no Spirits furnish'd to any One Except Genl. Nelson's Command, by Order of Mr. Wm. Claiborne, who Styles Himself, Director of the Stores, under my Care. The Flour in Bad

Order, Quality same, Have Dealt out, as Sparingly as Possible, to the Partys of Millitia passing this Way, which are many and Extremely pressing me for everything. This Moment Mr. Richd. Burnley, wants the Remainder of the Flour, and six hhds. Rum for Genl. Nelson, the Former Have Granted, but the Latter remains, for Your Determination; Knowing as You Observ'd to me, it is a Very Scarce Article. I can't Yet make up my Mind as to the Heavy Artillery. There is about 200 bbls. Corn Come up the River, which (one of Your Board thinking it necessary for Mr. Rose to have the quantity at Cumberland) mention to You.

I shall in Cases of Difficulty Apply to Your Excellency and in Everything Do the best I can, Being on all Occasions, wth Great Esteem, Your Most Obedt. Servt., J SYME

RC (Vi); addressed and endorsed.

From William Armistead

20th Jany. 1781.

Present State of the Shoemaking business under Mr. Mathew Anderson.

No materials on hand to carry on the business; nor to be procured without the ready money.

13 Soldiers employed and Standing idle.

3 hands employed for the day

Mr. Andersons Wages going on; together with house rent &c., the Shoes made, from the high Price of leather &c. and the hands being obliged to be idle from the Want of money to purchase that Article, are found to Cost as much as they may be bought for elsewhere.

From the above, I would take the liberty of Submitting to your Excellency whether the discontinuance of that business will not be proper. W ARMISTEAD

RC (Vi); addressed and endorsed.

To George Rogers Clark

SIR In Council January 20. 1781.

Having cause to entertain doubts from several Letters transmitted me, whether Mr. Jno. Dodge who was appointed to conduct a commerce with the Indians on behalf of this state has not been guilty of gross misapplication or mismanagement of what has been confided to him and the distance between him and us rendering it impracticable to call the examination before ourselves, you are hereby authorized and desired either by yourself or such persons as you shall appoint to enquire into any part of his conduct which you may have reason to suppose unjustifiable and if it be found so, to remove him from his office and take such measures as may be most effectual for bringing him to account and indemnifying the public against such malversations. Shou'd he be removed we think it unnecessary to appoint another in his stead.

I am, Sir, Your most obt. humble servant, TH: JEFFERSON

RC (WHi); addressed and endorsed. FC (Vi).

From George Rogers Clark

SIR Richmond Jany 20th 81

There is some probability of my demands on the Tresury being answered so as to Inable me to set out tomorrow if the necessary papers from your Excellency do not detain me which I Should be glad to know as Days are pretious.

I am with Esteem your very Hbl Servt., G R CLARK

RC (Vi); addressed and endorsed.

To George Rogers Clark

SIR Richmond Jan. 20. 1781.

I think every paper is now ready for you. They shall be delivered to you tomorrow morning if you will be so good as to call on me. I expect Colo. Gibson here tomorrow. Would you think it worth your while to stay a day to see him? I am with great esteem Sir your most obedt. servt., TH: JEFFERSON

RC (WHi); addressed and endorsed. Among the PAPERS ready for delivery to Clark was a duplicate, dated 19 Jan., of TJ's letter to Clark of 25 Dec. 1780, q.v.; see also TJ to George Rogers Clark, 22 Jan., with enclosure, below.

To the First Magistrate of Each County

SIR RICHMOND (IN COUNCIL) JANUARY 20, 1781.

THE invasion of our country by the enemy at the close of the late session of Assembly, their pushing immediately to this place, the dispersion of the publick papers, which for the purpose of saving them necessarily took place, and the injury done at the printing office, have been so many causes operating unfortunately to the delay of transmitting you the important act for supplying the army with clothes, provisions, and waggons, which I now enclose you. In the mean time, the days of execution are so far advanced that I am persuaded they must have passed over before it can be received in many counties. In this case, the only measure to be advised is, to adopt the earliest days possible. Could any legal scruples arise as to this, there would be no doubt that the ensuing Assembly influenced by the necessity which induced them to pass the act, would give their sanction to its execution, though at a later date than is prescribed. However the substance of the act is to procure supplies of beef, clothing, and waggons. The time of doing this is a circumstance only; and the principle is sound both in law and policy, that substance not circumstance is to be regarded. While we have so many foes in our bowels and environing us on every side, he is but a bad citizen who can entertain a doubt whether the law will justify him in saving his country, or who will scruple to risk himself in support of the spirit of a law where unavoidable accidents have prevented a literal compliance with it.

LET me exhort you therefore, sir, should this act come to hand so late as to prevent your proceeding to its execution by the time prescribed, to have it executed as early as possible. No man can say this will be an injury to him, because the times were affixed to compel an early compliance, the delay of which, some days, must rather be matter of indulgence.

PERSONS will be appointed to receive the waggons and appendages to be furnished by your county, who shall give you notice of the place of delivery in due time.

I have the honour to be, with great respect, sir, Your most obedient, and most humble servant, *Th: Jefferson*

Broadside (DLC); 2 other copies of same (Vi); all signed by TJ. See Swem, "Va. Bibliog.," 7274, which lists a similar letter, "no copy seen," under 24 Jan.; this entry, perhaps taken from the printer's records, doubtless refers to the above. FC (Vi); captioned: "To the first Magistrate in each County." Enclosure: "An act for supplying the army with clothes, provisions, and waggons," no copy of which has been located; printed in Hening, x, 338-43.

On 1 Jan. 1781, the House of Delegates ordered the public printer to print 200 copies of the act for supplying the army with provisions (JHD, Oct. 1780, 1827 edn., p. 79). The act provided that the "courts of the said counties . . . are hereby authorized and required for this particular purpose, to meet at the courthouses on some day between the twentieth day of January and seventh of February . . . and there assess and levy . . . a sufficient amount . . . to make payment" for the wagon, team, driver, and articles required. For an answer from one magistrate see Robert Ewing to TJ, 12 Feb. 1781.

From John Harmanson

Northampton, 20 *Jan.* 1781. In accordance with instructions, two vessels loaded with corn were sent off to Head of Elk, but off Tangier Island were taken by a 10-gun privateer. One was sent to New York, but was forced ashore by a hard northwest wind—most of corn recovered in fair condition. Other vessel, robbed of sails, was ordered to follow privateer into harbor. It fell so far behind that, at night, it escaped; but having only a mainsail and a broken boom, was forced by wind to run ashore on the bay side and was bilged. Damaged corn was saved, except for 100 bu., and was sold at public sale "for about 6. or 7 pound ℔ barrel." About 7,000 bu. corn and as much oats still on hand, and instructions are requested concerning disposal. Salt would have been sent if fleet had stayed out three more days, but will be sent in "a fine New Vessel" if the fleet goes out. There are 700 or 800 bu. of salt. Orders were expected earlier.

RC (Vi); 4 p.; addressed, in part: "℔ Favour of Mr. Williams"; endorsed; printed in CVSP, I, 450-1.

John Harmanson was commissioner of the provision law for Northampton co. (CVSP, II, 239).

To George Lyne

SIR In Council January 20th 1781

Considering the Public liable to pay Storage for the Articles mentioned in your Letter, this of Course puts the Business of receiving and delivering on the Keeper of the Store. As Rum may be had below, I shall hope Genl. Nelson will be able to procure [it] there for his Troops. Rum is wanted in this Quarter and after being brought so far it would seem bad Management to send it down again. Provisions may be delivered for the use of any Troops embodied or marching, but the other articles to be forwarded here as we agreed when you were with us. I should think it prudent to send your Waggons in Brigades and to appoint a trusty Waggon master.

T.J.

FC (Vi).

Lyne's letter to TJ to which this is a reply has not been located.

From George Muter, with Reply

SIR War office Jany 20. 1781.

I beg leave to inform your Excellency that Mr. Mattw. Anderson's time he engaged for is out, and the shop under his direction at a stand. I beleive he is willing to engage for sometime longer (if the shop can be properly supported) and I expect him here this forenoon.

Capt. Nathl. Irish (Continental commissary of military stores) sollicits your Excellency, for a supply of cloathing from the public store. He is in great necessity and can't get his money to enable him to purchase elsewhere.

Permitt me to mention to your Excellency the necessity of appointing a Commissary of military stores, with proper assistants, or authorised to appoint them. 'Twill be utterly impossible to have the arms properly collected and repaired, or the ammunition duely taken care of unless there is some person who can be depended on, whose only business it will be [to] manage the arms and ammunition. At the same time I beg leave to observe, that the post of Commissary of military stores, has not a single shilling of sallary annexed to it.

I have the honour to be Your Excellency's Most hl Servant,

GEORGE MUTER. C.

In Council Jan. 20. 1781.

The board are of opinion that Mr. Matthew Anderson's shop as a public one should be discontinued and that he should be engaged to work for the public such materials as they shall furnish at the old prices, to be paid in provisions in fixed proportions at the old prices also.

The discontinuance of the public store by act of assembly cuts short all questions about furnishing cloathing. TH: JEFFERSON

RC (Vi); addressed and endorsed; reply, in TJ's hand, written below Muter's letter. Tr of reply in War Office Journal (Vi).

MATTW. ANDERSON: Matthew Anderson was in charge of the shoe manufactory (*Official Letters*, II, 297). DISCONTINUANCE OF THE PUBLIC STORE: By an Act of Assembly passed at the Oct. 1780 session, "for making good the future pay of the army, and for other purposes," the public store was replaced by a clothier general, appointed by the governor (Hening, X, 373-5). NECESSITY OF APPOINTING A COMMISSARY: See George Muter to TJ, with enclosures, 19 Jan. 1781, and Muter to TJ, following.

From George Muter, with Reply

SIR War office Jany. 20. 1781

I have conferred with Capt. Irish. He thinks it not incompatible, for him to act as State Commissary of Military stores, at the same time that he is Continental Commissary, and is willing immedeatly to undertake that office. He requires a good assistant at an adequate sallary, and a right to appoint occasional assistants when necessity requires. On these conditions he will undertake for three months certain, and if it is thought proper to continue him, he will expect a reasonable sallary from the beginning of his acting; but if it is then found improper for him to continue, and that a separate commissary for the state should be appointed; he will give up immedeatly, and will not demand any pay for his services.

I have the honour to be your Excellency's most humble servant,

GEORGE MUTER. C.

In Council Jan. 20. 1781.

The board approve of employing Capt. Irish as herein proposed, and will allow five shillings a day old money to be discharged in the present money according to the price of tobacco formerly @ 20/ the hundred, and it's price at the time of paiment as settled by the last preceding valuation of the grand jury. They will allow an assistant who being of the military line shall have an additional allowance of four shillings by the day to be paid in the same way. They are of opinion that Capt. Spiller should for the time he served have the allowance herein before settled for Capt. Irish.

TH: JEFFERSON

RC (Vi); addressed and endorsed; reply, in TJ's hand, on verso; Tr of reply in War Office Journal (Vi).

A minute in the War Office Journal for the same day states that "Capt. Irish accepts of the appointment of Commissary of Military Stores, on the terms agreed to by the Governor and Council, and is this day appointed to that Office accordingly." CAPT. SPILLER: Under 22 Jan., a minute in the same Journal records that a warrant was issued to Capt. William Spiller "for his services as State Commissary of Military Stores from the 21st. of September 1780, to the 19th. of January 1781, inclusive." See also George Muter to TJ, 19 Jan. 1781.

From George Muter, with Reply

[*Richmond*] *20 Jan. 1781.* Encloses list of supplies for Capt. Read's troop which cannot be furnished by the quartermaster. Read "thinks he can procure the necessarys more readily and on cheaper terms in Maryland . . . clear of the expence of transportation." Suggests giving Read permission to purchase there and furnishing him with money. Countersigned: "In Council Jan. 20. 1781. An estimate being necessary of the sum these articles will cost before we can judge whether it can be furnished, we shall be glad of such an estimate. Th: Jefferson."

RC (Vi); 2 p.; addressed and endorsed; reply, in TJ's hand, written at bottom of page. Tr of reply in War Office Journal (Vi). Enclosure: James Cocke to George Muter, 18 Jan. 1781, q.v., above.

To Thomas Nelson

Dear General In Council January 20th 1781

I will send to Mr. Brown the Commissary the Paragraph from your Letter relative to Provisions with orders for him to take measures for Relief. At the same time I wish the Principal expenditures could be in Indian meal that the Flour might be kept as much as possible for the Summer's use. Majr. Hollier has no authority to make exchange [of] Prisoners with the enemy. The inclosed Proclamation will shew you the Principles on which [an exchange] will be approved, to wit that a Citizen shall be considered as a Soldier if he were taken in arms, embodied as a Soldier, and acting under the Command of his Officer. You will perceive that these Circumstances are necessary to distinguish from a Citizen engaged in his domestic or other Occupations. Any equal exchange made on these Principles and approved of by yourself shall be considered as valid.

T.J.

FC (Vi). Enclosure (missing): Proclamation concerning Paroles, 19 Jan. 1781, q.v.

YOUR LETTER RELATIVE TO PROVISIONS: Nelson's letter to TJ has not been located, nor has a letter from TJ to Brown, transmitting the paragraph mentioned.

From William Call

Sir Prince Geo. Jany 21. 1781

The very great demand for Arms for the Army has heitherto Prevented my making any application for any for this county. Probably there may be spare Arms out of order, if so, on having your approbation I will endeavour to get them repair'd at the Publick expence, could they be Sent over, in any of the publick Waggons, unless they could sooner be done in the hands of the publick artificer's. Amunition would also be wanting, which with the Arms I should Propose puting into the hands of the diffirent Captains to be deliverd out to the Men on any alarm, or to remain in their hands to be kept in order, and be ready when called for. Cartouch boxes will also be wanting.

I have the Honour to be with respect Sir Yr. Excellencys. mo. Obt H Svt,

Wm Call

RC (Vi); addressed and endorsed.

William Call was county lieutenant of Prince George co. (*Official Letters*, II, 344).

From George Rogers Clark

DR SR Richmond Jany 21 1781

Excuse the liberty I take in writing to you on a Subject that you might think would not Concern me so much as it Really does. As great part of my forces will be from Kentucky the appointment of the County Lieutenants is an object worthy my attention. I this day Learnt that Col. Christy hath Resignd the Lieutenancy of Jefferson County. I would beg leave to Recommend to you Col. Jno. Floyd an Inhabitant of the County as a Gentlemen that I am Convinced will do Honour to the appointment and known to be the most Capable in that County—a Soldier Gentlemen and a Scholar whom the Inhabitants from his actions have the Greatest Confidence in. I hope Sir that you will not put any unfavourable Construction on this Letter and beg leave to Subscribe my self your very Hbl. Servt, G R CLARK

RC (Vi); addressed and endorsed; in the margin opposite this recommendation of Floyd is the word "issued."

At the meeting of the Council on 22 Jan. a commission was "issued appointing John Floyd Gentn. County Lieutenant of the County of Jefferson." (*Va. Council Jour.*, II, 277). COL. CHRISTY: Probably William Christian; see John Floyd to TJ, 15 Jan. 1781.

From Sampson Mathews, with Jefferson's Instructions to George Muter

SIR Bowling-green 21st. Jany 1781

I am advanced this Far with the Militia From augusta (after having been at Fredricksburg four days) by order of Genl. Mulenburg. Colo. John Bowyer with about 220 Men From Rockbridge has Joined me this morning.

There is wanting Smiths vices, Files and some fine Steel For the Repair of the arms of the militia.

The Bearer Mr. Chas. Cocke will wait on your Excellency For an order For these articles which are very much wanting. I have the Honour to be with Much Esteem & Respect your Excellencys obedt. huml. Servt., SAMP. MATHEWS

If it be possible to furnish these articles, it is conceived to be very necessary, and we wish Colo. Muter to take immediate measures for that purpose. A person waits for them. TH: JEFFERSON

RC (Vi); addressed, in part: "Pr. Mr. Chas. Cocke Express"; endorsed; instructions to George Muter, in TJ's hand, written on verso of enclosed memorandum. Enclosure (Vi): "Memom. of files &c. wanting for the Gunsmith of Collo. Mathews Militia now on duty Imedeatly under his command & Colo. Jno. Bowgers do. from Rockbridge—2 Hand vices & one Bench Vice 2 Fetheredge Files. & 2. three square files do. 6 ℔. of good London or Germain Steel. January the 21st. 1781. Samp. Mathews Lieut of augusta."

From Thomas Newton, Jr.

SIR Surry Janry. 21. 1781.

Coll. Godfrey being so unfortunate as to have his only son taken prisoner is very unhappy on account of it, thinking his activity may occassion him to be ill treated; he was taken on board a vessel which was defended with the greatest bravery, and I can assure your Excellency of my own knowledge that the young Gentleman has been very active, and at all times appear'd on duty whenever the Enemy came in without waiting a particular turn. Several others were taken at the same time which if they cou'd be exchanged I doubt not they wou'd exert themselves in defence of their Country. I am Yr. Excellcy Most Obt. Servt., THOS NEWTON JUNR.

Names of the persons taken

Wm. Godfrey, Henry Whiting, Jno. Livingston, Jno. Cooke and Richd. Lee.

RC (Vi); addressed and endorsed.
See Matthew Godfrey to TJ, 6 Jan. 1781.

From John Christian Senf

SIR Cabbin Point Janury. 21st. 1781.

On my Return from below I received Your Excellency's two Letters, and have acquainted the Baron with the Contents of it, but the General has orderd me, that I first would go down with Him below to establish some Posts, which will probably take me five or Six Days.

As soon as I have done this Business, I shall wait directly on Your Excellency for Your further Orders.

I have the Honour to be with great Respect Your Excellency's most obedt. and most humble Servt., JN. CHRISTN. SENF
Colonel Engineer

RC (Vi); addressed and endorsed.
YOUR . . . TWO LETTERS: Only one of TJ's letters to Senf has been located, that of 15 Jan. 1781, q.v.

From Steuben

Sir Cabbin point 21st Jany. 1781.

The 19th. Inst. in the Afternoon the Enemy crossed Nansemond River at Sleepy hole ferry and Encamped on the opposite bank. Eight of their Vessels then lay at the mouth of the River and two of Goodrich's Privateers near the ferry, the Boats had fell down to the Fleet.

From all their movements it appears evident they mean to take post, at least for some time, in Portsmouth and its environs. The question naturally resulting is whether we have the means of forcing them from that position. The better to determine this I thought it necessary to have an interview with Genl. Nelson at Williamsburg, from whence I returnd yesterday Evening. He is of opinion with Colo. Senf who surveyd that Country and many other Officers acquainted with the ground, that we are not in a situation to undertake such an Enterprize.

Our Operations must therefore be confined to preventing the Enemies parties from making incursions into the Country on either Side of James River or should they undertake to come out with their whole force to render any enterprize of theirs difficult, always having in view the keeping open the communications across James River. The communication is at present established from Allens to Sandy point, that in case of any danger from the fleet the boats may be secured in upper Chippoake Creek.

The number of Troops necessary to be kept up for these purposes will be 2700 Regulars exclusive of the Volunteer Horse and Nelsons and Armands Corps of Cavalry. In this calculation I had nothing more at heart than to avoid all unnecessary expence to the state. I therefore reduced the 4000 Men I at first asked to this number, but this force must be kept compleat and I propose arranging it in the following manner.

The Volunteers }
Nelsons } Horse } on the South Side the River
Armands }
100 Light Infantry
1600 Infantry 8 Battalions

Colo. Griffins Horse
200 Light Infantry } on the North Side
800 Infantry in 4 Battalions

The Command on the Lines I have given Genl. Laws[on] who has with him 900 Infantry with the Volunteers and Nelsons Horse.

Two Regiments of 800 Men and Armands Corps I have left here till I determine whether or not I shall take a position lower down. I have orderd Genl. Muhlenberg here to take the Command of this Brigade and Genl. Nelson will keep the Command on the other side of the River. Genl. Weedon I have directed to remain at Fredricksburg to collect 1000 Stand of Arms with Ammunition and to make every other Arrangement necessary for having that number of Men Armed on the Least Alarm.

The Militia of the Counties adjacent to the River I would have remain at home ready to turn out on the Shortest notice of any movement of the Enemy and as many of the back Country Militia will bring their Arms I propose collecting all the Spare Arms and keeping them on Waggons ready to Arm any additional force we may call in.

Tomorrow I propose going to Smithfield [and] Suffolk to make the necessary Arrangements there and as I expect to find Genl. Muhlenberg here at my return I shall then have the honor of waiting on your Excellency at Richmond.

I cannot but look on our Situation as very critical and should think it very necessary to call together the Assembly that proper measures may be taken to prevent the loss of this State and thereby that of all the other southern States.

Dft (NHi); endorsed: "Copy to Gov Jefferson 21 Jany."

GOODRICH'S PRIVATEERS: See John Goodrich, Sr. to TJ, 20 Jan. 1777; Edmund Randolph to TJ, 22 Feb. 1778. For the location of SLEEPY HOLE FERRY, at the mouth of the Nansemond River; ALLENS, on the south side of the James; SANDY POINT, across the James from Allen's, at the mouth of the Chickahominy River, and UPPER CHIPPOAKE (Chippokes) CREEK, just above Allen's, see Fry-Jefferson Map.

To George Weedon

SIR Richmond Jan. 21. 1781.

I am very sorry we shall not be able to furnish you with a supply of lead until we receive some for which we have sent up the river. The Southern army has been entirely furnished from hence. Five tons were sent to the Northern army last fall. This had reduced our stock very low; and of what was left, one third was destroyed by the enemy. There remains on hand but a small parcel which is now making up at the laboratory. Should however the enemy's movements indicate an intention of visiting you, we will send you what we have, which I think may be done in time to supply the expenditure of what you have. The money press has not yet got to work. As soon as it does I shall be very glad to have money furnished for the purpose of enlisting men, which I consider as a very important one. I suppose it is impossible for you to engage them without the ready money. The bounty is 2000 dollars which should certainly be paid on demand. My last intelligence of the enemy was that their troops were on shore in the Isle of Wight, and their shipping at Newport's news and Hampton road.

I am with great respect Sir your most obedt. servt.,

TH: JEFFERSON

RC (A Midwestern Collector, 1945); addressed: "Brigadr. Genl. Weedon Fredericksburg"; endorsed.

To George Rogers Clark, enclosing Clark's Commission

SIR — In Council Jan. 22. 1781.

I do myself the pleasure of inclosing you a Brigadier General's commission. The laws having given us power to appoint a General officer only for special purposes, and not a perpetual one, has obliged us to express the particular occasion of this appointment. Besides this I thought it necessary to give you an exemplification of your former commission which was perpetual.

I wish you in every circumstance all possible success and felicity, and to beleive me to be with very sincere esteem Sir your most obedt. & most humble servt., TH: JEFFERSON

ENCLOSURE

The Commonwealth of VIRGINIA

To George Rogers Clarke Gentleman, greeting:

KNOW YOU that our GOVERNOUR, with the advice of the Council of State, doth constitute and appoint you *a Brigadier General of the forces to be embodied on*[1] *an expedition westward of the Ohio.* In Testimony whereof, these our Letters are sealed, with the Seal of the Commonwealth, and made Patent.

Witness THOMAS JEFFERSON, Esquire, our said Governour, at *Richmond*, the *twenty second* Day of *January* in the Year of our Lord One Thousand Seven Hundred and Eighty *one.*[2]

Th: Jefferson

RC (WHi); addressed: "Brigadier General Clarke Richmond"; endorsed. Enclosure (WHi): printed form, such as was used for commissioning officers of the militia, filled in by a clerk and signed by TJ; seal at foot of text.

THE LAWS . . . APPOINTMENT: Clark had desired a Continental commission, but the established rules did not permit the granting of such a commission to officers in state regiments (*George Rogers Clark Papers, 1771-1781*, p. cxlv).

[1] The words "of Militia in the County of" that appeared at this point in the printed form were struck out by the clerk.

[2] The word "one" is in TJ's hand.

From George Muter

[*Richmond, 22 Jan. 1781.* A minute in the War Office Journal (Vi) under date of 22 Jan. 1781 records two warrants to Capt. Edmund Read: (1) for £26,100, "on account for the pay due his Troop from the 1st. day of August 1780, to the 1st. day of January 1781 inclusive" (George Muter to the Auditors, 22 Jan. 1781, countersigned by TJ, in Contingent Fund Vouchers, Vi); (2) for £5,196, "on Account to purchase necessaries for his Troop in Maryland agreable to an estimate given in for that purpose"; also, a "Letter, to the Governor inclosing the abovementioned estimate and Warrants, and a petition to the Governor and Council from C[. . .] the prisoner." The second warrant to Edmund Read, the estimate, and the letter from Muter to TJ enclosing them, have not been located. The minute concerning the "petition . . . from C[. . .] the prisoner" is incomplete, and the petition has not been identified.]

From George Muter

[*Richmond, 22 Jan. 1781.* Minute in the Virginia War Office Journal (Vi), under date of 22 Jan. 1781: "Letter, to the Governor informing that Capt. John Allen of the State Artillery has lost his Commission, which he says was dated the 16th. day of April 1780. and, that he sollicits for a new one." Letter not located.]

From George Muter

[*Richmond*] *22 Jan. 1781.* Mr. Milton Ford is now here and ready to hire carpenters "for the works at the Forks of James River," and awaits instructions; his brother and father will assist him, if that is proper; Ford has previously been employed for the public, acting with "much industry and punctuality."

RC (Vi); 1 p.

From George Muter, with Reply

SIR War office Jany 22d. 1781.

Several Cannon that were cast at the Foundery have not been bored. Cannon are wanted for the Jefferson of those that have been cast at the Foundery, as also to comply with the contracts formerly made with individuals. Capt. Maxwell also wants Cannon for the Thetis: none for her have yet been cast.

The cannon cannot be bored 'till a boring mill is built and fitted, and no cannon can be cast 'till a moulding house is built and the foundery in some measure repaired. I therefore beg leave to submitt these matters to the consideration of your Excellency and the Honble Council.

I have the honour to be Your Excellency's Most hl servant,

GEORGE MUTER. C

In Council. Jan. 23. 1781.

We know not how guns come to be wanting for the Jefferson. As to the others we consider the repairing the Foundery, rebuilding the moulding house, and the boring mill (on a more simple plan) as works to be executed as soon as possible. Are there not some nine pounders on the Eastern shore belonging to the state?

TH: JEFFERSON

RC (Vi); addressed and endorsed; reply, in TJ's hand, written on verso of Muter's letter to TJ.

From Thomas Nelson

DEAR SIR Williamsburg Jany. 22. 1781

I am just favoured with yours of the 20th. Instant inclosing your Proclamation respecting those who have been paroled, which shall be strictly adhered to.

We have hitherto made use of Meal for the Soldiers, and shall continue this Practice as long as we can be regularly supplied with it; but it would be proper to have some Flour on hand for fear of a Disappointment in the other Article. I received a Letter from Mr. Page two Days ago, informing me that Col. Peyton could procure 240 Stands of fine Arms at Baltimore for £190 ℔ Stand, which is much below the Price allowed for them in this State. As we are in Want of Arms, I desired that they might be procured, but the Difficulty will be to pay for them. I am told that the Corn at Cumberland is to be carried over to Richmond. May I take the Liberty of suggesting to you the Expence which will attend the conveying this Grain from Cumberland to Newcastle by Water, and from Newcastle to Richmond by Land. A Gentleman well versed in these Matters assures me that it will exceed £100 ℔ Barrel, and after all the Corn will be scarcely fit for Use. I have been under the Necessity of ordering two Flat-Loads of it down to this Post, which I am told is spoilt. I would also take the Liberty of suggesting another Matter to you, that is the Necessity of calling the Assembly. From disagreeable Experience I am convinced that the Defence of this Country must not rest on the Militia under its present Establishment. They have been so much harassed lately that they would give nearly half they possess to raise Regulars, rather than be subject to the Distresses they feel at leaving their Plantations and Families. We have been obliged to call out the whole of the Militia from several Counties, some of whom I have not been able to discharge for Want of Men to relieve them. I am order'd by Baron Steuben to keep in this Neck 1000 or 1200 Men, and were I to discharge the Men who were on Duty the last Invasion, which I confess they have a Right to claim, I should not have one third of that Number. Many of the paroled Men of Elizabeth City have taken up Arms, and others will do so if they can be supported. This I am about to do with a light Corps.

There are many things which the Service requires to be done, which cannot be effected for Want of Money. If the State of the Treasury will admit of it, I must therefore request that the Quarter Master be furnished with some. Mr. Brooke, who is going to Richmond for the Purpose of drawing Money for the Artillery, may be safely entrusted with it.

I am, with the greatest Respect, dear Sir, Your mo: Obedt. & very hble Servt., THOS NELSON. JR. B.G.

RC (PHi).
See TJ's reply under date of 25 Jan.; also John Syme to TJ, 27 Jan. 1781.

From Matthew Pope,

enclosing Proposals for Better Regulating the State Medical Department

HONBLE. SIR Richmond Jany: 22d. 1781

I have taken the liberty to inclose your Excellency Proposals for establishing, and Regulating a Medical department in this State;

which appears to me at this time absolutely necessary. It is first intended for your own perusal and afterwards to make such use of as your Excellency shall think fit; thus much I am well assured of, that for want of some proper regulations the State is daily, and hourly, imposed upon: besides Sir to my knowledge many of the Servants of the public in the Hospital department are suffering for want of pay long since due them; the orderly, his wife, and Negro woman at York, who have been in the Service ever since July last have never received one single shilling, but have lived on the borrow ever since: the same circumstance attends the orderly &c. at this place. These people (tho honest) when they find they are neglected will in time be tempted to help themselves. Negro's are hired at a very extravagant day pay which might be hired by the Year for a fourth part of the Money: necessarys are purchased in time of Invasion for the Sick at a much higher rate than they might be, and when purchased are often misapplied. Should your Excellency think proper to lay the inclosed proposal before the Honble. Members that compose your Board, and they with you concur in Opinion that such an Appointment is necessary, and think me capable and deserving of it, I shall be ready in a few days to proceed on my Duty. Your Excellency will pardon the method I have taken in conveying the inclosed when I assure you my only motive (knowing your multiplicity of business) was to give you as little trouble as possible.

I have the Honour to be with the greatest Esteem & Regard Your Excellencys Most Respectful Servt., MATTW POPE

ENCLOSURE

Proposals for the better regulating and establishing a Medical department in this State humbly submitted to the consideration of His Excellency the Governour and the Honble. Members of Council.

That there shall be one Surgeon in Chief whose duty it shall be to attend the main army wherever posted in time of Invasion and to make proper provision for the Sick and Wounded who shall also be Director General of all the Hospitals and have the power of Appointing the different Surgeons to the Hospitals, Orderlys Nurses &c. and shall have power to displace all such as neglect their duty and appoint others. The said Director General shall have the superintendence and Regulations of all the Hospitals, Visiting them as often as occasion may require, pay all Accounts appertaining thereto [and] shall have power to purchase Medecines and all other necessarys for the support of the said Hospitals subject to the controul and directions of the Governour and Council. He shall also have power to sell such medecines as may become perishable and all others which may be spared. That the Director General shall keep regular Accounts of all the Medecines, Stores, utensils &c., belonging to the said Hospitals and State and make proper returns of them at such periods as the Governour and Council shall direct. By adopting a mode of this sort general satisfaction would be given to the Officers and Soldiers. The sick and wounded would be properly provided for and attended to and if the Director General did his duty would certainly save the State a very considerable expence which is now daily going on for want of some such appointment.

That the Chief Surgeon and Director General shall be allowed Shillings hard Money per day with forage for Two Horses and a Ration for himself and Servant.

RC (Vi); addressed and endorsed. Enclosure (Vi); in Pope's hand.

There is no record in the proceedings of the Council that TJ submitted Pope's proposals for consideration. However, on 1 Feb. 1781 the following entry appears in the *Va. Council Jour.* (II, 282-3): "Major General Baron Steuben having represented the necessity of making provision for the Militia in case of sickness, the Board advise that during the continuance of the Militia in service a chief Surgeon be appointed to attend the principal encampment; to make proper provision for the sick, and wounded, to appoint deputy surgeons to the principal corps acting separately, and assistants if they be found requisite; that he also employ all necessary attendants for the sick and wounded, that for the present, particularly, he appoint a surgeon to attend General Lawsons camp; and that Doctor Galt be considered as acting under him at General Nelson's camp; that he furnish from the medicinal Stores of the State whatever necessary medicines they contain, and apply thro' the commander in chief for what may be furnished by the Continental Stores. . . . Doctor Matthew Pope is appointed chief Surgeon, he providing, at his own expence, some person to perform his Duties at Richmond, during his absence." Pope had been acting, up to this time, as director of the hospital established for the militia at Richmond (same, p. 274; see also Memorial of Matthew Pope, 2 Apr. 1781).

From George Slaughter

SIR — Louisville January 22d. 1781.

I wrote you by express the 19th instant giving an account of the news brought to us by a prisoner that made his escape from the Shawneese Indians; to which I refer you, the account brought by him is so well authenticated by the inclosed Letters and deposition that I've thought proper to dispatch another express, in consequence of which have also sent another Messenger to Fort Jefferson to meet Major Linctot with orders to the commanding officer there to supply him with all the ammunition that can be possibly spared from that post with safety. Every thing here seems to be in confusion for want of a Court to swear in the Militia officers, and am apprehensive as there are but 4 members in the Country at present it will be some time before there can be a Court. In the mean time every man sems to do all that which he judges best.

I have the honor to be Yr Excellencies Mo Obt Huml servant,

George Slaughter

RC (Vi); addressed; endorsed: "Majr Slaughters Letter inclosg Sundry others." Enclosures not identified; among them may have been two letters from Linctot to Slaughter of 11 and 13 Jan. 1781 (Vi; printed in CVSP, I, 428, 432).

From Charles Dick, enclosing Statement of His Services in the Arms Manufactory at Fredericksburg

Sir Fredg. 23d January 1781

I received your Excellencys favour of the 15th. and shall punctually observe your Directions in case of Appearance of any Danger of the Enemy. It seems to be the Wish of every body, they wou'd at this Time attempt to come this Way, and I verily believe they wou'd never get back again.

I never intended to resign the Business of the Factory, as I had such a considerable Share in it's formation &c., and the pleasure of it's thriving to such a Degree for the public Benefit, cou'd I [have] been, even but allow'd a bare Maintainance for my fidelity and Services; But, True it is! Such Ingratitude gall'd me, And it was Modestly termed a Resignation, when the true Cause was, Our being Meanly cheated (pardon the Expression) out of two Years Services, and no Redress; As your Excellency will observe by the inclosed Matter of Fact.

I am now providing and contracting for the proper materials, and Provisions for the Factory on my own credit and Interest, for no body will trust the Public a farthing; And, shall have more Honour to be under your Excellency and Council's Appointment and Directions, not doubting but I shall be Supported with Money to carry on the Business with pleasure, and Benefit to the Public; for which purpose, I hope to be in Richmond very soon; and have the Honour to be Your Excellencys Most Obedt. Humble Servt.,

Chas. Dick

ENCLOSURE

Col. Fielding Lewis and Chas. Dick were appointed by the Convention in 1775 Commissioners to Form, Establish, and Conduct a Manufactory of Small Arms at Fredericksburg without any Salery annex'd, as it was unknown the Trouble they might be at.

The first Year being 1776, They accomplished the same after much Trouble and Attention, in puting the Factory on an extraordinary good footing; for which the Honble. House allow'd them 10/ Day each, then, equal to Gold or Silver amounting for the Year 1776 to Each. . . . . £182.10. Although they thought it not Adequate to their Services, they acquiesced.

For the year 1777 they were allow'd the same, and as the Money had received no great Depreciation they said nothing.

The Year 1778. They were allow'd £300 Each, from which deducting the Depreciation as settled by Congress amounts only to . . . . £54.18.

The Year 1779 Allow'd £1000. Each, only worth . . 43.

We have done the Business effectually with the greatest Dilligence and Integrity, to the great Benefit of the Public, We think it very hard to suffer so much, as it has not been in our power to make a bargain for Ourselves. We hope, the Honl. House will at least take our Services for these two last Years into Consideration, and grant Us a full Recompence.

The Subscriber his Whole Time being taken up in that Service only, has greatly injured Him. CHAS. DICK

RC (Vi); addressed, in part: "favour Mr. Jas. Maury"; endorsed. Enclosure (Vi); in Dick's hand.

Among the Contingent Fund Vouchers (Vi), there is an order to the Auditors, dated 31 Jan. 1781 and signed by TJ, "to issue a warrant to Mr. Charles Dick (one of the Commissioners of the Gun manufactory) for twenty five thousand pounds on account." See also TJ to Dick, 7 Feb. 1781, and, for a general discussion of Dick's conduct of the Fredericksburg arms factory, Kathleen Bruce, *Virginia Iron Manufacture in the Slave Era*, N.Y. and London, 1930, p. 31-9.

From James Hayes

SIR Richmond Jany. 23d. 1781.

I am sorry to be troublesome, but must beg leave to inform your Excellency, that the Warrant you were pleased to favor me with this day, is by far inadequate to the expence of a Horse, Paper, and other Articles necessary to compleat the Printing Apparatus intended for the use of this State.

As it is not probable such another opportunity may happen a considerable time to come, I could wish to have such a stock of Paper on hand, as may enable me to carry on both the Public and Private Business of the state in an extensive, accurate, and expeditious manner.

I am, with respect, Your Excellency's most Obt. Servant,

JAMES HAYES

RC (Vi); addressed and endorsed. An order to the auditors, dated 23 Jan. 1781 and signed by TJ, directs the payment of £15,000 to James Hayes (Contingent Fund Vouchers, Vi). See also James Hayes to TJ, 18 Jan. 1781.

Proclamation Convening the General Assembly

By his Excellency Thomas Jefferson esqr. Governor of the Commonwealth of Virginia

A Proclamation.

Whereas it is become necessary that the General Assembly be called together before the time to which they stand adjourned: I have therefore thought fit with the advice of the Council of State to issue this my proclamation, hereby appointing the first day of march next for the meeting of the said General Assembly, at which time their attendance is required at the Capitol in the Town of Richmond. Given under my hand and the Seal of the Commonwealth at Richmond aforesaid this 23d Day of Jany in the year of our Lord 1781 and of the Commonwealth the fifth.

TH: JEFFERSON

Engrossed copy (Vi); in a clerk's hand, signed by TJ, with seal; endorsed: "Proclamation for calling the Assembly. Jany 23d. 81." Printed in *Va. Gaz.* (D & N), 3 Feb. 1781. Swem ("Va. Bibliog.," 7272) lists a separate printing of the Proclamation under an assigned date of 29 Jan. 1781, attributing it to Dixon and Nicolson, with a note: "No copy seen. 100 copies printed." The Sabin entry (100205) is taken from Swem. No printed copy of this Proclamation has been found.

The Assembly convened on 1 Mch. but adjourned to the following day, not having a quorum until then. It remained in session until 22 Mch. The Journal of the Senate for this session is not known to be extant in print or MS. The MS Journal of the House is in Vi. Not printed at the close of the session, and not included in the 1827-1828 reprints of the *Journals*, it was printed for the first time in Virginia State Library, *Bulletin*, XVII, No. 1, Jan. 1928.

Circular Letter to Members of the Assembly

SIR   IN COUNCIL, at RICHMOND, JANUARY 23, 1781.

I AM sorry, after so long and laborious a session of Assembly, the publick exigencies should be such as to call for an earlier meeting of the members than was intended. A proclamation has been this day issued for convening you on the first day of March; and though that alone was necessary in point of formality, I could not deny myself the apprizing you by letter of those circumstances which have rendered the measure necessary, and which could not with propriety be explained in the publick proclamation. Such is the load of publick debt contracted by certificates, and such the preparations necessary for the ensuing summer, to enable us to meet our enemies in the north, south, east, and west, that before any considerable progress was made in paying the past, and providing for the future, the whole sums allowed to be emitted were engaged. It became a matter of certainty that within a few days we should be unable to move an express, repair an arm, or do any other the smallest thing, though the existence of the state should depend on it, for want of money. It was impossible to think of hazarding the state in this condition through the months of February, March, April, and probably May, while we have an enemy within our country, and others approaching it on every side.

Information also from the General Officers brought us assurance that our defence could not be rested on militia. Not to mention other circumstances, such we are assured is become their impatience already, that they would give any consideration to raise regulars, rather than be kept in service themselves. Though the Commanding Officer has determined to reduce them to 2700 infantry, there will be considerable difficulty in keeping that number in the field. Men and money therefore will be the subject of your deliberations.

I make no doubt but some legislative aid may also be rendered necessary for securing the execution of the acts for recruiting men and procuring beef, clothing, and waggons. The absence of the militia from their counties has thrown very great obstacles into the way of the former, and the latter was ingrafted on that as its stock. The destruction of one of the printing presses likewise, and injury done the other, has delayed the printing the latter act with the other papers necessary to be sent out, till it is become certain the days of setting it into a train of execution will be past before it will be received. The zealous citizen, unable to do his duty so soon as was prescribed, will do it as soon as he can; but the unwilling will find much room for objection, which the authority of the legislature alone will be able to remove.

Not apprehending that the Assembly, when convened at so unusual a season, will propose to go on general business, I have reason to hope that you will be detained here a few days only. Besides the general despatch which will ensue your punctual attendance on the day appointed, let me adjure it on the ground of the publick distress, which will accumulate from day to day in the most rapid progression, should the meeting be delayed by failure of the members to attend.

I have the honour to be, with the greatest respect, Sir, Your most obedient, and most humble servant, *Th: Jefferson*

Broadside (DLC); signed by TJ; Swem, "Va. Bibliog.," 7273; Sabin 100203. Swem lists this broadside under an assigned date of 29 Jan. 1781, attributing it to Dixon & Nicolson with the following note: "No copy seen. 100 copies printed." The Sabin entry is taken from Swem. FC (Vi); at head of text: "Circular to the Members of the General Assembly."

This letter was transmitted with the Proclamation Convening the Assembly, preceding. INFORMATION . . . FROM THE GENERAL OFFICERS: See Steuben to TJ, 21 Jan.; and Thomas Nelson to TJ, 22 Jan. 1781. SECURING THE EXECUTION OF THE ACTS FOR RECRUITING MEN AND PROCURING BEEF &C.: See TJ to the County Magistrates, 20 Jan.; and TJ to Nathanael Greene, 16 Jan. 1781.

From Rowland Madison

[*Without place*] *23 Jan. 1781.* Has expended the £500,000 which was furnished him when he was appointed quartermaster and commissary to "the Expedition intended to be Carried into the Country beyond the Ohio"; needs £300,000 to complete his contracts, and the success of the expedition depends on ready supplies. Unless sum needed is furnished immediately, "Contracts will be Defeated"; begs that "any failieur, That may happen in Consequence thereof may not, after this notice, be Attributed" to the writer.

RC (Vi); 2 p.; addressed and endorsed.
See TJ to Rowland Madison, 23 Dec. 1781.

From George Muter, with Reply

SIR War office Jany 23d. 1781.

Colo. Southall requires that his house (wanted for Mr. Anderson's shop) shall be returned to him in the same order it was in when the state has done with it; and also, that the price for the tobo. shall be the current price at the warehouses at this place at the time of paiment, and not the price settled by the grand jury. Those articles agreed to, he is willing the house shall be immediatly made use of, and the rent valued. As his requisitions are different from the terms of agreement with others, I beg for your Excellency's instructions.

There is one Thomas Reynolds (who is near here) who has for a considerable time worked as a bricklayer at the foundery, and was lately down with the volunters under Colo. Southall; when the enemy were on their march to this place (I am informed he was assisting in the removal of the arms at the foundery) he was taken by the enemy on the road to Westham and took a parole. He hopes that his case may be considered as somewhat different from that of the people described in your Excellency's proclamation, and wishes it may be enquired into, from an expectation that he wou'd not be considered in the same predicament with them, but allowed to remain: his services wou'd at this time be very usefull. As the poor man is very uneasy, I must beg leave to sollicit for your Excellency's instructions respecting him.

I have the honour to be Your Excellency's Most hl servt,

George Muter. C.

In Council Jan. 23. 1781

The board have no objections to fixing the price of tobo. to be paid in rent at the market price here instead of the price settled by the grand jury, only taking care that the valuers be apprized of this circumstance. They agree also to leave the house in the condition it now is, noting this also to the valuers.

The case of Thomas Reynolds seems worthy of consideration. Will Colo. Muter be pleased to take and communicate to us authentic information of the facts.

Th: Jefferson

RC (Vi); addressed and endorsed; reply, in TJ's hand, written on verso of Muter's letter.

Southall's house: On 20 Jan. Muter wrote to Turner Southall and James Anderson, public armorer, informing them that the Council had agreed to rent Southall's house for one year for James Anderson's use, the rent to be settled by two impartial men in tobacco "in old Money at 20/ ℔ hundred for Tobacco, payable in the present Money at the price of Tobacco settled by the Grand Jury, at the valuation last preceeding the payment" (War Office Letter Book, Vi). thomas reynolds: Muter enclosed his report on Reynolds in his letter to TJ of 30 Jan. 1781 (first letter), q.v. On 10 Feb. 1781 a warrant was issued to Reynolds for his services as a bricklayer at the foundry (War Office Journal, Vi).

From the Virginia Delegates in Congress

SIR [Philadelphia, 23? January 1781]

It is with much concern that we have learnt from your Excellency's, and the Baron de Steuben's letters to Congress, the misfortunes our Country has suffer'd from the Invasion under the command of the detestable Arnold, and that he has ventured with impunity even to our Capitol. We have some reason to Imagine that the same plan of operations which induced Clinton to send him there will occasion him to remain in our Bay, and continue that alarm to our State and Maryland, which he has so successfully begun, in order to Harrass our Military, increase our expenses, waste our resources, destroy our Magazines and Stores when he finds it practicable; and by thus distracting us, prevent our sending the necessary succours to the Southern Army. This Sr, is a game we are open to at every period of our short enlistments, and in a great measure exposed to, for want of a militia organized to take the field, a few gunboats or Galleys, and some good fortifications in the most advantageous situations on our Rivers, for defence. But this late event has rendered this so obvious, that we are fully persuaded our Country will now see the necessity of adopting arrangements very different from what have been of late trusted to. We have been anxiously expecting to hear that some steps were taken at Rhode Island, in consequence of our application to the Minister, but it is more probable you will hear before we do, should that event take place, which we have spared no pains to have accomplished; and of this we have little doubt should it be found practicable. Nothing new has happened here since we last wrote.

The Judge of the Admiralty of this State has given us notice that there are three negroes, Tom, Hester and Celia, confined in Joal here, in consequence of a condemnation of the vessel in which they were taken. They say they are the property of a certain Money Godwin of Norfolk in Virginia; that their Master went of with the British fleet under Leslie, and gave them permission to do the same, on which they went on board the vessel in which they were taken. If on enquiry your Excellency shall find these facts to be truly stated, we shall with pleasure execute your instructions for securing the slaves for those to whom shall be adjudged.

We have the honor to be, with the utmost respect yr: Excelly's most obt & humble Servants.

MS not located. Text from *Calendar of Virginia State Papers*, I, 454-5, where it is printed with the letters of 23 Jan., but with date "January 25d" in the margin on p. 454 and "January 23d" on p. 455; this text was carelessly transcribed from the (now missing) original, and has the following caption: "Jas: Madison jr: and Theod Bland (Delegates) to Gov: Jefferson."

From John Broaddus

HIS EXCELLENCY
SIR Jany. 24th. 1781.

I have lately received information from Col: Thornton that Mr. James Warren at Fredericksburg requests that we may procure what Pork or Stalled beef we can, and send to him, for which he says a reasonable price shall be paid, and that he shall have the money in a few days. Since the receipt of which information I have applyed to several persons that I expected might have such articles to spare, but not one of them wou'd agree to let me have any, without I cou'd let them know what price they were to have. Therefore unless I am enabled to do that, I hardly think I shall be able to get either Pork or stalled beef, but if such prices cou'd be fixed as shou'd reasonably satisfie the people, I believe I shou'd succeed. I have been told that some Commissaries have lately given eight dollars per pound for stalled beef, and that some persons that have Pork to sell, hold it at three hundred Pounds per hundred, but as these prices are only hearsay, I cannot affirm it for a truth. You will therefore please to fix such prices as you think proper, and send me your directions by my son who waits on you with this Letter. And as I always have, so shall still continue to do my true endeavour to comply with your Instructions to the utmost of my power.

I am, Sir, your most humble Servant, JOHN BROADDUS
Caroline County

P.S. I have wrote to Mr. Brown on the above subject and have also acquainted him with the number of beeves that I have collected &c.

RC (Vi); addressed and endorsed.

From Nathanael Greene

SIR Camp on Pedee January 24th. 1781.

I congratulate you on the success of the detachment under Genl. Morgan. They were attacked by 1100 British troops under Lt. Col. Tarlton on the 17th. Inst. whom they defeated entirely and with very little loss. I must beg you will permit me to refer you to Major Genl. The Baron de Steuben for the particulars.

I have appointed Major Hyrne of the S. Carolina line Deputy Commissary General of Prisoners and have directed him to march all the prisoners to Charlotville. I beg your Excellency will please to give the necessary orders for their reception. Genl. Stephens has them in Charge.

I am With respect and esteem Your Excellency's Most Obedient & humble Servant, NATH GREENE

P.S. Unless the State of Virginia immediately begins to collect the magazines of provision on the Roanoke, we shall absolutely starve in this Country. N.G.

RC (PHi). Tr (CSmH).

This brief announcement from Greene relates to one of the most complete American victories of the war—Morgan's defeat of Banastre Tarleton at "the Cowpens" in South Carolina on 17 Jan. 1781. Tarleton was a brilliant soldier with a long record of combat experience dating back to the beginning of the Revolution, but Morgan, through a simple ruse whose object was to convey to the enemy the idea that the Americans were being put to rout, led the numerically larger force into a trap, turned its flanks with cavalry and militia, and killed or captured almost the entire body. Of Tarleton's force of 1,150 (opposed by 940 under Morgan, including Pickens' command), some 600 were captured and over 200 were killed or wounded (Tarleton and a small remnant escaped); the American loss was 72 killed or wounded (see Carrington, *Battles of the Amer. Revolution*, p. 542-6; Edward McCrady, *History of South Carolina in the Revolution*; and the sketch of Tarleton in DNB). See also Stevens to TJ, 24 Jan. 1781.

From George Muter, with Reply

SIR War office Jany. 24. 1781.

The building the boring mill and the moulding house for the use of the foundery, being a separate matter entirely from the other works to be erected near the foundery, I am of opinion it will be unnecessary to wait for the arrival of Colo. Senf before they are contracted for, more particularly as from circumstances, the same situation and walls must be again made use of, and those houses will be the first wanted.

I have reason to beleive, I can contract for having the boring mill (and perhaps the moulding house) built immedeatly, and the mill wright's work done. And if your Excellency approves of it, I will appoint people to meet me for that purpose on Saturday next.

I have the honour of inclosing a list of Mr. Harmer's negroes, all of whom he offers to hire to the State.

The negroes at Warwick, I shou'd suppose will be certainly wanted, but of that I am not fully able to judge.

The negroes said to be at the foundery (James is missing) will certainly be wanted, if the works goe on; this will be the case with those said to be with Mr. Moody; and I imagine the shoemaker at Mr. Rose's, indespensibly necessary.

I cannot positively determine respecting the women and children, but I think if the women will answer the purposes for which women are wanted, and they can be got at a reasonable price with their children, it will be well to hire them. Women are wanted to cook and wash for the tradesmen; this I think, tho' apparently in addition to the expence, will be found truely a saving, as the men will be able, if so provided for, to attend more closely to their work.

Joe, if he shou'd be brought back, I should think could hardly be kept, as he is so averse to living in this part of the Country; therefore it wou'd hardly be proper to hire him.

I beg leave to mention to Your Excellency that the Honl. Mr. Jameison, offers to hire some negroes to work at the Foundery. [I think] it will be proper to hire them, as they will most certainly be wanted.

Permitt me to observe to Your Excellency, that if Mr. Smith is successfull in engaging armourers to come in to work, that it will be necessary some provision shou'd be made for their accomodation, particularly in lodging. How that is to be done, I can not pretend to say.

I have the honour to be Your Excellency's Most hl servant,

George Muter. C.

Since writing the above Capt. Thomas is come into this office, and he says the negroes or others in their room, will most certainly be wanted. I have the honour of inclosing a memorandum from Capt. Thomas, of some negroes that formerly belonged to inhabitants of Norfolk, that he thinks ought to have been disposed of under the law concerning escheats &c.

In Council Jan. 24. 1781.

The board approve of building the moulding house and boring mill on contract. A water wheel and shaft for boring a single gun at a time will suffice; the shaft being made capable of having a cogwheel put to it whenever we shall carry on the business to such extent as to require more than one borer. It will be well to avoid agreeing to advance any of the money or as little as possible. We are of opinion the negroes should be hired if practicable for reasonable hire. As many armourers as can be received into the shop here should be lodged in log huts to be built here; all others should have log huts for lodging and working built at the Foundery. We shall be obliged to Capt. Thomas to give notice to the Eschaetor of this county as to the slave Pompey. TH: JEFFERSON

RC (Vi); addressed and endorsed; TJ's reply, in his own hand, is on address leaf. Enclosures missing.

MR. HARMER'S NEGROES: See George Harmer to TJ, 25 Jan. 1781.

From George Muter

[*Richmond, 24 Jan. 1781.* Minute in the Va. War Office Journal (Vi) under this date: "Letter, to the Governor inclosing Mr. Mattw. Andersons proposals; and informing that he refuses the proposals made him, in consequence of the order of Council." This letter and its enclosure have not been found, but see Muter to TJ, 20 Jan. 1781.]

From Edward Stevens

SIR Camp Hick's Creek So. Carolina Jany 24th: 1781

Genl. Greene I make no doubt, has by the same hand that this goes by, informed you of the Glorious stroke that Genl. Morgan has given Tarlton. It affords me so much satisfaction that I can't forbear repeating to you (what I expect he has done) tho' perhaps not so fully, I not haveing the same means in my power. Tarleton was Detached with about Eleven Hundred Men, about Three Hundred of that number was Cavalry the whole of which was British Troops, to attack Morgan, Who retreated before him for Two or Three Days 'till he got to advantageous Ground near a Place called the Cow Pens. And on the 17th Inst. he Halted and Determind to Stand and give Battle, altho' his numbers were not quite so considerable as his antagonist. Tarleton accordingly attacked and after some contest, Our People made a charge which imedeately broke the Enemy and threw them into such confusion that they were never able to rally again and were persued upwards of Twenty Four Miles. They had Killed on the Field upwards of One Hundred among which was Ten or Twelve Officers, and Wounded Between Two and Three Hundred. Besides, Five Hundred and Two Privates, with Twenty Nine Officers, were taken Prisoners with Two Brass Field Pieces, Eight Hundred Stand of Arms, Travelling Forge, Thirty Five Waggons And all their Baggage which was very considerable. This was done with a loss on our Side of only Ten Men Killed and Fifty Five Wounded. Among the latter number were Three Subaltern Officers all Virginians and Two of them belonging to the Militia, One of which is feared will Die of his Wound. In my former Letters I informed you what Troops Morgans Command was composed of. They in General behaved well, Tho it adds greatly to my Satisfaction, that the Detachment of Virginia Militia under the imedeate command of Triplett is spoke of with the greatest applause for their behaviour that day. This I hope will wipe off some of the stain of the 16th August. I am truly unfortunate as I could not partake in doing of it, And am rendered now much more so as I have not the Smallest glimpse of hope left of doing any thing in that way with those men who are here under my imedeate command, As their times are Just about expireing, And I am ordered to march in the morning to take charge of the Prisoners and Conduct them to Virginia. I must endeavour to reconcile myself to my hard Fate. Colo. Washington of the Cavalry Distinguish[ed] himself in a Particular manner. He with only Fifty Horse charged the Enemy's Cavalry and drove them. Among the Prisoners are the noted Majr. McCarty of the 71st. who has done so much mischief in this Part of the Country by Fire &c. He and Colo. Tarleton were the only Two Field Officers in the Detachment. The Latter got off with a Wound on his Arm. If our Army here was in a Situation to take the advantage of this Stroke, Oh it might be made very glorious. Cornwallis with his main Body are still in the neighbourhood of Winsborough. With every sentime[nt] of esteem and respect I have the honour to be Your Excellency's Most Obedt. and very hum: Servt, EDWARD STEVENS

RC (Vi); addressed, in part: "Hond. by Majr. Giles"; on the address-leaf Edward Giles wrote the following memorandum: "Major Giles presents his compliments to Governor Jefferson and begs he would excuse his omitting to deliver him this Letter. He was so engrossed with the Pleasure of imparting good News, that he lost his Recollection"; Giles had been in the battle of Cowpens as aide de camp to Morgan and must, therefore, have given TJ an engrossing account of the victory. Tr (DLC).

TROOPS in MORGANS COMMAND: The return of militia enclosed in Stevens' previous letter to TJ, 14 Jan. 1781, has not been located; for a list of commissioned officers from Virginia at the battle of Cowpens, see Burk-Girardin, *Hist. of Va.*, IV, 477. MAJR . . . MCCARTY: I.e., Maj. Archibald M'Arthur, in command of the British 71st regiment (Henry Lee, *Memoirs of the War in the Southern Department*, Washington, 1827, p. 172; W. C. Ford, *British Officers in the American Revolution 1774-1783*, Brooklyn, N.Y., 1897).

From John Todd

MAY IT PLEASE YOUR EXCELLENCY Lexington 24 Jany. 1781

I recd. the inclosed Letters a few days ago; as they contain some Matters of Consequence I transmit them just as I recieve them.

They are written with a freedom which spares no Character and may with additional Letters which I expect you have recd. throw light upon our Situation in the Ilinois. Winston is Commandant at Kaskaskia, McCarty a Captain in the Ilinois Regiment who has long since rendered himself disagreeable by endeavouring to enforce Military Law upon the civil Department at Kohos.

The peltry mentioned by Winston as purloined or embeazelled by Montgomery was committed to their joint Care by me in Novr. 1779 and from the Circumstance of Col. Montgomery's taking up with an infamous Girl, leaving his Wife and flying down the River, I am inclined to believe the worst that can be said of him. Being so far out of the Road of Business I cannot do the State that Justice I wish by sending down his case immediately to the Spanish Commandants on the Missisippi.

A late Letter informed your Excellency of my Design of laying some Beef and Corn in Store for the Expedition planned last year. I expect to get 30 or 40 thousand Weight of Beef and two or three thousand Bushels of Corn on Better Terms then will be got any where in this Country. A Prisoner, Martin Wistill, taken spring was a year at Wheeling by the Shawanese, two weeks ago left his party, being 7 Shawanese, about half a Mile from Bryants Fort as they were stealing Horses. He says the Shawanese have built 4 Block Houses at Logans Town 12 Miles beyond the Pickaway, that they are much Distressed for want of provision and are keen for making an Attack next Spring upon the Kentucky Settlements, that Blackfish and Logan are dead &c. I am uneasy lest Crockett should not arrive timeously at Licking and many of our Settlers seem desirous to fly immediately to the south side of Kentucky lest he should not.

Two Certificates to Wm. Grant and Israel Grant dated the 16th this Inst. one for 627 Bushels Corn the other for 80 were signed by Jos. Lindsay, Commissary, and Countersigned. I wish the payments to be delayed till further Information to the auditors.

I have the Honor to be with the greatest Respect your Excellency's Most obedient & humble Servant, JNO TODD JR.

RC (Vi). Enclosures: Richard McCarty to John Todd, "Cascaskia," 14 Oct. 1780, printed in CVSP, I, 379-80; Richard Winston to John Todd, "Kaskaskias," 24 Oct. 1780, printed in same, p. 380-2.

McCarty's letter to Todd, enclosed, expresses complete disgust with the management of affairs at Kaskaskia, especially the transactions of one Col. De la Balme, a discontented Frenchman; the letter further states that "we are become the Hated Beasts of a whole people by Pressing horses, Boats, &c &c, Killing cattle &c &c, for which no valuable consideration is given: even many not a certificate, which is here looked on as next to nothing." Winston's letter reports that

Montgomery has gone off, carrying with him "Large Quantities of Provisions, Boats deeply Loaden, besides Five Black Slaves, for all which the Publick fund has suffered," and has left no accounts of his transactions; that the goods purchased by Lindsay are now in the possession of Lindsay and the "Illustrious Captain Dodge"; that "this part of the world is too far from Government to call people to account before it is too late"; and that De la Balme was "received by the Inhabitants Just as the Hebrews would receive the Masiah." (On Augustin Mottin De la Balme's career in the West, see *Ill. Hist. Colls.*, II, V, *passim.*)

From John Winston

SIR Hanover Court House Jany. 24 1781

The Command of the Louisa Militia having devolved on me in Consequence of Lt. Colo. Fontains absense; the wretched State in which I found this Militia in point of Amunition and accoutrements obliges me to trouble your excellency with this application to know where we can be furnished. We have neither Cartridge Boxes, Cartridges, or even paper for that purpose and but a small proportion of Powder and Lead. As to Arms we are tolerably well furnished, but unless the other deficiencies can be supplied it will be utterly impossible for these men to act with effect.

There are many other deficiencies which I have not enumerated and for information I beg leave to refer you to Ensign Parker the Bearer hereof.

If we can be supplied from Richmond I will send a Waggon forward from this place, and order it to meet us in Wmsburgh (if not before) to which place I am ordered with all possible dispatch by Genl. Muhlenberg. I have the Honour to be with all respect Your Excellency's most obt Servant, JNO. WINSTON

RC (Vi); addressed and endorsed.

From George Brooke, enclosing Lists of Paid and Unpaid Warrants

SIR Richmond January the 25. 1781.

By the inclosed list it will appear what sum of money hath been issued and paid away of the last Emission, also the amount of balances due on several Warrants lodged in the Office and partly paid. Those two sums will exceed the sum I was empowered to Emit by the last Assembly. I have also sent you a list of Warrants in the hands of other People but I am well satisfied there are many more, as those I have mentioned are such as I coud recollect and in the hands of persons in or near this place. I shall be obliged to you for your direction with respect to the balance of the money I was to emit and any others you may think necessary to give. Your Excellencys most obedient Servant, GEORGE BROOKE

ENCLOSURE

Warrants unpaid lodged in the Treasury. vizt.

David Ross balance	2,351,376	
Wm Armistead do	140,970	
Stephen Southall do.	41,870	
Chas Irving	10,000	
Granville Smith balances	25,380	
Edward Carrington do.	18,380	
Nathl Irish do	25,325	
	£2,613,301	
Cash Emitted	£4,650,000	
On hand	930,000	
	£3,720,000	
Paid away of the October Emission		£4,836,000
Warrants in the Office and partly paid vizt		
Mr. David Ross. balance	£2,351,376	
Capt. Nathl Irish	28,035	
Colo. Edward Carrington	18,380	
Granville Smith	25,380	
Carter Braxton Assignee of William Armistead	27,735	
Stephen Southall	41,870	
		2,492,776
		7,328,776

Warrants in the hands of Sundrys vizt.

William Armistead	464,243	
Capt. Edmund Reade	36,600	
Josias Moffet	21,545	
Patrick St Lawrence	31,141.4	
James Hays	15,000	
Charles Thomas	20,000	
Samuel Bealle, abt.	200,000	
John Hay, abt.	100,000	
John Reveley	9,000	
Charles Dick	50,000	
		947,529.4
		8,276,305

RC (Vi); addressed; endorsed: "Mr. Treasurers Letter 25 Jany 81." Enclosure (Vi).

There are in Vi, classified as "Contingent Fund Vouchers," over 300 orders to the state auditors during TJ's governorship. Most of them are in a clerk's hand and signed by TJ, although some are entirely in TJ's hand or bear additional instructions written by him. Not all of these communications, which are, in effect, letters of TJ to the auditors, will be printed in this edition. Numerous as they are, the file is far from complete; and the chief value of their inclusion would be to reveal, in some measure, the overwhelming amount of "paper work" which the governorship involved. A conscientious effort has been made to print all of the vouchers having significance or else to give their substance in the footnotes of letters to which they relate (e.g., see James Hayes to TJ, 23 Jan. 1781). Many of the orders to the auditors which will not be printed are routine issues of funds "on account" to officers like those whose names appear in the above enclosure, e.g., DAVID ROSS, commercial agent for the state; WILLIAM ARMISTEAD, commissary of stores; STEPHEN SOUTHALL, Continental deputy quartermaster; GRANVILLE SMITH, state deputy quartermaster; EDWARD CARRINGTON, quartermaster general for the southern department; NATHANIEL IRISH, Continental and state commissary of military stores; and CHARLES DICK, commissioner of the gun factory (*Va. Council Jour.*, II, *passim*).

From William Davies

SIR Chesterfield Jany. 25. 1781.

I found upon my return hither that all the troops, that marched from hence upon the arrival of the enemy, had by order of Baron Steuben come back to this station, from their utter inability to keep the field, from the want of almost every species of cloathing. Many men have not a remnant of cloathing larger than a good napkin to cover their nakedness, and a number of these are dependent upon others for a part of a blanket to shelter them at night from the cold. Your Excellency, if I remember right, informed me at Westham, that a number of blankets could be procured from Mr. Ross. I must solicit your Excellency to direct me by what means and from what places they may [be] brought hither. I am the more anxious on this head, as all the coarsest of the cloth, which we had lately received from Mr. Armistead, was given out among the men as blanketting, which was the only expedient the late emergency would admit for rendering the troops in any degree fit for the field, to oppose the incursion of the enemy. This coarse cloth is not yet unfit to be made up into garments, but soon will be, unless the arrival of a supply of blankets shall enable us to put it into the hands of the taylors for that purpose. Could this be speedily accomplished, we might do a great deal towards cloathing our men, as we can easily turn out from 8 to 10 coats of a day. This we are now doing of the best of the cloth, which we reserved for this use. The want of shirts and shoes is another distressing circumstance, and I must beg your Excellency's attention to it. Unless some method can be adopted for supplying the men, they had much better be dismissed altogether; they are not able to do any thing in the field, and near 60 of them too naked to do any thing in quarters, and every idea of training them for actual service has long since been laid aside.

These must be unpleasant truths, but it is my duty to represent them. I hope my conduct is too well known to your Excellency to admit the idea that I have ever neglected any thing in my power to guard against or to remedy the distressful situation of the troops who have been entrusted to my command. Give me leave, however, to say that a mistaken system has long prevailed in the mode of cloathing our men. Saving and preserving is almost as important as supplying in the first instance. A shoe after soaling will last almost as long as it did before, and a coat properly patched is nearly as useful to the soldier as a new one. Yet we have nothing given to us for these necessary purposes of repairing, and of course instead of mending our old clothes we are always asking for new. It is out of the power of your officers to remedy these things without the assistance of the State. Another great misfortune is the manner of issuing the cloathing. A good pair of stockings is given to a naked soldier today; he has no shoes and wears them out by the next week, and in a fortnight afterwards when his stockings are gone, he gets his shoes; Or perhaps he gets breeches, but no lining to them; a new coat or a fashionable hat, but has no shirt, or if he has, he is without breeches. By this means the country runs into debt, and the soldier is always uncomfortable, and utterly devoid of that military pride of appearance, so essentially necessary in every army. At present, however, some immediate assistance is absolutely necessary to preserve the lives of these men. Some of them are so naked that they have refused furloughs to go home to try to get cloaths, being ashamed as well as unable in their situation to travel at this season. There never will be a possibility of preventing desertions till men find it more comfortable to be soldiers, than has generally been the case of the Virginia line, aggravated as their reflections must be, when they observe the comparatively happy circumstances of the troops from other states. I have of late been endeavoring to draw off descriptive lists of the deserters, of whom I have had returns; and am now at the 170th. As soon as it is properly prepared I shall forward it to your Excellency. I intend to propose to the General, to give furlows for a limited time to all the men now here that will enlist for the war, pay them a part of their bounty now, and the remainder when they return. As they can be of no service till they are cloathed, and provision is with difficulty procured, I hope this proposal will not be thought ineligible. In the mean time I would submit it whether it will not be necessary to order a quantity of leather here for the purpose of mending shoes: we have tools and shoemakers of our own. I would also request that some money might be spared to pay the taylors, who have for these five months past made up almost all the cloaths our men have had. They are much discouraged for want of it, and many of them think they are working for nothing.

I hope to be excused for my prolixity, but must persevere in my applications as long as there remains any prospect of success. The extra expence of calling an equal number of militia into the field, would go far towards fitting these men for service, who if properly trained, might have been very useful on the late occasion, but as matters now stand are only a useless incumbrance upon the country.

I have the honor to be, sir, with the highest respect, your Excellency's most obedient and most humble servt.,

William Davies

RC (Vi).

From George Harmer

His Excellency the Governor, and Council

Gentlemen Richmond January 25. 1781

Permit me to return you my most sincere thanks for your past favors, and believe me much concerned that I should have occasion to make any further application to you at this time: but as I am informed by my friends, that I could reclaim many of my Negroes on application to the parties who have purchased them, for which purpose it will require a considerable Sum: (I suppose not less than One hundred thousand pounds to regain One half of the number at the price they were sold for) and as it is not in my power to advance any part of the said sum, without your additional kindness, may I presume to hope you will please to add another obligation to those already conferred on, Gentlemen, Yr Most dutiful & Most Humble Servant,

Geo. Harmer

RC (Vi); addressed: "His Excellency the Governor & Council of the Common-Wealth of Virginia"; endorsed.

your past favors: By an Act of Assembly passed in the May 1780 session George Harmer, who had "left Great Britain in expectation of receiving" the estate of John Harmer, "but the same being now escheated and sold," was allowed maintenance, payable "out of the sequestered profits of the . . . estate," subject to the approval of the Governor and Council, until his case should be reviewed (Hening, x, 301). On his part, Harmer signed a parole agreement (MS, Vi; printed in CVSP, I, 356). An Act passed in the Oct. 1780 session directed that the slaves sold under the Act concerning Escheats be restored to Harmer, "now a citizen of this commonwealth," on 10 Jan. 1781 (same, p. 371). Payment was made to Harmer by a warrant of 20 Feb. 1781; see TJ to the Auditors under that date.

From James Hunter

Sir — Fredericksburg. 25th. January 1781.

I received in course your excellency's favour of the 10th. currt. with an intimation of the supposed design of the enemy to come this way, and your advice to remove whatsoever would be most exposed to their attempts.

I beg permission to return your excellency my best thanks for this your kind attention to my concerns, and for the early notice your letter conveyed.

In consequence whereof, I immediately caused to be transported to a place of safety, such of the articles at my works as were made for the public use: being the camp kettles, axes, &c. ordered by Gen. Greene; some of the same and other things designed for the state; and a part of my own effects.

And though, for this purpose, I had no occasion to make use of your excellency's permission to impress waggons, the assistance afforded me by those belonging to the public, together with the service of my own teams having proved sufficient, I consider myself nevertheless as obliged by it; as I am by the directions given to Gen. Weedon to take measures for the protection of my works, which were fully complied with.

But it gives me concern to acquaint your excellency that it is not in my power to repair any of the arms sent me by Col. Muter, whose letter accompanying them came to hand yesterday; my workmen in that branch having all left me, and the manufactory of small arms being, of consequence, discontinued; but the orders before given by the state for other matters are going on with all possible expedition.

I have sent, by the bearer, Mr. Dick, the warrant granted me on the treasury, some time ago, for £50,000; of which I have not yet received payment; but beg I may now, as the reasons for obtaining it, and which I had the honour to lay before your excellency still subsist with undiminished force; and as I have also certificates from Gen. Gates of the delivery of sundries, manufactures of my works, furnished during the course of the last summer, for the use of the army under his command, to the amount of, at least, £130,-000., a considerable part of which is due for workmen's wages, provisions &c.

I have on hand a parcel of coarse woollens, sufficient for the cloathing of 150 or 200 men, which I would deliver, if the state has occasion for them, and receive in payment tobacco, inspected at the warehouses of Fredericksburg and Falmouth; at the price of £50 per hundred weight. If this should answer, you will be pleased to appoint somebody to examine into the quality, and to fix with me the prices of these goods.

I have the honour to be, with the most perfect respect, Sir, your excellency's very obedient and very humble servant,

James Hunter

RC (Vi); addressed; endorsed.

From George Muter, with Reply

[*Richmond*] *25 Jan. 1781.* Some "eight months men" who work in the laboratory consider themselves cleared from service and are with difficulty persuaded to work; Muter desires to know how they shall be dealt with. Mr. Ford wishes to know whether the persons who are to work at the fork of the James are to be furnished with provisions by the state, or whether money is to be advanced "to enable the undertaker to purchase provisions himself." TJ's reply follows: "Jan. 26. 1781. No law has discharged the eight months men from service but that which allows them to enlist for the war. It seems impossible to decide whether we are to find provisions for the workmen till we know whether the work be done by ourselves or by undertakers. At any rate it will be in our power to furnish provisions to be allowed for in some way or other. Th: Jefferson."

RC (Vi); 3 p.; addressed and endorsed; reply, in TJ's hand, written on verso of Muter's letter. Tr of reply is in War Office Journal (Vi).

Mr. Ford: See George Muter to TJ, 22 Jan. 1781 (third letter from Muter under that date).

To Thomas Nelson

Sir — Richmond January 25th 1781

I gave orders to Mr. Brown to send you a Sufficiency of Flour to fill up any Intervals which might happen between your Supplies of indian meal. We think the Stands of Arms you have directed to be purchased at Baltimore are a great Bargain if they be really good and will certainly find means of paying for them. The Corn at Cumberland was Continental Property having been delivered to Colo. Finnie long ago. On the present invasion we had that with other Public Stores moved up to New Castle as a Place of greater Safety. The other Stores indeed we meant to withdraw to other Places: but not the corn. However I learn that our Quarter Master has in his Distress for that Article been obliged to send for some of it for his Horses here, and we have lately ordered a considerable Number of Public Horses too poor for Service to be carried and fattened there; by which means we shall save so much of it to the Continent. We have determined to convene the Assembly on the first Day of March. The Printer will enable us to send out the Laws which require immediate Execution this week. I make no Doubt but by that Time you will have received either from their Counties or from Baron Steuben so many of the Militia meant to be retained as will enable you to discharge the others. Indeed the Baron Steuben means to reduce the number originally intended to 2,700 Infantry which will enable him to send back those of a greater Number of Counties. With Respect to the Paroled Men my sentiments are these. Had I unwarily entered into an Engagement which the Laws of my country would not permit me to fulfill, I should certainly deliver myself to the enemy to cancel that engagement and free my personal Honour from Imputation. Nevertheless if any of them chuse to remain and to perform freely all legal Duties, I do not know that Government is bound to send these People in to the Enemy. It is very different from the Case of a military Officer breaking his Parole who ought ever to be sent in. We deny the propriety of their taking Paroles from unarmed farmers. But as in any event the only justifiable Punishment of a Breach of Parole is Confinement, so should the enemy hang a single man for this Cause, we will instantly retaliate by hanging their Prisoners in equal number. This may be declared to the paroled men who you say are ready to take Arms. Mr. Granville Smith received yesterday a warrant for £20,000 for the contingent expences of your Camp, to be called out only on your order. As the money Press is not yet at work it will be some Days before he will get it. T.J.

P.S. Mr. Brown just informs us of your Application for Spirits. There is not a Hogshead belonging to the State, but very great Quantities are in the Hands of the Continental Commissaries. I have special Returns of upwards of twenty thousand Gallons delivered them by the Commissioners of the Provision Law, and no

Doubt great Quantities of which there is no return. As on actual invasions all reasonable expences are Continental, you are undoubtedly authorised to call on their Commissaries, or should you have a Doubt Baron Steuben will clear it up. A Mr. Lyon one of those Commissioners [Commissaries] at York can certainly supply you. I would observe to you that Baron Steuben informed me in Conversation that Spirit would not be allowed as a Part of the Daily ration but only on particular Occasions. T.J.

FC (Vi). THE PAROLED MEN: I.e., those who had accepted paroles from the invading British army; see TJ's Proclamation concerning Paroles, 19 Jan. 1781.

From the Officers of the Berkeley County Militia

SIR Berkeley County. Jany. 25th. 1781.

Colo. Swearingen the Leiutenant of this County laid before us some time ago, your Excellencys orders of the 24th. of December directing Two Hundred and Seventy five of the Militia of this County under proper officers to march Immediately to the falls of the Ohio, to join Colo. Clarke in an Expedition from thence. We beg leave to represent to your Excellency, that we have Seventy men now on duty from this County in the Southern army, which with the 68. we are to raise for the army, and the 275 now ordered into service, will make near one half of the Militia of this County fit for duty. From these Circumstances and the immense distance from here to the falls of the Ohio, being by the way of Fort Pitt, little less than a Thousand Miles, we are sorry to inform your Excellency that we have the greatest reason to beleive that those whose Tour it now is from this County will suffer any punishment, rather than obey our orders for their march. So general an opposition to orders of Government from such a number, we think of too much consequence at this Crisis, for us to proceed without informing your Excellency, of the difficulties with which the execution of those orders will be attended. We beg leave further to inform your Excellency that notwithstanding the great reluctance the People in General discover in complying with this order of Government, yet there are many young men in this County who having connections in the Kentucky Country, woud turn out as Volunteers on such an Expedition were they assured that they have no prospect of enriching themselves with the substance of a number now calld as Militia who would give every thing they have to a Substitute rather than undertake such a Tour. Would your Excellency therefore dispense with the Militia on this occasion and impower us to raise Volunteers we think it woud be in our power to procure such a number of men as would render their Country greater service on such an Expedition than the Two Hundred and seventy five taken from the Classes of the Militia. We wish your Excellency to beleive that it is exceedingly disagreeable to us to delay for a moment the Execution of your orders, but we flatter ourselves your Excellency will, upon examining the Gentleman who will deliver you this, fully Justify us. We have the Honour to be Yr. Excellency's most Obt. Hble servts.,

PHIL. PENDLETON Colo. 1st. B.M.
JOHN MORROW Colo. 2nd. B.M.
ROBERT CARTER WILLIS L. Colo. B.M.
WILLIAM MORGAN L. Colo. B.M.
GEO SCOTT. Majr. 1st. B. B.M.

RC (Vi); addressed, in part: "favd. by Majr. Hunter."; endorsed: "Berkeley Militia Letter Feby 81."

COLO. SWEARINGEN: Josiah? Swearingen (or Van Swearingen), county lieutenant of Berkeley from 1777 (Gwathmey, *Hist. Reg. of Virginians in the Revolution*). See TJ's reply, 16 Feb. 1781.

To John Winston

SIR Richmond January 25th 1781.

I am very sorry that your Militia by different Orders from a Succession of Persons should have been harrassed with marches to so little purpose. It was not intended by us that they should be called on at all. When I learnt however that they were come into Duty and were at Hanover Courthouse, I thought it best for them to join and remain with General Nelson till he should receive the Militia of those Counties meant to be retained in Service. As I expect Baron Steuben the Commander in chief to be here to Day or tomorrow, I do not chuse to give you any other order but to remain where you are until I shall have consulted with him and determined what you are to do, so as to save you any future unnecessary marching. As soon as this shall be settled between us, I will send you orders by express. TH JEFFERSON

FC (Vi).

To William Davies

SIR Richmond January 26th 1781

As for the outer Clothing for the Soldiers there is no early Prospect but from the 1495 yards of Cloth sent you some Time ago. We purchased 100 or 150 Blankets and 400 Pair of Stockings of Mr. Ross whom I desired in Presence of an Aid of Baron Steuben's to deliver them to the Order of the Baron. And the aid (Major Walker) promised to notify the Baron of this. There are some Blankets (perhaps 100) included in a Purchase from Mr. Braxton not yet come from York River. They shall be sent to you. Mr. Armistead will deliver to your order as much Linen as will shirt all your men if you can have it made up. Four hundred Shirts have been lately provided by Mr. Duncan Rose on Application from Baron Steuben. These should be first applied. Mr. Armistead has about 100 pr. of Shoes here which he will deliver you and being offered 100 pr. at Petersburg he is sending an Agent to make the Purchase who will call on you on his return and let you know where they lie. We expect a Couple of Waggons from Charlotsville with Leather. If you will let me know in Time what may suffice for mending Shoes, we will endeavour to spare it. Mr. Armistead has now some sole Leather which he will deliver you. I should suppose the shreds which might be saved by the Taylors would go far towards mending Cloaths. However it would be œconomy even to cut from the Pieces of the Cloth for this Purpose. Oznabrigs and Thread for the same Purpose shall be furnished you whenever you chuse to send for it. I join you in disapproving the Issues of Clothing by Piece meal and would wish it remedied as far as our Circumstances will admit. If you will state the Sum of money which will do to keep your Taylors in Spirits we will endeavour to have it furnished as soon as the Printer can resume the operation of emitting.

TH JEFFERSON

Cloathing which according to what precedes you either have or may have: 400 Suits of outer Cloathing (being the 1495 Yards of Cloth sent you) 400 Shirts from Petersburg what is deficient from hence. 100 pr. of Shoes from Petersburg. 100 pr. Do. from hence. 400 pr. Stockings from Mr Ross. From 200 [to 300] blankets, part now at Petersburg, the Rest at York River, Leather, Oznabrigs thread for mending from hence.

FC (Vi).

This letter was evidently sent to William Armistead, commissary of stores, who transmitted it to Davies on 27 Jan. with the following note (Vi): "The bearer will hand you a letter from His

Excellency the Governor, and is proceeding on to Petersburg to procure with the assistance of Mr. Elliott or King One hundred Pair of Shoes for your Troops, whether they can be had or not he is to call on you upon his return from hence to let you know. About 100 Pair more of Shoes may be had by application at Warwick to Mr. Anderson."

From John Pierce Duvall and James Neal

SIR January 26th 1781

In Consequence of a Commision to us Directed for a Justing and setling the Claimes to unpatened lands in the district of Monongalia, Youghagania and Ohio, the tenth day this Instant was appointed for proseeding to business, with a full Expectation that Col. Francis Peyton and Capt. George Meriweather would attend, but they have not yet arived, whereby the Business is detered and a great Uneasyness Created in the people under an apprehention that the limited time by law will Expire and there lands be liable to be taken by Treasury warnts agreable to the terms of the Commonwealth's land office. Therefore have requested us to send an Express to your Excellency preying that those two gentlemen may be removed and that Charles Martin and William Hayman Esqs. may be aded to the Commision whereby they hope that the Business may be done befor the Limited time Prescribed by law should Expire.

We are Your Excellencys Most Obedient Hubl. Servants,

JOHN PIERCE DUVALL
JAMES NEAL

NB Sir,

Whereas we have been under the Necessaty of paying the Express hope your Excellency will Give him an order on the Treasury for the sum of one thousand Eight hundred dollars being the sum agreed for.

JOHN PIERCE DUVALL
JAMES NEAL

RC (Vi); addressed and endorsed.

COMMISION . . . FOR A JUSTING AND SETLING THE CLAIMES: See the Bills for Establishing a Land Office and for Adjusting and Settling Titles, printed above under 8-14 Jan. 1778. On 5 Feb. the Council took the following action: "Charles Martin and William Hayman Esquires are appointed Commissioners for settling the titles of Claimers to unpatented Lands in the District of Monongalia Yohogania and Ohio, instead of Francis Peyton and George Meriwether Esquires, who have failed to undertake the execution of the said duties. Provided nevertheless that if the said Francis Peyton and George Meriwether shall have attended the execution of their said Office, before the said Charles Martin shall have qualified to this Commission, then the same shall become void; and if the one or the other only of the said Francis Peyton and George Meriwether shall have so attended, and the other failed, then this Commission to be void, as to the said William Hayman" (*Va. Council Jour.*, II, 286).

From Nathanael Greene

SIR Jan: 26th. 1781.

This will be handed by Lt. Colonel White who I have ordered to Virginia to compleat his Regiment. I must entreat your Excellency to give every possible assistance to forward so important a piece of business.

General Stephens [Stevens] marched his Militia yesterday for Virginia. I cannot do justice to my own feelings without mentioning to your Excellency the good order and regularity which was established by the General among his Militia. I hope I shall not again be under the necessity of discharging men from the State of Virginia on account of their short enlistments. But should the Militia be ordered into service in future perhaps no person could command them with more propriety.

I am With respect and esteem Your Excellency's Most Obedient Humble Servant, N GREENE

FC (MiU-C); in clerk's hand; endorsed: "To Govr. Jefferson Jan: 26h. 1781. Exd." Tr (CSmH).

From George Muter, with Reply

SIR War office Jany. 26. 1781

As the armoury at the foundery will probably be built on a different plan, from what was originally intended, when I contracted with Colo. Richd James, and, as he wishes to be clear of that contract, I have this day agreed with him that it shall be void.

Colo. James is willing still to work for the public, and will furnish plank and scantling deliverable at the fork or the foundery as may be wanted, but before he contracts he wishes to be fully informed of the manner in which he can *fully depend* on being paid. I have acquainted him with the mode that is adopted as far as it respects the value of the money, but I am unable to inform him of the time when he can rely on being paid, as I am unacquainted with the resources the state is at present possessed of, and the manner of applying these resources that has been adopted by the supreme executive. I have promised Colo. James to inform him (if possible) on Sunday, and must beg for information from your Excellency on that head.

I have the honour to be Your Excellency's most hl Servt,

GEORGE MUTER. C.

I do not suppose any considerable sum of money can be paid till after the meeting of assembly. TH: JEFFERSON

RC (Vi); addressed and endorsed; TJ's reply, in his own hand, is written below Muter's letter.

On 29 Jan. Muter wrote Richard James (Tr in War Office Journal, Vi), quoting TJ's reply in full and adding, "It is probable that but little money can be advanced before the meeting of the assembly, but that probably will be of no inconvenience as the meeting is so near."

From Thomas Nelson

[*Williamsburg*], *26 Jan. 1781.* Eight British vessels have been driven ashore, four of which it is supposed will not be gotten off again. The greatest advantage cannot be taken of their distress because the vessels are on a coast chiefly in British power.

MS not located. Text abstracted from an entry in Anderson Galleries, sale catalogue, 19-20 Jan. 1926 (James H. Manning Sale), lot 407; a 1-page A.L.S.

To the Virginia Delegates in Congress

GENTLEMEN Richmond January 26th 1781.

I shall now beg leave to answer your Letter of the first inst. which inclosed a Paper from Baron de Arendt. Mr. William Lee was some Time ago invested with a special Agency from this State, having received however no instructions from him of his having engaged any other Person to transact any Part of it, we are uninformed as to his Stipulations with Baron de Arendt. If he has left the particular one for twenty five Louis unfulfilled we think ourselves bound to discharge which we will do in such Sum of paper money as may purchase that quantity of hard money in Philadelphia, for there being no hard money here, there is no fixed exchange. If you will therefore settle this Sum with him we will make the Remittance either in money or by answering a Bill, or otherwise, as shall be most practicable. After a variety of Trials to effect the cloathing of our Troops and procuring of military Stores and failing in them all, a particular Institution has been adopted here for those Purposes. Into this Channel all our means must be turned to enable it to be effectual. Our Situation is too well known to suppose we have any thing to spare. It is therefore not in our Power to enter into the Commerce with Prussia proposed by the Baron de Arendt, however desirous we are of opening a Communication with that respectable State and willing under every other

Circumstance to effect it by great Sacrifices, were Sacrifices necessary. Should the Subject of Prussia chuse to adventure on Private Trade with our Citizens every Facility and encouragement in our Power will be certainly afforded. As the Speaker Harrison sets out within three or four Days for Philadelphia and can so much more fully explain to you by words the Steps taken for supporting our Opposition to the common enemy, I shall decline answering that Paragraph of your Letter and beg leave to refer you to him.

TH. JEFFERSON

P.S. We have no Letters of Marque left. Be so good as to send us some by the first Opportunity.

FC (Vi). This letter was conveyed to Philadelphia by Benjamin Harrison and was answered by the Delegates on 13 Feb. 1781, q.v.

From Arthur Campbell

SIR Washington Janr. 27th. 1781

Since writing my Letter of the 15th: Instant I am informed that the Indians have killed one of the settlers in Powells Valley and carried off 14 Horses belonging to a party of Men coming from Kentuckey. Whether this is done by Indians that had set out to War before our approach were known in the Towns; or it may be some of the Fugitives that have taken refuge in the adjacent Mountains for the conveniency of good Hunting to subsist their Families on, is not certain. Which ever it may be, this with their former successes near the same place, may encourage them to attempt further depredations, and so render the passage to Kentuckey exceeding unsafe. To prevent this, and to seek satisfaction for what is past I am raising a Company to patrole the Country adjacent to the Gap, and to begin the building the Fort your Excellency formerly ordered: and in order that our men may be well provided for the pursuit, I have taken the liberty to direct one half of the Company to act as Cavalry until the decision of the Executive is known respecting them. This Company with two Troops of Horse now a raising in Carolina to act on that frontier I hope will be sufficient to repel any force the Cherokees are now able to embody, should they be excited to continue the War. The method of impressing and appraising Provisions as directed by the Invasion Law, I believe will enhance its price much; could an industrious trusty man be found that would act as a Commissary great savings might be made, by having ready money. The Cherokee War, and other occurrences seems to have put an end to the raising Men in this, and Montgomery County to go to the Southward with Colo. William Campbell. The Botetourt men are gone on with the Major of the Regiment.

I am Your Excellencys Most Obedient Servant,

ARTHUR CAMPBELL

RC (Vi); addressed and endorsed.

From John Syme

SIR — New Castle 27th Jany 1781.

Having Several Matters to lay before your Excellency, I fully intended to Have Waited on You Yesterday; My indisposition prevents me, and I Know not Certainly when I can go Out.

Reflecting on the Business of Moving the Stores and from a thorough Conviction of being Right, as to Not Water bearing them, I wrote the Inclos'd Letter to Mr. Claiborne; He being on a Jorney, I immediatly Communicated the Same Sentiments to Mr. Watkins; You Have His Answer, by which you Will find it is Necessary, to Confirm what I Have Done, under Considerable Expence. I mean not this to Save Myself Trouble; If it is Desired, I will finish Here, and then proceed to the Same at Cumberland. The Prices of Waggonage and Freight &c. I am at a loss precisely to Ascertain, but Most Surely, the Removal of every bble Corn, Will be upwards of One Hundred Pounds, Under the present Plan, from Cumberland to Richmond. The large guns, More than four Hundred to this Place; How much from Hence to Your Town, or WestHam Can't Say; But Nearly Double what it Would be on my Plan which would loose me storage but Effect it Sooner, by far, than to bring them up this River. My Only Meaning is to transact these things with Propriety.

In consequence of your Message, by Mr. Granville Smith I sent You Sundry Expresses, which Hope Have been with You 'ere this, and Could Have furnish More but My Militia Were mostly Out. I Have Received a letter from Genl. Nelson to forward (as I understand it) One Half of the Men of this County to Him. Pray was not the Idea of Your Board only a fourth to remain in Service? I suppose the Same as to the Baron.

I can Scarcely set up, to Write, which Hope will Apologize for this Scrawl. I Have the Honor to be, Sir, Your Mo: Obedt. Servt,

J SYME

RC (Vi); addressed, in part: "By Waggon Master Cawthorn"; endorsed. Enclosure: John Syme to William Claiborne, dated "New Castle, 24th Jany. 1781" (Vi), in which Syme remarked: "In the two last Conversations I had with Governor and Council on the Subject of Waggoning the Stores to James River, forwarded to my Care by you, He was Pleas'd to Refer them to my Management. I Dare say you will think with me, that it does not quit Cost, to Water Bear Corn, Oats, &c. and be at the Expence of taking out of craft, Storage, and Loading Waggons Here, for Richmond, it being not much farther by Land from Cumberland to that place. . . . For the same reasons that Govern as to the Grain, will it not be proper to Carry the Artillery of Every Kind, from Cumberland by Land, as the placing them in, and taking out of Craft, I find both Difficult, and very Expensive."

YOU HAVE HIS [WATKINS'] ANSWER: Syme's letter to Watkins (missing) was acknowledged by John Watkins on the same day in a letter now in Vi dated "Cumberland 25th. Jany. 1780 [1781]." In commenting on Syme's communication, Watkins added: "I am at a loss what to say respecting the removal of the Country Stores from this place. I waited on his Excellency the 14th Instant at Richmond and his orders then was to have all the Stores removed to N. Castle with all possible expedition. As he did not ask me any questions respecting the expence attending such removal, I thought it would be forward in me to give my opinion about it. N. Castle I conceive wou'd be a more secure place than this. But the expences will be great of removing the Stores. A Waggon I suppose would make a trip from this to Richmond nearly as soon as from N. Castle, the distance from hence not being more than 4 Miles farther than from N. Castle. I am also told by the forage master that all the grain at this place will be wanted for the use of our Army below, in a short time. They make use he tells me of 120 barrs. per Week. I have sent about 1900. bus. to them already by Order G. Nelson. It is not my wish that the Country Stores should remain here, unless it should be the pleasure of the executive, for the Stores may be an object, that may induce the Enemy to come this way, and perhaps do me more damage than I may ever be able to repair. These Vessells are now at this place waiting for loads and in the morning I intended to begin to dispatch them. However, I will wait tomorrow for farther Orders and those I would wish to have from the Governor and Councill as I have these orders to deliver the whole." See Nelson to TJ, 22 Jan. and TJ's reply, 25 Jan.; also TJ to Syme, 31 Jan.; Syme to TJ, 1 Feb.; and TJ to Syme, 2 Feb.

From Robert Lawson

SIR Camp McKee's Mills Jan. 28th. 1781.

Hearing that the Enemy were again in our Country, and had penetrated as far as Richmond; I consider'd it as my duty to wait on Baron Steuben, who I was informed was at Petersburg, and recieve from him such command and orders as he was pleas'd to give.

The Baron thought proper to give me the command of a Brigade of Militia; and has after several previous movements, fix'd me as the Officer commanding the advanced Posts. As I am informed that he has repair'd to Richmond to communicate to the Executive body, the situation of our military affairs, I doubt not but that he will fully explain the motives, which induced him to take the positions, which the advanced Army now occupy. But lest the

Baron, from the multiplicity of business which surrounds his command, may not immediately recollect some material things respecting the Post which it becomes my duty more directly to attend to, I beg leave to trouble your Excellency with a state of such matters as my situation requires me to lay before you.

From it's being the fact, that this part of the Country has always been the scene of the incursive, and predatory war, which the Enemy has carried on in this State it follows, that the Inhabitants have been greatly distressed in the Article of Provision and forage and that our Army finds it a matter of great difficulty to procure the necessary supplies in this quarter. Having no money to purchase necessaries for the Army, and the mode of obtaining them by impressment only, renders the undertaking not only difficullt and dilatory but in every point of view, very disagreeable to the Officer, whose Authority must sanctify the procedure: but as the exhausted State of our money matters makes this mode (disagreeable as it is) indispensibly necessary we must prosecute it. I would wish however to suggest to your Excellency, that as Troops must be kept up in this quarter, to countenance desertion; give protection to the well affected; and prevent the Enemy from forageing extensively; that it is proper that we should have Magazines of Provision, and forage, established in such parts of the adjacent Country as may be least expos'd to the consequences of a quick movement of the Enemy, and so convenient to our Posts below at the same time, as to enable us to draw from thence the wanted supplies, without great delay or Expence. Major Newton who is kind enough to be assisting in this disagreeable business waits on your Excellency for your decision on the occasion, and he will give you such further information as you may require, especially as to the Places where Magazines can best be fix'd on.

The next object which I would wish to trouble your Excellency with is the diminished State of our Cavalry. Altho' a number of Gentlemen turn'd out as Volunteer Cavalry at the commencement of the Invasion, and have render'd all the service they could while on duty; still as they were mostly from Chesterfield, and the Militia of that County being reliev'd, they have claimd the right of being discharged also, and have gone to their respective habitations. Those who remain are not bound to stay any certain fix'd time, and may therefore insist whenever they please to be discharged. I need not comment on the inconvenience, and possibly mischief, which the Troops under my command might be expos'd to on this account. The Enemy are already strong in Cavalry; and they are moreover seizing upon the likely Horses in their reach, and augmenting this strength daily. Major Nelsons Horse, which are also under my command, do not amount to thirty men fit for duty; and both the Horses, and Men, are really, in general, objects of distress—The Men suffering for want of the Cloths, the Horses being so reduced as scarcely to be able to perform the duty of carrying their riders in a very moderate pace. To remedy this I would wish to suggest that if the Executive was to authorize raising of Volunteer Horse, it might in my conception be readily accomplish'd under a plan some what like this—They should chuse their Officers (under the rank of Field Officers) find their own Horses, Saddles, Bridles, Boots, and Caps, if to be procured, and be compell'd to serve for the space of six Months at least, should the Invasion continue so long; and be subject to the like Rules and Regulations in war, as govern the Continental Troops. On behalf of the Public they will furnish those who can't supply themselves with Pistols, Holsters, Valeesces, Pads, Swords, Caps, and Halters and pay a generous price for the Horses lost. Should this plan be carried into effect, I would beg leave to recommend the Officers who are now in service, as worthy of the confidence of their Country and whose active Zeal entitle them to hold military commissions in its service. I should imagine that this Country could easily subsist a body of Cavalry amounting to 150, or 200. Confident am I, that such a body properly equipt would render this Country essential services —indeed an Army laying near an Enemy who has a superior force in Cavalry must be ever subject to their insults, and very frequently to great injury.

I must close this Letter with a representation of the state of the Troops in this quarter; which must be distressing indeed to every friend to the present opposition, whose Heart is not callous to the feelings of Humanity.

We have no Tents; and are posted where we cannot have the benifit of Houses. The severity of the Season coming on daily, The Baron order'd us to build Hutts: but this cannot be done without proper Tools, and those we have not as yet been able to procure, altho the Quarter Master has been empower'd to impress them for this particular purpose. Indeed it is a lamentable fact that we have not as many Axes as are essentially necessary for the purpose of cuting Wood to make fires for the Men, who are decreasing my strength daily by sickness, occasion'd I am confident from their expos'd state to the severity of the excessive bad weather we have had in this quarter.

We want exceedingly ammunition Waggons, with proper military Chests, Cartridges, and almost every article of Camp Equipage. I am far from believing or expecting that the Stores on hand will yield ample supplies of those articles: but I trust Your Excellency will give the proper orders to supply the Militia under my command with whatever may be necessary to conduce either to their comfort or defence.

I have the honour to be with the greatest respect, Sir, Your Excellencys Mo. obedt. Servt., RO: LAWSON. B.G.M.

RC (Vi).

To the Auditors

In Council Jan. 29. 1781.

The Commonwealth of Virginia Dr. to A. Willy for Candells for the use of the Councill Chamber for Sealling Land pattens and Comisians &c. from Septem. the 1st 80 till December the 18. 80

	£30–0–0
to Cash Paid for [. . .] Coall	12–0–0
to do. January the 24	12–0–0
	£54–0–0

These services were performed on requisition of the Executive

TH: JEFFERSON

N in Contingent Fund Vouchers (Vi); TJ's confirmation of the account, in his hand, is on verso of invoice; endorsed.

From Theodorick Bland

DR. SR. [Philad]elphia Jany 29th. 1781

A French officer of the name of Dubuisson a Colonel in our Army and formerly aid to the Baron Du Kalb who was wounded in the Action near Cambden and taken Prisoner, has requested me to enclose the Contents of this to Your Excellency, which will fully explain his desire. Your Excellency, will be pleased to do in the affair, what you think Justice, Humanity and Policy dictate, and will be so obliging as to give as speedy an answer as circumstances will permit. I have the Honor to be Yr. Excelly's most obedt. & very H: Servt, THEOK. BLAND

RC (Vi); addressed: "His Excelly. Thos. Jefferson Esqr. Govr. of Virginia. Free Theok: Bland"; endorsed by a clerk: "Colo. Bland proposing an Excha. of Colo. Duby-song for Lt. Colo. Hamilton." Enclosures: (1) Dubuysson to Bland, Philadelphia, same date (Vi); (2) copy of a letter from Joshua Loring, British commissary general of prisoners, to Dubuysson, New York, 5 Nov. 1780 (Vi); (3) copy of letter from Abraham Skinner, Continental commissary general of prisoners, to Dubuysson, without place or date but written after 8 Nov. 1780 (Vi).

The proposal of DUBUISSON (Charles-François, Chevalier Dubuysson des Hays) that he be exchanged for Henry Hamilton was declined by TJ; see his reply to Bland, 9 Feb. 1781, and also George Washington to Abraham Skinner, 8 Nov. 1780 (*Writings*, ed. Fitzpatrick, XX, 324-5). On the Hamilton case generally, see TJ to Bland, 8 June 1779, and references there.

From Archibald Cary

HONORABLE SIR [29 January 1781]

I have calls on me which I must in a Few days comply with, for £16000 or thereabouts for my proportions towards raising the 3000 men. Mr. Rubsarnen Informs me he has a warrant on his and my account for about £40.000. He informs me, he has been apply'd to Worke over a Quantity of Powder taken out of the Canel. This Powder will require a large Quantity of Salt Peter, which without ready money can not be had. I assure you I have it not in my power to advance it, nor even to Pay the money for the Soldiers without receiving this Warrant, nor can we purchase Salt Peter, or even undertake the repreration of the Powder without it. This money has Great part of it been due a considerable time. Application has been made at the Treasury without effect. I hope therefore your board will give order that it be paid, as I shall think it exceeding hard to sell two or three Slaves to raise the money for the Publick, when the Publick owes me more than would answer the Demand on me. What I have due for Provisions, nigh £18.000 I wish now to have paid, as with it I design to pay as far as it will go, my Taxes.

I am Sir, with great Esteem Your Hble Servt.

MS not located. Text from *Calendar of Virginia State Papers*, I, 471, where it is printed without place or date among the letters of 29 Jan. 1781. This is a manifestly inaccurate transcription from the (now missing) original.

MR. RUBSARNEN: Jacob Rubsamen (see Rubsamen to TJ, 1 Dec. 1780). On 30 Jan. 1781 the Council requested the treasurer to emit, from the amount authorized by the Assembly, various sums to be applied as directed, among them, "twenty five thousand pounds to be applied in part paiment of a Warrant issued by the Auditors the 25th instant in favor of Mr. Jacob Rubsaman" (*Va. Council Jour.*, II, 281).

From Richard Claiborne

Sir Richmond. 29th January. 1781

I inclose your Excellency a Copy of the Arrangement proposed by Colonel Carrington and myself, and approved of by the Council, for the Quarter Master's Department in the Continental Line of this state; also a Copy of the prices established in Specie equal to Tobacco at Twenty Shillings pr. hundred weight, or other money equivalent; and a return of the assistant Deputy Quarter Masters.

Your Excellency will find that the state is now laid off into certain districts calculated for the Convenience of transportation both by Land and Water. Each District Comprehends a Certain number of Counties which are apportioned According to the Situation of the Principal Posts, and are to be under the influence of an assistant Deputy Quarter Master.

Among the duties of this department transportation is one, and is a heavy branch of business. To enable us to Answer the demands of the Service in this respect, your Excellency and Council were pleased to say, that the private property Waggons in the Senatorial Districts, should be thrown into Brigades and be under the derection of the Agent of the State for collecting the Supplies, to be called out to the aid of the Continental Quarter Masters, when the business of their office should render it necessary for them to apply.

By an Extract from the Journals of Congress I find that the Assistant Deputy Quarter Masters and Store keepers are to receive the Supplies from the state Agents, both in the forage and Commissarys line, and to have Store houses provided for their reception.

The Arrangements respecting these two points directed by Congress and the Legeslature of Virginia are so nearly conected that I feel myself interested in a very particular manner, that there should be a full explanation of it between the officers of my Department, and those of the line of State Commissioners. I beg your Excellency therfore for Copies of all the directions which have been issued or are intended to be issued from the Executive, to the state Agent which effect the business to be done between each Department, since it was commenced by Colonel Carrington and myself.

Upon a faithful discharge of the duties of the State Commissioners in a great measure depend the existance of the business under my direction. Collecting the Supplies from the Country, and furnishing the means for transporting them, are great and important objects, and demand Unwearied diligence in those employed to do the business. As a well-wisher to the Interest of my Country, and desirous to Answer the trust reposed in me, I have to beg your Excellency that you will veiw me as Acting from a Zeal to promote the Public Service; and to impress your officers with an Idea of the Necessity of meeting me and my officers in our endeavors. I hope we shall always be found willing and ready to join and assist in any Measure that may be calculated to give Success to the business.

One cannot proceed without the other, and from repeated assurances of my assistants I can venture to say they will perform their part.

I did myself the honor the other day to lay before your Excellency, a state of the Wages of persons to be employed in this Department, established in Specie or Tobacco or other Money equivalent by Colonel Carrington and myself, which met with your approbation. As this Matter is to be refered to the Quarter Master General I beg that the Executive will give their assent that it does not exceed Strict Justice to the Public, agreable to what is given generally, in this Country. I have enquired particularly of several Persons who are well Acquainted with the different Occupations Mentioned in the Estimate, and am well Assured that men cannot be had for less who will work willingly or do the business properly.

In carrying this Arrangement into operation I experience considerable delays in some points from the late distruction in the Press at this place. I have applied frequently to the Printer to have some Copies taken of the new plan from Congress for the Quarter Masters Department, but he is prevented by business from the Executive and the Acts of the late assembly. As the assistants cannot possibly go on without the System, I beg your Excellency to give directions to have it printed immediately.

I beg your Excellency for a Warrant on the Treasurer for half a Million of Pounds to be delivered to my Draughts as the Service of the Department under my direction may render necessary.

I have the honor to be With great respect and regard Your Excellencys most obedient Humble Servant, RD. CLAIBORNE
D.Qmr.S. Virga.

RC (Vi); addressed and endorsed. Enclosures: Copy of a Plan for the Quartermasters Department, printed above under 1 Jan. 1781; the copy of the prices established in specie and the return of the assistant deputy quartermasters have not been located.

See TJ to Claiborne, 3 Feb.; Claiborne to TJ, 7 Feb., and TJ's answer, 7 Feb. On 5 Feb. Claiborne informed Timothy Pickering that he had accepted the post of deputy quartermaster for Virginia and enclosed "a Copy of the Arrangement for this state made by Colo. Carrington and myself, and approved of by the Executive" (DNA: RG 93).

To Benjamin Harrison

SIR Richmond January 29th. 1781

Several matters of Public Importance resting on the Hands of the Executive to be transacted to the Northward, we beg Leave to avail ourselves of your Journey thither to get them settled, being satisfied they may be much better done on your verbal representations than by anything which may go in writing from us. The Trade has been carried on to a very small extent between this State and the Bermuda Islands. This was begun under a resolution of Congress permitting the exportation of a certain Quantity of Corn from this State to Bermuda. We required the Bermudians to come for it and to bring a bushel of Salt in exchange for every two of Corn. Our Distress for salt[1] increasing we continued the License and in the last Summer gave three Bushels of Corn for one of Salt. Some Tobacco also was allowed in exchange. But few vessels (I think not more than half a Dozen) have come on that Business. Whether the number may increase or not I cannot Say, but I think the Trade necessary and could wish its Continuance without Umbrage to Congress or the French minister. A Trade with vessels reporting themselves as from Neutral Ports but in truth as we believe from Ireland has also been winked at. This is more exceptionable on the Part of the States and their Allies and less advantageous to us. We have indeed received occasional Supplies of Cloathing from them, but we might have bought on nearly as good Terms in America and thereby avoided risking the mischiefs which may attend the Permission of Irish Importations. Should our Commercial Agent be Successful in his endeavours to supply our future Public wants, this powerful reason for tolerating the Trade will be removed. There will then remain no other Inducement to it, but as it will increase the quantity of goods imported into the State, but whether the Advantage be great or small we will willingly place this Commerce on whatever general Footing shall be thought requisite for the Good of the States and their Allies.

The removal of the Convention Troops was determined on by the Executive on the invasion of this State which took Place in the last Fall and was effected as to the British Division about 800 in Number. The Germans 1400 in Number being thought less dangerous were permitted to remain till Accomodations could be provided for them in Maryland. Congress having afterwards directed that they should not be removed and our Assembly that they should, the Executive are placed in a very disagreable Situation: we can order them to the Banks of Potowmac, but our Authority will not land them on the opposite Shore. Besides prohibiting the removal of those remaining here they have required us to furnish half the Provisions for those gone to Maryland. I beg leave to refer you to my Letters to the Board of War and to Governor Lee on this Subject a Copy of which is furnished you from whence you will see the grounds on which I have remonstrated against this latter Requisition and on which I should have remonstrated against the former also but that I wished to avail myself of your more forcible representation in Person.

A Mr. Patoun of Baltimore sent us some Cartridge Boxes. They were brought in a vessel of Mr. Braxtons to Annapolis where the vessel being sold they were left and I have heard nothing of them since. I must beg the Favour of you to get them brought on if possible. Any supply of the same Article as also of Cartridge Paper and Flints which the Board of war can send on are essentially wanting.

Penet & Co. of France sent us a quantity of Stores in a vessel called Le Comite. She was taken on her Passage, retaken and carried into Rhode Island where on Condemnation the one Half of our Part of her Cargoe has been decreed to us. I take the Liberty of putting into your Hands the Papers on this Subject. Our Delegates have been endeavouring to have them brought on but hitherto without Effect. The Salt indeed had better be sold there, but the Arms, Clothing and other Articles are so much wanting that we should be much obliged to you to adopt an effectual mode of having them brought hither immediately either by hiring a trusty Agent to go and bring them in waggons, attending them himself, or in any other way you find most practicable and expedient. Congress being considerably indebted to us in the Article of Powder I lately wrote to desire from five to ten Tons to be sent to this Place. It is essentially necessary that we send four tons more to Fort Pitt and that it be there by the 1st Day of March. The State with which you are furnished of our Advances of Powder to the Continent will inform you how far we have a right to make this Call. I must trouble you to procure from them at Baltimore if possible and if not then at Philadelphia the four Tons before mentioned and to send them under a trusty Person in waggons to Fort Pitt to be delivered to the Order of Colo. Clarke or other Person acting under him, the Residue or as much of it as can be got should be brought here at Continental Expence.

FC (Vi). Enclosures: Copy of TJ's letter to Thomas Sim Lee, 15 Jan. 1781; papers relating to the cargo of *Le Comité*, not certainly identifiable but see Samuel Nightingale to TJ, 22 Nov. 1780; Statement of Arms and Men in Service, 29 Jan. 1781.

YOUR JOURNEY: On 2 Dec. 1780 the House of Delegates "proceeded to consider the resolutions which lay on the table, for representing to Congress a state of the war in the south, and calling for aid from our sister States or European allies." The first resolution requested the Virginia delegates in Congress to move that a full representation of the situation in the South be placed before the French and Spanish governments. The second was passed in this form: "That the General Assembly will appoint some proper person to lay before Congress a clear state of the war in this quarter, the resources of this State in men, money, provisions, clothing, and other necessaries, and to solicit the necessary aids either from our sister States or European allies, and to concert with Congress, the minister of France, and General Washington, the proceedings necessary in the present conjuncture of affairs in the south" (JHD, Oct. 1780, 1827 edn., p. 35). Joseph Jones, a member of the House, gave a more intimate view of the aims of the Assembly in a letter to Madison, 2 Dec. (*Letters of Joseph Jones*, Washington, 1889, p. 59). The plan of a special envoy to Congress did not please Madison, who thought it expressed little confidence in the Virginia delegates in Congress; see his letters to Jones, 12 Dec. 1780, and to Pendleton, 16 Jan. 1781 (Burnett, *Letters of Members*, V, Nos. 540 and 610). But on 14 Dec. the resolutions passed, and on 22 Dec. the Assembly elected Speaker Benjamin Harrison to carry out the mission (JHD, Oct. 1780, 1827 edn., p. 51, 65, 76). Various delays kept Harrison from setting out, and he did not arrive in Philadelphia until 11 Feb. (TJ to Huntington, 15 Jan.; Harrison to TJ, 12 Feb.). On 13 Feb. a committee of six members of Congress (including Madison) was appointed to confer with Harrison; on the 15th the report on TJ's letter to Huntington, 15 Jan., respecting the Convention troops, was referred to the same committee; on the 19th the committee delivered in its report; and on the 20th the report was read and a series of resolutions was passed (JCC, XIX, 142, 148, 160, 176-8). Harrison on 19 Feb. reported fairly optimistically to TJ on the status of his mission; see his letter under that date. The principal measures agreed on by Congress were that (1) "the southern army be composed of all the regular troops, from Pensylvania to Georgia, inclusive," with a few exceptions; (2) that 400 wagons be procured and furnished for the southern army; (3) that the Board of War be ordered to furnish the southern army with 10,000 suits of clothes and various other military supplies and munitions in proportion; (4) that the executives of Delaware, Maryland, Virginia, and North Carolina concert plans for provisioning the southern army and for transporting the provisions procured. Copies of part of these resolutions were enclosed in Huntington's letter to TJ of 20 Feb. 1781. No action was taken on the important question of removing the Convention troops still in Virginia, but as a result of an appeal by Harrison to Pres. Huntington, 22 Feb. (Vi; printed in CVSP, I, 533-4), Congress resolved on 24 Feb. "That the Convention prisoners, now in Virginia, be removed into some State more northerly, and that the Board of War have them immediately put in motion for that purpose, and continue their march by the way [of] Knowland's ferry, until the farther order of Congress" (JCC, XIX, 193). See also Harrison's letter to Washington, 16 Feb. (Vi; printed in CVSP, I, 523-4), which was not answered until 27 Mch. because Washington had been conferring with the French commanders in Newport (Washington, *Writings*, ed. Fitzpatrick, XXI, 380-3); Washington was somewhat cooler than Congress to the Virginia proposals.

[1] The copyist wrote "Corn"; this has been corrected (in TJ's hand?) to "salt."

From the Officers of the Greenbrier County Militia

SIR Green Briar 29th. January 1781

A Letter from your Excellency of the 24th of December directing that 137 Men of the Militia of this County shou'd forthwith be raised and sent to the County of Kentucky to join Colo. Clarke, and serve under him this ensueing Summer on an Expedition against the Indians in Consequence of which We have given orders to Draft that Number together with Proper Officers to Command them, amounting to 146 effective Men; so large a number out of a Militia scarcely 550 strong lying in a County exposed to the daily inroads of the Indians, fill[s] us with much uneasiness about the dangers we are like[ly] to suffer from this weakening of our Militia, especially at a time when we cannot expect to be reinforced from any of the interiour Counties, shou'd any such danger arise. How much more then must our apprehension of Danger increase when we find that by an Act of Assembly we are to furnish 34 Men More for the Continental Army. It is with the utmost reluctance we address ourselves to your Excellency on this occasion (at a time when the necessities of the State require the utmost exertion of its members in its defence) to request that you will Prolong the Term in which we are to furnish said recruits, till the return of o[ur] Militia from Colo. Clarke, or at least till such time as [the]y have got into the Indian Country and may have drawn their attention to his operations. Assure yourself Sir we wou'd not have made this request but in consequence of the intreaties of the inhabitants here and the imminent danger to which we think these frontiers exposed, by thus drawing away the Militia. We shall continue to use all means to have the Militia ready as speedily as Possible, shou'd you think it improper to grant our request.

We are Sir Your most Obedt. Hble Servants,

ANDW. DONNALLY
SAML BROWN
ANDW. HAMILTON

RC (Vi); addressed and endorsed. See TJ's reply, 17 Feb. 1781.

Statement of Arms and Men in Service

[29 January 1781]

		Muskets in good repair	Muskets out of repair	Bayonets fitted	Cartouch boxes
1. How many arms have we in the state fit for service, bayonets &c.	In the magazines	68.	2273	159.	161.
	In the hands of the troops embodd. (to be retd to magazine)				
	Dispersed in counties much exposed	3315.			

2. How many have we lent N. Carolina since the war. How many since the invasion of S. Carolina	This shall be answered under Qu. 4. because we consider what have been sent Southwardly as sent into Continental service.

3. What stock of ammunition & military stores of all kinds have we in hand?

With what has N. Carolina been furnished?

Return of powder in the States magazines Nov. 20. 1780.

	Musket	Canon	Incertain which	Total
Fit for use	17,900℔.	16,200℔.	6,419℔.	40,519℔.
Wanted remanufacturing	3,980	3,000	5,780	12,760
Total	21,880	19,200	12,199	53,279
Destroyed by the enemy, as nearly as we can find & to be deducted			10,000	
				43,279

1779, Sep. 25. lent to Congress 22,960℔. powder of which perhaps 10,000℔. was their own 12,960
1780. June. 30. delivered to Colo. Finnie for the Southern service 10,000
22,960

The accounts of other ammunition sent to N. Carolina from the state magazines are among the papers lost. The fixed ammunition is remembered to have been somewhat short of 100,000 cartridges. How much more loose ammunition is not remembered.

4. How many arms had we from Congress? Were they complete stands? How many have been furnished Congress since the war?	Arms (most of them complete stands) carried into Continental service by		
	The 3d Virginia regiment	627	
	4th.	515	
	5th.	270.	
	6th.	673.	
	2d. state regiment	416	2501.
	Colo. Porterfeild's detamt. sent to S.C. 1780	200	
	Harrison's artillery	25	225
	2d. 10th. & 12th. none.		
	The 1st. 7th. 8th. 9th. 11th. 13th. 14th. 15th. & 1st. State from which I have no returns (forming an average from the 3d. 4th. 5th. 6th. 2d. State, & the 2d. 10th. & 12th. from which I have returns) may be supposed	2812.	2812
	Sent to S. Carola with Colo. David Mason in 1779.	1000	1000
	Sent to S. Carola with Genl. Scott's new levies in 1779.		
	Sent to N. Carolina in 1780. 2200 rampart arms & 1775 muskets & bayonets	3975	3975
	We received of Continental arms in 1779, one half of which were rampart arms	5000	
5. How many tents, or tent-cloth & other camp necessaries have we?	We had 230 tents in November last. They were delivered for the use of the militia & state troops during that invasion. After the invasion 75 were sent on with Colo. Green's corps; some were reserved for the troops at Chesterfd. C. H. and the rest are in use with the state troops & militia now in the feild in this state. We have not at present a sufficient number of camp-kettles, but very shortly shall have. We were disfurnished of our canteens by the militia which went to the Southward, and now have very few.		
6. What prospect have we of supplies of the above? Also blankets & cloth for Souldier's clothes?	We have no prospect of any supply of tent cloth. Camp-kettles we have it in our power to procure from Hunter's works. There are provided for the men at Chesterfeild C. house 400 suits of clothes, 400 pr. stockings, 200 pr. shoes, 800 shirts, & 200 blankets. The deficiency we have no means of providing, nor yet a single article for Colo. Buford's corps. Colo. Taylor's regiment is unclothed and no prospect of our cloathing them. Our Captives in Charlestown are in extreme distress, which nothing will enable us to relieve unless we could get permission to send tobacco to them.		

7. How many men have we in the feild? and how many that cannot act for want of necessaries? & what are their principal wants?

	for the war	for less terms, or terms not specified	Total
Gibson's regiment at Fort Pitt Sep. 22. 1780	61	117.	178.
Capt. Heath's company at F. Pitt, no return beleivd about		30.	30
Taylor's regiment of guards. Dec. 1. 1780		260.	260.
Colo. Harrison's regiment. no return but said to be about	60		60
Colo. Buford's command (cannot act for want of clothing)	500	500	500
Colo. Green's command	400	400	400
at Chesterfd. C. house	500	500	500
Gibson's State regiment (including Brent's 30. men) Jan. 22. 1781	182	40	222.
White's & Washington's horse. no return, but said to be about		300.	300
Majr. Nelson's horse		94.	94.
In captivity at Charlestown. May. 12. 1780		1392.	1392.
Militia in service in Carolina. Jan. 13. 1781		991.	
Militia in service in Virginia, to be reduced to		2700	

Summary view of this.

	In the Feild.	In Captivity	Total
Regulars	2544	1392	3936
Militia	3691		3691
Total	6235	1392	7627

8. What stock of provision. What are our resources, & expectations as to them.

I hope we shall be able to purchase about 3000 hogs. The act of assembly will furnish 3000 beeves. We have engaged 10,000 barrels of flour & can engage more if necessary. The returns of short forage under the specific tax the last year amounted to about 100,000 bushels, and I suppose may be reckoned the same this year. Whatever more may be wanting, can be procured under the provision law. We shall be

	very far short of the Continental demand in spirits & salt. The pork, beef, & flour abovementioned excludes what we are now consuming.
How far are you advised as to the wants of N. Carolina?	I have not the least information.

MS (Vi); entirely in TJ's hand. Endorsed: "Lre Speaker Harrison Jan. 29. 1781." Another MS (DLC: Washington Papers); in a clerk's hand, signed and dated by TJ: "Jan. 30. 1780."

Neither of the MSS has a caption, but the endorsement on MS (Vi) indicates that it was among the papers enclosed in TJ to Harrison, this date; and the presence of another copy, dated 30 Jan., in the Washington Papers, indicates that these data were also sent to Washington. The following minute appears in the War Office Journal (Vi) under 29 Jan. 1781: "Gave in to the Governor, a return of the State Garrison regiments and a list of the Officers; a return of Arms issued for Continental use and to the Militia &c., a return of the made up ammunition and lead on hand the 29th. inst. of November, and a return from Capt. Irish with remarks on some of them where it was necessary." The returns submitted by Muter, which have not been identified, were evidently requested by TJ in order to prepare the present document.

From Sampson Mathews

Cabin Point, 29 Jan. 1781. When at Ruffin's Ferry on 22 Jan., Mathews received orders from Gen. Muhlenberg to march to this point by way of Sandy Point, and "being detained three days there by wett, and Badness of the Boats," arrived this morning. Has been ordered to march tomorrow morning to Smithfield. Expected on his arrival to be supplied with tents and ammunition, but was disappointed; is sending Capt. Robert Gamble to request that "thirty six tents, one of which to be Large For myself and field officers and one For the Staff Department," be sent to Smithfield "without Loss of Time, as many of the militia are already Sick for want of Tents"; has issued his warrant to impress them or linen to make them. Is afraid the men will mutiny because the "march is So Severe" and the "duty on the Lines will add To the fatigue." Needs a surgeon and hopes Dr. Foushee—or, if he refuses, some other good surgeon—will join the rifle corps as soon as possible. The smith's tools and files have not arrived; hopes they can be sent at once because many of the rifles are out of order.

RC (Vi); 3 p.; partly illegible; addressed, in part: "Pr Capt. Robert Gambell"; endorsed.

To George Muter

SIR In Council Jan. 29. 1781.

The habitual drunkenness of Colo. Warneck renders him in the opinion of the board unfit to be longer trusted with the execution of the duties of an engineer. Should he chuse (on your intimating this to him) to resign, the board are disposed to give him what assistance they may justifiably: otherwise it becomes necessary that you take proper measures for trying him by a proper court in order to reduce him. I am Sir your very humble servt. TH: JEFFERSON

RC (Vi); addressed and endorsed.

COLO. WARNECK: Frederick Warneck (or Warnick) had been appointed "Engineer for the Service of this Commonwealth" on 18 Oct. 1777 (*Va. Council Jour.*, II, 12). About this time he fell into the hands of the enemy and gave a parole, the validity of which TJ questioned; see TJ to Steuben, 17 Feb., and proceedings of Council, 20 Feb. (*Va. Council Jour.*, II, 297).

From George Muter, with Reply

[*Richmond*] *29 Jan. 1781.* Encloses a certificate concerning payment of which the quartermaster wishes instructions. [*Reply:*] "Our Quartermaster is not to pay this difference. We have nothing to do with it. I think he had better take his remedy at law to obtain a just price. Th: Jefferson."

RC (Vi); 2 p.; addressed; endorsed: "Letter to the Govr. respecting the Q: Mr. applying to me about a Certif. from S: Southall. Jany. 29th. 1781." Reply, in TJ's hand, written below Muter's letter.

A minute in the War Office Journal (Vi) under this date records this letter as follows: "Letter, to the Governor respecting a certificate of Mr. Southall for additional waggon hire, which he expected the State Q: Mr. was to pay."

From George Muter

[*Richmond, 29 Jan. 1781.* Minute in the War Office Journal (Vi) under this date: "Letter, to the Governor respecting the issuing spirits to the Officers and Soldiers in the State Service, and an order enclosed for a hogshead of rum to be delivered Francis Graves, to be issued to the Officers, Soldiers, tradesmen &c. if he approves of it." Muter's letter and its enclosure have not been located. TJ's reply is dated 31 Jan. 1781, q.v.]

From George Muter

[*Richmond, 29 Jan. 1781.* Minute in the War Office Journal (Vi) under this date: "Letter, to the Governor inclosing Mr. Harmer's proposals for hiring his Negroes; and informing that I think the hire Mr. Jameson asks for his negroes reasonable." Muter's letter and its enclosures have not been located. On 1 Feb. Muter wrote to George Harmer: "I am informed by a member of the Council that your offer has been rejected by the Board, because they think the hire you ask for your Negroes *considerably too high*" (War Office Letter Book, Vi).]

To David Ross

SIR Richmond January 29th. 1781

As it will be necessary that every Proposition relating to the trading Department should in future be referred to you, I take the Liberty of inclosing the within extract to you. I am to desire with Respect to this as well as every other one to be sent you hereafter that you will not consider our Transmission of them as ever amounting to a Recommendation to enter into Treaty on them. If you shall think them worth no further notice, you will take no further notice of them. If otherwise you will do on them what you think best.

TH JEFFERSON

FC (Vi). Enclosed "extract" has not been identified.

On 23 Jan. the proceedings of the Council record that "Mr. David Ross having been desired to undertake the Office of commercial Agent, and having been in the exercise of that Office from the twenty seventh day of December last; The Board advise that his appointment be now entered, and be considered as having taken place from the said 27th day of December one thousand seven hundred and eighty" (*Va. Council Jour.*, II, 278). The commission was not sent to Ross until 2 Feb.; see TJ's letter to David Ross of that date.

From John Christian Senf

Richmond January 29th. 1781.

The Battery, which is to be errected upon Wind Mill Hill below the Old Battery at Hood's, according to the Plan, proposed by the Major General Baron de Steuben, will consist of Eight 24 or 18 pounder[s] and defended in the Rear by a strong Redoubt for Sixty Men and four or two Field pieces, mounted in the Angles in Parapet. A Barrack in the Center of the Redoubt, sufficient large for the Guarrison. The Magazines for Amunition and provision under the Barrack. A good Revettment, Ditch, Draw Bridge, Glacis on the Outside, and will be secured by all kind of Impediments, as Palisades, Abbatties, Wolftraps and Fougasses.

The Time, in which to execute the Worck, will depend on the Number of Labourers, Season and of furnishing the necessary

Materials. If the Worck is to be compleated in two Months time, it will require

Labourers

1 Master Carpenter and	With their necessary Tools
3 Carpenters	
1 Master Bricklayer and	
3 Assistants	
2 Blacksmiths	
—	
10	

40 Able Negroes as Pioniers furnish'd with
- 40 Spades
- 20 Hoes
- 10 Pick Axes
- 20 Axes
- 20 Fashine knifes
- 10 Wheel Barrows
- Some Trooing Lines and some Nails.

Materials

560,000 Bricks, which may be had near about Hoods from the Inhabitans, and the Guarrison may replace them again next Spring, without any further Expences to the Country.

82	12 Inch Timber, 22 feet long		May all be procured near Hoods.
45	———, ———, 30 ———		
8	———, ———, 10 ———		
600	8 Inch Palisades, 12 feet long		
200	Inch Bords ———		

A few Waggons or Boats and a few Necessarys for the Plattform, Draw Bridge and Joiners Worck may be easy furnish'd, in time the Main Worck is carried on.

An Addition of a Detachment of Soldiers at present in the Field, will finish in proportion the Worck the sooner.

JN. CHRISTN SENF
Coll. Engineer

RC (Vi); endorsed. Though there is no indication of the recipient of this letter, the endorsement is like that on other letters received by the executive at this period; it was probably first submitted to Steuben and by him transmitted to TJ.

See Steuben to TJ, 11 Feb., and TJ's reply, 12 Feb. 1781.

To Steuben

SIR Jany 29. 1781

I send you below a List of the Counties which were called on to make a part of the 4000 men for this invasion, tho' they were called into the field on the last invasion also. As your reduction of the 4000 to 2700 will enable you to discharge some of those Counties, I think it would be best that these below mentioned should be first discharged.

I have the honor to be with great esteem Sir Your mo: ob: & mo. hble Servt., TH: JEFFERSON

Amherst, Albemarle, Fluvanna, Goochland, Powhatan, Amelia, Brunswick, Dinwiddie, Chesterfield, Henrico.

Note. Rockbridge, Augusta, and Rockingham were also called down on the former invasion: but I apprehend it will not be proper to discharge them.

RC (NHi); in a clerk's hand, signed by TJ; endorsed. FC (Vi).

To John Banister

SIR In Council Janry. 30th. 1781.

I inclose you a letter from Colo. Meade, one of Baron Steuben's aids, by which you will perceive that a Mr. Hill of your county while commanding at Hood's has seized a work ox from a person in that neighbourhood contrary to the express orders and regulations of the Baron; it is further said that this violence was accompanied with insult which rendered it more injurious. While the public necessities oblige us to use force, for the supplies of our army, it is our duty to lay the practice under strict rules, to guard it against oppression and wanton injury, and to reprobate every thing like insult which might make the sufferer feel the act of violence more deeply. You will therefore be pleased to arrest the said Mr. Hill and have him tried by a court-martial. You are herewith informed what were the orders of Baron Steuben forbidding the act complained of.

I am Sir Your very huble Servt., T.J.

FC (Vi); at head of text: "County Lieut. of Dinwiddie." Enclosure not located. John Banister was county lieutenant of Dinwiddie from or before 1779 (*Va. Council Jour.*, II, 251; *Official Letters*, III, 165).

From Edward Carrington

SIR Richmond Jan. 30th. 1781

I did myself the Honor to attend at the Door of the Council Chamber yesterday with a view of Conferring with the Executive on the subject of purchasing the necessary Horses wanted from this State for the southern Army, but as I could not gain Admittance immediately, my business in other respects would not admit of my waiting. I now take the liberty of troubling your Excellency with my thoughts on the subject, and wish for the Executive to take them under consideration. The Army being destituate of Horses must have a supply by some Means or other: The principles on which the Laws of the State direct those Purchases to be made will evidently ruin us if we continue to make the purchases on them, as every Horse will cost three or four times his Value. I wish for something to be done for obtaining the Horses, and exempting the Public from such abuses. I apprehend that by classing the Horses we shall want, fixing a certain price to each Class, in Tobacco or Specie, and having it determined by indifferent People into which Class the Horse purchased shall be estimated would answer our purpose. The Executive may perhaps be scrupulous about their powers to make such an alteration in the execution of the Law, but I apprehend the pressing Necessity for such a Step must obtain the approbation of the Legislature. However I think, should the Executive not chuse to risk such a Step by Absolute authority, the measure might yet be effected by an Application to the different Counties through the same means th[at] the Waggon Act is to be executed in such a Manner, as to carry in some measure the weight of Authority without the real exertion of it. Suppose a request should be made by the Executive to the Counties, that each shall produce by the same mode pointed out for obtaining Waggons, two or three Horses? I really think such a request could not be disregarded. Any Conferences necessary on the subject may be had with Major Claiborne.

I have the Honor to be with much respect Yr. Excellencies Mo Obt ED. CARRINGTON

RC (Vi); addressed and endorsed.

The WAGGON ACT: "An act for supplying the army with clothes, provisions, and waggons," passed in the Oct. 1780 session of Assembly (Hening, X, 338-43).

From Linctot

au poste Vincenne 30 Janvier 1781

Jenvoye Mr. Vaucheret aupres de Votre Exelence pour Vous apprendre qua mon arivée au poste Vincenne et aux Illinois, Jai trouvé Les Nations Seauvage En Bonne Intilligense avec nous Exepte La Nation MiaMi. Jai Employé tout Le credit que Je pouvais avoir aupres Deux pour Les Exité a prendre patience Et de rester fidelle avec nous, mais Leur grande miserre ou Ils sont reduit poura par Les Exorbitant present que Les anglais Leurs offres Sans Cesse poura Les Engager a rompre avec nous Si on ne Leur fourni Les besoins necessaire quil Souffre de puis Longtems En restant fidelle avec nous. Cest pour cette raison que Jenvoye M. Vaucheret aupres de Votre Exellence pour obtenir Les Secours necessaire que Lon Leur fait Esperrer depuis Longtems.

Monsieur Vaucheret ne peut plus me fournir de Secour Il men a fourni autant que Sa fortune La permis. Jai tirre En Sa faveur Une Lettre De change de Vingt mille piastre gourdes que Je Vous prie Lui fournir pour Les Depenses absolument Necessaire Et pour Maintenir La tranquilité parmi Les Nations. Ces Le Dernier moyens que Je puisse Employer pour Soutenir Les Interrest des Etats Et Le Seul Moyens que Mes Services Vous Soyent agreable. Les Seauvages veulent bien attendre son retour Et mon promis me tenir Lamain Jusqua ce tems, cest pour quoy Jesperre que Votre Exellence me metra a même de continuer Mes Services En menvoyant SeSecours autrement Il ne Seroit Daucune Utilite pour Les Etats.

Jay Lhonneur destre avec respect Monsieur Votre tres humble obeisant serviteur, GODEFROY LINCTOT maj. Ind

RC (InHi); addressed: "Son-Excellence Le Gouverneur de La province De Virginie."

From George Muter

SIR War office Jany 30. 1781.

Permitt me to mention to your Excellency that a very large quantity of nails will be wanted for the public buildings. Nail rod was received yesterday, which came from Fredericksburgh, but nail makers are wanting. Mr. Anderson would not agree to the terms that were offered him.

The tradesmen that are willing to undertake public work, or to work for the public, require some thing to be done to satisfy them that they are not to be subject to militia duty and draughts, while employed for the public. My telling them that they will most assuredly be cleared, I find is not satisfactory. They require also a positive agreement respecting provisions.

I have the honour of inclosing a list of the canoes that were impressed. Mr. Price has also given certificates to the people, both for the canoes, and canoe men. It is not however yet known, how much, or in what manner, the people are to be paid on their certificates.

I have also inclosed a list of tools wanted for Moody's shop, as also a list of his people and their present employment.

Your Excellency will find inclosed, all the material information I have been able to obtain concerning Thomas Reynolds case.

I have made enquiry concerning Colo. Warneck; and have been informed by Mr. Galt that he heard him petition Genl. Arnold, not to carry him with him, but to let him remain on his parole; and that the General told him, as he was a foreigner (particularly a German for whom he said they had a great respect) he would permitt him to remain on parole. Mr. Galt cou'd not say with certainty, how Warneck got the parole he had signed into his possession.

I have the honour to be Your Excellency's most hl servant,

George Muter. C.

RC (Vi); addressed and endorsed. Enclosures: Statement of Robert Boush, Edward Valentine, and George Muter concerning Thomas Reynolds' actions during the invasion (Vi).

The LIST OF CANOES and the LIST OF TOOLS were probably not sent with the letter, for under date of 1 Feb. there is the following minute in the War Office Journal (Vi): "Sent down to the Council a return of Canoes impressed in the Service of the State Jany. 2d. 1781, and a list of Tools wanted for Mr. Moody's Shop. Answer to the above, from the Council. 'Mr. Price was empowered to impress Canoes at the time abovementioned: Mr. Moody's Articles should be procured.' " THOMAS REYNOLDS: The enclosed statements concerning Reynolds (see Muter to TJ, 23 Jan. 1781) declare that he had assisted in removing the arms from Westham; that he was later taken by the British when he was trying to join the Goochland militia; and that he had been for some time employed as a bricklayer at the foundry. COLO. WARNECK: See TJ to Muter 29 Jan., and to Steuben, 17 Feb. 1781.

From George Muter

Sir Jany. 30. 1781

The money (30,000 dollars) due me agreeable to act of assembly for depreciation, is with-held in consequence of my having an open account on the Auditor's books; kept open for upwards of three months at the requisition of the auditors, that I might pay some money due by the state to Mr. Jno. King of Petersburgh, and settle for the whole together. The ballance due from me, without paying Mr. King, is about £300, by my account; by the Auditors books in consequence of a mistake, the ballance wou'd be in my favour. I have a warrant for a quarter's sallary amounting to £4875 in my possession, which the Treasurer refuses to pay, in consequence of orders he has received from your Excellency.

In consequence of the treasurer's refusal to pay my warrant (as I owe some debts and cant think of borrowing) I shall be involved in considerable difficultys, unless your Excellency, thinks proper to releive me by issuing an order to the treasurer for that purpose, more particularly as I cant immedeatly settle my account, to enable me to draw my depreciation money, all my vouchers being in Albemarle. I must therefore request that you will please to issue an order to the treasurer in my favour, if it can be done with propriety, & am Your Excellency's most hl servt., GEORGE MUTER

RC (Vi).

From Charles Scott

Hadderells Point Jany. 30th. 1781

Your Excellency's favor by Capt. Blackwell without date together with bills to the amount of One thousand and eight pounds Sterlg., One hundred barrels of flour, four Hhds. of Tobacco, twenty Hhds. of Rum with sundry Articles of clothing, I have had the honor to receive. All which shall be dispos'd of agreeable to the directions enclos'd in your letter.

The following are the rates I have been able to procure for the goods sent from the State. The Bills have been sold without deduction, or on Par. The Tobacco for fifty five shills. Sterlg. pr. Hundred and the flour for thirty shills. Stg. p do. The Rum will be divided agreeable to the abovemention'd instructions.

I am sorry to inform you that I cannot with any degree of propriety give the certificate respecting the Arms &c. of the 5th. Regiment, when taken on Continental Establishment, not having recourse to my papers. I beg leave to refer your Excellency to Colo. Josiah Parker of Smithfield, who was at that time Commandant of the Regiment.

I have enclos'd the return You desir'd. The distance of situation between us and the non-commission'd Officers and Privates would not allow me to send you the particular names or to discriminate between the Number of each. What You recieve is the most exact that can be procur'd.

You will please to observe that amongst the commission'd Officers mention'd in the return, there are several who bear staff commissions in the line or Regiments—such are Brigade Inspectors, Pay Masters, Adjutants and Quarter Masters. These Gentlemen besides their posts in the line have had regular appointments to the other Offices and have conform'd to their duty.

It is wish'd that our supplies were greater, but being convinc'd of the desire of the state to serve us, We wait for a supply of Tobacco, for which I have receiv'd permission. I have enclos'd an Extract from my letter and the Commandant of Charlestown's Answer. We are sensible of the inconveniency of supplies as express'd in your letter; but We expect the permission enclos'd will obviate the difficulty.

I had forgot to mention that I had receiv'd some Medicine, and intend to have respect to the procuring of some more, if found necessary. You must be convinc'd from the return that the division of money will be trifling and that the chief dependency of comfort relies upon the arrival of fresh supplies or Tobacco which We are now permitted to receive and dispose of in any Quantity. We hope the length of time since We have been captur'd will be consider'd and the unavoidable necessity of being under obligations of debt for such things as the climate requires. As to my part, I made it my business to procure credit on my own Account, and distribu[te] to those in need, what Articles their situation or health demanded. But as this Matter is somewhat personal, I would chuse to leave it to the consideration of the State, when it is not requir'd on business of more importance.

I have the honor to be with great respect, Your mo. obedt. servt.,

CHS. SCOTT B.G. Virga. Line

RC (PHi). Enclosures: (1) The return of troops has not been found. (2) The other enclosure (Vi) was an extract from "a letter dated Hadderels point Jany. 30th. 1781. from B. Genl. Scott to Lieut. Colo. Balfour Commandant of Charlestown" asking permission that tobacco be sent to Charleston in sufficient quantity to pay the prisoners' debts and to make them comfortable during their captivity, together with an answer by "C Fraser Town Major" for the commandant that there was "no kind of objections to the request."

YOUR EXCELLENCY'S FAVOR: TJ's letter to Scott concerning supplies for the prisoners at Charleston, with its enclosures, has not been found; but see Charles Scott to TJ, printed at end of Dec. 1780. The enclosed extracts of Scott's letter to the commanding officer at Charleston and the reply to it were sent by TJ to William Phillips and were the subject of prolonged negotiations thereafter; see TJ to Phillips, 31 Mch.; to Steuben, 10 Apr.; and to the Virginia Delegates, 10 May 1781. See also Scott's supplementary letter of 2 Feb. 1781.

From the South Carolina Delegates in Congress

Philadelphia, 30 Jan. 1781. "Tho: Bee, Isaac Hobbe and Jno Mathews, Delegates from So Carolina, to Gov: Jefferson of Va. introducing William Parker, Esqr., one of the Treasurers of South Carolina, who goes to Virginia for the purpose of removing the Public Papers under his charge to some place of Safety, and requesting such aid be given him, as the circumstances may require."

MS not located. Summary quoted from CVSP, I, 475. The name "Isaac Hobbe" is, of course, an error; it should be Isaac Motte.

From Steuben

SIR Jany 30. 1781.

I enclose your excellency an abstract of the state of the forces of this State drawn from the Returns. By this you will observe that supposing no deficiency arises in the 3000 men voted and that the number now in the field does not diminish 1844 men will still be wanting of the Quota determined by Congress. With respect I am Your Excellency's Most obed. Servt, STEUBEN Maj. Gen.

MS not located. Text from A. H. Joline, *Meditations of an Autograph Collector*, N.Y. and London, 1902, p. 277. Enclosure not found.

From the Virginia Delegates in Congress

SIR Philada. Jany. 30th. 1781

We were honored yesterday with your Excellency's favor of the 15th. inst: inclosing Mr. Anderson's explanation of his letter to Capt. Trott, and that of the 18th. enclosing instructions as to the Mississippi and requesting sundry military supplies, in promoting which no exertions shall be omitted on our part. Your Excellency's letter to Congress on the subject of the Convention Prisoners and the unequal apportionment of the general resources with respect to the two great Departments was also received yesterday and referred to a Committee. The Resolutions of the General Assembly ceding the Territory N. West of the Ohio to the United States was laid before Congress at the same time. Although nothing has been yet done declaratory of their sense of them and although they are not precisely conformable to the recommendations of Congress on the subject, we flatter ourselves that the liberal Spirit which dictated them will be approved and that the public will not be disappointed of the advantages expected from the measure. We have pretty good though unauthenticated information that Maryland has already acceded to the federal Union.

Since the extinguishment of the Mutiny in the Pennsylvania line, some commotions founded on similar complaints have taken place in that [part] of New Jersey. But we have the pleasure to inform you that the prudent and seasonable remedies applied have re-established order and discipline among the troops.

We have the honor to be with the most perfect esteem & regard Yr. Excelly's. most obt. Servts.,

JOS. JONES
JAMES MADISON, JUNR.
THEOK. BLAND

RC (DLC: PCC, Portfolio 103); in Madison's hand, signed by all the delegates.

TJ's LETTER . . . ON THE SUBJECT OF THE CONVENTION PRISONERS: TJ to Huntington, 15 Jan. 1781. MARYLAND: On 30 Jan. the Maryland House of Delegates assented to "An act to empower the delegates of this State in Congress to subscribe and ratify the Articles of Confederation"; the Act was approved by the Senate on 2 Feb. and presented to Congress by the Maryland delegates on 12 Feb. 1781 (JCC, XIX, 138-40, where the Act is printed). COMMOTIONS . . . IN . . . NEW JERSEY: See Washington's letter to the President of Congress, 23 Jan. 1781, read in Congress on 29 Jan. (*Writings*, ed. Fitzpatrick, XXI, 135-6; see also Burnett, *Letters of Members*, v, No. 625, note 4).

From George Walls

Berkeley, 30 Jan. 1781. The terms of enlistment of the men in his regiment will expire in ten months, most of whom can be enlisted for the duration of the war for a "bounty of one third or perhaps less what is now given." The men can best be reenlisted now; "When they are Clear or nearly so of the Service it will be with great Difficulty and at a great expence they will be inlisted." If a sum of money can be sent with the bearer, Major Hunter, "between one and two Hundred good men may Certainly be got for the war."

RC (Vi); 3 p.; addressed (in part): "Favd by Majr Hunter"; endorsed. See Walls to TJ, 4 Feb. 1781, which is in part a duplicate of the present letter.

From George Elliott

[*Without place or date, ca. 31 Jan. 1781.*] Can no longer carry on the business under his direction and "must discharge all those imployed" unless he is granted a warrant for £41,525; is "Exceedingly unhappy for the Distress of his Creditors."

RC (Vi); 2 p.; signed: "George Elliott D Q M G"; addressed: "His Excellency Thomas Jefferson in Council"; endorsed: "Geo. Elliottes Letter. Jany 81." [*In another hand:*] "advance charged 31st Jany 1781."

To Robert Lawson

Sir Richmond Jan. 31. 1781.

I have conferred with Baron Steuben on the subject of forming a magazine of provision for your post: and intimated that behind the Blackwater, or Nottoway at farthest such a magazine would be safe, and if rendered unnecessary in this state by the removal of the enemy, would be convenient to Carolina. He disapproves of it, however. He has directed that no great collections of provision shall be made in that part of the country, and that the Commissaries shall furnish provisions to the army from three days to three weeks,[1] so as always to have that stock of provisions on hand and no more.

I cannot conceive how Majr. Nelson's cavalry are already reduced [to] sufferance for want of cloathing, when they have been cloathed since [their re]turn to this state during the present invasion.

[I have conferred] also with Baron Steuben on the plan you [proposed for] raising Volunteer horse. He seems unwilling to receive [any for a] shorter term than the [continuance of the invasion. Could they be ob]tained for that term on [the conditions you mention it would certainly] be more eligible. He pro[poses to supply the want of horse by per]mitting some of the militia-infant[ry to serve on horse back on] their own horses. I beleive also that we shall recall Capt. Reid's troop from Maryland. This troop is full. I hope you will be able to procure tools enough by impressing for building huts, as the destruction of our shops and tools here disa[bles us fr]om making them. Huts will be warmer than tents and therefore p[refera]ble as far as they can be used. But some tents ought certain[ly to] be with you and I should think might be had. There were betw[een two and] three hundred delivered out during the last invasion, of which seventy five went on to the Southward with Colo. Green's corps. The residue must still be remaining. I will have enquiry made for them.

I am with great respect Sir your most obedt. servt.,

Th: Jefferson

P.S. Since writing the above I have spoken with Mr. Newton. The powers under which provisions are impressed will suffice to form a magazine and as he seems to think that it [will] be sufficient if a few days provision be laid in I [think] the Commissaries may store so much [behind the] Blackwater. I am just informed there is [a prospect of raising horse here during] the invasion [to serve under the conditions of militia.]

RC (NcD); MS badly mutilated, missing portions of text supplied from FC; addressed: "General Lawson Mc.Kie's mills."; endorsed: "Govr. Jefferson to Gen. Lawson No. 6." FC (Vi).

On 28 Jan. Steuben wrote from Richmond to Lawson, in part as follows: "I have already spoke the Governor on sending a number of Militia horses, from the Counties below, and shall again urge the Matter. Major Nelsons Corps I have observed scattered over the Country, some with waggons and others with horses, and others without having any appearance of business at all. I should be glad all his corps now in this state might be together where they might be of service. As to those in Maryland I have consulted the Governor on and he says they can be sent for, but the Council must agree to it. He will propose it to them" (NHi). See Lawson to TJ, 28 Jan.

1 TJ inadvertently wrote "days."

To Sampson Mathews and John Bowyer

Sir — Richd. Janury. 31st. 1781

Every tent and all the tentstuff owned by the State were delivered during the last Invasion, 230 in the whole. Of these 75 were sent to the Southward, the remaining 155 are still somewhere. I have given orders to find in whose possession they are, and as soon as it is known I will inform Baron Steuben and communicate to him your want, which I make no doubt he will order to be first supplied; as it seems that those who being nearest the enemy's lines must frequently shift their quarters, should have what tents there are, those at a greater distance having it their power to build and remain in their Huts.[1] The application for ammunition must be to the Officer commanding where the main body lies. This is at present Genl. Mulenburg. We can only furnish ammunition to the Commanding Officer, and he orders the distribution. After secreting every store public and private, no tools can be got for you except a few files. The tools in our public Shops were mostly destroyed.

If you can procure tent-stuff by impressing it will be approved. You will give certificates to the owners and return me a list of the certificates. I will use my endeavours to prevail on Dr. Foushee or some other Surgeon to attend your Corps. T.J.

FC (Vi); at head of text: "Colos. Mathews and Bowyer."

1 The letter to Bowyer ends at this point. There is an asterisk in the margin of the MS, and the following note at the foot of the text: "Colo. John Bow[y]er to the word huts."

To J. P. G. Muhlenberg

Sir Richmond Jan. ⟨29⟩ 31. 1781.

Acquainted as you are with the treasons of Arnold, I need say nothing for your information, or to give you a proper sentiment of them. You will readily suppose that it is above all things desireable to drag him from those under whose wing he is now sheltered. On his march to and from this place I am certain it might have been done with facility by men of enterprize and firmness. I think it may still be done though perhaps not quite so easily. Having peculiar confidence in the men from the Western side of the mountains, I meant as soon as they should come down to get the enterprize proposed to a chosen number of them, such whose courage and whose fidelity would be above all doubt. Your perfect knowlege of those men personally, and my confidence in your discretion, induce me to ask you to pick from among them proper characters, in such number as you think best, to reveal to them our desire, and engage them [to] undertake to seize and bring off this greatest of all traitors. Whether this may be best effected by their going in as friends and awaiting their opportunity, or otherwise is left to themselves. The smaller the number the better; so that they be sufficient to manage him. Every necessary caution must be used on their part to prevent a discovery of their design by the enemy, as should they be taken, the laws of war will justify against them the most rigorous sentence. I will undertake if they are succesful in bringing him off alive, that they shall receive five thousand guineas reward among them, and to men formed for such an enterprize it must be a great incitement to know that their names will be recorded with glory in history with those of Vanwert, Paulding and Williams. ⟨*I shall be sorry to suppose that any circumstances may put it out of their power to bring him off alive after they shall have taken him and of course oblige them to put him to death. Should this happen, however, and America be deprived of the satisfaction of seeing him exhibited as a public spectacle of infamy, and of vengeance, I must give my approbation to their putting him to death. I do this considering him as a deserter from the American army, who has incurred the pain of death by his desertion, which we have a right to inflict on him and against which he cannot be protected by any act of our enemies. I distinguish him from an honourable enemy, who, in his station, would never be considered by me as a justifiable object of such an enterprize. In event of his death, however, I must reduce the reward proposed to 2000 guineas, in proportion as our satisfaction would be reduced.*⟩ The inclosed order from Baron Steuben will authorize you to call for and to dispose of any force you may think necessary to place in readiness for covering the enterprize and securing the retreat of the party. Mr. Newton the bearer of this, and to whom it's contents are communicated in confidence, will provide men of trust to go as guides. These may be associated in the enterprize or not as you please; but let that point be previously settled that no difficulties may arise as to the parties entitled to participate of the reward. You know how necessary profound secrecy is in this business, even if it be not undertaken.

Dft (DLC); without name of recipient; scored out and revised. In the present text only the most important deletion and the revision of the date have been included, the other alterations being matters of form rather than content. The enclosed order of Baron Steuben has not been located.

This letter has been frequently printed, usually without the deleted matter, and sometimes with George Rogers Clark named as the recipient. It was, however, undoubtedly addressed to Muhlenberg, Clark having already departed for the West; see TJ to L. H. Girardin, 14 Apr. and 12 May 1815; also Burk-Girardin, *Hist. of Va.*, IV, 457-9. No evidence has been discovered that Muhlenberg replied to the letter or that any efforts were made to carry the plan into execution, although Girardin's account, which was written with TJ's approval, implies that the letter was sent. For the reasons which may have prevented an attempt at the plan, see Wallace, *The Muhlenbergs of Pennsylvania*, p. 208-11; and Kimball, *Jefferson: War and Peace*, p. 151. VANWERT: Isaac Van Wart; see Van Doren, *Secret History*, p. 340-1. MR. NEWTON: This may have been the "Major Newton" referred to in Robert Lawson's letter to TJ of 28 Jan., q.v., since he was with TJ around 29-31 Jan. when the present letter was written; see TJ to Lawson, 31 Jan. For a similar attempt to capture Arnold, see Washington's letter to Major Henry Lee, 20 Oct. 1780 (*Writings*, ed. Fitzpatrick, XX, 223). Lee selected two men to carry out this enterprise. To one, a sergeant, he promised promotion. To the other he pledged "one hund. guineas, five hundd. acres of land, and three negroes." The sergeant, John Champe, "a very promising youth of uncommon taciturnity, and invincible perseverance," deserted under orders, entered New York, came before Sir Henry Clinton, and accidentally met Arnold in the streets, thus paving the way for a successful coup. He failed, however, and was imprisoned "till the troops under Arnold reached Virginia" (*Tyler's Quart.*, II [1920], 332). Despite the failure of this effort, Washington, so late as April 1781, still entertained hope that Arnold would be brought in (*Writings*, ed. Fitzpatrick, XXI, 447).

To George Muter

In Council Jany. 31st. 1781.

Being certified by Major Genl. Baron Steuban that the Continental rules are, that spirit shall not be issued, but to Troops on long marches, on duty in wet weather, or on fatigue duty, and that he has accordingly regulated the present issues to the Militia and troops in Service; It is the opinion of the Board, that Troops in the seperate service of the State, should be placed on the same footing with those under Continental Officers, and therefore that the regulation before mentioned be adopted by the State.

Tr in War Office Journal (Vi).

This letter, a reply to one of Muter's letters of 29 Jan., is quoted in full (including TJ's signature, which does not appear in the text here printed) in a letter from Muter to the "Commanding Officer of the State Garrison regt.," 31 Jan. (Tr in War Office Journal, Vi), with an explanation that the "original, of which the above is a Copy goes with the order (on the back of it) but I thought it necessary to advertise you of it."

From George Muter

SIR War office Jany. 31st. 1781.

The waggons are ready to start that are to carry out the necessarys for the forces in the Western department, and instructions with respect to the delivery of the goods they carry are wanted. I am incapable of even originating instructions, as I know no more of the matter, than that the goods are to be carried to Fort Pitt, but I am entirely ignorant of any thing farther. I am informed that Majr. Quirk has said, he cannot give the necessary instructions. I beg leave to add, that Mr. Rose informs me, the waggoners refuse to move, unless some spirits are furnished them, and a satisfactory provision made for their being paid. These are matters I do not know what to do in, therefore, have I been induced to mention them to your Excellency.

I have the honour to be Your most hle servant,

GEORGE MUTER. C.

RC (Vi).

A minute in the War Office Journal (Vi) under 31 Jan. records this letter as follows: "Letter, to the Governor informing that the Waggons are ready to start with the necessaries for Genl. Clarke's men."

From George Muter

[*Richmond, 31 Jan. 1781.* Minute in War Office Journal (Vi) under this date: "Letter to the Governor inclosing one, from Mr. Peter to me (just received) for his consideration, and one inclosed in that from Mr. Mead to Mr. Peter." Muter's letter has not been located. For enclosures, see TJ's reply, following, and notes there.]

To George Muter

In Council Jan. 31. 1781.

If Mr. Peters means to perform military and other duties required by the laws, as would have been, had he given no parole, he is at liberty to remain: if he does not mean this, he must deliver himself up to the enemy. TH: JEFFERSON.

RC (Vi); written on verso of Walter Peters to George Muter, 30 Jan. 1781 (see below); endorsed: "Walter Peters respecting his being a prisoner on parole & Govrs. answer Jany. 30th. 1781." Tr in War Office Journal (Vi); another Tr in War Office Letter Book (Vi).

MR. PETERS: Walter Peters was employed by the state at Hood's (see Muter to TJ, 8 Sep. 1780). On 26 Jan. 1781 Muter wrote "Walter Peters Esq: at Hoods inclosing a Warrant for ten thousand Pounds and informing him of the reason for not sending it before" (War Office Journal, Vi). On 30 Jan. Peters replied, stating, in part: "by the Enclos'd letter You will be able to judge of my present situation. I woud make personal aplication to his Excellency on the occasion, but my horses have been so harass'd . . . they coud not carry me to Richmd. in three days. I have done no Malitia duty this two Years on Account of my having the Gout and being short sighted, and I am still willing to pay my Clubb of all Publick Charges. Please take his Excellencys opinion on this matter" (Vi). The letter enclosed by Peters has not been located (see Muter to TJ, preceding).

George Muter to Levin Walker

[*Richmond*] *31 Jan. 1781.* There are a "number of deserters from the Continental Army, the State forces and the Navy of the State in the Counties of Accomack, and Northampton"; Walker is ordered to secure them and have them brought to Richmond. Letters to the county lieutenants of Accomack and Northumberland are enclosed requesting them to assist Walker. Letter and enclosures signed by Muter and countersigned by TJ.

Tr of letter and enclosures in War Office Letter Book (Vi).

In the Contingent Fund Vouchers (Vi) there is an order to the auditors, signed by Muter and countersigned by TJ, to pay Levin Walker £2000 to "defray his expences in collecting and securing deserters."

To Alexander Spotswood

SIR Richd. January 31st. 1781

I received your favour containing a proposition for raising a Legion for the defence of the State: As there are several parts of it which are beyond the powers of the executive to stipulate, I shall do myself the pleasure of laying it before the General Assembly whom we have been obliged to convene on the first of March next. The result of their determinations shall be immediately communicated to you. T.J.

FC (Vi).

YOUR FAVOUR: Spotswood's letter and the enclosed PROPOSITION have not been found. TJ transmitted the proposition to the House of Delegates, who referred it to a committee that reported on 8 Mch. An Act based on the plan was passed on 17 Mch.; and on 20 Mch. Spotswood was appointed brigadier general in command of the two legions (1,400 men) to be raised for defense of the state during actual or threatened invasions (JHD, Mch. 1781, Va. State Libr., *Bull.*, 1928, p. 12, 15-16 [Spotswood's plan printed in full], 21, 23, 36, 41-42; Hening, X, 391-3).

To John Syme

Sir   Janury. 31st. 1781. Richmd.

What induced the executive at first to remove the Stores from Cumberland up the river to Newcastle was the danger they would be in from the enemy who seemed to shew by their actions that the destruction of public Stores was a principal object. Their later movements seeming now to indicate no such danger, we shall decline removing the corn at all from Cumberland, and as the transportation by land from Cumberland here is so little more than from New Castle, we shall adopt the plan of bringing the cannon from Cumberland by land. The Shells, shot &c. being less important may remain untill they can be carried by water to whatever place they shall be wanting at. If all the rum and other Spirit is not come already; that should be brought directly. I am to thank you for your attention to this business and am with great respect,   T.J.

FC (Vi). See Syme to TJ, 27 Jan. and references there.

To George Weedon

Sir   Richmond Jan. 31. 1781.

I am glad that the Commissioners of the provision law in your neighborhood have agreed to lend their aid in furnishing you with provisions. They are certainly justifiable as that law has been reenacted by the assembly. As soon as a force began to collect at Fredericksburg I directed the Commissary Brown (who is authorized by the law to instruct the Commissioners in what is to be expected from them) to take immediate measures for procuring subsistence for those forces either by sending a deputy or applying to the Commissioners.

Your arrangements for the defence of Potowmac and Rappahanoc appear to have been judicious. Baron Steuben coming here soon after the receipt of your letter I referred to him to do in that what he should think best, as it is my wish to furnish what force is requisite for our defence as far as I am enabled, but to leave to the commanding officers solely the direction of that force. I make no doubt he has written to you on that subject.

I am with great respect Sir your most obedt. humble servt.,

Th: Jefferson

RC (A Midwestern Collector, 1945). FC (Vi).

From Edward Carrington

SIR Petersburg Feb. 1st. 1781.

I flattered myself that by the information I had given your Excellency of the Diversions making of the Provisions destined for Magazines for the Southern Army, I had effectually put a stop to so ruinous Measures, especially as I had been honored with a Letter from you, that they should be discontinued. However I find now so little regard paid to your Excellencys Orders, that even a parcel of hogs driven by Mr. Mason southwardly by the Advice of Genl. Smallwood and myself, have been ordered back by Mr. Brown for the purpose of supplying the Militia and I understand those are called back in Consequence of their having consumed most of the Hogs collected and which had not been yet driven outwards. I beleive it will not be necessary to say more to you on the Subject than amounts to information of the Facts. You certainly are apprised of the fatal Consequences that must arise from those Magazines being neglected, on which Genl. Greene is now calculating for the Existence of his Army the next Campaign. Your Excellency will excuse my sollicitations on this Subject as the General has confided to me his own Apprehensions on it. And I am just now honoured with a Message from him, praying that I shall give every Attention to having them formed as early as possible.

I have the honor to be with much respect & Esteem Your Mo. Obt. ED. CARRINGTON

RC (Vi); addressed and endorsed.

On 31 Jan. Carrington wrote to Steuben substantially as in the letter to TJ above, to which he added: "For Gods sake why does not Major Forsythe come in and regulate his Department? I some time ago wrote to the Governor on the subject, who promised that he would stop the misapplications. However, I find it still going on and I am very clear we shall have no Magazines laid in unless something is done to regulate Mr. Brown in his Office" (NHi). Carrington's earlier letter to TJ on the subject of misapplication of supplies is no doubt that of 13 Jan., to which TJ appended an order.

To William Davies

SIR Richmd. February 1st. 1781.

I suppose there is no hope of our getting hats for the soldiers. We will aid you anywise in our power towards getting caps made. Mr. Armistead receives 1800£ to be transmitted you for your tailors and sempstresses. He has received an order to deliver you all the leather he has (enough for about 300 or 350 pair three qr.

soals) and receives one now to make up the deficiency of 1500 pair as soon as we receive it from the Barracks.

I shall take measures for obtaining from Colo. Waggoner an explanation as to Mattenly's complaint, and if not satisfactory shall do what Justice further requires. T.J.

FC (Vi).

From William Davies

Sir Chesterfield Feby. 1. 1781.

Of the hundred pair of shoes expected from Petersburg, there came only 53, and those so bad that a day's wear will destroy them. If my wish could be had, they should be returned. For my part I will never direct the distribution of any of them to the men, unless it be to taylors and shoemakers, whose sedentary occupations will not admit of much walking.

There are a number of men belonging to the continent, among the taylors and shoemakers at Warwick. I think they would be of more service here, where they would be entirely subject to martial law, and be employed with our taylors and shoemakers.

I beg leave to observe to your Excellency that the *sub-cloathier*, as he is styled by Congress, is here. If I recollect right he is the proper officer thro' whose hands all issues of cloathing should pass. He is capable of being serviceable to us, but seems to have been forgot by the executive. I have often heard Mr. Armistead complain of the multiplicity of his business, and I would submit it to your Excellency, whether, considering the infirm state of Mr. Armistead's health, it would not be proper to employ Mr. Peyton (the cloathier's name) in such parts of the business as it is the duty of the sub-cloathier to perform.

There is the most urgent necessity for a number of nails or nail rods. We cannot finish the necessary buildings for the reception of cloathing, provision, military or quartermaster's stores, unless we are favored with your Excellency's assistance, which will be attended with a saving more important than the price of the nails.

I have the honor to be, sir, with the utmost respect, Your Excellency's most obedt hble servt., William Davies

P.S. I have forgot to observe to your Excellency that the 1495 yards you count upon as sufficient for 400 *suits* will make no more than 370 *coattees*. The cloth is only 2½ quarters wide, and it requires 3¾ yards to make one of these *coattees* or *jack coats*, as they are called. I should have imagined that the width as well as the length of the cloth would have been reported to your Excellency, as otherwise it is impossible to form a proper estimate of the quantity of cloathing that can be made of it.

RC (Vi); addressed and endorsed.

THE CLOTH IS ONLY 2½ QUARTERS WIDE: That is, 22.5 inches. Davies wrote Steuben on 1 Feb. that "the 1495 Yards of cloth which the Governor estimates as sufficient for 400 suits will only make 350 jack coats"; Steuben acknowledged this from Richmond on 2 Feb. and added: "Capt. North waited on the Executive with the letter. Their answer to it was, that anything in their Power should be done towards remedying the Complaints. The Camp Kettles shall be furnished" (both letters are in NHi).

To Thomas Sim Lee

SIR Richmd. Febry. 1st. 1781.

I am much obliged by your Excellency's favour of Janury. 5th. Joseph Shoemaker is a citizen of this State and has been an active mischeivous traitor. The dangers of escape on the road from Baltimore to this place, and from this place, where since our removal from Wmsburg no public jail has been yet erected, are so great as to induce me to suggest to your Excellency the trial and punishment of this offender under your laws, should he have committed any depredation within your State which they would punish capitally: and in this case I will on intimation from Your Excellency furnish you with proofs of his citizenship authenticated in any way which your Laws shall require. Should he not be amenable to justice under your Laws, or should he be acquitted on trial, I will on information thereof take immediate measures for having him received and brought hither.

I have been honoured with a letter from the Honorable Mr. Jenifer President of your Senate and Mr. Bruff Speaker of the house of Delegates, proposing that we should invite our Allies the French to take a post within our state convenient for the defence of Cheasapeake Bay, and desiring a communication on this subject with your Excellency. The difficulties on this head will certainly not arise with us. Should our Allies not have a certainty of obtaining and keeping a superiority of naval power in the American seas, they would probably think any post on the navigable waters of Cheasapeake liable to loss. As a discussion of this matter with the French Minister required full information to him of the various ports and grounds which they might think fitted for defence as well as for overlooking the Bay, of their conveniency to aid from the

Country and many other circumstances which might draw the correspondence, if on paper, to a great length, I have thought it best to desire the honble. Mr. Harrison Speaker of our house of Delegates who set out for Philadelphia two days ago, and who is perfectly acquainted with these circumstances, to speak with the French Minister on this subject, and to give him every information which may be necessary to determine his Opinion. I had during the last Summer taken the liberty of solliciting from him some Naval force to be stationed in our bay, and received hopes that it might be done, just when the Enemy now within this State, came into the bay. I am afraid the proof they have exhibited of the practicability of making inroads into our country when conducted with rapidity and aided by winds and waters, will rather discourage our Allies from hazarding much in any situation which may be pointed out.

I have the honour to be with every sentiment of esteem & respect Your Excellency's Most Obt. & mot. hble. sert., T.J.

FC (Vi).

On SHOEMAKER, a connection of the notorious Goodriches of Virginia, see Lee's letter of 5 Jan. here acknowledged; also frequent references in *Md. Archives*, XLVII, and CVSP, II-III. A LETTER FROM . . . MR. JENIFER . . . AND MR. BRUFF: Maryland General Assembly to TJ, 5 Jan. 1781. For TJ's earlier solicitation of the French Minister for SOME NAVAL FORCE TO BE STATIONED IN OUR BAY, see TJ to La Luzerne 31 Aug. 1780.

From Daniel Morgan

SIR Camp Sherels [Sherrill's] Ford catabaw River 1 Februy 1781

The British army are on the south side of the River and I with my Little Detachment on the other. I think they will attempt to cross this morning. Never the less, we have filled up all the fords and thrown every obstruction immaginable in their way, they are in force and I have about two hundred and thirty Reguler infantry, and about sixty horse, Genl. Davidson near five hundred Malitia. The inhabitents seem to make a stir, what they will do is unceartain, but I fear not much. Genl. Green arrived yesterday, he has ordered his little army to join us, they are not more than seventeen or eighteen hundred. This number and my detachment when join'd will be much inferior to the enemy, who must be Near three thousand, well supplyd and provided for, and our men almost Naked.

I am of opinion that Lord cornwallis fully intends to make a push through this state In order to make a junction on the roan oak or els whares, nor do I see what is to hinder him.

Great god what is the reason we cant Have more men in the

field—so many men in the country Nearby idle for want of employment. How distressing it must be to an anxious mind to see the country over Run and destroyed for want of assistance which I am realy afraid will be the case if proper exertion are not made use of. I have gained a little advantage through the tres[1] which would serve very well for a begining if we had force to follow it up. I have been so harassed and exposed this winter that I am entirely emmaciated. An old pain in my breast and Hip aceazed me so that shant be of much use in the field this winter—if [e]ver I am, but as I have been broke down in the services of my country shall bear the infirmitys of old age with more satisfaction.

I have the Honor to be sir Your obedt & very Hble Servt,

DANL MORGAN

RC (PHi); addressed: "His Excellency Thomas Jefferson Esqr Governor of Virga."; endorsed.

[1] The word may also be "tras," which Morgan may have intended for "trace," meaning *path* or *route*. Another though less likely reading is that the two preceding words were intended for "thicketty"; the region to which Morgan refers was known as Thicketty (or Thicketty Mountain). Whatever the correct reading of this word or words, there can be no doubt as to the meaning of the passage as a whole: the LITTLE ADVANTAGE to which Morgan so modestly referred was his brilliant victory at Cowpens on 17 Jan.

From George Muter, with Reply

SIR War office Feby 1st. 1781.

I have not been yet able to learn where or in whose possession any of the tents are except those (by the quarter masters return 49 in all) that have been delivered for the use of the State Garrison regiment: and Majr. Magill informs me that he is obliged to let his men use them at present for want of blanketts, there hardly being a blankett in the possession of one of his soldiers.

I have the honour to be Your Excellency's most humble servant,

GEORGE MUTER C.

In Council Feb. 1. 1781.

While troops are out in the open feild without cover, it is impossible to permit those under the cover of houses to use tents as blankets, were such an abuse admissible in any situation. It is therefore the opinion of the board that the tents within mentioned be immediately delivered to the State Quarter-master.

TH: JEFFERSON

RC (Vi); addressed and endorsed. TJ's reply, in his own hand, is on verso of Muter's letter. Tr of reply is in War Office Journal (Vi); another Tr is in War

Office Letter Book (Vi), where it is appended as an enclosure to a copy of Muter's letter to "The Commanding Officer of the S[tate] g[arrison] R[egiment]," i.e., Charles Magill, 3 Feb., ordering the tents to be turned over to the quartermaster.

From John Page

DEAR SIR [1 February 1781]

As I think it of Consequence that the Gentleman recommended should as speedily as possible receive his Commission, I have inclosed it by the first Conveyance I could procure. I think it proper to add that he served as a Captain in the Continental Army with Credit, and is esteemed as an excellent Officer, and was recommended by a full Court amongst whom was every field officer. I have not time to add more than that I am yrs. sincerely,

JOHN PAGE

RC (Vi); addressed and endorsed; without place or date, but undoubtedly written from Gloucester co., and the enclosure (certificate of the Gloucester county court's recommendation of "James Baytop Gent. as a proper person for Lieutenant Colonel," signed "C: Pryor D.C.C.") is dated 1 Feb. 1781.

Baytop was appointed; his military record is in Gwathmey, *Hist. Reg. of Virginians in the Revolution.*

From Robert Porterfield

Charleston, S.C. 1 Feb. 1781. Reports the death on 10 Jan. of his brother Col. Charles Porterfield, who was on his way from Camden to Charleston. During his brother's "almost five months extreme illness, The consequence of a wound he received on the 16th. of August near Camden, His necessary expences amounted to a considerable sum, for the purpose of defraying which, he borrowed of Lord Rawdon, Thirty Guineas which I have made myself answerable to his Lordship for as soon as may be in my power." Cannot raise such a sum in his present circumstances; asks TJ's assistance, which he thinks his brother's "services has merited from the Authority of the State, in whose employ he lost his life." If TJ should consider this an impropriety, then he requests loan of thirty guineas "in order that my faith with a Gentleman who granted, not only that, but many other favours to my Brother while in great distress may not be broken."

RC (Vi); 3 p.; addressed and endorsed; printed in CVSP, I, 479.

Robert Porterfield, capt., 7th Va. Line, had been captured at the battle of Camden, where his brother Charles was mortally wounded (Gwathmey, *Hist. Reg. of Virginians in the Revolution*). For TJ's action on the present appeal, see TJ to Granville Smith, 28 Feb. 1781.

From John Syme

New Castle, 1 Feb. 1781. Acknowledges TJ's letter of 31 Jan. Has heard that "Mr. Watkins (who is Very Anxious to Remove evry thing from Cumberland) has loaded 3 Vessells, now on their way with Shells, Shott &c. Shall they be Landed Here or Return'd?" In obedience to Gen. Nelson's orders, Syme has ordered out his lower battalion of militia, but doubts the propriety of the order, which interferes with recruiting and which allows a still longer exemption to the men of the upper battalion. Refers to TJ's observations "in your Publick Letter" and apologizes for his militia officers' neglecting to make returns. Since corn is so plentiful and wagonage so dear, proposes that as much forage as possible be consumed where it grows.

RC (Vi); 3 p.; addressed (in part): "By Mr. Jno. Cockburn"; endorsed. Printed in CVSP, I, 480-1.

YOUR PUBLICK LETTER: That is, TJ's letter to the County Lieutenants, 19 Jan. 1781.

From John Todd

MAY IT PLEASE YOUR EXCELLENCY Lexington 1st Feb. 1781

Accounts from all Quarters lead us to expect vigorous Measures from our Enemies the next Campain. I have just recieved Duplicates of Letters sent from our Officers of Ilinois to others at Louisville which inform that the Spanish and American Ilinois Settlements are preparing defensively for heavy Attacks. The Original Letters I hear are sent forward to your Excellency. On Conferring with Cols. Bowmans and Trigg We concluded it expedient to send 150 Men to Garrison the Mouth of Licking until Crockett shall arrive which we shall expect Weekly. We apprehended the Expence would be less to Government than to wait until the Enemy arrive at Settlements and better conduce to the Security of the People.

Inclosed are Recommendations for certain Officers in this County. Would there be any Impropriety in sending out some Blank Commissions as formerly? I would engage that no abuses be committed. There are many Vacancies for other Officers than those recommended whose Ranks are as yet unsettled.

I have the Honor to be with the greatest Respect Your Excellency's most Obedient & humble Servant, JNO TODD JR

RC (Vi); addressed (in part): "℗ Capt. Henderson"; endorsed. Enclosures not found.

From Vivian Brooking

SIR Am[elia] February 2. 1781

Pursuant to the Act for recruiting this States Quota of Troops to serve in the Continental Army I summond the Field Officers, four Senior Majistrates and Commissioners of the Tax, to meet at the Court House the last Day of January the Captains or other Commanding officers of the several Militia Companys also being required to attend. We met agreable to appointment but several Captains with their Subalter[n]s and chief of the Men belonging to their Companies, being out of the County in Actual Service, and no one appearing with a Roll, for them agreable to the said Act we adjourned the Meeting untill the fifteenth Instant, hoping, by that Time, the Officers and Men may return to the County, o[r that we] may obtain your Excellencys Advice in what Manner to proceed. I should also be proud to have your Advice, with regard to two of the Officers of this County which were arrested the 12th. Ulto. by Order of the General Baron Steuben. They have requested a Tryal but the Baron has not, as I have heard of, yet, ordered a Court. The Officers insist on the Right of being tryed as Militia Officers by the Court Martial of their County, and untill they are tryed or discharged, they hold themselves clear from all Duty and from the ensuing Draught. The Officers are Lt. Colo. Booker and Capt. Finney. I have given general Orders agreable to yours of the 19th. Ult. and shall endeavour to have them put in execution, as it has been my constant Desire, since in Office, to comply strictly with all Laws, Ordinances and Orders notwithstanding it has been my misfortune to fail, thro' the Inattention of some of the Inferior Officers. I am Sr. Your mot. obedt Servant,

V. BROOKING Co. Lt.

RC (Vi); addressed and endorsed.

YOURS OF THE 19TH ULT.: See TJ to the County Lieutenants, 19 Jan. 1781.

From Arthur Campbell

SIR Washington Febr. 2d. 1781

This moment I have the intelligence that a Body of Indians (supposed to be Cherokees) attacked Blackmores Fort on Clinch, took four Men prisoners and has carry'd off a considerable number of Horses. I must entreat the speedy attention of the Executive to my former proposals of a Garrison in Powells Valley; and on the banks of the Tenasee, as absolutely necessary for the preservation of the Southwestern frontier and keeping up the communication to Kentucky.

I am Sir Your most Obedient Humble Servant,

ARTHUR CAMPBELL

RC (Vi); addressed and endorsed. See Campbell to TJ, 7 Feb. 1781.

From Richard Claiborne

Richmond, 2 Feb. 1781. The manufactory of wagon harness has been established at Charlottesville so that the German workmen among the Convention troops could be employed; these men may be had on reasonable terms, and, if the Convention army is to be moved, as TJ "observed the other day," Claiborne wishes to be empowered to "engage as many of them as my business may require, and their Commander may approve of." The Act respecting wagons to be furnished for the use of the southern army authorizes the executive to direct where these wagons are to be delivered; Claiborne wishes to know the places to be so designated. Also wishes to know what he shall do when the teamsters' service, which is limited to one month under the terms of the Act, is completed. Has no power to draft teamsters, nor money to employ them.

RC (Vi); 4 p.; in a clerk's hand, signed by Claiborne; addressed and endorsed. Printed in CVSP, I, 483-4.

To William Davies

SIR In Council Febr. 2d. 1781.

I am very sorry the shoes and cloathing fall so far short of what we had reason to expect. Such of the former as are unfit for use had better be returned. We shall omit no opportunity of making up the whole deficiency. The Shoemakers and Taylors at Warwick receive orders to day to go to your post under a Mr. Thornbury's care, who is himself one of them. We shall be glad to have the services of the sub-clothier, provided he is from the nature of his appointment, or will make himself accountable to our Clothier for his issues: what we wish to guard against is the issuing our clothing under the orders of a Continental Clothier-general who might give them to other troops. I inclose you an Order for three hundred (long) wieght of nail rods.

I am with much respect Sr. yr. Mos. Obt. Sevt., T.J.

FC (Vi). Enclosure not found.

From Horatio Gates

SIR Berkeley County. 2d. February 1781

This Letter will be presented to Your Excellency by Lieut. Col: Darke, who is lately returned from a Tedious Captivity in New York; he is an excellent Officer to Command Rifle Men, in which Service, he is particularly, and I may add very superiorly Instructed. His tried Courage, and Strong Natural understanding, Join'd to his experience in the Back Wood, and Indian Wars, render him completely fitted to Command in the Partizan Line. I rejoice you are some what relieved from your troublesome Visitors; and should be much Obliged to you to know what They are now about. If They take Post at Portsmouth, as I have constantly suspected they would, they will not only annoy the Eastern Parts of North Carolina, but be continually harrassing, and Distressing all Virginia, and Maryland within their Reach, all which will Favour Lord Cornwallis in his Designs upon The Southern States. I now reckon Nine Thousand of The Enemys Regular Troops are employed in Virginia and the Two Carolina's. Surely it is high Time there was an Army of ours in The Field to oppose Them. When I say an Army, I mean a Body of Troops considerably Superior in Number to the British: well disciplined, well Armd, well Appointed, and in every Respect well provided for instantly commencing an Offensive Campaign. If Lord Cornwallis Conquers the Southern, and Eastern Parts of No: Carolina, and extends his Posts of Communication to Portsmouth, you must expect the weight of the War will penetrate into your Bowels, and Cause such an Inflamation there, as may (if Timely remedies are not applied) consume the Life Blood of the State. Have you cried aloud to Congress, and to *The Commander in Chief of The Army*, for Succour; have they Listen'd to your Cry? If they have not, are you doing the best thing for Yourselves? Military Wisdom has ever heretofore, been imputed to Virginia; is there a Rotteness in the State of Denmark? Find it out, and Cut it off. This is the Letter of One Chess Player to Another, not the Letter of General Gates, To Governor Jefferson; I am now at my unhappy private House, you are acting in the Busy Scene of Public Life, and in the most Exalted Station; in which I sincerely wish you all Honour and Success; Happiness, I know you cannot have.

When I was at Fredericksbourg,[1] Genl. Weedon, and Col. Grayson, told me the State had Ordered the Depreciation of the Currency to be made Good to the Continental Officers, for a certain

Limitted Time; and recommended it to me to apply for my due. I did so, by an Order on The Treasury for the Sum; which I requested Gen. Adam Stephen to receive for me, and bring it with Him from Richmond. He says, I am not consider'd in the Line of the State Troops, and must apply to Congress; as Gen. Stephen has lost my Order on the Treasurer, I must beg the Favor of you to direct Him to pay no Regard to my Order should it reach his Hands further than to deliver it to Your Excellency. Five Years Absence from my Farm, has so ruined my Fortune, with Other untoward Circumstances, that I am difficultied, to pay the Taxes demanded of me by Government; this induced me to wish to receive the Sum granted by the Legislature, in lieu of the Depreciation of The Currency. When the Season Softens, the Weather is Moderate, and the approach of the Sun tells me we must prepare for Action; I shall go to Philidelphia, and know, from the Lords who should be Lords Paramount, and who should deserve to be so, what is my Destination.[2] *Public Good*, has throughout this War, been my Polar Star. My Poverty, and my Zeal declare it; my Enemies, who are the Rich, and Cuning Beings of The Hour, write my Elegy by their Malice! but, Nil conscire sibi, nulla pallescere Culpa; yours ever most truely & Affectionately, HORATIO GATES

P.S. I shall be happy to hear from You by Mr Hunter, who carries the Executive a Petition from the County.

Dft? (DLC); in Gates' hand; endorsed: "To Govr: Jefferson 2d. Febry: 1781." RC (DLC); in an unidentified hand, signed by Gates. The MS believed to be a draft (despite its presence in the TJ Papers) is in nearly all respects a more reliable text than the recipient's copy, though the former lacks the postscript, which is here supplied from the latter.

A PETITION FROM THE COUNTY: This was the petition of the officers of the Berkeley County militia of 25 Jan., q.v.

1 RC reads: "Hanover Court House."

2 Interlined above "Doom," crossed out.

To Abner Nash

SIR Richmd. Feby. 2d. 1781.

As it is possible the Enemy may mean to continue in their present position at Portsmouth and thereby shut up all commerce through the bay of Chesapeake, it becomes necessary to make provision in time through some other channel, of Salt, cloathing and coverings for our Southern Army. South Quay presents itself as the most practicable port. We have found it necessary here to permit the exportation of corn *on public account* to procure Salt for public use. Vessels will therefore be freighted with this article from

South Quay, which as they must of necessity pass through your State, I hope will be permitted to pass freely; indeed could your Excellency give permission to Mr. Ross our commercial agent, to procure part of his loading of Corn in your State, it would save much transportation to us. The returns in salt will be in like manner to South Quay or directly up the Roanoke to the magazines desired to be established by Genrl Greene.

We hope within a short time to complete the equipment of the residue of our regulars (between 4 & 500) and to send them on to Genl. Greene, being determined to permit the body of plunderers in our State to divert as little as possible of our effectual aids from the Southern quarter. We shall oppose them with militia, and send our regulars to join the Southern army.

I have the honor to be with very great Esteem Yr. Excelncs. most Obt. & Mot. Hble Sert., T.J.

FC (Vi). SOUTH QUAY was located just north of the North Carolina boundary, on the Blackwater river, a branch of the Chowan; a customs office was established there "in consequence of the importance attached to the place during the Revolutionary . . . war" (Martin, *Gazetteer of Virginia*, 1836, p. 239).

From Abner Nash

DEAR SIR Col. Longs Feby. 2d. 1781.

I have this Moment on my way to Newbern received your Excellencys favour of the 16th. and thank you for the intelligence communicated. I am extreamly glad your loss has been so inconsiderable from the Enemys late invasion at the same time it is greatly to be lamented that you had not previous notice of their approach. [I am now Sir to acquaint Yr. Excellency that I have just received an account of the arrival of a British Fleet in Cape Fear River. The Account says Eight large ships had got over the Bar and a Considerable Number in the Offing. This invasion will I fear distress us very greatly, our Men in the lower parts of the Country being by frequent drafts almost intirely exausted of Armes. This invasion in another respect affects us greatly because if we shall not be able to check them in a short time they no doubt will open a communication with the Highland Settlement about 100 miles up the Cape Fear River. These men are at heart all Enemies. In short Sir there remains no doubt but that the reduction of this State is the immediate object of the British and I fear we shall be exposed to very great distress before we get rid of them. The regulars in this de-

partment are inconsiderable. They with the Western Militia I have no doubt will be able to repel any advances of Ld. Cornwallis, but how the poor unpractised and unarmed Militia of the lower parts without the aid of one regular will be able to restrain the progress of the Enemy lately arrived, I cant foresee.][1] It would be of the last importance and perhaps be the saving of this distressed state if Yr. Excellency could send to our Aid a few Hundred of your Mountain Heroes under their distinguished Commander Col. Campbell. I hope Yr. Excellency will take care of the Enemy at Portsmouth and not let them come into the N.E. part of our state by the way of the Great Bridge. I shall not fail to acquaint you from time to time of our situation and hope for a continuation of your Correspondence. Our assembly have now when it is almost too late, given me unlimited power. I could wish it were in more able hands but shall employ it for the public good to the best of my ability. With the highest esteem & respect I am Yr. Excellencys Most obt. & Hble servt.
A Nash

Excuse this scrawl writ in the utmost hurry.

RC (PHi); addressed and endorsed; in the date line, "Col. Longs" has been substituted for "Halifax," crossed out. An extract of this letter, containing its principal intelligence, was enclosed to Huntington and also to Washington in TJ's letters to them dated 12 Feb.; the copy sent to Washington is in DLC: Washington Papers.

TJ had received intelligence of the BRITISH FLEET IN CAPE FEAR RIVER before Nash's letter arrived; see TJ to Huntington and Washington, 8 Feb. 1781.

1 The part included in square brackets (supplied) was enclosed in TJ to Washington, 12 Feb. 1781, q.v.

From William North

Without place, 2 Feb. 1781. "The Baron's [Baron Steuben's] Sentiments with regard to the sick Militia are" that competent surgeons ought to be with Generals Muhlenberg, Lawson, and Nelson, and that sufficient quantities of medicine should be furnished each surgeon to enable him to treat the slightly sick. Those whose disorders "render them fit objects for the Hospital" may be sent to Chesterfield or, preferably, home, since there are now at Chesterfield too many sick for the surgeons to treat properly.

RC (PHi); 2 p.; signed "Wm North Aide de Camp"; addressed and endorsed.

Proclamation

Inviting Mercenary Troops in the British Service to Desert

By his Excy. &c. [2 February 1781]

A PROCLAMATION[1]

Whereas Congress considering that it had been the wise policy of these states to extend the protection of their laws to all those who should settle among them of whatever nation or religion they might be and to admit them to a participation of the benefits of civil and religious freedom, and that the benevolence of this practice as well as it's salutary effects had rendered it worthy of being continued in future times: that his Britannic majesty in order to destroy our freedom and happiness had commenced against us a cruel and unprovoked war, and unable to engage Britons sufficient to execute his sanguinary measures had applied for aid to foreign princes who were in the habit of selling the blood of their people for money and from them had procured and transported hither considerable number of foreigners; and it was conceived that such foreigners if apprised of the practice of these states would chuse to accept of lands, liberty, safety and a communion of good laws and mild government in a country where many of their friends and relations were already happily settled, rather than continue exposed to the toils and dangers of a long and bloody war, waged against a people guilty of no other crime than that of refusing to exchange freedom for slavery; and that they would do this the more especially when they should reflect that after they had violated every Christian and moral precept by invading and attempting to destroy those who had never injured them or their country, their only reward if they escaped death and captivity, would be a return to the despotism of their prince to be by him again sold to do the drudgery of some other enemy to the rights of mankind: and that our enemies[2] had thought fit not only to invite our troops to desert our service but to compel our citizens falling into their hands to serve against their country: did resolve that these states would receive all such foreigners who should leave the armies of his Britannic majesty in America and should chuse to become members of any of these states, and that they should be protected in the free exercise of their respective religions, and be invested with the rights privileges and immunities of natives as established by the laws of these states, and moreover that they would provide for every such person 50 acres of unappropriated lands in some of these states to be held by him and his heirs in absolute property:[3] I have therefore thought fit by and with the advice of the Council of state to issue this my proclamation hereby notifying more generally the said engagement of Congress, and further promising to all such foreigners who shall leave the armies of his Britannic majesty while in this state and repair forthwith to me at this place, that they shall receive from this Commonwealth a further donation of two cows, and an exemption during the present war from all taxes for the support thereof and from all militia and military service: and moreover that they shall receive a full compensation for any arms and accoutrements which they shall bring with them and deliver to the Commanding officer at any of the posts holden by our forces, taking his[4] receipt for the same.

Given under my hand &c.[5]

Dft (Vi); endorsed by a clerk: "Proclamation inviting foreigners to quit the british Service Feby 2d 1781." MS (Vi); an engrossed copy, corrected and signed by TJ and with seal affixed at foot of text; endorsed: "Proclamation Feby 2d 1781." Variations between Dft and engrossed copy are noted below; the numerous small revisions in Dft are not noted.

On 2 Feb. 1781 "His Excellency laid before the board the following proclamation & asked their advice thereupon and the same being read, the board highly approves thereof" (*Va. Council Jour.*, II, 283). TJ's Proclamation restated, on the part of Virginia and in somewhat amplified terms, the Proclamation of Congress, 14 Aug. 1776, inviting the German mercenary troops to desert the British service; see JCC, V, 653-5. TJ was the probable author of Congress' Proclamation, as he certainly was of the Proclamation issued by Congress on 27 Aug. 1776, which was directed to the officers of the mercenary forces and which is printed above, Vol. 1: 509; see the note there and also L. H. Butterfield, "Psychological Warfare in 1776: The Jefferson-Franklin Plan to Cause Hessian Desertions," Amer. Philos. Soc., *Procs.*, XCIV (1950), 233-41.

1 The engrossed copy has the following caption: "By His Excellency Thomas Jefferson Esqr. Govr. of the Commonwealth of Virga."

2 Preceding two words were interlined by TJ in Dft as a substitute for "the parliamt. of Gr. Brit.," deleted. This alteration proves that in composing the present draft TJ was for the most part copying directly from Congress' Proclamation of 14 Aug. 1776, which has "the parliament of Great Britain" at this point.

3 TJ here ended his quotation-paraphrase of Congress' Proclamation of 14 Aug. 1776, for that Proclamation ends at this point.

4 In Dft TJ wrote "their." It is corrected in an unidentified hand to "his" in both Dft and engrossed copy.

5 The last paragraph of the engrossed copy reads: "Given under my Hand and the Seal of the Common Wealth at Richmond this second day of February in the Year our Lord 1781: and of the Commonwealth the fifth."

To David Ross

SIR In Council February 2d. 1781.

I do myself the pleasure of inclosing your appointment as Commercial Agent to this State. The General Assembly have by their

Act declared that they will make good all your Engagements and thereby pledged the faith of the State to supply any deficiency of the Funds put into your hands or any accidental losses which may occur. To which I have only to add an assurance that every aid and facility shall be furnished you which are in the power of the Executive.

I am with much respect Sir Your most Obt. Huml Servant,

THO JEFFERSON

Tr (ViWC); written below Tr of the Commission, dated 23 Jan. 1781, appointing David Ross "Commercial Agent for this Commonwealth." FC and another Tr of the letter are in Vi.

See TJ to Ross, 29 Jan. 1781. THE GENERAL ASSEMBLY . . . BY THEIR ACT: An Act for the more effectual and speedy clothing of the army, under the terms of which Ross was appointed; it was passed at the Oct. 1780 session (Hening, x, 376-8).

From Charles Scott

SIR — Haddrils Point 2d. Feby. 1781

Since my address to Your Excellency of 30th. Ult. wherein I mention'd the Sail of the bills upon Parr, I find on the return of Lt. Colonel Clarke who was sent to Charles Town to Negotiate them; that a Deduction of 10 Pr. Cent. will be obliged to be allow'd for the want of their triplicate, which Never Came to hand here and I Suppose from some reason was detain[ed] in Virginia. Other disadvantages on the price of Necessaries, for the Soldiers will attend this omission; for I assure Your excellency the Soldiers Nakedness, and the Wants of the Officers in General, will by no means adm[it] of delaying the Sale of the bills; which I must sell at the loss of 10 P. Ct.—and Considering the Circumstances, I am convinced must be approved of.

I have the Honor to be Your Excellencys Mo. obt & mo. Hble. Servt., CHS. SCOTT. B.G. Virga. Line

RC (NN).

To Steuben

SIR — Feby. 2d. 1781.

General Arnold having left in the hands of Mr. Buchanan of this place twenty Guineas for purposes not approved of by us I am to beg leave to trouble you with the ordering it to be returned by flag.

I am with great respect Sir Your mo: ob: hble. Servant,

TH: JEFFERSON

RC (NHi); in a clerk's hand, signed by TJ; addressed to Steuben, but without indication of place; endorsed. FC (Vi).

Nothing else is known concerning this sum of money left by ARNOLD in the hands of MR. BUCHANAN of Richmond, but see Steuben to TJ, 15 Feb.

To John Syme

SIR Richmd. Febry. 2d. 1781.

Should any of the Stores be on their way up before my last order becomes notified to Mr. Watkins they had better be received and Stored at Newcastle than to be sent back. If your letter mentioned Genl. Nelsons call of your lower battalion, it escaped me. I must confer with Baron Steuben on the subject from whom whatsoever order is given will go to Genl. Nelson. The observation on the failure to make returns of their militia by the County Lieutenants was become necessary, as not more than ⅓ made any return at all. Mr. Smith the S.Q. [State Quartermaster] was instructed some time ago to go to New Castle and endeavour to procure fields in order to send his foot horses to, to be fattened with the public Corn there. I suppose him to be in the execution of this order. T.J.

FC (Vi).

To John Browne

SIR Richmond Feby. 3d. 1781

I have last night received such a representation of the condition the Southern Army, is like to be in, for want of provisions as to give serious apprehensions, that it may be obliged to retire into this State, and of course to draw the Southern enemy into it. It therefore becomes absolutely necessary that whatever pork can be procured, should be laid in on the Roanoke, and that the forces and posts within this State be subsisted on beef. For this purpose it will be proper that you immediately appoint a deputy in each county with orders to furnish you without delay with all the beef that can be eaten, and put up and prepare by feeding what may be necessary to continue the Subsistence of these posts through the winter.

I am Sir Your Humble Servt., TH. JEFFERSON

Tr (Vi); endorsed. FC and another Tr are in Vi.

The Council's proceedings of this day help to clarify the complex arrangements being made for provisioning the southern army: "The board on consideration that one Deputy Commissioner in each Senatorial District, under the Act of Assembly for reviving and amending the Act for procuring a supply of Provisions & other necessaries for the use of the army may not be sufficient to answer the purposes of the said Act; advise that Mr. Brown the Commissioner of the provision law, be directed to appoint a Deputy in each County, with instructions to procure immediately all the eatable beef possible; the said Deputy shall be allowed at the rate of 4,000 ℔ tobacco by the year, or its worth in paper money according to the valuation made by the grand Jury at the Court next before the date of their warrant" (*Va. Council Jour.*, II, 285). See the following letters to Browne and Claiborne. There is in Vi a letter from Browne to Francis Lee, 8 Feb. 1781, appointing Lee deputy commissioner for Warwick co. and outlining his duties in detail. For the charge that Browne had disregarded TJ's orders for supplying Greene's army, see Carrington to TJ, 1 Feb.

To John Browne

SIR — In Council Febry. 3d. 1781.

In my letter of this date directing the immediate appointment of your deputies in each County I omitted to desire you to instruct them to give notice without delay to the Court of their County of the place within their County at which they will receive the waggon team and other appendages provided by the Act for supplying the army with clothes, provisions and waggons: which waggon team and appendages they are immediately to deliver to the Continental Quarter Master, taking his receipt and certifying to you the cost of the whole that you may debt the Continent with it.

I am Sr. Your hbl. Sert., THS. JEFFERSON

FC (Vi). See note on preceding letter.

To Richard Claiborne

SIR — In Council Febry. 3d. 1781

The establishment of a Harness Manufacture in Albermarle, seems advisable, but the Barracks will be much better than Charlottesville, because the German commanding Officer may and probably will prohibit the men from leaving the Barracks.

The necessity of the most active exertions to procure provisions for our Army has obliged us to require Mr. Brown to appoint a Deputy in each County, instead of each Senatorial district, as formerly intended. The place of delivery of the Waggons and Teams shall be notified to the County Courts by these Deputies. It will probably be at their Offices.

I inclose you your Warrant for half a Million of pounds which I hope will enable you to procure drivers among other purposes which will require money from you.

I am &c., T. JEFFERSON

FC (Vi). Enclosure not found.
See Claiborne to TJ, 29 Jan., and Claiborne to Charles Pettit, following.

Richard Claiborne to Charles Pettit

SIR Richmond. 3d. February. 1781

I hope you will readily excuse me for not writing you before now, when I assure you, that nothing has kept me from it but a close confinement to public business; that I might be able to give you some certain information respecting the Quarter Master's department in this state. I expect you have, by this time, received Letters from Colonel Carrington, advising you of my Appointment of Deputy Quarter Master for the State of Virginia, and of the circumstances which led to it. It is unnecessary for me to repeat them, therefore I shall proceed to acquaint you with what I have done.

I inclose to you No. 1. a Copy of the arrangement made by Colonel Carrington and myself, and approved of by the Executive. In this you will find, that the Counties are apportioned to each principal Post as a District which is to be under the influence of an assistant Deputy Quarter Master, and that the disposition is calculated for the convenience of Land and Water transportation.

No. 2 is a Copy of some instructions from the Executive to Mr. John Brown, who is Commissioner of the Provision Law for the state, which, by comparing with my arrangement, you will find, that instead of the Continental Quarter Master applying to the Civil Authority in each County, the Deputy Commissioners of the provision Law in the Senatorial Districts, were to furnish all the means of transportation whenever it should be necessary for us to call for them. This plan might have done, but it would have been attended with great delays and expence, as the Senatorial Districts do not corrispond with mine, and the residence of the Deputy Commissioners might have been at too great a distance to answer the immediate demand of the Service.

No. 3 is an Extract from Governor Jeffersons Letter to me, of this day, which confines the means of transportation to be furnished by a single person within each County, so that the assistant Deputy Quarter Masters will call upon the County Commissioners in rotation.

I can assure you, Sir, that no business was ever Undertaken so destitute of means and Support, as the one in which I am engaged. Indeed it is as much as I can say, that the Department had an existance when I took charge of it. There was no System, no Officers, no Stores, nor no money; and what was still worse no credit with the People. You perhaps will ask then upon what principle, or what veiw did I undertake so arduous a task? I engaged from no other motive, than to promote the service of my Country. The Appointment was proposed to me by Baron Stuben and Colonel Carrington, at a time when the Idea of such a thing had never occured to me; and considering, that by persuing the same Line of diligence I had done in the department before, I might still be useful, I accepted the Commission.

The late invasion of this State, did me great injury! I was considerably advanced in my preparations for business, but the confusion into which the whole Country was thrown by the Enemy, almost unfixed every thing I had done. Myself, with what Officers I had appointed, were obliged to take the Field, and acted for the Troops until the Enemy returned to their Shipping.

I have now engaged all my assistants, and have them fixed at the principal Posts mentioned in the arrangement. No. 4 is a Return of their names. They are every one, Gentlemen of undoubted varacity and with whom I can chearfully serve; but they want instruction in this business. I have taken great pains in giving them every information that I am capable of, and have not the least doubt, if we are properly supported, strict justice will be done to the public, and the business will prosper. To give them the true sense of what a Quarter Master ought to be, will require some time, which I hope you will take into consideration, and not expect more from us than we are able to perform; for be assured, that the business was begun as tho' there had never been a Department before.

I am now prepared for business, but Sir, one thing is wanting to enable me to answer the purpose of my appointment. Money must be had! With this, in the hands of the Agents, in commencing our operations, we can restore public credit, and equip the Southern army in a short time. The Confidence of the people is lost in the public Officers, and we can only regain it by punctual payments. At present, myself and my Officers are held in a very favorable point of veiw, and the Merchants and others, with whom I have conversed, assure me, that they will spare any thing they have towards equiping the Army, if I can only put them in some sure way of getting paid for their goods. We are considered as having entered the Department, principally from a zeal for the service of our Country; and as I am conscious to myself that it is the Case, I beg you to help me to support this good character throughout the department, while I have the honor to hold it. You will recollect, Sir, that we are nearly all officers who have served with reputation in the army, and would beg that we may not forfeit a thing which is so dear to us, by entering into an employ, against which great jealousies and Suspicions have prevailed for a long time. By discharging our Contracts punctually at first, we shall establish our credit; and should money fail us after that, we could still proceed by giving Certificates in Specie or Tobacco, to be paid in that or other money equivalent; but at present, such Certificates would be ineffectual. The Merchant must have a return of his money to go on in trade, and it is vain to Attempt to persuade him to any thing contrary to his wishes, and to the prejudice of his interest. I have obtained a Warrant from the Executive on the Treasury of this state for five hundred thousand Pounds, but there is such large draughts before me that I despair of getting any in Season. I have applied frequently, but the Treasurer, who is a very good man assures me that the ten Million which was emitted by the last Assembly, is engaged, including my Warrant, and that it is not in his power to prepare the Money fast enough. The destruction in the press by the Enemy, and the Sett hours for business in the different Boards, are other causes of delay, which I see no likelihood of being removed. There is but one press which can be used; and that has the News papers, the Acts of Assembly, the advice and derections of the Executive, and many other things to print, so that Money hardly gets its portion of time. Nothing can be done by any Board here, except the Treasury, but between Nine O'Clock in the Morning, and 'till two O'Clock in the afternoon; after that all business ceases until the same hours the next day. You will not be Surprised then, that the Money is not signed in time, when it has to go through the hands of the Auditors, after being prepared by the Treasurer; neither will you think me tadious in the business, when I am connected with, and dependant upon men governed by such slow methods. Perhaps it may be right, but as I am of a different way of thinking at this time, I have mentioned the circumstances, that I may not be considered careless of the Public interest. I have only to repeat once more, that Money must be had, or all my endeavors, with those of my Officers, will be ineffectual, and we must fall under the disagreable censure of having undertaken what we were not able to perform. I feel the great weight which is upon my Shoulders, and in behalf of all who have done me the honor to engage with me, I look up to you for Support. It is not with a Veiw of accumulating wealth that we have undertaken the business, but from a zeal to serve our Country. Be good enough then, to enable us to give a Spring to the business at first, and I have not the least doubt but we shall rise Superior to every difficulty which is before us.

Public credit is so far exhausted here, that I am obliged to make my own personal property liable for houses to Answer the demands of the Service. I beg that you will consider this matter in time, as the money becomes due the 1st. day of January next and be prepared to secure me from Suffering. Had I not have done this, I could not have proceeded in the business but relaying upon my Supporters for timely aid, I did not hesitate to render every assistance in my power.

I have received from Major Forsyth, the method of keeping the Accounts and Returns, addressed to him as Deputy Quarter Master for the state of Virginia, from your Office. In my first Circular Letter to the Assistants, I enjoined upon them in a very Particular manner, the necessity of engaging, as a Clerk, a person well Acquainted with Accounts and Bookkeeping, that the rendering clear and distinct Accounts, was a matter, which I should require particularly of them, and that they should make it one of their first Objects. I am sensible they will do their utmost to give satisfaction; but I am doubtful it will be a difficult task to get persons capable of performing such a matter, as the business of Speculation is too predominant in this part of the Country. There are very few who do not make more in the common trading way, than we can possibly give them from the Public. It was a fortunate circumstance, that I engaged Commissioned Officers to fill the Department; but some of them begin to say already, that if they cannot be enabled to do speedy justice to those with whom they make Contracts, they cannot remain in the business. The Officers from having been in the state Line for a long time, were deprived of service when those Regiments were reduced, and not being reconciled to lead a life of dissipation, did me the honor to enter the Department, or [as?] the Sallery which is allowed by the System was not Sufficient to induce other good men, who were in private business, to engage. However, I shall do my utmost to have the Accounts and returns rendered in Season and as correct as lies in my power.

The State is almost destitute of every kind of Stationary. Blank Books are not to be had. I beg you to send me ten Setts for the Accounts and Returns, which will be appropriated to my Office, and the Nine assistant Deputy Quarter Masters. Be kind enough to send some Paper, wax, Inkpowder and wafers, as they are not to be had here.

I have the honor to be, with great respect and esteem your most obedient Humble Servant, RD. CLAIBORNE D Q Mr St Virga.

Tr (DNA: RG 93); in a clerk's hand; at foot of text: "A Copy." This copy may have been sent to Quartermaster General Pickering. The enclosures transmitted with the recipient's copy (not found) were presumably the following: (1) The Carrington-Claiborne Plan for the Quartermaster's Department in Virginia, printed above under 1 Jan. 1781; (2) a letter from TJ to John Browne, possibly the missing letter of instructions enclosed in TJ to Browne, 1 Jan., q.v.; (3) extract of TJ's letter to Claiborne of 3 Feb., stating that Browne is to appoint a deputy in each county instead of each senatorial district (what appears to be the original of this enclosure, in a clerk's hand, is in OFH); and (4) a list of Claiborne's assistants in the state quartermaster's department, not found.

Charles Pettit, of New Jersey, was assistant quartermaster general of the Continental army from Mch. 1778 to June 1781 (DAB). The present letter to him from the newly appointed Continental deputy quartermaster for Virginia is included in full because it is not only closely interrelated with TJ's correspondence with the Continental and state quartermasters at this period, but because it furnishes a vivid (but biased) picture of conditions in Virginia between the British invasions in early 1781.

From William Davies

SIR Chesterfield Feby. 3. 1781.

Inclosed I transmit copies of the resolution of Congress and the opinion of the board of war of this state with your Excellency's order respecting Captain Peyton the sub or state clothier. I think there has not yet been much reason to apprehend so great an over proportion of cloathing would be in his hands, as to induce the Continental Cloathier General to direct a distribution of it to other troops, and I know it is the inclination and, I conceive from the ordinance, it is the duty too, of the State Clothier to hold himself accountable to the Executive for his application of any cloathing he may receive, excepting only such articles as may be delivered to him by the Continental Clothier General. This has been Captain Peyton's practice hitherto, as he informs me, and he desires me to ask your Excellency whether you have any other or further instructions to give him relative to the discharge of his duty. Your Excellency may be assured that much waste has resulted from the issue of cloathier's stores to other persons than the sub cloathier. It is a matter within my certain knowledge that cloth sufficient for 40 or 50 coats has been issued sometimes to one and sometimes to another, and very little other security for the proper application of it than the integrity of persons who were strangers. Confident of the importance of the issues to the army going always thro' one certain channel, I would respectfully submit it whether it would not be necessary during the present division of the Virginia line, that a deputy, (perhaps an officer) should be appointed either for the troops here or those to the southward. If the deputy should, in the first instance, be ordered to the southward, all the cloathing intended for the Virginia troops might be delivered to the Sub cloathier here, who should, agreeably to your Excellency's directions, send forwards to the southern army equitable proportions of such issues from the State store, to be delivered to his deputy there. This deputy as well as the Sub cloathier himself, should be required to settle with the regimental cloathiers, to whom they respectively may have issued cloathing, always within one month after such issues were made. The deputy within another month should settle with the Sub cloathier, and the Sub cloathier every three months or oftener with the State agent or commissary of stores. Unless some such mode is adopted, I can assure your Excellency, (and I speak it from a good deal of experience) that you will never be able to learn what becomes of your cloathing: and it is more particularly necessary now, as from the unhappy deranged state of the Virginia line, the whole are obliged to act by detachment. I mention an officer as being the most proper person to be the clothier's deputy, because he will be more attentive to the interests of the troops than another would be, and because he may be had at less expence, especially as there are several regimental paymasters, who from the reduction of the several regiments, are out of employ tho' they do not conceive themselves out of office. One of these might very easily be engaged for this business. I would farther respectfully submit it to your Excellency, whether it would not be necessary for a settlement to be had by Mr. Armistead immediately, for all the cloathing issued for the use of the soldiery, at least for the last year; that a more equal and systematic method may be in future pursued, and justice done to all. Other lines of the army are much better regulated than the Virginia line is or appears likely to be in this particular; and I know full well, from what I have often seen, that if any cloathing has been sent on to the southward, and no appointment, similar to what I have proposed, has taken place, that you will find with your greatest exertions you will never be able to obtain an adequate knowledge either of the quantities of cloathing actually issued to the men or the manner of its being executed. Checks are necessary to make men diligent and careful as well as to make them honest, and there is at present hardly any thing of the kind in the army, except the excellent establishment of inspection, of which Baron Steuben is at the head. Should your Excellency have no copy in your possession of the other parts of the ordinance of Congress, of which the inclosed is an extract, I will at your request transmit one. I shall add no further than to express my sentiments drawn from long observation, that double the quantity of cloathing is or at least has been destroyed in the army, than would have been the case had the officers been often and regularly called to account for the application of the cloathing that has passed thro' their hands, and put into the possession of the soldier. A great deal has been underhandedly sold by the men, and no account being required of the officer, he therefore pays no attention to the men. Another great cause of our distresses has been the want of materials to mend our cloaths; but this your Excellency seems disposed to prevent in future.

The Artificers from Warwick are not yet arrived. I hope your Excellency will favor the men with a few more hats or leather caps at any rate. I keep up all the cloathing I receive, till every thing can be delivered at once. It will be great saving in the end to have tent poles made. Without them the tents will be ruined in a fortnight. I must remind your Excellency of my application for a little money for my taylors, and some to pay for making shirts. I have no answer upon that subject. It is of consequence to the soldiery and the state too for this matter to be decided. It is impossible for the men to move without.

I have the honor to be Sir, with the highest respect, your Excellency's most obedt. humble servt., William Davies

RC (Vi); addressed and endorsed. Enclosures: Presumably (1) copy of resolve of Congress, 29 Sep. 1779, issuing a warrant of $400,000 for obtaining clothing for the Virginia troops in Continental service (printed in JCC, XV, 1125); (2) copies of instructions of the Va. War Office to John Peyton, clothier general for the state, 8 Nov., and TJ's approval thereof, 9 Nov. 1779 (printed above under their respective dates).

On the present date the Council directed William ARMISTEAD "to give Bond and good security, in penalty of a hundred thousand weight of tobacco, for the due and faithful discharge of his office as Clothier general" for Virginia (*Va. Council Jour.*, II, 285).

To David Geddes

Sir Richmond Febr. 3d. 1781

Our prisoners in N. York being at present much distressed for a sum of money amounting to 14,492 hard dollars, it would make me very happy should you have present occasion to sell draughts to that amount for paper money at the rate of exchange current at that time with you. Your draughts on me expressing the rate of exchange and accompanied with a certificate from the American

Officer commanding at the post that such is the rate current at that market shall be honoured on sight to that amount. Any preference which you may give us in the purchase of your bills on equal terms, and any anticipation of the ordinary periods of your draughts will be considered as an evidence of that accomating [accommodating] disposition, so worthy of being cultivated as it tends to make all parties happier, and as entitling the corps of which you are generally, or yourself personally to a reciprocation of kind office. Your answer informing me whether anything can be done in this business will oblige Sir, Yr. mst. Obt. & Mst. hble. St., T.J.

FC (Vi); captioned: "Mr. Geddis Paymaster to the Convention Troops." Enclosed, with the letter following, in TJ's letter to James Wood of this date, q.v.

See *Va. Council Jour.*, II, 285, and Geddes' reply to the present letter, 24 Feb. 1781.

To James Hamilton and O. C. A. Mengen

SIR Richmd. Febry. 3d. 1781.

I do myself the pleasure of inclosing you an extract of a letter I received from Majr. Genl. Phillips containing a proposition for the mutual accommodation of the Captives on both sides; I shall be very happy if it can be carried into execution, tho' to bring it within our power it will be necessary that we furnish the mony of the State, and receive credit for it in gold and silver at the exchange which shall be current at market. Our prisoners at New York are now peculiarly distressed for a sum of mony amounting to 14,492 hard dollars. Should it be convenient for you to call for any sum of paper money for the use of the troops in Albermarle, your draughts on me expressing the rate of exchange and accompanied with a certificate from the American commanding officer at the same place, that such is the rate current at that market, shall be honoured on sight to that amount. My anxiety for the assistance of my Countrymen in New York induces me to add further, that any preference which you may by this means give us in the purchase of your bills on equal terms, and any anticipation of the ordinary periods of your draughts which you may think proper to use for our accommodation on the present occasion, will be considered as one of those kind offices which, as they tend to make all parties happier, it is our desire to cultivate and to multiply on our part. Your answer informing me whether anything can be done in this business will oblige Sir Your mst. obt. & mst. hbl. Svt., T.J.

FC (Vi); captioned: "Genl. Hamilton & Colo. Mingen." Enclosure: Presumably an extract from William Phillips' letter to TJ of 28 Nov. 1780, q.v. Separate letters were no doubt addressed to Hamilton, commanding officer of the British Convention prisoners, and to Otto Carl Anton Mengen, commanding officer of the German Convention prisoners (see Riedesel, *Memoirs*, II, 270, &c.); and both letters were enclosed in TJ's letter to James Wood of the present date.

See Hamilton's reply, 24 Feb. 1781.

Agreement with George Harmer for the Public Use of Slaves

In Council February 3d. 1781.

The Board agree to give thirty thousand weight of Tobacco for the within Slaves one year: and if Mr. Harmer takes them away on the 10th. of October, or at any time between that and the end of the year, he shall allow a Credit for a part of their cloathing and taxes proportioned to the time wanting to make up the compleat year. If they be withdrawn on Account of an Invasion, a Similar deduction is to be made for their Wages, Cloathing and taxes. Payment to be made half yearly.

TH JEFFERSON

Tr (Vi); endorsed in several hands: "Govern. & Council's agreemt. for Negroes 3 Februy. 1781 to commence 10 Jany. past. Mr. Harmers Papers 1781 Settled."

See Muter to TJ, 24 Jan., and Harmer to TJ, 25 Jan. 1781. The War Office Journal (Vi) has a minute under 3 Feb. 1781 stating that Harmer has been informed of these terms "and requesting him to inform, if the terms the Governor offers are agreable."

From George Muter, with Reply

SIR

War office Feby 3d. 1781.

I beg leave to inform your Excellency, that Capt. Irish received orders yesterday from Barron Steuben to be ready in three days to proceed to North Carolina, where he is to remain. This will immedeatly leave the state without a commissary of military stores, which (if not quickly remedied) will be productive of confusion and inconvenience.

I have the honour of enclosing a warrant in favour of Jno. Ellis for your Excellencys approbation. He has been a considerable time kept out of his money, and hopes by means of the warrant to be enabled to pay his taxes.

I have the honour to be Your Excellency's most hl servant

GEORGE MUTER. C.

Mr. Harmer begs to know the determination of your Excellency and the Honorable Council on his proposal of yesterday, relative to the hiring his negroes.

In Council Feb. 3. 1781.

Col. Muter will be pleased to look out for an active attentive officer to undertake the duty of Commissary of military stores.

TH: JEFFERSON

RC (Vi); addressed and endorsed. TJ's reply, in his own hand, is at foot of text. Enclosure not found, but the War Office Journal (Vi) has an entry under this date reading: "Warrant, to John Ellis for Nine hundred & twenty two Pounds ten Shillings due him for services performed & sundry articles furnished to the States Foundery in the year 1779. Account for the same & Manager's certificate lodged in this Office."

From George Muter

[*Richmond, 3 Feb. 1781.* Minute in the War Office Journal (Vi) under this date: "Letter to the Governor inclosing a Scheme presented to me by Dr. Pope (which I think reasonable) for paying the orderly's at the Hospitals, for consideration." Letter not located. The enclosure (Vi) is a 1-page memorandum, signed "M[atthew] P[ope]" and endorsed "Hospitals Dr. Pope," proposing that "The Orderlys and their Wifes who Act as Nurses to the Public Hospitals shall be allow'd from Jany. 1st. 1780 Twenty five Dollars Pr. Week Currency with the usual advantages heretofore allowed up to the last payment, and from the last payment in future so long as they shall be thought necessary five Shillings hard Money Pr. day" without privileges.]

To George Muter?

enclosing Terms for Rebuilding the Boring Mill

In Council Feb. 3. 1781.

The board approve of letting the building on the within terms, only postponing the advance of the money mentioned till the raising of the house. They recommend the providing the works for boring a single cannon at a time only, which will probably render all geer unnecessary except a water wheel. The size of the house should be reduced so as only to comprehend the works and leave necessary room for the workmen: or if raising a house on the old walls will render this as cheap, as building a smaller house on new walls, the spare room should be applied to some other purpose.

TH: JEFFERSON

ENCLOSURE

Boring mill 45 feet long 30 feet wide and 8 feet pitch, to be raised on the old walls.

Nails and Trees for the plank and scantling to be furnished, he to furnish timber for shingles himself. The work to be valued by two men indifferently chosen (if they disagree they to chose [a] third) when it is done, and to be paid in tobacco at 20/ pr. hundred, or in current money agreable to the valuation of the grand jury, at the last time preceeding the date of the warrant for paiment.[1]

One third of the price of building the house, to be paid in provisions valued in the same manner as the building. One third of the remainder of the price of building to be paid in money when the work is begun and one third of the provision another third at raising, and the remainder at finishing the house. Mr. Crow to keep 8 hands at least constantly at work and to begin on or before the 8th. of February next; and shou'd he be furnished with any timber or plank by the state, it is to be valued and deducted out of the price of the house in the same manner as the work is to be valued.

RC (Vi); written on verso of the enclosure. Without indication of addressee, but the enclosed terms for rebuilding the boring mill, without date, are apparently in George Muter's hand and must have been transmitted by him to TJ shortly before the Council acted; see Muter's letters of 22 and 24 Jan. 1781.

Letters from Turner Southall to Muter, 18 and 23 Feb. 1781 (in Vi), report that Mr. Nathaniel Crow is willing to proceed with the rebuilding "as soon as the terms for doing so are known" (printed in CVSP, I, 525, 534). Among the Contingent Fund Vouchers (Vi) is an order, signed by George Muter, countersigned by TJ, and endorsed as executed, to issue £1,000 to Anthony Crowe "in part of the price of building the boring mill at the foundery."

[1] Preceding six words substituted in TJ's hand for "time of payment," deleted.

From Thomas Nelson

Williamsburg, Feb. 3, 1781

I have visited the Posts below this Place, and am happy in informing your Excellency that the paroled People require nothing but Assistance to make them very spirited Friends to their Country. They have in general destroyed their Paroles, and have formed a very fine Company to join the Troops sent down. The Troops at present under my Command are altogether from the Counties whose Militias are directed to be discharged. . . . Having observed that the Country sustained a very great Loss in Hides from the Want of a proper Person to take Charge of them, I have directed all from this Port, and below to be deliverd to Mr. Plume, a good Tanner and very honest Man.

MS not located. Text (extracts only) from Walter R. Benjamin, *The Collector* (N.Y.), July 1948, item M1382, where the letter is described as an A.L.S., 1 p., sm. 4to.

THE PAROLED PEOPLE: Those who had accepted paroles from the invading force under Benedict Arnold; see TJ's Proclamation concerning Paroles, 19 Jan. 1781.

To Thomas Newton

SIR Richmond Febry. 3d. 1781.

The judge of the Admiralty of Pensylvania has given notice to our Delegates in Congress that there are three Negroes, Tom, Hester and Celia confined in jail in Philadelphia in consequence of a condemnation of a vessel in which they were taken. They say they are the property of a certain Money Godwin of Norfolk, that their Master went off with the British Fleet under Leslie, and gave them permission to do the same, on which they went on board the Vessel in which they were taken. I shall be much obliged to you to enquire and inform me whether these facts be true, or whether their master be in the State still. I am &c., T.J.

FC (Vi); at head of text: "Colo. Thos. Newton."

From Timothy Pickering

SIR Newburgh Feby. 3d. 1781.

I am this moment honoured with your Excellency's letter of the 15th ulto. informing of the appointment of Major Claiborne to be deputy quarter master for the state of Virginia. This was unexpected, and I fear may produce some difficulty.

In consequence of your Excellency's letter of November 21st, informing me of your having written to Major Forsythe, offering him the place of DQM for Virginia, and his own application to me for the appointment, I wrote to Major Forsythe, assuring him of my approbation. He was then at Philadelphia. The next day (Decr. 15th) I wrote also to your Excellency, expressing my satisfaction with your intentions respecting Major Forsythe. On the 25th of Decr. Colo. Pettit A.Q.M.G. wrote to me, informing of Major Forsythe's having applied to him for money as D.Q.M. in consequence of your Excellency's letter making him a tender of the office, of which he declared his acceptance. Colo. Pettit applied to the Treasury Board accordingly, and furnished Major Forsythe with the forms of accounts &c. An extract from this letter is inclosed.

I supposed Major Forsythe was deputy commissary of purchases for Virginia at the time your Excellency tendered him the office of D.Q.M. but that you deemed him competent to both offices, seeing the supplying provisions depended almost solely on the state. If there be an incompatibility in the two offices, the appointment should doubtless rest with Major Claiborne; otherwise, I conceive, Major Forsythe has a just claim to it. I beg leave however to submit the matter to your Excellency's decision. I have a regard for both the gentlemen; and hope the affair will be adjusted to their mutual satisfaction.

I was happy to hear from Genl. Greene that he had appointed a gentleman of Lieut. Colo. Carrington's talents and industry deputy quarter master for the southern army: but Colo. Carrington has totally mistaken his authority in conceiving that he had a right to interfere in the appointment of a single officer of a state; and Major Claiborne can therefore derive no preference from such interference. The first page and the plan for the quarter master general's department is decisive in this respect, and shews by whom such *state* appointments are to be made.

I exceedingly regret that this business has occasioned so much trouble to your Excellency; had it been in my power I would most gladly have prevented it: and I beg leave to thank your Excellency for the patient attention you have given to it.

I have the honour to be with the greatest respect, Sir, your most obedt. servt.,

TIM: PICKERING QM

RC (Vi); in a clerk's hand, signed by Pickering; addressed: "(Public Service) His Excellency Governour Jefferson Virginia. Colo. Miles will be pleased to forward this from Phila. T. Pickering QMG. by post or otherwise"; endorsed. Tr (DNA: RG 93, Pickering's Letter Book). Enclosure (filed with the letter in Vi): "Extract of a Letter from Colonel [Charles] Pettit AQMG dated Philadelphia Decr. 25th. 1780," stating that Pettit had some time ago been shown a letter from TJ to Forsyth "requesting him to accept the office of DQM for that state, and has since informed me that he has accepted it"; and that Forsyth had been given instructions and funds for carrying out his duties. (TJ's letter of appointment to Forsyth has not been found.)

The letters here mentioned as exchanged between Pickering and TJ are printed above under their dates, except TJ's to Pickering, 21 Nov. 1780, not found.

From John Tyler

SIR Charles City Feby. 3d—'81.

I receiv'd your Summons by Express, and shall pay due attention thereto, as soon as my little domestic affairs are brought into order[1] again. After a long application to business in the Assembly it's reasonable to suppose I wish'd to have enjoy'd a few weeks at home; but one day did not pass before we were invaded, and all who liv'd near the River were obliged to retire to a more secure situation with their Families in order to render more Service when occasion required than could have been done otherwise. I hope therefore, that although my neglect of Duty is not justifiable, my peculiar situation will at least be an excuse for it.

In ten or twelve days I expect to be in Richmond, unless your Excellency may think fit to demand my Attendance sooner. I am with the highest regard your Excellency's Most obedient Servant,

JOHN TYLER

RC (Vi); addressed and endorsed.

YOUR SUMMONS BY EXPRESS: See TJ's circular letter to Members of Assembly, 23 Jan. 1781, q.v.

[1] The words "little domestic affairs" and "order" are heavily underscored, probably by someone other than Tyler.

To Peter Wagener

SIR Richd. Febry. 3d. 1781.

The inclosed is an Extract from a letter written to me by Colo. Davies who commands at Chesterfield Court-house. I make no doubt you are able to state this matter to our satisfaction, and while duty impels me to require it on behalf of the souldier, my own wishes concur perfectly in affording you an opportunity of justifying yourself by placing this transaction in its true light.

I am with much respect Sr. Yr mst. obt. hbl. sert.,

THOS. JEFFERSON

FC (Vi); captioned: "Colo. Waggoner." The letter from Davies, of which an extract was enclosed by TJ, has not been found, but it was the one to which TJ replied on 1 Feb., q.v. See also TJ to Davies, 6 Mch. 1781.

Peter Wagener, county lieutenant of Fairfax, signed his name in the form we have used, and is listed in Gwathmey's *Hist. Reg. of Virginians in the Revolution* under this spelling.

To James Wood

SIR Richmond Feby. 3d. 1781.

The inclosed letters will sufficiently explain to you their object: I shall be much obliged to you to endeavour to negociate the purchase of bills therein proposed with all the expedition you can. It is natural to expect that the demand for such a sum will raise the exchange to a certain degree. We have no right to expect to force the ordinary course of things and must therefore submit to it. Should a higher exchange be insisted on than has been before currently given you will be pleased to certify the last current rate of exchange, by which we shall judge of the reasonableness of the rise.

I am with much respect Sir Your mo. obedt. & mo. hble. Servt.,

TH: JEFFERSON

RC (MHi); without indication of addressee, but endorsed in Wood's usual manner. FC (Vi); captioned: "Colo. Wood"; notation of alternative addresses at foot of text: "Colo. Wood at the barracks in Alberl. or at Fredk. town in Maryland. Colo. Wood or in his absence Colo. Taylor at the barracks." Enclosures: TJ's letters to Geddes and to Hamilton and Mengen of the present date, qq.v.

To George Muter

[*Richmond, 4? Feb. 1781.* Minute in War Office Journal (Vi) under date of 5 Feb.: "Letter from the Governor received yesterday requiring Mr. Moody to be directed to make seventy five tent poles, and ten Wheelbarrows immediately: four of Mr. Moodys men to go to Hoods: four more to be employed in making carriages: Application to be made to the Officers of the State Artillery to come in to be instructed by Capt. Groar; and informing of the number of Cannon wanted immediately to be mounted." Letter not located, but the War Office Journal contains various entries under 5 Feb. indicating that these orders were carried out. On Groar (Groer, &c.) see also TJ to Muter, 23 Nov. 1780.]

From Meriwether Smith

DEAR SIR Fredericksburg, Feb: 4h: 1781.

I am on the road to Philadelphia, and have just Time to acquaint you that I have received Letters from De francy dated at Bourdeaux informing me that he should find no Difficulty in complying with the Contract he had made with this State; and that I might expect him in the Spring of the Year.

He earnest requests me to press the providing of the Tobacco for his Ships, as Nothing but Dispatch can render the Trade here beneficial to his Friends. I entreat you, my dear Sir, to be attentive to this Circumstance, as I am convinced in my Mind that Notwithstanding our other Endeavours, we shall find this the Chief Source from whence our Supplies will flow, and the only one on which we may with certainty depend. M. de Beaumarcha[is] continues still disposed to serve America and will prosecute his first Plan. The fault will be ours, so far as we are concerned, if we do not turn it to our Advantage.

The Loss of Charles town and the Reports wh[ich] were industriously circulated, that it had been given up by Lincoln and that Congress were disposed to make Peace with Britain on any Terms, have served to embarrass our Affairs in France, as the Ministry were much alarmed on the Occasion; having before, for some Time, entertained Suspicions of such a Design.

De francy writes me that he shall be out with ten Ships well armed, two of which will be of the Line.

I rejoice with you on Morgan's late Success—tis a great Affair and will be very important I apphrehend in its Consequences. Without it, I suspect that Genl. Green would have found himself shortly [in a] very perilous Situation. This will give Spirits to the People, strengthen our Hands and give us *Time* which I beleive we want.

The Speaker left this place Yesterday. My Carriage is broken down, but I shall proceed to Morrow.

I am with great Esteem & Regard, Dr Sir, Yr: most obedt. hble Servt.,

M: SMITH.

RC (Vi); addressed and endorsed.

DE FRANCEY: See Agreement with De Francy, 11 May 1780.

From George Walls

Berkeley, 4 Feb. 1781. The time of the men in the regiment to which Walls belongs will expire in less than twelve months, but "I am Certain they Cou'd be cheafly all inlisted for the war" and with less expense if they were asked to engage now rather than later. Requests a sum of money by "the bearer Majr. Hunter" in order to obtain these enlistments.

Tr (Vi). This letter is puzzling. First, it appears to be a recipient's copy and is found among the Executive Papers; it is, however, endorsed (in part): "Copy." Second, it is in large part a duplicate of Walls' letter to TJ of 30 Jan.: both were identical in substance and both were carried by Major Hunter. The explanation may be that Hunter, who carried several other communications (see Gates to TJ, 2 Feb.), was delayed in setting out, Walls thereupon took advantage of the delay to redraft his letter, and, through mistake, Hunter brought away both the versions of 30 Jan. and 4 Feb., the latter being copied before disappearing. But this is conjectural.

To the Auditors

In Council Feb. 5. 1781.

The bearer hereof Lewis Duval came express from Monongalia on necessary business.

TH: JEFFERSON

RC (Vi: Contingent Fund Vouchers); endorsed (in part): "£657." On the face of TJ's note are the following calculations in another hand:

"350 miles coming	700
Do. returning	700
1 Days Attendce	60
	1460 @ 14/.
	3
	£4380
	219
	657"

A separate note accompanies TJ's note and reads as follows: "Ms. Auditors I am well Acquainted with the distance from here to the Monongalia and I think it is three hundred and fifty Miles the way most commonly traveled to Mr. Duvals House. John Madison jr."

To the Auditors

GENTLEMEN Feby. 5. 1781.

Be pleased to issue to Colo. George Matthews, a Warrant for three thousand pounds upon account of expences on his way from the northward to this State on business of our prisoners in New York.

By Advice of Council. TH: JEFFERSON

RC (Vi: Contingent Fund Vouchers); in a clerk's hand, signed by TJ; endorsed.

To the Auditors

GENTLEMEN Feby 5. 1781.

Be pleased to issue to Colonel John Syme a Warrant for one thousand five hundred pounds on account for removing public Stores.

By Advice of Council. TH: JEFFERSON

RC (Vi: Contingent Fund Vouchers); in a clerk's hand, signed by TJ; endorsed.

To the County Lieutenants of Dinwiddie and Essex

SIR Richmd. Febry. 5th. 1781.

I have received particular information that Richard Overby and Richard Wills two of Capt. Hardaway's company[1] of Militia of your county lately on duty below have deserted and carried off their arms; as they are triable by a Court-Martial of the Officers remaining in the field, I am to desire you to exert every effort to have them taken and when taken to send them under guard to Cabbin point or wherever else the principal encampm[ent] shall be.

I am with much respect Sir Your most Obt., T. JEFFERSON

FC (Vi).

1 A notation at foot of text indicates that in the letter to the county lieutenant of Dinwiddie the following should be substituted in place of the names of deserters from Essex co.: "Jesse Hood of Capt. Dixon's Company."

To William Davies

SIR Richmond Febr. 5th. 1781.

I am anxious to have secured for the detachment which is next to proceed Southwardly as many tents as will suffice for them, and to collect all the residue belonging to the State and send them down for the use of the Militia. Of 230 tents issued during the last invasion, I understand that 75 were sent on with Colo. Green's detachment, I find that about 28 were returned to this place, the rest I have reason to expect were delivered up at Petersburg, and I am informed that whatever were at that place were on the late approach of the enemy brought to Chesterfield Court House and moved from thence under your care. I shall be much obliged to you to inform me what number will be requisite for the detachment which is to go Southwardly, what number you have, and whether you know any thing of any others.

I am Sr. &c., T.J.

FC (Vi). See William Rose's Return of Tents, this date, below.

To George Gibson

SIR Richmond 5th. Febry. 1781.

The Executive are Shortly to proceed to the reformation of the State Forces according to a resolution of Assembly. As your commission is the oldest it is probable the Council will be of opinion that you are entitled to a continuance in command, and I think they will consider it as fortunate that they will be at liberty to continue you; from what passed in conversation when I had the pleasure of seeing you I apprehended you did not mean to remain in Service. I shall be very glad to know your wishes before We proceed to this business as I shoud be anxious to retain your Services if not entirely disagreeable to you, and if you were determined to retire that this might be effected on the footing you wou'd prefer. Your answer will oblige Sir Your very humble Servt.,

TH: JEFFERSON

Tr (Vi); at head of text: "Copy." The Tr is evidently in Gibson's hand; it was enclosed in a letter from Gibson to Gov. Thomas Nelson, dated at "Cumberld. County Pennsa.," 1 Aug. 1781 (Vi), which states that soon after receiving the letter above, and shortly before leaving Virginia, Gibson waited on TJ "and gave him the following reasons for the declining the Honor the Council intended to confer on me" in the following terms: "After a service of upwards of five years, during which I have received the approbation of His Excellency the Commander in chief and the General officers under which I have had the honor to serve, It is with heartfelt pain I conceive myself obliged to decline the acceptance of the Honor intended by Council, communicated in Your Excellencys letter of the 5th. Febry. I had determin'd from my first entering the Army not to quit the Service so long as I cou'd be of use, and that I cou'd continue without doing violence to my feelings. Notwithstanding I have remained in service since the Year 1777. under every disadvantage; against these injuries, I have remonstrated in the most respectful manner to the Legislature of this State, *without effect.* Promotions have been made which have affected the very partial and contracted Rank we have hitherto held. To continue therefore to serve wou'd be a tacit acknowledgment to the World that our complaints were frivolous, that We were destitute of Merit, and unfit for promotion. I wish therefore to retire for the Present from a service which hath been rendered truly disgusting not only to myself but also to the Corps I have had the Honor to serve with. If it is consistant with equity I wish to be considered A supernumeray Officer on the State establishment. Nor wou'd I leave the State at this Juncture but from a conviction that my family from my long long absence need my utmost assistance. If hereafter I can be of Service I shall conceive myself bound to pay implicit obedience to the Orders of this State of which I consider myself A subject and to which I have a strong local attachment." Continuing his letter to Nelson, Gibson added: "From the confusion which hath since ensued, from the rapid marches of the Enemy (which hath made my heart to ache more than once) It is probable the remembrance of So insignificant an Animal as I am may be buried in oblivion. I have therefore taken the liberty to Address Your Excellency, to tender my Poor services and to request I may not be exempted from the advantages accruing to Officers retiring Cum priviligio from service." Gibson was clearly copying from his letter to TJ when he quoted it to Nelson, but no such response to TJ's letter to him of 5 Feb. has been found, other than the present version.

The RESOLUTION OF ASSEMBLY in question, passed by the House of Delegates on 1 Jan. 1781, empowered the executive "to discontinue for the present, from actual service, such of the . . . officers who are supernumerary to the men composing at present the several regiments or corps on State establishment" (JHD, Oct. 1780, 1827 edn., p. 78); see also Gibson's letter to TJ, following, and Advice of Council, 6 Feb. 1781.

From George Gibson

Petersburg 5th. Febry 1781.

MAY IT PLEASE YOUR EXCELLENCY

Your favor of the 28th. ultimo did not come to hand before the 3rd. Inst. From its being folded into a small size or from the carelessness of the Bearer, it was found thrust in a letter from Your Excellency to A Gentleman of Dinwiddie County. I now do myself the Honor to transmit you a Return of the 1st Virginia State Regiment together with the Arms accoutrements Field equipage, Waggons, &c. being the State of the Regiment when we cross'd the Powtomack in September 1777 Also a return of the Arms we drew since the return of the Regiment to this State. I am sorry I had it not in my Power to send them sooner to you.

I was some time since honor'd with yours of the 14th. ultimo covering an Extract of a letter from His Excely. Genl. Washington which You desired might be communicated to the Officers of the two State Regiments. With the officers of the 2nd State Regiment I have not the least communication nor indeed am I acquainted with the Places of their residence. I am told Colo. Brent is at present at Annapolis Maryld. The greatest Part of the officers of the 1st. State Regiment are now in a service which from Its nature is truly Irksome. *The Command of undisciplined troops*, who as soon as they are taught their duty, are relieved by others with whom the Officers have the same trouble, So that in fact they are little better than Dril Serjeants. From these considerations it was with reluctance the Gentlemen accepted their appointments, and I am confident *Principle* alone induceth them to continue. I thought it therefore prudent to Keep them ignorant of the Determination of His Excelly. respecting them until they shall be relieved from their present engagements or until I have your positive Orders for making them acquainted therewith.

As I am unacquainted with the Acts of Assembly respecting the reduction of these regiments I shall esteem It a particular favor if You will please to acquaint me whether the Officers are to have the Emoluments of Half pay, Lands, Exemption from draughts.

I hope you will pardon the freedom I take in addressing you on this subject.

I have the Honor to be with the greatest Respect Your Obedt. Huml. Servt.,

GEO. GIBSON

RC (Vi); addressed and endorsed. Enclosures missing.

TJ's letters to Gibson of 14 and 28 Jan., here acknowledged, have not been found; the former evidently enclosed AN EXTRACT OF A LETTER FROM . . . GENL. WASHINGTON to TJ of 28 Dec. 1780, q.v., concerning Continental commissions for officers on the state establishment. See also TJ's letter to Gibson, preceding, and Advice of Council, 6 Feb. 1781, below. The GENTLEMAN OF DINWIDDIE has not been identified. Since the letter to Gibson was carried by the same person who bore the letter to the "Gentleman of Dinwiddie," the latter was probably written ca. 28 Jan. 1781. It may, therefore, have been the letter to Steuben of 29 Jan., since Steuben was then at Petersburg. It may also have been the letter to Robert Lawson of 31 Jan., since he was stationed in that vicinity. But most likely it was TJ's letter to John Banister of 30 Jan., for Banister, as county lieutenant of Dinwiddie, was certainly the leading citizen of the county and the one about whom such an allusion as that made by Gibson would have been readily understood by TJ.

From William Lewis

Osbornes, 5 Feb. 1781. Agreeable to TJ's instructions Lewis has "made Every Captain Acquainted what they have to do." There are now two vessels here that could take in military stores, and if required at Richmond they will be ordered up. Since contrary winds may keep Lewis and his force from getting to Hood's as soon as expected, provisions will be needed.

RC (Vi); 2 p.; addressed and endorsed; printed in CVSP, I, 490.

William Lewis was captain of an armed merchant vessel, the *Renown*, at this time lying in James River. Among the papers concerning the *Renown* in Vi (see note on TJ to William Lewis, 4 Mch. 1781), there is a copy of a letter from Steuben to "the Commodore, or Commanding officer of the Armed Merchant Vessells laying at or above Osbornes," 8 Jan. 1781, stating that it might be possible for the said vessels to take several enemy ships "lying in Appamatock" and requesting the officers to hold themselves in readiness for further orders. TJ's INSTRUCTIONS, referred to in the present letter but not found, may well have been subsequent orders relating to the same project.

To George Muter

[*In Council, 5 Feb. 1781.* War Office Journal (Vi) has the following entry under 5 Feb.: "Sent in to Council Mr. Milton Fords proposals for Building at the Fork of James River"; and on the following day the Journal enters the Council's answer of 5 Feb.: "Agreed to; Mr. Ford making due allowance for waggons, provisions or any other things furnished by the public, to be valued by the same persons who shall value the work." No other text located. Under date of 7 Feb. the *Va. Council Jour.* (II, 289) records "the sum of ten thousand pounds issued by Colonel Muter in favor of Milton Ford upon account." The War Office Journal under 7 Feb. records a warrant to Ford "for one thousand Pounds on Account in part payment for the Buildings he has contracted to erect for the State, at the fork of James River. Bond and Security lodged in this Office." And under 8 Feb. the same Journal records a "Certificate, that Milton Ford is engaged in building sundry houses for the State at the Fork of James River, and thereby cleared from Militia duty; and that his Brother Samuel Ford and John Jones are also engaged in the same Business with him and exempted also."]

From George Muter

[*Richmond, 5 Feb. 1781.* Va. War Office Journal (Vi) under this date records a "Letter, to the Governor respecting giving orders to Capt. Groar to remain sometime longer in this State." Letter not located, but see TJ to Muter, 23 Nov. 1780 and 4? Feb. 1781.]

From George Muter

War Office, 5 Feb. 1781. Lt. Col. Edmonds [Elias Edmunds] of the state artillery regiment is in Richmond for two days and desires to know if TJ has any orders respecting the regiment. Edmunds cannot make a return of the regiment, but his adjutant can, and Muter has written the adjutant for that purpose. One company of the regiment is serving with the southern army under Capt. [Christopher] Roane, whom Edmunds recommends strongly for continuation in service. "He also recommends Lt.   Browne of the state artillery (who is now in town) to be employed as an assistant Commissary of military stores for the state, and to be instructed by Capt. Grear [Groar]." Browne is willing to undertake the post and "desirous of being instructed."

RC (Vi); 2 p.

William Rose's Return of Tents, with Addenda by Jefferson

[5 February 1781]

A List of Tents delivered the Army & Militia during the last & present Invasion.

1780.		
Octo. 3d.	delivered to Stephen Southall for Genl. Muhlenburg	Tents 23
7	To Jno Carpenter QMS for the Garrison Reg.	48
31	To Ben Sharp sejt. for Colo Harrisons ditto	10
Nov. 4	To Richd Philips for Continental use. militia[1]	15
5	To Jno Hord QMS. militia[1]	45
7	To Wm Jones QM for major Magills corps	14
	ditto Magill for his use a horsemans tent	1
	To Capt Eddin 1 ditto	1
9	To Colo Spotswood 1 ditto	1
10	To Jno Royall Lt. for Colo Lawsons volunteers	20
16	To Capt Higginbothan for the Augusta militia. delivd. here to Southall[2]	7
	To Capt Christian for the Amherst ditto	7
	Capt Harrises for for ditto	5
17	To James Barret capt for ditto	7
24	To Wm. Barnet ensign for capt Morrison's compy Amherst Volunteers	9
	To Wm. Ingram for capt Johnsons compy Orange militia	17
		total 230. tents

Wm Rose DQMG

Of the 48. delivd to John Carpenter[3]

28. were retained for the State garrison regimt.
20. used by the militia annexed to that regimt. delivd. up at
—— Petsbg.
48.
14. to Jones disposed of as the 20

Besides the within, 14. of thick duck were compleated by Rose Feb. 3. 1780. which with 22. of those in possn. of Sta. gar. reg. were ordd. to be delivd to Capt. Gamble for the militia to be issd by ord. of Bar. Steub. or commdg. off. at principal encampmt. Feb. 5.

MS (DLC); apparently in William Rose's hand and signed by him, with insertions and additions by TJ as noted below.

See TJ to Davies, this date, above.

[1] This word inserted by TJ.

[2] Preceding four words inserted by TJ.

[3] All that follows Rose's signature is in TJ's hand.

To the Auditors

GENTLEMEN Feby 6. 1781.

Be pleased to issue to Doctor Pope a Warrant for seven thousand pounds upon Account as Director of the public hospitals.

By Advice of Council. TH: JEFFERSON

RC (Vi); in a clerk's hand, signed by TJ; endorsed.

See the Council's resolution of 1 Feb. 1781 respecting the state medical department and personnel (*Va. Council Jour.*, II, 282-3).

From Jonathan Clarke

SIR Albermarle Barracks Feby: 6: 1781.

I had the honor of writeing to your Excellency on the 8th: ultimo when I mention'd, that I had ascertain'd the quantity of Provisions due to the Convention Troops, to the satisfaction of the Issuing Commissary and that he had certify'd it to Mr. Hawkins the purchasing Commissary and that he was going the next day to Richmond for the money.

I now pray leave to acquaint you Sir, that Mr. Hawkins is return'd to this place without the money and he informs me that altho' he thought himself warranted to pay those arrears at the time he went down the Country and intended to have done it, but upon seeing Major Forsyth who was the Principal in his department, he finds it necessary to have your Excellency's orders to do it; therefore I take the liberty to enclose you, Sir, an account of the Provisions due agreeable to the returns of each Regiment which I lodged in the hands of Mr. Dickinson the Issuing Commissary, which he examined and found right, also copy of his certificate to Mr. Hawkins and copy of Mr. Hawkins's acknowledgement of having received that Certificate, and I pray the favor of your Excellency to give the necessary orders to compleat this bussiness which is the only object that detains me here to my very great disadvantage.

Mr. Hawkins also mention'd the rate at which the Provisions were to be paid. I told him I tho't the price which he at present gives would be the only government, if your Excellency's opinion coincides with mine, I also pray the favor of you to give instructions upon this head.

I have the honor to be very respectfully Sir Your Excellency's most obedient Humble: Servt:, JONA: CLARKE

Senior Commissary of the Convention Army

RC (Vi); endorsed: "J Clarke, Commissary Convention Army." Enclosures (filed with the letter in Vi): (1) "An Account of Provision due to the Convention Army. Meat commencing Septr: 13th: 1780. and Flour October 23d: and ending Novr: 17th: 1780. each date inclusive"; in Clarke's hand, listing the Convention troops by units and tabulating the amount of flour and meat due each unit; totals are 79,203 lb. flour, 193,095 lb. meat; this tabulation is printed in CVSP, I, 493-4. (2) Tr of a letter to Joseph Hawkins signed by "Elijah Dickinson, A[ssistant] C[ommissary] Issues, Barracks," 8 Jan. 1781, stating that "The within quantity of Provisions . . . are due to the Convention Troops agreeable to returns lodged in my hands"; below Dickinson's letter is Tr of statement signed "Jos[eph] Hawkins, A[ssistant] C[ommissary] P[risoners]," without place or date: "I acknowledge to have received a Copy of the above Certifcate."

See Hawkins to TJ, 30 Dec. 1780; Clarke to TJ, 8 Jan.; TJ to Clarke and also to Hawkins, 7 Feb. 1781.

From William Harrison

Yohogania County, 6 Feb. 1781. Received TJ's "Instructions" on 25 Jan., together with the cash sent by Col. Richard Campbell, for purchase of provisions and building boats; proceeded at once on the business but finds it out of his power to have provisions and boats ready before 1 June since both beef and most of the materials for boats, particularly iron, must be carried over the mountains. "The Commandant at Pittsburg has promised to furnish me some Tools of the Continental Store and Informed me that there was about fifty Light Batteaux at Fort Pitt which might be had by an Order from the Board of War, which I think is Much better Calculated for those Rivers than Bargus[1] as they will run over Shoals where a Keel'd Vessel must be Carried." The beef will require salt, which Harrison is not authorized to purchase. "The Cash Deliver'd me by Col. Campbell being nearly expended and the Inhabitants have been allready so much Impos'd on in this Country by the Contractors for the United States that it will be out of my power to do any thing without Cash."

RC (Vi); 3 p.; addressed (in part): "By Col Nevill"; endorsed. Printed in CVSP, I, 493.

TJ's INSTRUCTIONS to Harrison have not been found; they embodied part of the plan for mounting George Rogers Clark's offensive against Detroit; see TJ's letters of 23-25 Dec. 1780.

[1] The word appears to be "Bargus" or "Bargers" and may have been intended to be "Barges." It seems clear, however, that Harrison was here discussing the relative merits of the two types of craft that came to be known as flatboats and keelboats.

From Joseph Jones

DEAR SR. Phila: 6th. Febry 1781

We yesterday received information that General Parsons with a party of our Troops had passed over to Morrisana, attacked the Enemies Post there, burnt about 40 barracks, a quantity of Forage and brought off 52 prisoners. The bridge of Boats which the Enemy had over Harlem River was also destroyed. A late New York paper mentions the sailing of three ships of the line of the French Squadron at R. Island and that part of Graves Fleet had put to Sea in pursuit of them. If this intelligence be true it is probable you have already or will soon hear of them in the Chesapeake. Mr. Dunlap informed me this morning he had not heard from Mr. Hays these five weeks and that every thing necessary for prosecuting the business under the latter upon his coming up with some Cash to bear the expence of transporting them to Virga. should be forwarded in a week after his arrival and that He was surprised Mr. Hays was not come and that he had been so long without hearing from him. I mention this to your Excellency that if any thing on the part of the Executive is necessary to be done towards forwarding this matter it may be attended to and the Press got as soon to work as possible. Respectfully I am Yr. Exlys. obed Servt., JOS: JONES

P.S. Maryland has certainly acceded to the Confederation.

RC (Vi); endorsed.

MR. DUNLAP . . . MR. HAYS: John Dunlap and James Hayes, printers; see TJ to the Virginia Delegates in Congress, 31 Aug. 1708; also Hayes to TJ, 18, 23 Jan.; and the Virginia Delegates' letter to TJ, 20 Feb. 1781.

To George Muter

[*Richmond, 6? Feb. 1781.* War Office Journal (Vi) has the following entry under 6 Feb.: "Letter, from the Governor, enquiring what Camp Kettles were brought from Fredericksburg and how disposed off: whether the Waggons have returned that went for leather, and if Cartouch boxes were making." Not located.]

From George Muter

[*Richmond, 6 Feb. 1781.* War Office Journal (Vi) has the following entry under this date: "Letter, to the Governor in answer to one received from him this day, mentioning that no Camp Kettles were ready at Fredericksburg as I was told. I had no Letter by the Waggons. I have had no returns respecting Cartouch boxes, nor information respecting the Waggons sent for leather, but I will enquire and inform his Excellency as soon as possible." Not located; but in War Office Letter Book (Vi) is a copy of a letter of 7 Feb. from Muter to the state quartermaster general asking him to report to TJ on the kettles and wagons.]

From George Muter

[*Richmond, 6 Feb. 1781.* War Office Journal (Vi) has the following entry under this date: "Letter, to the Governor informing of Major Magill's intention of setting off in a few days for the Southern Army." Not found.]

From George Muter

[*Richmond, 6 Feb. 1781.* War Office Journal (Vi) has the following entry under this date: "Letter, to the Governor inclosing a Copy of a list received from Mr. Vowles; of the State Artillery Officers, with Mr. Vowles's Letter to me for his Excellencies perusal." The enclosed list of officers has not been found, but Henry Vowles' letter transmitting it to Muter, dated "Falmouth, Jany. 30th. 1781," is in Vi and is, in part, as follows: "The inclos'd is an accurate Return of the Officers belonging to the Regiment of State Artillery. I am exceeding sorry it is not in my power to furnish you with such a Return as you call for, respecting the Soldiers. I can only Account for those that March'd to Join the Southern Army, of whom there are only thirty . . . left, including the Non-commissioned Officers, the others having serv'd the time of their enlistments and got their discharges. Those remaining . . . are to serve during the War. A few days before I marched to the Southward, I transmitted to his Excellency the Governor, a particular Return of the Regiment wherein I particularized those who were to remain in the State, from those destin'd for the Southern expedition; perhaps that return is in existence; if it should not, Capt. Moody certainly can furnish you with a state of those left under his Command. I was unfortunate enough to lose most all the Papers respecting the Regiment with my Baggage, in that unfortunate Action near Cambden. . . ." Vowles' recollection about the return furnished TJ was quite accurate: there is in DLC: TJ Papers, 5:713, a tabulation dated 2 Apr. 1780 covering the years 1780-1782 and showing the "Different periods at which the terms of service expire of the State Artillery, who are under marching orders"; of the 310 men listed, the terms of all save thirty-two were to have expired before Mch. 1781. Vowles' return of 30 Jan., however, did not arrive in time for inclusion in the Returns of the State Regiments of 6 Feb., q.v. Vowles was adjutant of Edmunds' state artillery regiment (Gwathmey, *Hist. Reg. of Virginians in the Revolution*).]

From George Muter

[*Richmond, 6 Feb. 1781.* War Office Journal (Vi) has the following entry under this date: "Letter, to the Governor inclosing two accounts from Colo. Gibson's regiment, and desiring instructions relative to them as they are entirely new to me in their nature." Neither letter nor enclosure located.]

Advice of Council respecting Consolidation of the State Regiments

In Council February 6th 1781.

The board proceeded to take into consideration the resolution of General Assembly of the 1st. of January 1781. which is in these words to wit "Whereas the regiments on State establishment are greatly reduced in their numbers of men insomuch that most of the Officers belonging to them are without employment: the General Assembly taking the same into their consideration and sensible of the merit of the said Officers of whose Services they cannot now be availed for want of men induced by the exigencies of the State *have resolved* that the Governor with advice of Council be desired to discontinue for the present from actual service such of the said Officers who are supernumerary to the men composing at present the several Regiments or [Corps] on State establishment" and the returns of [the 1st. and 2d.] State regiments and State garrison regiment wher[eby] it appears that there are of the 1st. State regiment 192 non commissioned Officers and privates, of the 2d. State regiment 30 and of the State Garrison regiment 176. Whereupon they advise the Governor that the whole non commissioned Officers and privates of the said regiments be consolidated into one, to be divided into seven Companies and commanded by the oldest Lieutenant Colonel and Major and the seven eldest Captains, Lieutenants and ensigns of the said three regiments, and that all other the Officers of the said regiments be discontinued for the present from actual service as supernumeraries. And having no return of the regiment of Artillery but receiving information that there are not more men remaining thereof than will form a Company the greater part of which if not the whole are at present in actual service to the Southward under Captain Roane, they advise that the same be continued in service under his command as a Company until the expiration of their enlistments and that all others the Officers of the said Regiment be discontinued for the present from actual service as supernumeraries. ARCHD: BLAIR C.C.

MS (Vi); in Archibald Blair's? hand and designated by him "(A Copy)." MS mutilated; missing matter has been supplied from *Va. Council Jour.*, II, 287. Enclosed in TJ's letter to Speaker R. H. Lee, 1 Mch. 1781, q.v., and endorsed: "[Go]vernors Letter Stating sundry Matters March 2d: 1781. Referred to the Committee of the Whole House on the State of the Commonwealth."

See TJ to George Gibson and Gibson to TJ, both dated 5 Feb. 1781; see also Returns of the State Regiments, same date.

From Granville Smith, with Jefferson's Instructions to George Muter

SIR 6th. February 1781.

The enclosed is from Mr. Thomas respecting his purchase of canoes, and finding the prices much higher than what your Excellency calculated on, you will please to direct me whether I shall instruct him to continue his purchases, or not: also under whose care and direction the four that have come to Westham are to be put. I am Your Excellency's Obt. Hble. Servt.,

G. SMITH Ast.Q.M.Gl.

In Council Feb. 6. 1781.

Colo. Muter will be pleased to order the Overseer of the Foundery negroes or such other person as he thinks proper to receive and take care of the canoes brought and to be brought to Westham until a house can be built for them and the matter arranged. Chains and a lock or locks should be provided. TH: JEFFERSON

RC (Vi); addressed and endorsed. TJ's note to Muter is in his own hand below Smith's letter. Enclosure (Vi): Joseph Thomas to Granville Smith, 21 Jan. 1781, in which Thomas reported that he had bought only four tobacco canoes and had sent them to Westham.

Returns of the State Regiments

[6 February 1781 and after]

	Colonel	Lt. Col.	Majr.	Captn.	1st. Lts.	2d. Lts.	Ensns.	Serjt. Majrs.	Q. M. Serjts.	Serjts.	Dr. & Fifes		Rank and File: for the War.	Rank and File: for shorter terms.	Rank and File: for terms not specified.	Total N. Commd. & Privates
First State regiment Nov. 18. 80.	1.	1.	1.	3.	8		1.	1.	1.	10.	11.		152	17.		192
Second State regiment Nov. 18 80	1.	1.	1.	1.									30			30
State Garrison regiment Jan. 19. 1781.	1.	1.	1.	1.	4.		2.	1.	1.	14.	9.				151.	176
Regiment of artillery.																
Illinois regiment.																
Western regiment.																
Regiment of guards. Dec. 1. 80.	1.		1.	6.	4.		5.	1.	1.	11.	2.				223.	238.

Roll of the officers of the State regiments, State garrison regimt.[1]

Name.	rank	date of Commn.	promotion since	corps.	situation.	residence.
George Gibson.	Colo.	1777. June. 5.		1st. Sta. reg.		
William Brent.	Colo.	1779. Jan. 1.		2d. Sta. reg.		
George Muter.	Colo.	1779. Nov. 8.		Sta. Gar. reg.		
John Allison.	Lt. Col.	1777. June 11.		1st. Sta. reg.		Alexandria
Charles Dabney	Lt. Col.	1777. Jan. 23.		2. S. R.		
Chas. Porterfeild	Lt. Col.			S. G. R.		
Thomas Meriwether.	Majr.			1. S. R.		Caroline.
John Lee.	Majr.	1778. Feb. 1.		2. S. R.		
Charles Mcgill.	Majr.	1780 Feb. 26.		S. G. R.		
Wm. Hoffler.	Cap.	1777. Jan. 9.		1. S. R.	Supy.[2] May. 1.	
Thos. W. Ewell.	Cap.	31.		1. S. R.		
Windsor Brown.	Cap.	Feb. 28.		1. S. R.		Alexandria.
Thos. Hamilton.	Cap.	Mar. 3.		1. S. R.		Alexandria.
Abner Crump.	Cap.	May 10		1. S. R.		New-Kent.
Henry Dudley	Cap.	Sep. 1.		2. S. R.		
Thos. Armistead.	Cap.	1778. Apr. 6.		1. S. R.		
Charles Ewell	Cap.	June 1.		1. S. R.		Prince William
Augustine Stabb.	Cap.	Sep. 10		2. S. R.		
Machere[3] Boswell	Cap.	Sep. 15		2. S. R.		
John H. Holt	Cap.	Sep. 29.		1. S. R.		Chesterfield.
John Hudson	Cap.	Oct. 1.		2. S. R.		
William Long	Cap.	1779. Jan. 1.		2. S. R.		
William Campbell	Cap.	1779. Jan. 16		1. S. R.		K. & Queen.
James Moody	Cap.	Apr. 30		2. S. R.		
Nathanl. Welsh	Cap.	May. 1.		2. S. R.		
Angus Rucker.	Cap.	July 3.		1. S. R.		Culpeper.
Thos. H. Drew.	Cap.	July 3.		S. G. R.		

Roll of the officers of the State regiments (continued)

Name.	rank	date of Commn.	promotion since	corps.	situation.	residence.
John Mcelhany	Cap.	Aug. 25		2. S. R.		
John Fleet	1st. Lt.					
George Triplett	1st. Lt.	1777. Sep. 12.		1. S. R.	Supy May. 1.	
Chas. Yarbrough.	1st. Lt.	1778. Feb. 1.		1. S. R.		
Frederic Woodson	1st. Lt.	June. 1.		1. S. R.		Henrico.
John Fleet	1st. Lt.	Sep. 10.		2. S. R.		
Isaac Holmes	1st. Lt.	Sep. 15		2. S. R.		
Elliott Rucker.	1st. Lt.	July 11.		1. S. R.		Culpeper.
John Hardyman	1st. Lt.	Sep. 24.		2. S. R.		
Benj. Edmondson	1st. Lt.	1779. Jan. 1.		2. S. R.		
Chas. Russell.	1st. Lt.	1779. Jan. 16.		1. S. R.		K. Wm.
O. Davenport.	Lt.	Jan. 22.		S. G. R.		
Thos. Bryant.	Lt.	Jan. 23.		S. G. R.		
John Vaughan.	Lt.	Jan. 24.		S. G. R.		
Wyatt Coleman.	1st. Lt.	Apr. 1.		1. S. R.		Culpeper.
Levin Walker	1st. Lt.	Apr. 30.		2. S. R.		
John Baylor	1st. Lt.	May. 1.		2. S. R.		
David Mann.	Lt.	July. 1.		S. G. R.		
James Kennedy.	Lt.	July 20.		S. G. R.		
Thos. White	1st. Lt.	Aug. 13.		1. S. R.		Pr. William.
Thos. Quarles	1st. Lt.	Aug. 24.		2. S. R.		
John Marston.	1st. Lt.	July. 3.		1. S. R.		Charles city
Samuel Cary	1st. Lt.	Aug. 25.				
Thomas Hayes	2d. Lt.	1778 Oct. 22.				
John Russel	2d. Lt.	1778. Dec. 7.		1. S. R.		Caroline.
Churchill Gibbs.	2d. Lt.	Dec. 7.		1. S. R.		Culpeper.
Wm. Broddus.	2d. Lt.	Dec. 7.		1. S. R.	Supy. May. 1.	
James Harper.	2d. Lt.	Dec. 7.		1. S. R.		Alexandria.

Roll of the officers of the State regiments (continued)

Name.	rank	date of Commn.	promotion since	corps.	situation.	residence.
Wm. Slaughter.	2d. Lt.	Dec. 7.		1. S. R.		Culpeper.
Wharton Quarles	2d. Lt.	1779. Jan. 2.				
Pratt Hughes.	2d. Lt.	1779. Jan. 16.		1. S. R.		Culpeper.
William White.	2d. Lt.	Apr. 1.		1. S. R.		Caroline.
William Vaughter	2d. Lt.	June. 1.		1. S. R.		Culpeper.
En. Berry	Ensign.	1780. Apr. 1.		S. G. R.		
R. Boush.	Ensn.	June 13.		S. G. R.		

A Roll of the officers of the Regiment of artillery.

Name.	rank	date of Commn.	promotion since	corps.	situation.	residence.
Thomas Marshall	Colo.	1777. Oct. 9.		Artillery		
Elias Edmonds.	Lt. Col.	1780. Apr. 16.				
John Mazaret.	Majr.	1780. Apr. 16.				
Edwd. Moody	Cap.	1777. Nov. 6.				
James Bradley.	Cap.	1778. Jan. 31.				
Thomas Clay.	Cap.	1779. June 30				
Gideon Johnston.	Cap.	1779. Aug. 10				
Samuel Blackwell	Cap.	1779. Dec. 19				
Christophr. Roan.	Cap.	1780. Feb. 15.				
Wm. Spiller	Cap.	Apr. 13.				
John Allen	Cap.	17.				
John Williams.	Cap.	18.				
Wm. Thompson.	Cap.	19.				
Peter Kemp.	Cap.	23.				
Thos. Marshall.	Cap.	23.				
Humphrey Marshall	Cap. Lt.					

A Roll of the officers of the Regiment of artillery (continued)

Name.	rank	date of Commn.	promotion since	corps.	situation.	residence.
Robert Cowne	do.	1779. Dec. 19.				
John Quarles	do.	do.				
Yancey Lipscombe	do.	1780. Jan. 20				
Henry Vowles	do.	Feb. 15				
Wm. Oliver	do.	Apr. 12				
Sewell Edenburgh.	do.	13.				
Bernard Lipscombe	do.	17.				
John Scott	do.	20				
James Cleverius	do.	23.				
Walter Graham.	do.	23.				
Cary Wiatt	1st. Lt.	1779. Nov. 19.				
Nathanl. Rice	do.	do.				
Walter Scott	do.	1780. Jan. 20				
Robert Brown	do.	Apr. 12				
J. M. Marshall	do.	13.				
Austin Cowne	do.	16.				
John Turner	do.	20.				
Saml. Butler	do.	23.				
Wm. Ballard.	do.	23.				
John Spencer.	do.	23.				
John Yates.	2d. Lt.	Feb. 11.				
Chas. Vowles	do.	12.				
Josiah Valentine	do.					

MS (DLC); 4 p.; entirely in TJ's hand. These tabulations of officers and men of the several state regiments must have been compiled, at least in part, before the Advice of Council of this date (see above). The returns for the 1st and 2d state regiments and the state garrison regiment are the same in the Advice and the present tabulation. However, as was made clear by the letter of Adjutant Henry Vowles of 30 Jan. (which arrived in time to be transmitted by Muter to TJ on 6 Feb., q.v.), no return for the artillery regiment was available owing to the destruction of the regimental papers at the battle of Camden. But in that letter Vowles sent a list of the officers which, though now missing, was obviously used by TJ in compiling the above "Roll of the Officers of the Regiment of artillery"; on 12 Feb. Vowles wrote again to Muter, saying: "I received yours respecting the Officers &c. of Artillery and sent forward the Return the next Day by (as I thought) a very safe hand, which I expect you have received before this" (Vi).

1 "Regimt of artillery" struck out.

2 That is, supernumerary.

3 Perhaps "Machen."

From Patrick St. Laurence

Richmond, 6 Feb. 1781. Having taken to the southward a quantity of iron and steel "purchased at Headquarters for the use of the public" at the cost of £31,141, and having, in the expectation of prompt payment of this sum by the state treasury, agreed to return with three wagonloads of dry goods for the troops, St. Laurence desires of TJ a special order to the treasury for payment of the abovementioned sum. Encloses, for TJ's approval, his pass for returning with the wagons; mentions "the Enormous expence I am daily at attending for the Money."

RC (Vi); addressed and endorsed. Enclosure missing.

From George Washington

SIR Head Quarters New Windsor February 6th. 1781.

I am much obliged to your Excellency for your letter of the 10th. of January, giving me an account of the enemy's incursion into your state. Baron De Steuben has informed me of their successive operations to five miles below Hoods. It is mortifying to see so inconsiderable a party committing such extensive depredations with impunity: but considering the situation of your state, it is to be wondered you have hitherto suffered as little molestation. I am apprehensive you will experience more in future: nor should I be surprized if the enemy were to establish a Post in Virginia till the season for opening the Campaign here. But as the evils you have to apprehend from these predatory incursions are not to be compared with the injury to the common cause and with the danger to your state in particular, from the conquest of those states southward of you, I am persuaded the attention to your imediate safety will not divert you from the measures intended to reinforce the Southern Army and put it in a condition to stop the progress of the enemy in that Quarter. The late accession of force makes them very formidable in Carolina—too formidable to be resisted without powerfull succours from Virginia: and it is certainly her policy as well as the interest of America to keep the weight of the War at a distance from her. There is no doubt that a principal object of Arnolds operations is to make a diversion in favour of Cornwallis, and to remove this motive by disappointing the intention, will be one of the surest ways to remove the enemy.

We have just received an account that the enemy's fleet employed in blocking that of our allies at Rhode Island has lately suffered severely by a storm. One seventy four is said to have been stranded and intirely lost on the East End of Long Island—another (some accounts say two others) dismasted and towed into Gardners Bay—and a ninety driven to sea in great distress. I expect every moment a confirmation and the particulars of this agreeable intelligence.

I have the honor to be with sentiments of perfect respect and the warmest esteem, Your Excellency's Most Obedient and Humble servant, GO: WASHINGTON

RC (Vi); in the hand of George Augustine Washington, signed by George Washington; addressed; franked: "Go: Washington"; endorsed. Dft (DLC: Washington Papers).

From the American Philosophical Society

Held at Philadelphia For Promoting Useful Knowledge

SIR Philadelphia Feby 7. 1781

The American Philosophic society on the 5th of January last held their first annual election under the act of incorporation by the General Assembly of Pennsylvania, and I have it in charge to inform your Excellency, that they have elected you a Councellor for two years. The powers of the Council are to "be described, fixed and determined by the statutes, laws, regulations and ordnances of the said society hereafter to be made" of which you will have due notice.

The members of this society flatter themselves, that the benevolent and liberal objects of it will induce you to give it your countenance and assistance and enable them to shew to posterity that in the midst of a bloody and unparalled war, where every moment was indeed precious, men of the first imminence in America cherished the arts and sciences and dedicated a part of their time to Philosophy.

I have the honor to be with great respect Your Excellency's Most obedient and very humble servt., T MATLACK Secy. P.S.

Officers elected the "*first Friday in January*" 1781
Presidt. Dr Benjn Franklin
Vice Presidents. Dr Bond, D Rittenhouse and Jas Wilson
Secretaries. Dr Ewing, Own. Biddle, T Matlack and Revd. W White

Councellors. Geo Bryan, Thos McKean, DeMarbois and Charles Thomson . . . . } 3 years

Revd. Dr Duffield, Govr Livingston, Govr Jefferson and Dr Witherspoon . . . } 2 years

Dr Ezra Stiles, M Clarkson, J B Smith and John Lukens . . . . } 1 year

Curators, Coll Nicola, Du Simitiere and Dr Duffield
Treasurer F Hopkinson.

RC (MHi); in Timothy Matlack's hand; addressed: "His Excellency Thomas Jefferson Esqr. Governor of the State of Virginia"; endorsed by TJ: "American Philosoph. Society."

The records of TJ's early relations with the American Philosophical Society, with which he was to be long and fruitfully associated, are imperfect and confusing. His name first appears in the Society's MS Minutes under date of 17 Dec. 1779. The entry reads as follows:

"letters from the Revd. Mr. Maddison, President of William & Mary's College in Virginia containing a Series of meteorological observations by his Excellency Governor Jefferson and himself seperately for an year and a half; likewise a set of Experiments on what are called the 'sweet springs.' Mr. Rittenhouse is desired to thank both those gentlemen in the name of the Society for these favors, and to request a continuance of their valuable correspondence."

No minutes are preserved for a meeting of the Society on 21 Jan. 1780, when (according to a notice in the *Penna. Packet*, 27 Jan.) TJ, Rev. James Madison, George Washington, La Luzerne, Marbois, John Jay, Henry Laurens, John Adams, Generals St. Clair, Wayne, and Steuben, Alexander Hamilton, Timothy Matlack, and eight other new members were elected. In consequence, some of those in this list were elected again at various times, and possibly TJ himself was. If TJ was notified of his election at this time, neither the notification nor his acknowledgment has been found. (The newspaper notice of the meeting on 21 Jan. 1780 is reprinted in full in Gilbert Chinard, "Jefferson and the American Philosophical Society," Amer. Philos. Soc., *Procs.*, LXXXVII [1943], p. 264.)

On 5 Jan. 1781, as the present letter states, TJ was elected a councillor of the Society for a two-year term. TJ acknowledged this honor in a letter addressed to Matlack on 18 Apr. 1781, q.v.; and on the following 20 Dec. he wrote Charles Thomson (who had on 5 Jan. 1781 been elected a councillor for a three-year term) asking information as to "the particular duties of that office" and requesting Thomson's opinion whether the answers TJ was preparing to some of Marbois' Queries concerning Virginia (q.v. above under date of 30 Nov. 1780) might not be "a proper tribute to the Philosophical society." See Thomson's reply, 9 Mch. 1782.

Thus TJ, whose "aversion . . . to being counted as a drone in any society" was deep and sincere, seized the first opportunity that offered to promote the aims of the American Philosophical Society; but the record of his election to membership is still puzzling. Among his personal papers now in MHi there remain two diplomas of membership in the Society, both reproduced in the present volume. One of these is signed by Benjamin Franklin as president of the Society and by the other officers serving in 1786; its only date is the date when it was filled in and attested, 20 Jan. 1786. According to Mrs. Gertrude D. Hess, assistant librarian of the Philosophical Society (communication to the editors, 23 June 1944), Franklin on this date signed a number of membership diplomas for members who had been elected during the years Franklin was abroad. For example, the diploma for Ebenezer Hazard was signed by Franklin on this day but bears at its lower left-hand corner the date 19 Jan. 1781, the actual date of Hazard's election (see *Early Procs.*, p. 110). If TJ's case is parallel with Hazard's, the 1786 diploma merely confirmed TJ's election, the date of which, not being recorded in the Society's Minutes, was not known five years later and was therefore not entered on the document. This is a plausible explanation and would be acceptable but for the presence and nature of the other diploma. This, though an identical engraved form, is designated a "Copy" in respect to the data supplied in the spaces left blank in the text; i.e., the recipient's name and office, the signatures of President Franklin and the other officers, and, most important, the date when originally issued and attested. TJ is here named "Governor of the State of Virginia" instead of "Minis[ter Pleni]potentiary to the Court of France" as in the 1786 diploma; the officers and witnesses are named as of Jan. 1781 (see *Early Procs.*, p. 110); and the date of issuance and attestation is given as 20 Jan. 1781, which is certainly an error. The date when the copy was made is known because the verso of the diploma bears an affidavit (MHi) that reads and is signed as follows: "The Certificate issued by the American Philosophical Society held at Philadelphia for promoting usefull Knowledge, of which the foregoing is a true Copy, having miscarried, I have caused the Seal of their Corporation to be annexed to the said Copy, that it may serve in place of the Original. Given under my hand this twenty fourth day of March one thousand Seven Hundred and Ninety one. Davd. Rittenhouse President. Attested R: Patterson Jona Williams J Secretarys."

Evidently TJ at about the time he first attended a meeting of the Society (1 Mch. 1791; *Early Procs.*, p. 192), though he had in his possession the diploma actually signed by Franklin on 20 Jan. 1786 (which may or may not point to a second, otherwise unrecorded election), desired proof of his earlier election to the Society, and the certified copy was therefore issued to him on 24 Mch. 1791. If the original had "miscarried," as Rittenhouse stated, it is difficult to see how it could have been copied unless, as is highly unlikely, a duplicate was retained by the Society. The 1791 document is presumably a reconstruction rather than a copy of the lost diploma, and the most likely explanation of its date (20 Jan. 1781) is that it is an error by transposition for 21 Jan. 1780, the true date of TJ's election. Perhaps TJ himself supplied the date of his election to Rittenhouse; the error as it appears on the diploma could have been his, Rittenhouse's, or the engrossing clerk's.

From Arthur Campbell

SIR Abingdon Febr. 7th. 1781

It now appears that the Indians that attacked Blackmores Fort, as mentioned in my last, were a small party of Shawanese headed by our noted enemy Logan.

The last Travelers that came from Kentucky came thro Cumberland Gap safe, having on their way made no discoveries of Indians. Some attention of Government to former means proposed, I am convinced may bring about a Peace; or make the war with the Cherokees a light work. I am now peculiarly anxious on that head, as a late pressing application of General Greene, for the aid of the Mountain Men, will not be so effectually answered; until the apprehensions of danger from the Indians, may in some measure be remov'd. Not an ounce of the Powder your Excellency formerly promised is come to hand, nor can I hear any thing of it. The flints is much needed. From information that I believe may be depended on, the destruction of the Works at the Lead-Mines are an object the Tories have in view early in the Spring.

I am Sir Your most Obedient Servt., ARTHUR CAMPBELL

RC (Vi); addressed (in part): "By Capt. Sullivan"; endorsed.
MENTIONED IN MY LAST: Campbell to TJ, 2 Feb. 1781, q.v.

From Richard Claiborne

SIR Richmond. 7th Feby. 1781

I do myself the honor to inclose to your Excellency, a copy of the estimate of supplies to be furnished from this State for the equipment and support of the Southern Army the ensuing Campaign.

I am sensible of the urgent necessity there is for the things being provided without loss of time, and beg leave to request the Executive to consider how far it will be in their power to assist me. The articles specifically obtained through the Civil Authority will enable me to carry on my business for some time, with the money which I am to receive from the Treasury; but should I be obliged to purchase them with money, the sum granted me by the Executive is small, compared with the prices which things bear at present, and the great expence of Waggon-hire, and the pay of persons to be employed.

I beg an answer from your Excellency to that part of my Letter of the 27th of January which respects the pay to be allowed to persons employed. I find that the Eighteen pence which is to be given to Waggoners, agreable to the Estimate, is too small. I believe it will be necessary to increase it to two shillings and sixpence.

I have the honor to be Your Excellency's Most obedient Humble Servant,

RD. CLAIBORNE
DQMR. S. VIRGA.

RC (Vi); endorsed. Enclosure missing.

MY LETTER OF THE 27TH OF JANUARY: Missing, but Claiborne, in his letter to TJ of 29 Jan., stated that he had "the other day" laid before TJ "a state of the Wages of persons to be employed in this Department" and that this had met with TJ's approval. See TJ's reply to the present letter, following.

To Richard Claiborne

SIR Richmond Febry 7th. 1781.

We were not able to proceed to the consideration of the prices proposed to be given in your department till we could get a late arrangement of our own which interfered with some articles of you[rs]. This we got to day, and have come to the determination inclosed. Your first article we omitted because we give but two thirds of the allowance there proposed; the 2d because we have no such persons, the 3d and 6th. because people fit for these offices are so very rare, that we are obliged to make our bargains with them as we can: the 4th. 5th. 7th. and [8th] articles we have raised knowing from experience that those people cannot be got for the prices you propose.

By an estimate which we have made of the cost of the articles contained in your requisition of this day we find they will cost 6,358,000 pounds: the bare naming of such a sum with your knowledge of the State of the Treasury will suffice to satisfy you that it would be chimerical for us to say we would procure those articles. It is our duty to make the most of the public money by applying it in the first instances to the supplying the greatest wants. On this view we can only endeavour to furnish money for such and so many of the articles therein stated as are most essentially necessary.

I am Sr. &c &c &c, T.J.

Pay of persons to be employed, and Waggons hire ℔ day.

		Specie	or ℔s. Tobo.
1	Assistant Deputy Quarter Master's	15/.	75
2	Clerks and Store Keeper's	12/.	60
3	Superintendant of Artificers	10/.	50
4	Artificers best kind	4/.	20
5	Common Do.	3/.	15
6	Superintendant Boatwrights	10/.	50
7	Boat Wrights best kind	5/.	25
8	Common Do.	4/.	20
9	Waggon conductors	5/.	25
10	Waggoners	1/.6	7½
11	Labourers, good	1/.6	7½
12	Express riders	2/.6	12½
13	Four horse Team and Drivers	10/.	50
14	Two horse Team and Drivers	7/.6	37½

FC (Vi). The pay schedule which follows the letter is quite clearly a copy of the schedule submitted by Claiborne before its revision by the Council as described in TJ's letter. For the schedule as revised by the Council, see TJ to Muter, this date, from which it appears that the Council raised items 10 and 11 in addition to those named above by TJ.

To Jonathan Clarke

Sir Richmond Febry 7th. 17[81]

By a letter from Mr. Hawkins Commissary at the Barracks I find that the deficiences in the issues stated in your account are not agreed to by him. If you will be pleased to settle this matter with him, I shall be glad to receive such an account of these deficiences as is acknowledged on both sides. I take this occasion also to inform you that the account you were pleased to trans[mit] me before has been lost by accident. I am Sr. Yr. very hbl. svt., T.J.

FC (Vi). A LETTER FROM MR. HAWKINS: Dated 30 Dec. 1780, q.v.; see also Jonathan Clarke to TJ, 6 Feb., and TJ to Joseph Hawkins, 7 Feb. 1781.

To William Davies

Sir In Council Febry. 7th 1781.

It was our intention that the tools should go with the workmen and hope they have accordingly gone. I have enquired of Mr. Armistead as to the giving a yard of linen for making shirts at Petersburg. He says it was never done by him; but that Colo. Elliot the Continental Q.M. had given the price of a yard of linen. Mr. Armistead's allowance for the white linen shirts is 30 dollars. There is no cloathing at Petersburg under our order; from a hint in your letter you seem to expect that the men of the State regiments are transferred to the continent. This is not the case. On the contrary such of them as are gone to the Southward will be recalled, to be employed as garrison. We approve of your having 30 or 40. shirts of the coarse linen made for the purpose of shifting the patients in the hospital. Before the receipt of yours of the 5th I had inclosed the regulations proposed to be made in the Clothier's department for your observations.

I am with much respect Sr Yours &c &c, Thos. Jefferson

FC (Vi). YOURS OF THE 5TH: Not found, but this may be an erroneous reference to Davies' letter of 3 Feb. 1781, q.v.

To Charles Dick

Sir Richmond Febry. 7th. 1781.

I was willing to hope from your letter to me that you would still consent to conduct the gun factory at Fredericksburg; in the hurry of business while you were here I omitted to ask you particularly, for which reason I think myself obliged to send you the inclosed resolution, and inform you that the Executive have reappointed you to that business and hope your continuance in it. Colo. Lewis's state of health we understand has induced him to decline the further care of it.

I am with much esteem, &c &c &c, T.J.

FC (Vi). Enclosure not found, but see Dick's reply, 26 Feb. 1781.

YOUR LETTER TO ME: Dated 23 Jan. 1781, q.v.

To Benjamin Harrison

SIR Richmond Febry. 7th. 1781.

The inclosed papers will sufficiently explain themselves to you. They were put into my hands by Colo. Matthews together with a requisition from Congress to furnish 14492 hard dollars to pay the debts of our prisoners in New York. Were we permitted to send produce, we could do it for less than half of what the hard dollars will cost us, and I think such articles might be selected from the within, especially when that of coal is added (which Colo. Mathews assures me will be done) as would do neither good to the enemy nor injury to us. Coal sells in N. York at six guineas the chauldron. Colo. Mathews assures me that the Enemy have never experienced the least inconvenience from a want of provisions since he has been in captivity; that indeed before the arrival of the Cork fleet they began to be apprehensive, but he thinks they have now near a twelve months provision. Taking this into consideration with the great alleviation of the maintenance of our prisoners which it should bring to us, perhaps you could negotiate a permission to us to send some of these articles to New York and Charlestown.

I am &c &c., T.J.

FC (Vi). Enclosures not identified, but see Harrison's answer, 19 Feb. 1781.

COLO. MATTHEWS: Doubtless George Mathews, lt. col., 9th Va. Line, who had recently been exchanged (Gwathmey, *Hist. Reg. of Virginians in the Revolution*). See TJ's letters to Wood, Geddes, Hamilton and Mengen, 3 Feb.

To Joseph Hawkins

SIR Richmond Febry. 7th. 1781

Finding by your letter of the 30th. of December that the justice of Commissary Clarke's account of the deficiences in the issues [of] provision to the Convention Troops is not acknowledged by you; be pleased to make me a return of those deficiences according to what you suppose to be right.

I am Sr. &c &c &c &c, T.J.

FC (Vi). See Jonathan Clarke to TJ, 6 Feb., and TJ to Clarke, 7 Feb. 1781.

To James Hunter

SIR Richmond Febry. 7th. 1781

By the Loss of many of our papers we find ourselves unable to say how stand our orders with you for camp-kettles. We shall be glad however, whatever they be, that you now furnish us with one thousand for the separate use of the State and to be called for by my order only.

I am Sr. &c., T.J.

P.S. We will send 2 waggons a week hence for camp-kettles and continue them going backward and forward on the same business if you can make them fast enough till we get our whole number.

T.J.

FC (Vi). See Hunter's reply, 20 Feb. 1781.

From Joseph Martin

SIR Febr. the 7th 1781

I hope you will Excuse the shortness of this as I accedenttally met the Barer on the Road having no more paper Can only inform your Excellency that I have in my Care 15 Indian prisoners and 12 others that Come in of their own Choice Expecting to be maintaind by the publick. Should be glad you would Direct me what is to be Done with them and in what manner they are to be supported. Part of those that Came in have Renderd singular services to the states and are still Willing to Do so. If approvd of by you I Can send one of them to the Nation who will Return with Certain Inteligance by which means we shall have it in our power to Counteract their hostile Intentions or Treat with them which Ever your Excellency shall think best as I am Convincd I Can Draw part if not all of the old Towns to our Interest as they find they have been Decieved once more by the English. The Hanging Maw in open Council Declard against the Warr and Told them if they attemptd to Join the English he would Immediately Remove himself and his Town and live amonst the white people which he attempted by sending a flag to us but some of our Disorderly men Kill'd the Two fellows that Brought the flag which prevented our speaking to the Hanging Maw but I Believe it is still in my power to Bring him in with all his Town which Consists of about 400 souls and if approvd of by Government I think they would be Willing to live at the Island till the End [of] this Warr. I Beg you will let me Know what is to be Done as soon as possible.

I am Sr your most ob Svt, JOS MARTIN

RC (Vi); addressed.

HANGING MAW: A prominent Cherokee chief; see Hodge, *Handbook of American Indians*, and numerous references in both Swem, *Index*, and *N.C. State Records*. THE ISLAND: Doubtless Long Island of Holston; see Martin to TJ, 12 Dec. 1780. See also TJ's reply to the present letter, 19 Feb. 1781.

To Richard Morris

SIR Richmond Febry. 7th. 17[81]

Tho' I consider our last appointment of you as having put the business prescribed by the inclosed resolution into a course of execution, I think it necessary in point of formality to inclose it to you and to repeat my wishes for as expeditious a settlement of the accounts of the Commissioners of the Provision Law and Agents of the Specific tax as can be had. I am with much respect Sir Yrs &c &c, T.J.

FC (Vi). Enclosure not identified.

Morris had been appointed to settle the accounts of the commissioners of the provision law; see his letter to Gov. Nelson, 6 Aug. 1781, CVSP, II, 297.

To George Muter

	Specie	
Artificers of the best kind	5/. or	25 ℔. tobacco
Common Do.	3/9	18¾
Boat wrights of the best kind	7/6	37½
Common Do.	5/.	25
Waggon Conductors	5/.	25
Waggoners	2/6	12½
Labourers good	2/	10
Express riders	2/6	12½

4 horse teams and drivers	10/.	50.
2 horse teams and drivers	7/6	37½

SIR In Council Feby 7. 1781.

It being necessary that there should be an agreement in the prices given by the Continental and State Quartermasters, you will be pleased to order the State Q.M. not to exceed the above rates of daily hire in any future contracts. Those Contracts already in existence we are not at liberty to reduce. I am Sir Yr. very hble Servt,

TH: JEFFERSON

RC (Vi); in a clerk's hand, signed by TJ; endorsed. FC (Vi). Tr in War Office Journal (Vi). The schedule of pay for employees of the state and Continental quartermasters' departments is a revision of a schedule submitted by Claiborne; see TJ to Claiborne, this date.

From George Muter

SIR War office Feby. 7. 1781.

I have a letter from the quarter master, in which he informs me "That the cartridge blocks at Moody's shop as well as those that were in his possession, were all destroyed by the enemy; and that since then he has not been able to procure a single workman to make more: but that he will use every exertion in his power to push a bussiness so essential at this critical period. He cannot assign any reason for the delay of the waggons that went to Charlott'sville, and supposes that the leather probably was not ready. When the waggons arrive he will inform immedeatly.

Permitt me to observe, that Mr. Braxton's letter to the gentleman in whose hands he expects the Cartouch boxes at Annapolis are, is still here. I have the honour to be Your Excellency's most humble servant,

GEORGE MUTER. C.

RC (Vi); addressed and endorsed. A LETTER FROM THE QUARTER MASTER: William Rose, "DQMG.," to Muter, without place, 7 Feb. 1781 (Vi). THE CARTOUCH BOXES AT ANNAPOLIS: See TJ's letter to Benjamin Harrison, 29 Jan.

From Thomas Nelson

DEAR SIR Williamsburg Feby 7th 1781

In consequence of your Letter to me to assist Captain Joel with a Vessel for an enterprize against the Enemy's Fleet, I gave him an order to the Commissioner of the Navy on the Subject; but he not being at the Yard, the Person who acts under him; has deliver'd the Dragon Ship of which I never was inform'd until last night. I immediately orderd her back to the Ship Yard, because in my opinion, it is risking too much, and because she is particularly appropriated by act of Assembly, so that my powers do not extend to allotting her for any such enterprize. My Idea was that he should have taken some old Hulk that would not have been any loss to the State should the enterprize fail, of which (between friends) there is almost a certainty, it being known to all the lower County and probably to the British before this day. If as he has gone so far, you chuse he should prosecute his scheme, the Dragon shall be deliver'd to him again.

I am Dear Sir Your Obedt Servt, THOS NELSON jr. B.G.

I have discharg'd the militia that were down on the last Invasion. Numbers have deserted and others from various circumstances have been permitted to go home so that the force on this side is much short of what was allotted. Neither the Caroline nor Essex militia have been call'd out. They would afford a good reinforcement.

RC (NN). On JOEL and his ENTERPRIZE, see TJ to Nelson, 16 Jan. 1781, and references there.

From David Ross

SIR Arrowfield 7 February 1781

By Borrowing and purchasing I have procured a sufficient quantity of Canvass for the 100 tents You mentioned for Colo. Buford also some Cloth which shall be sent to Richmond immediately.

I shall be glad to receive the several Estimates mentioned when I was at Richmond. I am sorry to inform you that the prospect of obtaining supplies becomes every day more discouraging.

Every body I see from the lower Country seem Confident that the Enemy mean to continue at Portsmouth as long as they can hold it. This will enable them to annoy the trade of North Carolina more than ever—add to this another fleet of their ships have entered Cape Fear River. We had this information yesterday at Petersburg. Last night I received a letter from General Parsons from Halifax which confirms it. He says eight ships had got over the Bar and many others laying off that 'tis suposed to be a Reinforcement to Ld. Cornwallis under the command of G Prevost.

I am with great Respect Your Most huml servant,

David Ross

RC (Vi); addressed and endorsed. GEN. PARSONS: General Thomas Persons of North Carolina. Ross forwarded Persons' letter to TJ; see TJ to Huntington, 8 Feb.

To Steuben

Sir In Council Febry. 7th. 178[1]

The bearer hereof Colo. Gaines a militia Officer in the County of Amherst being desirous to become qualified in fact for the command he holds in his county, has applied to us to be permitted to serve on such a footing as will place it in his power to acquire a knowledge of his duty, asking nothing but rations and forage; while others, offended at the preference given to Officers formerly of the Line, have resigned commissions the duty of which they were not qualified to discharge; this Gentleman more laudably determines to learn those duties. This spirit we wish to encourage because produced by a due temperement of modesty and patriotism. New therefore as the undertaking is, I must beg the favor of you to find some means of disposing not only of him but of any others who may apply for the same purpose, so as to put it in their power to acquire the knowledge necessary to enable them to act in their proper command hereafter. The rations and forage allowed them shall be at the expence of the State.

I am with much respect Sir Yors., &c. &c.

Thomas Jefferson

FC (Vi). COLO. GAINES: Probably Daniel Gaines, listed as "Major and Colonel" in Gwathmey, *Hist. Reg. of Virginians in the Revolution.*

To Steuben

Sir Richmond Febry. 7th. 1781.

The inclosed Letter contains the first notification the Executive have received of the existence of any such cases as that of Lieut. Warm[an] therin stated. Exclusive of the justice of his claim, the express reserva[tion] by the board of Officers of the rights of all those in his situation, seems to place him on the footing on which he would have been, had his Commission been actually made out instead of that of whatever officer was substituted in his place. As you are proceeding to a new Arrangement of our Line, I have taken the liberty of referring Lieut. Warman with the inclosed Letter to you to claim his rank. Should there be, contrary to the expectations of the Executive, such reasons against his claim and in favor of his Competitor, as in your Judgement should decide this point against Lieut. Warman, I shall be obliged to you for a communication of them; and in the mean time to keep the question open.

I have the Honor to be with very great Esteem & respect, Yr. Mst. Ot. Hbl. St., T.J.

FC (Vi). Enclosure not found.

LIEUT. WARMAN: Thomas Warman, captured at Germantown, Oct. 1777, and exchanged in Dec. 1780; he is listed as a captain in 3d Va. Line, Nov. 1778, by Gwathmey, *Hist. Reg. of Virginians in the Revolution*; and he furnished a circumstantial account of his record and losses in two letters to Gov. Thomas Nelson, 9 and 14 Aug. 1781 (CVSP, II, 306, 327).

From the Subaltern Officers
of the Guard Regiment at Albemarle Barracks

Albemarle Barracks, 7 Feb. 1781. "We the Subalterns of the Regiment of Guards beg leave to lay before your Excellency our grievencies Respecting our Rank. We have been in the Said Regiment for two years, and, some of us have been intitled to promotions for upwards of twelve months from many Resignations and other circumstances." Knowing that Col. [Francis] Taylor has written to TJ on the subject, the officers have waited patiently for an answer but received none. They now wish their case may be considered or they cannot continue in service, "as there is three company in the Regiment Commanded by Subalterns only. We think that every lieutenant is intitled to a Captaincy and each Ensign to a Lieutenancy."

RC (Vi); 2 p.; signed by Lts. Saml. O. Pettus, John Taylor, Richd. Paulett, and Ensigns Jesse Paulett, Nichs. Meriwether, William Kennedy (all the names appear to be in the hand that drew up the petition); addressed and endorsed. Printed in CVSP, I, 496.

On the officers' GRIEVENCIES see Francis Taylor to TJ, 30 Dec. 1780 and 8 Feb. 1781; James Wood to TJ, 9 Feb.; TJ to Taylor and also to Wood, 13 Feb. 1781.

To the Virginia Delegates in Congress

GENTLEMEN Richmond Febry. 7th. 1781.

The Courier d'Europe a vessel from Penet & Coy. [Company] having on board military stores for this state was chased into Boston by the enemy in the Summer of 1779. They were principally Artillery Stores, too bulky and heavy for us to think of bringing them on by land. By the loss of our papers we are unable to furnish an invoice of them but they are in the hands of a Mr. J. Bradford in Boston who I suppose can furnish you with one. If you can get them on board any part of the French Fleet which may at any time be coming here, it would be eligible: otherwise I would beg the favour of you to have them disposed of to the best advantage for the public.

I am with very great respect and esteem Gentn. Your most Obt. & Most humbl. St., T.J.

FC (Vi).

J. BRADFORD: John Bradford, "continental agent at Boston" (JCC, XV, 1131). This affair dragged on for a long time; see Bradford to Madison and Jones, 20 Mch. 1782, and Madison, Bland, and Jones to Gov. Harrison, 23 Apr. 1782 (CSVP, III, 104, 137).

From William Davies

SIR Chesterfield Feby. 8. 1781.

Your several favors came to hand yesterday, but neither the tools nor the taylors are yet arrived. I never knew whose property the tools were, whether public or private, and the taylors, belonging to the State Garrison regiment, are countermanded by Major McGill, as Mr. Thornbury informs me. If it is disagreeable or inconvenient to their officers, I would not wish their men to come, tho' I do not doubt they would do considerably more here than they did at Warwick. If I was mistaken with respect to the men of Gibson's and Brent's regiments, it was an error I was led into by Baron Steuben, who I fancy entertained the same idea. There are some of them now here, and if they are not to belong to the continent, I would wish to get rid of them, excepting only such as are tradesmen. At your Excellency's request I will send them to any place you may appoint. As for the idea of applying them as garrisons, I do not profess myself a competent judge of its utility. If it is intended they should garrison forts, good men will undoubtedly be necessary; but if they are to be employed only as guards to stores or magazines, a corps of invalids would probably answer every purpose full as well in the interior parts of the country. Many men might be usefully employed in such a corps, whom we are now obliged to discharge. There are officers too, who from their years, infirmities or wounds, might be willing, if properly supported to take charge of such a corps.

There will be wanting for the detachment one marquee, 11 horsemen's tents and 65 soldiers' tents. We have exactly 65 here, but no marquee besides mine, nor any horsemen's tents, and 3 or 4 of the soldiers' are not so good as I can wish. The only tents that I know of besides, are 21 at Powhatan court house. I beg leave to observe to your Excellency the amazing waste which results from the irregular discharge of the militia. In addition to 230, which were issued by the State quarter masters, there were 108 which were made here and issued on the former and the present calls, but 86 are the whole that I know any thing, exclusive of 28 that were returned to Richmond and the 75 with Col. Green's detachment.

I have been so exceedingly hurried, that I have not had sufficient time to attend so fully to the clothing arrangements, as I could wish. I would remark that the soldiers pay is so small, and so very badly paid to them, that it would be robbing themselves for the country to over value the cloathing the soldiers may buy: if they are debited at a high price they should be credited at the same rates justice requires it. The plan in contemplation of the Executive is good as far as it goes, tho' it seems more immediately to have for its object the securing the monies the soldiers may owe for their purchases of cloathing: but this will not answer the purpose fully, and I have therefore taken the liberty to enclose a few obser[v]ations and additions to the plan, with some forms, that, if executed, will have a very advantageous effect.

I think the post of Deputy clothier of too high importance to be left to the Sub-clothier. I think it would be full as well if he was appointed by the Executive upon a recommendation from the officer commanding at the post, where the deputy is to serve. I would beg leave to suggest another matter to your Excellency, that the regimental paymasters, who are our only clothiers, do not hold themselves bound to take charge of any other stores of cloathing than the bounty allowed by Congress, and altho' they have in general undertaken it for the sake of the soldiers yet perhaps it will be very reluctantly executed, if they receive no kind of compensation for the extra services the proposed plan requires. The allowance of a small gratuity I have great reason to believe, would be amply reimbursed by the great saving which will follow the execution of the design.

I have the honor to be, sir, with the highest respect, Your Excellency's most humble servt, William Davies

RC (Vi); endorsed. No enclosure found.

YOUR SEVERAL FAVORS: TJ had written Davies on 2, 5, and 7 Feb.

From Horatio Gates

Berkeley County, 8 Feb. 1781. Letter introducing James McAlister, county commissioner and issuing commissary in "this Districkt," who waits on TJ for "Directions in regard to His Future Conduct." Gates recommends him as "a good and Faithfull Servant of The Public."

RC (NHi); addressed and endorsed.

To Samuel Huntington

SIR Richmond Feb. 8. 1781.

I have just received intelligence which though from a private hand, I beleive is to be relied on, that a fleet of the enemy's ships have entered Cape Fear river, that eight of them had got over the Bar and many others were laying off; that it was supposed to be a reinforcement to Ld. Cornwallis under the command of Genl. Prevost. This account which had come through another channel is confirmed by a letter from Genl. Parsons at Halifax to the Gentleman who forwards it to me. I thought it of sufficient importance to be communicated to your Excellency by the stationed expresses. The fatal want of arms puts it out of our power to bring a greater force into the feild than will barely suffice to restrain the adventures of the pitiful body of men they have at Portsmouth. Should any others be added to them, this country will be perfectly open to them by land as well as by water.

I have the honour to be with all possible respect Your Excellency's most obedt. & most humble servt., TH: JEFFERSON

RC (DLC: PCC, No. 71, II); addressed; endorsed: "Letter from Govr. Jefferson Feby 8th. 1781. Read 20th." FC (Vi); captioned: "Genl. Washington & the President of Congress." Tr (DLC).

The PRIVATE HAND through whom TJ received a report of the British fleet in Cape Fear River was David Ross; see his letter to TJ, 7 Feb. The present letter was not noted in the Journals of Congress as received and read, unless (as seems likely) it is the same as "a letter, of 9 [Feb.], from the governor of Virginia" which was read on 19 Feb. (JCC, XIX, 175) and of which no other record has been found. See also Huntington's reply, 25 Feb.

From Samuel Huntington

SIR Philadelphia February 8. 1781.

Your Excellency will receive enclosed, two important Acts of Congress of the 3d and 7th Instant,

Recommending to the several States as indispensably necessary, that they vest a Power in Congress to levy for the Use of the United States, a Duty of five per cent, ad Valorem at the Time and Place of Importation, upon all Goods, Wares and Merchandize of foreign Growth and Manufacture which may be imported in to any of the said States from any foreign Port, Island or Plantation after the first Day of May, 1781, except Arms &c. as therein expressed. Also a like Duty on all Prizes and Prize Goods.

The Monies arising from the said Duties to be appropriated to the Discharge of the Principal and Interest of the Debts already contracted, or which may be contracted on the Faith of the United States for supporting the present War, and the Duties continued until the said Debts are finally discharged.

You will observe from the Tenor of the Resolves that if any one or more of the States immediately pass a Law vesting in Congress the Powers requested, it cannot take Effect or operate to any Purpose until all the States that are not prevented by the Events of the War, shall have passed similar Laws. That is, at present, all the States except South Carolina and Georgia, and when all the other States have passed the necessary Laws, the Monies arising from the Duties are to be applied to their Benefit, exclusive of the remaining States, unless such States shall pass similar Laws the first Session after the Events of the War will admit of the assembling their Legislatures: and Congress have not the least Doubt of their Compliance as soon as Circumstances shall put it in their Power.

The Necessity of the Debts and Imposts being raised under one general and uniform Direction, is an Idea that will readily suggest itself.

I am specially directed to urge the Necessity of immediately calling the Assembly, if not already convened, for the Purpose of vesting Congress with the Powers mentioned in the enclosed resolutions.

Although it may be improbable any Person not particularly acquainted with the daily Business in Congress should have an adequate Conception of the Difficulties and Embarrassments that arise for Want of some certain and permanent Fund to support the national Credit, yet I doubt not, the Wisdom Knowledge and Penetration of the respective Legislatures will view those Embarrassments as very great.

It ought to be remembred that Loans are not to be obtained without some permanent Fund established at least to pay the annual Interest punctually.

That, in the present State of our Finances, the Army must be in a great Measure immediately supported by the States separately, in a precarious Manner and perhaps very unequally; and a Train of Embarrassments too obvious to need Enumeration, must ensue which have already been felt in a Degree and must greatly increase.

I have only to add that it will be of Importance to transmit to Congress the A[cts that] may be passed in Consequence of the enclosed R[esolves] as soon as possible.

I have the Honor to be with every Sentiment of Esteem & Respect your Excellency's most obedient & most humble servant,

SAM. HUNTINGTON President

P.S. I have been honourd with your Excellency's dispatches of January 10th: 15th: 17th: and 18th also of the 25th of Decemr.

RC (Vi); in a clerk's hand, signed and with postscript in Huntington's hand. FC (DLC: PCC, No. 15). Enclosures (filed with the letter in Vi): Copies attested by Charles Thomson of the resolves of 3 [but in this copy misdated 5] and 7 Feb. 1781 described in the letter; these are printed in JCC, XIX, 112-13, 124-5.

From Edward Stevens

SIR North Carolinia Guilford County Febry. 8th. 1781.

I wrote you by Major Giles from the Camp at Hickes Creek the 24th. January. I then informed you I was under marching Orders to take charge of all the Prisoners at Salisbury. I marched on the evening of the 25th. after which there came on Violent Rains which raised the Waters in Such a manner as it made my march Two days longer than it otherwise would have been.

When I got within Twelve miles of Salisbury on the night of the 1st. Inst. and not before I heard how things were going with Morgans Party, by Major Burnett Genl. Greenes Aid D. Camp, who came from Salisbury to my Camp, about midnight and informed me the enemy was as near Salisbury as I was, And Desired me from the General to push as fast as Possible for the Tradeing Ford on the Yadkin about Seven miles from Salisbury, which I accordingly did and when I got their I found Genl. Morgan and his Party crossing. What Publick Stores was removed was at this place to Cross. The Great Quantity of Rain that fell the night before raised the River in such a manner as made it difficult to Cross even in Boats. General Greene with a small Party of Horse was still at Salisbury, Pushing out the remainder of the Stores from that place to the Tradeing Ford which was effected that night, except some few old musketts which was unfit for Service. The day before this the Prisoners under a Guard of Militia of this State was pushed over the River and Continued on their march to Virginia. On the evening of the 3rd Inst. the enemy appeared at the River tho by this time we had Compleated Crossing all to a Waggon or Two and those they paid Pretty dear for, as there was a Party of Virginia Rifflemen of about a Hundred under the Command of Major Campbell, and a small party of North Carolinia Militia Horse was formed in ambush to receive them with Orders to give them a fire or Two and then Disperse down the River and Cross in Canoes which they executed very well and with but a very Triffleing loss on their part.

It perhaps may be some what mistereous to you, General Greens being with Morgan. Two days after I left his Camp, he got information of Cornwallis destroying his Waggons and heavy Baggage and making his whole Army a Light Core [Corps]. He expected what would follow and imedeately ordered the Troops under his imedeate Command to be put in motion and he with a small escort of Horse made Instantly to Morgan.

The rebuff the Militia met with in attempting to Prevent the enemy from crossing the Catawbor was unluckey as it has been a means of dispersing them. General Davidson who that day was Killed or Badly wounded and fell in the hands of the enemy will be a great loss to the uper part of No. Carolinia. After crossing the Yadkin we could not have Paraded a greater Force than Eight Hundred for Action if even that Including Militia and all and a great part of that number was the Militia under me whose times were out. I saw the greatest necessity of these men remaining a few days till the Troops from General Greens Camp could get up, and this the General requested of me to endeavour to bring about. I had them paraded and addressed them on the Subject. But to my great mortification and astonishment scarce a man would agree to it, And gave for answer he was a good Soldier that Served his time out. If the Salvation of the Country had depended on their staying Ten or Fifteen days, I dont believe they would have done it. Militia wont do. Their greatest Study is to Rub through their Tower [Tour] of Duty with whole Bones. It was Absolutely necessary that the Troops should remain at the River till the Baggage and Stores could get out of the way. I therefore was obliged by compulson to detain them a day, And on the night of the 4th. Inst. the whole force moved of from the River.

I left General Greene and the small party with him halted about Seventeen miles from Guilford Court House on the road leading to the Yadkin, where he intended to remain till Joined by the Troops from Hickes Creek who were in about Twenty miles of him and on his left Flank.

These men under me are so exceeding anxceous to get home, it is allmost impossible to Keep Them together. What makes me more desireous of Keeping them together is on account of their Arms, As I wish to get them to some Secure and Convenient place to have them Stored. And General Greene wishes to have all the Stores and Magazines fixed on the North side and uper parts of the Dan River. When the Arms are lodged I will Advise you of it. The Neighbourhood of Pittsylvania old Court House I have at this time in View to lodge them, tho there will be no great number of them, As those of the sick and Invaleads were left at Hickes Creek and a part of them must go on to guard some Prisoners we have with us to the Barracks.

Cornwallis must have had several objects in View in this rapid move of his, Two of which must have been the retaiking the Prisoners and the Dispersing of Morgans party. The latter he nearly effected and if he remained inactive after Tarltons Drubing he certainly would have had all that Country on him.

On the morning of the 7th. Inst. he had not crossed the Yadkin nor do I expect he has any intention of doing it, to remain any time, as I think he must be sensible of the Precarious Situation he Stands in without Crossing, that is provided the Country would exert her Strength. If he should cross the greater part of his Supplies must come from the other side for he cannot get Supplyed on this. The River then would be such a Barrear between his Army and the well affected Counties of Roan [Rowan] and Mecklingburg that they would cutt of the Supplies from him in that Quarter. We are informed the People in them Counties are gathering very fast under Genl. Sumpter who is near Charlotte.

General Pickins who lived in the Neighbourhood of Ninty Six is gone round their to see what he can do with the Inhabitants in that Quarter.

The People of South Carolina if they wish it, can never have a better Opportunity of extrecating themselves from the Tyranny they have lately experienced.

What a reflection is it on us to let a Body of not more than Four or Five Thousand men, hold possession and march through such an extent of Country. Cornwallis it is said has only about Three Thousand men with him. I think he will if he finds the People begin to turn out with Spirit and in large numbers, file of to his right, and move down the Peedee Keeping his left Covered by that River, and about the Cheraws form a Junction with the Party that is landed at Wilmington. This retreat I am afraid will derange our Supplies of Provision in such a manner, altho they were before only from hand to mouth, that our Army must Suffer greatly before things can get into a Proper Train again, And as we have lost the most Plentifull part of the Country, I am Doubtfull whether the remains of this State can at any rate Support such a Force as will be Absolutely Necessary to Prevent the reduction of the whole State.

When I left Hickes Creek the General allowed all the married men of the 8h. Months men to be Discharged. They were Generally very Poor, and of course very Naked for Cloths, many of them large Familys and had they not have been Discharged now they could not have made a Crop the insueing Year, and that would have been total ruin to them. They have done Pritty good Penance for their falt. All the Young men are Continued, there was about a Hundred of them, And Proper Officers are left to take charge of them. With the greatest respect I am Your Excellencies most Obedt. & Very hum. Servt., EDWARD STEVENS

RC (PHi). Tr (DLC); endorsed (in part): "(Copy)."

It is difficult for the editors to maintain a dispassionate objectivity when confronted with the kind of letters that Edward Stevens and Daniel Morgan wrote—letters that must also have been heart-warming to Thomas Jefferson during these critical first days of February 1781. The present letter of Stevens (typical of all that came from his pen) and the equally superb one that Morgan wrote to TJ on 1 Feb., q.v., were written during the most difficult moment of one of the greatest campaigns of the Revolution—Greene's masterly retreat before Cornwallis. In their descriptive powers, their sound sense, their exalted patriotism, their instinct for essentials, their blunt and unerring way of striking at weaknesses (both their own and their enemies'), the writers of these letters had much in common. They were both natural leaders of men, born of humble origins. Both were stanch patriots. Both spelled atrociously and wrote superbly. No one in America could more justifiably have uttered the eloquent appeal that Morgan voiced a few days after his victory over Tarleton: "Great god what is the reason we cant Have more men in the field." And no more penetrating observation was made by an American commander during the Revolution than Stevens' comment: "Militia wont do. Their greatest Study is to Rub through their Tower of Duty with whole Bones." The editors, moved by such eloquence, expressed at a time when one of the writers was "aceazed" by an old pain in hip and breast that caused him to think himself "broke down in the service of my country" and when another, driven to exhaustion, led men who did not share his belief that the "Salvation of the Country" should be put above all private interest, feel that such letters deserve a better fate than to be buried among thousands of others without appreciative comment.

From Francis Taylor

SIR Barracks Feby. 8. 1781.

The greater part of the Soldiers of the Regiment of Guards, claim discharges, saying they were enlisted only to serve at this place, and as they have been removed that their engagement is complied with. They have been very troublesome, but hope they will be more satisfied hereafter, especially if they can get cloathed. I think 400 yards of Cloth would (with some they have received) make each Soldiers Suit, and I hope Mr. Martin may get that quantity, with Hats and Stockings.

The Subaltern Officers complain of the injustice of their not being promoted. The Number of Officers when we came here was 9 Captains 7 Lieutenants and 6 Ensigns. At present 4 Captains, 3 Lieutenants and 3 Ensigns, and about two thirds the number of Soldiers. Our being ordered to march prevented my sending down the damaged Arms, and since our return thought I had better wait your further orders, as I hear some of the Armourers went off with the Enemy. There is here several pieces of a kind of Flannel which came with the cloth, intended for Linings for Soldiers Coats, and some damaged Stockings, which are not fit to be issued to the men. I have desired Mr. Martin to mention them to you and ask what had best be done with them.

The Officers were very badly provided with blankets when they came here, and most of them drew one or two, and by accidents they have lost some and worn others. They wish a price to be fixed on them, as it is not in their power to replace them and that they will pay for them.

I am apprehensive of wanting provision soon, having very little Beef and no flour or meal in Store, and I believe none engaged by the Commissary.

I flatter myself with hopes that Mr. Martin will not be disappointed in getting money for us, the whole Regiment being greatly in debt and in want.

I am Sir Your obedient Servt, FRAS. TAYLOR

RC (Vi); addressed (in part): "Favour of Mr. Martin"; endorsed.

See letter from the Subaltern Officers at the Barracks to TJ, 7 Feb.; also TJ's reply to the present letter, 13 Feb. 1781.

MR. MARTIN: Hudson Martin, a former Continental officer and currently paymaster to the regiment of guards at the Albemarle Barracks (Gwathmey, *Hist. Reg. of Virginians in the Revolution*; War Office Jour., Jan.-June 1781 (Vi), p. 39).

To George Washington

Richmond, 8 Feb. 1781. This letter is identical in substance with TJ's letter to Huntington of this date, q.v.

FC (Vi); captioned: "Genl. Washington & the President of Congress." Tr (DLC); a defective press copy.

Agreement with James Anderson for Nailers

Richmond Feby. 9th. 1781.

I have Nine lads thats Nailors, which the State may have for one Year at 2/3 Specie Pr. Day, they lads must be fed Clothed Washing and lodgeing fiting for Apprentises. Eight of those lads shall make Twenty five Thousand Nails pr. Week. JAMES ANDERSON

In Council Feb. 9. 1781.

The board agree to engage the above persons for one year on the terms above proposed on the condition that when not necessary to be employed in making nails, they shall do such other smith's work as they are able to do. TH: JEFFERSON

MS (Vi); in Anderson's hand, followed by the Council's approval in TJ's hand; endorsed.

Anderson's proposals were submitted to George Muter and by him communicated to the executive; there are copies of Anderson's paper and the Council's determination in War Office Journal (Vi) under 10 Feb. 1781.

To Theodorick Bland

SIR Richmond Febry. 9th. 1781.

I received yesterday your letter inclosing that of Colo. Dubuysson. It gives us great pain that we are not able to do what is desired by that gentleman. I shall not rest this merely on the determination of the Executive not to exchange Govr. Hamilton at all while matters on our frontier are situated as at present, a determination founded as well on the possibility of real injury he would be enabled to do as on the apprehensions which the Western Country entertain of his eager enmity against us and influence with the savages. It is well known that the whole Line of Officers belonging to Virginia and North Carolina were taken some months before the captivity of Colo. Dubuysson, and stand previously entitled to exchange on the just principle of regular rotation. Exchanges out of turn have already given great disgust, not only to those who have been passed by, but to the Officers in general who find themselves exposed to the danger of a like insult. I leave to yourself, Sir, to judge what would be the complaints were we to consent to the exchange in question, passing over a whole army whose Officers stand first entitled; these complaints would be the more distressing as they would be founded in justice, and would admit no possibility of answer. The same reasons are good against a parole exchange of such extent as the one proposed. I hope therefore that Colo. Dubuysson will see this matter in it's proper light and be satisfied that nothing but a sense of its being clearly against our duty prevents our concurrence in a measure leading so much to his relief and which is stated as eventually interesting to the family of Baron de Kalb, to whom gratitude would induce us to render every service reconcilable to that justice which is due to others. I am &c. &c. &c.,

Ts. Jefferson

FC (Vi).

YOUR LETTER: Dated 29 Jan. 1781; see note there for COLO. DUBUYSSON'S communication. On the case of GOVR. HAMILTON generally, see TJ to Bland, 8 June 1779, and references there. Having by this time gone to New York on parole, Hamilton was exchanged on 4 Mch., and on 27 May 1781 he sailed for England (Hamilton's "Report," *George Rogers Clark Papers, 1771-1781*, p. 206).

From Theodorick Bland

Sir — Philadelphia Feby. 9th 1781

The Delegates some time ago transmitted to Your Excellency officially an account of their application to the Minister of France to interpose his interest with Monsr. de Ternay to induce him to detach a frigate of the Fr: Squadron at Rhode Island, to convey the Arms belonging to our state which came in the Comite, thither in safety. Since which my Personal application, singly, has been unremitted to prevail by the same Channel, to have a line of Battle ship and one or two frigates sent into our Bay, but I have redoubled these applications and enforced them with the strongest Arguments I could address ever since the Sailing of Arnold from New york, having been always apprehensive that his design was on our Country. I am now happy to inform your Excellency, that in Consequence of our Joint application the Arms are on boad a frigate intended to be sent as above mentiond; and of enclosing you a Copy of a letter from the Count De Rochambeau which was this day received by Congress, through General Washington; besides which the Minister of France has communicated to me, and Charged me with Secrecy to every Soul, but your Excellency, with whom he wishes it to remain inviolate untill executed, that Mr. Des Touches the Present Commander in Cheif of the French Fleet, has determined to put to Sea (in consequence of the disaster that has happend to the British Fleet, which gives him a Superiority) and either Give Battle to, or Block up the British fleet in Gardner's Bay in either of which cases he is determined to send one or two Ships of the line and two frigates into our Bay. An Express being about to set off tomorrow I thought it necessary to give your Excellency this Intelligence that every preparation might be made by land, as well as that Pilots might be orderd with the Utmost secrecy and dispatch to attend at the Capes for their arrival, should fortune favor us in this Critical and interesting affair as we expect. Your Excellency will be not less aware of the importance of being prepared on land to cooperate with these vessels should they arrive, than of sending on board proper pilots and Conductors, with every necessary intelligence of the Situation, state and strength of the Enemy by land and Sea as also the most convenient stations and Harbors for the Ships of our ally in Case of necessity. I cannot conclude my letter without taking notice how much we are indebted to his Excellency the Chevalr. de La Lucerne for the frankness with which he has Concurred and the cordiality with which he is enclined to promote every measure that we have Jointly, and I have individually had the honor to proprose to him for the good of the common Cause, and for the particular benefit and relief of our State. I have the honor to be with the greatest Sincerity Dr. Sr. Yrs. most affectionately, THEOK: BLAND

RC (Vi); endorsed. Enclosure: Copy (Vi, in Bland's hand) of a letter from Rochambeau to Washington, "New Port Jany [2]9th," informing him that a storm had grounded two British ships of the line and a frigate; "the Chevalier des Touches is waiting for more exact intelligence to go out with his whole fleet"; hopes that at last Destouches will be able "to send one man of War with two frigates to Cruize before Chesapeake bay to break the Communication from New York to the South." De Tilly had sailed 9 Feb. but Rochambeau did not write Washington of this until three days later, obviously because of a desire for secrecy (*Writings*, ed. Fitzpatrick, XXI, 197).

The Delegates' ACCOUNT OF THEIR APPLICATION TO THE MINISTER OF FRANCE has not been found. See, further, Joseph Jones to TJ, 10 Feb. 1781. Bland and the other Virginia delegates were not the only ones to urge that French naval assistance be sent to the Chesapeake. "On the first notice of the storm and its ill effects," wrote Washington to President Huntington on 26 Feb., "I intimated to the French General [Rochambeau] the possibility and importance of improving the opportunity in an attempt upon Arnold. When I received a more distinct account of the damage sustained by the British fleet (which was a long time coming to me) I immediately put in motion as large a part of my small force here as I could with any prudence spare to proceed under the command of the Marquis De la Fayette to the head of Elk; and made, without delay, a proposal for a cooperation in Chesapeak-bay, with the whole of the fleet of our allies and a part of their land force. Before my proposition arrived, in consequence of an application to him, through the Chevalier De la Luzerne, Mr. Des touches had sent the force I have already mentioned to Chesapeak bay" (*Writings*, ed. Fitzpatrick, XXI, 197, 301-302). The application to La Luzerne was doubtless that made by Bland and the other delegates.

From Beesly Edgar Joel

SIR Williamsburg Feby. 9th 1781.

In consequence of your Letter, and approbation I proceded with the utmost rapidity to this place. After a delay of five or six days, (the usual fatality attending our service) for Captain Maxwell, I wrote to General Nelson pointing out the necessity of expidition in an affair of this nature; and obtain'd an Order on the Ship-Yard, to be supplyed with such necessarys, and workmen, as I should demand. I found no vessel here but the *dragon*, which had lain many month under water; by the advice of, and Assurance of Mr. Cole she was totally unfit for service, I by the assistance of the Commanding Officer of the Navy proceded to raise her up, and in five days had the pleasure to see her in forwardness for the intended service. Contrary winds detain'd me in the river untill the 6th. Ult. when having procured a Pilot I got under way to run out, but was by his ignorance, and inattention run on the Bar where she lay three days. During this time, forgetting the station in which *I have hitherto* moved, but anxious only for the service of a country in whose cause I have engaged, and who have suffer'd so much disgrace by the *present procedings* of the Enemy, I cond[escended] *even* to the meanest employments of a common Sailor, sharing in every fategue, and injuring my constitution which you can easy immagine is none of the most indelicate. Hitherto I had informed Genl. Nelson of my procedings both by Letter, and by Mr. Cole. You cannot immagine my surprise, when yesterday Just as I was going down, (after having remain'd without rest for three nights on service) to receive the inclosed. You must pardon Sir, the freedom I am going to take in a few observations my duty to myself obliges me to make.

It is Sir generally the case, when a man animated perhaps by a spirit, more enterprizing than the most part of his Fellow creatures; puts himself in the Front of danger, he meets with every obstruction which *delay*, or want of Judgment can throw in his way.

General Nelson was no stranger to my conduct. If he disaproves of it; why not stop it in the Bud? But at the instant when ev'ry thing was prepar'd, and I ensured of success was going to proced on an enterprize, beyond the resolution of every one; to be thus stop't is surly strange! and must cast a shade on me which to prevent, you must allow me, to give to the Public a circumstantial account of my conduct; of my Offer, assiduity, exertion, and design, that the People of *this country* may see, I dared to serve them, And the Enemy in their laugh at the abortion of the scheme, may not Join *my* name to the objects of their ridicule. Schemes out of the common Line, either for the danger, or singularity of the attempt, untill crown'd with success is beyond the comprehension of the vulgar. But from you or Genl. Nelson who move in more exalted spheres other steps are to be expected. If this prevention of my proceeding, issues from a doubt of my success, I can convince the world of the falacy of *their* arguments who pretend to deny it. The Dragon is now from the preparations made in her unfit for any other service; I shall anxiously wait for your orders to go down with her, and allow me to observe if succesfull she will be of more service than the whole fleet have hither to been, which now lays, and I fear will remain so totally unprepared, and useless. The World must now be a judge of my intentions. *Virginia* must acknowledge that without an Idea of reward I have offer'd myself a victim for her service, satisfied should I escape with honor I hope to throw on her. Let them know this and then Judge whether such a design deserves encouragement or obstructions.

I have the honor to be with *unfeigned* respect your Ob. H Svt.,

B: EDGAR JOEL

RC (Vi); addressed: "On Service His Excellency the Governor"; endorsed.

YOUR LETTER: Joel may refer here to TJ's letter to Nelson, 16 Jan., q.v.; see also Nelson to TJ, 7 Feb.; TJ to Nelson, 13 Feb.; TJ to Joel, 14 Feb. 1781.

To Paul Loyall

SIR — In Council Feby. 9th 1781

The Board having further considered the application you were pleased to make for Arms for the Virginia Militia at the North West Bridge, are of opinion, that the chief direction of the Military operations against the Enemy in this State being in Baron Steuben; it will be improper to make any order until consultation with him. The Militia embodied in this State having been put under his command, it is probable that any orders which may go out on this subject may go from him. I shall take the earliest opportunity of consulting with him a[nd] of having done immediately whatever shall be concluded. I beg you to give the fullest assurances to the people of Princess Anne and Norfolk that no Efforts of which we are capable, shall be spared to rescue them from the hands of the Enemy so soon as we shall be in condition to do it.

I am &c &c &c, THOMAS JEFFERSON

FC (Vi).
On Paul Loyall, of Norfolk, at this time a member of the Senate, see a note in *Official Letters*, II, 329. TJ took up Loyall's request in a letter to Steuben, 17 Feb., q.v.

From George Muter

[*Richmond, 9 Feb. 1781.* A minute in the War Office Journal (Vi) under this date reads as follows: "Letter, to the Governor informing him of Sheet Tin, to be sold at Vendue to day, which is wanted for the State, but that Mr. Armistead says he is unable to purchase, for want of Money." Not located.]

From Edmund Randolph, with a Memorandum by Jefferson

SIR February 9. 1781.

As your excellency and the council probably have not access to Vattel, on whose doctrines this hasty answer is founded, I shall inclose the paragraph from his work, which treats of the right of soldiery to booty. They seem to amount to this: that booty does in strictness belong to the commonwealth; but that late usage has divided it among the captors, military stores excepted. Now I believe, but cannot affirm, that congress have distributed captures in conformity to this usage. Whether this state has made a declaration of a like nature in favor of the army, or, if none such exists, whether the continental rule ought to be adopted here, or whether horses do not fall within the description of military stores, I must refer to your board, as better judges. I trust, that I am correct, when I suppose, that there is no just distinction in this instance between regulars and militia.

No similar conclusion, however, is drawn from the above with respect to the unarmed peasantry: who seem to stand in the following predicament. They are in truth parties to the war, and in that view possessed unquestionably a right of capture, before the law of arms was modelled upon the present customs of Europe. As to the enemy that right still exists, but they are liable to be hanged, as robbers, if taken. Vattel conceives, that private citizens are prohibited from making captures by a kind of tacit law of the state, not by the law of nations. He says indeed, that "custom actually authorizes, nay even obliges all subjects of whatever rank to *secure* the persons and things belonging to the enemy, when they fall into their hands." This gives no right of property in what is taken. And yet it is Every day's practice for private persons to retain a ship which they have captured, if another with a commission should not lay His hands upon it before condemnation: And such property, as horses, belong to the takers without the formality of a condemnation. I presume that the same restriction as to military stores will apply to unarmed citizens and soldiers equally. But I do not pretend to say, whether Vattel or daily practice shall prevail.

I have the honor to be yr. excys. mo. ob. serv:,

EDM: RANDOLPH.

[*Below the text, in TJ's hand:*]

The opinion of the board is that these horses (of the property of the enemy) belong to the captors; that they be lodged with the Q.M. till the captor makes his right of capture appear before the Commissioner of the W[ar] Office.

RC (Vi). Enclosure (filed with the letter in Vi): 3-page extract in clerk's hand, with interlineations by Randolph, from Vattel's *Law of Nations* concerning booty; Vattel's opinion was that title to both lands taken (conquest) and movable things captured (booty) vested in the sovereign; he further asserted, however, that the sovereign might, and by custom did, grant the troops what share of the booty he pleased. This extended to things found on enemy soldiers fallen in battle, to the pillage of a camp, and even to the plundering of a town, but not to "artillery, military stores, magazines, and convoys of provision or forage which are applied to the wants and use of the army." Randolph challenged this exception (as to unarmed citizens) in the letter following; see also TJ to Nelson, 10 Feb. 1781.

From Edmund Randolph

DEAR SIR Friday P.M. [9 February 1781]

Reflecting upon what I wrote this morning respecting the capture, made by the unarmed countrymen, I am inclined to think, that I was inaccurate. As well as I recollect, Vattel was said to be against their claim; but that daily usage was in favor of it. So far perhaps he is right.

But if they have title to what they take; it is certainly wrong to affirm, that military stores are to be excepted. For they seem to be excepted in the case of a soldier, only because he has devoted himself, by his engagement, to his country, and the time spent in the acquisition of the booty would be so much withdrawn from the public service. Sed aliter with a peasant.

I am Dr Sir with sincere respect yr. mo. ob. serv:,

EDM: RANDOLPH

RC (Vi); addressed and endorsed.

See preceding letter and note. Randolph was mistaken in arguing that Vattel's exception of military stores was due to the reason assigned; actually the exception was argued by Vattel as being justified not because of the time the soldier spent "withdrawn from the public service," but because artillery, magazines, &c. were needed "for the wants and use of the army" as a whole —an argument that would apply to unarmed citizens as well as to soldiers. The Governor and Council made no such distinction as to the status of the captor.

From John Smith

SIR Frederick, Feby. 9th. 1781

Your excellencys orders for a draught of two hundred and eighty five men from the militia of this county to serve in an expedition under Col. Clarke, have been executed, so far as to direct the men to be held in readiness, agreeable to the time appointed by Col. Clarke. As I know that many difficulties will arise in compelling these men to march and an equal aversion to the expedition prevailing in the other Counties, I can but inform you of the small probability there is of the mens being obtained. Should the draught be executed and the men be ready to march, I cannot procure twenty Guns in the county to arm them with, and to march without, would render no service; of this I inform'd Col. Clarke who says that Arms may be procured from philadelphia and requested I would inform your excellency of it. Major Hunter from Berkeley will deliver this. I have inform'd him of the sentiments of the County and beg leave to refer you to him for further information. I have the honor to be Sir Your excellency's obt. Servt.,

JOHN SMITH Cy. Lt. Fk.

RC (Vi); endorsed.

YOUR EXCELLENCYS ORDERS: See TJ to the County Lieutenant of Frederick (John Smith), 24 Dec. 1780. See also TJ's reply (To the County Lieutenants of Berkeley and Frederick, 16 Feb. 1781).

From James Wood

SIR Charlottesville 9th. Feb. 1781.

Since the Return of the German Troops to the Barracks a Great Proportion of the Regiment of Guards Conceive their times of

Service from the Tenor of their enlistments are expired. I have never been Able to learn what the Instructions to the Recruiting Officers were, but from their Certificates Granted to the men they have Certainly Acted very improperly. I have Directed Copies of these Certificates to be made Out, and have the Honor of inclosing them with Colo. Taylors Remarks; and must beg that you will Come to a Detirmination On them, as I have been in Constant Expectation of a mutiny, or the whole going Off, and which Prevents Me from Visiting the Post at Frederick Town. I think the whole of them wou'd reinlist for a Limited time not exceeding Twelve Months. Our Prospect of supplies of Provisions are Very Alarming, and have wrote Mr. Commissary Browne On the Subject.

I have the Honor to be wth. Respect Sir, Yr Excellency's Very Obt. Servt., J WOOD.

RC (Vi); endorsed. The enclosed certificates are missing; they had been sent to Wood by Francis Taylor in a letter dated at the Barracks, 5 Feb. 1781 (Vi; substance printed in CVSP, I, 490); Taylor's letter was also doubtless enclosed in the present letter, for it bears an endorsement in the same hand as that on Wood's letter and on others received by TJ at this time. The postscript of Taylor's letter reads: "I think if the Soldiers were well Clad they would be much better Satisfied, they have generally been Enlisted 2 years and have received but little more than one years allowance of Cloathing."

From Robert Andrews

Williamsburg, 10 Feb. 1781. "The City of Williamsburg having procured a Waggon, Team &c. as ordered by Act of Assembly," Andrews desires to know to whom they shall be delivered.

RC (Vi); endorsed (in part): "From the Revd Robt. Andrews."

The ACT OF ASSEMBLY in question was an Act of the Oct. 1780 session for supplying the army with clothes, provisions, and wagons; see Hening, X, 388-43.

From George Rogers Clark

DR SIR Winchester Feby 10th 1781.

Before my arrival at this Post I met with Mr. Randolph from Pittsburg. Col. W. Harrison is Exerting himself to Compleat the Purchases ordered, Great Incouragement given by Most Persons of Note N of the Allegany Pensylvanians, as well as Virginians. Col. Crawford now with me says their is no danger of their not turning out or a failiour of provition, but no possibility of its being Ready by the time appointed. I am Extreamly anctious to get to Pittsburg but doubt it will be some Days before I can leave this place. Am Sorry that some of the officers of Berkely Cty appear to be backward in furnishing men. Before this Reaches you you must have Received a Petition from them. I guess the purport by Letters from their Lieutenant. They want arms. Men they have. The officers of Frederick appear Rather desirous to Incourageing the Expedition but I doubt Cannot arm their men. I have Learn[t] that a number of Rifles lay in Philadelphia. If they Could be procured they might be brought to this place in a few weaks by the Cty Lieuts Receiving orders in Consequence. Its Truly surprising to me that those Gentlemen should undertake to dictate for Government or Remons[tra]te against her orders. I wish we may not here-[after] feel the fatal effects of such Conduct. Col. Crawford who will hand you this is Capable and hath already been of Great Service to us in the Department of Pittsburg whare we have a pleasing Prospect at present. I wish it was the Case hear then would be but little doubt of Suckecess. I begin to fear the want of men but the Idea of a disappointment is so disagreable to me that if the Authority and Influance that I have with Every Exertion that can be made will Carry my point I shall Certainly do it without[1] your orders for the Enterprise is Countermand[ed] or a failiour in the supplies I am to Receive which I hope will not be the Case.

I am Sr your Very Hb. Servant, G R CLARK

RC (Vi); addressed: "His Excellency the Governor of Virginia Richmond Col. Crawford"; endorsed by a clerk; also on back is a notation in TJ's hand: "redoubt & block house."

SOME OF THE OFFICERS OF BERKELY CTY: See letter from the Officers of the Berkeley County Militia, 25 Jan. 1781. THEIR LIEUTENANT: Josiah Swearingen was the county lieutenant of Berkeley.

1 This sentence, more involved than is usual in Clark's direct style, becomes clearer when it is understood that "without" is used in the sense of "unless."

To Nathanael Greene

SIR Richmond Feb. 10. 1781.

I now do myself the pleasure of transmitting you information on the several heads of your requisitions. I am sorry that full compliance with them has appeared impracticable. Every moment however brings us new proofs that we must be aided by our Northern brethren. Perhaps they are aiding us, and we may be uninformed of it. I think near half the enemy's force are now in Virginia and the states South of that. Is half the burthen of opposition to rest on Virginia and N. Carolina? I trust you concur with us in crying aloud to Congress on this head.

I sincerely rejoice with you on Genl. Morgan's late important success. Besides the real loss sustained by the enemy in the force they were moving against us, it will give us time to prepare for the residue. The prisoners taken on that occasion I shall certainly take the liberty of handing on Northwardly through this state. For the reasons for doing this I beg leave to refer you to the inclosed.

Doctr. Brownson received £75,000 equal to £1000 specie. For the balance he must wait until the assembly meets. They are called together on the 1st. of the ensuing month. I hope they will then determine to make up their quota of men fully. I have the pleasure to inform you that we have reason to expect during the two ensuing months very full supplies of all necessaries for our army from France, on a contract we had made the last spring. I hope too that their escort is such as not only to render their entrance secure but to promise something further. I have the honour to be with very great esteem & respect Sir Your most obedt. & most humble servt,

TH: JEFFERSON

RC (N). FC (Vi). Enclosures not found.

YOUR REQUISITIONS: Presumably those printed above under date of 20 Nov. 1780.

From Nathanael Greene

SIR Guilford Court house Feb: 10h 1781

Your Excellency's favor of the 16h Ulto. is before me.

The enemy are in the vicinity of Moravian towns and are advancing with great rapidity.

Our force is so inferior that every exertion in the State of Virginia is necessary to support us. I have taken the liberty to write Mr. Henery to collect 14 or 1500 Volunteers to aid us.[1]

I must refer your Excellency to the Honble. the Baron de Steuben for particulars. The Army are marching towards Boyds ferry on Dan river.

I am With great esteem & respect Your Excellency's Most Obedient Servant, NATH GREENE

RC (Vi); in an aide's hand, signed by Greene; endorsed. FC (MiU-C). Tr (CSmH).

MR. HENERY: Patrick Henry; Greene's letter to him, of the present date, is printed in part in William Johnson, *Sketches of the Life and Correspondence of Nathanael Greene*, Charleston, 1822, I, 447. I MUST REFER YOUR EXCELLENCY TO . . . STEUBEN: Greene's letter to Steuben, of the present date, is among the Steuben Papers in NHi; it gives detailed reasons why Greene has been obliged to retreat and asserts: "The interest of America is so nearly connected with the operations of this Campaign that prudence makes it necessary to avoid the present moment of action to strike a blow hereafter that may be decisive and important. My expectations on this head will rest chiefly on Virginia, so that your exertions to assist me from that quarter will become more necessary." Steuben transmitted a copy of Greene's letter (not found) to TJ on 15 Feb. (see Steuben's letters of that date).

[1] This sentence appears at the beginning of the second paragraph in FC and Tr, neither of which mentions the size of the volunteer force requested.

To John Harmanson

SIR Richmond Febry. 10th. 1781

I am sorry that the inattention of the Continental Officer Colo. Finnie and Major Forsythe to whom the provisions on your shore were transferred, should have given so much trouble to you and to us. We have interfered merely to save it to the Continent. On the same principle we must advise you to keep whatever will keep till you can get information from one of those Gentlemen what shall be done with it. What will not keep had better be sold. I expected the Bacon had been taken away by the flag to Charlestown. As it is not you had better sell it to the best advantage. The Salt we shall be glad of on this shore, as formerly desired if you can get a safe opportunity of sending it over.

I am Sr. &c &c &c, THOS. JEFFERSON

FC (Vi). See Harmanson to TJ, 20 Jan. 1781.

From Joseph Jones

Philadelphia, 10 Feb. 1781. More information is now available on the movements of the "French Ships from R. Island and the Detachment of Graves's Fleet in search of them." Four frigates left Newport before the storm of 22 Jan.; two 74's and a frigate were dispatched from British fleet to intercept them. Both were exposed to the storm, but two British ships of the line have suffered, one being stranded on Montauk Point, and the French ships are safely back at Newport. This will probably give the French naval superiority. "Whether *we* shall receive any assistance in consequence of this Event will be soon manifested." In view of this possibility, measures must be concerted on our part for cooperation. Rejoices on "the important success of Genl. Morgan."

RC (Vi); 3 p.; addressed as "Private" and franked by Jones; endorsed; printed in CVSP, I, 503-4. See Theodorick Bland to TJ, 9 Feb. 1781.

From George Muter

[*Richmond, 10 Feb. 1781.* War Office Journal (Vi) contains the following entry under this date: "Letters, to the Governor inclosing a list of Mr. Andersons men that lost their bedding, and an order to the Commissary of Stores to furnish what is wanted Viz. eight beds, eight Sheets and twenty Six Blankets as soon as the circumstances of the public Store will permit of it. The order is returned Countersigned by the Governor and forwarded to Mr. Anderson." Not located.]

From George Muter, with Reply

[*Richmond, 10 Feb. 1781.* War Office Journal (Vi) contains the following entries under this date: "Letter, to the Governor inclosing a list of some men that Mr. Ford has engaged that are now down with the Militia, whom he wishes to have Authority to send for."

Answer to the above:

"In Council February 10th. 1781. The Executive never had an Idea of withdrawing workmen from the Militia in service to do these works, nor can consent to do it." Muter's letter and enclosure not located; no other text of TJ's reply found.]

To Thomas Nelson

Dear Genl. In Council Febry. 10th. 1781.

Information having been given the Board that sundry Horses of British property, having been left by the Enemy, were taken by our Militia or un-armed Citizens, and a question made whether they belong to the Commonwealth or the Captor, we are of opinion that they should be yeilded to the Captor. It is thought however where any possible doubt can arise who was the Captor, that the Horse should be put in the Hands of the State Quartermaster, and the party or parties claiming make their right appear to the Commissioners of the War Office. As this question as far as we are informed concerns only persons under your command, I take the liberty of communicating it to you.

Your disposition of the Hides of Slaughtered Beeves is approved of. I am sorry any loss has been incurred in that article before.

We made it the subject of enquiry on the former Invasion and from the reports made to us, had reason to believe all had been taken care of. The oil is almost of as much importance as the Hide. The Waggons which were sent to Fredericksburg for camp-kettles, found none ready made. Mr. Hunter is making more and other Waggons will go off for them within three or four days. As fast as they are brought we shall endeavour to send them to the Militia. It would be well for us to be informed what number you have.

I am with great respect &c, T. JEFFERSON

FC (Vi). See the two letters from Edmund Randolph to TJ, 9 Feb. 1781.

From William Preston

SIR Lead Mines Feby. 10th. 1781.

Mr. Carter Just now delivered me your Excellency's Letter with the other Papers for this County committed to his Care. I shall do all in my Power to comply with the Instructions I have received, as well as the Acts of Assembly; but I am doubtful it will be sometime before I can attempt it. Lord Cornwallis with his Army having proceeded so far into the State of North Carolina that the Militia of Washington and Montgomery are called for, I have therefore given express Orders for all the Effective Officers and men in this County to meet me at this Place next monday and Tuesday, to march out to the relief of the People in the upper Counties in No. Carolina bordering on this state, where it is believed the british Troops are now ravaging the Country, unless they bend their Course towards Petersburg, which some of the Carolina Officers, now here, believes will be the Case.

As the Washington Militia had the first Notice I make no doubt but they will March on Monday next. These troops are to continue one Month on Duty after they arrive at head Quarters; as soon as they return, or should the necessity of their going into Carolina cease, I shall immediately proceed to the Draught for the Continental Service. But should the Orders I have given to draw out our Militia be countermanded, while the Enemy are so nigh to this Country, the opportunity might be forever lost. If any further Intelligence from the southard worth notice, should come to hand I shall communicate it to your Excellency by the Express on his return from Washington.

I am your Excellencys most Obedt Servt., WM. PRESTON

RC (Vi); addressed (in part): "℔ Express"; endorsed.

YOUR EXCELLENCY'S LETTER WITH THE OTHER PAPERS FOR THIS COUNTY: TJ's circular to the County Lieutenants, 19 Jan. 1781, q.v., enclosing copy of Act for recruiting Virginia's quota of troops for the Continental army, &c.; Preston was county lieutenant of Montgomery.

From Richard Claiborne

SIR Richmond. 11th. February 1781.

As I am altogether unacquainted whether your Excellency does business on the Sabbath or not, I hope I shall be excused for addressing you this Morning, because it is respecting a matter in which I am particularly interested for the whole Department, and for the Southern army.

Your Excellency and Council were pleased to inform me by letter of the 7th. that it would be chimerical for you to attempt to procure the whole of the Articles stated in the Estimate; but would endeavour to furnish money for such and so many of them, as are most essentially necessary.

Your Excellency will observe that among the most weighty articles, there are five hundred thousand bushels of Corn and Oats, to be laid in at the Magazines on Dan River, from Boyd's ferry upwards. That I might not be burthensome to the Treasury, for money, I Substituted Certificates, of which the inclosed is a Copy, but I am really doubtful, they will meet with but a poor reception. The People have been so much imposed upon by Certificates, that the very name of such a thing is obnoxious to them; so that I have very little hopes of doing any thing without money. Could I be Supplied with grain for the Southern Army by the Specific tax, the scattered manner from which it must be collected, and transported to our Magazines upon Dan, would be more expensive, than to purchase at once in the Southern Counties. I beg for information respecting this matter; and how far the Specific grain will be applied to the Quarter Masters Department in the Continental line of this State.

Your Excellency may rest assured, that none of the Articles stated in the estimate, shall be purchased, but such as are indispensably necessary. At the same time, I am sorry to say that the prices of every thing are so enormous in the present currency, that the half million will go but a small way in procuring them.

I have the honor to be With great respect and regard Your Excellency's Most Obedient Humble Servant,

RD. CLAIBORNE DQMr. S. Virga.

RC (Vi); in a clerk's hand, signed by Claiborne; endorsed. Enclosure not found. It should be noted that in referring to the amount of grain requested, Claiborne spelled out the total: FIVE HUNDRED THOUSAND BUSHELS. Edward Carrington later claimed, in an indignant letter, that TJ had magnified his figures tenfold and that he had requested only fifty thousand bushels (see Carrington to TJ, 24 Feb., TJ's reply, 3 Mch., and Carrington's apology, 31 Mch.).

To George Muter

TH: J. TO COLO. MUTER. Feb. 11. 1781.

I shall be much obliged to Colo. Muter to settle finally with Warneck to-day if possible the question he was so good as to undertake to put to him.

RC (Vi); addressed by TJ: "Colo. Muter"; endorsed.
See TJ to Muter, 29 Jan., and Muter's two letters of the present date.

From George Muter

SIR Feby 11. 1781.

Warneck should have called on me yesterday, but failed: I shall goe after him in a few minutes.

I have just received a letter from Majr. North (one of the Barron's aids) informing me that the Barron desires me to send 400℔ of pistol powder, 2000℔ of lead and 600 flints to Suffolk immedeatly to be delivered to Genl. Muhlenberg. I have sent to the Quarter Master for the State to make (if possible) provision for sending off these articles immedeatly, at the same time I have requested of Mr. North to inform me, if there is any officer to whom the ammunition can be delivered here, or any covered waggon belonging to the Continent (as there is none that I know of the property of State) to send the powder in.

The Barron's *orders* at present requiring a different mode of delivering the amunition from that heretofore used, and which in the present circumstances of affairs in the State, will occasion much difficulty, I must beg for Your Excellency's opinion how I ought to act. In the mean time as I am anxious to do every thing in my power to promote the good of the service, I shall take every measure I can to comply with the Barron's orders from the State only, if that must be done. I beg leave to observe however that there is a field commissary of Military Stores (Majr. Pryor) who I beleive is in town, and I shou'd suppose him to be the proper officer to receive and forward the amunition required.

I have the honour to be Your Excellency's Most hl Servant,

GEORGE MUTER

RC (Vi); addressed and endorsed. A LETTER FROM MAJR. NORTH: Dated 11 Feb., without place (Vi; printed in CVSP, I, 505).

From George Muter

Sir Feby 11. 1781

I have been in search of Warneck but can-not find him. He shall certainly wait on your Excellency and the Council to morrow forenoon, that his affair may be determined finally, if he is in this place.

I have the honour of inclosing a note to the Commissary of Stores to provide some tacks for covering two waggons that want only covering with canvas to fitt them for taking in the ammunition, the wooden work being already done.

Since writing the above, I have received your Excellency's note. I am now at Mr. Rose's but he is not at home. I believe the waggons mentioned above, must be those he meant, I have hear'd of no other, and they were ordered to be fitted some time agoe, the want of tacks (I am told now) has prevented their being compleated. For fear I shou'd be mistaken in the waggons, I shall goe immedeatly to Mr. Smith's to get what information I can there respecting them, and trye every possible means to push off the ammunition quickly.

I have the honour to be Your Excellency's most hl Servt.,

George Muter

RC (Vi). Enclosure not found, but an entry in War Office Journal (Vi) under this date records an order to "the Commissary of Military Stores, or Henry Clayton" to deliver the powder, lead, and flints mentioned in Muter's first letter of this date; another entry in the same records an order to the officer commanding at the Quarters of the State Guard Regiment to send a sergeant and two men as a guard for these supplies.

Your Excellency's note: Apparently not TJ's note of this date printed above, but another (not found), in answer to Muter's first letter of this date.

From David Ross

Sir Arrowfield 11 February 1781.

I Have the honor of receiving your favour of the 8th. instant, and am greatly relieved to see so fair a prospect of an abundant supply of necessary Stores in the Spring.

I Shall be glad to know if you are Confined to any particular Warehouses and what Warehouses for the delivery of Mr. De francey's Tobacco.

When tis convenient to furnish me with the necessary Estimates shall be glad to receive them.

The Enemy's ships that entered Cape Fear River, landed about 500 troops who were join'd by a number of disaffected. By the latest Accounts they had penetrated about 40 miles. Their aim apeared to be the magazine at Kingston from which place they were about 20 miles distant. This party is said to be under the Command of a Majr. Craig.

I am with great regard Sir Your most huml Servant,

DAVID ROSS

RC (Vi); addressed and endorsed.
YOUR FAVOUR OF THE 8TH.: Not found, but see TJ to Ross, 2 Feb. 1781.

To Granville Smith

SIR Richmond Febry. 11th. 1781.

Forty slaves will be wanting two months to execute a defensive work at Hood's: You will therefore go out yourself immediately and endeavour to hire them. Apply in the first instance to those persons who having houses on the river above that place are more immediately interested in it's defence. I have been told that Mr. Carter, Colo. Ricd. Randolph and Mr. Bowler Cooke particularly have offered to furnish a number of Hands. It is labourers only that we want to that amount, for which if good and in proportion for those which are indifferent, the worth of ten pounds payable a day in paper money according to the last valuation of the Grand Jury preceding the payment shall be allowed. Besides these you are desired to engage one master Bricklayer and three assistants. The Labourers must be at Hoods on Monday the 19th. inst., the Bricklayers when called for. T.J.

FC (Vi). On the DEFENSIVE WORK AT HOOD'S see Senf to TJ, 29 Jan.; Steuben to TJ, 11 Feb. 1781; and numerous allusions in the letters that follow.

To Steuben

SIR Richmond Feb. 11. 1781.

Having been informed about a week ago that the troops nearest to the enemy's lines were much in want of ammunition waggons I have had two made ready, which are now sent to your orders. I think it was Genl. Lawson particularly who applied for these waggons.

I have the honour to be with much esteem & respect Sir Your most obedt. humble servt., TH: JEFFERSON

RC (PHi); addressed by TJ: "The honble. Majr. Genl. Baron Steuben or in his absence the Commanding officer at Cabbin point. with two covered waggons"; endorsed.

From Steuben

Sir [11 February 1781]

Immediately after my arrival in this State Colo. Senf represented to me the necessity of establishing a Battery at Hoods and some other trifling works in the vicinity of James River. His opinion appearing to me to be well grounded, I did not hesitate a moment to submit it to your Excellency. I am informed you laid it before the Assembly but that it was not taken into consideration.

The last Invasion and a more perfect knowledge of the ground convinced me still further of the necessity[1] of erecting a Battery at the above place covered by a Redoubt with a Block house the whole to contain about 60 Men and to cost about 12 or 1500 Dollars Specie. I accordingly laid before your Excellency and the Council a plan of the Work proposed with an Estimation of the expence and the Articles necessary to finish it in Six Weeks and I was happy in finding it approved. The most important Article required was 40 Negroes and 10 Artificers and If I understood your Excellency these were to be furnished by the five nearest Counties and to be at the Spot the 7 Inst. I therefore orderd Colo. Senf to Hoods on that Day to receive the Workmen and tools and to begin the Work.

At my Return from Cabbin point I was much surprized at Colo. Senfs informing me that he had not been furnished with any workmen and that Government had declared they had it not in their power to furnish any and in consequence I orderd him to Return to Richmond.

Three weeks are now Elapsed Since the Enemy went down the River. In this time the Work could have been half finished. If Government think the Work unnecessary [or if] they have it not in their [power?][2] I have only to beg they would for my own Justification give me their Opinion in writing. I must beg your Excellency to consider that the shamefull opposition made to the last incursion of the Enemy falls in some measure on me as the Commanding Officer in the state and I cannot but reckon it among my misfortunes to have been here at the time. My wish is to prevent a Repetition of the Disgrace but as I can do nothing without the Assistance of the Government, I must beg your Excellency to give me Answer to this that I may have it in my power to Justify my own Conduct.

Dft (NHi); endorsed: "Copy to Gov Jefferson 11 Feby 81." Original is faded and in places only semi-legible.

Steuben's indignant letter on Virginia's failure to fortify HOODS on the James has been cited more than once as an indictment of TJ's competence as governor. For the history of the affair see TJ to Speaker Harrison, 30 Nov., transmitting Senf's earliest and now missing plan for the fortification; Steuben to TJ, 15 Dec. 1780, inquiring what action had been taken by the Assembly; Senf to TJ, 29 Jan., submitting a revised plan; TJ's answer to the present letter, 12 Feb.; TJ to Granville Smith, same date; Archibald Cary to TJ, 13 Feb.; TJ to Turner Southall and others, 15 Feb.; TJ to John Allen, 16 Feb.; John Allen to TJ, 12 Mch. 1781.

One of the reasons, undoubtedly, that Steuben felt angry over the failure to fortify Hood's promptly was the fact that he had already told Washington that it would be done promptly. On 1 Feb. he wrote as follows: "The governor has called the Assembly who are to meet the 1st of March and I propose endeavoring to get some better Arrangements made with their Militia, tho' from the very dispersed situation of the Inhabitants and their [being] almost wholly disarmed, this Country will always be more defenceless than any of the Northern states. I have proposed to have a Battery with a redoubt and blockhouse built at Hoods for the defence of the River. The Governor and Council have agreed to the proposal and it will be begun in a few days" (Steuben had first written "a short time" and then struck it out; Steuben to Washington, 1 Feb., NHi). A few weeks later Steuben again committed himself in advance by writing to Washington that everything was in readiness for Lafayette's expedition. This of course was very far from being the case and in proportion as TJ's efforts failed to meet the conditions already described by Steuben as accomplishments, his anger mounted.

[1] In a corresponding, but deleted, passage in Dft, Steuben employed the expression "absolute necessity."

[2] Portion of text missing at foot of page; it may be that more than one word is missing.

To the Auditors

GENTLEMEN Feby. 12. 1781.

Be pleased to issue to Mr. John Walker a Warrant for three thousand pounds upon Account.

By Advice of Council. TH: JEFFERSON

RC (Vi: Contingent Fund Vouchers); in a clerk's hand, with Walker's name filled in and signed by TJ; endorsed.

Advice of Council

respecting Purchase of Gunpowder, with a Warrant for the Purchase

Feb. 12. 1781.

The Executive will advance £20,000 to Messrs. Lewis and Thornton on the 12th. of March, and will agree to the terms proposed in Mr. Lewis's letter of Feb. 6. 1781. reserving a liberty to pay for the powder in tobacco @ 20/ the hundred or it's worth in paper money as valued by the grand jury next preceding paiment.

TH: JEFFERSON

Mar. 5. 1781.

The Executive will take five tons or so much of it as shall be ready by the last of July next. TH: JEFFERSON

GENTLEMEN April 2. 1781.

Be pleased to issue to Messrs Lewis and Thornton a Warrant for twenty thousand pounds in advance for a quantity of Gun powder to be furnished by them to the State.

By Advice of Council. TH: JEFFERSON

Three notes to the Auditors (Vi: Contingent Fund Vouchers), of several dates but apparently all sent on 2 Apr. 1781. The first two are in TJ's hand on the recto of a small slip of paper; the third, in a clerk's hand, signed by TJ, is on verso. There is a separate endorsement sheet bearing notations in more than one hand: "2d April 1781 Mess. Lewis & Thornton £20000 On Acct. Exd."

MR LEWIS'S LETTER OF FEB. 6. 1781: This letter (in Vi) was written by John Lewis, without place, and addressed "To Colo. John Harvie Richmond." Lewis and his partner Thornton state that they will "furnish one Ton of Powder at four Shillings Specie ℔r. pound and what ever quantity more we make we will take Five Shillings ℔ pound Specie. . . . I expect our mill will get to work by the middle of April and think we can make Eight hundred weight powder per week"; they will, however, require £20,000 immediately to purchase supplies. This letter was submitted by Harvie to the Council, and below the text is a copy of the Council's decision (the first note printed above) and also a note by TJ identical with the second note printed above.

From John Baylor

SIR Newmarket Feb: 12 1781

Hoping that you may have supplyed yourself with an American Atlas, in the space of six or eight Months, You will please to deliver to General Weedon's Care, my Atlas. I have the Honor to be Your Excellency's most Ob: & H: Sert, JOHN BAYLOR

RC (Vi); addressed; endorsed (in part): "Requesting the return of his American Atlas."

To John Browne

SIR Richmond Feby. 12th. 1781

You will be pleased to provide in the neighbourhood of New Castle flour and stalled[1] beef for 50,000 rations to be applied to no use but on my special order that these are meant to be applied. The beef must be kept ready for Slaughter at the Shortest warning.

THOS. JEFFERSON

FC (Vi).

The proceedings of Council this day explain this order; the rations were to be gathered "in case of any french forces coming this way" (*Va. Council Jour.*, II, 291).

[1] That is, stall-fed.

To John Browne

SIR — Richmond Febry. 12th. 1781

As the time for receiving the specific tax is approaching, you will be pleased to instruct your deputies in the several Counties to receive all the articles except the tobacco and to apply them to the general purposes of the Commissary's and Quarter Master's departments. I inclose you orders on the Commissioners and Commissaries of the specific tax of the several counties to authorize your calling for those articles. I am Sr. &c &c &c, T.J.

FC (Vi). Enclosures not found.

From Arthur Campbell

SIR — Washington Febr. 12th. 1781

Late dispatches from General Greene and various Letters from Officers in Carolinia entreats the aid of the Mountain Militia, and I have taken the liberty once more to order them out notwithstanding their circumstances ill suits such a tour now. Matters yet unsettled with the Cherokees, and the Northwards already begun to annoy us; but altho, we have these, and other difficulties to combat with, I believe the County will turn out with its usual ardor. Why cannot the eastern Militia act in the same manner. Surely they have the most property to fight for. In truth, Sir, it wounds our feelings to learn, that the safety of our Country cannot be trusted to the natural defence thereof.

I am Sir your Obedient Servant, ARTHUR CAMPBELL

RC (Vi); addressed and endorsed.

From Robert Ewing

SIR — Bedford febr. 12th 1781

I had not the Honour to Receive your favor till Late the 6th instant; then without Loss of time; throu the favor of Col. Leftwitch; my self and son without charge; summond a full court as by Law Required; to meet the 9th. Tho None Met; but four; three Justices's and the above field officer being one. The Reasons Not yet Known, except the active Colo. James Calaway then call'd upon with a guard to Receive the British prisoners on his Line. Wee directed such orders as to put the act to purchass the waggon &c. compleat in execution, and then with the same court thought it expedient, according to the spirit of Law: tho Not Literaly so: with the present pressing call &c. to direct farther that the Beef and clothing act with out Loss of time should be put in execution allso. Wee hope to have your Excellencys Aprobation, and could Wish to Remove future scruple the ensuing assembly may confirm what in such cases May have been dun for the publick good &c.

I wish to Let your Excellency Know that as the Late Honorable assembly thought fit to place: all Last taxes on property assessable in specie only: and pased over Luxeries and current money: the Reason Not yet Known; causes Much Murmering.

I have the Honour to be with the greatest Respect and esteem Sir your Excellencys Mo. obt and very Hble Servt, ROBT EWING

RC (Vi); addressed and endorsed. No attempt at repunctuation has been made, since the meaning is clear and since Ewing's method of punctuation is, to say the least, unconventional.

YOUR FAVOR: TJ's circular to the Magistrates of each county, 20 Jan. 1781, q.v.

To Benjamin Harrison

SIR Richmd. Feby. 12th. 1781

Colo. John Gibson is appointed to go as next in Command under Genl. Clarke on the business communicated to you. As Colo. Gibson is now here he will return to Fort Pitt by the way of Baltimore to see the powder sent on, and prevent any danger of it's stopping by the way. Be so good as to lodge at Goddard['s] the Printer in Baltimore a line to Colo. Gibson informing him in what state the procuring of the powder is. He will call there for it.

That your information may be perfect as we can render it, I am to inform you that the three Months Militia under Genl. Stevens in North Carolina, their number not known, are discharged, having served their term out. For Southern news I beg leave to refer you to the President of Congress, who has a letter from Baron Steuben giving information of the events in the Neighbourhood of Genl. Greene, and one from myself as to the movements of the Enemy at Cape Fear. Arnold remains quiet. Colo. Dundass came out the first instant with 500 Men towards Suffolk. Genl. Lawson went down towards him with an equal number, whereon Dundass returned in the Night. They are drawing their shipping into shallow Water and have a large vessel from N York cut down so as to mount twenty 24 pounders on one Deck.

I am &c &c &c, T.J.

FC (Vi); captioned: "Speaker Harrison." TJ wrote two letters to Pres. Huntington on THE MOVEMENTS OF THE ENEMY AT CAPE FEAR, 8 and 12 Feb. 1781, qq.v.

From Benjamin Harrison

SIR Philadelphia Feby. 12. 1781

I arrived at this place late in the evening of yesterday after a most disagreable journey, which has been considerably lengthend by the great difficulty I found in exchanging state money for Continental, and with all my trouble I fear I have not procured as much as will support me. I am just return'd from the board of war who have given me an order for four ton of powder. As you were not particular in the kind that would be wanted, I have taken it one half in musket the other in cannon Powder, which I suppose will be about the proportion that will be wanted for the service for which it is intended. I have no doubt of getting it on the way in a day or two, as the board are giving me every assistance in their power. I think you would do well to advise Colo. Clarke as soon as possible of its being on the way, that he may send an escort to meet it, as the board informs me there is some danger of its being distroy'd on the way without it, there being a conside[rable] body of disaffected people in that quarter. The Expence of transportation I must pay out of the money you entrusted me with, there being not a shilling in the Continental Treasury; The new Congress money for this State and the Jerseys pass at seventy five for one, whilst that of Virginia will only bring thirty seven and a half, and will not do even that, but from the Speculators, a set of men that nothing but necessity shall cause me to deal with. I shall endeavour if possible to exchange the money with the public, and have some little expectations of succeeding. The continental powder at Baltimore amounted only to 2500 wt. I therefore thought it better to take the whole here. I much fear no great success will attend my Embassy, it appearing to me that Congress can not command Men, or if they had them, have they any quantity of necessaries to furnish them for the field. There is great abundance of cloathing in this Town, but it can't be procured without money or tobacco, nor will the latter do, unless the Enemy leave our country, yet would it not be well that Ross should send an agent here if I can't procure them, to try the Experiment; of my success you shall have immediate notice. I am with great esteem and respect Your most obedient and most Humble Servant, BENJA HARRISON

RC (Vi); endorsed. MY EMBASSY: On Harrison's special mission to Congress see TJ to Harrison, 29 Jan. 1781, and references there. AN ORDER FOR FOUR TON OF POWDER: See Harrison to TJ, 19 Feb. and references there.

To Samuel Huntington

SIR Richmond February 12th. 1781.

The enclosed extract of a letter from Governor Nash which I received this day being a confirmation of the intelligence I transmitted in a former letter, I take the liberty of handing it forward to your Excellency. I am informed through a private channel on which I have considerable reliance, that the Enemy had landed five hundred Troops under the command of a Maj. Craig, who were joined by a number of disaffected; that they had penetrated forty miles: that their aim appeared to be the Magazine of Kingston, from which place they were about twenty Miles distant.

Baron Steuben transmits to your Excellency a Copy of a letter from Genl. Greene, by which you will learn the events which have taken place in that quarter since the defeat of Colo. Tarlton by Genl. Morgan. These events speak best for themselves and no doubt will suggest what is necessary to be done to prevent the successive losses of State after State to which the want of Arms and a regular Soldiery seem more especially to expose those in the South.

I have the honor to be with every sentiment of respect Your Excellency's Most obedient & Most Humbl Servt.,

TH: JEFFERSON

RC (DLC: PCC, No. 71, II); in a clerk's hand, signed by TJ; endorsed: "Letter from Govr Jefferson Feby 12th. 1781. Read 20th." Enclosure: Extract of letter from Abner Nash, 2 Feb., printed above. FC (Vi). Tr (DLC); with caption and signature by TJ. TJ sent an identical letter to Washington on this date.

A PRIVATE CHANNEL: See David Ross to TJ, 11 Feb. 1781. A LETTER FROM GENL. GREENE: Both Washington and Huntington interpreted the words "Baron Steuben transmits" as meaning that TJ was enclosing Greene's letter to Steuben. Washington on 26 Feb. wrote Huntington that Greene's letter "appears from the manner of Governor Jeffersons speaking of it to be an interesting one" and added that "it was not among Your Excellency's dispatches. I should be happy to be favoured with a sight of it, as I have no letter from General Greene since that containing an acct. of Morgans affair" (*Writings*, ed. Fitzpatrick, XXI, 302); to this Huntington replied that through "some mistake of the Governor's Secretary, [Greene's letter] was not inclosed in his

Dispatches to me and has never come to Hand" (DLC: Washington Papers, Huntington to Washington, 2 Mch. 1781). Actually, Steuben sent the letter directly to Washington, who received it on 26 Feb. and acknowledged it the next day (*Writings*, ed. Fitzpatrick, XXI, 310).

From George Muter

War Office [*Richmond*], *12 Feb. 1781*. Mr. John Henderson, from Albemarle, is with Muter and offers to rent to the public a sawmill he has charge of that is erected on [John] Harvie's land, or he "will furnish plank at the point of fork" at reasonable prices. Transportation from the mill to Point of Fork is five miles by land and thirty by water. Muter desires instructions.

RC (Vi); 1 p.

From Duncan Rose

Richmond, *12 Feb. 1781*. Has obtained "a final settlement" with the auditors but is "in want of the amount of the Inclosed warrant out of the Ballance due me from the Publick, and understand that no money will be paid to private individuals on warrants drawn by the Auditors without being countersigned by Your Excellency. . . . I hope this request will be granted by your Honorable Board when it is consider'd that I have invariably advanced the Publick every shilling I could command from time to time."

RC (Vi); 2 p.; addressed and endorsed. Enclosure not found, but the Council on this day approved a warrant in favor of Duncan Rose in the sum of £10,000 (*Va. Council Jour.*, II, 291).

From David Ross

SIR Arrowfield 12th. February 1781.

I am just now honour'd with your favour of this date. This morning I despatch'd a Waggon with a parcel of Tent stuff and Cloth nearly enough for Colo. Bufords troops. I have an agent at South quay in search of blankets and some other woolens. I expect an answer to day.

I shall exert my best endeavours to procure the articles Your Excellency mentions. As well the Credit as the interest of the State is engaged, that their troops should take the field like Soldiers.

I often hear it mentioned in a transient Manner that the troops at Chesterfield Courthouse are very Naked, destitute of every thing almost. About next wednesday I shall have occassion to send as far as Alexandria on Account of the Tobacco purchase and mean to take that opportunity to look for such articles as cannot be procured this way. If there be any other articles wanted than what you've mention'd, 'tis probable you may know by that time. I will wait upon you for that purpose. I have Wrote to two men below that carry on a Shoe factory to considerable extent to know what quantity they can deliver weekly. You seem'd uncertain how the State was provided with that article.

I am much affraid hats cannot be got. Caps I expect must be made for the men. I have been with Mr. Harrison about his blankets. He has got Copy of an Invoice and bill of Lading for the blankets but has no advice of the arrival of the ship; I have engaged the Blankets and urged him in the most pressing manner to send to Maryland in search of them.

I am happy to see by your Excellency's letter that we continue successfull to the Southward. I have heard nothing worth mentioning since my last.

I am with the greatest Regard Your most huml Servt,

David Ross

RC (Vi); addressed (in part): "favour of Colo. Zinf [Senf]"; endorsed. TJ's favour of this date has not been found.

To Steuben

Sir In Council Feby. 12. 1781.

I have been honored with your letter of yesterday's date. Your representation of the importance of erecting a small Work at Hoods was considered by the Executive as an evidence of your friendly attention to the defence of the State and was by them as you desired laid before the Assembly. The Assembly, pressed in time, did not, as far as I am informed, take it under consideration. The invasion which took place just before their rising prevented any thing further being done till the departure of the Enemy from this place, and the return of the Executive to it. The proposition of undertaking the Work which you then again renewed was approved of by them, and they determined to procure if possible the several Articles necessary for carrying it into immediate execution according to the plan and estimate prepared.[1] I think however you misapprehended us when you understood it was agreed that the 40 Negroes and 10 Artificers required should be furnished by the five nearest Counties and be at the spot on the 7th. inst. It does not occur to me or to any

Gentleman of the Council that the 7th. or any other day was fixed on for their assembling: and that we could not have agreed[2] that the 40 Negroes and 10 Artificers should be furnished by the five nearest Counties may be deduced from the conversation which you will recollect to have passed between us the Evening before you last went to Cabin-Point. You informed me you meant to call for 20 Militia from each of the [five][3] circumjacent Counties to come to Hoods with their Hoes and Axes to erect the Work but to notify to them at the same time that you would receive 10. Negroes in their room: and you asked me whether you must apply to Government for authority to do this. I answered that such an application would produce no effect, as it had been the subject of conversation at the Council Board that day, and the Board was of opinion we had no right to call out the Militia to do fatigue duty. You then replied you would do it of your own authority and throw yourself on the Assembly for a justification. I repeat this conversation thus particularly to satisfy you that we could not have agreed that the five neighbouring Counties should produce these Labourers and of course that we stand discharged of having failed to fulfill such an Agreement. The Executive have not by the laws of this State any power to call a freeman to labour even for the Public without his consent, nor a Slave without that of his Master. Sensible of this, when we first proposed to undertake this Work, as you meant that Colo. Senf should superintend it, I desired him to search among our Artillery Officers for one whom he would chuse to conduct it under his direction and that this Officer should immediately proceed to hire the Slaves in the Neighbourhood of Hoods, where I thought it more likely the people would be willing to hire as the Work respected their safety more immediately. He did so, and sent a Capt. Allen on this Business. In a subsequent Journey to Petersburg Colo. Senf informed me that he had himself engaged 8 or 10. Four carpenters were assigned to Colo. Senf at this place, the several Articles of Tools (except Hoes, fascine knives and barrows) were procured for him here, a boat to carry them down and [I][3] took for granted that they went. The two Black-smith's are ready at this place when wanted. What success Capt. Allen has had is not reported to me. The Executive are far from thinking this Work unnecessary; nor yet that it will be out of their power to furnish the necessaries for erecting it. Yet they may possibly be disappointed in their expectations of engaging voluntary labourers, the only means in their power. Sensible that a necessary Work is not to be abandoned because their means are not so energetic as they could wish them and on the contrary that it is their duty to take those means as they find them and to make the most of them for the public Good, they propose to pursue this work, and if they cannot accomplish it in a shorter, they will in a longer time.

From a review of these circumstances, I hope you will be persuaded that any delays which may have occurred have been produced by circumstances which it was not in our power to controul, and not from either a want of attention, or inclination to the work.

I have the honor to be with great respect Your most obedt. Servt.,

TH: JEFFERSON

RC (NHi); in a clerk's hand, signed and addressed (without place) to Steuben by TJ; endorsed. FC (Vi).

On the proposed SMALL WORK AT HOODS, see Steuben to TJ, 11 Feb., to which the present letter is a reply.

1 Corrected (though not in TJ's hand) in RC from "according to a plan and estimate prepared by Colo. Senf," which is also the reading in FC. (Senf's plan is printed above, 29 Jan. 1781.)

2 This word is underlined in FC.

3 This word is in FC but was carelessly omitted in RC.

From George Lee Turberville

Post at Sandy Point Feby. 12th. 1781

MAY IT PLEASE YOUR EXCELLENCY

I am this moment informed that the guard sent to Richmond with the British Prisoners (consigned by Genl. Nelson's order, to the care and direction of Baron Steüben) have been Furlough'd by your Excellencies order. It has reduced me to a situation not a little disagreeable, as I am now commanded by Genl. Nelson to return them to Williamsburg, and from the Delay of the guard I am unable to ascertain where they may at this period be station'd. I flatter myself that your Excellency will be pleased to give me timely instructions, or in what manner I am to proceed in regard to them, that is whether I must weaken this Post, (already too intolerably weak) by sending a detachment to Richmond to conduct them to Wmsburg. or whether I may expect that Your Excellency will cause them to be conducted by some other party, agreeable to the Baron's desire that Genl. Nelson might endeavour to effect an exchange of them. The Post I command at is of very great importance as the Principle station to effect a communication with the counties on the North and South Sides of James river. I am at present reduced to the small number of Seventy effectives which when I consider that the counties of Hanover and Henrico compose the Regiment really astonishes me. Desertion is so prevalent that at least

Sixty have left the Post since I occupy'd it, altogether (I beleive) actuated by pusillanimity and fear that they were to pass the River and come to immediate Action. This post (unless I am speedily recruited) cannot be depended on as secure. Cou'd it be possible to reinforce it by any Edict from your Excellency I make no doubt but the Feild Officers in the Abovenamed counties will receive your Excellencies command immediately to dispatch the Furlough'd Soldiers with Deserters to me.

I am totally at a loss how to punish Desertion at present. As the State Militia Laws are expired I am induced to think that they may be tried and punished according to the Martial Law by Congress established. Your Excellencies opinion on this head as well as any mode by which that worst of Military evils may in some measure be cured will render essential service.

I hope your Excellency will excuse the length of this Epistle. I have the honor to be with becoming respect Yr Excellency's Most Obedt. Servant, GEO. LEE TURBERVILLE Major

There is a material post that ought to be occupied about four miles from this place. 'Tis impossible that infantry can do it. If twelve horse might by your Excellencies Order be raised by impress and Swords alone furnished I coud mount them immediately. The post I mean is Dancing point from whence James Town may be seen. GLT

RC (Vi); addressed and endorsed. See TJ's reply, 13 Feb.

To George Washington

Richmond, 12 Feb. 1781. This letter is identical in substance with TJ's letter of this date to Samuel Huntington, q.v.

RC (DLC: Washington Papers); 2 p.; in a clerk's hand, signed by TJ; endorsed (in part): "recd 28u. Ansd. 21st March." Tr (DLC). Printed from Tr in HAW, I, 291-2. Enclosure: Abner Nash to TJ, 2 Feb. 1781, extract (DLC: Washington Papers); this letter is printed in full above under its date and the part included in the extract is there identified. A PrC of the extract, in a clerk's hand, is in DLC: TJ Papers.

To Daniel Brodhead

SIR Richmd Feby. 13th. 1781

I have duly received your favor by Colo. Gibson. I am sorry to learn there is any scarcity of provisions in your settlement. Nevertheless I must suppose it too numerous to be at any time under a difficulty to support so moderate a Garrison as yours, if the means of drawing provisions from the people are furnished you. I apprehend your wants proceed rather from deficiences of mony than of provisions, in which case our purchases will scarcely affect you as the forbearing them would not increase your stock of money: however from what Colo. Gibson tells me I have reason to hope that animal food will in a great measure be procured on the South side of the boundary. Genl. Washington's Letter transmitted you by Genl. Clarke will no doubt have satisfied you how earneastly he espouses the service on which that Gentleman is ordered and that it is his desire he should receive from you every aid of men and necessaries which you can help him to. I rely for your cordial execution of this desire on your Zeal for the common cause as well as your respect for the wishes of the Commander in Cheif. Colo. Gibson at my request with his regiment is ordered by Majr. Genl. Baron Steuben on the same service.

I am &c., T.J.

FC (Vi); captioned: "Colo. Broadhead." This letter was transmitted by John Gibson; see TJ to Gibson, this date.

YOUR FAVOR BY COLO. GIBSON: Brodhead to TJ, 17 Jan. 1781, q.v. GENL. WASHINGTON'S LETTER TRANSMITTED YOU BY GENL. CLARKE [George Rogers Clark]: Washington to Brodhead, 28 Dec. 1780; see note on Washington to TJ of that date. Steuben on 3 Feb. had ordered Gibson to form the remainder of his regiment in two companies and to bring them to Richmond (Steuben to Gibson and Steuben to Brodhead, both dated 3 Feb. and both in NHi).

From Archibald Cary

DEAR SIR Ampthill 13th Febuary 1781

I hope you will Excuse the Fredom I Venture at, In recommending any Publick Matter, and I hope you will; The Baron Dined with me Yesterday, and the Conversation Turnd, on the Defence of our River on which he Mentioned a Fort at Hoods, which would he was Confident prevent any Ships Coming by. This Morning Col: Self [Senf] Came here in Quest of the Baron who had gone on to the Courthouse, the Colonel shewed me a Plan of the Workes he proposed to erect from both the Gentlemen I was told application had been made for Labourers and Artificers to Accomplish this business, but that the Executive altho fully Satisfied of the Utility of the Measure had it not in their Power to procure them, and I Make no doubt of its being so from the Plan they May have Taken. It is this reason which Induces Me to offer my Advice, and I think it will Succeed.

That you Appoint in the Countys on the River above that Place Some one Person of Interest in Each County, who Shall Apply to the Wealthy People to represent this Matter to them, and to Indeavour to Hire or otherways Git a Negro or more from Each, who Shall be at the place on a Certain day to begin and Finish the Worke. 50 or 60 I think may be procured by this Means, and I am told a Month or 6 Weeks with that Number will Compleat the business. My ill Health prevents my Undertakeing it in My County, Majr. Goode is a Person I would recommend, Southall for Henrico, Col: Banister for Dinwiddie, Col. Starke and Mr. Tyler Can inform who will be proper in Prince George[1] and Charles City. As to what Tools may be Wanted, I judge the Publick will Supply. If they Cannot, the Same Gentlemen May Apply for them. Col: Self Informs me there is an officer on the spot to receive the People.

I think the Interest of Every Man on or near the River, and indeed of the Publick so much at Stake on the Compleation of this Worke that a doubt does not remain with me but the People may be procured. What have we to prevent a Second Visit from the British Troops, our Troops all below, they may put theirs on board their Ships at Night and run up the River burn and Plunder as they Come and be again Imbarked before it will be Possable for our Men to March up, and if they do not so Act, they want wisdom. I Set out with apolagiseing for this letter And I Am Convinced you will Conclude it proceeds from a Right Cause, the Interest of my Country.

I Am Sir Your Most Obedt. and afft Hble Servt.,

ARCHIBALD CARY

P.S. Perhaps a letter Addressed from the Executive to the People in the hands of the Gentlemen who you may appoint would be of Great use.

RC (Vi); addressed (in part): "Pr Mr Randolph"; endorsed.

TJ carried out the plan proposed by Cary; see letter to Turner Southall and others, 15 Feb. On the affair of the FORT AT HOODS, see Senf to TJ, 29 Jan., and references there.

[1] Above "Prince George" TJ interlined "Colo. Call," who was among those addressed by TJ on 15 Feb.

To George Rogers Clark

SIR In Council Feb. 13. 1781.

Still having at heart the success of the expedition at the head of which you are placed, we have obtained leave from Baron Steuben for Colo. J. Gibson to attend you as next in command, and of course to succeed to your offices in the events of your death or captivity which however disagreeable in contemplation yet as being possible it is our duty to provide against. I have further added my most pressing request to Colo. Broadhead that he permit Colo. Gibson's regiment to be added to your force for the expedition, a request which I hope will be succesful as coinciding with the spirit of Genl. Washington's recommendations. Colo. Gibson is to go by Baltimore to see the powder conveyed to Fort Pitt. The articles which were to be sent from this place to Frederic county were duly forwarded a few days after you left us. I wish you laurels and health and am with esteem & respect Sir Your mo. ob. hble. servt.

Dft (Vi); endorsed (in part): "Entered." RC (WHi); in a clerk's hand, signed and addressed by TJ: "Brigadr. Genl. Clarke Fort Pitt"; endorsed in later hands. FC (Vi).

See TJ's letters to John Gibson and Daniel Brodhead, this date.

To Jonathan Clarke

SIR Richmond Febry. 13th. 1781.

As I expect to see Majr. Forsythe here within a few Days I must beg leave to postpone a definitive answer to your Letter 'till I am informed whether he has any and what objections to your demand, after which I will do myself the pleasure of writing you on the Subject. T.J.

FC (Vi). YOUR LETTER: Dated 6 Feb. 1781, q.v.

To John Gibson

SIR Febry. 13th. 1781. Richmond

Having obtained leave from Majr. Genl. Baron Steuben that you should concur in an expedition across the Ohio under the command of Genl. Clarke, I am to desire that you will in the first place take Baltimore in your way, at which place I have reason to beleive four tons of powder have been furnished us by the Continental Board of War which we mean for this expedition. The obtaining this powder was to be negotiated by the Speaker Harrison who has been desired to lodge a letter at Mr. Goddard's the printer in Baltimore enabling you to take it under your care, yet it is possible it may have been furnished at Philadelphia instead of Baltimore, and that you may be obliged to take that in your route. In any event you will please to find it out and see it safely conveyed to Fort Pitt and delivered to Genl. Clarke as the event of the expedition depends on his receiving this Supply. I send by you a letter to Colo. Broadhead desiring that your regiment may be joined in this expedition to Genl. Clarke's force, in which I hope to be gratified. You will take that or any other command which Genl. Clarke shall assign you. In the events of Genl. Clarke's death or captivity your rank and our confidence in you substitute you as his successor in the command; in which case you will prosecute the expedition under the instructions given to Genl. Clarke.

I am &c &c &c, T.J.

FC (Vi); at head of text: "Colo. Jo. Gibson."
A LETTER TO COLO. BROADHEAD: TJ to Daniel Brodhead, this date, q.v.

To Nathanael Greene

[*Richmond, 13 Feb. 1781.* Minute in *Va. Council Jour.*, II, 292: "Tuesday February 13th 1781 . . . Letters of this date from the Governor to General Greene, Colonel John Gibson, and Colonel Brodhead, on the Subject of the Western Expedition . . . being read, are approved, and ordered to be registered." No such letter from TJ to Greene has been found and none of this date was acknowledged by Greene. It is probable that the clerk of the Council mistakenly wrote "Greene" while intending to write "Clark," since TJ on 13 Feb. wrote George Rogers Clark "on the Subject of the Western Expedition." The letter to Clark and all others concerning the Western expedition are transcribed in the Executive Letter Book, but there is no file copy of a letter to Greene of this date.]

From James Henry

SIR King and Queen Feb. 13th. 1781

I was lately on the E. Shore, and there I discovered that the 2 fine Gallies destin'd for that Station, were not only abandoned, but in a way very soon to be totally lost to the publick. They ly ashore, greatly injured by the Worms; the smaller Cannon, either stolen, or borrowed, and put on board Vessels which depart from thence and never return; the small Rigging and other apparel, from time to time imbezzled, and, I much fear, the very Hulls will be soon cut away for the sake of the iron. Under these Circumstances, it would certainly be more eligible to sell all at once, and Save something, than lose all. They tell me the Sails and Rigging, Cables and Anchors would produce a considerable Sum, and perhaps the very Hulls would sell for something worth attention. The Ordnance and Stores, I presume, ought to be retained.

As I intend soon to go to that Country again shortly, if you think it adviseable to do any thing with them; my Son waits on you to receive the Orders or any other for that Country, which I will take care to deliver to the concerned. I am Sir, Your Excellency's most obedt Servt., JAS. HENRY

RC (PHi); addressed and endorsed. See TJ's reply, 14 Feb.

To Linctot

SIR In Council Febry. 13th. 1781.

I received two Days ago your favor of Decemr. 5. 1780 from Fort Pitt. It was the more acceptable as I had not before heard of you after your departure for that place on your way from Wmsburgh and had really entertained fears that some accident had befallen you. The Letter you mention to have written informing me of your proceedings never came to hand and of course could not be answered. I having nothing to recommend but the General office of preserving peace with such of the Indians whose conduct has not rendered chastisement necessary: peace and friendship with them is our desire and their interest. I am sorry that the events and continuance of the war have more and more increased our inability to furnish you with those necessaries for the Indians which would facilitate the purposes of your mission to them. We have now the fullest assurance of regular and plentiful supplies of cloathing, arms, and military stores for our armies without requiring payment from our great Ally. Should this not be extended to supplies suitable to your department, it will leave us enabled to furnish those supplies ourselves; yet you cannot be too strenuous in preparing the minds of the Indians for disappointments and wants in these Articles should they happen contrary to our hope, and considering as the principal reward of their sufferings a hearty and cordial friendship with us, with free commerce and plentiful supplies on the restoration of peace. I wish you success in your endeavours and much health, and am with much respect &c, T.J.

FC (Vi).

From George Muter, with Reply

SIR War office Feby 13. 1781

I have never seen the law that exempts people employed for the public from militia duty &c., therefore I take the liberty of inclosing a note from Wm. Stone and Thos. Stone, for your Excellency's determination. They I beleive have contracted with Mr. Moody for making wheels and waggons, tho' I have nothing from Mr. Moody at present to show for it; and wish to have something to show, to satisfy the County Lieutenant of Henrico that they are exempted.

I must beg leave to mention to your Excellency, that the Clerk in this office is ordered by the County Lieutenant of Henrico, to hold himself in readiness to goe down in the militia immediatly to march from this County. From my not having seen either the former law that exempted the clerks of the board of war from militia duty, nor the act of last assembly to that purpose, I know not what is to be done in the present case, tho' I am sensible of the inconveniences that will arise, if he is carried off from the office.

I have the honour to be Your Excellency's most hl servant,

GEORGE MUTER C

Feb. 13. 1781.

The act of assembly exempts all artificers in public service from military duty provided they be engaged *for 6. months at least*. This proves that they must be employed in public work alone, and of course will not exempt every person who happens to undertake to furnish the public with work by the peice.

When the clerk of the War office shall be under marching orders I will give him a furlough. TH: JEFFERSON

RC (Vi); addressed and endorsed. Enclosure not found. TJ's note, in his own hand, is on a blank page of Muter's letter. Both letters are entered in War Office Journal (Vi) under this date.

From George Muter, with Reply

War Office [*Richmond*], *13 Feb. 1781.* Encloses an attestation of three soldiers enlisted for the war who have applied to Muter for a certificate for their bounty money. Muter desires to know what the bounty for such enlistments is. Below the text are two undated notes in TJ's hand:

"The bounty for Continental enlistments for the war is 2000 dollars *to be charged to the United States* and the recruiting money to the officer is 180[1] dollars of which 80 are to be charged to the United states. Th: Jefferson."

"The bounty on state enlistments (that is in the state regiments) is 750 dollars only, the recruiting money 150 dollars, the whole paiable by the state. Th: Jefferson."

RC (Vi); 2 p.; addressed and endorsed; cover also bears arithmetical calculations.

1 This figure is uncertain; it is written above another figure, crossed out.

To Thomas Nelson

Sir In Council Febry. 13th. 1781

Your suspension of Capt. Joel's enterprise against the Enemy's fleet seems to have been well grounded. It was become so universally known, as to leave little doubt of the Enemy's being apprised of it and of course prepared against it. Capt. Maxwell had some time before informed me that the Dragon had been devoted to this purpose. He at the same time assured me he had found it impossible to sell her as desired by the Assembly, and that she was not worth more than 50 pounds old money. This occasioned my acquiescence under her new destination. As she is ready prepared as a fire-ship and it is possible that future occasion may arise for using her as such against the present enemy, I think it will not be amiss to suffer her to remain in the yard ready to be so applied.

We are very anxious, if it be possible, to avoid calling in a relief of Militia from fresh Counties untill the draught be over, as it is found impossible to execute the law where a great proportion of Militia is absent, and every thing is to be considered as calamitous which prevents the raising a permanent force of Regulars.

I am sir with great Esteem &c, T.J.

FC (Vi). capt. joel's enterprise: See TJ to Nelson, 16 Jan. 1781, and references there.

From John Christian Senf

"*At Coll. Cary's*" [*Ampthill*, *Chesterfield co.*], *13 Feb. 1781.* Was at Manchester last night, but too late to cross the river; is now on his way to see Steuben at Chesterfield Courthouse; will return to Richmond for TJ's orders tonight. "Mr. Ross intends to set off with me for the Fork of James River the Day after to morrow, if No Contra Orders."

RC (Vi); 2 p.; signed: "Senf"; addressed and endorsed.

To Steuben

SIR Richmd. Febry. 13th. 1781.

The inclosed resolutions of Congress of Janry. 8th. and Aprl. 9. 1777 under which Capt. Heth's independant company at Fort Pitt were raised, will inform you of a condition to which they seem entitled of not being removed from that Station without their consent: the subsequent one of Octor. 3d. 1780 incorporates them in positive terms into the troops of the State. The former resolutions were probably not recollected at the time. The footing on which therefore they seem to stand rightfully is to remain at Fort Pitt if they chuse it; but as it was the desire of Congress that they should be annexed to some of our regiments and Colo. J. Gibson thinks they would rather join his than remain at Fort Pitt after losing their own Officers, I beg leave to refer to you whether it might not be proper that you should order so many of them to be annexed to that regiment *as should be willing to join it*. This, while it pays due respect to a solemn engagement with those people, will probably effect the wish of Congress in reducing that as well as other detached Corps to some regular form.

I have the honor to be with great respect Sr. Yr. Mo: obt. & mst. hbl. St., T. JEFFERSON

FC (Vi). Enclosures (not found): Copies of resolves of Congress, 8 Jan. and 9 Apr. 1777, 3 Oct. 1780; see Henry Heth to TJ, 13 Jan. 1781, and note describing these resolves.

To Steuben

SIR Richmond, Feby. 13th. 1781.

That the reformation of the troops of the Continent and State now on hand may be complete, I beg leave to inclose you a return of Col. Taylors regiment of guards. They are enlisted most of them to serve only during the continuance of the Saratoga troops in Albemarle. Their numbers being two hundred thirty eight, noncommission'd and private, I suppose they should be reduced to four companies and officered accordingly. However as they are in Continental employ I beg leave to submit to you the forming them on the general model. Col. Taylor who commands the regiment will carry into execution any orders you may think proper to give. If there be any other circumstances necessary for your information I shall take pleasure in communicating them on receiving information what they are.

I have the honor to be with great respect, Sir, Your Mo. obedt. & mo. hble Servt., Th: Jefferson

RC (NHi); in a clerk's hand; corrected, signed, and addressed by TJ to Steuben at Petersburg. Enclosure missing. FC (Vi).

To Francis Taylor

Sir Richmond Febry 13th. 1781.

The claim of the souldiers to discharges is by no means well founded as many of their enlistments were during the continuance of the Convention troops in this State, and others during their continuance in Albermarle. No occasional exit from the County with an intention to return can be considered as having broken off their continuance in the County and determined the enlistments. As however I conceive that these troops will be removed, I wish it were possible to re-inlist these men for the war. The bounty allowed is 2000 dollars. The Treasury indeed is not at this time in condition to advance any money; but as the Assembly meets within three weeks for this very purpose I hope that within a somewhat longer space it will be replenished; this will in a great measure disappoint Mr. Martin's present application for money during the same interval. We have it not in our power to furnish the cloathing required at present. I have formerly mentioned to you the provision made last Summer by the Executive to obtain cloathing. I have now the pleasure to assure you that I have received late information that it will certainly be with us during the course of the two ensuing months and so escorted as not to fear a capture. The arrival of this will furnish all our troops plentifully.

Congress having determined newly to model their forces, the Baron Steuben is now he[re on th]at business. The Ass[embly] have directed the Executive to have the same done as to the State-troops. Your regiment being in Continental service will be submitted to Baron Steuben: till this be done, which however will be done within a few Days, no promotions can take place. Be so good as to inform the Gentlemen of your Regiment who wrote to me on this subject that it will not be in my power to give an answer to their Letter till this arrangement is made. Some workmen in your neighbourhood will I beleive receive orders to take some of your damaged Arms. Be pleased to let them have those which require the greatest repairs and let the rest be boxed and sent here immediately. Mr. Mar[tin] will consult with Mr. Armistead what is to be done with the damaged cloathing; the price of the blankets used by the officers must be settled with the same gentleman. Mr. Brown received money about a fortnight ago sufficient to lay in animal food for your post for three months. Meal he is enabled to provide under the provision law. T.J.

FC (Vi). This is a reply to Taylor's letter of 8 Feb., q.v. THE GENTLEMEN OF YOUR REGIMENT TO ME: See their letter, or petition, under 7 Feb. 1781.

To George Lee Turberville

SIR Richmd. Febry. 13th. 1781

Your information that I had ordered furloughs to the Guard which brought up prisoners was without foundation as I never have in a single instance given or ordered a furlough. I consider it as my duty to furnish the number of men required by the Commanding Officer, to provide them as far as our circumstances enable us, and to leave to him and those acting under him the direction of them: this prevents me from taking any steps on the other parts of your letter relating to the post at Dancing Point, horsemen &c. The deserters of the Militia are punishable by being sentenced by a Court Martial to six months service as regulars. The Continental rules of War are unfortunately not in force with the Militia while serving in their own State. I am with respect &c, T.J.

FC (Vi).

YOUR INFORMATION: See Turberville to TJ, 12 Feb. 1781. I NEVER HAVE . . . ORDERED A FURLOUGH: But see TJ to Muter of this date (first letter), in which TJ promised to grant Muter's clerk a furlough when the clerk received marching orders.

From the Virginia Delegates in Congress

SIR Philada. Feby. 13th. 1781

By the Speaker Harrison who arrived here the day before yesterday we were honored with your Excellency's favor of the 26th. Ulto. We shall communicate your answer to the Baron d'Arendt, and if his claim against the State be supported by proper evidence shall take the best steps in our power to discharge it.

A Vessel just arrived from Cadiz has brought Congress two letters from Mr. Carmichael, from one of which dated Madrid Novr. 28th. 1780. the following is extracted: "From the best information I have been able to collect I am sorry to tell you, that the nation (British) will be able to borrow the sum demanded for the expenditures of 1781. which with the usual note of credit at the end of the session will amount to 16 Millions sterling at least. The scheme of the Ministry to effect this is not yet public but I am told it will be on similar conditions to that of the present year. 92,000 men are voted for the marine, and I have reason to think a considerable reinforcement will be sent early to the Southward and that agreeable to a proposition of Sr. J. Amherst the Enemy means to occupy and fortify strongly a port near the Mouth of Chesapeak from which, with a strong Garrison and naval force, they hope to interrupt the navigation of the bay and by frequent incursions prevent the States of Maryland and Virginia from sending supplies of men &c. &c. to the Carolinas. Among the troops mentioned to be embarked there are three regiments of Light Dragoons. Your servants nearer G.B. will however give you more accurate information. I am persuaded that our Ally will take early measures for defeating these designs. This latter information is derived indirectly from conversations with men in a situation to be well informed." Private letters by the same conveyance add that the blockade of Gibraltar was continued with great vigor, and that the Garrison began to be severely distressed.

We have the honor to be with great respect & esteem Yr. Excelly's. obt. Huml. Servants,

JOS: JONES
JAMES MADISON JUNR
THEOK. BLAND JR

RC (Vi); in Madison's hand, signed by the three delegates, and addressed and franked by Madison; endorsed.

The letter from William CARMICHAEL in Madrid, here quoted, is printed in full in Wharton, *Dipl. Corr. Amer. Rev.*, IV, 164-8.

From the Virginia Delegates in Congress

SR. Philadelphia Feby. 13 1781

We are Just informd from Genl. Varnum a Member now in Congress from Rhode Island that he has received Certain Intelligence that the Culloden of 74 Guns is drove on Shore and all her Crew except 17 men Perishd. The London of 90 Guns is driven out to Sea dismasted and two other 64 Gun Men of War Were dismasted entirely and all their Guns thrown over board in the late storm. Since writing the above We have procured the account from Genl. Varnum in his own hand, which We have the Honor to Enclose. It is moreover added that on hearing the above the Enemy at N. York sent orders to Arnold to retreat from Virginia. Heavenly Storm. We are Yr. Exlys Most obedt. Sevts,

JOS: JONES

THEOK. BLAND

RC (Vi); in Bland's hand, signed by him and Jones, and addressed and franked by Bland; endorsed. Enclosure not found.

To James Wood

SIR Richmond Febry. 13th. 1781

I have laid before the Council the several Certificates you were pleased to inclose to me. They are very clear that an enlistment to serve untill the prisoners should be removed from Albermarle can by no fair construction be deemed at an end by any occasional crossing of the line with an intention to return. A man is not said to be removed from his residence by taking a journey from it. You will find endorsed on two Certificates an Opinion of the Board in favour of the parties. We cannot enlist men for 12 months but shall be glad to reinlist these for the War as I have no doubt but the Germans will be removed. Mr. Browne about a fortnight ago received money to purchase 3 months animal food for the Germans. Meal he is authorized by the provision law to procure. T.J.

FC (Vi). Enclosures not found, but see Wood to TJ, 9 Feb., in which they were transmitted to TJ and to which this letter is a reply.

To James Henry

SIR Richmond Febry. 14th. 1781

The Gallies of which you are so kind as to give me information have been the subject of great misconduct in the Officers. They were first abandoned by Officers and men, and all their Apparel and furniture left with themselves exposed to depredation. On information of this last summer, we ordered Commodore Baron to bring one of them over to the Western shore, to bring the other to the Bay side of the Eastern shore from whence it might occasionally cooperate with our other Vessels, and to proceed against Officers and Men for abandoning them. This however has not been done and from our present situation cannot be done. I will therefore ask the favor of you and give you Authority to have every thing belonging to these Vessels of a movable nature stored in some safe place in the Hands of an honest Person, and the Hulls to remain as they are 'till we can be authorized to sell or enabled to repair them. We shall also be obliged to you to obtain for us information who has plundered any part of their appurtenances, who has borrowed, and who dared to lend them. I am with great Esteem and many thanks for your information Sr. yors. &c &c &c, T.J.

FC (Vi). See James Henry to TJ, 13 Feb., to which this is a reply.

From Edmund Massingbird Hyrne

New London, Va., 14 Feb. 1781. On departing from Greene's headquarters, Hyrne was instructed to march the prisoners now under his command "into such part of Virginia as your Excellency should direct for their residence; but the alarming accounts of the Enemy's approach induc'd me to push them on towards Stanton without halting, as I at first intended, for your instructions." Is to march from hence this morning and wishes to receive TJ's orders at Staunton. Also desires to know who the deputy commissary of prisoners is in this state, and wishes him to be instructed to make immediate returns of all the prisoners in Virginia, so that "they may be collected, if necessary, and register'd in one book; the exceeding irregularity which has hitherto prevaild with regard to Prisoners, makes this step necessary." "Considerable numbers" of prisoners escaped during Hyrne's rapid march through Henry and Bedford cos.; they are no doubt concealed in the country; suggests that an order be given "for collecting them." Hyrne will apply to the county lieutenant at Staunton for a guard.

RC (Vi); 3 p.; signed: "Edmd: Massbd: Hyrne Dep. Comy: Genl: of Prisoners"; addressed; endorsed.

To Beesly Edgar Joel

Sir Richmond Febry. 14th. 1781.

I am sorry that any circumstances have arisen to occasion the laying aside the enterprise which you had undertaken, bold in itself and, if succesful, advantageous. As it was however, pretty certain that the enemy had received notice of it, there seemed little hope of it's success for the present with however bold a hand it might have been conducted. Attempts of this kind have been generally deemed to depend for their issue on surprise. A little notice enables the enemy to withdraw from their pen or parry their approach. To prosecute them after such notice is to sacrafice the lives of the brave men who conduct [them,] better reserved for other occasions; of these circumstances Genl. Nelson to whom we refered the direction altogether, was better able to judge than we were at this distance. Some time hence perhaps the enemy may be again taken napping and the vessel being reserved in her present condition will give an opportunity of effecting whatever may be undertaken. The risk to which you had meant to expose yourself has furnished full proof of your zeal for our cause and will doubtless excite those sentiments of gratitude in every breast which it merits. I beg leave to take this occasion of testifying mine and of assuring you that I am with much respect Sir Yr. &c &c &c, T.J.

FC (Vi). This letter is a reply to Joel's of 9 Feb., q.v.; see also TJ to Nelson, 16 Jan. 1781.

To George Muter

SIR Richmond Febry. 14th. 1781

I must beg the favor of you to have immediate measures taken for the following purposes.

To send some of the worst Arms to Fredericksburg to be repaired at the Factory and by Mr. Hunter and to bring all the Camp kettles in readiness.

To have five ton of powder brought from Baltimore at Continental expence to replace what we have lent them and to bring our Cartouch boxes.

To have all the lead at the mines or at Winston's brought down.

To send up James river to purchase 20 or 30 of the best Tobacco canoes on the river.

To have battery carriages made ready for 8 of the 18 ℔[er]s which are here. Baron Steuben proposes to place them immediately at Hood's. I have informed him there are 24℔[er]s at S. Quay. Perhaps the carriages should be made fit for these should he prefer them.

To order Mr. Armistead to deliver 60 oznabrigs shirts to Baron Steuben's order for Armand's Corps.

To find a proper person to send out to collect gunsmiths.

To find a proper person to send out to collect carpenters and to superintend them at work.

To fix temporary shops in the mean time here at Westham and collect at these places all the Military Stores not in use elswhere.

To set persons to making cartouch boxes.

To send to Albermarle for leather.

I am &c., T.J.

FC (Vi).

From George Muter

[*Richmond, 14 Feb. 1781.* War Office Journal (Vi) contains the following entry under this date: "Letter to the Governor, in consequence of an application made to me from Major Magill, respecting the Soldiers of the State Garrison Regiment that served in the Southern Army, informing him they have received no pay for the time they served there, and petition his Excellency to advance pay for them on Account of the Continent." Not located.]

From the General Assembly of North Carolina

SIR Halifax February 14th. 1781.

The General Assembly of North Carolina by joint Resolve of both Houses, have directed us to lay before your Excellency the Situation of the Affairs of this State, which since the Commencement of the War with Britain have not been at a more critical Period. Lord Cornwallis irritated with the Blow struck at one of his principal Partizans by General Morgan hath penetrated into the Heart of the State with rapidity, at a Time our Militia were indulged with a small Respite, that the Regular Army might have a larger Supply of Necessaries, and at a Time our Legislature were preparing a System of regular Defence.

General Greene not being in Force for Action hath thought proper to retreat to the Dan, where he may be more properly reinforced to make Resistance, in the mean while we are wholly exposed to the enterprizing Genius of his Lordship, either to march through this State to join Arnold in Virginia before our Strenth can be collected or else form a Junction with him in this, thereby attempting our Subjugation which hath long been his Object. About three Weeks past near Five hundred British landed at Cape-Fear and have taken Possession of Wilmington, against whom our Governor hath marched with the lower Militia; we are drawing forth the Force of the other parts of the State, and mean to level it at Cornwallis under Major General Caswell.

However surrounded by a restless and troublesome Enemy, we are determined to defend this State to the last Extremity, and we flatter ourselves, our Northern Friends to whom we are already greatly indebted, will not be idle Spectators of the Conflict; through you Sir, we address our ancient Sister Virginia, that she will send us such further Succours and Aid as she can spare, not injuring her own internal defence: we need not suggest to your Excellency the Policy of fighting an Enemy from Home; if he is once suffered to arrive the Militia in general intent on saving their Property will not continue in Arms, while this and their Families are their principal Object. Near the Route of the Enemy, this we unfortunately experience, which no doubt will be your Case should you suffer them to penetrate into Virginia; but the Spirit of our Militia who are not immediately overwhelmed with the British Torrent is great, are now collecting in all Quarters, who we flatter ourselves if further countenanced by you will greatly teaze his Lordship, and so circumscribe him, that at length he must fall an easy Prey to General Greene or them. We are greatly distressed for Arms, the late Defeat near Camden deprived us of a great many of this essential Article which we cannot replace; we request your Excellency to furnish us as many you have not immediate use for.

We have the Honor to be with the highest Respect Your Excellencys most obedient humble Servants, ALEX. MARTIN S S.

THOS. BENBURY S C

RC (Vi); in a clerk's hand, signed by Martin and Benbury; endorsed (in part): "Lr. frm N. Carolina Assembly."

MILITIA . . . NEAR THE ROUTE OF THE ENEMY: For further comment based on experience that militia near the scene of invasion were less to be depended upon than those from a distance, see James Innes to TJ, printed above under date of 21 Oct. 1780.

From George Elliott

Petersburg, 14 Feb. 1781. By a letter from TJ of 6 Dec. 1780, Elliott was directed to furnish wagons for the purpose of moving Col. [John] Green's troops to the south; he received from Capt. Thomas Claiborne a wagon and three horses valued at £12,350 Virginia currency, and gave Claiborne a certificate therefor.

RC (Vi); 2 p.; addressed; endorsed (in part): "charged 15th. feby 81." TJ's letter to Elliott of 6 Dec. 1780 has not been found.

From George Rice

Richmond, 14 Feb. 1781. The distress of the quartermaster's department at Albemarle Barracks, where Rice has acted as assistant since its establishment, has become so great for want of money "that I think it my duty as a publick officer to lay a plain and full state of the matter before your Excellency." The lack of money has involved Rice in a load of debts that he has been unable to pay, and his creditors "have thereby suffered one hundred ℔ Cent in the depreciation of our money by such delay of payment. Notwithstanding this Circumstance, I do assert and an Inspection of the Accounts will prove it, that the people have Supply'd Provisions, Waggonage and Forage at a Cheaper rate than they have been procured in any other part of this Commonwealth." Rice furnishes comparative figures. "Upon the late Emission of money all Publick Creditors expected to have their old debts paid off so as to be prepared for the Collectors in the Gathering of Taxes. Their disappointment in this expectation has raised a violent clamour against me in particular and the Justice of the Publick in General, and now haveing occasion to ask their immediate assistance I must expect only to be answered with upbraidings. . . . If the old debts could be fully paid up a Credit might be again obtained, but whilst those remain largely in Arrear the Creditors minds from the want of their money is kept in perpetual irritation and seeing Sums paid for Articles at the moment Supplied and costing double and Treble the rate for which they furnish'd of the same Kind increases their ill temper and occasions a backwardness even in those who are the most disposed to promote the Welfare and interest of their Country." Encloses an estimate of the sum due his department, namely £360,000; if the treasury cannot furnish an advance now, an authoritative promise of early payment "would quiet the most Clamourous and Enable me to give much more effectual Aid to the publick wants than what I otherwise can possibly do." Rice sets out this evening for the Barracks and will gladly bear any commands to that post.

RC (Vi); 4 p.; addressed and endorsed. At foot of first page of text, in TJ's hand, is this note: "Rice assured we would pay when able."

From John Banister

Without place or date [*15? Feb. 1781*]. Encloses receipt for £5,250 "advanced for the Equipment of the Volunteer Horse in Lawsons Corps under an Express promise that I would be reimbursed the Succeeding Week." Necessities are now so urgent that he hopes for early payment of this and also $2,700 "advanced the other day for Catrige Boxes."

RC (Vi); 2 p.; undated; addressed and endorsed. Enclosure missing; see TJ's reply, 17 Feb., which virtually fixes the date of the present letter as 15 Feb.

From Lewis Burwell

Mecklenburg Feb 15th 1781

Your Excellency will I make no doubt be informed before you get this of the near approach of Lord Cornwallace with the British Army. I last night received information that the enemy were at Boyds Ferry on Dan River Halifax County. I have order'd out all the Militia of this County but I can assure you that we have little or no Amunition and I fear not a hundred Guns in the County. The People would fight and endeavour to defend this Country but their whole cry is for arms. Genl. Green they say is on this side the River but I suppose he will be obliged to retreat. I shall reinforce him with what Men I can arm and you may depend I will exert every nerve to save my Country but our Situation is truly deplorable as we shall not only feel the first stroke from the British army but be exposed to be plunder'd by the Damned Tories. I am with all due respect your Excellencys most obt Servant, LEWIS BURWELL

RC (Vi); addressed and endorsed.

To the County Lieutenants of Washington and Certain Other Counties

SIR Richmond Febry. 15. 1781.

I have just received intelligence from Genl. Greene that Lord Cornwallis, maddened by his losses at the Cowpens and George town, has burnt his own Waggons to enable himself to move with facility, and is pressing forward towards the Virginia line, Genl. Green being obliged to retire before him with an inferior force. The necessity of saving Genl. Green's Army and in doing that the probability of environing and destroying the Army of the enemy induce me to press you in the most earnest terms, in the instant of receiving this to collect one [1] of your Militia, and send them forward well armed and accoutred under proper Officers to repair to the orders of Genl. Greene wherever he shall be. By this movement of our enemy he has ventured his all on one stake. Our stroke is sure if the force turns out which I have ordered and without delay. In such a crisis expedition decides the event of the contest. Reflecting that it depends in a great measure on your personal exertions in effecting a rapid junction of your men with Genl. Green whether the Southern war be terminated by the capture of the hostile Army or entailed on us by permitting them to fix in our bowels, I cannot beleive you will rest a moment after receiving this untill you see your men under march. They must be subsisted on their way on whatever can be furnished by any person holding public provision or by impressing under the invasion law, returning to the Auditors lists of the certificates they give, or by taking provisions with them: for which they shall be allowed by way of rations.

This order necessarily interrupts the execution of the draught law. It would be too oppressive on those spirited men who shall now turn out, to have that law carried into execution, when they should not be on the spot to act for themselves. I would therefore advise you to postpone it untill their return and I will undertake to lay it before the Assembly which is shortly to meet who I cannot doubt will approve of the suspension and allow the execution of the Law at a future day.

Should the approach of danger and your public spirit have already called any Men from your county to the aid of Genl. Greene, they will be counted in lieu of so many of the number now ordered.

T. JEFFERSON

P.S. It is possible that you may have made such progress already in the draught as to render the immediate completion of it not only practicable but more eligible to the people on the whole than to discontinue it now and resume it hereafter. In this case use your own judgment and act for the best.

	whole	half	fourth			
Washington	829	414	207			
Montgomery	750	375	187			
Botetourt	589	294	147		Under this letter	1564
					Chestd. C.H.	400
		1083	541	1083	Riflemen below	800
				481		
						2764
Henry	1004	502	251	1564	of whom 1883 would	
Pittsylvania	924	461	230		be riflemen	
		963	481			
		2046	1022			

FC (Vi); at head of text: "Several County Lieuts." RC to William Preston (county lieutenant of Montgomery) is in Vi (in a clerk's hand, signed by TJ; endorsed); it calls for one fourth of the Montgomery militia.

INTELLIGENCE FROM GENL. GREENE: The *Va. Council Jour.* under the present date (II, 293) has this entry: "The Members present taking under their consideration General Greenes Letter wherein he mentions his being obliged to retire before Lord Cornwallis, who is pressing forward towards the Virginia line, advise the Governor to write to the County Lieutenants of Washington Montgomery, Botetourt, Henry & Pittsylvania pressing them immediately to send a fourth part of their respective Militias to the aid of General Greene: and to write to Baron Steuben informing him of this measure, & leaving to his judgment the propriety of reinforcing General Greene from the army below." The references to Greene's recent letter here and elsewhere may seem puzzling, for Greene in his short letter to TJ of 10 Feb., q.v., does not mention retiring before Cornwallis and other details recited in the present and other letters of this date; nor had TJ at the time of writing the present letter seen copies of Greene's letters addressed to Washington and Steuben that did give these details (see letters exchanged between TJ and Steuben, 15 Feb., below).

But the explanation may be that TJ had received the full and accurate report from Stevens of 8 Feb. at the time he received Greene's of 10 Feb. (i.e., the night of 14 Feb.) and that he therefore could cite details that apparently came from Greene but actually derived from another source. In any case TJ certainly understood more from Greene's letter than Greene put in it (see TJ to Steuben, 15 Feb., first letter).

1 The tabulation at foot of FC indicates that this blank was to be filled by "half" in the letters to Washington, Montgomery, and Botetourt, and by "fourth" in the letters to Henry and Pittsylvania. However, in the letter to Preston (of Montgomery co.), TJ himself inserted "fourth" in the blank; see TJ to Steuben, 15 Feb.

From Nathanael Greene

Camp at Boyds ferry on the Dan River
Feb 15th 1781

Sir

I wrote your Excellency a short letter at Guilford Court house, and referd you to my letter to Baron Stuben respecting the movements of the enimy. Since then the enimy have been pressing our rear every day. We have crossed the Dan, and I am apprehensive they will cross it above us, at the horse ford. If they should they will oblige us to cross the Stanton branch of the Roanoke. Our Army is so great an object with Lord Cornwallis, and the reduction of the Southern States depend so much upon it, that I think it highly probable he will push us still farther; and I am not without my apprehensions that he will oblige us to risque a general action, however contrary to our wishes or interest, which cannot fail to prove ruinous to the Army as our force is but little more than one half the enemies, and there are few or no Militia that have joined us on our March, or at least not more than one or two hundred.

Should the enemy cross the Dan,[1] and not be able to bring us to action, I imagine they will recross it and fall down the Country to Hallifax; which place I am taking measures to have fortified, to prevent their taking post there. But your Excellency will not take this for granted; for it is by no means certain, that Lord Cornwallis will not push through Virginia. It is to be lamented that so little a force should march through an extent of Country of several hundred Miles without a check. Unless our Army is greatly reenforced I see nothing to prevent their future progress. If the Militia is called out let them be put under Continental officers, that are or have been in service. One half the force officerd in this way, will give more effectual support, than double their numbers upon the common footing, in which the Militia take the field.

Cavalry are so essential to the service as well to prevent the enemy from ravaging the Country on their march as to prevent their penetrating it, that I wish your Excellency to take the most effectual measures for fitting up the first and third Regiments of Dragoons; and I must beg leave to observe to your Excellency that the occasion is so pressing, that I think horses and every thing else necessary to their equipment, should be taken in any manner which will complete the business in the most speedy and effectual manner.

The Country is inevitably lost unless decided Measures are taken. You will consider the necessity and act accordingly. I have not time to enter into a farther detail of matters, being pressed on every side with a multiplicity of business, and almost fatigued to death having had a retreat to conduct for upwards of 200 Miles Manouvering constantly in the face of the enemy, to give time for the Militia to turn out and to get off our Stores. In addition to the common difficulties incident to all retreats we have had several large rivers to cross and the enemy at our heels before we could get over.[2] Necessity has and will oblige me to take many measures to effect the removal of our Stores contrary to the established laws of the different States; the occasion must justify the measure, and I trust the Legislature will make charitable allowances accordingly. The Army is all that the States have to depend upon for their political existence. I trust therefore whatever is necessary to its support will meet their approbation.

I am with great respect Your Exy Mot Ob. Hb St, N GREENE

Dft (MiU-C); endorsed. Tr (CSmH).

The SHORT LETTER from Greene to TJ is that dated 10 Feb., q.v. Greene's LETTER TO BARON STUBEN, of the same date (RC in NHi), was transmitted to TJ by Steuben apparently on 15 Feb.; see Steuben's letter of this day, below.

1 Following deleted in Dft at this point: "Lord Cornwallis will cross the State of Virginia and attempt a junction with General Arnold."

2 Following deleted in Dft at this point: "We have been obliged also to cover all our Stores that have been coming up for three Months past which has been attended with incredible difficulty."

From Robert Lawson

SIR Colo. Bannisters Feb 15th 1781.

I am this far on my return Home. I am concern'd that the bad state of my Health should make it necessary to obtain the Baron's permission, to leave my command on the lines, until I could get it again establish'd.

I left McKee's Mills the 13th. Inst. in the Afternoon. When I came from thence, the Enemy were still in Portsmouth: their Post at the Great Bridge they retain. They have foraged but once at any distance from Portsmouth, and I doubt not but that The Baron hath related to your Excellency, the Contents of my Letter to him on that occasion. I am confident their whole strength exceeds not 1500 effectives.

Our advanced Post is near Halls; consisting of nearly 350 Riflemen under Colo. Matthews, with about 150 pick'd Musqueteers under Major Dick, with some Light Horse. The want of a respectable body of Horse cramps the movements of our Light Infantry greatly.

The Evening I left McKee's Mills, I received a Letter from General Gregory, from North Carolina, who informs me that he had about 250 Effectives (only) and that he expected daily, a reinforcement of about 300 more from Carolina; That he much wanted Flints, and some other military appendages; and hoped I could supply him. I was very sorry this was not in my power, as we are badly supply'd with those Essential Articles. His Letter I shew'd General Muhlenburg.

I also received a Letter at the same time, and from the same place (North West Bridge) from Colonels Godfrey, and Thoroughgood, informing, that the number of Militia collected by them, from the Counties of Norfolk and P. Ann was inconsiderable, with which number they had join'd General Gregory, but at the same time, they acquainted me, that there was a body of Militia collected in P. Ann, who had prevented the Enemy from foraging, in small bodies, and that they had gain'd several small advantages over their foraging parties; and operated as a great check upon them in that quarter.

General Gregorys Position is a very defensible one and he has 4 Pieces of Cannon with him: and as his parties are frequently out, they check the Enemies foraging parties sent out from the Great Bridge.

I am sorry to inform Your Excellency that our militia feel, rather too severely, the want of Hutts, Tents, or some covering to shelter them from the inclemency of the weather. It is a real fact that Axes, or other implements for erecting Hutts, cannot be procured, or it is very Certain, that the Persons employ'd to impress them make this Report to me.

I have been ever since I return'd from the Army (at the close of the Campaign in 1777) employ'd by this State, more or less, in some military Capacity or the other. I have never drawn a shilling from my Country for any claim that I had a right to make on this

Account. It is true my services have not been sensibly felt by the State. It has been my misfortune ever to be so situated, as to want the means of rendering such essential service, as every body feels from obtaining an advantage in battle over our Enemy. But it is also as certain a Truth, that altho' this was to me a mortifying fact, yet my Expences have been great. I wish my fortune would supply a fund, equal to my Inclination to serve my Country! I say not this, from Vanity, or ostentation. The impartial part of my Countrymen, who know me, will acquit me of either.

I have now taken the Liberty to draw upon the Treasury for £5,000. And altho' that sum will go but a little way towards defraying my Expences, still as I am so very sensible of the exhausted state of our finances, I chose not to draw for a larger one.

So soon as my Health will permit I hope to rejoin my command. I have the honour to be with the greatest respect, Sir, Your Excellencys Mo. Obedt. hum Servt., Ro: Lawson B.G.M.

RC (Vi); endorsed. *Va. Council Jour.*, II, 295, has the following entry under date of 17 Feb. 1781: "The Auditors are desired to issue to General Lawson a Warrant for five thousand pounds upon account."

To Charles Lynch

Sir Richmond Febry. 15. 1781.

The rapid approach of Ld. Cornwallis renders it necessary for us to made a sudden and effectual opposition. If you can raise any body of Volunteers and proceed immediately to oppose the enemy either by joining Genl. Greene or falling in with any other forces embodied, you will render essential service. I therefore pray you to do it, taking the command of the men yourself, and having such subordinate officers as shall be agreeable to the people and yourself. Subsist the men by calling on any Persons holding public Provisions, or by impressing under the Provision Law and returning a list of the certificates given, to the Auditors, or by furnishing themselves with provisions for which they shall be allowed by way of rations.

I am with much Esteem Sr your most obedt. St., T.J.

FC (Vi).

From George Muter

War Office [*Richmond*], *15 Feb. 1781.* Encloses a letter just received from Capt. Browne [Windsor Brown]. Since Capt. Irish will probably remain in the state, is it TJ's wish that Irish continue to act as commissary of military stores for the state? Muter does not doubt Irish's ability and application, yet is "apt to think a seperate Commissary for the state may be proper." Desires TJ's instructions.

RC (Vi); 2 p. Enclosure (Vi): Windsor Brown to Muter, Petersburg, 13 Feb. 1781, signifying his willingness to accept the office of commissary of military stores for the state. See TJ's reply, following.

To George Muter

[*Richmond*, *15 Feb. 1781.* An entry in the War Office Journal (Vi) under this date reads as follows: "The Governor, with the advice of the members present of the Council, there not being a Board, directs me to write to Capt. Browne, that he agrees to his being appointed Commissary of Military Stores, but that no sallary can be fixed at present for the Office." Not located. Muter's letter to Capt. Windsor Brown in pursuance of TJ's advice is dated the same day, and a file copy is in War Office Letter Book (Vi). See further, Muter to TJ, with reply, 19-20 Feb. 1781.]

From George Muter

[*Richmond*, *15 Feb. 1781.* The War Office Journal (Vi) contains the following entry under this date: "Letter to the Governor mentioning that it is Doctor Leiper's opinion that the sick be immediately removed from the house they are now in, and that the Quarter Master can procure one for that purpose, until the hospital is finished; and mentioning the necessity of retaining Doctor Leiper at this place, as there is a number of sick soldiers and no person to attend them if he goes down in the Militia." Not located.]

From Thomas Read

SIR Charlotte 15. February 1781.

By an express Received yesterday from the Honorable Paul Carrington Esqr. enclosing two others from Cols. Coleman and Cock of Halifax, information was given me that Lord Cornwallis with his Main Army were on their March to the borders of Virginia, and were then within thirty five Miles of Boyd's ferry on Dan River.

I have thought proper to Order out part of our Militia to Reinforce General Morgan who is said to be in the front of Cornwallis and have retreated across Dan.

I thought it a duty incumbant on me to give you this early intelegance. Any Orders you have to give respecting the Militia in this Quarter, the bearer of this Mr. Watkins will take Charge of em.

I am Your Excellency's Most Obt. St., THOMAS READ

RC (Vi); addressed (in part): "favr. Mr. Watkins"; endorsed.

From John Christian Senf

SIR Richmond Febry. 15th. 1781.

I have spoke to Coll. Mutter about the Vessel which the Commissary send to Cabbin Point with provision, and was to be stopp'd at Hoods, but he says the Vessel had been given up three Months ago to the Commissary's Use, and was neither fit for that Business.

The Quartermaster is not arrived yet, and Coll. Mutter thinks, that he will have very little Success. Would it not be good to send in the Meantime to the County Lieutnants too? And should there be to many Negroes, some of them may be discharg'd again. An Order to the Commissary will be necessary, to send some provisions to Hoods, as there is non to be had the other Side of the River.

Your Excellency will likewise kindly remember, to send an Instruction to the Officer commanding at Hoods, for stopping and to examen all Vessels going or coming.

I take the Liberty to hand to Your Excellency a Copy of my State Apointment, as Lieut. Col. and few Months after was promoted to the rank of Colonel, and took Command of a considerable Body of Militia in that State.

If no further Commands I shall go to Day to Chesterfield Courthouse to the Baron, and return tomorrow to here.

With the greatest Respect and Estime I have the Honour to be Your Excellency's Most obedt. and most humble Servant,

SENF Coll. Engineer

RC (Vi); addressed and endorsed. In the margin beside the first paragraph TJ has added this memorandum: "Joshua Poythress of Blandford has 2. Schooners or flats" (see TJ to John Allen, 16 Feb.). Enclosure not found, but see note on Senf's military career under Gates' letter to TJ, 4 Oct. 1780; also TJ to Senf, 21 Feb., and Senf to TJ, 26 Feb. 1781.

To Turner Southall, Robert Goode, John Banister, William Call, and William Greene Munford

Sir Richmond Febry 15. 1781.

For the future protection of the Stores and Country on James River it has been thought necessary to erect a defensive work at Hood's. Among other requisites forty labouring Slaves are wanting for two months. After trying the exertions of the ordinary Officers to procure them we have been able to procure 13 only, who are to be at the place on Monday next. I must therefore resort to the aid of the zealous Citizens in the Counties round about that post to endeavour to prevail on the people to spare labourers. Give me leave to beg your assistance in this way and to rely on you for procuring on the best terms you can within your County six able labouring slaves to be at Hoods immediately and to continue there two months. To this be so good as to add the further favor of informing me from time to time of your success.

I am with great Esteem Sir &c, T.J.

FC (Vi). At head of text: "Colo. Turner Southall Henrico Majr. Goode Chesterfield Colo. Bannister Dinwiddie Colo Call Prince George [*blank*] Chas. City." The recipients are more satisfactorily identified in *Va. Council Jour.*, II, 293; see also Archibald Cary to TJ, 13 Feb., and the general note on the problem of fortifying Hood's under Steuben's letter to TJ, 11 Feb. 1781.

To Steuben

Sir Richmond Feby. 15th. 1780 [1781].

I received last night a letter from Genl. Green referring me for particulars to you. However he gives me enough to convince me that reinforcements of Militia must be sent him. I think the most speedy and effectual reinforcement would be the Militia of Rockbridge, Augusta, Rockingham and Shenandoah now encamped below, provided they can be induced to go willingly. The length of their march heretofore and having been some time in service seems to give them a right to be consulted. I leave the detaching them to the aid of Genl. Green to your better judgment. Should you approve of it and think it necessary to call other militia to take their place, I will order others. Besides this reinforcement to Genl. Green, I propose to order from Washington, Montgomery and Botetourt 540 (riflemen) and from Pittsylvania and Henry 480

These will want Arms. To these add the detachment at Chesterfeild Court House. I send out to-day the Orders to Washington, Montgomery, Botetourt, Pittsylvania and Henry. If you would advise any more, and think they can be armed, more shall be sent.

I have the honor to be with great respect, Sir, Your Mo. Obedt. hble. Servt., TH: JEFFERSON

RC (NHi); in a clerk's hand; corrected, signed, and addressed by TJ to Steuben at "Chesterfd. C. House"; endorsed. FC (Vi).

A LETTER FROM GENL. GREEN: Greene to TJ, 10 Feb. 1781.

From Steuben

SIR Chesterfield Co. He. 15 feby 81

General Muhlenberg has just forwarded me the inclosed Letters. What can have given rise to a correspondence of this nature I cannot say. It was contrary to my wish or desire. I shall be glad to know your Excellencys pleasure respecting the Exchange proposed by Genl. Arnold, both the Prisoners belonging to the State.

I inclose a Receipt for the Twenty Guineas sent in agreable to your desire.

I am extremely anxious to get off the Detachment for the Southard. I inclose an exact state of what Cloathing we can have ready here, and I must intreat your Excellency to take such measures as will insure us the remainder by the day fixed. I need not point out the necessity of our exertions. The inclosed Copy of Genl. Greens Letter will suffice.

There seems to be a difficulty in getting the shirts made up. This surprizes me especially after Colo. Carey informd me had wrote Mr. Armstead offering to make a large number I think 150 and was never honord with an Answer. I am convinced many private families would gladly assist.

I shall give the necessary direction for Arranging Colo. Taylors Regiment in the manner you mention.

Dft or FC (NHi); in the hand of an aide; endorsed: "Copy to Governor Jefferson feby 15." The enclosures, except for "The inclosed Copy of Genl. Greens Letter" to Steuben of 10 Feb. (RC, NHi; see also note on Greene to TJ, 10 Feb.), have not been fully identified, though it is certain that one was a (missing) letter from Arnold to Robert Lawson of 12 Feb. in which Arnold proposed "to exchange Colonel Werneck taken at Westham and two of the Gentlemen you mention for Lieut. Col. Elligood and the two soldiers of Colonel Simcoe's Regiment" (Arnold to Muhlenberg, 23 Feb., NHi). Arnold himself had apparently initiated this proposed exchange of prisoners, but Lawson had written to Steuben on 24 Jan. that this was in his opinion only a pretext and that he was "rather inclined to think that he [Arnold] wished to know where our outposts were and what movements we were making"; Lawson had therefore stopped the British flag at Suffolk, answered Arnold's letter non-committally, and reported the whole matter to Steuben, who approved Lawson's course, declared that he had no intention of entering upon a general exchange of prisoners, and said that there were only three persons that he wanted to exchange at that time—"Parson Hurt, Capt. Pearce, and Mr. Cocke" (Lawson to Steuben, 24 Jan.; Lawson to Arnold, 24 Jan.; Steuben to Lawson, 28 Jan., all of which are in NHi; see also TJ to Steuben, second letter of 17 Feb., for an apparent variation in the spelling of the names of the men and for a further note concerning the outcome of these negotiations).

On the subject of the TWENTY GUINEAS it is worth noting that Steuben had just issued orders forbidding any flags to be sent to the British when he received TJ's letter of 2 Feb. requesting that the money be returned, a request with which he complied (TJ to Steuben, 2 Feb. and the following in NHi: Steuben to Lawson, 6 Feb.; Muhlenberg to Steuben, 12 Feb.). COLO. TAYLORS REGIMENT: For TJ's proposal, see Taylor to TJ, 8 Feb. and TJ's letters to Taylor and Steuben, 13 Feb.

To Steuben

SIR — Richmond Feb. 15 1781.

I am glad my proclamation has offended Arnold: it proves it to be right. The exchange of the prisoners must await a board of Council, which I doubt having immediately. I will have every thing done which can be done here for providing the deficient clothing.

Doctor Pope set out about three days ago for Genl. Muhlenberg's camp, with powers to employ assistants, so that I hope there will be no want of Surgeons.

I am with much respect Sir Your most obedt. servt.,

TH: JEFFERSON

RC (NHi); addressed: "The honble. Majr. Genl. Baron Steuben Chesterfd. C. house"; endorsed.

Major John Graves Simcoe, writing from Portsmouth on 14 Mch., gave the following estimate of TJ's proclamation of 19 Jan. concerning paroles: "Your pretended Governor has absolved the Inhabitants of this Colony from their voluntary Paroles, authorizing Breach of Faith in the profligate, and by penalties enforcing it on the more Virtuous, and has rendered Virginian Probity a bye Word to Posterity. These, Sir, are Acts of Barbarism; they are the growth of Rebellion, and I trust they will remain its Monopoly" (Simcoe to Parker, 14 Mch. 1781, NHi). Simcoe was usually temperate in expression; hence, in the absence of Arnold's comment on TJ's proclamation, Simcoe's remarks may be taken as a pale reflection of his commander's opinion. It is important to note that TJ's proclamation accused the British of violating the law of nations in issuing paroles to unarmed citizens and that the opinion of Simcoe and other British officers treated TJ's proclamation as a violation of the law of the realm, the one being based on a concept of war between sovereigns and the other on the assumption that the conflict was a rebellion. Hence there was no common ground from which to view the legality of the act Simcoe complained of, though in such matters as the conduct of flags by which these and other completely conflicting opinions had to be interchanged, the laws and customs of nations were tacitly accepted and acted upon by both sides.

From Steuben

SIR Chesterfield 15th: Feby. 1781

I am this moment favord with your Excellencys Letter of this date. I had before transmitted you Copy of General Greens Letter to me with a state of our wants for compleating the Detachment destined for the Southard.

I agree with your Excellency that the Militia of Rockbridge Augusta Rockingham and Shenandoah would be the most speedy reinforcement to General Green, but they must first be reliev'd by others—the force we now have below is as weak as can be kept not to endanger this part of the Country. The sooner the Commanding Officers of the above Militia can be consulted, the better and if they are willing to go your Excellency will please to order them relieved.

The Militia of the other Counties you mention being in the Vicinity would be a good addition could they be Armed, but how this is to be done I am at a loss to Say. We have not an Arm to spare here. With General Muhlenberg and Nelson we [may] perhaps find sufficient to Arm the Men who [are to] relieve those below who go southard.

As to calling out more Militia as we cannot Arm them it would be in Vain, and I dread the consequence that the calling out so many will have in delaying the grand object of compleating our Army. With respect & Esteem I am Sir Your Excellencys Most Obedt. & Very hum Sert.,

STEUBEN Maj: Gen.

RC (Vi); in an aide's hand, signed by Steuben; addressed and endorsed. Dft (NHi); in the same aide's hand. RC contains several small errors of repetition and omission which have been corrected from Dft.

TJ's LETTER OF THIS DATE must be the first of the two sent to Steuben that are printed above. COPY OF GENERAL GREENS LETTER TO ME WITH A STATE OF OUR WANTS: Greene to Steuben, Guilford Court House, 10 Feb. 1781, copy enclosed in Steuben's first letter to TJ of the present date, q.v.

From George Lee Turberville

Sandy Point Feby. 15th. 1781

MAY IT PLEASE YOUR EXCELLENCY

A Dragoon now waits an answer to my letter of the 13th. inst.

A Flag is here at present detain'd by me till Baron Steuben's order can return. Lieut. Hare who is the Officer is very anxious to see your determination in regard to the restitution of property. 'Tis for that purpose he is come up.

I have the honor to be your Excellency's Obedient Sert.,

GEO LEE TURBERVILLE Major

RC (Vi); addressed: "Public. his excellency Thomas Jefferson esquire, governour of Virginia Richmond. by express"; endorsed.

This is the first document in a long series relating to a British FLAG vessel, commanded by LIEUT. HARE which touched off a violent controversy among the military and civil authorities in Virginia. Because of the complicated questions at issue, to say nothing of the animosities engendered during the critical weeks of February and March, the editors have decided to present the entire matter in as completely documented a form as possible. This will be done in the following manner. All letters to or from TJ about the subject will be printed in their proper chronological order in Volumes 4 and 5. All other letters exchanged among Arnold, Mrs. Byrd, Hare, Turberville, Steuben, Nicholas, Nelson, Innes, Walker, and others will be presented as Appendix I, Vol. 5: "The Affair of Westover"—the designation by which TJ referred to the episode in one of his letters. The key document to the entire affair is missing, though the editorial note in the Appendix to Vol. 5 offers some deductions concerning its contents. MY LETTER OF THE 13TH: No doubt Turberville's letter to TJ, 12 Feb. q.v. YOUR DETERMINATION IN REGARD TO THE RESTITUTION OF PROPERTY: see note to Steuben to TJ 21 Feb. (first letter of that date).

To James Wood

SIR Richmond Feb. 15. 1781.

I have just received information from Genl. Greene that Ld. Cornwallis, maddened by his losses at the Cowpens and George town has burnt his own waggons to enable himself to move with facility and has pressed forward as far as the Moravian towns, Genl. Greene being obliged to retire before him with an inferior force. We are endeavouring to gather a force around him from which I hope he will not escape; nevertheless as the event is hastening on, 'till it be in some measure known, I think it will not only be prudent for you not to leave your present post, but to hold the Convention troops and guards in readiness to march at a moment's warning. I would also advise that you recall Capt Reed's troop, as it may be more useful with you if it be necessary to remove the Germans, and will be wanting here, should their removal be not necessary.

I am with much esteem Sir Your most obedt. humble servt,

TH: J.

RC (Frederick M. Dearborn, New York City). FC (Vi).

To John Allen

SIR Richmond Febry. 16. 1781

It having been concluded to build a defensive work at Hoods under the direction of Colo. Senf, I am to desire the favor of you to see to the execution of it according to his instructions. Thirteen Labourers will be with you on Monday next. Besides these I have written to Colo. Southall of this County, Colo. Banister of Dinwiddie, Colo. Call of Prince George and Colo. Munford of Charls. City to procure each of them six and send them to you as soon as procured. Carpenters went from this place, and Colo. Senf informed me there were smiths at the place. Of the 13 Slaves who will be with you on Monday, one belonging to Mr. Ryland Randolph is a bricklayer. I shall endeavour to have three or four more bricklayers engaged. Vessels being wanting to transport your bricks and lime, I must get you to go out to procure them on hire if you can, and if not they must be taken. Colo. Senf mentions two Schooners or flats belonging to Joshua Poythress at Blandford which would suit; these or such others as are proper you will engage. If Lime cannot be got nearer to you I expect it may be had at Petersburg and this place. Being informed you have no provisions I give orders now to the Commissary on that head. As Colo. Senf will be with you occasionally you will be pleased to apprize me from time to time of your wants to carry on the work.

I am your hbl. Sert., THOS. JEFFERSON

FC (Vi).

On the DEFENSIVE WORK AT HOODS see Steuben to TJ, 11 Feb. 1781. JOSHUA POYTHRESS (FC erroneously has "Johua"): The information about his boats must have been given to TJ by Senf orally; see note on Senf to TJ, 15 Feb.

To Richard Claiborne

SIR Richmond Febry. 16. 1781

Baron Steuben being very desirous to have as large [a] collection of Boats made as possible and joined to those he now has at Sandy Point, You are hereby authorized to impress all boats proper for the transportation of troops in James or Appamattox rivers (excepting only one horse Boat at every ferry, and such cases of extreme hardship as in your discretion you shall think should exempt the parties from this order). You will of course take the usual methods for appraising the Vessels and their use by the day. When seized you will have them carried to Sandy Point or wherever else the other Boats shall be and delivered to the commanding Officer there. I am &c &c &c, T.J.

FC (Vi). TJ later informed Steuben that the Council had not authorized him to impress armed boats on the James; see TJ to Steuben, 16 Feb. (third letter) and Claiborne's reply to TJ, 17 Feb.

From Richard Claiborne

SIR Richmond. 16th. Feby. 1781.

Some of the assistant Deputy Quarter Master's have made application to me to know whether they and the persons employed under them, are subject to the insuing draft of this State. I am likewise informed that my Name, with some of my Officers are inroled, and that it is the intention of the Court to comprehend us in the Draft. This is a step which I cannot think justifiable, as it should have been known in the first place who of us were Commissioned Officers and who not. It is agreable to my Ideas that the *persons* of all Continental Officers and others engaged in that Line, whether in Commission or not, are exempt from Militia duties and drafts of any kind whatsoever during that employ. If the property is taxed I admit we should bear a proportion, but if the *person* is taken away, the public business must suffer. As to my own part I am not uneasy in this matter because of my Commission in the Line, but Your Excellency will foresee the bad consequences of depriving me of a useful man at this important time, when all that we can do will not nearly be sufficient to answer the demands made for the southern Army. This is not all. The department must be supported, and considerable supplies must come from us for the Troops in the state. I beg Your Excellency to give directions upon this subject in time, that the further operation of my plan may not be delayed.

I have the honor to be with much respect Your Excellency's Most obedient Servant,

RD. CLAIBORNE
D Q Mr. S. Virga.

RC (Vi); in a clerk's hand, signed by Claiborne; endorsed. A signed copy is also in Vi, and a Tr in NHi: Steuben Papers.

To the County Lieutenants of Berkeley and Frederick

SIR Richmond Febry. 16. 1781.

I have with exceeding distress of mind received information that the service to which the Militia of the Counties of Frederick and Berkely have been called Westwardly is so disagreeable as to render it probable that that call will be very imperfectly obeyed. A knowledge that an extensive combination of Indians had been formed to come on our frontier early in the spring induced us to prevent them by striking the first stroke. The Counties Westward of the Allegany were called on in the first place, and their numbers not sufficing, it was concluded to make them up by a call on some of the Counties on this side of the Allegany. Those of Hampshire, Berkely, and Frederic were deemed the most proper as being nearest to Pittsburg and farthest from the Southern war. The expedition if carried to the greatest extent would end by the last of June. Should this expedition be discontinued, the Savages will be spread on our whole Western frontier: in that case not a man can be brought during the whole Summer from the Western side of the Blue-ridge; and what will be the consequence of leaving the Army of Ld. Cornwallis and the Army at Portsmouth to be opposed by the lower Country only, I had rather the friends of their Country should reflect than I foretell. We are all embarked in one bottom, the Western end of which cannot swim while the Eastern sinks. I am thoroughly satisfied that nothing can keep us up but the keeping off the Indians from our Western quarter; that this cannot be done, but by pushing the war into their Country; and that this cannot be attempted but with effectual aid from those three counties. This reasoning is simple, and the conclusion of it melancholy. A hope is held out to us that an aid as effectual can be obtained from your County by the engaging of Volunteers to go instead of the militia. Trusting to this assurance and the zeal of your people which never before has failed us, I will so far throw our safety on them, as to revoke the orders for their peremptory march as militia and depend on their sending a sufficient number of Volunteers. These Volunteers must proceed according to the orders given as to the militia except that some extention of time must be admitted. This I leave to your discret[ion]. Be punctual in advising Genl. Clarke and myself from time to time of your progress and expectations.

I am with much respect Sr. Yor. most obt. hble Sert., T.J.

P.S. [to the Frederic Lieutenant][1] I rely on you in every event to send forward to Pittsburg under a proper escort the Stores sent on to you from different places as advised in my original letter.

FC (Vi).

See TJ's original orders to these county lieutenants, 24 Dec. 1780; letter from the Officers of the Berkeley Militia, 25 Jan.; and letter from John Smith, county lieutenant of Frederick, 9 Feb. 1781.

[1] Brackets in MS.

To the County Lieutenant of Hampshire

SIR Richmond Febry. 16. 1781.

The inclosed letter is founded on representations received from the Counties of Frederic and Berkely. I have not heard that the same aversion to the service has arisen in your county, and I am led to hope it has not from many considerations: Lest it should however, and you should be delayed by sending here, I inclose you a copy of my letter to the County Lieutenants of the other Counties and leave to your discretion to conduct yourself as pointed out to them, if absolute necessity requires it; if on the contrary you find that the former requisitions of government will be complied with, I am to assure you the public safety needs it indispensably, and to desire that in such case you will keep this letter unmentioned.

I am with much respect Sr. &c, T.J.

FC (Vi). The enclosure (not found) was a copy of TJ's letter of this date to the county lieutenants of Berkeley and Frederick, preceding.

From Robert Lawson

SIR P. Edward Feb. 16th. 1781.

I yesterday was inform'd on my way home, that General Green had retreated to Dan River, being inferior to Cornwallis in his number of Men, who was pushing after him with great avidity, and that Gl. Green had call'd upon the most convenient Counties to turn out the Militia to his Aid. Among one of the Counties that are call'd upon is this. The Militia have met to day at the Court House (where I now am) and I am confident that I could march the whole of them, that are at all able to do military duty, were they properly arm'd, but as they are not arm'd, I have thought it most eligible to send only such as have such arms as may serve until better can be procur'd. The rest of the Militia I have order'd to hold themselves in readiness to march at a moments warning, should it be consistent with your Orders. I have form'd a Company of Riflemen (pick'd Men) consisting of 24 Rank and file, and have order'd them to march with all possible speed to General Green. A Company of about that number with very good Guns (not musquets) march'd from this County last Evening under Capt. Moore. And I have collected as many more Guns, as will enable me to march another Company early Tomorrow—in all about 100 Men. If Arms &c. can be procur'd, I'll engage to march the whole force of this County if necessary. I have sent down an Express to your Excellency in order to recieve particular Orders, as to the forming, arranging, and marching the Militia in this quarter. As Genl. Muhlenberg commands the Militia below, I wish for yours, and the Barons approbation, to take command of the Militia in this quarter, as I know them pretty generally, and am well acquainted with the Country and the roads leading thro' it—especially as it is the earnest desire of the people that this should be the Case.

I must beg leave to suggest to Your Excellency, that it is necessary that the tenor of my Commission should be alter'd. You'll recollect that my Commission gave me command over the Volunteers only: As such a body exists no longer, I must sollicit Your Excellency, if agreeable to the Honorable board, that a new Commission be made out giving me command in the Militia, dated at the time my Volunteer one pass'd the board. I hope no objection can be form'd against this request of mine particularly as the Honble. Major Gl. The Baron de Steuben hath been pleas'd to confer on me the command of all the Troops on the Southern Side of James River, had it been convenient to me to continue at the post below. Altho' my Health is still impair'd, I cannot reconcile it to my feelings to stay at home, when a vindictive, and cruel Enemy are making such rapid strides towards the Heart of our Country.

You'll be pleas'd to inclose me the necessary Commission with your full instructions, which I shall literally, and chearfully fulfill so far as within my power.

I hope the Express will be dispatchd as quick as may be.

I have the honor to be with great respect Sir, Your Excellencys Most Obedt. Servt, RO: LAWSON B.G.M.

RC (Vi).

To James Maxwell

SIR Richmond Febry. 16. 1781.

The arrival of a French naval force will render it necessary for us to put into immediate order for service and to man every Vessel we have capable of rendering any service. You will therefore be pleased to have this done, and to have the Vessels kept in readiness to move at a moment's warning. You are also desired, having left this matter in a proper train, to proceed yourself and examine the different armed Vessels in James River which in your opinion might be of service in an enterprize on the British fleet in Elizabeth river, to report to us their condition and to endeavour to engage them to enter into that Service.

I am with much respect Sr. Yr. &c &c., T.J.

FC (Vi).

On 15 Feb. TJ received word "of the arrival of a 64 gun ship and two frigates in our bay, being part of the fleet of our good ally at Rhode island" (to Huntington, 17 Feb.; see further details in letter to Gates, 18 Feb.). This small squadron, detached from the French fleet at the moment it achieved a temporary superiority over the British naval force in North America (see Theodorick Bland to TJ, 9 Feb.), was commanded by Capt. Arnaud Le Gardeur de Tilly in the *Eveillé*. Its mission was to destroy the British vessels supporting Arnold's forces at Portsmouth, but as TJ told Huntington in the letter quoted above, the French line-of-battle ship could not get into the Elizabeth River, into which the British vessels had withdrawn. De Tilly did not dare to stay long in Virginia waters, for fear of being bottled up in his turn; and in a letter to TJ of 19-20 Feb., Gen. Nelson reported that the French squadron had sailed. It returned to Rhode Island but soon came back with the larger force under Destouches and Viomesnil that was assigned to support Lafayette in the effort to destroy the British army and capture its commander. Destouches' fleet, however, never reached its destination, for it met a British fleet under Arbuthnot off the Virginia Capes, fought an inconclusive engagement on 16 Mch., and retired northward. These events are the subject of a great deal of the correspondence that follows in February and March; see also *My Campaigns in America: A Journal Kept by Count William de Deux-Ponts, 1780-81*, ed. Samuel A. Green, Boston, 1868, p. 21-8. On De Tilly specifically, see Contenson, *La Société de Cincinnati de France*, p. 213.

To Thomas Nelson

SIR Richmond Febry. 16. 1781

I am very anxious to prepare for cooperating with our Allies, and for providing for their support. For the former purpose measures are taking as agreed on this moment in a conference with Baron Steuben. For the latter we suppose York town the most effectual to prepare as an Assylum for their Vessels. Colo. Senf comes down with instructions to point out what may be done there in a short time; the Baron will send Colo. Harrison or some other artillery officer to superintend the execution of what he shall plan; and I must resort to your influence to take such measures as may call in a sufficient number of labourers with their tools to execute the Work. Whatever you do for this purpose shall be approved by us. The County of Gloster alone can probably furnish many hands. Those in the Neck I trust will also be forwarded. I am &c, T.J.

FC (Vi). See note on preceding letter.

From Stephen Southall, enclosing Order

Without place or date [*16? Feb. 1781*]. Has settled with several persons whose wagons were employed in Continental service "at the Price then allowed by the Continent which did not exceed twenty pounds, and on the Presumption of the Enclosed Order from you I did in some measure promise them the same pay as was allowed by this state." Having given certificates to these people for the deficiency of their pay, Southall now finds that Mr. [Duncan] Rose has denied payment and "told the bearers if I did not Answer the payment for them to Bring suit against me." Wishes instructions. Enclosure: "Let the Q Master settle with these people at as low a hire as will give them tolerable satisfaction and if it is disallowed by Congress, this state will indemnify him, by paying the difference between what he shall be allowed by Congress and what he shall have Actually paid under his direction. (A Copy) Th Jefferson."

RC (Vi); 3 p., including enclosed copy of TJ's authorization (date unknown) in Southall's hand; addressed; endorsed (in part): "Feby 81."

See TJ's reply, 17 Feb., and Southall's second letter on the same subject, 17? Feb.

From Turner Southall

Richmond, *16 Feb. 1781.* Part of the militia of this county being called on to march, the case of Thomas Smith came before the court-martial, which determined that it did not have a power, consistent with the law, "to Exempt him from his Tour." Smith was advised, however, to apply to TJ, since both he and his clerk are "employed in the Settlement of the Public Accounts," and it appears that his presence is "much wanted in that business." Southall remembers a bill introduced in last Assembly that exempted Smith, but, though it passed in the House, it never came back from the Senate.

RC (Vi); 2 p.; addressed and endorsed.

Thomas Smith was appointed "Agent for Trade" on 3 Dec. 1777; and on 3 Aug. 1781 "An exemption from Military Duty was granted to Mr. Thomas Smith to the end that he may employ himself in settling the public accounts against the United States" (*Va. Council Jour.*, II, 40, 245, 370).

To Steuben

SIR Richmond Feb. 16. 1781.

I received the inclosed letter last night and took the liberty of informing Colo. Loyauté that I would let you know of the offer of his services and that he is here, as you could best judge in what line they might be useful.

I have the honour to be with much respect Sir your most obedt. sert., TH: JEFFERSON

RC (NHi); endorsed. Enclosure not found. On LOYAUTE (variously spelled), see R. H. Lee to TJ, 11 May 1778; TJ to Weedon, 12 Jan. 1781. If TJ wrote Loyeauté at this time, the letter has not been found.

To Steuben

SIR Feb. 16. 1781.

I think from every enquiry we shall find it impossible to get hats for the men at Chesterfeild. Could not a cap of cloth be made to answer? The grenadiers I beleive wear such. If you think it would do, could you help us to a model?

I am with much respect Sir your most obedt. sert.,

TH: JEFFERSON

RC (NHi); addressed by TJ, but without place; endorsed.

To Steuben

SIR Feb. 16. 1781.

I make no doubt from what passed in council in your presence you were led to beleive as I was that I should be advised to impress immediately all armed vessels in James river to cooperate with the French force. The board however decide against an impress, so that I am only to endeavor to engage the willing. I mention this to you that nothing more may be expected than is likely to be obtained from this measure.

I have the honour to be with much respect Sir Your most obedt. sert., TH: JEFFERSON

RC (NHi); addressed by TJ, but without place; endorsed. See Claiborne to TJ, 17 Feb. and note there.

To John Banister

DR. SIR Richmond Febry 17. 1781

Your letter was put into my hands on the evening of the day before yesterday by a young Gentleman whom I informed that it could not be answered till the meeting of Council the next day, and desired he would attend with the receipt which he said he had, for it was not inclosed in the letter as you mentioned. He did not call again. I laid your letter before the council: As far as our money will hold out they are desirous of paying, particularly monies advanced or due to Artificers, or for necessaries for the Army. Of this nature is your Advance for the cartridge boxes. What the other part of the demand was for, they are not particularly informed. They wish however to know before any order is made, the articles for which these monies are paid, by whose order, and to whom the articles have been delivered. As there remained yesterday but 40,000 pounds in the Treasury and every day brings considerable calls, I hope you will be so kind as to furnish the specification desired before this be drawn out. Should it however be otherwise it will be but ten days to the meeting of the Assembly when I hope a replenishment of the treasury will take place.

I am &c &c, T.J.

FC (Vi). YOUR LETTER: Banister's undated letter printed above under 15? Feb., q.v. Banister was paid on 17 Mch. (*Va. Council Jour.*, II, 311).

To Arthur Campbell

SIR Richmond Feby 17th. 1781.

I have received your several favours by Mr. Lathim and am much pleased at the happy issue of the expedition against the Cherokees. I wish it to be used for the purpose of bringing about peace, which under our present circumstances is as necessary for us as it can possibly be to them. If you can effect this a right should be reserved of building a fort at the confluence of Holston and Tannissee: a matter which we must refer to Congress as it lies not within our boundary. The prisoners you have taken had better be kept for the purpose of exchanging for any of ours taken by them. Should any surplus be on hand at the conclusion of peace they should be given up. Nancy Ward seems rather to have taken refuge with you. In this case her inclination ought to be followed as to what is done with her. As by our Laws the pay of Militia is made the same with that of the Continental troops, and that by a resolution of Congress is to be in the new money of Mar: 18. 1780, or in old money at 40 for 1. I apprehend you will be paid at that rate. By a late arrangement the Commissary is directed to have a Deputy in every County. I hope that by their means the Militia may henceforward be better supplied with provisions when proceeding on an expedition. The fort at Powell's Valley you will please to proceed on. We approve of the company you have raised for patrolling against the Indians and garrisoning the fort.

I am with much respect Sir Your Most obedt. Servt.,

TH: JEFFERSON

Tr (DLC: PCC, No. 71, II); signed by TJ and transmitted in his letter to Huntington of this date; endorsed. FC (Vi). Tr (DLC).

YOUR SEVERAL FAVOURS: Presumably Campbell's letters of 15, 27 Jan., 2 Feb. 1781.

To Richard Claiborne

SIR

Richmond, Feby. 17th. [1781]

I have submitted your Letter of yesterday to the consideration of the Gentlemen of the Council, who are present. It is thought that as the Letter of the Draft Law has left it to the Militia Officers to determine who are the proper Subjects of the Law, so the exemptions specifyed by the Law itself imply that no others shall be allowed. Whether the Staff Officers of the Continent or State are entitled to exemptions was proper for the determination of the Legislature: The Executive therefore do not intermeddle with it.

I am Sir your mo: Obt. Servt., TH: JEFFERSON

Tr (Vi); in the hand of a clerk in Claiborne's office and endorsed: "Governor's Answer." Another Tr, presumably sent to Steuben by Claiborne, is in NHi. FC (Vi); this and the preceding Tr have the date in full.

From Richard Claiborne

SIR

Richmond 17th. Feby 1781.

I have received Your Excellency's Warrant of Yesterday for impressing the Boats on James and Appomattox Rivers, to be sent to Sandy Point.

I should chearfully proceed in the business this Morning but Your Excellency well knows the difficulty of executing such a matter without a considerable party of Armed Men. Experience has taught me that it is impracticable, unless the things are taken and secured with a Guard. I can only apply to your Excellency for this assistance in James River; and the instructions which I shall give for the other River, will be sent to Chesterfeild Court-house for another party.

I am Your Excellency's Most Obedient Humble Servant,

RD. CLAIBORNE D Q Mr. S. Virga.

RC (Vi); in a clerk's hand, signed by Claiborne; addressed and endorsed. At foot of text, in TJ's hand: "Gave order to Capt. Price for officer & 20 men."

TJ's action in this case is puzzling in the light of his letter to Steuben of 16 Feb. (third letter of that date) in which he indicates that the Council had "decided against an impress." His letter to Claiborne of 16 Feb. had authorized impressment and he had issued a warrant for that purpose; moreover, this authorization had been laid before the Council and approved (*Va. Council Jour.*, II, 294); there is no evidence that the Council rescinded this action. It is possible, of course, that the Council could have reconsidered or clarified its intent after TJ had written to Claiborne and before he wrote to Steuben on 16 Feb. But if so, there seems no satisfactory explanation for TJ's present authorization of troops for impressment except on two grounds: (1) the Council had again reversed itself, or (2) TJ had decided deliberately to disregard the Council's decision not to impress. Whatever the explanation, it is to be wondered at that TJ gave Claiborne military aid in making impressments of boats when he later refused to order the militia to aid in impressing horses (see TJ to Steuben, 10 Mch.). On 17 Feb. Claiborne pointed out to Steuben that it was needless to attempt to seize boats except by force, and added: "Agreeable to a warrant from the Governor in consequence of your application to him, I have given instructions to an officer and party of men which I accidentally procured on their way through this town [Richmond] to impress the Boats on James River"; Claiborne enclosed orders in blank for Steuben to issue to another impressment party to seize boats in Appomattox river (NHi).

From Richard Claiborne

SIR 17th. Feby. 1781

Lieutenant Lambert is the Commanding Officer of a party of Men to impress the Boats on James River. It is necessary that his Men should be armed. I have referred him to your Excellency for orders in this matter, as my Commission does not authorize me to direct in any such thing. I have the instructions agreeable to your Excellencys Warrant ready.

I have the honor to be Yr. Excellency's Obt. hble Servt,

RD. CLAIBORNE D Q Mr. S. V.

RC (Vi); addressed and endorsed. YOUR EXCELLENCYS WARRANT: TJ to Claiborne, 16 Feb.; see also Claiborne's earlier note to TJ of this day.

To the County Lieutenants

of Loudoun, Fairfax, Prince William, and Fauquier

SIR Richmd. Febry. 17. 1781.

You will be pleased immediately on receipt of this, to order one fourth of your Militia to be assembled and marched without delay to Wmsburg under proper field officers, Captains, and subalterns. Send as many riflemen among them with their rifles as can be had, and of the rest let every man bring a good musket and accoutrements who has one. Let them proceed first to Fredericksburg where we shall endeavour to have such armed as bring no Arms of their own; from thence they must proceed to Wmsburg. They will be subsisted as directed by the Invasion law, only that where any public provisions can be had, it would be better they should draw than impress. A baggage Waggon must come for every 75 men, to remain in duty as long as the Men do.

I am &c &c &c.

FC (Vi). These militia were ordered into service at Steuben's request; see *Va. Council Jour.*, II, 295.

To Horatio Gates

DEAR GENERAL — Richmond Feb. 17. 1781.

The situation of affairs here and in Caroline[1] is such as must shortly turn up important events one way or the other. By letter from Genl. Greene dated Guilford C. house Feb. 10. Ld. Cornwallis rendered furious by the affair at the Cowpens and surprise of George town had burnt his own waggons to enable himself to move with facility, had pressed on to the vicinities of the Moravian towns and was still advancing. The prisoners taken at the Cowpens were saved by a hair's breadth accident, and Greene was retreating. His force 2000 regulars and no militia, Cornwallis's 3000. Genl. Davidson was killed in a skirmish. Arnold lies still at Portsmouth with 1500 men. A French 64. gun ship and 2 frigates of 36 each arrived in our bay three days ago. They would suffice to destroy the British shipping here (a 40., four frigates and a 20) could they get at them. But these are withdrawn up Elizabeth river which the 64. cannot enter. We have ordered about 700 riflemen from Washington Montgomery and Bedford and 500 common militia from Pittsylva. and Henry to reinforce Genl. Greene, and 500 new levies will march from Chestfd. C. H. in a few days. I have no doubt however that the Southwestern counties will have turned out in greater numbers before our orders reach them. I have been knocking at the door of Congress for aids of all kinds, but especially of arms ever since the middle of summer. The Speaker Harrison is gone to be heard on that subject. Justice indeed requires that we should be aided powerfully. Yet if they would repay us the arms we have lent them we should give the enemy trouble tho' abandoned to ourselves.—After repeated applications I have obtained a warrant for your advance money £18,000 which I put into the hands of Mr. McAlister to receive the money from the Treasurer and carry it to you.

I am with very sincere esteem Dr Genl. Your friend & servt,

TH: JEFFERSON

Dft (DLC). [1] Thus in Dft.

To Nathanael Greene

SIR Richmond Febry. 17. 1781

In the moment of receiving your letter of the 10th. I issued orders to the Counties of Washington, Montgomery, Botetourt and Bedford for seven hundred and odd riflemen and to those of Henry and Pittsylvania for four hundred and odd of their Militia. Yet my trust is that neither these nor the adjacent counties have awaited orders, but that they have turned out and will have joined you in greater numbers than we have directed. The reinforcement from Chesterfd. Court House cannot march these ten days. I shall be glad if you will call on the neighboring County Lieutenants for any succours which you may want, and circumstances forbid to be delayed. A minute communication of events to us will be very necessary as we wish as far as we are able to increase the opposing force, if that already ordered shall be insufficient. This change of position has thrown us into great doubt where to collect our provisions.

Two days ago I received notice of the arrival of a 64 gun ship and 2 frigates of 36 each, part of the French fleet at Rhode Island. Having yet had no communication of the views of the Commanding Officer (Commodore Tilly) I cannot say to what measures this aid will lead. They are equal to the destruction of the British Vessels could they get at them, but these are drawn up into Elizabeth River into which the 64 cannot enter. I am &c.

P.S. Since writing the above we are told Ld. Cornwallis has advanced to the Roanoke. I am in consequence issuing orders to embody every man between this and that for whom a firelock can be procured and that they march to join you.

FC (Vi).

To Samuel Huntington

SIR Richmond Feby 17. 1781.

By a Letter from General Greene dated Guilford C. House Feby.

10. we are informed that Ld. Cornwallis had burnt his own waggons in order to enable himself to move with greater facility and had pressed immediately on. The prisoners taken at the Cowpens were happily saved by the accidental rise of a Water course which gave so much time as to withdraw them from the reach of the enemy. Ld. Cornwallis had advanced to the Vicinities of the Moravian towns and was still moving on rapidly. His object was supposed to be to compel General Greene to an action, which under the difference of force they had would probably be ruinous to the latter. General Greene meant to retire by the way of Boyds ferry on the Roanoke. As yet he had lost little or no stores or baggage, but they were far from being safe. In the instant of receiving this intelligence we ordered a reinforcement of militia to him from the most convenient counties in which there was a hope of finding any arms. Some great event must arise from the present situation of things which for a long time will determine the condition of southern affairs. I shall direct the prisoners of the Cowpens to be marched on through this State to such place as you shall please to determine on for their station.

Arnold lies close in his Quarters. Two days ago I received information of the arrival of a 64 gun ship and two frigates in our bay, being part of the fleet of our good ally at Rhode island. Could they get at the British fleet here they are sufficient to destroy them. But these being drawn up into Elizabeth river, into which the Sixty four cannot enter, I apprehend they could do nothing more than block up the river. This indeed would reduce the enemy as we could cut off their supplies by land: but the operation being lengthy would probably be too dangerous to the auxiliary force. Not having as yet had any particular information of the designs of the french commander I cannot pretend to say what measures this aid will lead to.

Our proposition to the Cherokee chiefs to visit Congress for the purpose of preventing or delaying a rupture with that nation was too late. Their distresses had too much ripened their alienation from us, and the storm had gathered to a head when Major Martin got back. It was determined to carry the war into their country rather than await it in ours, and I have it in my power to inform you, that thus disagreeably circumstanced the issue has been successful. The Militia of this State and north Carolina penetrated into their country, burnt almost every town they had amounting to about 1000 houses in the whole, destroyed 50,000 bushels of grain killed 20 and took 17 prisoners. The latter are mostly women and

Children. I inclose your Excellency the particulars as reported to me. Congress will be pleased to determine on Colo. Campbells proposition to build the fort at the confluence of the Holston and Tanissee.

I have the honor to be with great respect Your Excellency's Mo. obdt. & Most hble. Servt., TH: JEFFERSON

P.S. Since writing the above I receive information which tho' not authentic, commands attention, that Ld. Cornwallis had got to Boyd's ferry on the Staunton branch of Roanoke on the 14th. I am issuing orders in consequence to other counties to embody and march all the men they can arm. In this fatal situation without arms there will be no safety for the Convention troops but in their removal, which I shall accordingly order. The prisoners of the Cowpens were at New London (Bedford Court house) on the 14th.

RC (DLC: PCC, No. 71, II); in a clerk's hand, signed and with postscript in TJ's hand; endorsed: "Letter from Gov. of Virginia Feby. 17. 1781. Read 26. Referred to Mr Sharpe Mr M[eriwether] Smith Mr [Joseph] Jones." Enclosures: (1) A report of the recent campaign against the Cherokees; though not found, this was presumably a copy of Arthur Campbell's letter to TJ of 15 Jan., q.v.; (2) copy of Arthur Campbell's letter to George Muter, Washington co., 16 Jan., detailing his plans for establishing "a Post on the Tenasee, in order to secure our late advantages in the Cherokee Country"; RC in Vi, printed in CVSP, I, 438-9; Tr in DLC: PCC, No. 71, II; (3) copy of TJ's letter to Campbell, 17 Feb., also in PCC, No. 71, II, and printed above. FC (Vi); at head of text: "The Presdt. of Congress & Genl. Washington"; and at foot of text: "Genl. Washington leaving out the last two sentences & the sentence about the march of prisoners."

OUR PROPOSITION TO THE CHEROKEE CHIEFS: See entry for TJ's (missing) letter to Huntington, 10 Oct. 1780. Though the committee appointed by Congress on the present letter does not appear to have reported, the postscript, concerning the removal of THE CONVENTION TROOPS, was referred to a separate committee; this was a subject that had been under previous consideration (as a result of Benjamin Harrison's urgent appeal earlier this month); and on 3 Mch. Congress reached a determination embodied in Huntington's letter to TJ of 4 Mch., q.v.

From James Maxwell

SIR State Yard Feby: 17th: 1781

In answer to Yours of Yesterdays date I am to inform your Excellency that General Nelson haveing sent me word of the Arival of A French Fleet the Jefferson and Tempest are immediately geting ready under the Command of Captains Markham and Travers and are now endeavouring to get Voluntairs at Williamsburg for this service. I have also ofered Mr. Joel the command of the Louis Gally (for the present) provided he can get 20 Men and Your Excellency Aproves of it and [wo]uld also Add the Tarter and Safe Guard to the Above if A [proba]bilaty of geting Men. I hope to be able to have matters [in] such A Situation as to leave this in the Morning, and proceed up James River in search of such Vessels as You have described when shall immediately wait on You, haveing some Millitary Articles to dispatch down to our Navy.

I am with great Respect Your Excellencys Most Obedt. and most humble Servt:, JAS: MAXWELL

RC (Vi); addressed and endorsed.

To the Officers of the Greenbrier County Militia

GENTLEMEN Richmd. Febry. 17. 1781

I am fully sensible of the pressure of the several calls which are made on your County for Militia and for regulars at the same time, and should not have been induced to urge the first of these at the time we did, but to counteract and prevent movements meditated against you by the savage enemy in the West. I beg you to believe also that these calls are not made on your county alone. At present they are nearly general through the whole Counties; we have to oppose the Indians in the North West, Ld. Cornwallis in the South, and Arnold in the East. However in consideration of the dangers to which you will be exposed on the departure of your Militia; I will undertake to approve of your postponing the raising your regular recruits 'till the expedition under Genl. Clarke may be supposed to have advanced so far as to leave no danger of molestation to your county from the Indians; and will lay this before the assembly to obtain a legislative sanction.

I am Gentlemen with much respect &c.

FC (Vi). At head of text: "Colos. Andw. Donelly, Saml. Brown, & Andw. Hamilton of Green Bri[er]."

This letter is a reply to a letter signed by these officers and dated 29 Jan. 1781, q.v.

To Thomas Read

SIR Richmond Febry. 17. 1781.

I had received two days ago information from Genl. Greene of the advance of Ld. Cornwallis and immediately ordered about 1200 men from Washington, Montgomery, Botetourt, Bedford, Henry and Pittsylvania. Besides this I trusted that the Militia of other

Counties immediately in their way would turn out with Spirit. If this be done I hope a very good account will be rendered of Ld. Cornwallis. Your calling forth the whole strength of your County and the same measure by every County Lieutenant would be greatly approved to obtain so great an object. We did not call on your Counties particularly, because they had been called to Portsmouth, but every extra exertion of spirit will be very serviceable. Where Situations may shift every moment so rapidly I can only leave you to your own discretion recommending the most strenuous exertions to oppose the Enemy.

I am with great respect Sr. Yr. &c.

FC (Vi). At head of text: "Colo. T. Read of Charlotte." See Read to TJ, 15 Feb. 1781.

To Stephen Southall

SIR Richmond Febr. 17. 1781

An extreme throng of business prevented my answering your Letter yesterday. The order then given of which you sent me a copy, was not a general order but a special one in behalf of the bearers whoever they were. I think it was in the case of the waggoners employed by Majr. Pierce at Baltimore who had made them a special promise. It is certainly just that all should receive a reasonable price for their Waggons. Twenty pounds at that time was but 6/8 old money, which is but little more than the half of what waggon hire used to be; and that article for very good reasons should be higher now than formerly. The waggoners whom you have referred to Mr. Rose were employed by the Continent. Why should not the Continent pay them the just and full price? Why should this State undertake to pay the difference between the price you allow and that which would be just and be under the disagreeable necessity of urging an allowance of it in future? We think it unreasonable and therefore forbade our Quartermaster to pay that difference except in the single instance before mentioned where the Waggoners had been engaged on the faith of the State. Major Claiborne allows now 50℔ of Tobo. a day: why not allow it in earlier instances? The people have a right to recover the true worth of their Services, and no doubt the laws have provided them a remedy. I suppose I have mentioned to one or two of them that the remedy must be against the person employing or impressing them.

I am Sr. &c., THOS. JEFFERSON

FC (Vi). See Stephen Southall to TJ, 16? Feb., and Southall's second letter on the same subject, following, apparently written before this reply was received.

From Stephen Southall

Without place or date [*17? Feb. 1781*]. Alludes to his (Southall's) letter of the day before describing the difficulty of settling the accounts of people who had transported stores to the southern army. "The Bearer hereof is a person Who has been much distressed by having his Waggons taken from him for which Services he has only received the 20£ allowed by Congress," and he therefore begs TJ to order [Duncan] Rose to pay him what is still due him.

RC (Vi); 2 p.; addressed (but without bearer's name) and endorsed. Evidently written before receipt of TJ's answer, preceding, to Southall's letter of 16? Feb. 1781.

To Steuben

SIR Richmond Feb. 17. 1781.

Mr. Loyall from the post at the North west Bridge representing to me that about 400 of the militia of Princess Anne and Norfolk are embodied, that they annoy the enemy considerably, restraining their foraging parties, and checking their motions (which latter circumstance is confirmed by letter from Genl. Lawson) but that they are dispirited for want of some communication with the main army on the Northern end of the Dismal, and meditating to lay down their arms, I submit to yourself the propriety of establishing a line of riders from Genl. Gregory's camp to such of your posts as you shall think proper. Your order (if you think proper) to Colo. Elliot the feild Quartermaster will suffice to effect this. I have taken the liberty of referring Mr. Loyall to you. He will also speak with you on the subject of arms. But as those already embodied, are armed, I cannot but doubt the expediency of sending any from our stock under present circumstances. I order the Commissary to send a deputy to subsist these men on the East of the Dismal. Every circumstance of notice will keep up their spirits: and if the enemy can be restrained from foraging below Portsmouth as well as above, they will be less easy in their situation. I am with much respect Sir Your most obedt. servt., TH: JEFFERSON

RC (Vi); endorsed. FC (Vi). See TJ to Paul Loyall, 9 Feb. 1781.

To Steuben

Sir Richmd. Febry. 17. 1781

I have laid before the Council the proposition for exchanging two of the British souldiers for Mr. Hurst and Mr. Locke, on condition that we give Colo. Alligood for Colo. Warner [Warneck]. I am sorry the enemy should annex impossibilities to their proposition, as it seems to throw on us the refusal to exchange. Colo. Alligood has been proposed in exchange for Colo. Matthews, a full colonel who has been in captivity ever since the Battle of German town. Warner is only a Lieutenant Colonel taken the other day, if he were taken at all, of which no evidence has come to my knowledge. Both rank and turn therefore prohibit this part of the exchange. I have the honor &c &c.

FC (Vi).

COLO. ALLIGOOD: Jacob Ellegood (variously spelled), of Rosehall on the Lynnhaven River, Princess Anne co., was a substantial landowner and justice of his county who remained loyal to the crown, raised troops in his neighborhood in support of Gov. Dunmore in 1775, and was given command of them as colonel; at some time prior to 29 Feb. 1776 he was captured, and in Nov. 1780 Gen. Phillips proposed that he be exchanged for COLO. MATTHEWS (John Mathews, col., 9th Va. Line); Ellegood was paroled in Apr. 1781 and after the Revolution settled in the Province of New Brunswick (VMHB, XIV [1907], 252; XXX [1922], 373-4; *Tyler's Quart.*, V [1923-1924], 144; numerous references in *Va. Council Jour.*, I-II; William Phillips to TJ, 28 Nov. 1780). COLO. WARNER: This is almost certainly a mistaken reference to Frederick Warneck (see TJ to Muter, 29 Jan., and reply, 30 Jan. 1781). Under date of 20 Feb. the *Va. Council Jour.*, II, 297, contains the following entry: "Lieutenant Colonel Warnick, Engineer to the Commonwealth, acknowledging himself to have been taken by the enemy and producing a Copy of the Parole he gave; the board advise, that the said Parole be submitted to a board of Officers to declare their Opinion whether an Officer giving one in such a form should not be remitted into the hands of the enemy; that the same may be cancilled; or whether any, and what other proceedings, should be had thereon."

TJ's clerk also probably erred in putting down the names of MR. HURST and MR. LOCKE, for Steuben must have been referring to these two when he approved an exchange of "Parson Hurt, Capt. Pearce, and Mr. Cocke" (Steuben to Lawson, 28 Jan., NHi). On 18 Feb. Steuben sent to Muhlenberg "the Governors answer to the proposition for exchanging Colo. Elligood" and at the same time wrote a letter to Simcoe concerning another exchange. Arnold refused the terms offered and on 26 Feb. Muhlenberg reported to Steuben: "I have sent him [Arnold] the Governors Answer relative to the exchange proposed between Colo. Elligood and Warneck, which I suppose will end the negotiations for exchanging" (Steuben to Muhlenberg, 18 Feb.; Steuben to Simcoe, 18 Feb.; Arnold to Muhlenberg, 23 Feb.; Muhlenberg to Steuben, 26 Feb.; and Lawson to Steuben, 28 Jan., all of which are in NHi).

To Steuben

Sir Richmond Feb. 17. 1781.

I have this moment received intelligence that Ld. Cornwallis continues his rapid approach and there is reason to beleive he was at Roanoke on the 14th. This information is not authentic, yet it comes in such manner as to command some attention. I have therefore thought it expedient to order every Man of the Counties of Powhatan, Cumberland, Amelia, Lunenburg and Brunswick who has a firelock or for whom one can be procured to be embodied and marched immediately to join Genl. Greene and those of the Counties of Chesterfd. and Dinwiddie to be embodied but not marched till further orders which they may receive at the moment of embodying better adapted to actual circumstances. I am aware of the possibility that my information my be premature, yet as it's truth is equally possible and the consequences of disregarding it might be so much more fatal I think it my duty to take this measure. Your most obedt. humble servt., TH: JEFFERSON

RC (NHi); addressed and endorsed. FC (Vi); dated 18 Feb., obviously an error. Steuben acknowledged the present letter on 18 Feb. as TJ's "Letter of Yesterday."

From Steuben

Chesterfield Court House, 17 Feb. [*1781*]. Capt. Morris, "a prisoner of War belonging to the State of Georgia," has applied to Steuben for money to enable him to proceed to Philadelphia. Steuben cannot furnish money but hopes TJ can, since Morris "has furnished the Continent with large sums, and wishes to settle his accounts with the board of war, in Congress."

RC (Vi); 2 p.; in an aide's hand, signed by Steuben; addressed and endorsed.

To George Washington

Richmond, 17 Feb. 1781. This letter is identical in substance with that sent by TJ to Huntington this day, q.v., except that the last sentence in the first paragraph and the last two sentences in the paragraph before the complimentary close in the letter to Huntington are not in the letter to Washington.

RC (DLC: Washington Papers); 4 p.; in a clerk's hand, signed and with postscript in TJ's hand; endorsed (in part): "Ansd. 21st. March." FC (Vi); same as that to Huntington of this date, which contains notation of sentences omitted in the copy sent to Washington. Tr (DLC).

To the County Lieutenant of Augusta

SIR Richmond Febry. 18. 1781

Before the receipt of this letter I expect you will have furnished Mr. Hyrne Depty. Comsy. Genl. of Prisoners with a guard for the safe custody of the prisoners taken at the Battle of the Cowpens. You will be pleased to continue that guard on duty with the prisoners untill releived by one from Shenandoah as ordered.

I [am] with much respect, &c.

FC (Vi).

To the County Lieutenants of Chesterfield and Dinwiddie

SIR Richmond Febry. 18. 1781

Not knowing where the very rapid march of Ld. Cornwallis may terminate, I think it necessary to desire that every man of your Militia who has a firelock or for whom one can be procured by impressing or otherwise be immediately embodied under proper Officers. I do not herein give orders for their march because you are so convenient that you can without it's causing but little delay give me notice when your men are embodied, and I may then give you orders suited to the actual situation of things at the time. I am with much respect Sr. &c.

FC (Vi). Another FC (Vi). These have identical texts, but variant captions. The first is headed: "County Lieuts. of Chesterfield & Dinwiddie." The second is headed: "County Lieut. or Commanding Officer of Chesterfield Militia." Since both are transcribed in the Executive Letter Book (the first at p. 119 and the second at p. 122), and since it is unlikely that TJ dispatched two identical letters to the county lieutenant of Chesterfield on 18 Feb., this curious duplication was an apparent error. Two possible explanations occur: (1) the second FC was intended for the commanding officer of some county other than Chesterfield and the clerk, in transcribing, made an error in the caption on p. 122; and (2) the clerk simply erred in repeating the text in the Executive Letter Book, forgetting that he had already transcribed such a text. Either error is understandable on a day when the executive office must have been operating under an exceptional "throng of business," as TJ put it. The second appears to be the more likely explanation, for if such a text had been intended for some other county in addition to the two mentioned, the clerk, following usual practice, would no doubt have added the name of that county to the caption of the text on p. 119, instead of wasting time in making another copy.

To the County Lieutenants of Lunenberg, Amelia, Powhatan, Cumberland, and Brunswick

SIR Richmd. Febry. 18. 1781

Not knowing where the very rapid march of Ld. Cornwallis may terminate I think it necessary to desire that you immediately assemble the whole of your Militia who have arms, or for whom they can be procured by impressing or otherwise and march them with proper officers without delay to join Genl. Greene who by the last intelligence had crossed the Dan at Boyd's ferry and was retreating before the enemy. The emergency is so extreme that I must rely on your losing not a moment's time in executing this order. I shall be glad to be informed of the numbers you equip and time of their march. I am with much respect &c.

FC (Vi). On p. 118 of the Executive Letter Book, this FC precedes FC of TJ's letter to Steuben, printed above under date of 17 Feb.; in that letter the FC was dated 18 Feb. and the RC dated 17 Feb., which Steuben on 18 Feb. acknowledged as TJ's "Letter of Yesterday." However, the reply of Vivian Brooking, county lieutenant of Amelia, 20 Feb., acknowledges TJ's letter of 18 Feb.; hence the RC (not found) of the present letter was also dated 18 Feb. This must also have been true of the letters to the county lieutenants of Powhatan, Cumberland, Lunenberg, and Brunswick.

To the County Lieutenant of Shenandoah

SIR Richmd. Febry. 18. 1781.

The prisoners taken at the Battle of the Cowpens being to pass under the conduct of Mr. Hyrne or Mr. Boush Commissaries of Prisoners, they will be attended by the guard at present with them as far as Shenandoah Court House. There you will be pleased to have assembled such guard and at such time as either of these Gentlemen shall fix on, which guard must see them safely over the Potowmack. I am with much respect, &c.

FC (Vi). The original was enclosed to Edmund M. Hyrne in a letter to him of this date, q.v.

To Nathanael Greene

SIR Richmond Feb. 18. 1781.

The very interesting situation of Southern affairs with respect to our state at this crisis, and the multiplicity of your business which alone must forbid me to hope a very frequent communication from you, have induced me to send on the bearer Majr. McGill to give us from time to time notice of the movements of the two armies and other important occurrences that we may be able to adapt to them the measures to be taken by us. The zeal, discretion, and good sense which have recommended Majr. McGill to us for the execution of this office, will render him worthy of any countenance and civilities you shall think proper to shew him. Give me leave to hope also that you will trust him with any communications which you may think not improper to be made to us, of which we shall endeavor to make the best use for the common good.

I have the honor to be with very great respect Sir Your most obedient & most humble servt., TH: JEFFERSON

RC (MiU-C); addressed by TJ: "The honble. Majr. Genl. Greene by Majr. McGill." See TJ to Charles Magill, this date.

To Nathanael Greene

SIR Richmond Feb. 18. 1781

I have this moment received your favor of the 15th. from Boyd's ferry. I had heard yesterday of the approach of the Ld. Cornwallis, gave orders in consequence for embodying so many of the militia between this place and that as could be armed and of this gave you information in a letter of yesterday's date. I hoped at the same time that the militia would not await my orders, and by the letters I receive I trust they have not. I sincerely wish you may be able to find it practicable to avoid a general action till you can be sufficiently reinforced with militia which I am sure you will be as far as arms can be found. I have no doubt you know and avail yourself of the Continental arms which passed on not long since, and of those lodged by Genl. Stevens at Pittsylvania Court house. The moment I hear Cornwallis has crossed the Dan I shall order every man to be embodied on this side river within a reasonable distance who can be armed. I shall attend as far as shall depend on me to what you recommend as to officering the militia and mounting the cavalry. As to yourself I would advise that you make no scruples about property so far as it is wanting for the public; only give orders that the owners be furnished with proper documents that they may be reimbursed.

I am with much esteem Sir Your most obedt. servt,

TH: JEFFERSON

P.S. Take horses to mount your cavalry, and I will undertake to have it justified.

RC (Munson-Williams-Proctor Institute, Utica, N.Y.); addressed by TJ: "The honble. Majr. Genl. Greene." Postscript is written in margin.

To Edmund Massingbird Hyrne

SIR Richmd. Febry. 18. 1781

I have just received your favor of the 14th. inst. from New London, and expect this will find you at Staunton. I formerly advertised Congress of the necessity of sending these prisoners on Northwardly, and have again yesterday given them notice that the rapid approach of Ld. Cornwallis who was at Boyd's ferry on the 14th., rendered it necessary to send on both these and the Convention prisoners without delay. The whole would form a great object for Lord Cornwallis and nothing between him and them but an unarmed Country abounding with disaffected. The Deputy Commissary of prisoners in this State is Mr. Boush at Winchester. You will be pleased to take such measures for delivering the prisoners to him as you think best, either conducting them that far yourself, or sending for him to meet you. I suppose you have a guard on them at present which may attend them to Shenandoah C. H. I inclose a letter to the County Lieutenant of Shenandoah to have such guard ready there and at such time as you shall direct who may attend them to Potowmack. Before you get that far you will doubtless receive the orders of Congress fixing their ultimate destination. For provisions I can only refer you to the Commissioners of the provision Law in the several Counties through which you will pass, tho' if they cannot furnish you, the Commissary attending you must impress, giving certificates of the Articles seized and their Value, and returning to the Auditors a list of the certificates given.

FC (Vi). At head of text: "Mr. Hyrne Comissy. Prisoners." Enclosure: TJ to County Lieutenant of Shenandoah, this date, printed above.

To Charles Magill

SIR Richmond Febry. 18. 1781

The situation of Southern affairs having become very interesting to this State, I am to desire the favor of you to proceed without delay to the head Quarters of Genl. Greene, to remain there or at any other place, from which you shall think the best intelligence may be obtained. You will be pleased to communicate to me the interesting movements of both Armies, the calls which shall be made on our Counties for supplies of me[n], provisions and other things, how these calls are complied with, what shall appear to be the spirit of the people, what is doing in the rear of Ld. Cornwallis and such other facts as you shall think important. There is a line of stationed Expresses from hence to Genl. Greene's Camp, which you will put into motion whenever you shall have any thing to communicate. You would do well to enquire of Colo. Elliot at Petersburg, the particular places at which these Expresses are stationed, to visit and rectify any thing amiss in them as you pass along. Your Expences in this service shall be borne by the public.

FC (Vi). **See TJ to Nathanael Greene, this date (first letter), which was conveyed to Greene by Magill.**

From Thomas Nelson

[Williamsburg, 18 February 1781]

A Flag vessel from the enemy, in which was Lieut. Hare formerly detained at Hampton, has been stopped at Sandy point. The inclosed papers will inform you of the business and the extraordinary Conduct he has observed. His abuse of Characters in this State has been general and his Expressions concerning your Excellency have been such, as from any other mouth but that of an enemy and at the same time a person of very little consequence in any point of view would be extremely injurious. His insinuations were that you had received Gold from New York. I mention this, not as a Circumstance which can affect you but which may perhaps in him be deemed justly a violation or an unwarrantable abuse of his flag. An officer who was sent on board saw in the Fire something which had the appearance of Letters just consumed.

Immediately on receiving information of the arrival of a French Squadron in our bay I went down to Hampton and the day before yesterday went on board the Commodores Ship in the road a few minutes after she Anchored. The Squadron consists of one Sixty four Gun Ship and two Frigates of 36 Guns each. Their present station is a little below Sewells point where when joined by some of our Vessels of smaller size they will be able completely to block up Eliza. river. More than this it will not be in their power to perform, there not being a sufficient Depth of Water, for the largest Ships, in Eliza. river. They are very anxious that something should be done immediately, thinking it unsafe to continue long in their present Station, as vessels from the enemy's Fleet at Portsmouth have shipped out which are supposed to be dispatched for New York. The Commodore proposed that, until we should be ready to cooperate with them he should cruize off the Capes, by which means he would intercept supplies, distress the enemy, and consult his own safety, should a Superior British Force arrive. I declined giving my opinion though Circumstances considered, I thought such Conduct would be prudent. This fleet brings Intelligence that three seventy fours of the enemy's Northern Fleet were lost, rendered useless, and missing. The Culloden of 74 Guns, a Copper bottomed Ship was entirely lost, the American was missing, and the Bedford dismasted and no means of repairing her. This renders the French Fleet superior in that Quarter.

Tr (NHi); in an unidentified clerk's hand; endorsed and with the following at head of text: "Extract of a Letter from General Nelson to The Governor." Enclosures: Not identified, but see Turberville to TJ, 15 Feb.

Nelson received INFORMATION OF THE ARRIVAL OF A FRENCH SQUADRON at three a.m. 15 Feb.; Lt. Col. Charles Dabney, commanding the posts below Williamsburg, wrote Nelson on 14 Feb. that the fleet of De Tilly had arrived and Nelson immediately forwarded the news to Steuben, who he thought was in Richmond but who actually was at Chesterfield. Nelson's early morning letter to Steuben (of which there are three copies in NHi, along with Dabney's) reflects the exultation that he felt at this apparent opportunity to capture Arnold and his forces, a feeling tempered on the following day by De Tilly's prudence: "I have the happiness to enclose you a Copy of a Letter from Colo. Dabney who commands the lower posts. What you expected has taken place. I give you joy with all my soul. Now is our time. Not a moment ought to be lost. I intended to have cross'd James River this day, but I shall first wait on the French Commodore and then cross to afford you every assistance in my power. I have represented to the Governor the Necessity for dispatch in our operations. There will be no occasion now for the boats I had engag'd." The last sentence appears to be significant; it may refer to TJ's plan to capture Arnold. For on 14 Feb. Nelson wrote Steuben from Williamsburg: "I have at length procur'd two Vessels proper for the business you entrusted me with. One of them is at York, the other in Kingston Parish Gloster County. As I shall cross the River tomorrow I would advise that the Gentlemen who are to go in the Boats be recommended, one of them to Mr. Reynolds at York, the other to Colo. Peyton of Gloster County, who will give them every assistance" (NHi). If these boats were not employed for the scheme to capture Arnold, it is not clear what other purpose they could have had that would have been rendered obsolete by the arrival of De Tilly's ships. It is to be noted also that the two boats engaged by Nelson were located in waters controlled by the British. Certainly it would appear that the most promising method of carrying out TJ's plan to bring Arnold off by a small party would have been to have a few Virginians from the lower counties (perhaps some who had given paroles) approach Arnold's headquarters by water, endeavor to get him aboard one of the vessels on some pretext, and then put off. Once clear of the British forces at Portsmouth, the rest would have been easy. The fact that Nelson had reported to TJ that the "paroled People require nothing but Assistance to make them very spirited Friends of their Country" and that Nelson had been selected to manage the ill-starred attempt of Captain Joel to lead a fire-ship against the enemy fleet may lend some weight to these conjectures (see Nelson to TJ, 3 and 7 Feb.). No letter from Nelson to TJ between 7 Feb. and 18 Feb. has been found; however, it is likely that the letter in which Nelson "represented to the Governor the Necessity for Dispatch in our operations" was written immediately after he had received Lt. Col. Dabney's letter—that is, in the early morning of 15 Feb.

From Steuben

SIR Chesterfield Co. Ho. Feby. 18. 1781

I am favord with your Excellencys Letter of yesterday and submit whether it would not be prudent to order the prisoners removed from the Barracks at Albermarle.

I have the honor to be Your Excellencys most Obed Servt,

STEUBEN Maj: Genl:

RC (Vi); in an aide's hand; addressed and endorsed.

YOUR EXCELLENCYS LETTER OF YESTERDAY: Evidently the third letter from TJ to Steuben printed above under 17 Feb. In view of Steuben's unremitting criticism of the Virginia government, his advice concerning the Convention PRISONERS is interesting. On the same day that he wrote the above letter, Steuben sent letters to Washington in part as follows: "If Cornwallis should continue to push in as rapidly as he has done or if Arnold should receive a reinforcement of 1500 Men, I fear that this State will not make much more resistance than No. Carolina has done. Every thing here is in confusion. The state is totally destitute of Arms, and by bad management of almost everything else necessary for defense. The Executive power is so confined that the Governor has it not in his power to procure me 40 Negroes to work at Hoods. In fact . . . I fear that without some speedy assistance our affairs in this quarter will go very badly. I have submitted to the Governor whether it would not be proper to remove the prisoners from Charlottesville" (Steuben to Washington, 18 Feb., NHi). Before Steuben made his suggestion about the prisoners, TJ had already acted: on 15 Feb., immediately on receipt of the inadequate information Greene had sent him, TJ directed James Wood to be prepared to remove the prisoners from Albemarle at an instant's notice; and on 18 Feb., whereas Steuben was merely advising that it be considered, TJ ordered immediate withdrawal.

To James Wood

SIR Richmond Febry. 18. 1781.

Ld. Cornwallis's approaches are so rapid that we know not where they will terminate. He was at Boyd's ferry on the 14th. inst. Without arms as our Countrymen are there is no safety for the Convention troops but in their removal; you will therefore be pleased to remove them in the instant of receiving this, only allowing them time to pack their baggage that it may follow them in Waggons. As the prisoners taken at the Cowpens will be [at] Staunton by the time this reaches you, and will proceed on along that valley, I think it most advisable that you should keep below the Blue Ridge: but of this you will judge yourself. Time does not allow me to send you formal warrants for taking provisions: I can therefore only give you this general authority to issue such warrants yourself. I have given notice to Congress of this measure who will no doubt send you orders at what place these people shall end their journey.

I am with much respect &c &c.

FC (Vi).

To George Rogers Clark

SIR Richmond Feby 19. 1781.

I received your Letter on the subject of the backwardness of the militia of Berkeley and Frederic to proceed Westwardly and had before received representations from the Counties. This circumstance was the more mortifying as we were informed from various quarters that should we persist in the order it would produce an open disobedience. Many Circumstances concurred to render it prudent to avoid this: the presence of two armies of the enemy within the State induced us to wish to prevent every thing like commotion or opposition to Government in every part of it. As therefore the representations were accompanied with hopes held out of raising a respectable number of Volunteers the board thought it prudent to accept of that offer. These two Counties were relied on for 560 men: on view of this disappointment we obtained an order from Baron Steuben for Colo. John Gibson with his regiment and Heths company (about 200 regulars) to be added to your command: an addition of more worth of itself perhaps than those militia, more especially if any number of volunteers should go. I hope too you will receive greater numbers from Kentucky than we counted on, and aids from the french settlements. We are apt to hope what we much wish, and perhaps this is my case.

The inclosed papers give us real concern as they hold out reason to apprehend great abuses in the Western quarter. I transmit them to you to have strict enquiry made (not by yourself for your time is otherwise better engaged, but) by such persons of known integrity and Character as you shall appoint. We do not know what to do with the bills of which Major Slaughter speaks. Indeed I wish such an enquiry could take place and that the persons you appoint would give their sanction to every bill.

The suggestions against the Gentleman who went to Kaskaskias under promise of availing you of it's resources and strength are of such a nature as to merit attention and delicate enquiry. I am sure you will keep your attention alive as to every thing of this kind and will use decision where decision is found necessary.

I am with much esteem & respect Sir Your most obedt & mo: hble Servt.,

TH: JEFFERSON

RC (WHi); in a clerk's hand, signed by TJ; endorsed: "From Government Govr. Jefferson Feby: 19 1781"; also bears an abstract of contents by Lyman C. Draper. One of the enclosures must have been a copy of George Slaughter's letter to TJ, 17 Jan. 1781, q.v.; no others have been identified. FC (Vi).

YOUR LETTER ON THE . . . BACKWARDNESS OF THE MILITIA OF BERKE-

LEY AND FREDERIC: Dated 10 Feb. 1781; see also TJ's letter to the county lieutenants of Berkeley and Frederick, 16 Feb. 1781. For the results of the ENQUIRY ordered by TJ into the conduct of Commissaries Shannon and Moore, see George Slaughter to TJ, 13 Apr. and 14 Apr. 1781.

To the County Lieutenant of Chesterfield

SIR Richmond Febry. 19. 1781.

As I have hopes that 280 men of your County may arm themselves, and I do not think it proper that a greater number should be sent from thence, you will be pleased to order that number of the most effective men to proceed to Watkin's Mills at which place they shall receive further orders, as soon as further intelligence shall enable me to point them properly. I am Sr. &c &c.

FC (Vi).

To Nathanael Greene, Enclosing Warrant to Impress Horses

SIR Richmd Febry 19. 1781.

I wrote you in haste yesterday by the return of your express in answer to your letter of the 15th. Majr McGill not being able to set out till this morning, furnishes me with an opportunity of inclosing you regular blank powers of impress to be directed to such persons as you shall think proper for impressing horses for your dragoons.

When we ordered out the militia from the several counties, we ordered them to go properly officered, as we had no certainty of there being any regular officers ready to command them. There is now a great collection of regular Officers at Chesterfld C. H. met for the purpose of arranging our line and discharging it of supernumeraries. As there are not regulars for even those who will remain in the service to command, I shall submit to Baron Steuben whether, besides requesting all those who shall be declared supernumerary to go to you, it may not be expedient to send those also who tho' remaining of the Line cannot have a present command for want of men. If these go, it will be in your power to permit such of the militia officers to return home as chuse it, and forming the men into small battalions to dispose of both regular and militia officers as you please. Baron Steuben has availed himself at Suffolk of the regular officers by forming the militia into regiments of 400 each, and dividing the regiment into two battalions of 200 each. This gave room for the regular Officers, who of course commanded those of the militia of the same rank; however this and every other plan is submitted to yourself. I have the honor to be with very great esteem, Sr. &c.

ENCLOSURE

To

The first and third regiments of Virginia Continental dragoons being in want of many horses, and the approach of the British army under Ld. Cornwallis rendering it necessary that they should be fully mounted in order to prevent the enemy from ravaging the country and to cut off their supplies, and it being certain that such horses in the way of the enemy as shall not be applied in defence of the State will be taken by them and emploied against it, you are hereby authorized according to such instructions as you shall receive from Majr. Genl. Greene, to proceed and impress for the purpose of mounting the said dragoons, so many good horses as he shall direct, confining yourself to the neighbourhood and probable route of the enemy. You will have these horses appraised according to law and give certificates thereof to the owners, returning to me a list of the certificates you shall give, stating therein the names of the owners, prices and dates. Given under my hand and the seal of the Commonwealth, at Richmond the 19th. Day of February 1781.

TH: JEFFERSON

FC (Vi). Enclosure (CtY); in a clerk's hand, signed by TJ. There is a typescript of the present letter in DLC: TJ Papers, 7:1109 that must have been made from the RC (not found); this typescript describes the letter as an "L.S., 2 pages, quarto, 'Richmond, Feby. 19, 1781.' "

From Benjamin Harrison

SIR Philadelphia Feby. 19th. 1781

When I did my self the pleasure of writing to you I fully expected the Powder would have been sent off the next day to fort Pitt, but the Q. Master assures me that with his utmost efforts he was not able to procure waggons till this day, and now only to go as far as Carlisle, for which place they set out this Evening. He thinks there will be no difficulty in getting it on immediately from thence as that country abounds in waggons. I wish the delay may not be attended with bad consequences; be that as it may I could not prevent it.

The Committee to whom I was refer'd carry in their report this day; I have been treated with the greatest politeness by them and Congress, and have every reason to expect they will grant me full as much as I asked, but I foresee very great difficulty in their carrying their resolutions into effect, they being extremely poor and their credit but low; some difficulties will arise on the removal of the Convention troops, tho' I expect the opposers of the measure will be overruled, as the objections only come from this State and Maryland. The other members of Congress that I have seen are convinced of the necessity of its being immediately done and will I am persuaded order it accordingly. I have also succeeded in the business of supplies, as far as it can be done on this side the water, being promis'd the most favourable representation of the matter and given to understand, that there is little doubt of our obtaining what we have asked; but this it is wished may be kept a secret as far as the nature of the thing will admit of.

I had some conversation with the French minister on the subject of the Bermuda and Irish trades. He seems extremely averse to their being permitted, and thinks it will prove injurious to the common cause. I shall leave these matters to our Delegates who I am confident will use their endeavours to have them put on a proper footing. The Arms &c. carried into Rode Island have been some time on board a French Frigate to be sent to York Town, if she can possibly get there, if not, I have requested of the Minister to have them landed at New castle on this river, and shall have what money I shall have left with the Delegates to forward them on to Fredericksburg; we have pretty certain accounts that a ship of the line belonging to Arburthnots fleet is lost, and three others dismasted which will give such a superiority to the French, that they may if they please render us very essential service in Virginia, and I think you may expect soon to see them.

Your favor of the 7th Instant came to hand late yesterday. I made the request of the officers known to some of the members of Congress, and was inform'd by them that Congress had before had the subject under consideration, and had refused it, looking on it as an absolute breach of faith, yet as the Virga. Delegates think with me, that articles may be sent, that can not give offence to our allies except that it opens a road to private adventurers they have agreed to prepose the thing again, I have therefore put the papers into their hands.

The long expected Paul Jones arrived here yesterday. The spirits of a man never were raised higher than mine were when I heard he was in the river; but a sad reverse took place when certainly inform'd, that he had not one article of cloathing. What occasions this great disappointment time must discover. We shall derive little comfort from the knowledge, if the delay brings ruin with it, and may not that be the case if our soldiers cannot be cloathed; This Town abounds with cloth, but the only way Congress can obtain it is on credit, and as I before said theirs is but at a low ebb. Perhaps I might prop it if I had power so to do, by plighting the faith of Virga. that if it was not paid in six months that we would do it in Tobacco, I mean as far as two thousand suits of cloaths would cost, which it appears to me should absolutely be obtaind at any expence. I can scarce refrain from making the experiment knowing the advantage my country would reap by my success, and would certainly do it, if I did not know there were some who wish to censure me and lower me in the Eyes of my country men, and there is no greater field for malevolence to work in, than going beyond the powers entrusted to me. I am in hopes Congress will determine on the report in a Day or two. As soon as I have made enquiry what can be done in the article of Cloathing I shall set out on my return, and take annapolis in my way, and if the Cartouch boxes are to be found will forward them on to Fredericksburg. I have the Honor to be with every sentiment of Esteem Your most Obedient and most Humble Servant,

BENJA HARRISON

RC (Vi).

On Harrison's mission in Philadelphia, see TJ to Harrison, 29 Jan., and Harrison's earlier report, 12 Feb. 1781. THE POWDER to be sent to FORT PITT was for the proposed expedition of George Rogers Clark against Detroit. On this subject there are in Vi two documents that supplement Harrison's letter. The first of these is a one-page MS containing five receipts signed by different persons, all dated 17 Feb. 1781 and all made out to Col. Benjamin Flower acknowledging receipt of a total of 129 casks of powder containing a net weight of 6015 pounds of powder which the several signers promised "to deliver to Col. Benjn. Harrison or his Order." The second of these documents is a letter from Samuel Hodgdon to Benjamin Harrison, "Comy Genls Office Carpenters hall Chesnut street," 19 Feb., in which Hodgdon informed Harrison that "the five waggoners that you directed the Quarter Master to send, to the Magazine to be loaded with powder for the state of Virginia," had been laden with "Three tons and Eighty-four pounds Net—being as much it seems as they can carry"; that the commissary at Carlisle was able to receive and deposit the powder, but that he was by no means able to "get it on—and without a Special Order from the Quarter Master here accompanies it—it may lay their this six Months"; Hodgdon's letter is printed in CVSP, I, 528.

To Joseph Martin

SIR Richmond Febry. 19. 1781.

In our present circumstances peace with the Cherokees is desirable to us on our own accounts as it always was on theirs; you will therefore take such measures to effect this as you think best. Should you find it most likely to preserve peace, we should approve of your removing such of the Nation as you can draw off to the Island or any where else within their own unceded territory: Those who are with you, maintain as well as you can; for aid herein apply to the Deputy Commissaries of Washington and Montgomery Counties. Treat the prisoners well, exchange them for any of our people taken by the Cherokees as far as necessary, and when peace shall be made give up the surplus if any. I am &c.

FC (Vi). See Martin's letter to TJ, 7 Feb. 1781, to which this is a reply.

From George Muter, with Reply

War Office [*Richmond*], *19 Feb. 1781*. "Capt. Browne [Windsor Brown] attends to know the detirmination of your Excellency and the Hon. Council respecting his acting as Commissary of military stores." All that remains to do is to fix his "allowance," and since he is soon to be reduced to half pay as an officer, that allowance should be "the more liberal."

In Council Feb. 20. 1781.

The board approves of the appointment of Capt. Browne as Commissary of military stores with the allowance given to Capt. Irish his predecessor. TH: JEFFERSON

P.S. The allowance to Capt. Irish was fixed by the day, but it was and is meant that exclusively of this the Commissary shall be allowed his reasonable expences while travelling on the duties of his office. TH: JEFFERSON

RC (Vi); addressed and endorsed. TJ's answer, in his own hand, is on a blank page of Muter's letter. Tr of TJ's answer is in War Office Journal (Vi). In War Office Letter Book (Vi), under 20 Feb., are copies of Muter's letters to Windsor Brown and Nathaniel Irish notifying them of the Council's action.

See Muter to TJ, 15 Feb., and reply under same date.

From Thomas Nelson

DEAR SIR Williamsburg Febry 19. 1781

Commodore Tilly having determined to sail with the first fair Wind, the Enemy will be left at Liberty to make use of all the Advantages which their Command of the Water gives them over us. They will probably be inclined, for some Losses they have sustained since the Arrival of the French Squadron, to wreak their Vengeance on the Parts of the State most exposed. Hampton and the adjacent Country have particular Reason to dread the Effects of their Resentment, having furnished our Allies with Pilots, and testified the greatest Readiness to afford them every other kind of Assistance. It gives me the utmost Pain that I find myself unable to give them the Protection they merit; the Force at present under my Command amounting to not more than four hundred Effectives. The Militia from Albemarle and Fluvanna are much distressed for Want of clothing, and ought to be relieved if it can be done. By Col. Senf I wrote this Morning to Commodore Tilly, requesting that he would assist the State with Arms or any military Stores he may be able to spare from his Captures or otherwise, and engaging that the State will make him whatever Return he may think proper. I hope this Step will not be disapproved of by Government. Amongst the Enemy's Vessels taken, 8 in Number, are the Lord Cornwallis and another Privateer. Other Prizes of greater Importance were expected.

I am, dear Sir, with the greatest Respect, Your mo: Obedt. & very hble. Servt., THOS NELSON JR. B.g.

Febry. 20. By Intelligence received last Night, the French Fleet had fallen below the old Fort on Point Comfort. The Prizes they have sent round to York, and I fear from our present Weakness they will not be safe there. T.N.

RC (John Work Garrett Library, Baltimore, 1946; now MdBJ); addressed and endorsed. An extract of this letter was enclosed in TJ's letter to Steuben, 20 Feb. 1781.

From David Ross

SIR Richmond 19 February 1781.

I Have just now the offer of about 400 pr. Soldiers Stockings. Altho I understand that Overalls are at present substituted in place of Stockings for the troops at Chesterfield Courthouse, I take the liberty of mentioning them to You as tis probable the Southern Army now returned to Virginia may have occaision for some supplies more especially as they will for some time be exposed to severe duty.

I trouble You with the enclosed State of the Cloathing &c. to be furnished for the troops which will give You an idea when they can march.

If Ld. Cornwallis has any substantial objects in view from his extraordinary movements it may be presumed he has good reason to expect another Army Sent from N York. In that Case Petersburg would Not be safe and I have directed that some Prisoners which I have in that Neighborhood should be sent up to the Fork.

I am with great regard Sir Your most huml Servant,

David Ross

I am to give an Answer as to the Stockings immediately.

RC (Vi); addressed and endorsed. The "enclosed State of the Cloathing &c." was transmitted to Steuben in TJ's letter of 20 Feb. and has not been found.

To Steuben

Sir Richmond Feb. 19.

The prisoners in Albemarle were ordered to be removed immediately giving them time only to pack their baggage that it might follow them in waggons. Those taken at the Cowpens which were at New London on the 14th. inst. were likewise ordered Northwardly by the way of Staunton keeping above the Blue ridge while the Conventioners pass below it. These orders were issued at the same time with those for embodying the militia and have been notified to Congress and Genl. Washington.

By a letter from Count Rochambeau to Genl. Washington a copy of which is transmitted me, it appears that some French frigates were out cruising from Newport, that two 74s. and a frigate were sent out by the British to take them, that a storm came on which drove one of the 74s ashore on Montuck [Montauk] point and obliged the other to put back into Gardner's bay dismasted, and the frigate also to put back tho' without injury, and forced the French frigates back to port which they reached in safety; that this accident had given the French fleet a superiority whereon the Chevalr. de Touche [Destouches] was determined to send a line of battle ship and two Frigates to cruize off the capes of Chesapeake and break off the communication between New York and Charlestown. This letter is dated Jan. 9. We are therefore to suppose the French vessels now here to be come in consequence of the above and to hope they are in no danger.

I am with much respect Sir Your most obedt. humble servt.,

Th: Jefferson

P.S. I have heard nothing from Genl. Nelson or Commodore Tilly.

RC (NHi); endorsed. Enclosure (not found): Rochambeau to Washington, 9 Jan. 1781; an extract is printed in CVSP, I, 425-6.

To Steuben

SIR — Richmond Feby. 19. 1781

The inclosed is an extract of a letter from Genl. Greene to me. As the Gentlemen of the Army whom he wishes to take Command of the Militia who shall join him are now pretty generally collected with you for the purpose of arranging the line; on which Arrangement it is probable some will become supernumerary I submit to you whether it would not be agreeable to Genl. Greene if you could prevail on all the Gentlemen who shall become supernumerary and as many of those who tho remaining of the line have not a present Command of Regulars, to join Genl. Greene without delay on the present important occasion and take such Commands as he shall assign them. You will be pleased to act in this as you shall think best.

I have the honor to be with great respect Sir Your most obedt & most humbl Servt.,

TH: JEFFERSON

RC (NHi); in a clerk's hand, signed and addressed by TJ to Steuben at "Chesterfd. Court house"; endorsed.

EXTRACT OF A LETTER FROM GENL. GREENE: This was that part of Greene's letter to TJ of 15 Feb. in which Greene remarked: "If the Militia is called out let them be put under Continental officers, that are or have been in service." On 23 Feb. Steuben's aide-de-camp, Major William North, wrote to Greene as follows: "The Virginia Line give him [Steuben] the Greatest Trouble. The Arrangement is nearly completed and they are continually applying for leaves of absence. An extract of your letter to the Governor was published in orders, and they were *ask'd* to Join You—and had the Baron *commanded* he knew it would have been of no Effect. Six signed their names but afterwards excused themselves. Gen. Nelson is sick, Lawson at home. Arnold in Portsmouth. The Assembly to meet 1st March. Rendezvous opened. Officers to be sent to receive the recruits. Government to be harrassed 'till they cloath the men they raise. The Baron wishes to be with you. He had rather Obey in an Army, than Command in Virginia" (North to Greene, "Moors Ordinary," Prince Edward co., 23 Feb.; an extract from Steuben's General Orders of 19 Feb., addressed to Colonel Davies, is in Vi). The discontent of the Virginia officers, and their requests for leaves may have been Steuben's fault in some measure. The arrangement of the Virginia Line on the Continental Establishment, to be carried out in accordance with the resolution of Congress of 21 Nov., had been ordered by Steuben on 20 Dec. to take place at Chesterfield court house on 10 Feb. (broadside, NHi, "By the General's Command P. S. Du Ponceau. Aide-de-Camp"). Most of the officers assembled on the date specified, but Steuben remained in Richmond until 11 Feb. and then adjourned the meeting to Petersburg for the 18th. On top of this he insisted on returning Weedon to service despite the fact that Weedon had been in retirement for three years. This move was strongly protested by the Board of Virginia Field Officers on 18 Feb., who pointed out that "confusion, disgust, and resignations . . . followed such irregularities" and threatened to send their protests to Congress, to Washington, and to Greene (Board of Virginia Field Officers to Steuben, 18 Feb.; two letters from Davies to Steuben on 10 Feb. and one on 11 Feb.; Steuben to Davies, 11 Feb., all in NHi). This arrangement of the Virginia Line, as well as the animosities engendered by Steuben's inept handling of "The Affair of Westover" (see Appendix I, Vol. 5), must have been in large part responsible for the feeling against Steuben that caused Davies to write Greene somewhat later: "The Baron has unfortunately become universally unpopular, and all ranks of people seem to have taken the greatest disgust at him, and carry it to such a length as to talk of applying to Congress for his recall. A very little, however, has raised all this clamour; but at all events his usefulness here is entirely over" (Davies to Greene, 17 June, NHi). It should be noted that Davies was head of the Board of Virginia Field Officers that had protested Weedon's return and that he enjoyed Steuben's confidence probably as much as any other Virginia officer.

From Steuben

SIR Chesterfield Ct Ho. 19th. feby 1781

I have the honor to inclose your Excellency Copy of a Letter I have just received from General Greene.

The absolute necessity of supporting him and consequently of calling out the Militia makes me extremely apprehensive that it will prevent the drafting the Recruits. The time fixed for this is the 10 of March. Before this time there may be a necessity of ordering out a part of every County. Should this happen not a Recruit will be drafted and our whole dependance will be on Militia.

This consideration urges me to submit to your Excellency if it would not be proper to order the Lieutenants of those Counties whose Militia are now at home to draft their Recruits immediately. If you approve this the Officers are ready and shall be sent to the places of Rendezvous immediately.

With great regard & respect I am Your Excellencys most Obedt Servt., STEUBEN Maj: Gen.

RC (Vi); in an aide's hand, signed by Steuben; endorsed. Dft (NHi); heavily scored out, interlined, and partly illegible. Enclosure (Vi): Greene to Steuben, "Camp Irwins Ford on Dan River," 15 Feb. 1781; printed in CVSP, I, 519.

The enclosed LETTER . . . FROM GENERAL GREENE gives more detailed information on the movements of Greene and Cornwallis than Greene supplied in his letter to TJ of the same date. It also enclosed "an Account of the Enemy's Strength, and the formation of their Army, also of our own force, by which you may see [our] critical Situation"; TJ stated in his letter to Gen. Lawson of 25 Feb. that "the State of Genl. Greene's force" had been withdrawn from Greene's letter while it was in transit.

From John Teackle

Accomac County, 19 Feb. 1781. Has addressed three letters to TJ, the last in October, acquainting him with "the deplorable situation" of the two galleys "on this Shore," but has had no answer. "By your Advice to me, in Council last June, you did not authorise me to intermeddle with 'em, Only to furnish with Provision, and Superintend such Repairs as should be directed." The vessels are exposed to the enemy and have also suffered injury from "our internal foes. . . . I would again beg leave to say, that unless a very speedy Sale, is made of the Vessells and some Perishable Articles, they will be of little Value to the State. . . . Indeed I fear some of the Officers have connived at the Country's Property, being applyed to private emolument. I would Recommend You, to Mr. Thomas Evans (who will hand you this) for a full State of the Vessells, and by him hope to be informed of your Excellency's Pleasure, on that head."

RC (Vi); 2 p.; addressed and endorsed.

John Teackle (Teacle, Teagle, &c.) had been a member of the House of Delegates for Accomac, 1778-1779 (Swem and Williams, "Register of the General Assembly of Va."). None of his earlier letters to TJ has been found.

From Charles Thomson

Secretary's Office [*Philadelphia*], *19 Feb. 1781.* Encloses twenty-four blank commissions, with blank bonds and instructions, for private armed vessels. "You will please to give orders that the bonds when Executed be returned into this Office." Others may be obtained upon application.

RC (Vi); 1 p.; in a clerk's hand, signed by Thomson; addressed and endorsed; printed in CVSP, I, 526. Enclosures not found.

To the Auditors

GENTLEMEN Feby. 20. 1781.

Be pleased to issue to Mr. George Harmer a Warrant for ten thousand pounds on Account of his Subsistence agreeably to Act of Assembly in his case made.

By Advice of Council. TH: JEFFERSON

RC (Vi: Contingent Fund Vouchers); in a clerk's hand, signed by TJ; endorsed. See Harmer to TJ, 25 Jan. 1781.

From John Banister

DEAR SIR 20 Feby. 1781

I am happy in having anticipated your order respecting the Arms, having before directed the Captains to collect every effective Fire lock in the County to a proper Place on the Road leading to Taylor's Ferry, but I fear when the best endeavours are used few will be the Number, as this collection has repeatedly been made to arm the continental Soldiers sent from hence, and I cannot help observing how unjust it is in Congress not to assist us with Arms when we have to contend singly with the greatest part of the british Army. The Men of this and all the Counties between this Place and the Enemy are highly animated in their Country's Cause and I am convinced would turn out to a man if they Could be armed. I got information yesterday of about Sixty Muskets that were sent by Elliot to be repaired, but finding nothing has been done I have ordered them into other hands; as soon as they are repaired and those collected from the People you shall be informed of the Number. Convinced of the impossibility of collecting the Beef tax in this County I have agreed to accept of the People the same quantity of Pork which is more advantageous to the publick and less difficult for the individual.

You will pardon me for suggesting that now is the time to strike a blow on the british Army, and that the thing should be rendered as certain as Numbers can make it. The hotspur Cornwallis is followed by a number of Savages from the Creeks. Judge what distress the poor defenceless inhabitants must experience as they pass thro' their Country. I am dear Sir with perfect esteem your mo obedt. & mo. hble. Servant, J BANISTER

RC (Vi); addressed and endorsed. YOUR ORDER RESPECTING THE ARMS: As Banister was county lieutenant of Dinwiddie, this may refer to TJ's letter to the county lieutenants of Chesterfield and Dinwiddie, 18 Feb. 1781.

From Vivian Brooking

Amelia, 20 Feb. 1781. Received TJ's letter of 18 Feb. this evening and will endeavor to execute the orders therein, but there will be difficulty because "the Militia has been embodied on this Alarm, and disbanded last Night, as we had not received any Orders from you or Requisition from the Commanding Officers of the Neighbouring Counties." Brooking also received a letter this day from an Amelia militia officer on duty near Portsmouth "desiring me to apply to your Excellency that the Men from this County may be releived as others have been, which I hope you will be pleased to order as soon as convenient."

RC (Vi); 2 p.; addressed (in part): "Pr. Mr. Jno. Casay Express"; endorsed. TJ's letter to which this is an answer was addressed to the County Lieutenants of Lunenberg, Amelia, and certain other counties, 18 Feb.

From Jonathan Clarke

Charlottesville, 20 Feb. 1781. Since last writing to TJ, Clarke has received a letter from Brig. Gen. [James] Hamilton "acquainting me that it was not agreeable to Maj. Gen. Phillips that the Convention Troops should receive money for the Provisions due to them, and therefore he wishes that the Germans should receive the Provisions here and the British at Frederick Town."

RC (Vi); 2 p.; addressed and endorsed.
Clarke's earlier letter is dated 6 Feb. 1781.

From George Elliott

DEAR SIR Petersburg Feby 20 1781

I am this moment Call'd on by the Barron Steuben to furnish four Expresses to ride Between General Gregories Posts and Suffolk. I am at a Very Great Loss to Know what mode to take for Horses for the Different Express Riders. As its for the field Business I expect Majr. Claiborne Wont Interfeiar in it. The practice of Impressing horses is Attended with Double the expense that Buying would be, for in the first place Seldom Proper Horses Can be got that way as we Are frequently Obligd to take the first we come at and in Cases of this Kind the Horses is Always Vallued at much more than they are Worth for Since this Invation I have had Some Impres'd by the Orders of the Barron which have been Vallued to fourteen thousand pounds Tobo: Some of Which are now in the Service and must be till Others Can be got to Supply their places and those Horses for Cash might be Bought for Six thousand Pounds. What we Could Return we have and the Damage of Some have been Vallued to one thousand pounds by men on their Oaths, and with Respect to the propriety of Pressing at any Rate I am at a Loss about as I Have Never Been furnish'd with any Law Respecting it. Majr. Claiborne has Directed me to have the whole of them Returnd but it is Out of my Power to Comply With it fully. Armongs Core [Armand's Corps] is mounted on Some of them and Some of them in the Barons family, others Now below With the Army as Express &c. Pray Sir, Be Kind Enough to Give me Your Immediate Advice or Directions in This Matter Which Will Greatly Releive Your Most Obedt: Huml Servt:

GEO: ELLIOTT Field. Q: Master.

P.S. I forgot to mention Some of the people absolutely refuse to take their Horses and Intend to petition the Assembly for payment. Yrs. G.E.

RC (Vi); endorsed.

From Commissary Benjamin Harrison

[*South Branch of Potomac*, *20 Feb. 1781.* Summary in CVSP, I, 529: Is employed by Maj. William Harrison, under instructions from the executive, in purchasing provisions and building boats. The scarcity of beef on the western side of the "Allegania Mountain" has obliged him to come to this country to procure the necessary supply, but he finds that not a sixth part can be gotten. This condition of things must continue until the vegetation will admit of pasturage. Desires instructions. MS not found. See William Harrison to TJ, 6 Feb. 1781.]

From James Hunter

SIR Stafford, 20th. February. 1781.

In reply to your excellency's inquiry how far the orders that have been given for camp kettles, to be made at my works, are complied with, and in what manner those made have been disposed of, I beg leave to inform you, that the order given last summer for 1000, to be furnished for the particular use of the state, is now fully compleated and the greater part of them, including in the number the 400 received by Colo. Zane, by virtue of your excellency's order to that effect, have, at different times, been delivered; and for more full satisfaction on this head, I shall direct my manager to make out an exact specification of the number furnished at each time, to whom delivered, and an account of what remain on hand; which paper shall be transmitted to your excellency.

We are now engaged in fabricating a parcel, together with some other things, by the direction of Gen. Greene, and for the use of his army; nevertheless, the order your excellency has last given for 1000 additional ones to be immediately got ready, for the separate service of the state, shall be particularly regarded; all possible dispatch used for it's completion, and your excellency made acquainted with our progress in the execution of it; be assured no cautions within the compass of my power shall be wanting, where the public good is concerned.

And on this occasion, I cannot forbear to testify to your excellency the great regret I felt, that I was unable to render fit for service the muskets sent to this place some weeks ago at a time too when they were so much wanted. But the making and repairing of small arms we prosecuted to so considerable an extent at my works has been for some time past discontinued, for want of workmen, all those employed in this service having left me principally because by an act of the legislature they were rendered subject to militia duty, draughts, &c. from which they had always enjoyed an exemption; altho' if that privilege could again be restored, I have no doubt that the works in this branch might be resumed to the great benefit of the state; and although, with respect to myself, I never derived any emolument from their continuance, but the contrary, yet as I am fully persuaded of the utility they would be of to the public at this time especially in case the exemption I before mentioned could be granted to the artificers and to the writers employed there, which last, it must be obvious are also indispensibly necessary at such works and if I could receive such countenance from your excellency as should be thought reasonable, I would attempt to set them on foot once more.

Or should it be judged more conducive to the public advantage to have them carried on for and by the state, rather than for the account, and under the eye of an individual, I will most readily assent to it, and require nothing for the use of the buildings which before served my people for this purpose, or for the use of such tools as I have that can be serviceable.

Nor do I stand singly in this opinion of their usefulness; when I last saw Gen. Greene, he expressed his concern, that a work, which might be rendered of such general service, should be suffered to sink into disuse; and promised, should it ever be revived, to send to it such artificers as it should be in his power to procure.

I have the honour to be, with perfect respect, Sir, Your excellency's obedient and humble servant, JAMES HUNTER

RC (Vi); in a clerk's hand, signed by Hunter; addressed and endorsed.

YOUR EXCELLENCY'S INQUIRY: TJ to Hunter, 7 Feb. 1781. THE WRITERS EMPLOYED THERE: By "writers" Hunter must have meant clerks; see CVSP, I, 531.

From Samuel Huntington

Philadelphia, 20 Feb. 1781. Encloses a resolve of Congress of this day "relative to compleating the quota of troops for the southern army and furnishing them with the necessary supplies." TJ's letters of 8 and 12 Feb. have been received.

RC (Vi); 2 p.; in a clerk's hand, signed by Huntington; addressed and endorsed. Enclosure (Vi): Two resolutions of Congress, 20 Feb. 1781, attested by Charles Thomson; by these Congress requested that the states south of Pennsylvania furnish their supplies for the southern army promptly; that these states and Pennsylvania complete their quotas of troops and send them southward; and that the governors of Delaware, Maryland, Virginia, and North Carolina agree upon a plan for supplying the southern army with provisions; the resolutions are printed in CVSP, I, 531. FC (DLC: PCC, No. 15).

See note on TJ's letter to Benjamin Harrison, 29 Jan. 1781.

From John Nicholas

[Sandy Point, 20 February 1781]

Agreeable to Colo. Innes's order to Major Turberville previous to my coming here, I examined Lt. Hare's Papers, in which I found the enclosed letter which gives me the greatest unhappiness to expose; but with the same hand ever devoted to the service of the Fair, I tenderly let fall the greater weight of my Country's good; but must still undivested of partiality for so tender a Character, beg she may be first informed of the strict necessity of such a Step, which if painted thro' my witnessing duty, I am convinced she will pardon—Hare informs me this Letter passed when the Army was at Westover.

Tr (NHi); in Turberville's hand? This Tr occurs at the top of a sheet on which another extract is copied (see following letter from Nicholas to TJ) and bears this caption: "Extract of a letter from Colo. John Nicholas dated Sandy Point Feb: 20. 1781."

From John Nicholas

[ca. 20 February 1781]

Since I wrote last I have discovered many other Letters from Mrs. Byrd which exasperates me in such a manner that I have determined to keep the one I mentioned to you secure with the rest for my own justification and untill I hear from you shall act agreeable to the dictates of my own reason. As Majr: Tuberville was so imprudent as to suffer Hare to go to Westover and as I have made discoveries on our part which tend to the injury of America I doubt not but some thing as great on the other may be brought to view. I therefore put off all feemale respect for the present and send Maj. Tuberville to Westover that all property presents &c. &c. from the enemy may be returned to the Vessell and the whole Correspondence between that Lady and the Enemy fairly investigated.

J.N.

RC (Vi); without place or date and signed only with initials; endorsed: "Colo. Nicholas Lr. Feby 81." Tr (NHi). This letter and the preceding were evidently enclosed in TJ's letter to Steuben of 22 Feb. On this whole subject see Turberville's letter to TJ, 15 Feb. 1781.

To Steuben

Sir Richmond Feby. 20. 1781.

I inclose you a report from Mr. Ross of the Cloathing provided and his prospect of further provision. The procuring Hats or leather

Caps still appears desperate, so that unless some substitute can be thought of I know not what will be done. There are no Hats I am told among the Cloathing come from the Northward.

I wrote you that after having called certain numbers from Washington, Montgomery, Botetourt, Henry and Pittsylvania I had called out all the Militia who could be armed of the Counties of Cumberland, Powhatan, Chesterfield, Dinwiddie, Amelia, Lunenburg and Brunswick to oppose Lord Cornwallis; Prince Edward was not called on because we knew them to have actually marched. Mecklenburg, Charlotte and Hallifax were so near the Enemy that we knew they must be in the feild before any Orders could reach them. So far the draught had been no more disturbed than it had been before by Arnold's invasion, except as to the five Counties of Washington &c. first named. It is not in our power to anticipate the time of draughting in the other Counties as you propose. The law gives certain times for raising Men voluntarily till the expiration of which no draught can take place. For this reason we have wished to avoid as much as possible calling on the Counties north of James River where the draught is as yet undisturbed untill we shall hear that Ld. Cornwallis has actually crossed the Dan, because that Act will decide that he means to penetrate this Country. Nevertheless if you think it advisable we will order Militia to a certain extent to be embodied on the North side of James River; and I shall be obliged to you for your opinion on this subject.

[I find by the inclosed papers which have passed between a Lt. Hare calling himself a Flag, and Capt Turberville that a vessel of the Enemy has come under very suspicious circumstances to Sandy point. What was her errand, to whom addressed, or whether she had passports from any of the Commanding Officers at the Posts in the Neighbourhood of the Enemy, are circumstances on which these papers give me no information: yet they appear material in fixing the real Character of this Vessel. It seems improper that under pretence of being Flags their Vessels should be permitted to penetrate our Rivers to their sources. This matter being within your line, and depending on usages with which you are better acquainted than we are, I wish to remit it altogether to yourself to have done what is right. A communication of what you determine will oblige me, as I am to write to Genl. Nelson on the subject.][1]

I also transmit you an extract of Gen. Nelson's letter on the subject of the French Ships here. I should think with him their cruizing off the Capes attended with safety to them, and great service to the American Cause by intercepting the Communication between New

York and Charles Town. But whether at this crisis till Ld. Cornwallis movements are decided the one way or the other, it be not of very great moment to retain Arnold in his present Quarters by the presence of a force sufficient to destroy his Navy if he withdraws from it, I would submit to your better Judgment. On this too I will ask your opinion as Genl. Nelson expects my answer.

I have the honor to be with very great respect Sir Your most obedt humbl Servt,
TH: JEFFERSON

RC (NHi); in a clerk's hand, signed by TJ; endorsed. Enclosures not found; one was a return of clothing sent in David Ross' letter to TJ, 19 Feb.; others were letters exchanged between Hare and Turberville concerning the controversial flag-of-truce vessel (see Turberville to TJ, 15 Feb.); and still another was an extract from Thomas Nelson's letter to TJ of 19 Feb., q.v. FC (Vi).

I WROTE YOU: TJ to Steuben, 17 Feb. 1781.

[1] There is in NHi a one-page sheet with various extracts of letters, of which the part in brackets (supplied) is one; others are from letters of Steuben to TJ, 21 and 25 Feb., and TJ to Steuben 22 Feb., qq.v.

From John Syme

New Castle, 20 Feb. 1781. The £1,500 ordered by the Council to be paid to Syme "for Waggonage of Stores" is quite inadequate for his "Cash ingagements"; needs £1,000 more. "Col. [John] Nicholas Writes Me He Has Your Directions, for releiving my Militia, from the Lower Battallion, Now On Duty, without Asertaining the Numbers"; Syme desires more exact information. Congratulates TJ "on the Arrival of arms and amunition, from the North."

RC (Vi); 3 p.; addressed (in part): "By Mr. Cockburn"; endorsed.

MY MILITIA: Syme was county lieutenant of Hanover (*Official Letters*, III, 155, note, 166).

From the Virginia Delegates in Congress

SR. Philadelphia Feby. 1781

Since our last in which we informd Your Excellency of the Arrival of Col: Harrison in this City, his Applications to Congress have been referd to a Special Committee, and the necessary Steps are takeing to Answer the wishes and wants of the Southern States, and of our State in particular as far is practicable in the present Situation of affairs. We doubt not but that Gentleman will give you full Information of the Progress he has made in the Special Business for which he has been Sent.

We are happy to Inform you of the Arrival of Capt. Paul Jones in the Ariel, from France. This event would have been a much more pleasing one had he brought the cloathing so long and anxiously expected. His Cargo is however by no means useless as it Consists of about thirty Ton of Powder. It is Conjectured that by this time Count D'Estaing is arrived in the West Indies with twenty two sail of the Line, and we are in great Hopes before this reaches you that a Ship of the Line from the fleet of our Allies in Rhode Island and three frigates will be in our Bay in order to cooperate with our Troops, in taking ample Vengeance on Mr. Arnold, for his treasons, perjuries, Robberies and depreadations, accounts being received in this Town that they saild from Rhode Island immediately after the storm and that Monsr. Des touches had taken effectual measures to Block up the Remaining Vessels of the Enemy in Gardners Bay. We have Sanguine hopes that this Expedition will not be fruitless, and that our Allies will find us in a Condition effectually to cooperate with them, as their aid will enable us to draw our whole force to a point. One of the frigates above mentiond will bring the Arms and Stores which were retaken in the Comite; which will perhaps not be an unseasonable aid. We have enclosed Your Excellency two New York Papers for your perusal containing Arnolds account of his Victories and Captures.

Mr. Hays informed us this morning he should be ready to set out for Virginia with the printing materials in about a week. We are with great respect Your Excelcys obed Servts.,

JOS: JONES

JAMES MADISON JUNR.

P.S. Since writing the above we have authentic information that one seventy four with two Frigates and a Cutter sailed from Rhode Island on the eigth for Chesapeake Bay.

RC (Vi); in Joseph Jones' hand, signed by him and Madison; endorsed. Enclosures not found. Burnett, who prints a portion of this letter, gives convincing reasons for assigning it the date of 20 Feb. (*Letters of Members*, V, No. 660, note 2).

OUR LAST: The first letter from the Delegates under date of 13 Feb. 1781. On the mission of COL: HARRISON, see TJ to Benjamin Harrison, 29 Jan. 1781. On MR. HAYS (i.e., James Hayes) and the PRINTING MATERIALS, see TJ to the Virginia Delegates, 31 Aug. 1780; Hayes to TJ, 18, 23 Jan.; Joseph Jones to TJ, 6 Feb. 1781.

From James Wood, Enclosing a Petition from Certain Men in Colonel Armand's Corps

SIR Charlottesville 20th Feb. 1781 11 Oclock A.M.

I this Instant Received Your letter of the 18th. Instant, and have given Orders for the immediate March of the Convention Troops, without their Baggage, as we have but a very few Waggons at the Post. The Troops have been Without Meal for Six Days Past, and but a very small Quantity of Beef On hand, so that I foresee the Greatest Difficulty, Indeed an Impossibility of Procuring Provisions by the Mode you Mention, in Consideration of which, I have Dispatched Ben. Calvert Express, in Expectation that the Money Received by Mr. Brown for the Use of this Post Should be immediately Sent to enable Me to Subsist the Troops. I Received an Express from Frederick Town Yesterday, informing me that the Troops had been without Animal food for Eight Days and that they had Drawn but One Pound of Flour in that time, so that I am fully Persuaded that the State of Maryland is Altogether Unable to Subsist the Troops, and will not Receive the Germans; My Own Idea of the Proper Mode of Accomodating them at the Present would be to Divide them between Winchester, Martinsburg, and the Warm Springs where there is a Number of Vacant Houses. If you shou'd Approve this I hope you will Signify it and impower Me to take Possession of the empty Houses at the Warm Springs. I shall stay here 'till the Return of the Express, in Order to forward the Straglers, and shall then follow with the Greatest Expedition.

Colo. Mingen Appears to be highly Pleased with the Proposal of Purchasing their Bills, and will Write you On the Subject. I find that the Exchange has risen Considerably. The last Considerable Purchase of Specie from them was at 100 for One about three weeks Ago. Small Sums Since have been Negotiated at 120. At Present they ask 500 Dollars for a Guinea. For Bills the Highest that has been given was 18/ to the Guinea Paid in Specie, or Paper at the Exchange of 100 for One. There is a Number of Speculators Tampering with them at this time from Pennsylvania; if any thing is Done it must be Suddenly, as they are now in the Greatest want of Money. Indeed I am afraid that the Movement will Oblige them to take the Offers which Have been Made them. I have Just Received Colo. Mingen's Letter which I have the Honor to inclose. Sometime ago Nine Germans were sent here from Richmond, I understood by the Baron Steuben. They have been Closely Confined ever since. The Inclosed Letter is from them. They are under great Apprehensions of being Delivered to their Own Officers. I really believe they wish to Remain in the Country, and I think wou'd be usefull Labourers. I Pray Your Excellency to inform Me what I am to do with them. They will Remain with the Guard which Must be left to take Care of the Tanyard Stores[1] Invalids &c. Colo. Taylor thinks that a Number of his Men Could be enlisted for three years, to Serve under their Own Officers in the Continental Army, and wishes to Know whether such Officers who Raised them, Could have rank in the Army.

I have the Honor to be Sir Yr. Excellencys Very Obt Servt,

J Wood

P.S. I have lately Received information that Genl. Hamilton had received Orders not to receive any money for Deficiencies of Rations, which Determined me not to give your Last Letter to Mr. Clark.

ENCLOSURE

We your petitioners begs leave to lay before your Excellency Our distressed Situation at present. We are in a Very Open Guardhouse, and Without Money Cloathing or Blankets. We are Deserters from Burgoins Army, and We Enlisted in Colo. Armongs [Armand's] Regiment for two Years and We Served two Campaigns To the North, and one to the South, Each of Which We Was on The Enemies Loins [Lines], Which Shues We are friends to America Or Might have Deserted then, if We Chosed. When Our Enlistments Was Expired, Our Colonel Was Gone to the Northward and We Appoid [Applied] to the Major of the Said Regiment but he Said he Could Not Give Us Our discharges, As he did not know for What Time We Ware Enlisted for. We then Applied to the other Officers, and they Said they had no Right to Discharge us and likewise Told Us that the Colonel Never intended to Return, and they Mostly Resigned. So We did Not know What to do. We then Came to Majr. Genl. Barron Destuban [Steuben] for Our Discharges, Who Sent Us to Richmond, and then to Petersburg, and had one Shot And three Others Received One hundred Lashes Each as Deserters, and then Sent Up here, to Albl. Barracks. We are now Throne of by Our people, and if Not taken Under Your Excellencies protection as Citisens and Soldiers We Shall be The Most Reached of All Beings. We have Served the Country Faithfully, and are Willing to do it Again, if Your Excellency Will please to have Us taken Out of this Misirable Place, and Your Petitioners Will Ever pray for Your Excellencys Protection.

RC (Vi); endorsed. Enclosures: (1) Petition of Certain Men in Colonel Armand's Corps, printed herewith from the MS in NHi; MS lacks signatures (perhaps on a missing leaf), and its cover bears the following notations in two or three different hands: "A Ptition To Governor Jefferson Petition Armands Men"; it was transmitted to Steuben by TJ in a letter of 21 Feb. (2) O. C. A. Mengen to Wood or to TJ; not found, but see TJ to James Hamilton and O. C. A. Mengen, 3 Feb. 1781. TJ also enclosed in his letter of 21 Feb. to Steuben an extract of that part of Wood's letter pertaining to the "Nine Germans" (NHi).

YOUR LAST LETTER TO MR. CLARK: Presumably Jonathan Clarke is meant; TJ's most recent letter to him that has been located is that of 13 Feb. 1781.

[1] Tr of extract in NHi reads "Tanyard Horses," a clerical error.

From Richard Claiborne

SIR Richmond 21st. Feb: 1781.

By a letter from Mr. Elliott at Petersburg, I am informed that there is in the possession of Mr. McNeal, Assistant to Mr. Ross at that place, a considerable quantity of Duck proper for Tents. The difficulty of procuring this article, for want of Money, obliges me to beg of your Excellency that a part of it may be delivered to Mr. Elliott, as he can have it made up immediately. There are Twenty five pieces particularly mentioned, to be sent up to Mr. Armstead; but as we have a factory there, and it will save transportation, I should be glad to take the whole.

I beg your Excellency likewise for an order on the Deputy Quarter Master General of the State for a Quantity of Wire for the Marquees and Tents, as it cannot be procured in Petersburg.

I have the honor to be with much respect Yr. Excellency's Most obt. Humble Servant RD. CLAIBORNE

D Q Mr. S. Virga.

RC (Vi); addressed and endorsed.

To William Davies

SIR Richmd Febry. 21. 1781

The want of a board of Council prevented our taking up the final arrangement of the Clothier's duties till yesterday, the paper I sent you having contained only what was proposed to be agreed on. Unfortunately no copy of it was retained, so that I am obliged to ask the favor of you to return it if you still have it.

We have here a large number of undressed deer-skins, and no person who can dress them: if you have any body who can do it, we shall very gladly send them to you, leather breeches being much wanted for the Cavalry.

I am with much respect Sir &c.

FC (Vi). THE PAPER I SENT YOU: See TJ to Davies, 7 Feb., and Davies' reply to the present letter, 23 Feb. 1781.

To George Elliott

SIR In Council Febry. 21. 1781.

The establishment of a Line of riders between Genl. Gregory's Camp and Suffolk is very necessary. I would advise you to purchase horses for that purpose at any rate almost, rather than to impress. But if you cannot purchase they should be impressed. I think it would be better, whether you purchase or impress, that it be done in the neighbourhood of the enemy as much as possible, because horses are cheapest there and these are in danger of being taken by the Enemy & used against us.

I am Sr. yrs. &c, T.J.

FC (Vi); at head of text: "Colo. George Elliott."

From James Innes

SIR Williamsburgh. Feby 21st 1781.

The present distressed Situation of the militia, under my Command induces me, to address your Excellency on their behalf. The most of them are totally destitute of the necessary cloathing to protect them from the Inclemency of the weather. They are lousy dirty and ragged, and from those Circumstances becoming every day more sickly. In addition to this such a spirit of disquietude prevails among the poorer Class, whose Corporeal Labours are necessary to sustain their families that I have been, and still am apprehensive of a mutiny, unless some assurances can be given of a speedy relief. I have sent up Capt. Richeson (in whom I repose much Confidence) personally to report to you the wretched Situation of the troops which compose my Regiment. The Evil consequences which would flow from a mutiny of the militia in our present Circumstances, induces me, contrary to my Ideas of military Discipline to adopt a temporizing Conduct. I have prevailed on the troops to wait patiently your Excellencys Answer, which I supposed would be the prospect of relief in some given time.

The enclosed Letter furnishes the latest advices we have had of the french Squadron. Capt. Edden's [Samuel Eddins'] Company of Artillery with two field pieces are detached to York, to give protection to the prizes sent to that post by Commodore Tilly.

General Nelson is at present confined to his Chamber with a violent pleurisy, by whose Request during his Indisposition, I have taken Command of the troops in this Quarter. I am still, tho' I have been in service from the Commencement of the Invasion, without a Commission. I only mention this Circumstance to your Excellency, as in case of capture I should be very hardly treated.

I immagine ere this you have heard of the black affair at Westover.

I have the honor to be very respectfully yr. most obt sert.,

JAS: INNES Colo. Commg.

RC (Vi); endorsed. Enclosure: Sans to Nelson, 21 Feb. 1781, printed below. THE BLACK AFFAIR AT WESTOVER: See note on Turberville's letter to TJ, 15 Feb.; also TJ's reply to the present letter, 22 Feb.

From Lafayette

SIR New Windsor february the 21st 1781.

I Am the More flatterd By the Command Which His Excellency General Washington Has Been Pleased to Intrust to Me, As Independant of the General Good that May Be Hoped from this Expedition, It seems to Promise An Opportunity to Gratify the High Sense I Have of My Personal obligations to the State of Virginia.

I Shall from time to time Inform Your Excellency of the Movements of the Continental detachment that Has Marched from this Place. They Will Be Precipitated As Much As I Can, And I'll Have the Honor of Writing to Your Excellency from Philadelphia Where I intend to Precede the troops.

Begging Leave to Refer You to the letter of the Commander in Chief, And To Express the desire I Have to Be Honord With A line from Your Excellency, I shall only Add that With the Most Ardent Zeal to do Any thing in My Power Which May promote the Wishes of Your Excellency, and With Every Sentiment of the Highest Respect I Have to Honor to Be Your Excellency's Most Humble And Most Obedient Servant, LAFAYETTE

RC (Vi); endorsed: "La Fayette's Letter Recd March 1. [*In another hand*:] cop'd."

THE COMMAND WHICH . . . GENERAL WASHINGTON HAS BEEN PLEASED TO INTRUST TO ME: Lafayette had been ordered to make a forced march with a detachment of Continental troops from the Hudson to Virginia in order to cooperate with a French naval squadron against the British army and its supporting naval force at Portsmouth; Lafayette's ardent hope was to capture Benedict Arnold, commanding the British in Virginia. See Washington to Lafayette, New Windsor, 20 Feb., enclosing instructions, Washington, *Writings*, ed. Fitzpatrick, XXI, 253-6; Washington to TJ, 21 Feb., below; Gottschalk, *Lafayette and the Close of the Amer. Rev.*, ch. IX; and the letters exchanged between Lafayette and TJ in March. The present letter, contrary to its endorsement, was received by TJ on the last day of February; see *Va. Council Jour.*, II, 300, and TJ's letters of 28 Feb. 1781.

To George Muter

SIR In Council Febry. 21. 1781

I take the liberty of transmitting to you the inclosed advice of Council that proper measures may be taken for notifying it for ascertaining what officers remain on duty and calling them to take command at the several posts where men are stationed. I should be glad also that there should be an inspection return made to me of the state of the men. I am &c., T.J.

FC (Vi). Enclosure (missing): Presumably a copy of the Advice of Council printed above under 6 Feb. 1781.

To Thomas Nelson

DR. GENL. Richmd. Febry. 21. 1781.

I received your letter of the 18th. the night before last and deferred answering it till I could confer with Baron Steuben which I had an opportunity of doing yesterday evening. He shewed me a letter from Monsr. Tilly from which and the information of his aid who went down, we suppose the French squadron sailed on a cruise yesterday morning. They will however be within our call, and therefore we think it proper to go on with the preparations for enabling us to make an attempt on the Enemy, and for affording an asylum to any of the ships of [our] Ally which may at any time Come to us. I put into his hands the papers relative to Mr. Hair and he will give orders on the subject: he seems to consider him as no flag, but a prisoner. As to Mr. Hair's calumnies on individuals of this State among whom I am one, I consider them as honorable testimonials; it is their known practice to bribe whom they can, and whom they cannot to calumniate. They have found one scoundrel in America, and either judging from that or their own principles they would pretend to beleive all are so. If pride of character be of worth at any time, it is when it disarms the efforts of malice. What a miserable refuge is individual slander to so glorious a Nation as Great Britain has been.

I spoke to Baron Steuben some time ago for a return of the number of Militia from each County which have been on duty and how long. As Militia duty becomes heavy it becomes also our duty to divide it equally. I have waited for this to order out releifs, which cannot be done on sure grounds without it. You will oblige me by having such a return made from your quarter as soon as possible.

I am sincerely sorry to hear of your indisposition. Wishing it speedily removed I am with much esteem. &c.

P.S. Is Capt. Kelly necessarily employed with you? If he can be spared we are desirous of employing him particularly in another effort to bring the Cannon from South Quay. The 24 ℔s are wanting immediately to be mounted at Hood's. If he can proceed on this, he must come here.

FC (Vi).

The letter from MONSR. DE TILLY, signed Le Gardeur de Tilly and dated 17 Feb., is in NHi. Nelson's secretary, the Rev. Robert Andrews, had written Steuben on 19 Feb. that Nelson was confined with such a severe cold as to require "great care . . . to keep it from becoming pleurisy." He also stated that the French commander expected to sail with the first fair wind, and added: "Genl. Nelson wishes to know whether your Designs with respect to York are still to be pursued"; the next day Andrews reported that Nelson was so much worse that he was "no longer able to do any business" and that he had turned over the command to Col. Innes. Steuben replied in part as follows: "Notwithstanding the french fleet is to sail the first fair wind, My desires with respect to York are to be pursued"; the reference to "York" is probably to the same subject as TJ's previous reference to PREPARATIONS FOR . . . AN ATTEMPT ON THE ENEMY (Andrews to Steuben, 19 and 20 Feb.; Steuben to Nelson, 20 Feb., all in NHi). For the PAPERS RELATIVE TO MR HAIR (Hare) and for his CALUMNIES ON INDIVIDUALS, particularly on TJ, see Turberville to TJ, 15 Feb. and Nelson to TJ, 18 Feb.

Sans to Thomas Nelson

York 21st feby 1781

I've the pleasure of informing you of the arrival of the eight prizes taken by the french Commodore Mr. Le Gardeur de tilly. They are all under the direction of Mr. Cottes which been appoint'd Commander of the prize Brig Cornwallis. Also the french Squadron [lyes] now at anckor at Linheaven Bay Between Horse Shoe and the Cap Henry. It Seems that they will enter Soon this River; the officer tells me one of the frigates will be order'd to Cruse in the Bay. The Same officer is order'd to remain here till further ord[ers. Therefore] if you have any thing to inform of M[r. de Tilly] please to foreward your letter by my M[essenger.]

I take the liberty of applying myself to you for to get of you an order to take four Guns 4 pounders and 100 Boulets which are down water Side, belonging to the state. As they make use of five cannons of mine and my Brig being blocked up in Pianketank by six privateers, I thought that the State wou'd approve the lending of 'em till I might get my Cannons. My Captain came last night, who inform'd me that I shou'd loose my Brig, if Cou'd not Send assistance immediately. So distress'd as I am I hope you will not refuse me.

I remain with respect Sir Your very Huml. Servt., SANS

RC (Vi); addressed: "To his Excellency General Nelson Williamsburg"; endorsed. Enclosed in James Innes' letter to TJ of this date.

To John Christian Senf

SIR In Council Febry. 21. 1781.

I do myself the pleasure of inclosing you the advice of Council for your appointment as finally settled. The Law which authorizes them to appoint an Engineer, restrains the rank to that of a Lieut. Colonel, and restrains also the circumstance of actual command. The resolution of Council is silent as to your continuance in Office after the War, because they are apprised of nothing which might induce an idea of the Office being discontinued at that period at which in their expectation it will become most usefull, as we shall then become most able to fortify the several posts requisite for defence. Your acceptance of this appointment will give me very real pleasure, and as soon as notified a Commission shall be made out. I am with respt. &c.

FC (Vi).

The Council's order for the appointment of Senf as "Engineer to this Commonwealth; with the rank, pay and emoluments of a Lieut Colonel" from 1 Jan. ("as he has been actually serving the State as Engineer during the present invasion") is printed under 20 Feb. in *Va. Council Jour.*, II, 297. Senf declined; see his answer, 26 Feb., and also note on Gates' letter to TJ, 4 Oct. 1780.

To Steuben

SIR Richmond Febry. 21. 1781.

I received from Mr. Armistead yesterday afternoon a Copy of the receipt for the 117 blankets. He excuses himself for the error in calling them 155 from having spoken by memory. I did not observe till I delivered it to you that the Certificate of the delivery of Mr. Ross's blankets (105 I think they were) wanted a date. I know however that they were delivered about the same time with those from Mr. Armistead. There will still remain 90 unaccounted for which will be worth enquiry.

An hundred pair of shoes are now in Mr. Armisteads hands ready to be delivered.[1]

The inclosed Letter from the Continental Director of the Hospital at Fredericksburg being proper to be transmitted to whatever person has succeeded Doctor Rickman either in his office generally or in the Custody of the Continental Medicines and being uninformed who that person is, I take the liberty of submitting it to your order.

I have the honour to be with great respect Sir Your most obedt. & most humble servt, TH: JEFFERSON

RC (NHi); in a clerk's hand, with complimentary close, signature, and address (without place) in TJ's hand. Enclosure not found. FC (Vi).

1 This sentence is not in FC.

From Steuben

SIR Chesterfield Court House 21st feby [1781]

As the Detachment of Continental Troops will march from Chesterfield on the 25th Inst. I wish to Join to them the Militia of this County and Dinwiddie. For this purpose they must be assembled at Dinwiddie Court house, and there wait my Orders. If you have no Objection to this Plan, an Express must immediately be dispatch[ed] to inform them, as part of the Chesterfd. Militia are on their march to Goods Bridge.

Excepting the two Regiments I have Ordered Gen. Weedon to form, and march to Williamsbg. I think the Militia[1] on the North Side James River should not be call'd out 'though they may be ordered to hold themselves in Readiness.

In addition to the Papers You inclosed me relative to Mr. Hare, I last night received a letter from him, and an other from Major Tuberville.

As the Circumstances attending the affair may not be known to Your Excellency a detail of them may be necessary.[2] Soon after the fleet left Westover, and previous to the Order of Goverment that no partial requisitions should be made for Property taken by the Enemy; I granted Mrs. Byrd a flag for the purpose of receiving her Negro's &c.[3]

I informed the person who went with the flag, that if Arnold would not send them,[4] he might send a flag when he pleased, with Mrs. Byrds Property, and that I would give his flag a pasport.

It seems Mr. Hare has come on that Business. From all the Papers,[5] and from evry Circumstance relating to the Affair: I find Mr. Hare has acted with the greatest impropriety, though he has not given sufficient Warrant for making him a Prisoner:[6] his Pasport Copy of which is inclosed, is from the Commanding Officer of the Navy on this Station, and perfectly Proper.[7]

As he has not brought all the Property which was taken from Mrs. Byrd doubtless he has Goods, or something else on board his Vessell as a Compensation for what still is in the hands of the Enemy belonging to Mrs. Byrd. [Whether those Goods shall be received by her, or not, I conceive to be a matter only to be determined by Government.[8] Was the same case to happen in Europe, the Suffering person; especially as she is a female and a widow, would be allowed to receive them.

If leave shall be Given to land what Mr. Hare may have brought, I shall Order his Vessell to Westover. If not she will be Ordered down the river immediately.][9]

I beg Your Excellencys Answer as an Express must be sent the moment I receive it.

I am with respect Your Excellencys Most Obedient

STEUBEN Maj. Gen.

RC (Lloyd W. Smith, Madison, N.J., 1946); addressed; endorsed. The enclosed copy of Lt. Hare's passport has not been found. Dft (NHi); in an aide's hand and with numerous deletions and interlineations, the more important of which are noted below. Dft is headed: "Ampthill 21 Feby 1 o'clock AM."

Concerning MRS. BYRD and the FLAG, see Turberville to TJ, 15 Feb. and references there. For the order that NO PARTIAL REQUISITIONS SHOULD BE MADE FOR PROPERTY TAKEN BY THE ENEMY, see TJ's letter to Nicholas, 10 Jan. Subsequent to this, the Council had issued the following order, which is probably the one to which Steuben referred: "The Enemy in the detention or restitution of Slaves having been governed by a distinction between such proprietors as have borne arms or otherwise been active, and those who have not; and the practice leading to the most dangerous and fatal consequences; it is the unanimous determination of the board that no flag for the purpose of sollicitimg a restitution of plundered property from the enemy, shall be again permitted" (*Va. Council Jour.*, II, 285; 3 Feb. 1781). For Steuben's orders of 1 Feb. and 1 Mch. forbidding flags to be sent in to the enemy, see Appendix I, Vol. 5: "The Affair of Westover." Even as late as 23 Feb., however, Arnold felt it necessary to write to Muhlenberg as follows: "To prevent unnecessary applications for Negroes in future, I beg leave to observe, that none will be returned to persons in Arms, or Office, in which class I consider all persons in the Militia liable to be called forth to Arms. When Widows, Orphans, or persons not under the above description, wish to have their Negroes returned, it will be necessary for them to have their property ascertained (as mentioned above) under oath, which authenticated Certificate being sent in by any person with a Flag, who can fix upon the Negroes claimed, they shall be immediately delivered up" (Arnold to Muhlenberg, Portsmouth, 23 Feb., NHi).

1 Dft reads: "I think with you that the Militia" &c.

2 This sentence does not appear in Dft.

3 Dft reads: "a few days after Arnold left Mrs. Byrds, she applyed to me for a Flagg to go down the river if Possible to recover the Property which Arnold had taken from her. Previous to the Resolution of Govt that no flagg should be sent, I gave her a Flagg." (The words "Previous to the Resolution . . . should be sent" are interlined.)

4 Dft reads: "would not return Mrs. Byrd's Property."

[5] Dft adds at this point: "now before me."

[6] Dft reads: "I find Mr. Hare to have acted with great impropriety, though he has not gone so far as to do any thing which may justify us in making him a prisoner."

[7] Instead of the preceding three words, Dft has the following: "of which I send a Copy, & in every respect he is a Flagg of truce."

[8] The following was deleted in Dft: "though as an American war is carried on very different from one in Europe, I can be no judge in the affair."

[9] There is in NHi a one-page sheet with various extracts of letters, of which the part in brackets (supplied) is one; others were from letters of Steuben to TJ, 25 Feb., and TJ to Steuben, 20 and 22 Feb., qq.v.

To Steuben

SIR Richmond Feb. 21. 1781.

I will immediately dispatch the orders you desire to the militia of Chesterfeild and Dinwiddie. Your favor of this day being put into my hands after the adjournment of Council I cannot answer as to Mrs. Byrd's property till tomorrow.

I take the liberty of inclosing you some papers relative to the nine men sent to the barracks in Albemarle, on which you will please to give any orders you think proper.

I am this moment informed by a militia officer who left Genl. Greene about noon of the 19th. that he was then at Halifax Court H. and the enemy still beyond the Dan, supposed to be making preparations to cross. Not many militia had yet joined Genl. Greene. He had received an express from Colos. Campbell and Shelby that they had crossed the mountain with 1000 men, and desiring orders; and that 700 men from Pittsylvania and Henry were on their march. I do not know this man; so give it you as it comes to me. I am with much respect Sir Your most obedt. humble servt,

TH: JEFFERSON

RC (NHi); addressed by TJ: "The honble. Majr. Genl. Baron Steuben Ampthill." The principal enclosure was the Petition of Certain Men in Armand's Corps, printed above as an enclosure to Wood's letter to TJ, 20 Feb.

From George Waller

SIR Henry County Feaby. 21st. 1781.

This evening, I recievd yours of The 15th. Instant, wherein you Call for The Assistance of our Militia, to the Aid of Gen. Greene, against Lord Cornwallis. I have the satisfaction to Inform You, that our Militia, has before this time Joind General Greene [at] headquarters. The approach of the enemy Towards this state, Appeared to Alarming To await your commands, which I am In hopes will be agreeable news. The County Lieutenant marchd this Militia Under the Command, of a Colonel which I beleive Containd more then the Number You Call for, from this County. I flatter my self that the next Account You receive of Cornwallis will be more to Your Satisfaction. I am just informed from Good Authority that Colos. Preston Crocket Shelby and Cammel from the Western is on march, to join Gen. Greene. Business of a Publick Nature, since the marching of our Militia, has Cald the County Leiutenant from home.

We shall in every respect pay due regard To Your Advice, to comply with as near as is Possible. The hospitall of the wounded and Sick of Gen. Morgans &c is at Present at Our Court house, with some Military Stores.

I am Sir yr. Obdt & Hbbl. Servt., GEO. WALLER. Majr M

PS The Account of Assistance from the western Waters I am in hopes will not retard the March of Others. G W

RC (Vi); endorsed.

From George Washington

SIR Head Quarters New Windsor 21st: Feby. 1781.

I do myself the honor to communicate, to your Excellency, a circumstance which I hope will be followed by the most Salutory consequences to the State of Virginia in particular, and which may ultimately have the happiest effect upon the interests of America in general.

The Chevalier des Touche, commanding His most Christian Majestys Squadron in the harbour of Newport, finding himself enabled, since the late misfortune which happened to the British Fleet in Gardiners Bay, to make a detachment, has dispatched a Ship of the Line of 64 Guns and three Frigates to Chesapeak, in hopes of finding there and destroying the Fleet under the direction of Arnold. The French Ships sailed the 9th. inst. from Newport with a fair Wind. They have taken on board a quantity of Arms and Cloathing[1] which had arrived there on account of the State of Virginia.

It is more than probable, that these Ships will have arrived in the Chesapeak, before my letter reaches you, but should they be retarded by adverse Winds or other accidents, your Excellency's need not be told that the most profound secrecy will be necessary on such an occasion, for should the least hint escape, and Arnold come to the knowledge of it, he would not hesitate to take the opportunity of pushing out of the Bay. The Ships once arrived at their Stations, the matter becomes of public notoriety without any disadvantage.

From an apprehension that the enemy may take such a position as will enable them to defend themselves and their shipping without a land cooperation, and knowing that Militia cannot be depended on for the vigorous measures that it may be necessary to pursue, I have put a respectable detachment from this Army in motion. It is commanded by Major Genl. the Marquis de la Fayette. It will proceed by land to the Head of Elk, at which I calculate it will arrive by the 6th. of March at farthest, and will fall down the Chesapeak in Transports.

I have written to the Baron de Steuben by this conveyance, given him the foregoing intelligence, and some directions relative to the position which he is to take with the Militia, collecting Magazines &c.

It will be highly necessary that an immediate, safe and expeditious communication should be opened between the Commanding Officers of the French Squadron and the Commanding Officer on Shore. In this, and every other measure tending to promote the public good, I am confident of your Excellency's assistance, and I have desired the Baron to make application to you in every case where your countenance may be wanting. The Marquis de la Fayette, who is the Senior Officer, will take the command upon his arrival.

I recollect but one thing further, which will require your Excellency's more immediate attention, and that is, the business of providing the most experienced and trusty Bay and River Pilots (should it not have been done before this reaches you) and sending them to the commanding Officer to be forwarded to the Fleet. This trouble must necessarily devolve upon your Excellency or some Gentlemen appointed by you, because our Officers, being Strangers, might be imposed upon in this most material point.

With the highest Sentiments of Respect and Esteem I have the honor to be Your Excellency's Most obt. and humble Servt.,

Go: Washington

P.S. Should you have occasion to write to the Marquis de la Fayette, let your first letter go by land under cover to the Qr. Mr. to the

Head of Elk. Any subsequent ones by Boats to the same place, because they will meet the transports in the Bay.

RC (Vi); in Tench Tilghman's hand, signed by Washington; addressed to TJ at Richmond and franked by Washington; endorsed: "Genl Washingtons Letter Feby 21. 81 recd Feby 28. 1781." Dft (DLC: Washington Papers); also in Tilghman's hand.

1 The word "Ammunition" was deleted in Dft and "Cloathing" interlined.

To James Wood

SIR Richmd Febry. 21. 1781

We consent to the dividing the Germans between Winchester, Martinsburg and the Berkely springs till further orders as proposed by you. I must get the favor of you to know from Colo. Mingen what sum of money by the fortnight they will have occasion for, and it shall be sent either to the Barracks in Albermarle to any Agent whom they shall leave there to settle their affairs or to their new Quarters, (in fact the meeting of the assembly on Thursday sen'night is relied on to furnish us with money of which we have not at present one shilling). I will send to Baron Steuben the petition from the 9. Germans: in the mean time you will do well to leave them as you propose under guard at the Barracks. We think our powers do not extend to the enlisting the men of the regiment of guards on the terms mentioned in your letter.

Mr. Browne informs me he sent 93,000 pounds to Mr. Jos. Hawkin[s] three days ago, and will send the like sum by the bearer.

FC (Vi).

THE 9. GERMANS: See Wood's letter to TJ, 20 Feb., and its enclosure.

To William Yates

SIR Richmond Febry. 21. 1781

It is become necessary that we ascertain the number of arms which we sent into Continental service with our regiments. As the only authentic information must come from you, I must beg the favor of you to make a return to me of the number of Arms sent on in the hands of regiments while you were Muster Master. I must pray also that this be without delay. I am &c., T.J.

FC (Vi).

To John Browne

Sir Richmond Feby. 22. 1781

New London, Staunton, Winchester, and Fredericksburg being appointed as places of rendezvous for the new Levies, if you have not Deputies already at those Posts, or in the Counties, you will be pleased to appoint them with instructions to furnish the Recruits with Provisions during their stay at the Rendezvous, and on their march from it. The Bearers hereof are going to Winchester to receive the Recruits, and will carry your appointment for that Post if you have [not] before made it. I am Sir yr. &c &c.

FC (Vi).

To James Innes

Sir In Council Febry. 22. 1781.

I had written the inclosed before Capt. Richeson arrived. I transmit it open through you for your perusal. I am very sorry that the men first called into the field have not been releived: but it has proceeded from the want of such a return as is mentioned in my letter and for which I applied some time ago to Baron Steuben, who has had hopes of furnishing it. You will readily be sensible that where any County shall have sent but half the quota called for, they have performed but half their Tour and ought to be called on again: Where any County has furnished their full complement, they have performed their full Tour and it would be unjust to call on them again 'till we shall have gone through the Counties. Militia duty becoming burthensome it is our duty to divide it as equally as we can. Upon the receipt of such a return a releif shall be ordered: and in the mean time the arrival of the Militia mentioned in the inclosed may enable you to permit those who have been longer on duty to return home.

On the present invasion the favour was asked of Baron Steuben to arrange the commands on principles laid down by the Executive, being the same determined on Leslie's invasion. We have awaited the receipt of his arrangement to issue Commissions: this alone is the [reason] why not a single commission has issued during the Invasion.

I will take care to remind the Baron of the want of his report and in the mean time should any gentleman have the misfortune to be captured not a moment shall be lost in sending him a commission.

The affair of Westover has been communicated to me so imperfectly that I am still ignorant of it. I know that a flag is detained at Sandy point, and have heard of letters between the Conductor and a person of his connection up the River: But their import I have never heard. I understand that I am particularly indebted to Mr. Hair for his Eulogiums. Indeed I think them the best certificate of my whiggism did my country want such a certificate at this day. I am with much esteem &c &c.

FC (Vi). The enclosure that TJ sent unsealed was undoubtedly the letter from TJ to Thomas Nelson of 22 Feb., following.

The AFFAIR OF WESTOVER: TJ cannot have been wholly ignorant of this episode, for Steuben had given him a detailed account, written in the early hours of 21 Feb., and TJ had replied the same day.

To Thomas Nelson

DR. GENL. Richmd. Febry. 22. 1781.

We sent expresses on the 17th instant to call down a fourth part of the militia of the Counties of Loudon, Fauquier, Prince William and Fairfax (about 1090) with orders to march immediately to Wmsburg. Genl. Weedon followed these orders to hasten their execution. These Counties are indeed distant, but they had been some time held in readiness; so that I hope they will afford an early and very substantial reinforcement. The moment however that I receive from you a return of the numbers who have served with you from the several Counties as desired in my letter of yesterday: it will be in my power to order reinforcements from counties more convenien[t] without doing injustice. Your application to Commodore Tilly for arms meets our approbation. I inclose you an extract of a letter from our delegates in Congress. Should Arnold not be recalled by positive orders, he may possibly come up Appamatox either to attempt a junction with Ld. Cornwallis or to divert our reinforcements to Genl. Greene, and place him between two fires. Ld. Cornwallis had not crossed the Dan on the 19th. Our accounts of the militia turning out to reinforce Genl. Greene are flattering. They seem in every place to have anticipated our orders.

I am with much respect &c., T.J.

FC (Vi). Enclosure not found; presumably it was an extract of one or the other of the letters addressed to TJ by the Virginia Delegates in Congress, 13 Feb. 1781.

To Steuben

SIR In Council Feby. 22d. 1781.

[Whether restitution of the identical property taken from Mrs. Byrd might be permitted seems to be a question unnecessary now to be determined by the board as Mr. Hare the Conductor of the flag does not pretend to have brought the identical property, but goods in compensation of it; and to what amount we are uninformed. This kind of compensation we think can by no means be permitted. Let the instances be multiplied, and a very small metamorphosis in the nature of the transaction, degenerates it into commerce. This is the opinion of the board independent of the influence which would have been produced on it by the intercourse supposed in the inclosed Letters, from Colo. Nicholas. What will be the result of the investigation set on foot we know not: You will be pleased to give any orders which may be rendered necessary by this new matter.][1]

I have the honor to be with great respect Sir your most obedt. & most humble servt., TH: JEFFERSON

P.S. I am daily pressed to order reliefs to the militia below which I am unable to do till I receive the returns of the numbers which the several counties have already had and kept in the feild.

RC (NHi); in a clerk's hand, with complimentary close, signature, and postscript in TJ's hand; endorsed.

The INCLOSED LETTERS from Nicholas were presumably those of 20 and ca. 20 Feb., qq.v.

[1] There is in NHi a one-page sheet with various extracts of letters, of which the part in brackets (supplied) was one; others were from letters of Steuben to TJ, 21 and 25 Feb., and TJ to Steuben, 20 Feb., qq.v.

From Garret Van Meter

SIR Hampshire 22d. February 1781

I have to acknowledge the receipt of your Excellencys letters of the 24th. December and 19th. January, both of which came to my hand the 13th. Instant. As Colo. Enoch Innis, who has your Excellency's Commission as County Lieutenant, has never qualified himself to act under his Commission, the command has consequently devolved on me; I have also received the Act of Assembly for recruiting this States Quota of Troops to serve in the Continental Army. Likewise Twenty Five Thousand Pounds for procuring provisions and for the Detachment of our Militia who are required to join Colo. Clark.

From the late arrival of these important papers Your Excellency will readily suggest that it will be impossible to comply with them, within the limited time, nevertheless, I shall take every prudent step, in order that every part of your Orders may be executed. For this purpose I have given the necessary orders to the Officers, I have likewise appointed a Commissary and Quarter Master, who will procure provisions and means of transportation to Fort Pitt. I have no certain account where Colo. Clark is, nor have I heard from that Gentleman since the receipt of your Excellency's letter. I have complied with your Orders respecting the Proclamations, and in short with every other requisition in both your Excellency's letters so far as time would admit.

I enclose you a return of one of the Battalions of this County. The others I have not yet had a proper return of from the Officers, but believe it to be nearly of equal strength with the former. I have the Honour to be Your Excellency's very obdt. Servt.,

GARRET VN: METER

RC (Vi); addressed and endorsed. Enclosure missing.

To Frederick Victor

SIR In Council Febry. 22d. 1781.

I have laid the inclosed depositions before the Council. However just and proper your anxiety may be to wipe away the aspersions thrown on you, yet it seems a matter on which the Executive cannot take up on these papers; nor could with propriety take up at all where no complaint has been lodged. Perhaps the proceedings of Courts of enquiry may come properly before them: but there does not appear to have been a Court of enquiry in the present instance, nor can such a Court be held but on the conduct of an officer. The Board is not informed whether you be an officer or not—if not the supposed offences [are] only cognizable in a civil court. I take the liberty therefore of remitting the papers into your hands, & am Sr. &c., T. JEFFERSON

FC (Vi). Enclosures not found.

To the Virginia Delegates in Congress

GENTLEMEN In Council Feby 22d. 1781.

The object of the inclosed Memorial of Messrs. Stodder, Kerr and North being attainable by Congress only and proper to be the subject of a representation from them I take the Liberty of transmitting it to you that Justice may be done to the parties interested.

I have the honor to be with great respect Gentlemen Your mo. ob. Hble Servant, TH: JEFFERSON

P.S. We are and have long been without Letters of Marque.

RC (DLC: PCC, No. 71, II); in a clerk's hand, signed by TJ; endorsed: "Feby. 22nd. 1781 Letter from Govr. Jefferson of Virginia. Read 26th." Enclosed Memorial of Stodder, Kerr, and North (complaining, as citizens of Virginia, that a trading vessel owned by them had been captured by the British in the neutral harbor of St. Martin) is in DLC: PCC, No. 41, IX; on motion of Madison and Meriwether Smith, 26 Mch. 1781, the Memorial and related papers were transmitted to John Adams "to represent the case to which they relate to their High Mightinesses the States General of the United Provinces of the Netherlands, and to claim such redress for the memorialists as justice and the law of nations require" (JCC, XIX, 312). FC (Vi). Tr (DLC); signed and endorsed by TJ.

From Mary Willing Byrd

SIR Westover, February 23, 1781.

Having heard from Major Turberville, that he had sent to inform you of the arrival of Mr. Hare, and the business on which he came; and that the answer he received was, you left that matter to the commanding officer, I thought it unnecessary for me to give you the trouble, at that time, of writing to you on the subject of his business, for two reasons; it was my determination not to keep the things brought by Mr. Hare in the Flag, without first consulting the Executive. This Mr. Meade and many other persons had often heard me say. In a letter I wrote immediately on his coming up to the Baron, I informed him some articles were brought for me, and assured him I had not the least inclination to keep them, if the Executive did not approve of it. The other reason was, I did not know the whole amount of the articles, and wished when I wrote, to be able to write fully on the subject. Think not, sir, that I had anything to do with Mr. Hare's coming from Sandy Point to Westover. I knew nothing of it, and beg the favor of you to suspend your opinion of my conduct, until I have an opportunity of vindicating it.

The officers have acted so confusedly that I dare believe you have had but a very imperfect account of the whole affair, and I am by no means capable of giving a proper one of it, I think.

I think I am called on say something on the subject, as a duty I owe myself, the public in general, and you in particular as Supreme Magistrate of this State. Baron Steuben thinks me accountable to the civil, and not to the military power for my conduct; and to that

I appeal for justice. Mr. Hare came up by the Baron's permission, on a Flag, granted by General Arnold, for the purpose of bringing up such negroes as he chose to return. This permission was given before your order was sent to General Nelson, respecting negroes. I flattered myself that I could have served my neighbors, and with this view, wrote by a flag, and by the advice of one of your most particular friends, a man of most excellent judgment, and express approbation of every person I have seen.

I hear Mr. Hare has forfeited his flag, been made a prisoner and searched. Among his papers was found a letter written by myself, while the fleet lay at Westover, I think in answer to a message I received from Captain Evans, by a little gentleman whom he was very fond of, a relation of his. I do not recollect the contents of this letter, but am easy about it, for [as] my heart never dictated aught that was dishonorable, so my pen could never have expressed anything that I could not justify. If policy had not forbid it, I owe too much to my honor to betray my Country.

Indeed, sir, you may rely on my veracity when I assure you, that no action of my life has been inconsistent with the character of a virtuous American.

I cannot express violent, enthusiastic opinions, and wish curses [and] distruction on the meanest individual on earth. It is against my religion. I wish well to all mankind, to America in particular. What am I but an American? All my friends and connexions are in America; my whole property is here—could I wish ill to everything I have an interest in?

My honor is dearer to me than my life; let not my Countrymen attempt to injure me further. The All-seeing eye of our gracious God, will revenge the innocent and the helpless. I pray that he will forgive my persecutors, and enable them to show as much virtue as I have done when they have as great a tryal. He that will show more let him cast the first stone. I flatter myself I have raised myself in the esteem of the British, by showing them that I had a perfect love for my country.

I hope you will pardon the trouble I give you. I mean to address you not only as the Governor, but as an acquaintance, whom I have experienced kindness and some friendship from, to ask your advice (Colonel Harrison is from home), what will be the proper steps for me to take in this affair. I know a law passed sometime ago, which I looked over in a cursory manner, importing what was treason. I never conceived that there was an object up the river, to lead the enemy near my habitation, therefore I did not attentively read the law. No person gave me warning of their approach. I had no time to send anything out of the way of the privateers, which were what I was afraid of.

When the officers landed, I received them according to my idea, with propriety. I consulted my heart and my head, and acted to the best of my judgment, agreeable to all laws, human and divine. If I have acted erroneously, it was an error in judgment and not of the Heart. As Pope expresses it, "One self-approving hour will outweigh the praises of millions." The force of this sentiment I now fully experience. I mean not by this to show contempt for the good opinion of the public. I value it highly, but would rather know I merited it, than know I had it.

If you, sir, will have the goodness to furnish me with that law, and your opinion on it, I shall be extremely obliged to you. I hope to prove myself worthy of your kindness. If any unavoidable things have happened that the law forbids, I cannot doubt the justice of the legislative body, that they will pass another in my favor, when I have an opportunity of making my innocence appear.

Every good man must have been shocked when they heard of the *savage* treatment I have met with. This cannot be called *Liberty*. I do not know who has been in fault. I am convinced, sir, that you have had no share in these bare[1] actions; and [I] should not do that great man, Baron Steuben, justice, if I did not declare that I was convinced, that the whole of his conduct was perfectly amiable, and that he was incapable of giving orders that would authorize such rash, such indecent, horrid conduct, as I have met with.

I have the honor to be, sir, your most obedient, humble servant,

M Byrd

MS not located. Text from *American Historical Record*, ed. Benson J. Lossing, II (1873), 467-9, where it is printed without indication of provenance. The brackets in the present text are in Lossing's text.

A LAW PASSED SOMETIME AGO: The Act defining treason was passed at the Oct. 1776 session (Hening, IX, 168). It stipulated that "if a man do levy war against this commonwealth in the same, or be adherent to the enemies of the commonwealth within the same, giving to them aid or comfort in the commonwealth or elsewhere, and thereof be legally convicted of open deed by the evidence of two sufficient and lawful witnesses, on their own voluntary confession," this should constitute treason, punishable by death and forfeiture of lands and chattels. For other letters on "The Affair of Westover," see Appendix I, Vol. 5.

[1] No doubt this is an error in transcription or printing for "base."

From William Davies

Chesterfield, 23 Feb. 1781. Because of his "present constant hurry," Davies has been unable to find "the plan for the cloathier's department";

will forward it as soon as he can find it. The deerskins can be dressed at Chesterfield if the men who understand doing it are permitted to stay.

RC (Vi); 2 p.; addressed and endorsed.

From Thomas Gaskins

HONL. SIR Northumbld. Febry. 23rd. 1781

You'l Receive this by Mr. John Gordon who promises to take down with him the proceedings of our Court martial in September Last in regard to the Rioters then in our County. It appears we have been much blaimed by some for our proceedings, but I hope upon the matter being fully inq[uired into] they'l find we have done well. The reason we took the rioters in for 18 months was to incourage them to come in. Those that stood out had not that benefit and there are many now out and some have gone over to the Enemy, by geting on boad of some of there Vessells. I also inclose you one Coppy of an advertizement for your further information. Almost the whole County was inflaim'd. I had given orders a day or two before the draft to five or six Captains to furnish a number of men to oppose those that mutinied but to my great suprise few or none appeard in our favor and the Very men I most Confided in appear'd in arms against us. I think I can say with truth that our Little Company of Volinteers and mostly of them officer[s] not more than 32 in number behaved well by Subduing almoste a whole County, and the proceedings of the Courtmartial we thought was for the best to incourage the outlying rioters to Come in. I am Honl. Sir yr moste obedt & Very Humbl. Servt., THOS. GASKINS

P.S. For further particulars I refer you to bearer Mr. Gordon who Lives near the Courthouse and is well acquainted with the whole proceedings. T G

RC (Vi); addressed (in part): "favd. by John Gordon Esqre."; endorsed. Enclosure: (1) Proceedings of a series of courts-martial held in Northumberland co., 16-25 Sep. 1780, on certain men who resisted the draft; printed in part in CVSP, I, 535-6; (2) the "Coppy of an advertizement" (or notice) is in Gaskins' hand (Vi), is dated 18 Sep. 1780, and is signed by Gaskins as county lieutenant of Northumberland co.

In the ADVERTIZEMENT alluded to, Gaskins stated that a number of persons on 14 and 15 Sep. had "entered into a most Criminal & unlawful Combination to prevent the due Execution of an Act of the last Session of Assembly for furnishing this States Quota of Troops to the Continental Army"; that at a court martial held on 16 Sep. a number of persons had been "Condemned to be Soldiers for the War," thirty-nine of whom were named in the notice; and that all militia officers and others were required to search for and apprehend those who had resisted the draft.

From John Mazaret

Prince Edward Court House, 23 Feb. 1781. Distress of troops serving under Mazaret; three officers and twenty men have not received a farthing of money or an article of clothing since last March "—they are all as naked as when they were born." Sends Capt. Lt. Rice to TJ "in hopes of some relief." After a six-week retreat Mazaret arrived at Prince Edward on the 20th with "5 pieces of Artillery, two Howitzers, 20 waggons loaded with amunition and all the heavy Baggage."

RC (Vi); 2 p.; addressed (in part): "favd. by Capt. Rice"; endorsed.

From George Muter, with Reply

War Office [Richmond], 23 Feb. 1781. Encloses two accounts for the expenses of Capt. Sansum in collecting and bringing over eighteen-month men from the Eastern Shore. As Sansum's authority was derived from Col. Webb, Muter does not know how to act in his case, especially since other officers have been and are now employed in collecting those men and deserters in that region, "in consequence of my being informed there were a considerable number." Answer follows: "In Council Feb. 23. 1781. If Capt. Sansum did not act under authority from this state, it does not appear to us that his expences can be borne by this state. Th: Jefferson."

RC (Vi); 2 p.; addressed and endorsed. TJ's reply, in his own hand, is at foot of text. Enclosures missing.

From Edmund Randolph

SIR Feby. 23. 1781.

I beg leave to remind your excellency of the situation of John Dean, a supposed fugitive from the lead mines, in defiance of the condition of his pardon. It is probable, that the actual abandonment of the place of labour will not be fixed upon him: 'tho' nothing can be more satisfactory, than that he had made preparations for flight. I say this upon the information of Colo. Lynch. Now I refer it to the executive with great deference, whether a pardon would not be adviseable in these circumstances? For the force of such a condition, 'tho' strictly legal, may be weakened, should a jury, whose tenderness is fortunately excessive in most cases, and would perhaps be extravagant in one, like this, where the prisoner has already suffered something from hard service, and much more from a painful imprisonment, bring in a verdict of acquittal. Such a discussion in favor of a criminal might impress the world with an opinion, that the power of pardoning conditionally was reprobated by a formal adjudication.

I should have addressed you, Sir, on this subject, before the present moment, had I not conceived, that his offence called for some exemplary suffering. This he has already experienced from the weight of his chains, and the other severities of a gaol. His parents are honest, decent, and industrious people: himself too stupid by nature, to be skilful in any of the nice branches of villainy, and scarse equal to the crime, which he committed, of being the bearer of a wretched counterfeit to the auditors for payment.

If it should seem necessary to word a pardon in this instance in a manner, expressive of the case, and forbidding a belief, that the violation of such conditions will not be punished, I shall readily conform to your instructions, being, Sir with absolute respect yr. mo. ob. serv:,

EDM: RANDOLPH

RC (Vi); addressed; endorsed (in part): "Mr. Attorneys Lr."

On 26 June 1780 the Council had taken the following action on the case of John Dean: "Jno. Dean, who lately made his escape from Jail after having obtained a pardon on condition to serve 3 years in the lead mines, being now in confinement the Govr, is advised not to withdraw his pardon provided the said Dean will proceed to the mines and serve his time out" (*Va. Council Jour.*, II, 260). There is no evidence that the Council acted upon Randolph's recommendation.

From Steuben

Ch[esterfield] Co. Ho. 23 Feb. 3 oClock PM

Till it is decided whether Cornwallis will cross the Roanoke or not we ought at all events to be prepared for the worst for which purpose we may have occasion for the troops under the command of Colo. Innes to cross the James River and I shall send orders for him to hold him self in readiness to move at a moments notice. But previous to such a movement (if it should take place) it will be necessary to take some steps to protect the Counties of Elizabeth Warwick and York from any incursion of the Enemy. At Gloucester is a Magazine of 7 or 800 Stand of Arms which can be distributed to the Militia of these three Counties. This militia should be ordered to take arms on the first notice from the governor and I request that your Excellency will make choice of a Colonel of the Militia, who is capable to take command there.

Dft (NHi); in an aide's hand; endorsed.

On 23 Feb. Steuben wrote the following interesting comment to Greene: "The departure of the French Vessells has destroyed all hopes of Success in an Attempt on Portsmouth. I have not, however, countermanded the preparations. . . . All this has not diverted my attention one moment from you. I have not ceased tormenting the Governor for the Cloathing for the troops at this place, but with all my importunity I do not think I should have been able to have Equipped them these 6 Weeks if a quantity of stores had not arrived from the Northward. From these I have drawn such Articles as I was deficient in and shall thereby be enabled to send off the detachment the 25th inst. The Governor informs me the militia on the frontiers towards you are all ordered out, by his Account you must have a Reinforcement of at least 2000 Men" (Dft in NHi; in part identical letters were also sent to Washington and the Board of War; Steuben no doubt referred to TJ's letter to him of 20 Feb.).

From John Banister

Without place or date [*before 24 Feb. 1781*]. Cannot send more than 100 men into the field with arms; but if arms could be had, "I suppose half our Militia would cheerfully turn out." At Petersburg are 400 good Continental arms. Desires instructions.

Tr (NHi). At head of text: "Copy of a Letter to the Governor from Colo. Banister." This is the copy enclosed in TJ's letter to Steuben of 24 Feb.

To John Banister

Sir In Council Febry. 24. 1781.

The arms you mention being Continental, they are subject to the orders of Baron Steuben. I have therefore sent him a copy of your letter and begged him to send you by this conveyance such orders as he thinks proper. As he is anxious that the reinforcement should be respectable I make no doubt he will order the Arms.

My letters mentioning that the detachments should go under proper officers were meant to direct such officers of the militia as the invasion law has prescribed in proportion to the numbers sent.

I am with great esteem &c.

FC (Vi).

From Edward Carrington

Sir Camp Wyleys 5 Miles So: Side of Dan Feb. 24th. 1781.

Major Claiborne has inclosed me a Copy of your Excellencies Letter on the Subject of the Estimate I left with him to be complied with in Virginia. I find the Executive have estimated the Amount of the Sum which will be requisite to comply with my Claims, and that the Greatness of it fixes the Impossibility even of an Attempt.

It is true, in forming the Estimates, I did not consult the finances of the State, but, as was my duty, the Equipment of the Army, and I expected that its being out of the Power of the State to compleat the requisitions, would not have prevented an Attempt to comply with them, as far as could be done. However I own I did not think the Estimate, carried to the full Extent, would exceed the Abilities of the State. The Sum indeed mentioned in your Excellencies Letter is excessive, and I am not surprised it should be so, when I find by a State of your Affairs sent to Genl. Greene, you have magnified the Estimate in one Article ten fold, and perhaps the same Circumstance attends the Estimation on some of the other Articles. I estimated for fifty thousand Bushels of Grain; in your Excellencies State to General Greene, it is called five hundred thousand. I should be glad the Executive would revise their Estimation, and perhaps after correcting those Errors, the Estimation may be reduced to a Sum not so alarming as has appeared.

I believe my Estimate contains very few Articles which are not already in the Country, and I apprehended that a State engaged in raising Men, would be as sollicitous to equip and support them in the field, as to enlist them; Virginia has already experienced the fatal Consequences of not paying an equal Regard to both those points. My Estimate is meant for the Virginia line, supposing the New Establishment to be compleat in Men. If it is too large it is not my fault, but that of Congress in calling on her for more men than she could raise and equip. If this Quota of Troops is not to be compleated, by so much as that will be deficient, by so much may my Estimate be deficient also. How far the former will fall short of the Requisition of Congress, your Excellency is better able to judge them myself and that deficiency may govern you with respect to my Estimate. Whatever assistance Major Claiborne is to receive from the Executive, I wish him to be possessed of as early as possible, that the Recruits may be equipped for the field as they come out.

I have the Honor to be With much respect Your Mo. Obt.

Ed. Carrington D.Q.M.S.A.

RC (Vi); in a clerk's hand, signed by Carrington; addressed and endorsed.

On this matter of the ESTIMATES, see TJ's letters to Claiborne of 7 Feb.; to Carrington, 3 Mch.; to Greene 10 Feb.; also Claiborne's letters to TJ of 7 and 11 Feb.; and Carrington's to TJ, 31 Mch.

To the County Lieutenants of James City and Certain Other Counties

SIR [24 February 1781]

Be pleased to order to on receipt of this of the militia of your County to remain on duty only till releifs ordered from Counties less exposed shall arrive. I hope this call will be thought less heavy on your County as we would avoid calling on it to perform a full tour of duty, and only wish them to serve during those short intervals between the necessary discharge of the militia and arrival of releifs. I am Sir &c.

FC (Vi). At head of text: "Cout. Lieuts. James City, York, Warwick, Elizth. city & City of Wmsburg." Date established from TJ's letter to Innes of this date; see also *Va. Council Jour.*, II, 299.

From David Geddes

Frederick Town [*Md.*], *24 Feb. 1781.* Has this moment received TJ's letter of 3 Feb. "and have to inform you that Paper Money at any rate will not answer here at present." The Assembly having called in all Continental money, little of any kind is to be had, and people will accept nothing but specie or bills. If an opportunity later occurs of "facilitating the business in the manner you prescribe," Geddes will give TJ timely notice of it.

RC (Vi); 1 p.

From James Hamilton

SIR Frederick's Town 24th Feby. 1781

I have the honor of receiving Your Excellencies Letter of the 3d Instant, with an extract from Major Genl. Phillips's Letter, which by adhering to, in Your ordering any Sum from one to five thousand Pounds in Specie to be paid Mr. Geddes here for the use of the Troops of Convention, I shall immediately Write to New York, that Your Prisoners may receive an equivalent Sum there, payable to those only, you shall please Direct it to be given.

My Orders are such, that I cannot receive the Sum Mention'd in Your Letter in any other Manner.

I have the Honor to be Sir Your Excellencies Most Obedt. And Most Humble Servant, JAS. HAMILTON

RC (Vi); endorsed.

To James Innes

SIR Richmod. Feby. 24. 178[1]

Having not yet received a General return of the men in service from the respective Counties, and time they have served, which might enable me to order releifs, from those Counties from which they ought to come, I must refer to your discretion to govern yourself by actual circumstances, and if you find a discharge of any of the militia with you necessary that you call from the Counties of York and James City and those below them a sufficient number to replace them, and to remain on duty untill I shall be enabled to order a releif, or until the arrival of the militia from the Northern Counties ordered a week ago, on which event those you call in, and any others now in service may be discharged. The call on the Counties near Wmsburg. will I hope be thought less oppressive as we have not at any time required them to perform full tours of duty, but only to make first opposition untill a force can be collected from Counties less exposed and to fill up those chasms between the discharge of some and arrivals of others which happen at times.

I am with much respect &c &c &c.

FC (Vi). Tr (NHi); enclosed in TJ's letter to Steuben of this day.

From James Innes

SIR Williamsburgh Feby 24th 1781.

The Return you require was sent from this post to the adjutant General, above nine Days since. But that I suppose having miscarried from the villainy of the Express riders (every one of whom, that I am acquainted with ought to suffer Death) I herewith transmit a second Account of the two Regiments stationed at and below this place. I can with truth assure your Excellency that I never within the Compass of my short existence experienced so much real anxiety as has fallen to my lot for a few Days past, on account of the mutinous spirit that prevails among the militias on Service in this Quarter. The promise of reliefs has appeased them for a time and I hope they will remain quiet until actual reliefs do arrive.

General Nelson desires me to remind your Excellency that in a few Days legislative Duty will call us from our Commands. He requests that you would inform the Baron of this Circumstance that officers may be timously sent down to supply our places. I have the honor to be most respectfully Yr Excellency's most obt Servt,

JAS INNES Colo Commt.

RC (Vi); endorsed. Enclosure missing, but for TJ's copy of Innes' return see Return of Militia by Counties, printed at end of February 1781.

Innes wrote Steuben on 26 Feb. advising that he would have to leave Williamsburg in a day or so to attend the General Assembly, and added: "I have mentioned this Circumstance to the Governor, requesting he would Communicate it to you that an officer might be timously sent down to take my place" (Innes to Steuben, 26 Feb., NHi).

From Littleberry Mosby

SIR Powhatan Febry. 24th 1781.

Agreeable to the Instructions given by you I sent all the Men that cou'd be furnished with Armes, which Amounted to one Hundred and Six Rank and file, under the Command of Captains Hughes and Williamson. Majr. Thomas Harris being Sick stay'd at Home; tho I think the Captains will prove Sufficient for the Command they will have as they are two Gentlemen I have a great Opinion off. Our Militia has been kept so long in the field when Called below, and So Soon ordered out Again after their Return has prevented our puting the Recruiting Act in Motion. The divisions are Made Out but the Court Martial Was of Opinion that they shou'd not be given to the persons Appointed to Recruit Untill the Men Now ordered to the Assistance of Gen. Green Returns.

I am Sir with the greatest Respect yr. most Obedt., L. MOSBY

RC (Vi); addressed and endorsed.

To Steuben

SIR In Council Feby 24. 1781.

I have received repeated information that the nakedness of the Militia on service near Wmsburg and want of Shoes is such as to have produced murmurings almost amounting to mutinies and that there is no hope of being able longer to keep them in service. The precedent of an actual mutiny would be so mischevious as to induce us to beleive an accomodation to their present temper most prudent, and therefore to send to Colo. Innes a Letter of which the inclosed is a Copy. In the mean time it is out of my power to order releifs on any fixed rule without such a return as mentioned in the Letter. As soon as I shall receive such a return new calls shall be made to replace the numbers you wished to have on the north side of James River independently of those from the Northern counties who were meant to be free for other service. I must therefore trouble you to exercise your authority in such manner as to produce me returns of the kind desired. This is the more necessary to be done speedily lest the same spirit should begin to shew itself in General Muhlenburg's camp. You will judge from the temper of these Militia, how little prospect there is of your availing yourself of their aid on the South side of the river should you require it.

I inclose you the copy of a letter from Colonel Bannister County Lieutenant of Dinwiddie. I have taken the liberty of referring him to you as to the arms, and the bearer who carries my Letter, will also carry any orders you please to give as to them. The size of his detachment it seems will depend on the Arms he can procure.

I have the honor to be with very great respect Sir Your mo: ob: hble. Servt., TH: JEFFERSON

RC (NHi); in a clerk's hand, signed by TJ; endorsed. Enclosures: TJ to Innes, this date; Banister to TJ, without date, printed above under the present date. FC (Vi).

From Steuben

SIR Chesterfield Court Ho. 24 feby 81

I set out tomorrow with the Detachment from hence for Dinwiddie Court Ho. from whence my movements will be wholly directed by those of the Enemy. The necessary instructions are given to General Muhlenbg who will keep the Command at Suffolk.

Colo. Innes with the Troops under his Command is orderd to pass the River and take post at Cabbin point till further orders. Genl. Weedon is orderd to march without delay to Hanover Co. Ho. where he will receive such orders as circumstances may render necessary.

As it is uncertain whether or when I shall return I recommend to your Excellency the Arrangements which Colo. Senf is instructed to lay before you.

Colo. Meade is gone to Sandy point to make the necessary Enquiry respecting the Flag. His report will determine my Conduct in that Affair. with great respect I am Yr. Excellencys Most Obedt St.

Dft (NHi); in an aide's hand; endorsed.

THE ARRANGEMENTS WHICH COLO. SENF IS INSTRUCTED TO LAY BEFORE YOU: On 24 Feb. Steuben wrote Senf in part as follows: "You will lay before

Government the necessity of the following arrangements being immediately made—1st. The necessary number of workmen must be employed in mounting on travelling carriages the Brass Cannon at New Castle and Cumberland. This must be done as soon as possible. It would be better to repair two at a time, in order to have at least some of them ready in a short time. Three or four carriages must be made to transport heavy ordnance. The Garrison destined for Hoods shoud be ordered there as soon as possible. They may be of service and may be instructed in making fashines Gabions &c. and in case of need they will be ready to construct them" (Steuben to Senf, 24 Feb., NHi).

From James Wood

SIR Charlottesville 24th. Feb. 1781.

Since I had the Honor of Writing you the 20th. Instant I have been informed that there is a Number of Prisoners of War at Winchester, that Provisions are Scarce and hard to be Procured in that Neighbourhood, and that the whole Houses are taken up. If this shou'd be the Case, it will be Necessary for me to Send a part of the Germans to Stovers Town or Shepherds Town, Neither of which will be Very Inconvenient to the Others. I have the Honor to be with Great Respect and Esteem, Sir Yr. Excellency's Very Obt. Servt., JAMES WOOD

RC (Vi); addressed and endorsed.

Preliminary indexes will be issued periodically for groups of volumes. A comprehensive index of persons, places, subjects, &c. arranged in a single consolidated sequence, will be issued at the conclusion of the series.

Preliminary indexes will be issued periodically for groups of volumes. A comprehensive index of persons, places, subjects, etc., arranged in a single consolidated sequence, will be inserted at the conclusion of the series.

The Papers of Thomas Jefferson is composed in Monticello, a type specially designed by the Mergenthaler Linotype Company for this series. Monticello is based on a type design originally developed by Binny & Ronaldson, the first successful typefounding company in America. It is considered historically appropriate here because it was used extensively in American printing during the last thirty years of Jefferson's life, 1796 to 1826; and because Jefferson himself expressed cordial approval of Binny & Ronaldson types.

Composed and printed by Princeton University Press. Illustrations are reproduced in collotype by Meriden Gravure Company, Meriden, Connecticut. Paper for the series is made by W. C. Hamilton & Sons, at Miquon, Pennsylvania; cloth for the series is made by Holliston Mills, Inc., Norwood, Massachusetts. Bound by the J. C. Valentine Company, New York.

DESIGNED BY P. J. CONKWRIGHT

THE TEXT of this book [illegible] is composed in Monticello, a [illegible] designed by the Mergenthaler Linotype Company for this series. Monticello is based on a type design originally developed by Binny & Ronaldson, the first successful typefounding company in America [illegible] the most [illegible] American printing during the last decades of Jefferson's life [illegible] 1800 and [illegible] Jefferson himself expressed a [illegible] for Binny & Ronaldson types.

Composed and printed by the Princeton University Press. Illustrations are reproduced in collotype by Meriden Gravure Company, Meriden, Connecticut. Paper for the [illegible] Hampshire [illegible] Monadnock [illegible] Holliston Mills, Inc., Norwood, Massachusetts. Bound by the J. C. Valentine Company, New York.

DESIGNED BY P. J. CONKWRIGHT